MrExcel
LIBRARY

Excel® 2016
VBA and Macros

Bill Jelen

Tracy Syrstad

800 E. 96th Street
Indianapolis, Indiana   46240

Contents at a Glance

Excel® 2016 VBA and Macros

ISBN-13: 978-0-7897-5585-8
ISBN-10: 0-7897-5585-8

Library of Congress Control Number: 2015950785

Printed in the United States of America

5   18

Trademarks

Warning and Disclaimer

Special Sales

For information about buying this title in bulk quantities, or for special sales opportunities (which may include electronic versions; custom cover designs; and content particular to your business, training goals, marketing focus, or branding interests), please contact our corporate sales department at corpsales@pearsoned.com or (800) 382-3419.

For government sales inquiries, please contact governmentsales@pearsoned.com.

For questions about sales outside the U.S., please contact international@pearsoned.com.

Editor-in-Chief
Greg Wiegand

Acquisitions Editor
Joan Murray

Development Editor
Charlotte Kughen

Managing Editor
Sandra Schroeder

Project Editor
Mandie Frank

Copy Editor
Kitty Wilson

Indexer
Ken Johnson

Proofreader
Dan Knott

Technical Editor
Bob Umlas

Editorial Assistant
Cindy Teeters

Designer
Chuti Prasertsith

Compositor
Trina Wurst

Contents

About the Authors

Bill Jelen, Excel MVP and the host of MrExcel.com, has been using spreadsheets since 1985, and he launched the MrExcel.com website in 1998. Bill was a regular guest on *Call for Help* with Leo Laporte and has produced more than 1,900 episodes of his daily video podcast, *Learn Excel from MrExcel*. He is the author of 44 books about Microsoft Excel and writes the monthly Excel column for *Strategic Finance* magazine. Before founding MrExcel.com, Bill Jelen spent 12 years in the trenches—working as a financial analyst for finance, marketing, accounting, and operations departments of a $500 million public company. He lives in Merritt Island, Florida, with his wife, Mary Ellen.

Tracy Syrstad is a Microsoft Excel developer and author of eight Excel books. She has been helping people with Microsoft Office issues since 1997, when she discovered free online forums where anyone could ask and answer questions. Tracy found out she enjoyed teaching others new skills, and when she began working as a developer, she was able to integrate the fun of teaching with one-on-one online desktop sharing sessions. Tracy lives on acreage in eastern South Dakota with her husband, one dog, two cats, one horse (two, hopefully soon), and a variety of wild foxes, squirrels, and rabbits.

Dedications

For Robert K. Jelen
—Bill Jelen

For Marlee Jo Jacobson
—Tracy Syrstad

Acknowledgments

Thanks to Tracy Syrstad for being a great coauthor.

Bob Umlas is the smartest Excel guy I know and is an awesome technical editor. At Pearson, Joan Murray is an excellent acquisitions editor.

Along the way, I've learned a lot about VBA programming from the awesome community at the MrExcel.com message board. VoG, Richard Schollar, and Jon von der Heyden all stand out as having contributed posts that led to ideas in this book. Thanks to Pam Gensel for Excel macro lesson #1. Mala Singh taught me about creating charts in VBA, and Oliver Holloway brought me up to speed with accessing SQL Server. Scott Ruble and Robin Wakefield at Microsoft helped with the charting chapter.

My family was incredibly supportive during this time. Thanks to Mary Ellen Jelen, Robert F. Jelen, and Robert K. Jelen.

—Bill

Juan Pablo Gonzalez Ruiz and Zack Barresse are great programmers, and I really appreciate their time and patience showing me new ways to write better programs. Chris "Smitty" Smith has really helped me sharpen my business acumen.

Thank you to all the moderators at the MrExcel forum who keep the board organized, despite the best efforts of the spammers.

Programming is a constant learning experience, and I really appreciate the clients who have encouraged me to program outside my comfort zone so that my skills and knowledge have expanded.

And last, but not least, thanks to Bill Jelen. His site, MrExcel.com, is a place where thousands come for help. It's also a place where I, and others like me, have an opportunity to learn from and assist others.

—Tracy

We Want to Hear from You!

As the reader of this book, *you* are our most important critic and commentator. We value your opinion and want to know what we're doing right, what we could do better, what areas you'd like to see us publish in, and any other words of wisdom you're willing to pass our way.

We welcome your comments. You can email or write to let us know what you did or didn't like about this book—as well as what we can do to make our books better.

Please note that we cannot help you with technical problems related to the topic of this book.

When you write, please be sure to include this book's title and author as well as your name and email address. We will carefully review your comments and share them with the author and editors who worked on the book.

Email: feedback@quepublishing.com

Mail: Que Publishing
          ATTN: Reader Feedback
          800 East 96th Street
          Indianapolis, IN 46240 USA

Reader Services

Visit our website and register this book at quepublishing.com/register for convenient access to any updates, downloads, or errata that might be available for this book.

As corporate IT departments have found themselves with long backlogs of requests, Excel users have discovered that they can produce the reports needed to run their businesses themselves using the macro language *Visual Basic for Applications* (VBA). VBA enables you to achieve tremendous efficiencies in your day-to-day use of Excel. VBA helps you figure out how to import data and produce reports in Excel so that you don't have to wait for the IT department to help you.

What Is in This Book?

You have taken the right step by purchasing this book. We can help you reduce the learning curve so that you can write your own VBA macros and put an end to the burden of generating reports manually.

Reducing the Learning Curve

This Introduction provides a case study about the power of macros. Chapter 1, "Unleashing the Power of Excel with VBA," introduces the tools and confirms what you probably already know: The macro recorder does not work reliably. Chapter 2, "This Sounds Like BASIC, So Why Doesn't It Look Familiar?" helps you understand the crazy syntax of VBA. Chapter 3, "Referring to Ranges," cracks the code on how to work efficiently with ranges and cells.

Chapter 4, "Looping and Flow Control," covers the power of looping using VBA. The case study in this chapter demonstrates creating a program to produce a department report and then wrapping that report routine in a loop to produce 46 reports.

Chapter 5, "R1C1-Style Formulas," covers, obviously, R1C1-style formulas. Chapter 6, "Creating and Manipulate Names in VBA," covers names. Chapter 7, "Event Programming," includes some great tricks that use event programming. Chapters 8, "Arrays,"

INTRODUCTION

and 9, "Creating Classes and Collections," cover arrays, classes, and collections. Chapter 10, "Userforms: An Introduction," introduces custom dialog boxes that you can use to collect information from a human using Excel.

Excel VBA Power

Chapters 11, "Data Mining with Advanced Filter," and 12, "Using VBA to Create Pivot Tables," provide an in-depth look at Filter, Advanced Filter, and pivot tables. Report automation tools rely heavily on these concepts. Chapters 13, "Excel Power," and 14, "Sample User-Defined Functions," include dozens of code samples designed to exhibit the power of Excel VBA and custom functions.

Chapters 15, "Creating Charts," through 20, "Automating Word," handle charting, data visualizations, web queries, sparklines, and automating Word.

Techie Stuff Needed to Produce Applications

Chapter 21, "Using Access as a Back End to Enhance Multiuser Access to Data," handles reading and writing to Access databases and SQL Server. The techniques for using Access databases enable you to build an application with the multiuser features of Access while keeping the friendly front end of Excel.

Chapter 22, "Advanced Userform Techniques," shows you how to go further with userforms. Chapter 23, "The Windows Application Programming Interface (API)," teaches some tricky ways to achieve tasks using the Windows API. Chapters 24, "Handling Errors," through 26, "Creating Add-ins," deal with error handling, custom menus, and add-ins. Chapter 27, "An Introduction to Creating Office Add-Ins," provides a brief introduction to building your own JavaScript application within Excel. Chapter 28, "What's New in Excel 2016 and What's Changed," summarizes the changes in Excel 2016.

Does This Book Teach Excel?

Microsoft believes that the ordinary Office user touches only 10% of the features in Office. We realize that everyone reading this book is above average, and MrExcel.com has a pretty smart audience. Even so, a poll of 8,000 MrExcel.com readers showed that only 42% of smarter-than-average users are using any 1 of the top 10 power features in Excel.

I regularly present a Power Excel seminar for accountants. These are hard-core Excelers who use Excel 30 to 40 hours every week. Even so, two things come out in every seminar. First, half of the audience gasps when they see how quickly you can do tasks with a particular feature, such as automatic subtotals or pivot tables. Second, someone in the audience routinely trumps me. For example, someone asks a question, I answer, and someone in the second row raises a hand to give a better answer.

The point? You and I both know a lot about Excel. However, I assume that in any given chapter, maybe 58% of the people have not used pivot tables before and maybe even fewer have used the Top 10 Filter feature of pivot tables. With this in mind, before I show how to automate something in VBA, I briefly cover how to do the same task in the Excel interface. This book does not teach you how to make pivot tables, but it does alert you when you might need to explore a topic and learn more about it elsewhere.

CASE STUDY: MONTHLY ACCOUNTING REPORTS

This is a true story. Valerie is a business analyst in the accounting department of a medium-size corporation. Her company recently installed an overbudget $16 million enterprise resource planning (ERP) system. As the project ground to a close, there were no resources left in the IT budget to produce the monthly report that this corporation used to summarize each department.

However, Valerie had been close enough to the implementation to think of a way to produce the report herself. She understood that she could export general ledger data from the ERP system to a text file with comma-separated values. Using Excel, Valerie was able to import the general ledger data from the ERP system into Excel.

Creating the report was not easy. As in many other companies, there were exceptions in the data. Valerie knew that certain accounts in one particular cost center needed to be reclassed as expenses. She knew that other accounts needed to be excluded from the report entirely. Working carefully in Excel, Valerie made these adjustments. She created one pivot table to produce the first summary section of the report. She cut the pivot table results and pasted them into a blank worksheet. Then she created a new pivot table report for the second section of the summary. After about three hours, she had imported the data, produced five pivot tables, arranged them in a summary, and neatly formatted the report in color.

Becoming the Hero

Valerie handed the report to her manager. The manager had just heard from the IT department that it would be months before they could get around to producing "that convoluted report." When Valerie created the Excel report, she became the instant hero of the day. In three hours, Valerie had managed to do the impossible. Valerie was on cloud nine after a well-deserved "atta-girl."

More Cheers

The next day, Valerie's manager attended the monthly department meeting. When the department managers started complaining that they could not get the report from the ERP system, this manager pulled out his department's report and placed it on the table. The other managers were amazed. How was he able to produce this report? Everyone was relieved to hear that someone had cracked the code. The company president asked Valerie's manager if he could have the report produced for each department.

Cheers Turn to Dread

You can probably see what's coming. This particular company had 46 departments. That means 46 one-page summaries had to be produced once a month. Each report required importing data from the ERP system, backing out certain accounts, producing five pivot tables, and then formatting the reports in color. It had taken Valerie three hours to produce the first report, but after she got into the swing of things, she could produce the 46 reports in 40 hours. Even after she reduced her time per report, though, this is horrible. Valerie had a job to do before she became responsible for spending 40 hours a month producing these reports in Excel.

VBA to the Rescue

Valerie found my company, MrExcel Consulting, and explained her situation. In the course of about a week, I was able to produce a series of macros in Visual Basic that did all the mundane tasks. For example, the macros imported the data, backed out certain accounts, made five pivot tables, and applied the color formatting. From start to finish, the entire 40-hour manual process was reduced to two button clicks and about 4 minutes.

Right now, either you or someone in your company is probably stuck doing manual tasks in Excel that can be automated with VBA. I am confident that I can walk into any company that has 20 or more Excel users and find a case just as amazing as Valerie's.

The Future of VBA and Windows Versions of Excel

Several years ago, there were many rumblings that Microsoft might stop supporting VBA. There is now plenty of evidence to indicate that VBA will be around in Windows versions of Excel through 2036. When VBA was removed from the Mac version of Excel 2008, a huge outcry from customers led to its being included in the next Mac version of Excel.

XLM macros were replaced by VBA in 1993, and 23 years later, they are still supported. Microsoft is making strides toward providing a JavaScript alternative to VBA, but it appears that Excel will support VBA for about another 23 years.

Versions of Excel

This fifth edition of *VBA and Macros* is designed to work with Excel 2016. The previous editions of this book covered code for Excel 97 through Excel 2013. In 80% of the chapters, the code for Excel 2016 is identical to the code in previous versions. However, there are exceptions. For example, the new AutoGroup functionality in pivot tables adds new options that were not available in Excel 2013.

Differences for Mac Users

Although Excel for Windows and Excel for the Mac are similar in terms of user interface, there are a number of differences when you compare the VBA environment. Certainly, nothing in Chapter 23 that uses the Windows API will work on the Mac. That said, the overall concepts discussed in this book apply to the Mac. You can find a general list of differences as they apply to the Mac at http://www.mrexcel.com/macvba.html. Development in VBA for Mac Excel 2016 is far more difficult than in Windows, with only rudimentary VBA editing tools. Microsoft actually recommends that you write all of your VBA in Excel 2016 for Windows and then use that VBA on the Mac.

Special Elements and Typographical Conventions

The following typographical conventions are used in this book:

- *Italic*—Indicates new terms when they are defined, special emphasis, non-English words or phrases, and letters or words used as words.
- `Monospace`—Indicates parts of VBA code, such as object or method names.
- **`Bold monospace`**—Indicates user input.

In addition to these typographical conventions, there are several special elements. Each chapter has at least one case study that presents a real-world solution to common problems. The case study also demonstrates practical applications of topics discussed in the chapter.

In addition to the case studies, you will see Notes, Tips, and Cautions.

> **NOTE**
> Notes provide additional information outside the main thread of the chapter discussion that might be useful for you to know.

> **TIP**
> Tips provide quick workarounds and time-saving techniques to help you work more efficiently.

> **CAUTION**
> Cautions warn about potential pitfalls you might encounter. Pay attention to the Cautions; they alert you to problems that might otherwise cause you hours of frustration.

Code Files

As a thank-you for buying this book, we have put together a set of 50 Excel workbooks that demonstrate the concepts included in this book. This set of files includes all the code from the book, sample data, additional notes from the authors, and 25 bonus macros. To download the code files, visit this book's web page at http://www.quepublishing.com or http://www.mrexcel.com/getcode2016.html.

Next Steps

Chapter 1 introduces the editing tools of the Visual Basic environment and shows why using the macro recorder is not an effective way to write VBA macro code.

Unleashing the Power of Excel with VBA

1

The Power of Excel

Visual Basic for Applications (VBA) combined with Microsoft Excel is probably the most powerful tool available to you. VBA is sitting on the desktops of 750 million users of Microsoft Office, and most have never figured out how to harness the power of VBA in Excel. Using VBA, you can speed the production of any task in Excel. If you regularly use Excel to produce a series of monthly charts, for example, you can have VBA do that task for you in a matter of seconds.

Barriers to Entry

There are two barriers to learning successful VBA programming. First, Excel's macro recorder is flawed and does not produce workable code for you to use as a model. Second, for many who learned a programming language such as BASIC, the syntax of VBA is horribly frustrating.

The Macro Recorder Doesn't Work!

Microsoft began to dominate the spreadsheet market in the mid-1990s. Although it was wildly successful in building a powerful spreadsheet program to which any Lotus 1-2-3 user could easily transition, the macro language was just too different. Anyone proficient in recording Lotus 1-2-3 macros who tried recording a few macros in Excel most likely failed. Although the Microsoft VBA programming language is much more powerful than the Lotus 1-2-3 macro language, the fundamental flaw is that the macro recorder does not work when you use the default settings.

With Lotus 1-2-3, you could record a macro today and play it back tomorrow, and it would faithfully work. When you attempt the same feat in Microsoft Excel, the macro might work today but not tomorrow. In 1995, when I tried to record my first Excel macro, I was horribly frustrated by this. In this book, I teach you the three rules for getting the most out of the macro recorder.

No One on the Excel Team Is Focused on the Macro Recorder

As Microsoft adds new features to Excel, the individual project manager for a feature makes sure that the macro recorder will record something when you execute the command. In the past decade, the recorded code might work in some situations, but it often does not work in all situations. If Microsoft had someone who was focused on creating a useful macro recorder, the recorded code could often be a lot more general than it currently is.

I once asked the project managers if they had a mission statement for the macro recorder. I asked them, "Are you trying to record code that will actually work or just trying to reveal the objects and methods so the person recording the code has to do more research to figure out how to use the commands?" The responses made me believe that no one at Microsoft actually cares about the macro recorder.

It used to be that you could record a command in any of five ways and the recorded code would work. Unfortunately, today, if you want to use the macro recorder, you often have to try recording the macro several different ways, until you find a set of steps that records code that reliably works.

Visual Basic Is Not Like BASIC

Two decades ago, the code generated by the macro recorder was unlike anything I had ever seen. It said this was "Visual Basic" (VB). I have had the pleasure of learning half a dozen programming languages at various times; this bizarre-looking language was horribly unintuitive and did not resemble the BASIC language I had learned in high school.

To make matters worse, even in 1995 I was the spreadsheet wizard in my office. My company had forced everyone to convert from Lotus 1-2-3 to Excel, which meant I was faced with a macro recorder that didn't work and a language that I couldn't understand. This was not a good combination of events.

My assumption in writing this book is that you are pretty talented with a spreadsheet. You probably know more than 90% of the people in your office. I also assume that even though you are not a programmer, you might have taken a class in BASIC at some point. However, knowing BASIC is not a requirement—it actually is a barrier to entry into the ranks of being a successful VBA programmer. There is a good chance that you have recorded a macro in Excel, and there's a similar chance that you were not happy with the results.

Good News: Climbing the Learning Curve Is Easy

Even if you've been frustrated with the macro recorder, it is really just a small speed bump on your road to writing powerful programs in Excel. This book teaches you not only why the macro recorder fails but also how to change the recorded code into something useful. For all the former BASIC programmers in the audience, I decode VBA so that you can easily pick through recorded macro code and understand what is happening.

Great News: Excel with VBA Is Worth the Effort

Although you probably have been frustrated with Microsoft over the inability to record macros in Excel, the great news is that Excel VBA is powerful. Absolutely anything you can do in the Excel interface can be duplicated with stunning speed in Excel VBA. If you find yourself routinely creating the same reports manually day after day or week after week, Excel VBA will greatly streamline those tasks.

The authors of this book work for MrExcel Consulting. In this role, we have automated reports for hundreds of clients. The stories are often similar: The IT department has a several-month backlog of requests. Someone in accounting or engineering discovers that he or she can import some data into Excel and get the reports necessary to run the business. This is a liberating event: You no longer need to wait months for the IT department to write a program. However, the problem is that after you import the data into Excel and win accolades from your manager for producing the report, you will likely be asked to produce the same report every month or every week. This becomes very tedious.

Again, the great news is that with a few hours of VBA programming, you can automate the reporting process and turn it into a few button clicks. The reward is great. So hang with me as we cover a few of the basics.

This chapter exposes why the macro recorder does not work. It also walks through an example of recorded code and demonstrates why it works today but will fail tomorrow. I realize that the code you see in this chapter might not be familiar to you, but that's okay. The point of this chapter is to demonstrate the fundamental problem with the macro recorder. You'll also learn the fundamentals of the Visual Basic environment.

Knowing Your Tools: The Developer Tab

Let's start with a basic overview of the tools needed to use VBA. By default, Microsoft hides the VBA tools. You need to complete the following steps to change a setting to access the Developer tab:

1. Right-click the ribbon and choose Customize the Ribbon.
2. In the right list box, select the Developer check box, which is the eighth item.
3. Click OK to return to Excel.

Excel displays the Developer tab, as shown in Figure 1.1.

Figure 1.1
The Developer tab provides an interface for running and recording macros.

The Code group on the Developer tab contains the icons used for recording and playing back VBA macros, as listed here:

- **Visual Basic**—Opens the Visual Basic Editor.
- **Macros**—Displays the Macro dialog, where you can choose to run or edit a macro from the list of macros.
- **Record Macro**—Begins the process of recording a macro.
- **Use Relative References**—Toggles between using relative or absolute recording. With relative recording, Excel records that you move down three cells. With absolute recording, Excel records that you selected cell A4.
- **Macro Security**—Accesses the Trust Center, where you can choose to allow or disallow macros to run on this computer.

The Add-ins group provides icons for managing regular add-ins and COM add-ins.

The Controls group of the Developer tab contains an Insert menu where you can access a variety of programming controls that can be placed on the worksheet. See "Assigning a Macro to a Form Control, Text Box, or Shape," later in this chapter. Other icons in this group enable you to work with the on-sheet controls. The Run Dialog button enables you to display a custom dialog box or userform that you designed in VBA. For more on userforms, see Chapter 10, "Userforms: An Introduction."

The XML group of the Developer tab contains tools for importing and exporting XML documents.

The Modify group enables you to specify whether the Document Panel is always displayed for new documents. Users can enter keywords and a document description in the Document Panel. If you have SharePoint and InfoPath, you can define custom fields to appear in the Document Panel.

Understanding Which File Types Allow Macros

Excel 2016 offers support for four file types. Macros are not allowed to be stored in the .xlsx file type, and this file type is the default file type! You have to use the Save As setting for all of your macro workbooks, or you can change the default file type used by Excel 2016.

The available files types are as listed here:

- **Excel Workbook (.xlsx)**—Files are stored as a series of XML objects and then zipped into a single file. This creates significantly smaller file sizes. It also allows other applications (even Notepad!) to edit or create Excel workbooks. Unfortunately, macros cannot be stored in files with an .xlsx extension.

- **Excel Macro-Enabled Workbook (.xlsm)**—This is similar to the default .xlsx format, except macros are allowed. The basic concept is that if someone has an .xlsx file, he will not need to worry about malicious macros. However, if he sees an .xlsm file, he should be concerned that there might be macros attached.

- **Excel Binary Workbook (.xlsb)**—This is a binary format designed to handle the larger 1-million-row grid size introduced in Excel 2007. Legacy versions of Excel stored their files in a proprietary binary format. Although binary formats might load more quickly, they are more prone to corruption, and a few lost bits can destroy a whole file. Macros are allowed in this format.

- **Excel 97-2003 Workbook (.xls)**—This format produces files that can be read by anyone using legacy versions of Excel. Macros are allowed in this binary format; however, when you save in this format, you lose access to any cells outside A1:IV65536. In addition, if someone opens the file in Excel 2003, she loses access to anything that used features introduced in Excel 2007 or later.

To avoid having to choose a macro-enabled workbook in the Save As dialog, you can customize your copy of Excel to always save new files in the .xlsm format by following these steps:

1. Click the File menu and select Options.
2. In the Excel Options dialog, select the Save category from the left navigation pane.
3. Open the Save Files in This Format drop-down and select Excel Macro-Enabled Workbook (*.xlsm). Click OK.

> **NOTE**
>
> Although you and I are not afraid to use macros, I have encountered people who freak out when they see the .xlsm file type. They actually seem angry that I sent them an .xlsm file that did not have any macros. Their reaction seemed reminiscent of King Arthur's "You got me all worked up!" line in *Monty Python and the Holy Grail*. Google's Gmail has joined this camp, refusing to show a preview of any attachments sent in the .xlsm format.
>
> If you encounter someone who seems to have a fear of the .xlsm file type, remind them of these points:
>
> - Every workbook created in the past 30 years could have had macros, but in fact, most did not.
>
> - If someone is trying to avoid macros, she should use the security settings to prevent macros from running anyway. The person can still open the .xlsm file to get the data in the spreadsheet.
>
> With these arguments, I hope you can overcome any fears of the .xlsm file type so that it can be your default file type.

Macro Security

After a Word VBA macro was used as the delivery method for the Melissa virus, Microsoft changed the default security settings to prevent macros from running. Therefore, before we can begin discussing the recording of a macro, it's important to look at how to adjust the default settings.

In Excel 2016, you can either globally adjust the security settings or control macro settings for certain workbooks by saving the workbooks in a trusted location. Any workbook stored in a folder that is marked as a trusted location automatically has its macros enabled.

You can find the macro security settings under the Macro Security icon on the Developer tab. When you click this icon, the Macro Settings category of the Trust Center is displayed. You can use the left navigation bar in the dialog to access the Trusted Locations list.

Adding a Trusted Location

You can choose to store your macro workbooks in a folder that is marked as a trusted location. Any workbook stored in a trusted folder will have its macros enabled. Microsoft suggests that a trusted location should be on your hard drive. The default setting is that you cannot trust a location on a network drive.

To specify a trusted location, follow these steps:

1. Click Macro Security in the Developer tab.
2. Click Trusted Locations in the left navigation pane of the Trust Center.
3. If you want to trust a location on a network drive, select Allow Trusted Locations on My Network.
4. Click the Add New Location button. Excel displays the Microsoft Office Trusted Location dialog (see Figure 1.2).
5. Click the Browse button. Excel displays the Browse dialog.
6. Browse to the parent folder of the folder you want to be a trusted location. Click the trusted folder. Although the folder name does not appear in the Folder Name box, click OK. The correct folder name will appear in the Browse dialog.
7. If you want to trust subfolders of the selected folder, select Subfolders of This Location Are Also Trusted.
8. Click OK to add the folder to the Trusted Locations list.

> **CAUTION**
>
> Use care when selecting a trusted location. When you double-click an Excel attachment in an email message, Outlook stores the file in a temporary folder on your C: drive. You will not want to globally add C:\ and all subfolders to the Trusted Locations list.

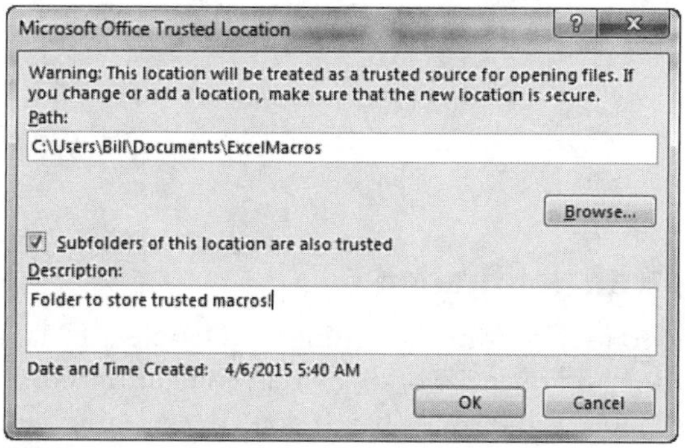

Figure 1.2
Manage trusted folders in the Trusted Locations category of the Trust Center.

Using Macro Settings to Enable Macros in Workbooks Outside Trusted Locations

For all macros not stored in a trusted location, Excel relies on the macro settings. The Low, Medium, High, and Very High settings that were familiar in Excel 2003 have been renamed.

To access the macro settings, click Macro Security in the Developer tab. Excel displays the Macro Settings category of the Trust Center dialog. Select the second option, Disable All Macros with Notification. A description of each option follows:

- **Disable All Macros Without Notification**—This setting prevents all macros from running. This setting is for people who never intend to run macros. Because you are currently holding a book that teaches you how to use macros, it is assumed that this setting is not for you. This setting is roughly equivalent to the old Very High security setting in Excel 2003. With this setting, only macros in the Trusted Locations folders can run.

- **Disable All Macros with Notification**—The operative words in this setting are "with Notification." This means that you see a notification when you open a file with macros and you can choose to enable the content. If you ignore the notification, the macros remain disabled. This setting is similar to Medium security setting in Excel 2003 and is the recommended setting. In Excel 2016, a message is displayed in the Message Area indicating that macros have been disabled. You can choose to enable the content by clicking that option, as shown in Figure 1.3.

- **Disable All Macros Except Digitally Signed Macros**—This setting requires you to obtain a digital signing tool from VeriSign or another provider. This might be appropriate if you are going to be selling add-ins to others, but it's a bit of a hassle if you just want to write macros for your own use.

- **Enable All Macros (Not Recommended: Potentially Dangerous Code Can Run)**—This setting is similar to the Low macro security setting in Excel 2003. Although it requires the least amount of hassle, it also opens your computer to attacks from malicious Melissa-like viruses. Microsoft suggests that you not use this setting.

Figure 1.3
The Enable Content option appears when you use Disable All Macros with Notification.

> ⚠ SECURITY WARNING   Macros have been disabled.   [Enable Content]

Using Disable All Macros with Notification

It is recommended that you set your macro settings to Disable All Macros with Notification. If you use this setting and open a workbook that contains macros, you see a security warning in the area just above the formula bar. If you are expecting macros in this workbook, click Enable Content. If you do not want to enable macros for the current workbook, dismiss the security warning by clicking the *X* at the far right of the message bar.

If you forget to enable the macros and attempt to run a macro, Excel indicates that you cannot run the macro because all macros have been disabled. If this occurs, close the workbook and reopen it to access the message bar again.

> **CAUTION**
>
> After you enable macros in a workbook stored on a local hard drive and then save the workbook, Excel remembers that you previously enabled macros in this workbook. The next time you open this workbook, macros are automatically enabled.

Overview of Recording, Storing, and Running a Macro

Recording a macro is useful when you do not have experience writing lines of code in a macro. As you gain more knowledge and experience, you will record macros less frequently.

To begin recording a macro, select Record Macro from the Developer tab. Before recording begins, Excel displays the Record Macro dialog box, as shown in Figure 1.4.

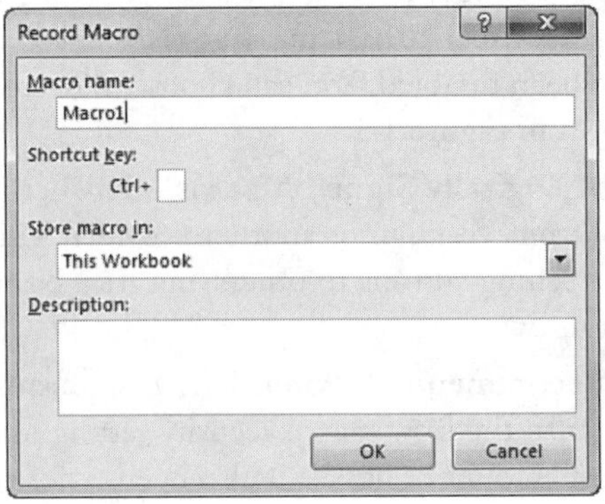

Figure 1.4
Use the Record Macro dialog box to assign a name and a shortcut key to the macro being recorded.

Record Macro

Macro name:
Macro1

Shortcut key:
Ctrl+

Store macro in:
This Workbook

Description:

[OK]   [Cancel]

Filling Out the Record Macro Dialog

In the Macro Name field, type a name for the macro. Be sure to type continuous characters. For example, type **Macro1** without a space, not **Macro 1** with a space. Assuming that you will soon be creating many macros, use a meaningful name for the macro. A name such as FormatReport is more useful than one like Macro1.

The second field in the Record Macro dialog box is a shortcut key. If you type a lowercase j in this field and later press Ctrl+J, this macro runs. Be careful, however, because Ctrl+A through Ctrl+Z (except Ctrl+J) are all already assigned to other tasks in Excel. If you assign a macro to Ctrl+B, you won't be able to use Ctrl+B for bold anymore. One alternative is to assign the macros to Ctrl+Shift+A through Ctrl+Shift+Z. To assign a macro to Ctrl+Shift+A, you type Shift+A in the shortcut key box.

> **CAUTION**
>
> You can reuse a shortcut key for a macro. For example, if you assign a macro to Ctrl+C, Excel runs your macro instead of doing the normal action of copy.

In the Record Macro dialog box, choose where you want to save a macro when it is recorded: Personal Macro Workbook, New Workbook, or This Workbook. It is recommended that you store macros related to a particular workbook in This Workbook.

The Personal Macro Workbook (Personal.xlsm) is not a visible workbook; it is created if you choose to save the recording in the Personal Macro Workbook. This workbook is used to save a macro in a workbook that opens automatically when you start Excel, thereby enabling you to use the macro. After Excel is started, the workbook is hidden. If you want to display it, select Unhide from the View tab.

> **TIP**
>
> It is not recommended that you use the personal workbook for every macro you save. Save only those macros that assist you in general tasks—not in tasks that are performed in a specific sheet or workbook.

The fourth box in the Record Macro dialog is for a description. This description is added as a comment to the beginning of your macro.

After you select the location where you want to store the macro, click OK. Record your macro. For this example, type Hello World in the active cell and press Ctrl+Enter to accept the entry and stay in the same cell. When you are finished recording the macro, click the Stop Recording icon in the Developer tab.

> **TIP**
>
> You can also access a Stop Recording icon in the lower-left corner of the Excel window. Look for a small white square to the right of the word *Ready* in the status bar. Using this Stop button might be more convenient than returning to the Developer tab. After you record your first macro, this area usually has a Record Macro icon, which is a small dot on an Excel worksheet.

Running a Macro

If you assigned a shortcut key to your macro, you can play it by pressing the key combination. You can also assign macros to a button on the ribbon or the Quick Access Toolbar, form controls, or drawing objects, or you can run them from the Visual Basic toolbar.

Creating a Macro Button on the Ribbon

You can add an icon to a new group on the ribbon to run your macro. This is appropriate for macros stored in the Personal Macro Workbook. Icons added to the ribbon are still enabled even when your macro workbook is not open. If you click the icon when the macro workbook is not open, Excel opens the workbook and runs the macro. Follow these steps to add a macro button to the ribbon:

1. Right-click the ribbon and choose Customize the Ribbon.

2. In the list box on the right, choose the tab name where you want to add an icon.

3. Click the New Group button below the right list box. Excel adds a new entry called New Group (Custom) to the end of the groups in that ribbon tab.

4. To move the group to the left in the ribbon tab, click the up arrow icon on the right side of the dialog several times.

5. To rename the group, click the Rename button. Type a new name, such as **Report Macros**. Click OK. Excel shows the group in the list box as Report Macros (Custom). Note that the word *Custom* does not appear in the ribbon.

6. Open the upper-left drop-down and choose Macros from the list. The Macros category is fourth in the list. Excel displays a list of available macros in the left list box.

7. Choose a macro from the left list box. Click the Add button in the center of the dialog. Excel moves the macro to the right list box in the selected group. Excel uses a generic VBA icon for all macros.

8. Click the macro in the right list box. Click the Rename button at the bottom of the right list box. Excel displays a list of 180 possible icons. Choose an icon. Alternatively, type a friendly label for the icon, such as Format Report.

9. You can move the Report Macros group to a new location on the ribbon tab. Click Report Macros (Custom) and use the up and down arrow icons on the right of the dialog.

10. Click OK to close the Excel Options dialog. The new button appears on the selected ribbon tab.

Creating a Macro Button on the Quick Access Toolbar

You can add an icon to the Quick Access Toolbar to run a macro. If a macro is stored in the Personal Macro Workbook, you can have the button permanently displayed in the Quick Access Toolbar. If the macro is stored in the current workbook, you can specify that the icon should appear only when the workbook is open. Follow these steps to add a macro button to the Quick Access Toolbar:

1. Right-click the Quick Access Toolbar and choose Customize Quick Access Toolbar.

2. If your macro should be available only when the current workbook is open, open the upper-right drop-down and change For All Documents (Default) to For *FileName.xlsm*. Any icons associated with the current workbook are displayed at the end of the Quick Access Toolbar.

3. Open the upper-left drop-down and select Macros from the list. The Macros category is fourth in the list. Excel displays a list of available macros in the left list box.

4. Choose a macro from the left list box. Click the Add button in the center of the dialog. Excel moves the macro to the right list box. Excel uses a generic VBA icon for all macros.

5. Click the macro in the right list box. Click the Modify button at the bottom of the right list box. Excel displays a list of 180 possible icons (see Figure 1.5). Choose an icon from the list. In the Display Name box, replace the macro name with a short name that appears in the tooltip for the icon.

6. Click OK to close the Modify Button dialog.

7. Click OK to close the Excel Options dialog. The new button appears on the Quick Access Toolbar.

Figure 1.5
Attach a macro to a button on the Quick Access Toolbar.

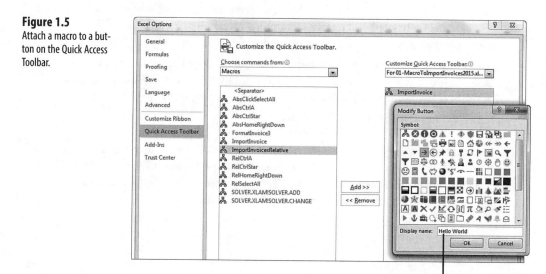

Enter the ToolTip here

Assigning a Macro to a Form Control, Text Box, or Shape

If you want to create a macro specific to a workbook, you can store the macro in the workbook and attach it to a form control or any object on the sheet.

Follow these steps to attach a macro to a form control on the sheet:

1. On the Developer tab, click the Insert button to open its drop-down list. Excel offers 12 form controls and 12 ActiveX controls in this one drop-down menu. The form controls are at the top, and the ActiveX controls are at the bottom. Most icons in the ActiveX section of the drop-down look identical to an icon in the form controls section of the drop-down. Click the Button Form Control icon at the upper-left corner of the Insert drop-down.

2. Move your cursor over the worksheet; the cursor changes to a plus sign.

3. Draw a button on the sheet by clicking and holding the left mouse button while drawing a box shape. Release the button when you have finished.

4. Choose a macro from the Assign Macro dialog box and click OK. The button is created with generic text such as Button 1.

5. Type a new label for the button. Note that while you are typing, the selection border around the button changes from dots to diagonal lines to indicate that you are in Text Edit mode. You cannot change the button color while in Text Edit mode. To exit Text Edit mode, either click the diagonal lines to change them to dots or Ctrl+click the button again. Note that if you accidentally click away from the button, you should Ctrl+click the button to select it. Then drag the cursor over the text on the button to select the text.

6. Right-click the dots surrounding the button and select Format Control. Excel displays the Format Control dialog, which has seven tabs across the top. If your Format Control dialog has only a Font tab, you failed to exit Text Edit mode. If this occurred, close the dialog, Ctrl+click the button, and repeat this step.

7. Use the settings in the Format Control dialog to change the font size, font color, margins, and similar settings for the control. Click OK to close the Format Control dialog when you have finished. Click a cell to deselect the button.

8. Click the new button to run the macro.

Macros can be assigned to any worksheet object, such as clip art, a shape, SmartArt graphics, or a text box. In Figure 1.6, the top button is a traditional button form control. The other images are clip art, a shape with WordArt, and a SmartArt graphic. To assign a macro to any object, right-click the object and select Assign Macro.

Figure 1.6

Assigning a macro to a form control or an object is appropriate for macros stored in the same workbook as the control. You can assign a macro to any of these objects.

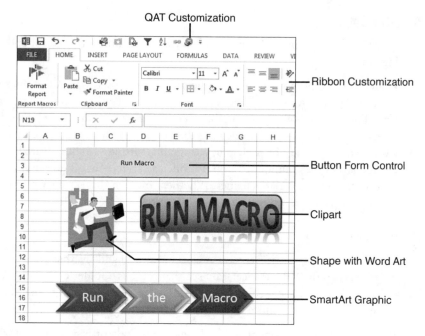

QAT Customization

Ribbon Customization

Button Form Control

Clipart

Shape with Word Art

SmartArt Graphic

Understanding the VB Editor

If you want to edit a recorded macro, you do it in the VB Editor. Press Alt+F11 or use the Visual Basic icon in the Developer tab.

Figure 1.7 shows an example of a typical VB Editor screen. You can see three windows: the Project Explorer, the Properties window, and the Programming window. Don't worry if your window doesn't look exactly like this because you will see how to display the windows you need in this review of the editor.

Figure 1.7

The VB Editor window.

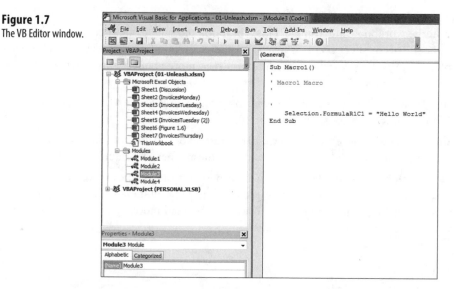

VB Editor Settings

Several settings in the VB Editor enable you to customize this editor and assist you in writing your macros.

Under Tools, Options, Editor, you find several useful settings. All settings except for one are set correctly by default. The remaining setting requires some consideration on your part. This setting is Require Variable Declaration. By default, Excel does not require you to declare variables. I prefer selecting this setting because it can save time when you create a program. My coauthor prefers to change this setting to require variable declaration. This change forces the compiler to stop if it finds a variable that it does not recognize, which reduces misspelled variable names. Whether you turn this setting on or keep it off is a matter of your personal preference.

The Project Explorer

The Project Explorer lists any open workbooks and add-ins that are loaded. If you click the + icon next to the VBA Project, you see that there is a folder containing Microsoft Excel objects. There can also be folders for forms, class modules, and standard modules. Each folder includes one or more individual components.

Right-clicking a component and selecting View Code or just double-clicking the components brings up any code in the Programming window. The exception is userforms, where double-clicking displays the userform in Design view.

To display the Project Explorer window, select View, Project Explorer from the menu or press Ctrl+R or locate the bizarre Project Explorer icon just below the Tools menu, sandwiched between Design Mode and Properties Window.

To insert a module, right-click your project, select Insert, and then choose the type of module you want. The available modules are as follows:

- **Microsoft Excel objects**—By default, a project consists of sheet modules for each sheet in the workbook and a single ThisWorkbook module. Code specific to a sheet such as controls or sheet events is placed on the corresponding sheet. Workbook events are placed in the ThisWorkbook module. You read more about events in Chapter 7, "Event Programming."

- **Forms**—Excel enables you to design your own forms to interact with the user. You'll read more about these forms in Chapter 10.

- **Modules**—When you record a macro, Excel automatically creates a module in which to place the code. Most of your code resides in these types of modules.

- **Class modules**—Class modules are Excel's way of letting you create your own objects. They also allow pieces of code to be shared among programmers without the programmer's needing to understand how it works. You read more about class modules in Chapter 9, "Creating Classes and Collections."

The Properties Window

The Properties window enables you to edit the properties of various components such as sheets, workbooks, modules, and form controls. The properties list varies according to what component is selected. To display this window, select View, Properties Window from the menu, press F4, or click the Project Properties icon on the toolbar.

Understanding Shortcomings of the Macro Recorder

Suppose you work in an accounting department. Each day you receive a text file from the company system showing all the invoices produced the prior day. This text file has commas separating the fields. The columns in the file are Invoice Date, Invoice Number, Sales Rep Number, Customer Number, Product Revenue, Service Revenue, and Product Cost (see Figure 1.8).

Figure 1.8
The Invoice.txt file.

```
invoice - Notepad
File  Edit  Format  View  Help
InvDate,InvNbr,RepNbr,CustNbr,ProdRevenue,ServRevenue,ProdCost
06/05/2017,123829,S21,C8754,538400,0,299897
06/05/2017,123830,S45,C4056,588600,0,307563
06/05/2017,123831,S54,C8323,882200,0,521726
06/05/2017,123832,S21,C6026,830900,0,494831
06/05/2017,123833,S45,C3025,673600,0,374953
06/05/2017,123834,S54,C8663,966300,0,528575
06/05/2017,123835,S21,C1508,467100,0,257942
06/05/2017,123836,S45,C7366,658500,10000,308719
06/05/2017,123837,S54,C4533,191700,0,109534
```

Each morning, you manually import this file into Excel. You add a total row to the data, bold the headings, and then print the report for distribution to a few managers.

This seems like a simple process that would be ideally suited to using the macro recorder. However, due to some problems with the macro recorder, your first few attempts might not be successful. The following case study explains how to overcome these problems.

CASE STUDY: PREPARING TO RECORD A MACRO

The task mentioned in the preceding section is perfect for a macro. However, before you record a macro, think about the steps you will use. In this case, the steps are as follows:

1. Click the File menu and select Open.

2. Navigate to the folder where Invoice.txt is stored.

3. Select All Files (*.*) from the Files of Type drop-down list.

4. Select Invoice.txt.

5. Click Open.

6. In the Text Import Wizard—Step 1 of 3 dialog, select Delimited from the Original Data Type section.

7. Click Next.

8. In the Text Import Wizard—Step 2 of 3 dialog, clear the Tab key and select Comma in the Delimiters section.

9. Click Next.

10. In the Text Import Wizard—Step 3 of 3 dialog, select General in the Column Data Format section and change it to Date: MDY.

11. Click Finish to import the file.

12. Press the Ctrl key and the down arrow key to move to the last row of data.

13. Press the down arrow one more time to move to the total row.

14. Type the word **Total**.

15. Press the right arrow key four times to move to column E of the total row.

16. Click the AutoSum button and press Ctrl+Enter to add a total to the Product Revenue column while remaining in that cell.

17. Click the AutoFill handle and drag it from column E to column G to copy the total formula to columns F and G.

18. Highlight row 1 and click the Bold icon on the Home tab to set the headings in bold.

19. Highlight the total row and click the Bold icon on the Home tab to set the totals in bold.

20. Press Ctrl+* to select the current region.

21. From the Home tab, select Format, AutoFit Column Width.

After you have rehearsed these steps in your head, you are ready to record your first macro. Open a blank workbook and save it with a name such as MacroToImportInvoices.xlsm. Click the Record Macro button on the Developer tab.

In the Record Macro dialog, the default macro name is Macro1. Change this to something descriptive like ImportInvoice. Make sure that the macros will be stored in This Workbook. You might want an easy way to run this macro later, so enter the letter **i** in the Shortcut Key field. In the Description field, add a little descriptive text to tell what the macro is doing (see Figure 1.9). Click OK when you are ready.

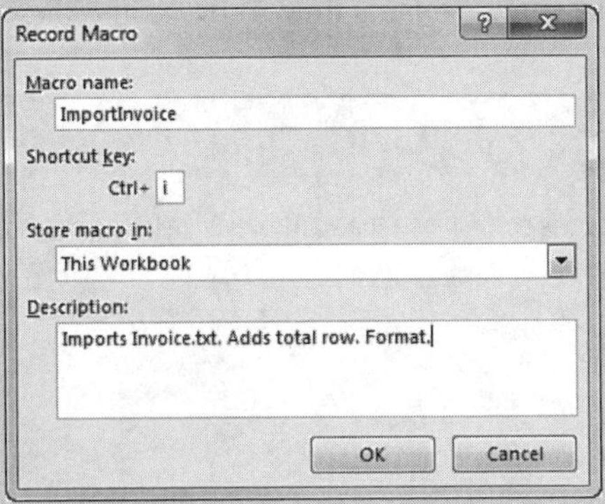

Figure 1.9
Before recording the macro, complete the Record Macro dialog box.

Recording the Macro

The macro recorder is now recording your every move. For this reason, perform your steps in exact order without extraneous actions. If you accidentally move to column F, type a value, clear the value, and then move back to E to enter the first total, the recorded macro will blindly make that same mistake day after day after day. Recorded macros move fast, but there is nothing like watching the macro recorder play out your mistakes repeatedly.

Carefully execute all the actions necessary to produce the report. After you have performed the final step, click the Stop Recording button in the Developer tab of the ribbon.

Examining Code in the Programming Window

Let's look at the code you just recorded from the case study. Don't worry if it doesn't make sense yet.

To open the VB Editor, press Alt+F11. In your VBA project (MacroToImportInvoices.xlsm), find the component Module1, right-click the module, and select View Code. Notice that some lines start with an apostrophe; these are comments and are ignored by the program. The macro recorder starts your macros with a few comments, using the description you entered in the Record Macro dialog. The comment for the keyboard shortcut is there to remind you of the shortcut.

> **NOTE**
> The comment does *not* assign the shortcut. If you change the comment to be Ctrl+J, it does not change the shortcut. You must change the setting in the Macro dialog box in Excel or run this line of code:
>
> ```
> Application.MacroOptions Macro:="ImportInvoice", _
>                Description:="", ShortcutKey:="j"
> ```

Recorded macro code is usually pretty neat (see Figure 1.10). Each noncomment line of code is indented 4 characters. If a line is longer than 100 characters, the recorder breaks it into multiple lines and indents the lines an additional 4 characters. To continue a line of code, type a space and an underscore at the end of the first line and then continue the code on the next line. Don't forget the space before the underscore. Using an underscore without the preceding space causes an error.

> **NOTE**
> The physical limitations of this book do not allow 100 characters on a single line. Therefore, the lines are broken at 80 characters so that they fit on a page. For this reason, your recorded macro might look slightly different from the ones that appear in this book.

Figure 1.10
The recorded macro is neat looking and nicely indented.

```
Sub ImportInvoice()
'
' ImportInvoice Macro
' Import Invoice.txt. Add Total Row. Format.
'
' Keyboard Shortcut: Ctrl+i
'
    Workbooks.OpenText Filename:="G:\2016VBA\SampleFiles\invoice.txt", Origin:= _
        437, StartRow:=1, DataType:=xlDelimited, TextQualifier:=xlDoubleQuote, _
        ConsecutiveDelimiter:=False, Tab:=False, Semicolon:=False, Comma:=True _
        , Space:=False, Other:=False, FieldInfo:=Array(Array(1, 3), Array(2, 1), _
        Array(3, 1), Array(4, 1), Array(5, 1), Array(6, 1), Array(7, 1)), TrailingMinusNumbers _
        :=True
    Selection.End(xlDown).Select
    Range("A11").Select
    ActiveCell.FormulaR1C1 = "Total"
    Range("E11").Select
    Selection.FormulaR1C1 = "=SUM(R[-9]C:R[-1]C)"
    Selection.AutoFill Destination:=Range("E11:G11"), Type:=xlFillDefault
    Range("E11:G11").Select
    Rows("1:1").Select
    Selection.Font.Bold = True
    Rows("11:11").Select
    Selection.Font.Bold = True
    Selection.CurrentRegion.Select
    Selection.Columns.AutoFit
End Sub
```

Consider that the following seven lines of recorded code are actually only one line of code that has been broken into seven lines for readability:

```
Workbooks.OpenText Filename:="C:\somepath\invoice.txt", _
        Origin:=437, StartRow:=1, DataType:=xlDelimited, _
        TextQualifier:=xlDoubleQuote, ConsecutiveDelimiter:=False, _
        Tab:=True, Semicolon:=False, Comma:=True, Space:=False, _
        Other:=False, FieldInfo:=Array(Array(1, 3), Array(2, 1), _
        Array(3, 1), Array(4, 1), Array(5, 1), Array(6, 1), _
        Array(7, 1)), TrailingMinusNumbers:=True
```

Counting this as one line, the macro recorder was able to record the 21-step process in 14 lines of code, which is pretty impressive.

> **NOTE**
> Each action you perform in the Excel user interface might equate to one or more lines of recorded code. Some actions might generate a dozen lines of code.

Test Each Macro

It is always a good idea to test macros. To test your new macro, return to the regular Excel interface by pressing Alt+F11. Close Invoice.txt without saving any changes. MacroToImportInvoices.xls is still open.

Press Ctrl+I to run the recorded macro. It should work beautifully if you completed the steps correctly. The data is imported, totals are added, bold formatting is applied, and the columns are made wider. This seems like a perfect solution (see Figure 1.11).

Figure 1.11
The macro formats the data in the sheet.

	A	B	C	D	E	F	G
1	InvDate	InvNbr	RepNbr	CustNbr	ProdRevenue	ServRevenue	ProdCost
2	6/5/2017	123829	S21	C8754	538400	0	299897
3	6/5/2017	123830	S45	C4056	588600	0	307563
4	6/5/2017	123831	S54	C8323	882200	0	521726
5	6/5/2017	123832	S21	C6026	830900	0	494831
6	6/5/2017	123833	S45	C3025	673600	0	374953
7	6/5/2017	123834	S54	C8663	966300	0	528575
8	6/5/2017	123835	S21	C1508	467100	0	257942
9	6/5/2017	123836	S45	C7366	658500	10000	308719
10	6/5/2017	123837	S54	C4533	191700	0	109534
11	Total				5797300	10000	3203740

Running the Macro on Another Day Produces Undesired Results

After testing the macro, be sure to save your macro file to use on another day. But suppose that the next day, after receiving a new Invoice.txt file from the system, you open the macro and press Ctrl+I to run it, and disaster strikes. The data for June 5 happened to have 9 invoices, but the data for June 6 now has 17 invoices. The recorded macro blindly added the totals in Row 11 because this was where you put the totals when the macro was recorded (see Figure 1.12).

For those of you working along using the sample files in this book, follow these steps to try importing data for another day:

1. Close Invoice.txt in Excel.

2. In Windows Explorer, rename Invoice.txt to be Invoice1.txt.

3. In Windows Explorer, rename Invoice2.txt to be Invoice.txt.

4. Return to Excel and the MacroToImportInvoices.xlsm workbook.

5. Press Ctrl+I to run the macro with the larger data set.

This problem arises because the macro recorder is recording all your actions in Absolute mode by default. As an alternative to using the default state of the macro recorder, the next section discusses relative recording and how it might get you closer to the desired solution.

Figure 1.12
The intent of the recorded macro was to add a total at the end of the data, but the recorder made a macro that always adds totals at row 11.

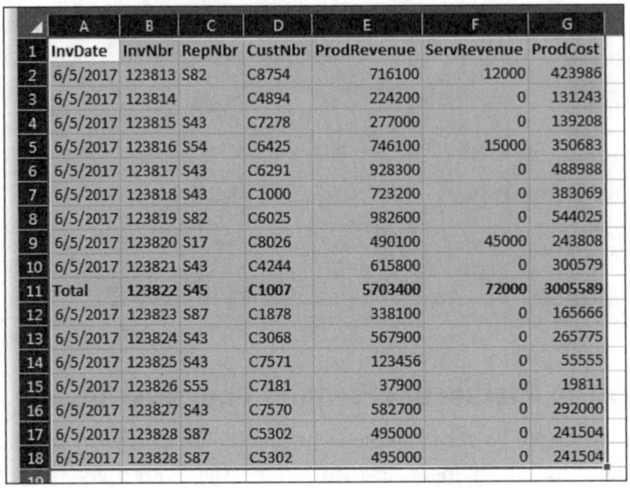

	A	B	C	D	E	F	G
1	InvDate	InvNbr	RepNbr	CustNbr	ProdRevenue	ServRevenue	ProdCost
2	6/5/2017	123813	S82	C8754	716100	12000	423986
3	6/5/2017	123814		C4894	224200	0	131243
4	6/5/2017	123815	S43	C7278	277000	0	139208
5	6/5/2017	123816	S54	C6425	746100	15000	350683
6	6/5/2017	123817	S43	C6291	928300	0	488988
7	6/5/2017	123818	S43	C1000	723200	0	383069
8	6/5/2017	123819	S82	C6025	982600	0	544025
9	6/5/2017	123820	S17	C8026	490100	45000	243808
10	6/5/2017	123821	S43	C4244	615800	0	300579
11	Total	123822	S45	C1007	5703400	72000	3005589
12	6/5/2017	123823	S87	C1878	338100	0	165666
13	6/5/2017	123824	S43	C3068	567900	0	265775
14	6/5/2017	123825	S43	C7571	123456	0	55555
15	6/5/2017	123826	S55	C7181	37900	0	19811
16	6/5/2017	123827	S43	C7570	582700	0	292000
17	6/5/2017	123828	S87	C5302	495000	0	241504
18	6/5/2017	123828	S87	C5302	495000	0	241504

Possible Solution: Use Relative References When Recording

By default, the macro recorder records all actions as *absolute* actions. If you navigate to row 11 when you record the macro, the macro will always go to row 11 when the macro is run. This is rarely appropriate when dealing with variable numbers of rows of data. The better option is to use relative references when recording.

Macros recorded with absolute references note the actual address of the cell pointer, such as A11. Macros recorded with relative references note that the cell pointer should move a certain number of rows and columns from its current position. For example, if the cell pointer starts in cell A1, the code `ActiveCell.Offset(16, 1).Select` would move the cell pointer to B17, which is the cell 16 rows down and 1 column to the right.

Although relative recording is appropriate in most situations, there are times when you need to do something absolute while recording a macro. Here's a great example: After adding the totals to a data set, you need to return to row 1. If you simply click row 1 while in Relative mode, Excel records that you want to select the row 10 rows above the current row. This works with the first invoice file but not with longer or shorter invoice files. Here are two workarounds:

- Toggle relative recording off, click row 1, and then toggle relative recording back on.
- Keep relative recording turned on. Display the Go To dialog by pressing F5. Type **A1** and click OK. The Go To dialog gets recorded as always, going to the absolute address you typed, even if relative recording is turned on. A variation of this method is used in the following case study.

In the next case study, let's try the same task as before, this time using relative references. The solution will be much closer to working correctly.

CASE STUDY: RECORDING A MACRO WITH RELATIVE REFERENCES

Let's try to record the macro again, this time using relative references.

Note: If you are following along with the sample files, complete these steps:

1. Close Invoice.txt in Excel.
2. Rename Invoice.txt as Invoice2.txt.
3. Rename Invoice1.txt as Invoice.txt.
4. Return to the MacroToImportInvoices.xlsm workbook.

In the Developer tab, choose Use Relative References to toggle on relative recording. This setting persists until you turn it off or until you close Excel.

In the workbook MacroToImportInvoices.xlsm, record a new macro by selecting Record Macro from the Developer tab. Give the new macro the name ImportInvoicesRelative and assign a different shortcut key, such as Ctrl+J.

Repeat steps 1 through 11 in the previous case study to import the file and then follow these steps:

1. Press Ctrl+down arrow to move to the last row of data.
2. Press the down arrow key one more time to move to the total row.
3. Type the word **Total**.
4. Press the right arrow key four times to move to column E of the total row.
5. Hold the Shift key while pressing the right arrow key twice to select E11:G11.
6. Click the AutoSum button.
7. Press Shift+spacebar to select the entire row. Type Ctrl+B to apply bold formatting to it.
8. Press F5 to display the Go To dialog.
9. In the Go To dialog, type A1:G1 and click OK. Even though relative recording is turned on, any navigation through the Go To dialog box is recorded as an absolute reference. Press Ctrl+Home to move to cell A1.
10. Click the Bold icon to set the headings in bold.
11. Press Ctrl+* to select all data in the current region.
12. From the Home tab, select Format, AutoFit Column Width.
13. Stop recording.

Press Alt+F11 to go to the VB Editor to review your code. The new macro appears in Module1, below the previous macro.

If you close Excel between recording the first and second macros, Excel inserts a new module called Module2 for the newly recorded macro.

```
Sub ImportInvoicesRelative()
' ImportInvoicesRelative Macro
' Import. Total Row. Format.
' Keyboard Shortcut: Ctrl+J
```

```
Workbooks.OpenText Filename:="C:\data\invoice.txt", _
    Origin:= 437, StartRow:=1, DataType:=xlDelimited, _
    TextQualifier:=xlDoubleQuote, ConsecutiveDelimiter:=False, _
    Tab:=False, Semicolon:=False, Comma:=True, Space:=False, _
    Other:=False, FieldInfo:=Array(Array(1, 3), Array(2, 1), _
    Array(3, 1), Array(4, 1), Array(5, 1), Array(6, 1), _
    Array(7, 1)), TrailingMinusNumbers:=True
Selection.End(xlDown).Select
ActiveCell.Offset(1, 0).Range("A1").Select
ActiveCell.FormulaR1C1 = "Total"
ActiveCell.Offset(0, 4).Range("A1:C1").Select
Selection.FormulaR1C1 = "=SUM(R[-9]C:R[-1]C)"
ActiveCell.Rows("1:1").EntireRow.Select
ActiveCell.Activate
Selection.Font.Bold = True
Application.Goto Reference:="R1C1:R1C7"
Selection.Font.Bold = True
Selection.CurrentRegion.Select
Selection.Columns.AutoFitSelection.Font.Bold = True
End Sub
```

To test the macro, close Invoice.txt without saving and then run the macro with Ctrl+J. Everything should look good, and you should get the same results as with the macro you created with the macro recorder.

The next test is to see whether the program works on the next day when you might have more rows. If you are working along with the sample files, close Invoice.txt in Excel. Rename Invoice.txt to Invoice1.txt. Rename Invoice2.txt to Invoice.txt.

Open MacroToImportInvoices.xls and run the new macro with Ctrl+ J. This time, everything should look good, with the totals in the correct places. Look at Figure 1.13. Do you see anything out of the ordinary?

If you aren't careful, you might print these reports for your manager. If you did, you would be in trouble. When you look in cell E19, you can see that Excel has inserted a green triangle to tell you to look at the cell. If you happened to try this back in Excel 95 or Excel 97, before SmartTags, there would not have been an indicator that anything was wrong.

When you move the cell pointer to E19, an alert indicator pops up near the cell. This indicator tells you that the formula fails to include adjacent cells. If you look in the formula bar, you will see that the macro totaled only from row 10 to row 18. Neither the relative recording nor the nonrelative recording is smart enough to replicate the logic of the AutoSum button.

Imagine that you had fewer invoice records on this particular day. Excel would have rewarded you with the illogical formula =SUM(E6:E1048574), as shown in Figure 1.14. Since this formula would be in E7, circular reference warnings appear in the status bar.

Note: To try this yourself, close Invoice.txt in Excel. Rename Invoice.txt to Invoice2.txt. Rename Invoice4.txt to Invoice.txt.

Figure 1.13
The result of running the Relative macro.

	A	B	C	D	E	F	G
1	InvDate	InvNbr	RepNbr	CustNbr	ProdRevenue	ServRevenue	ProdCost
2	6/5/2017	123813	S82	C8754	716100	12000	423986
3	6/5/2017	123814		C4894	224200	0	131243
4	6/5/2017	123815	S43	C7278	277000	0	139208
5	6/5/2017	123816	S54	C6425	746100	15000	350683
6	6/5/2017	123817	S43	C6291	928300	0	488988
7	6/5/2017	123818	S43	C1000	723200	0	383069
8	6/5/2017	123819	S82	C6025	982600	0	544025
9	6/5/2017	123820	S17	C8026	490100	45000	243808
10	6/5/2017	123821	S43	C4244	615800	0	300579
11	6/5/2017	123822	S45	C1007	271300	0	153253
12	6/5/2017	123823	S87	C1878	338100	0	165666
13	6/5/2017	123824	S43	C3068	567900	0	265775
14	6/5/2017	123825	S43	C7571	123456	0	55555
15	6/5/2017	123826	S55	C7181	37900	0	19811
16	6/5/2017	123827	S43	C7570	582700	0	292000
17	6/5/2017	123828	S87	C5302	495000	0	241504
18	6/5/2017	123828	S87	C5302	495000	0	241504
19	Total				3527156	0	1735647
20							

Figure 1.14
The result of running the Relative macro with fewer invoice records.

	A	B	C	D	E	F	G
1	InvDate	InvNbr	RepNbr	CustNbr	ProdRevenue	ServRevenue	ProdCost
2	6/8/2017	123850		C1654	161000	0	90761
3	6/8/2017	123851		C6460	275500	10000	146341
4	6/8/2017	123852		C5143	925400	0	473515
5	6/8/2017	123853		C7868	148200	0	75700
6	6/8/2017	123854		C3310	890200	0	468333
7	Total				0	0	0

If you have tried using the macro recorder, most likely you have run into problems similar to the ones produced in the previous two case studies. Although this is frustrating, you should be happy to know that the macro recorder actually gets you 95% of the way to a useful macro.

Your job is to recognize where the macro recorder is likely to fail and then be able to dive into the VBA code to fix the one or two lines that require adjusting to have a perfect macro. With some added human intelligence, you can produce awesome macros to speed up your daily work.

If you are like me, you are cursing Microsoft about now. We have wasted a good deal of time over a couple of days, and neither macro works. What makes it worse is that this sort of procedure would have been handled perfectly by the old Lotus 1-2-3 macro recorder introduced in 1983. Mitch Kapor solved this problem 33 years ago, and Microsoft still can't get it right.

Did you know that up through Excel 97, Microsoft Excel secretly ran Lotus command-line macros? I found this out right after Microsoft quit supporting Excel 97. At that time, a number of companies upgraded to Excel XP, which no longer supported the Lotus 1-2-3 macros. Many of these companies hired us to convert the old Lotus 1-2-3 macros to Excel VBA. It is interesting that in Excel 5, Excel 95, and Excel 97, Microsoft offered an interpreter that could handle the Lotus macros that solved this problem correctly, yet its own macro recorder couldn't (and still can't!) solve the problem.

Never Use AutoSum or Quick Analysis While Recording a Macro

There actually is a macro recorder solution to the current problem with recording an Auto-Sum. It is important to recognize that the macro recorder will never correctly record the intent of the AutoSum button.

If you are in cell E99 and click the AutoSum button, Excel starts scanning from cell E98 upward until it locates a text cell, a blank cell, or a formula. It then proposes a formula that sums everything between the current cell and the found cell.

However, the macro recorder records the particular result of that search on the day that the macro was recorded. Rather than record something along the lines of "do the normal Auto-Sum logic," the macro recorder inserts a single line of code to add up the previous 98 cells.

Excel 2013 added the Quick Analysis feature. Select E2:G99; open Quick Analysis icon that appears below and to the right of a rectangular selection; choose Totals, Sum at Bottom; and you get the correct totals in row 100. The macro recorder hard-codes the formulas to always appear in row 100 and to always total row 2 through row 99.

The somewhat bizarre workaround is to type a SUM function that uses a mix of relative and absolute row references. If you type =SUM(E$2:E10) while the macro recorder is running, Excel correctly adds code that always sums from a fixed row two down to the relative reference that is just above the current cell.

Here is the resulting code, with a few comments:

```
Sub FormatInvoice3()
Sub FormatInvoice3()
' FormatInvoice3 Macro
' Import. Total. Format.
' Keyboard Shortcut: Ctrl+K
Workbooks.OpenText Filename:="C:\Data\invoice.txt", _
    Origin:=437, StartRow:=1, DataType:=xlDelimited, _
    TextQualifier:=xlDoubleQuote, ConsecutiveDelimiter:=False, _
    Tab:=False, Semicolon:=False, Comma:=True, Space:=False, _
    Other:=False, FieldInfo:=Array(Array(1, 3), Array(2, 1), _
    Array(3, 1), Array(4, 1), Array(5, 1), Array(6, 1), _
    Array(7, 1)), TrailingMinusNumbers:=True
Selection.End(xlDown).Select
ActiveCell.Offset(1, 0).Range("A1").Select
ActiveCell.FormulaR1C1 = "Total"
ActiveCell.Offset(0, 4).Range("A1").Select
Selection.FormulaR1C1 = "=SUM(R2C:R[-1]C)"
Selection.AutoFill Destination:=ActiveCell.Range("A1:C1"), _
    Type:=xlFillDefault
ActiveCell.Range("A1:C1").Select
ActiveCell.Rows("1:1").EntireRow.Select
ActiveCell.Activate
Selection.Font.Bold = True
Application.Goto Reference:="R1C1:R1C7"
```

```
    Selection.Font.Bold = True
    Selection.CurrentRegion.Select
    Selection.Columns.AutoFit
End Sub
```

This third macro consistently works with a data set of any size.

Four Tips for Using the Macro Recorder

You will rarely be able to record 100% of your macros and have them work. However, you will get much closer by using the four tips listed in the following subsections.

Tip 1: Turn on the Use Relative References Setting

Microsoft should have made this setting the default. Turn the setting on and leave it on while recording your macros.

Tip 2: Use Special Navigation Keys to Move to the Bottom of a Data Set

If you are at the top of a data set and need to move to the last cell that contains data, you can press Ctrl+down arrow or press the End key and then the down arrow key.

Similarly, to move to the last column in the current row of the data set, press Ctrl+right arrow or press End and then press the right arrow key.

By using these navigation keys, you can jump to the end of the data set, no matter how many rows or columns you have today.

Use Ctrl+* to select the current region around the active cell. Provided that you have no blank rows or blank columns in your data, this key combination selects the entire data set.

Tip 3: Never Touch the AutoSum Icon While Recording a Macro

The macro recorder does not record the "essence" of the AutoSum button. Instead, it hard-codes the formula that resulted from pressing the AutoSum button. This formula does not work any time you have more or fewer records in the data set.

Instead, type a formula with a single dollar sign, such as =SUM(E$2:E10). When this is done, the macro recorder records the first E$2 as a fixed reference and starts the SUM range directly below the row 1 headings. Provided that the active cell is E11, the macro recorder recognizes E10 as a relative reference pointing directly above the current cell.

Tip 4: Try Recording Different Methods if One Method Does Not Work

There are often many ways to perform tasks in Excel. If you encounter buggy code from one method, try another method. With 16 different project managers on the Excel team, it is likely that each method was programmed by a different group. In one of the case studies in this chapter, one task involved applying AutoFit Column Width to all cells. Some people might press Ctrl+A to select all cells. Others might press Ctrl+*. Since Excel 2007, the code generated by Ctrl+A when pressed in Relative mode does not work. The Ctrl+* code is very old and continues to work in all cases.

Next Steps

Chapter 2, "This Sounds Like BASIC, So Why Doesn't It Look Familiar?" examines the three macros you recorded in this chapter to make more sense out of them. When you know how to decode the VBA code, it will feel natural to either correct the recorded code or simply write code from scratch. Hang on through one more chapter. You'll soon learn that VBA is the solution, and you'll be writing useful code that works consistently.

This Sounds Like BASIC, So Why Doesn't It Look Familiar?

2

I Can't Understand This Code

As mentioned in Chapter 1, "Unleashing the Power of Excel with VBA," if you have taken a class in a procedural language such as BASIC or COBOL, you might be confused when you look at VBA code. Even though VBA stands for *Visual Basic for Applications*, it is an *object-oriented* version of BASIC. Here is a bit of VBA code:

```
Selection.End(xlDown).Select
Range("A11").Select
ActiveCell.FormulaR1C1 = "Total"
Range("E11").Select
Selection.FormulaR1C1 = _
    "=SUM(R[-9]C:R[-1]C)"
Selection.AutoFill _
    Destination:=Range("E11:G11"), _
    Type:=xlFillDefault
```

This code likely makes no sense to anyone who knows only procedural languages. Unfortunately, your first introduction to programming in school (assuming that you are over 40 years old) would have been a procedural language.

Here is a section of code written in the BASIC language:

```
For x = 1 to 10
    Print Rpt$(" ",x);
    Print "*"
Next x
```

If you run this code, you get a pyramid of asterisks on your screen:

```
*
 *
  *
   *
    *
     *
      *
       *
        *
         *
```

If you have ever been in a procedural programming class, you can probably look at the code and figure out what is going on because procedural languages are more English-like than object-oriented languages. The statement `Print "Hello World"` follows the verb–object format, which is how you would generally talk. Let's step away from programming for a second and look at a concrete example.

Understanding the Parts of VBA "Speech"

If you were going to write code for instructions to play soccer using BASIC, the instruction to kick a ball would look something like this:

```
"Kick the Ball"
```

Hey, this is how you talk! It makes sense. You have a verb (*kick*) and then a noun (*ball*). The BASIC code in the preceding section has a verb (`Print`) and a noun (the asterisk, `*`). Life is good.

Here is the problem: VBA doesn't work like this. In fact, no object-oriented language works like this. In an object-oriented language, the objects (nouns) are most important, hence the name: object-oriented. If you were going to write code for instructions to play soccer with VBA, the basic structure would be as follows:

```
Ball.Kick
```

You have a noun (`Ball`), which comes first. In VBA, this is an *object*. Then you have the verb (`Kick`), which comes next. In VBA, this is a *method*.

The basic structure of VBA is a bunch of lines of code with this syntax:

```
Object.Method
```

Needless to say, this is not English. If you took a romance language in high school, you will remember that those languages use a "noun–adjective" construct. However, no one uses "noun–verb" to tell someone to do something:

```
Water.Drink
Food.Eat
Girl.Kiss
```

That is why VBA is confusing to someone who previously took a procedural programming class.

Let's carry the analogy a bit further. Imagine that you walk onto a grassy field, and there are five balls in front of you. There are a soccer ball, basketball, baseball, bowling ball, and tennis ball. You want to instruct a kid on your soccer team to "kick the soccer ball."

If you tell him to kick the ball (or `ball.kick`), you really aren't sure which one of the five balls he will kick. Maybe he will kick the one closest to him, which could be a problem if he is standing in front of the bowling ball.

For almost any noun, or object in VBA, there is a collection of that object. Think about Excel. If you can have one row, you can have a bunch of rows. If you can have one cell, you can have a bunch of cells. If you can have one worksheet, you can have a bunch of worksheets. The only difference between an object and a collection is that you add an *s* to the name of the object:

`Row` becomes `Rows`.

`Cell` becomes `Cells`.

`Ball` becomes `Balls`.

When you refer to something that is a collection, you have to tell the programming language to which item you are referring. There are a couple of ways to do this. You can refer to an item by using a number. For example, if the soccer ball is the second ball, you might say this:

`Balls(2).Kick`

This works fine, but it could be a dangerous way to program. For example, it might work on Tuesday. However, if you get to the field on Wednesday and someone has rearranged the balls, `Balls(2).Kick` might be a painful exercise.

A much safer way to go is to use a name for the object in a collection. You can say the following:

`Balls("Soccer").Kick`

With this method, you always know that it will be the soccer ball that is being kicked.

So far, so good. You know that a ball will be kicked, and you know that it will be the soccer ball. For most of the verbs, or methods in Excel VBA, there are *parameters* that tell *how* to do the action. These parameters act as adverbs. You might want the soccer ball to be kicked to the left and with a hard force. In this case, the method would have a number of parameters that tell how the program should perform the method:

`Balls("Soccer").Kick Direction:=Left, Force:=Hard`

When you are looking at VBA code, the colon–equal sign combination (`:=`) indicates that you are looking at parameters of how the verb should be performed.

Sometimes, a method will have a list of 10 parameters, some of which are optional. For example, if the `Kick` method has an `Elevation` parameter, you would have this line of code:

`Balls("Soccer").Kick Direction:=Left, Force:=Hard, Elevation:=High`

Here is the confusing part: Every method has a default order for its parameters. If you are not a conscientious programmer, and you happen to know the order of the parameters, you can leave off the parameter names. The following code is equivalent to the previous line of code:

```
Balls("Soccer").Kick Left, Hard, High
```

This throws a monkey wrench into our understanding. Without :=, it is not obvious that you have parameters. Unless you know the parameter order, you might not understand what is being said. It is pretty easy with Left, Hard, and High, but when you have parameters like the following:

```
ActiveSheet.Shapes.AddShape type:=1, Left:=10, Top:=20, _
    Width:=100, Height:=200
```

it gets confusing if you instead have this:

```
ActiveSheet.Shapes.AddShape 1, 10, 20, 100, 200
```

The preceding line is valid code. However, unless you know that the default order of the parameters for this Add method is Type, Left, Top, Width, Height, this code does not make sense. The default order for any particular method is the order of the parameters as shown in the Help topic for that method.

To make life more confusing, you are allowed to start specifying parameters in their default order without naming them, and then you can switch to naming parameters when you hit one that does not match the default order. If you want to kick the ball to the left and high but do not care about the force (that is, you are willing to accept the default force), the following two statements are equivalent:

```
Balls("Soccer").Kick Direction:=Left, Elevation:=High
Balls("Soccer").Kick Left, Elevation:=High
```

However, keep in mind that as soon as you start naming parameters, they have to be named for the remainder of that line of code.

Some methods simply act on their own. To simulate pressing the F9 key, you use this code:

```
Application.Calculate
```

Other methods perform an action and create something. For example, you can add a worksheet by using the following:

```
Worksheets.Add Before:=Worksheets(1)
```

However, because Worksheets.Add creates a new object, you can assign the results of this method to a variable. In this case, you must surround the parameters with parentheses:

```
Set MyWorksheet = Worksheets.Add(Before:=Worksheets(1))
```

One final bit of grammar is necessary: adjectives. Just as adjectives describe a noun, *properties* describe an object. Because you are an Excel fan, let's switch from the soccer analogy to an Excel analogy. There is an object to describe the active cell. Fortunately, it has a very intuitive name:

```
ActiveCell
```

Suppose you want to change the color of the active cell to red. There is a property called `Interior.Color` for a cell that uses a complex series of codes. However, you can turn a cell to red by using this code:

```
ActiveCell.Interior.Color = 255
```

You can see how this can be confusing. Again, there is the *noun-dot-something* construct, but this time it is `Object.Property` rather than `Object.Method`. How you tell them apart is quite subtle: There is no colon before the equal sign. A property is almost always set equal to something, or perhaps the value of a property is assigned to something else.

To make this cell color the same as cell A1, you might say this:

```
ActiveCell.Interior.Color = Range("A1").Interior.Color
```

`Interior.Color` is a property. By changing the value of a property, you can make things look different. It is kind of bizarre: Change an adjective, and you are actually doing something to the cell. Humans would say, "Color the cell red," whereas VBA says this:

```
ActiveCell.Interior.Color = 255
```

Table 2.1 summarizes the VBA "parts of speech."

Table 2.1 Parts of the VBA Programming Language

VBA Component	Analogous To	Notes
Object	Noun	Examples include cell or sheet.
Collection	Plural noun	Usually specifies which object: `Worksheets(1)`.
Method	Verb	Appears as `Object.Method`.
Parameter	Adverb	Lists parameters after the method. Separate the parameter name from its value with `:=`.
Property	Adjective	You can set a property (for example, `activecell.height=10`) or store the value of a property (for example, `x = activecell.height`).

VBA Is Not Really Hard

Knowing whether you are dealing with properties or methods helps you set up the correct syntax for your code. Don't worry if it all seems confusing right now. When you are writing VBA code from scratch, it is tough to know whether the process of changing a cell to yellow requires a verb or an adjective. Is it a method or a property?

This is where the macro recorder is especially helpful. When you don't know how to code something, you record a short little macro, look at the recorded code, and figure out what is going on.

VBA Help Files: Using F1 to Find Anything

Excel VBA Help is an amazing feature, provided that you are connected to the Internet. If you are going to write VBA macros, you absolutely *must* have access to the VBA Help topics installed. Follow these steps to see how easy it is to get help in VBA:

1. Open Excel and switch to the VB Editor by pressing Alt+F11. From the Insert menu, select Module.

2. Type these three lines of code:

```
Sub Test()
    MsgBox "Hello World!"
End Sub
```

3. Click inside the word `MsgBox`.

4. With the cursor in the word `MsgBox`, press F1. If you can reach the Internet, you see the Help topic for the `MsgBox` function.

Using Help Topics

If you request help on a function or method, the Help topic walks you through the various available arguments. If you browse to the bottom of a Help topic, you can see a great resource: code samples under the Example heading (see Figure 2.1).

It is possible to select the code, copy it to the Clipboard by pressing Ctrl+C, and then paste it into a module by pressing Ctrl+V.

After you record a macro, if there are objects or methods about which you are unsure, you can get help by inserting the cursor in any keyword and pressing F1.

Figure 2.1
Most Help topics include code samples.

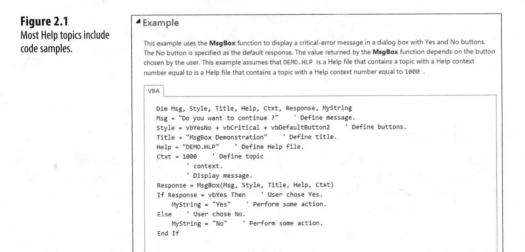

▲ Example

This example uses the **MsgBox** function to display a critical-error message in a dialog box with Yes and No buttons. The No button is specified as the default response. The value returned by the **MsgBox** function depends on the button chosen by the user. This example assumes that DEMO.HLP is a Help file that contains a topic with a Help context number equal to is a Help file that contains a topic with a Help context number equal to 1000 .

```
VBA

Dim Msg, Style, Title, Help, Ctxt, Response, MyString
Msg = "Do you want to continue ?"    ' Define message.
Style = vbYesNo + vbCritical + vbDefaultButton2    ' Define buttons.
Title = "MsgBox Demonstration"    ' Define title.
Help = "DEMO.HLP"    ' Define Help file.
Ctxt = 1000    ' Define topic
        ' context.
        ' Display message.
Response = MsgBox(Msg, Style, Title, Help, Ctxt)
If Response = vbYes Then    ' User chose Yes.
    MyString = "Yes"    ' Perform some action.
Else    ' User chose No.
    MyString = "No"     ' Perform some action.
End If
```

Examining Recorded Macro Code: Using the VB Editor and Help

Let's take a look at the code you recorded in Chapter 1 to see whether it makes more sense now that you know about objects, properties, and methods. You can also see whether it's possible to correct the errors created by the macro recorder.

Figure 2.2 shows the first code that Excel recorded in the example from Chapter 1.

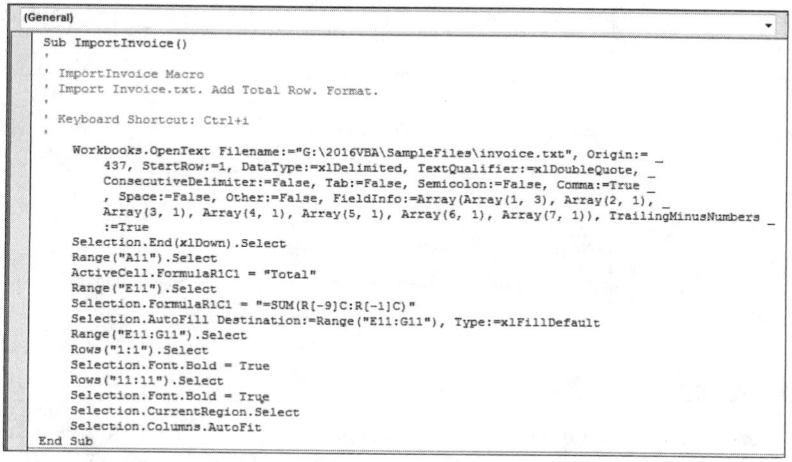

Figure 2.2

Recorded code from the example in Chapter 1.

```
(General)

Sub ImportInvoice()
'
' ImportInvoice Macro
' Import Invoice.txt. Add Total Row. Format.
'
' Keyboard Shortcut: Ctrl+i
'
    Workbooks.OpenText Filename:="G:\2016VBA\SampleFiles\invoice.txt", Origin:= _
        437, StartRow:=1, DataType:=xlDelimited, TextQualifier:=xlDoubleQuote, _
        ConsecutiveDelimiter:=False, Tab:=False, Semicolon:=False, Comma:=True _
        , Space:=False, Other:=False, FieldInfo:=Array(Array(1, 3), Array(2, 1), _
        Array(3, 1), Array(4, 1), Array(5, 1), Array(6, 1), Array(7, 1)), TrailingMinusNumbers _
        :=True
    Selection.End(xlDown).Select
    Range("A11").Select
    ActiveCell.FormulaR1C1 = "Total"
    Range("E11").Select
    Selection.FormulaR1C1 = "=SUM(R[-9]C:R[-1]C)"
    Selection.AutoFill Destination:=Range("E11:G11"), Type:=xlFillDefault
    Range("E11:G11").Select
    Rows("1:1").Select
    Selection.Font.Bold = True
    Rows("11:11").Select
    Selection.Font.Bold = True
    Selection.CurrentRegion.Select
    Selection.Columns.AutoFit
End Sub
```

Now that you understand the concept of Noun.Verb or Object.Method, consider the first line of code that says Workbooks.OpenText. In this case, Workbooks is an object, and OpenText is a method. Click your cursor inside the word OpenText and press F1 for an explanation of the OpenText method (see Figure 2.3).

The Help file confirms that OpenText is a method, or an action word. The default order for all the arguments that can be used with OpenText appears in the gray box. Notice that only one argument is required: Filename. All the other arguments are listed as optional.

Optional Parameters

The Help file can tell you if you happen to skip an optional parameter. For StartRow, the Help file indicates that the default value is 1. If you leave out the StartRow parameter, Excel starts importing at row 1. This is fairly safe.

Now look at the Help file note about Origin. If this argument is omitted, you inherit whatever value was used for Origin the last time someone used this feature in Excel on this computer. That is a recipe for disaster. For example, your code might work 98% of the time. However, immediately after someone imports an Arabic file, Excel remembers the setting for Arabic and thereafter assumes that this is what your macro wants if you don't explicitly code this parameter.

Figure 2.3
Part of the help topic for the `OpenText` method.

Parameters			
Filename	Required	String	Specifies the file name of the text file to be opened and parsed.
Origin	Optional	Variant	Specifies the origin of the text file. Can be one of the following **XlPlatform** constants: **xlMacintosh**, **xlWindows**, or **xlMSDOS**. Additionally, this could be an integer representing the code page number of the desired code page. For example, "1256" would specify that the encoding of the source text file is Arabic (Windows). If this argument is omitted, the method uses the current setting of the **File Origin** option in the **Text Import Wizard**.
StartRow	Optional	Variant	The row number at which to start parsing text. The default value is 1.
DataType	Optional	Variant	Specifies the column format of the data in the file. Can be one of the following XlTextParsingType constants: **xlDelimited** or **xlFixedWidth**. If this argument is not specified, Microsoft Excel attempts to determine the column format when it opens the file.
TextQualifier	Optional	XlTextQualifier	Specifies the text qualifier.
ConsecutiveDelimiter	Optional	Variant	**True** to have consecutive delimiters considered one delimiter. The default is **False**.

Defined Constants

Look at the Help file entry for `DataType` in Figure 2.3, which says it can be one of these constants: `xlDelimited` or `xlFixedWidth`. The Help file says these are the valid `xlTextParsingType` constants that are predefined in Excel VBA. In the VB Editor, press Ctrl+G to bring up the Immediate window. In the Immediate window, type this line and press Enter:

```
Print xlFixedWidth
```

The answer appears in the Immediate window. `xlFixedWidth` is the equivalent of saying 2 (see Figure 2.4). In the Immediate window type `Print xlDelimited`, which is really the same as typing 1. Microsoft correctly assumes that it is easier for someone to read code that uses the somewhat English-like term `xlDelimited` than to read 1.

Figure 2.4
In the Immediate window of the VB Editor, query to see the true value of constants such as `xlFixedWidth`.

```
Immediate
  Print xlFixedWidth
   2
  Print xldelimited
   1
```

If you were an evil programmer, you could certainly memorize all these constants and write code using the numeric equivalents of the constants. However, the programming gods (and the next person who has to look at your code) will curse you for this.

In most cases, the Help file either specifically calls out the valid values of the constants or offers a hyperlink that opens the Help topic showing the complete enumeration and the valid values for the constants (see Figure 2.5).

One complaint with this excellent Help system is that it does not identify which parameters are new to a given version. In this particular case, `TrailingMinusNumbers` was introduced in Excel 2002. If you attempt to give this program to someone who is still using Excel 2000, the code does not run because Excel does not understand the `TrailingMinusNumbers` parameter. Sadly, the only way to learn to handle this frustrating problem is through trial and error.

If you read the Help topic on `OpenText`, you can surmise that it is basically the equivalent of opening a file using the Text Import Wizard. In step 1 of the wizard, you normally choose either Delimited or Fixed Width. You also specify the file origin and at which row to start. This first step of the wizard is handled by these parameters of the `OpenText` method:

```
Origin:=437
StartRow:=1
DataType:=xlDelimited
```

Figure 2.5
Click the hyperlink to see all the possible constant values. Here, the 10 possible `xlColumn-DataType` constants are revealed in a new help topic.

XlColumnDataType Enumeration (Excel)

Office 2013 | Other Versions ▾
Specifies how a column is to be parsed.

▲ Version Information

   Version Added: Excel 2007

Name	Value	Description
xlDMYFormat	4	DMY date format.
xlDYMFormat	7	DYM date format.
xlEMDFormat	10	EMD date format.
xlGeneralFormat	1	General.
xlMDYFormat	3	MDY date format.
xlMYDFormat	6	MYD date format.
xlSkipColumn	9	Column is not parsed.
xlTextFormat	2	Text.
xlYDMFormat	8	YDM date format.
xlYMDFormat	5	YMD date format.

Step 2 of the Text Import Wizard enables you to specify that your fields be delimited by commas. Because you do not want to treat two commas as a single comma, the Treat Consecutive Delimiters as One check box should not be selected. Sometimes, a field may contain a comma, such as "XYZ, Inc." In this case, the field should have quotes around the value, as specified in the Text Qualifier box. This second step of the wizard is handled by the following parameters of the `OpenText` method:

```
TextQualifier:=xlDoubleQuote
ConsecutiveDelimiter:=False
```

```
Tab:=False
Semicolon:=False
Comma:=True
Space:=False
Other:=False
```

Step 3 of the wizard is where you actually identify the field types. In this case, you leave all fields as General except for the first field, which is marked as a date in MDY (Month, Day, Year) format. This is represented in code by the `FieldInfo` parameter.

The third step of the Text Import Wizard is fairly complex. The entire `FieldInfo` parameter of the `OpenText` method duplicates the choices made on this step of the wizard. If you happen to click the Advanced button on the third step of the wizard, you have an opportunity to specify something other than the default decimal and thousands separators, as well as the setting Trailing Minus for Negative Numbers.

> **TIP**
>
> Note that the macro recorder does not write code for `DecimalSeparator` or `ThousandsSeparator` unless you change these from the defaults. The macro recorder does, however, always record the `TrailingMinusNumbers` parameter.

Remember that every action you perform in Excel while recording a macro gets translated to VBA code. In the case of many dialog boxes, the settings you do not change are often recorded along with the items you do change. When you click OK to close the dialog, the macro recorder often records all the current settings from the dialog in the macro.

Here is another example. The next line of code in the macro is this:

```
Selection.End(xlDown).Select
```

You can click to get help for three topics in this line of code: `Selection`, `End`, and `Select`. Assuming that `Selection` and `Select` are somewhat self-explanatory, click in the word `End` and press F1 for Help. A Context Help dialog box appears, saying that there are two possible Help topics for `End`—one in the Excel library and one in the VBA library.

If you are new to VBA, you might not know which Help library to select. Select one and then click Help. In this case, the `End` Help topic in the VBA library is talking about the `End` statement, which is not what you need.

Close Help, press F1 again, and select the `End` object in the Excel library. This Help topic says that `End` is a property. It returns a `Range` object that is equivalent to pressing End+up arrow or End+down arrow in the Excel interface (see Figure 2.6). If you click the blue hyperlink for `xlDirection`, you see the valid parameters that can be passed to the `End` function.

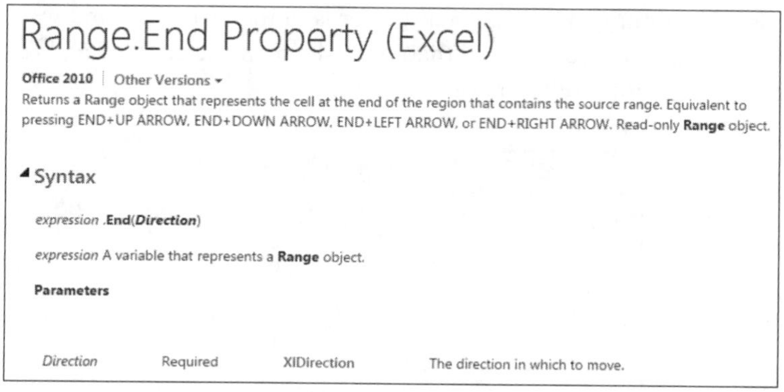

Figure 2.6
The correct Help topic for the End property.

Range.End Property (Excel)

Office 2010 | Other Versions ▾

Returns a Range object that represents the cell at the end of the region that contains the source range. Equivalent to pressing END+UP ARROW, END+DOWN ARROW, END+LEFT ARROW, or END+RIGHT ARROW. Read-only **Range** object.

◢ Syntax

expression **.End(*Direction*)**

expression A variable that represents a **Range** object.

Parameters

Direction	Required	XlDirection	The direction in which to move.

Properties Can Return Objects

Recall from earlier in this chapter that the basic syntax of VBA is `Object.Method`. Consider the line of code currently under examination:

```
Selection.End(xlDown).Select
```

In this particular line of code, the method is `Select`. The `End` keyword is a property, but from the Help file, you see that it returns a `Range` object. Because the `Select` method can apply to a `Range` object, the method is actually appended to a property.

Based on this information, you might assume that `Selection` is the object in this line of code. If you click the mouse in the word `Selection` and press F1, you will see that according to the Help topic, `Selection` is actually a property and not an object. In reality, the proper code would be `Application.Selection`. However, when you are running within Excel, VBA assumes you are referring to the Excel object model, so you can leave off the `Application` object. If you were to write a program in Word VBA to automate Excel, you would be required to include an object variable before the `Selection` property to qualify to which application you are referring.

In this case, the `Application.Selection` can return several types of objects. If a cell is selected, it returns the `Range` object.

Using Debugging Tools to Figure Out Recorded Code

The following sections introduce some awesome debugging tools that are available in the VB Editor. These tools are excellent for helping you see what a recorded macro code is doing.

Stepping Through Code

Generally, a macro runs quickly: You start it, and less than a second later, it is done. If something goes wrong, you do not have an opportunity to figure out what the macro is doing. However, using Excel's Step Into feature makes it possible to run one line of code at a time.

To use this feature, make sure your cursor is in the procedure you want to run, such as the `ImportInvoice` procedure, and then from the menu select Debug, Step Into, as shown in Figure 2.7. Alternatively, you can press F8.

Figure 2.7
Using the Step Into feature enables you to run a single line of code at a time.

The VB Editor is now in Break mode. The line about to be executed is highlighted in yellow, with a yellow arrow in the margin before the code (see Figure 2.8).

Figure 2.8
The first line of the macro is about to run.

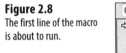

In this case, the next line to be executed is the `Sub ImportInvoice()` line. This basically says, "You are about to start running this procedure." Press the F8 key to execute the line in yellow and move to the next line of code. The long code for `OpenText` is then highlighted. Press F8 to run this line of code. When you see that `Selection.End(xlDown).Select` is highlighted, you know that Visual Basic has finished running the `OpenText` command. At this point, you can press Alt+Tab to switch to Excel and see that the `Invoice.txt` file has been parsed into Excel. Note that A1 is selected.

NOTE If you have a wide monitor, you can use the Restore Down icon at the top right of the VBA window to arrange the window so that you can see both the VBA window and the Excel window. (Restore Down is the two-tiled-window icon between the Minimize "dash" and the Close Window *X* icon at the top of every window.)

This is also a great trick to use while recording new code. You can actually watch the code appear as you do things in Excel.

Switch back to the VB Editor by pressing Alt+Tab. The next line about to be executed is `Selection.End(xlDown).Select`. Press F8 to run this code. Switch to Excel to see that the last cell in your data set is selected.

Press F8 again to run the `Range("A11").Select` line. If you switch to Excel by pressing Alt+Tab, you see that this is where the macro starts to have problems. Instead of moving to the first blank row, the program moves to the wrong row.

Now that you have identified the problem area, you can stop the code execution by using the Reset command. You can start the Reset command either by selecting Run, Reset or by clicking the Reset button on the toolbar (it is a small blue square next to icons for Run and Pause). After clicking Reset, you should return to Excel and undo anything done by the partially completed macro. In this case, you need to close the Invoice.txt file without saving.

More Debugging Options: Breakpoints

If you have hundreds of lines of code, you might not want to step through each line one at a time. If you have a general idea that a problem is happening in one particular section of the program, you can set a breakpoint. You can then have the code start to run, but the macro breaks just before it executes the breakpoint line of code.

To set a breakpoint, click in the gray margin area to the left of the line of code on which you want to break. A large maroon dot appears next to this code, and the line of code is highlighted in brown (see Figure 2.9). (If you don't see the margin area, go to Tools, Options, Editor Format and choose Margin Indicator Bar.) Or select a line of code and press F9 to toggle a breakpoint on or off.

Figure 2.9
The large maroon dot signifies a breakpoint.

```
    Selection.End(xlDown).Select
 |  Range("A11").Select
    ActiveCell.FormulaR1C1 = "Total"
    Range("E11").Select
●   Selection.FormulaR1C1 = "=SUM(R[-9]C:R[-1]C)"
    Selection.AutoFill Destination:=Range("E11:G11"), Type:=xlFi
    Range("E11:G11").Select
    Rows("1:1").Select
```

Next, from the Start menu select Run, Run Sub or press F5. The program executes but stops just before running the line in the breakpoint. The VB Editor shows the breakpoint line highlighted in yellow. You can now press F8 to begin stepping through the code.

After you have finished debugging your code, remove the breakpoints by clicking the dark brown dot in the margin next to each breakpoint to toggle it off. Alternatively, you can select Debug, Clear All Breakpoints or press Ctrl+Shift+F9 to clear all breakpoints that you set in the project.

Backing Up or Moving Forward in Code

When you are stepping through code, you might want to jump over some lines of code, or you might have corrected some lines of code that you want to run again. This is easy to do when you are working in Break mode. One favorite method is to use the mouse to grab the yellow arrow. The cursor changes to a three-arrow icon, which allows you to move the next line up or down. Drag the yellow line to whichever line you want to execute next. The other option is to right-click the line to which you want to jump and then select Set Next Statement.

Not Stepping Through Each Line of Code

When you are stepping through code, you might want to run a section of code without stepping through each line, such as when you get to a loop. You might want VBA to run through the loop 100 times so you can step through the lines after the loop. It is particularly monotonous to press the F8 key hundreds of times to step through a loop. Instead, click the cursor on the line you want to step to and then press Ctrl+F8 or select Debug, Run to Cursor. This command is also available in the right-click menu.

Querying Anything While Stepping Through Code

Even though variables have not yet been discussed, you can query the value of anything while in Break mode. However, keep in mind that the macro recorder never records a variable.

Using the Immediate Window

Press Ctrl+G to display the Immediate window in the VB Editor. While the macro is in Break mode, ask the VB Editor to tell you the currently selected cell, the name of the active sheet, or the value of any variable. Figure 2.10 shows several examples of queries typed into the Immediate window.

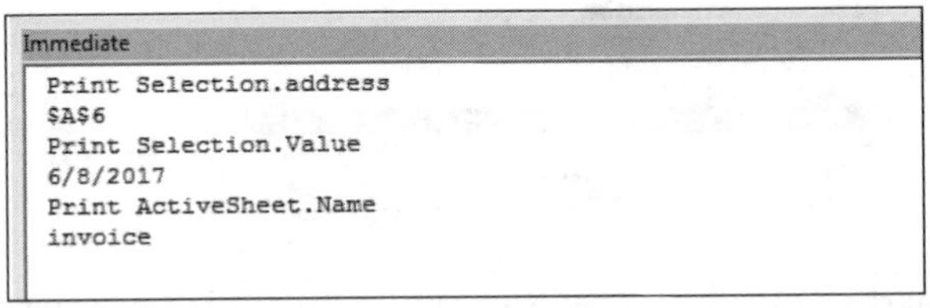

Figure 2.10
Queries that can be typed into the Immediate window while a macro is in Break mode, shown along with their answers.

```
Immediate
Print Selection.address
$A$6
Print Selection.Value
6/8/2017
Print ActiveSheet.Name
invoice
```

Instead of typing `Print`, you can type a question mark: `? Selection.Address`. Read the question mark as, "What is."

When invoked with Ctrl+G, the Immediate window usually appears at the bottom of the code window. You can use the resize handle, which is located above the blue Immediate title bar, to make the Immediate window larger or smaller.

There is a scrollbar on the side of the Immediate window that you can use to scroll backward or forward through past entries in the Immediate window.

It is not necessary to run queries only at the bottom of the Immediate window. For example, if you have just run a line of code, in the Immediate window you can ask for the `Selection.Address` to ensure that this line of code worked.

Press the F8 key to run the next line of code. Instead of retyping the same query, click in the Immediate window anywhere in the line that contains the last query and press Enter.

The Immediate window runs this query again, displays the results on the next line, and pushes the old results farther down the window. In this case, the selected address is $E$11:$G$11. The previous answer, `$E$11`, is pushed down the window.

You can also use this method to change the query by clicking to the right of the word `Address` in the Immediate window. Press the Backspace key to erase the word `Address` and instead type `Columns.Count`. Press Enter, and the Immediate window shows the number of columns in the selection.

This is an excellent technique to use when you are trying to figure out a sticky bit of code. For example, you can query the name of the active sheet (`Print Activesheet.Name`), the selection (`Print Selection.Address`), the active cell (`Print ActiveCell.Address`), the formula in the active cell (`Print ActiveCell.Formula`), the value of the active cell (`Print ActiveCell.Value` or `Print ActiveCell` because `Value` is the default property of a cell), and so on.

To dismiss the Immediate window, click the X in its upper-right corner.

> **NOTE**
> Ctrl+G does not toggle the window off. Use the X at the top right of the Immediate window to close it.

Querying by Hovering

In many instances, you can hover the cursor over an expression in code and then wait a second for a tooltip to show the current value of the expression. This is incredibly helpful when you get to looping in Chapter 4, "Looping and Flow Control." It also comes in handy with recorded code. Note that the expression that you hover over does not have to be in the line of code just executed. In Figure 2.11, Visual Basic just selected E1:G1, making E1 the active cell. If you hover the cursor over `ActiveCell.FormulaR1C1`, you see a tooltip showing that the formula in the active cell is `"=SUM(R[-9]C:R[-1]C)"`.

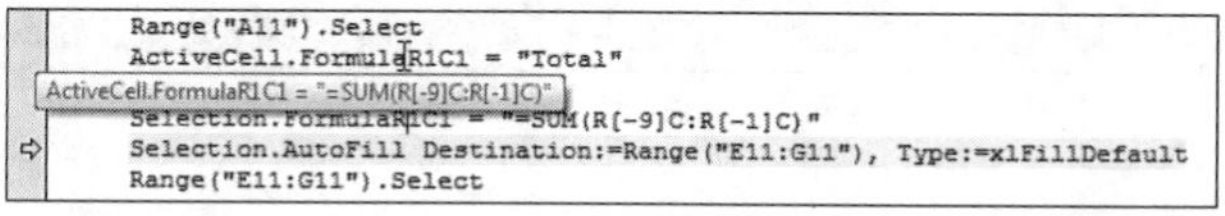

Figure 2.11
Hover the mouse cursor over any expression for a few seconds, and a tooltip shows the current value of the expression.

```
Range("A11").Select
    ActiveCell.FormulaR1C1 = "Total"
ActiveCell.FormulaR1C1 = "=SUM(R[-9]C:R[-1]C)"
    Selection.FormulaR1C1 = "=SUM(R[-9]C:R[-1]C)"
    Selection.AutoFill Destination:=Range("E11:G11"), Type:=xlFillDefault
    Range("E11:G11").Select
```

Sometimes the VBA window seems to not respond to hovering. Because some expressions are not supposed to show values, it is difficult to tell whether VBA is not displaying a value on purpose or whether you are in the buggy "not responding" mode. Try hovering over something that you know should respond, such as a variable. If you get no response, hover,

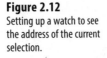

click into the variable, and continue to hover. This tends to wake Excel from its stupor, and hovering works again.

Are you impressed yet? This chapter started by complaining that VBA doesn't seem much like BASIC. However, by now you have to admit that the Visual Basic environment is great to work in and that the debugging tools are excellent.

Querying by Using a Watches Window

In Visual Basic, a watch is not something you wear on your wrist; instead, it allows you to watch the value of any expression while you step through code. Let's say that in the current example, you want to watch to see what is selected as the code runs. You can do this by setting up a watch for Selection.Address.

From the VB Editor Debug menu, select Add Watch. In the Add Watch dialog, enter Selection.Address in the Expression text box and click OK (see Figure 2.12).

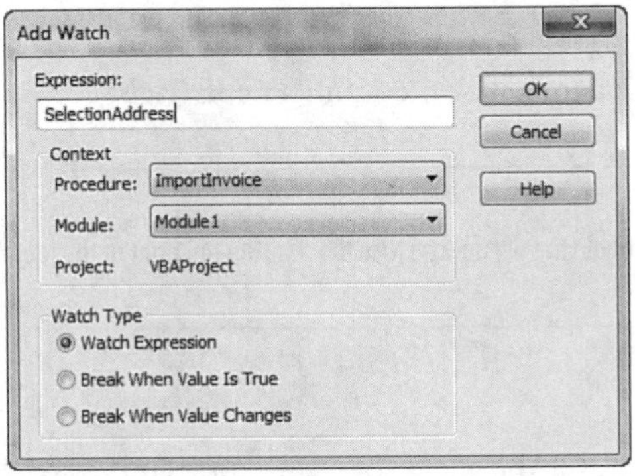

Figure 2.12
Setting up a watch to see the address of the current selection.

![Add Watch dialog box with Expression field showing "Selection.Address", Context section with Procedure "ImportInvoice", Module "Module1", Project "VBAProject", and Watch Type options: Watch Expression (selected), Break When Value Is True, Break When Value Changes. OK, Cancel, and Help buttons.]

A Watches window is added to the busy Visual Basic window, usually at the bottom of the code window. When you start running the macro, import the file and press End+down arrow to move to the last row with data. The Watches window confirms that Selection. Address is $A$18 (see Figure 2.13).

Figure 2.13
Without having to hover or type in the Immediate window, you can always see the value of watched expressions.

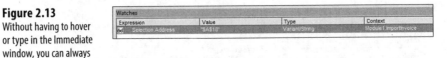

Press the F8 key to run the code Rows("1:1").Select. The Watches window is updated to show that the current address of the Selection is now $1:$1.

In the Watches window, the value column is read/write (where possible)! You can type a new value here and see it change on the worksheet.

Using a Watch to Set a Breakpoint

Right-click any line in the Watches window and select Edit Watch. In the Watch Type section of the Edit Watch dialog, select Break When Value Changes. Click OK.

The glasses icon changes to a hand with triangle icon. You can now press F5 to run the code. The macro starts running lines of code until something new is selected. This is very powerful. Instead of having to step through each line of code, you can now conveniently have the macro stop only when something important has happened. A watch can also be set up to stop when the value of a particular variable changes.

Using a Watch on an Object

In the preceding example, you watched a specific property: `Selection.Address`. It is also possible to watch an object such as `Selection`. In Figure 2.14, when a watch has been set up on `Selection`, you get the glasses icon and a + icon.

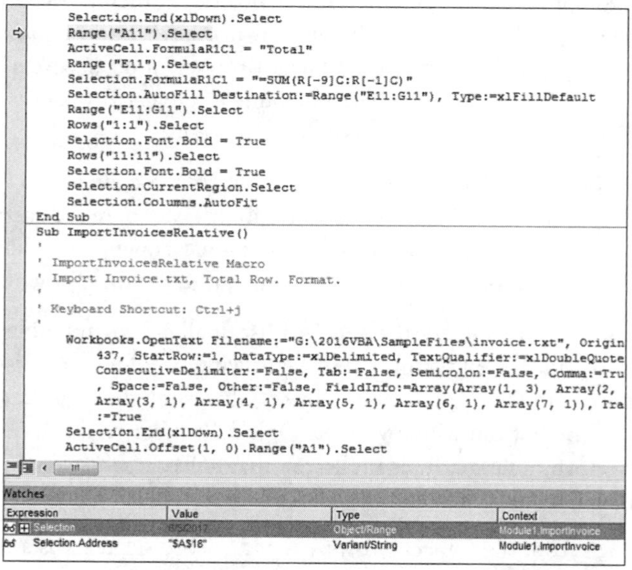

Figure 2.14
Setting a watch on an object gives you a + icon next to the glasses.

```
        Selection.End(xlDown).Select
        Range("A11").Select
        ActiveCell.FormulaR1C1 = "Total"
        Range("E11").Select
        Selection.FormulaR1C1 = "=SUM(R[-9]C:R[-1]C)"
        Selection.AutoFill Destination:=Range("E11:G11"), Type:=xlFillDefault
        Range("E11:G11").Select
        Rows("1:1").Select
        Selection.Font.Bold = True
        Rows("11:11").Select
        Selection.Font.Bold = True
        Selection.CurrentRegion.Select
        Selection.Columns.AutoFit
    End Sub
    Sub ImportInvoicesRelative()
    '
    ' ImportInvoicesRelative Macro
    ' Import Invoice.txt, Total Row. Format.
    '
    ' Keyboard Shortcut: Ctrl+j
    '
        Workbooks.OpenText Filename:="G:\2016VBA\SampleFiles\invoice.txt", Origin_
            437, StartRow:=1, DataType:=xlDelimited, TextQualifier:=xlDoubleQuote_
            ConsecutiveDelimiter:=False, Tab:=False, Semicolon:=False, Comma:=Tru_
            , Space:=False, Other:=False, FieldInfo:=Array(Array(1, 3), Array(2,_
            Array(3, 1), Array(4, 1), Array(5, 1), Array(6, 1), Array(7, 1)), Tra_
            :=True
        Selection.End(xlDown).Select
        ActiveCell.Offset(1, 0).Range("A1").Select
```

Watches			
Expression	Value	Type	Context
Selection	[R9C11]	Object/Range	Module1.ImportInvoice
Selection.Address	"$A$18"	Variant/String	Module1.ImportInvoice

By clicking the + icon, you can see all the properties associated with `Selection`. When you look at Figure 2.15, you can see more than you ever wanted to know about `Selection`! There are properties you probably never realized are available. You can also see that the `AddIndent` property is set to `False` and the `AllowEdit` property is set to `True`. There are useful properties in the list, and you can see the `Formula` of the selection.

In this Watches window, some entries can be expanded. For example, the Borders collection has a plus next to it, which means you can click any + icon to see more details.

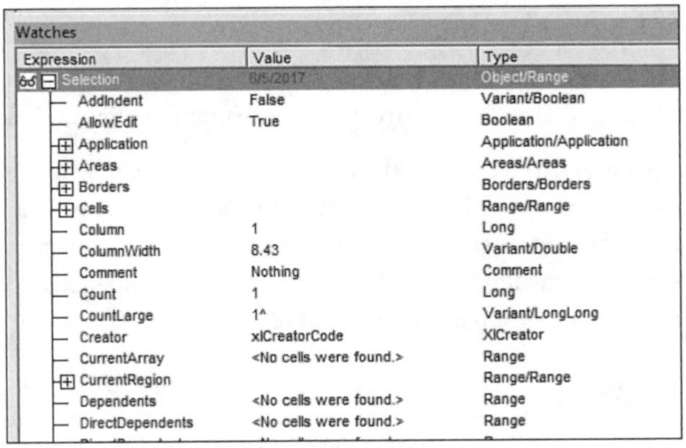

Figure 2.15
Clicking the + icon shows a plethora of properties and their current values.

Watches		
Expression	Value	Type
⊟ Selection	8/5/2017	Object/Range
─ AddIndent	False	Variant/Boolean
─ AllowEdit	True	Boolean
⊞ Application		Application/Application
⊞ Areas		Areas/Areas
⊞ Borders		Borders/Borders
⊞ Cells		Range/Range
─ Column	1	Long
─ ColumnWidth	8.43	Variant/Double
─ Comment	Nothing	Comment
─ Count	1	Long
─ CountLarge	1^	Variant/LongLong
─ Creator	xlCreatorCode	XlCreator
─ CurrentArray	<No cells were found.>	Range
⊞ CurrentRegion		Range/Range
─ Dependents	<No cells were found.>	Range
─ DirectDependents	<No cells were found.>	Range

Object Browser: The Ultimate Reference

In the VB Editor, press F2 to open the Object Browser, which lets you browse and search the entire Excel object library. I've previously owned large Excel books that devoted 400-plus pages to listing every object in the Object Browser. You can save a tree by learning to use the more-powerful Object Browser. The built-in Object Browser is always available at a press of F2. The next few pages show you how to use it.

When you press F2, the Object Browser appears where the code window normally appears. The topmost drop-down currently shows <All Libraries>. There are entries in this drop-down for Excel, Office, VBA, and each workbook that you have open, plus additional entries for anything you check in Tools, References. For now, go to the drop-down and select only Excel.

In the left window of the Object Browser is a list of all classes available for Excel. Click the `Application` class in the left window. The right window adjusts to show all properties and methods that apply to the `Application` object. Click something in the right window, such as `ActiveCell`. The bottom window of the Object Browser tells you that `ActiveCell` is a property that returns a range. It also tells you that `ActiveCell` is read-only (an alert that you cannot assign an address to `ActiveCell` to move the cell pointer).

You have learned from the Object Browser that `ActiveCell` returns a range. When you click the green hyperlink for `Range` in the bottom window, you see all the properties and methods that apply to `Range` objects and, hence, to the `ActiveCell` property. Click any property or method and then click the yellow question mark near the top of the Object Browser to go to the help topic for that property or method.

Type any term in the text box next to the binoculars and click the binoculars to find all matching members of the Excel library. Methods appear as green books with speed lines. Properties appear as index cards, each with a hand pointing to it.

The search capabilities and hyperlinks available in the Object Browser make it much more valuable than an alphabetic printed listing of all the information. Learn to make use of the Object Browser in the VBA window by pressing F2. To close the Object Browser and return to your code window, click the X in the upper-right corner.

Seven Tips for Cleaning Up Recorded Code

Chapter 1 gave you two tips for recording code. So far, this chapter has covered how to understand the recorded code, how to access VBA help for any word, and how to use the excellent VBA debugging tools to step through your code. The remainder of this chapter presents seven tips to use when cleaning up recorded code.

Tip 1: Don't Select Anything

Nothing screams "recorded code" more than having code that selects things before acting on them. This makes sense in a way: In the Excel interface, you have to select row 1 before you can make it bold.

However, this is done rarely in VBA. There are a couple of exceptions to this rule. For example, you need to select a cell when setting up a formula for conditional formatting. And it is possible to directly turn on bold font to row 1 without selecting it.

To streamline the code the macro recorder gives you, in many cases you can remove the part of the code that performs the selection. The following two lines are macro recorder code before it has been streamlined:

```
Cells.Select
Selection.Columns.AutoFit
```

You can streamline the recorded code so it looks like this:

```
Cells.Columns.AutoFit
```

There are a couple of advantages to doing this streamlining. First, there will be half as many lines of code in your program. Second, the program will run faster.

To do this streamlining, after recording code, highlight from before the word `Select` at the end of one line all the way to the dot after the word `Selection` on the next line and press Delete (see Figures 2.16 and 2.17).

Figure 2.16
Select from here to here...

```
    Range("E11:G11").Select
    Rows("1:1").Select
    Selection.Font.Bold = True
    Rows("11:11").Select
    Selection.Font.Bold = True
    Selection.CurrentRegion.Select
    Selection.Columns.AutoFit
End Sub
```

Figure 2.17
...and press the Delete key. This is Cleaning Up Recorded Macros 101.

```
    Selection.End(xlDown).Select
    Selection.Offset(1, 0).Select
    Range("A11").FormulaR1C1 = "Total"
    Range("E11").FormulaR1C1 = "=SUM(R[-9]C:R[-1]C)"
    Range("E11").AutoFill Destination:=Range("E11:G11"), Type:=xlFillDefault
    Rows("1:1").Font.Bold = True
    Rows("11:11").Font.Bold = True
    Range("A1").CurrentRegion.Columns.AutoFit
End Sub
```

Tip 2: Use `Cells(2,5)` Because It's More Convenient Than `Range("E2")`

The macro recorder uses the `Range()` property frequently. If you follow the macro recorder's example, you will find yourself building a lot of complicated code. For example, if you have the row number for the total row stored in a variable, you might try to build this code:

```
Range("E" & TotalRow).Formula = "=SUM(E2:E" & TotalRow-1 & ")"
```

In this code, you are using concatenation to join the letter *E* with the current value of the `TotalRow` variable. This works, but eventually you have to refer to a range where the column is stored in a variable. Say that `FinalCol` is 10, which indicates column J. To refer to this column in a `Range` command, you need to do something like this:

```
FinalColLetter = MID("ABCDEFGHIJKLMNOPQRSTUVWXYZ",FinalCol,1)
Range(FinalColLetter & "2").Select
```

Alternatively, perhaps you could do something like this:

```
FinalColLetter = CHR(64 + FinalCol)
Range(FinalColLetter & "2").Select
```

These approaches work for the first 26 columns but fail for the remaining 99.85% of the columns.

You could start to write 10-line functions to calculate that the column letter for column 15896 is WMJ, but it is not necessary. Instead of using `Range("WMJ17")`, you can use the `Cells(Row,Column)` syntax.

Chapter 3, "Referring to Ranges," covers this topic in complete detail. However, for now you need to understand that `Range("E10")` and `Cells(10, 5)` both point to the cell at the intersection of the fifth column and the tenth row. Chapter 3 also shows you how to use `.Resize` to point to a rectangular range. `Cells(11, 5).Resize(1, 3)` is E11:G11.

Tip 3: Use More Reliable Ways to Find the Last Row

It is difficult to trust data from just anywhere. If you are analyzing data in Excel, remember that the data can come from who-knows-what system written who-knows-how-long-ago. The universal truth is that eventually some clerk will find a way to break the source system and enter a record without an invoice number. Maybe it will take a power failure to do it, but invariably, you cannot count on having every cell filled in.

This is a problem when you're using the End+down arrow shortcut. This key combination does not take you to the last row with data in the worksheet. It takes you to the last row with data in the current range. In Figure 2.18, pressing End+down arrow would move the cursor to cell A7 rather than the true last row with data.

One better solution is to start at the bottom of the worksheet and look for the first non-blank cell by using this:

```
FinalRow = Cells(Rows.Count, 1).End(xlUp).Row
```

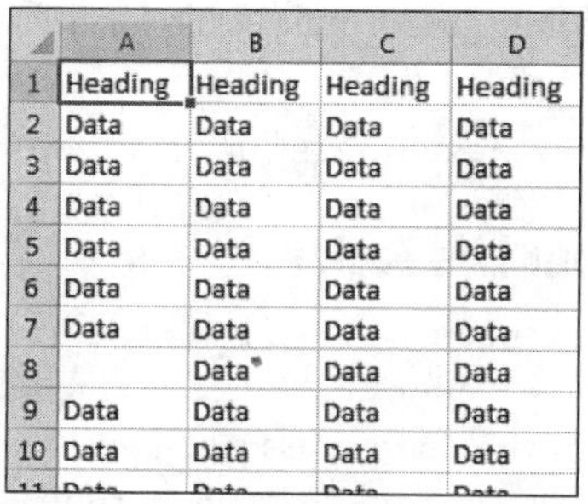

Figure 2.18
End+down arrow fails
in the user interface
if a record is miss-
ing a value. Similarly,
End(xlDown) fails
in Excel VBA.

▲	A	B	C	D
1	Heading	Heading	Heading	Heading
2	Data	Data	Data	Data
3	Data	Data	Data	Data
4	Data	Data	Data	Data
5	Data	Data	Data	Data
6	Data	Data	Data	Data
7	Data	Data	Data	Data
8		Data	Data	Data
9	Data	Data	Data	Data
10	Data	Data	Data	Data
11	Data	Data	Data	Data

This method could fail if the very last record happens to contain the blank row. If the data is dense enough that there will always be a diagonal path of non-blank cells to the last row, you could use this:

```
FinalRow = Cells(1,1).CurrentRegion.Rows.Count
```

If you are sure that there are not any notes or stray activated cells below the data set, you might try this:

```
FinalRow = Cells(1, 1).SpecialCells(xlLastCell).Row
```

The xlLastCell property is often wrong. Say that you have data in A1:F500. If you accidentally press Ctrl+down arrow from A500 you will arrive at A1048576. If you then apply Bold to the empty cell, it becomes activated. Or, if you type Total and then clear the cell, it becomes activated. At this point, xlLastCell will refer to F1048576.

Another method is to use the Find method:

```
FinalRow = Cells.Find("*", SearchOrder:=xlByRows, _
    SearchDirection:=xlPrevious).Row
```

You will have to choose from these various methods based on the nature of your data set. If you are not sure, you could loop through all columns. If you are expecting seven columns of data, you could use this code:

```
FinalRow = 0
For i = 1 to 7
        ThisFinal = Cells(Rows.Count, i).End(xlUp).Row
        If ThisFinal > FinalRow then FinalRow = ThisFinal
Next I
```

Tip 4: Use Variables to Avoid Hard-Coding Rows and Formulas

The macro recorder never records a variable. Variables are easy to use, but just as in BASIC, a variable can remember a value. Variables are discussed in more detail in Chapter 4.

It is recommended that you set the last row that contains data to a variable. Be sure to use meaningful variable names such as FinalRow:

```
FinalRow = Cells(Rows.Count, 1).End(xlUp).Row
```

When you know the row number of the last record, put the word *Total* in column A of the next row:

```
Cells(FinalRow + 1, 1).Value = "Total"
```

You can even use the variable when building the formula. This formula totals everything from E2 to the `FinalRow` of E:

```
Cells(FinalRow + 1, 5).Formula = "=SUM(E2:E" & FinalRow & ")"
```

Tip 5: Use R1C1 Formulas That Make Your Life Easier

The macro recorder often writes formulas in an arcane R1C1 style. However, most people change the code back to use a regular A1-style formula. After reading Chapter 5, "R1C1-Style Formulas," you will understand that there are times when you can build an R1C1 formula that is much simpler than the corresponding A1-style formula. By using an R1C1 formula, you can add totals to all three cells in the total row with the following:

```
Cells(FinalRow+1, 5).Resize(1, 3).FormulaR1C1 = "=SUM(R2C:R[-1]C)"
```

Tip 6: Copy and Paste in a Single Statement

Recorded code is notorious for copying a range, selecting another range, and then doing an `ActiveSheet.Paste`. The `Copy` method as it applies to a range is actually much more powerful. You can specify what to copy and also specify the destination in one statement.

Here's the recorded code:

```
Range("E14").Select
Selection.Copy
Range("F14:G14").Select
ActiveSheet.Paste
```

Here's better code:

```
Range("E14").Copy Destination:=Range("F14:G14")
```

Tip 7: Use `With...End With` to Perform Multiple Actions

If you are making the total row bold with double underline and a larger font and special color, you might get recorded code like this:

```
Range("A14:G14").Select
Selection.Font.Bold = True
Selection.Font.Size = 12
Selection.Font.ColorIndex = 5
Selection.Font.Underline = xlUnderlineStyleDoubleAccounting
```

For four of these lines of code, VBA must resolve the expression `Selection.Font`. Because you have four lines that all refer to the same object, you can name the object once at the top of a `With` block. Inside the `With...End With` block, everything that starts with a period is assumed to refer to the `With` object:

```
With Range("A14:G14").Font
        .Bold = True
        .Size = 12
        .ColorIndex = 5
        .Underline = xlUnderlineStyleDoubleAccounting
    End With
```

CASE STUDY: PUTTING IT ALL TOGETHER: FIXING THE RECORDED CODE

Using the seven tips discussed in the preceding section, you can convert the recorded code from Chapter 1 into efficient, professional-looking code. Here is the code as recorded by the macro recorder at the end of Chapter 1:

```
Sub FormatInvoice3()
Workbooks.OpenText Filename:="C:\Data\invoice.txt", Origin:=437, _
    StartRow:=1, DataType:=xlDelimited, TextQualifier:=xlDoubleQuote, _
    ConsecutiveDelimiter:=False, Tab:=False, Semicolon:=False, _
    Comma:=True, Space:=False, Other:=False, FieldInfo:=Array(_
    Array(1, 3), Array(2, 1), Array(3, 1), Array(4, 1), _
    Array(5, 1), Array(6, 1), Array(7, 1))
Selection.End(xlDown).Select
ActiveCell.Offset(1, 0).Range("A1").Select
ActiveCell.FormulaR1C1 = "Total"
ActiveCell.Offset(0, 4).Range("A1").Select
Selection.FormulaR1C1 = "=SUM(R2C:R[-1]C)"
Selection.AutoFill Destination:=ActiveCell.Range("A1:C1"), Type:= _
    xlFillDefault
ActiveCell.Range("A1:C1").Select
ActiveCell.Rows("1:1").EntireRow.Select
ActiveCell.Activate
Selection.Font.Bold = True
Application.Goto Reference:="R1C1:R1C7"
Selection.Font.Bold = True
Selection.CurrentRegion.Select
Selection.Columns.AutoFit
End Sub
```

Follow these steps to clean up the recorded macro code:

1. Leave the `Workbook.OpenText` lines alone; they are fine as recorded.

2. Note that the following line of code attempts to locate the final row of data so that the program knows where to enter the total row:

   `Selection.End(xlDown).Select`

   You do not need to select anything to find the last row. It also helps to assign the row number of the final row and the total row to a variable so that they can be used later. To handle the unexpected case in which a single cell in column A is blank, start at the bottom of the worksheet and go up to find the last used row:

   ```
   ' Find the last row with data. This might change every day
   FinalRow = Cells(Rows.Count, 1).End(xlUp).Row
   TotalRow = FinalRow + 1
   ```

3. Note that these lines of code enter the word `Total` in column A of the total row:

   ```
   ActiveCell.Offset(1,0).Select
   ActiveCell.FormulaR1C1 = "'Total"
   ```

Better code uses the `TotalRow` variable to locate where to enter the word `Total`. Again, there is no need to select the cell before entering the label:

```
' Build a Total row below this
Cells(TotalRow,1).Value = "Total"
```

4. Note that these lines of code enter the `Total` formula in column E and copy it to the next two columns:

```
ActiveCell.Offset(0, 4).Range("A1").Select
Selection.FormulaR1C1 = "=SUM(R2C:R[-1]C)"
Selection.AutoFill Destination:=ActiveCell.Range("A1:C1"), Type:= _
    xlFillDefault
ActiveCell.Range("A1:C1").Select
```

There is no reason to do all this selecting. The following line enters the formula in three cells:

```
Cells(TotalRow,5).Resize(1, 3).FormulaR1C1 = "=SUM(R2C:R[-1]C)"
```

(The R1C1 style of formulas is discussed in Chapter 5.)

5. Note that the macro recorder selects a range and then applies formatting:

```
ActiveCell.Rows("1:1").EntireRow.Select

ActiveCell.Activate

Selection.Font.Bold = True

Application.Goto Reference:="R1C1:R1C7"

Selection.Font.Bold = True
```

There is no reason to select before applying the formatting. These two lines perform the same action and do it much more quickly:

```
Cells(TotalRow, 1).Resize(1, 7).Font.Bold = True
Cells(1, 1).Resize(1, 7).Font.Bold = True
```

6. Note that the macro recorder selects all cells before doing the `AutoFit` command:

```
Selection.CurrentRegion.Select
Selection.Columns.AutoFit
```

There is no need to select the cells before doing the `AutoFit`:

```
Cells(1, 1).Resize(TotalRow, 7).Columns.AutoFit
```

7. Note that the macro recorder adds a short description to the top of each macro:

```
' ImportInvoice Macro
```

You have changed the recorded macro code into something that will actually work, so you should feel free to add your name as author to the description and mention what the macro does:

```
' Written by Bill Jelen. Import invoice.txt and add totals.
```

Here is the final macro with all the changes:

```
Sub FormatInvoiceFixed()
' Written by Bill Jelen. Import invoice.txt and add totals.
```

```
Workbooks.OpenText Filename:="C:\Data\invoice.txt", Origin:=437, _
    StartRow:=1, DataType:=xlDelimited, TextQualifier:=xlDoubleQuote, _
    ConsecutiveDelimiter:=False, Tab:=False, Semicolon:=False, _
    Comma:=True, Space:=False, Other:=False, FieldInfo:=Array(_
    Array(1, 3), Array(2, 1), Array(3, 1), Array(4, 1), _
    Array(5, 1), Array(6, 1), Array(7, 1))
FinalRow = Cells(Rows.Count, 1).End(xlUp).Row
TotalRow = FinalRow + 1
Cells(TotalRow, 1).Value = "Total"
Cells(TotalRow, 5).Resize(1, 3).FormulaR1C1 = "=SUM(R2C:R[-1]C)"
Cells(TotalRow, 1).Resize(1, 7).Font.Bold = True
Cells(1, 1).Resize(1, 7).Font.Bold = True
Cells(1, 1).Resize(TotalRow, 7).Columns.AutoFit
End Sub
```

Next Steps

By now, you should know how to record a macro. You should also be able to use Help and debugging to figure out how code works. This chapter provides seven tools for making the recorded code look like professional code.

The next chapters go into more detail about referring to ranges, looping, and the crazy but useful R1C1 style of formulas that the macro recorder loves to use.

Referring to Ranges

A *range* can be a cell, a row, a column, or a grouping of any of these. The RANGE object is probably the most frequently used object in Excel VBA; after all, you are manipulating data on a sheet. Although a range can refer to any grouping of cells on a sheet, it can refer to only one sheet at a time. If you want to refer to ranges on multiple sheets, you must refer to each sheet separately.

This chapter shows you different ways of referring to ranges, such as specifying a row or column. You'll also find out how to manipulate cells based on the active cell and how to create a new range from overlapping ranges.

The Range Object

The following is the Excel object hierarchy:

```
Application > Workbook > Worksheet >
Range
```

The Range object is a property of the Worksheet object. This means it requires that a sheet be active or else it must reference a worksheet. Both of the following lines mean the same thing if Worksheets(1) is the active sheet:

```
Range("A1")
Worksheets(1).Range("A1")
```

There are several ways to refer to a Range object. Range("A1") is the most identifiable because that is how the macro recorder refers to it. However, all the following are equivalent when referring to a range:

```
Range("D5")
[D5]
Range("B3").Range("C3")
Cells(5,4)
Range("A1").Offset(4,3)
Range("MyRange") 'assuming that D5 has a
'Name of MyRange
```

Which format you use depends on your needs. Keep reading....It will all make sense soon!

Syntax for Specifying a Range

The `Range` property has two acceptable syntaxes. To specify a rectangular range in the first syntax, specify the complete range reference just as you would in a formula in Excel:

```
Range("A1:B5")
```

In the alternative syntax, specify the upper-left corner and lower-right corner of the desired rectangular range. In this syntax, the equivalent statement might be this:

```
Range("A1", "B5")
```

For either corner, you can substitute a named range, the `Cells` property, or the `ActiveCell` property. The following line of code selects the rectangular range from A1 to the active cell:

```
Range("A1", ActiveCell).Select
```

The following statement selects from the active cell to five rows below the active cell and two columns to the right:

```
Range(ActiveCell, ActiveCell.Offset(5, 2)).Select
```

Named Ranges

You probably have already used named ranges on your worksheets and in formulas. You can also use them in VBA.

Use the following code to refer to the range `"MyRange"` in Sheet1:

```
Worksheets("Sheet1").Range("MyRange")
```

Notice that the name of the range is in quotes—unlike the use of named ranges in formulas on the sheet itself. If you forget to put the name in quotes, Excel thinks you are referring to a variable in the program. One exception is if you use the shortcut syntax discussed in the next section. In that case, quotes are not used.

Shortcut for Referencing Ranges

A shortcut is available when referencing ranges. The shortcut involves using square brackets, as shown in Table 3.1.

Table 3.1   *Shortcuts* **for Referencing Ranges**

Standard Method	Shortcut
Range("D5")	[D5]
Range("A1:D5")	[A1:D5]
Range("A1:D5, G6:I17")	[A1:D5, G6:I17]
Range("MyRange")	[MyRange]

Referencing Ranges in Other Sheets

Switching between sheets by activating the needed sheet slows down your code. To avoid this, refer to a sheet that is not active by first referencing the `Worksheet` object:

```
Worksheets("Sheet1").Range("A1")
```

This line of code references Sheet1 of the active workbook even if Sheet2 is the active sheet.

To reference a range in another workbook, include the `Workbook` object, the `Worksheet` object, and then the `Range` object:

```
Workbooks("InvoiceData.xlsx").Worksheets("Sheet1").Range("A1")
```

To use the `Range` property as an argument within another `Range` property, identify the range fully each time. For example, suppose that Sheet1 is your active sheet and you need to total data from Sheet2:

```
WorksheetFunction.Sum(Worksheets("Sheet2").Range(Range("A1"), _
    Range("A7")))
```

This line does not work. Why not? Although `Range("A1"), Range("A7")` is meant to refer to the sheet at the beginning of the code line (Sheet2), Excel does not assume that you want to carry the `Worksheet` object reference over to these other `Range` objects and assumes that they refer to the active sheet, Sheet1. So what do you do? Well, you could write this:

```
WorksheetFunction.Sum(Worksheets("Sheet2").Range(Worksheets("Sheet2"). _
    Range("A1"), Worksheets("Sheet2").Range("A7")))
```

But this not only is a long line of code but also difficult to read! Thankfully, there is a simpler way, using `With...End With`:

```
With Worksheets("Sheet2")
    WorksheetFunction.Sum(.Range(.Range("A1"), .Range("A7")))
End With
```

Notice now that there is a `.Range` in your code, but without the preceding object reference. That's because `With Worksheets("Sheet2")` implies that the object of the range is the worksheet. Whenever Excel sees a period without an object reference directly to the left of it, it looks up the code for the closest `With` statement and uses that as the object reference.

Referencing a Range Relative to Another Range

Typically, the `Range` object is a property of a worksheet. It is also possible to have `Range` be the property of another range. In this case, the `Range` property is relative to the original range, which makes for unintuitive code. Consider this example:

```
Range("B5").Range("C3").Select
```

This code actually selects cell D7. Think about cell C3, which is located two rows below and two columns to the right of cell A1. The preceding line of code starts at cell B5. If we assume that B5 is in the A1 position, VBA finds the cell that would be in the C3 position relative to B5. In other words, VBA finds the cell that is two rows below and two columns to the right of B5, which is D7.

Again, I consider this coding style to be very unintuitive. This line of code mentions two addresses, and the actual cell selected is neither of these addresses! It seems misleading when you are trying to read this code.

You might consider using this syntax to refer to a cell relative to the active cell. For example, the following line of code activates the cell three rows down and four columns to the right of the currently active cell:

```
Selection.Range("E4").Select
```

I mention this syntax only because the macro recorder uses it. Recall that when you recorded a macro in Chapter 1, "Unleashing the Power of Excel with VBA," with relative references on, the following line was recorded:

```
ActiveCell.Offset(0, 4).Range("A2").Select
```

This line found the cell four columns to the right of the active cell, and from there it selected the cell that would correspond to A2. This is not the easiest way to write code, but it is the way the macro recorder does it.

Although a worksheet is usually the object of the `Range` property, occasionally, such as during recording, a range may be the property of a range.

Using the `Cells` Property to Select a Range

The `Cells` property refers to all the cells of the specified `Range` object, which can be a worksheet or a range of cells. For example, this line selects all the cells of the active sheet:

```
Cells.Select
```

Using the `Cells` property with the `Range` object might seem redundant:

```
Range("A1:D5").Cells
```

This line refers to the original `Range` object. However, the `Cells` property has an `Item` property that makes the `Cells` property very useful. The `Item` property enables you to refer to a specific cell relative to the `Range` object.

The syntax for using the `Item` property with the `Cells` property is as follows:

```
Cells.Item(Row,Column)
```

You must use a numeric value for `Row`, but you may use the numeric value or string value for `Column`. Both of the following lines refer to cell C5:

```
Cells.Item(5,"C")
Cells.Item(5,3)
```

Because the `Item` property is the default property of the `Range` object, you can shorten these lines as follows:

```
Cells(5,"C")
Cells(5,3)
```

The ability to use numeric values for parameters is particularly useful if you need to loop through rows or columns. The macro recorder usually uses something like `Range("A1")`.

Select for a single cell and Range("A1:C5").Select for a range of cells. If you are learning to code only from the recorder, you might be tempted to write code like this:

```
FinalRow = Cells(Rows.Count, 1).End(xlUp).Row
For i = 1 to FinalRow
    Range("A" & i & ":E" & i).Font.Bold = True
Next i
```

This little piece of code, which loops through rows and bolds the cells in columns A through E, is awkward to read and write. But how else can you do it? Like this:

```
FinalRow = Cells(Rows.Count, 1).End(xlUp).Row
For i = 1 to FinalRow
        Cells(i,"A").Resize(,5).Font.Bold = True
Next i
```

Instead of trying to type the range address, the new code uses the Cells and Resize properties to find the required cell, based on the active cell. See the "Using the Resize Property to Change the Size of a Range" section later in this chapter, for more information on the Resize property.

You can use the Cells properties for parameters in the Range property. The following refers to the range A1:E5:

```
Range(Cells(1,1),Cells(5,5))
```

This is particularly useful when you need to specify variables with a parameter, as in the previous looping example.

Using the Offset Property to Refer to a Range

You have already seen a reference to Offset when you recorded a relative reference. Offset enables you to manipulate a cell based on the location of another cell, such as the active cell. Therefore, you do not need to know the address of the cell you want to manipulate.

The syntax for the Offset property is as follows:

```
Range.Offset(RowOffset, ColumnOffset)
```

For example, the following code affects cell F5 from cell A1:

```
Range("A1").Offset(RowOffset:=4, ColumnOffset:=5)
```

Or, shorter yet, you can write this:

```
Range("A1").Offset(4,5)
```

The count of the rows and columns starts at A1 but does not include A1.

If you need to go over only a row or a column, but not both, you don't have to enter both the row and the column parameters. To refer to a cell one column over, use one of these lines:

```
Range("A1").Offset(ColumnOffset:=1)
Range("A1").Offset(,1)
```

Both of these lines mean the same, so the choice is yours. If you use the second line, make sure to include the comma so Excel knows that the 1 refers to the ColumnOffset argument. Referring to a cell one row up is similar:

```
Range("B2").Offset(RowOffset:=-1)
Range("B2").Offset(-1)
```

Once again, you can choose which one to use. It is a matter of readability of the code.

Suppose you have a list of produce in column A, with totals next to the produce items in column B. If you want to find any total equal to zero and place LOW in the cell next to it, do this:

```
Set Rng = Range("B1:B16").Find(What:="0", LookAt:=xlWhole, _
    LookIn:=xlValues)
Rng.Offset(, 1).Value = "LOW"
```

When used in a Sub and looping through a data set, it would look like this:

```
Sub FindLow()
With Range("B1:B16")
    Set Rng = .Find(What:="0", LookAt:=xlWhole, LookIn:=xlValues)
    If Not Rng Is Nothing Then
        firstAddress = Rng.Address
        Do
            Rng.Offset(, 1).Value = "LOW"
            Set Rng = .FindNext(Rng)
        Loop While Not Rng Is Nothing And Rng.Address <> firstAddress
    End If
End With
End Sub
```

The LOW totals are noted by the program, as shown in Figure 3.1.

Figure 3.1
Find the produce with zero totals.

	A	B	C
1	Apples	45	
2	Oranges	12	
3	Grapefruit	86	
4	Lemons	0	LOW

> **NOTE** Refer to the section "Object Variables" in Chapter 4, "Looping and Flow Control," for more information on the Set statement.

Offsetting isn't only for single cells; you can use it with ranges. You can shift the focus of a range over in the same way you can shift the active cell. The following line refers to B2:D4 (see Figure 3.2):

```
Range("A1:C3").Offset(1,1)
```

Figure 3.2
Offsetting a range:
`Range("A1:C3").`
`Offset(1,1).`
`Select.`

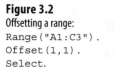

Using the `Resize` Property to Change the Size of a Range

The `Resize` property enables you to change the size of a range based on the location of the active cell. You can create a new range as needed. This is the syntax for the `Resize` property:

```
Range.Resize(RowSize, ColumnSize)
```

To create the range B3:D13, use the following:

```
Range("B3").Resize(RowSize:=11, ColumnSize:=3)
```

Here's a simpler way to create this range:

```
Range("B3").Resize(11, 3)
```

But what if you need to resize by only a row or a column—not both? You don't have to enter both the row and the column parameters.

To expand by two columns, use either of the following:

```
Range("B3").Resize(ColumnSize:=2)
```

or

```
Range("B3").Resize(,2)
```

Both lines mean the same thing. The choice is yours. If you use the second line, make sure to include the comma so Excel knows the 2 refers to the `ColumnSize` argument. Resizing just the rows is similar. You can use either of the following:

```
Range("B3").Resize(RowSize:=2)
```

or

```
Range("B3").Resize(2)
```

Once again, the choice is yours. It is a matter of readability of the code.

From the list of produce, say that you want to find the zero totals and color the cells of the total and corresponding produce (see Figure 3.3). Here's what you do:

```
Set Rng = Range("B1:B16").Find(What:="0", LookAt:=xlWhole, _
    LookIn:=xlValues)
Rng.Offset(, -1).Resize(, 2).Interior.ColorIndex = 15
```

Figure 3.3
Resizing a range to extend the selection.

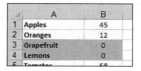

Notice that the `Offset` property first moves the active cell over to the produce column. When you are resizing, the upper-left-corner cell must remain the same.

Resizing isn't only for single cells; you can use it to resize an existing range. For example, if you have a named range but need it and the column next to it, use this:

```
Range("Produce").Resize(,2)
```

Remember, the number you resize by is the total number of rows/columns you want to include.

Using the `Columns` and `Rows` Properties to Specify a Range

The `Columns` and `Rows` properties refer to the columns and rows of a specified `Range` object, which can be a worksheet or a range of cells. They return a `Range` object referencing the rows or columns of the specified object.

You have seen the following line used, but what is it doing?

```
FinalRow = Cells(Rows.Count, 1).End(xlUp).Row
```

This line of code finds the last row in a sheet in which column A has a value and places the row number of that `Range` object into the variable called `FinalRow`. This can be useful when you need to loop through a sheet row by row; you will know exactly how many rows you need to go through.

> **NOTE** Some properties of columns and rows require contiguous rows and columns in order to work properly. For example, if you were to use the following line of code, 9 would be the answer because only the first range would be evaluated:
>
> ```
> Range("A1:B9, C10:D19").Rows.Count
> ```
>
> However, if the ranges were grouped separately, the answer would be 19. Excel takes the top, left-most cell address, A1, and the bottom, rightmost cell address, D19, and counts the cells in the range A1:D19:
>
> ```
> Range("A1:B9", "C10:D19").Rows.Count
> ```

Using the `Union` Method to Join Multiple Ranges

The `Union` method enables you to join two or more noncontiguous ranges. It creates a temporary object of the multiple ranges, which enables you to affect them together:

```
Application.Union(argument1, argument2, etc.)
```

The expression `Application` is not required. The following code joins two named ranges on the sheet, inserts the `=RAND()` formula, and bolds them:

```
Set UnionRange = Union(Range("Range1"), Range("Range2"))
With UnionRange
    .Formula = "=RAND()"
    .Font.Bold = True
End With
```

Using the `Intersect` Method to Create a New Range from Overlapping Ranges

The `Intersect` method returns the cells that overlap between two or more ranges. If there is no overlap, an error will be returned:

```
Application.Intersect(argument1, argument2, etc.)
```

The expression `Application` is not required. The following code colors the overlapping cells of the two ranges:

```
Set IntersectRange = Intersect(Range("Range1"), Range("Range2"))
IntersectRange.Interior.ColorIndex = 6
```

Using the `IsEmpty` Function to Check Whether a Cell Is Empty

The `IsEmpty` function returns a Boolean value that indicates whether a single cell is empty: `True` if empty, `False` if not. The cell must truly be empty for the function to return `True`. If it contains even just a space that you cannot see, Excel does not consider the cell to be empty:

```
IsEmpty(Cell)
```

Say that you have several groups of data separated by a blank row. You want to make the separations a little more obvious. The following code goes down the data in column A. When it finds an empty cell in column A, it colors in the first four cells of that row (see Figure 3.4):

```
LastRow = Cells(Rows.Count, 1).End(xlUp).Row
For i = 1 To LastRow
    If IsEmpty(Cells(i, 1)) Then
        Cells(i, 1).Resize(1, 4).Interior.ColorIndex = 1
    End If
Next i
```

Figure 3.4
Colored rows separating data.

	A	B	C	D
1	Apples	Oranges	Grapefruit	Lemons
2	45	12	86	15
3	71%	53%	82%	52%
4				
5	Tomatoes	Cabbage	Lettuce	Green Peppers
6	58	24	31	0
7	30%	43%	68%	1%
8				
9	Potatoes	Yams	Onions	Garlic
10	10	61	26	29
11	18%	19%	22%	82%

Using the `CurrentRegion` Property to Select a Data Range

`CurrentRegion` returns a `Range` object that represents a set of contiguous data. As long as the data is surrounded by one empty row and one empty column, you can select the data set by using `CurrentRegion`:

```
RangeObject.CurrentRegion
```

The following line selects A1:D3 because this is the contiguous range of cells around cell A1 (see Figure 3.5):

```
Range("A1").CurrentRegion.Select
```

This is useful if you have a data set whose size is in constant flux.

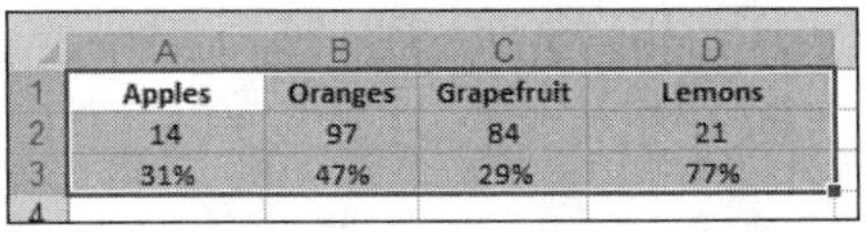

Figure 3.5
Use `CurrentRegion` to select a range of contiguous data around the active cell.

	A	B	C	D
1	Apples	Oranges	Grapefruit	Lemons
2	14	97	84	21
3	31%	47%	29%	77%
4				

CASE STUDY: USING THE SPECIALCELLS METHOD TO SELECT SPECIFIC CELLS

Even Excel power users might not have encountered the Go To Special dialog box. If you press the F5 key in an Excel worksheet, you get the normal Go To dialog box (see Figure 3.6). In the lower-left corner of this dialog is a button labeled Special. Click this button to get to the super-powerful Go To Special dialog box (see Figure 3.7).

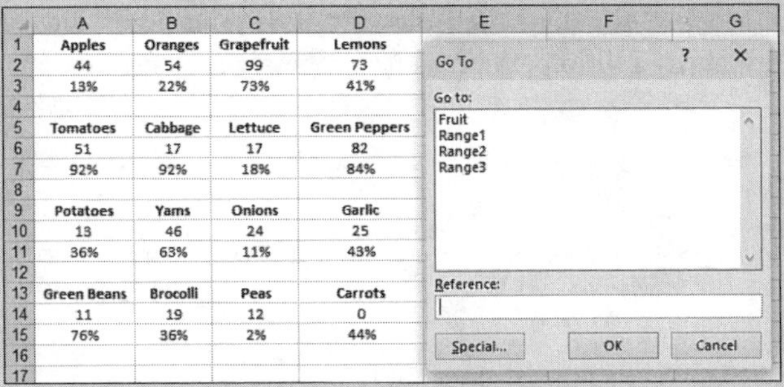

Figure 3.6
Although the Go To dialog doesn't seem useful, click the Special button in the lower-left corner.

In the Excel interface, the Go To Special dialog enables you to select only cells with formulas, only blank cells, or only the visible cells. Selecting only visible cells is excellent for grabbing the visible results of AutoFiltered data.

To simulate the Go To Special dialog in VBA, use the `SpecialCells` method. This enables you to act on cells that meet certain criteria, like this:

```
RangeObject.SpecialCells(Type, Value)
```

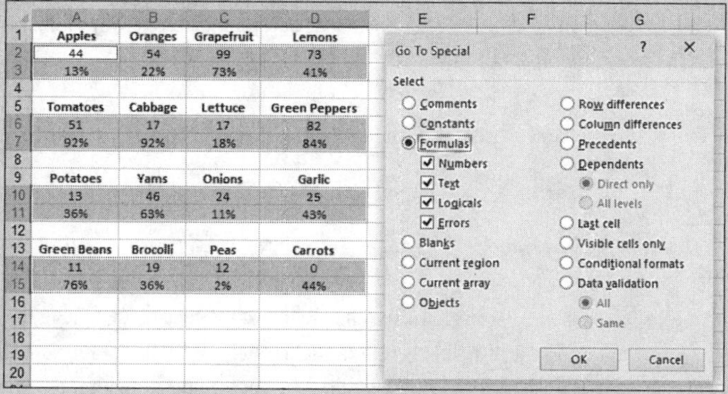

Figure 3.7
The Go To Special dialog
has many incredibly use-
ful selection tools, such as
one for selecting only the
formulas on a sheet.

This method has two parameters: `Type` and `Value`. `Type` is one of the `xlCellType` constants:

```
xlCellTypeAllFormatConditions
xlCellTypeAllValidation
xlCellTypeBlanks
xlCellTypeComments
xlCellTypeConstants
xlCellTypeFormulas
xlCellTypeLastCell
xlCellTypeSameFormatConditions
xlCellTypeSameValidation
xlCellTypeVisible
```

`Value` is optional and can be one of the following:

```
xlErrors
xlLogical
xlNumbers
xlTextValues
```

The following code returns all the ranges that have conditional formatting set up. It produces an error if there are no conditional formats and adds a border around each contiguous section it finds:

```
Set rngCond = ActiveSheet.Cells.SpecialCells(xlCellTypeAllFormatConditions)
If Not rngCond Is Nothing Then
    rngCond.BorderAround xlContinuous
End If
```

Have you ever had someone send you a worksheet without all the labels filled in? Some people think that the data shown in Figure 3.8 looks neat. They enter the Region field only once for each region. This might look aesthetically pleasing, but it is impossible to sort.

Figure 3.8
The blank cells in the
Region column make it
difficult to sort data sets
such as this.

	A	B	C
1	Region	Product	Sales
2	North	ABC	766,469
3		DEF	776,996
4		XYZ	832,414
5	East	ABC	703,255
6		DEF	891,799
7		XYZ	897,949

Using the `SpecialCells` method to select all the blanks in this range is one way to fill in all the blank region cells quickly with the region found above them:

```
Sub FillIn()
On Error Resume Next 'Need this because if there aren't any blank
'cells, the code will error
Range("A1").CurrentRegion.SpecialCells(xlCellTypeBlanks).FormulaR1C1 _
    = "=R[-1]C"
Range("A1").CurrentRegion.Value = Range("A1").CurrentRegion.Value
End Sub
```

In this code, `Range("A1").CurrentRegion` refers to the contiguous range of data in the report. The `SpecialCells` method returns just the blank cells in that range. This particular formula fills in all the blank cells with a formula that points to the cell above the blank cell. (You can read more about R1C1-style formulas in Chapter 5, "R1C1-Style Formulas.") The second line of code is a fast way to simulate doing a Copy and then Paste Special Values. Figure 3.9 shows the results.

Figure 3.9
After the macro runs, the blank cells in the Region column have been filled in with data.

	A	B	C
1	Region	Product	Sales
2	North	ABC	766,469
3	North	DEF	776,996
4	North	XYZ	832,414
5	East	ABC	703,255
6	East	DEF	891,799
7	East	XYZ	897,949

Using the `Areas` Collection to Return a Noncontiguous Range

The `Areas` collection is a collection of noncontiguous ranges within a selection. It consists of individual `Range` objects representing contiguous ranges of cells within the selection. If a selection contains only one area, the `Areas` collection contains a single `Range` object that corresponds to that selection.

You might be tempted to loop through the rows in a sheet and check the properties of a cell in a row, such as its formatting (for example, font or fill) or whether the cell contains a formula or value. Then you could copy the row and paste it to another section. However, there is an easier way. In Figure 3.10, the user enters the values below each fruit and vegetable. The percentages are formulas. The following line of code selects the cells with numeric constants and copies them to another area:

```
Range("A:D").SpecialCells(xlCellTypeConstants, xlNumbers).Copy _
    Range("I1")
```

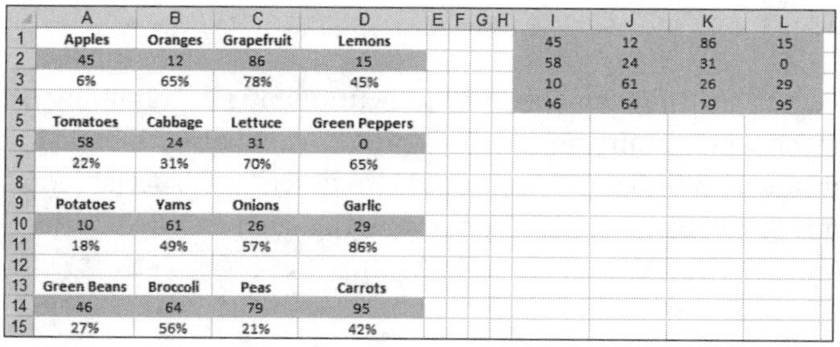

Figure 3.10
The `Areas` collection makes it easier to manipulate noncontiguous ranges.

	A	B	C	D	E	F	G	H	I	J	K	L
1	Apples	Oranges	Grapefruit	Lemons					45	12	86	15
2	45	12	86	15					58	24	31	0
3	6%	65%	78%	45%					10	61	26	29
4									46	64	79	95
5	Tomatoes	Cabbage	Lettuce	Green Peppers								
6	58	24	31	0								
7	22%	31%	70%	65%								
8												
9	Potatoes	Yams	Onions	Garlic								
10	10	61	26	29								
11	18%	49%	57%	86%								
12												
13	Green Beans	Broccoli	Peas	Carrots								
14	46	64	79	95								
15	27%	56%	21%	42%								

Referencing Tables

A table is a special type of range that offers the convenience of referencing named ranges. However, tables are not created in the same manner as other ranges. For more information on how to create a named table, see Chapter 6, "Creating and Manipulating Names in VBA."

Although you can reference a table by using `Worksheets(1).Range("Table1")`, you have access to more of the properties and methods that are unique to tables if you use the `ListObjects` object, like this:

```
Worksheets(1).ListObjects("Table1")
```

This opens the properties and methods of a table, but you can't use that line to select the table. To do that, you have to specify the part of the table you want to work with. To select the entire table, including the header and total rows, specify the `Range` property:

```
Worksheets(1).ListObjects("Table1").Range.Select
```

The table part properties include the following:

- `Range`—Returns the entire table.
- `DataBodyRange`—Returns the data part only.
- `HeaderRowRange`—Returns the header row only.
- `TotalRowRange`—Returns the total row only.

What I really like about coding with tables is the ease of referencing specific columns of a table. You don't have to know how many columns to move in from a starting position or the letter/number of the column, and you don't have to use a `FIND` function. Instead, you can use the header name of the column. For example, to select the data of the Qty column of the table, but not the header or total rows, do this:

```
Worksheets(1).ListObjects("Table1").ListColumns("Qty")_
    .DataBodyRange.Select
```

> **NOTE** For more details on coding with tables, check out *Excel Tables: A Complete Guide for Creating, Using, and Automating Lists and Tables* by Zack Barresse and Kevin Jones (ISBN: 978-1615470280).

Next Steps

Chapter 4 describes a fundamental component of any programming language: loops. If you have taken a programming class, you will be familiar with basic loop structures. VBA supports all the usual loops. That chapter also describes a special loop, `For Each...Next`, which is unique to object-oriented programming such as VBA.

Looping and Flow Control

4

Loops make your life easier. You might have 20 lines of macro code that do something cool one time. Add a line of code above and below, and suddenly your macro fixes a million rows instead of one row. Loops are a fundamental component of any programming language. If you've taken any programming classes, even BASIC, you've likely encountered a `For...Next` loop. Fortunately, VBA supports all the usual loops, plus a special loop that is excellent to use with VBA.

This chapter covers the basic loop constructs:

- `For...Next`
- `Do...While`
- `Do...Until`
- `While...Wend`
- `Until...Loop`

This chapter also discusses the useful loop construct that is unique to object-oriented languages: `For Each...Next`.

For...Next **Loops**

`For` and `Next` are common loop constructs. Everything between `For` and the `Next` is run multiple times. Each time the code runs, a certain counter variable, specified in the `For` statement, has a different value.

Consider this code:

```
For I = 1 to 10
    Cells(I, I).Value = I
Next I
```

As this program starts to run, you need to give the counter variable a name. In this example, the name of the variable is `I`. The first time through the code, the variable `I` is set to 1. The first time the loop is executed, `I` is equal to 1, so the cell in row 1, column 1 is set to 1 (see Figure 4.1).

Figure 4.1

After the first iteration through the loop, the cell in row 1, column 1 has the value 1.

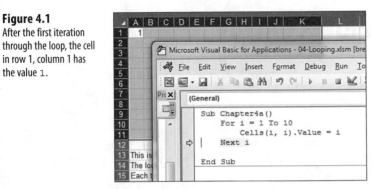

Let's take a close look at what happens as VBA gets to the line that says Next I. Before this line is run, the variable I is equal to 1. During the execution of Next I, VBA must make a decision. VBA adds 1 to the variable I and compares it to the maximum value in the To clause of the For statement. If it is within the limits specified in the To clause, the loop is not finished. In this case, the value of I is incremented to 2. Code execution then moves back to the first line of code after the For statement. Figure 4.2 shows the state of the program before it runs the Next line. Figure 4.3 shows what happens after the Next line is executed.

Figure 4.2

Before the Next I statement is run, I is equal to 1. VBA can safely add 1 to I, and it will be less than or equal to the 10 specified in the To clause of the For statement.

```
Sub Chapter4a()
    For i = 1 To 10
        Cells(i, i).Value = i
    Next I
        i = 1
End Sub
```

Figure 4.3

After the Next I statement is run, I is incremented to 2. Code execution continues with the line of code immediately following the For statement, which writes a 2 to cell B2.

```
Sub Chapter4a()
    For i = 1 To 10
        Cells(i, i).Value = i
    Next i               i = 2
End Sub
```

The second time through the loop, the value of I is 2. The cell in row 2, column 2 (that is, cell B2) gets the value 2.

As the process continues, the Next I statement advances I up to 3, 4, and so on. On the tenth pass through the loop, the cell in row 10, column 10 is assigned the value 10.

It is interesting to watch what happens to the variable I on the last pass through Next I. Before running the Next I line, the variable contains 10. VBA is now at a decision point. It adds 1 to the variable I. I is now equal to 11, which is greater than the limit in the For... Next loop. VBA then moves execution to the next line in the macro after the Next statement (see Figure 4.4). In case you are tempted to use the variable I later in the macro, it is important to realize that it will be incremented beyond the limit specified in the To clause of the For statement.

Figure 4.4

After incrementing I to 11, code execution moves to the line after the Next statement.

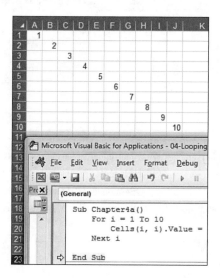

The common use for such a loop is to walk through all the rows in a data set and decide to perform some action based on some criteria. For example, to mark all the rows with positive service revenue in column F, you could use this loop:

```
For I = 2 to 10
    If Cells(I, 6).Value > 0 Then
        Cells(I, 8).Value = "Service Revenue"
        Cells(I, 1).Resize(1, 8).Interior.ColorIndex = 4
    End If
Next i
```

This loop checks each item of data from row 2 through row 10. If there is a positive number in column F, column H of that row has a new label, and the cells in columns A:H of the row are colored using the color index 4, which is green. After this macro has been run, the results look as shown in Figure 4.5.

Using Variables in the For Statement

The previous example is not very useful in that it works only when there are exactly 10 rows of data. It is possible to use a variable to specify the upper/lower limit of the For statement. This code sample identifies FinalRow with data and then loops from row 2 to that row:

```
FinalRow = Cells(Rows.Count, 1).End(xlUp).Row
For I = 2 to FinalRow
    If Cells(I, 6).Value > 0 Then
        Cells(I, 8).Value = "Service Revenue"
        Cells(I, 1).Resize(1, 8).Interior.ColorIndex = 4
    End If
Next I
```

Figure 4.5
After the loop completes all nine iterations, any rows with positive values in column F are colored green and have the label ServiceRevenue added to column H.

▲	A	B	C	D	E	F	G	H	I
1	InvoiceDate	InvoiceNumber	SalesRepNumber	CustomerNumber	ProductRevenue	ServiceRevenue	ProductCost		
2	6/8/2015	123829 S21		C8754	21000	0	9875		
3	6/8/2015	123834 S54		C7796	339000	0	195298		
4	6/8/2015	123835 S21		C1654	161000	0	90761		
5	6/8/2015	123836 S45		C6460	275500	10000	146341	Service Revenue	
6	6/8/2015	123837 S54		C5143	925400	0	473515		
7	6/8/2015	123841 S21		C8361	94400	0	53180		
8	6/8/2015	123842 S45		C1842	36500	55000	20696	Service Revenue	
9	6/8/2015	123843 S54		C4107	599700	0	276718		
10	6/8/2015	123844 S21		C5205	244900	0	143393		
11									

> **CAUTION**
>
> Exercise caution when using variables. What if the imported file today is empty and has only a heading row? In this case, the `FinalRow` variable is equal to `1`. This makes the first statement of the loop essentially, say, `For I = 2 to 1`. Because the start number is higher than the end number, the loop does not execute at all. The variable `I` is equal to `2`, and code execution jumps to the line after `Next`.

Variations on the `For...Next` Loop

In a `For...Next` loop, it is possible to have the loop variable jump up by something other than 1. For example, you might use it to apply greenbar formatting to every other row in a data set. In this case, you want to have the counter variable `I` examine every other row in the data set. Indicate this by adding the `Step` clause to the end of the `For` statement:

```
FinalRow = Cells(Rows.Count, 1).End(xlUp).Row
For i = 2 to FinalRow Step 2
    Cells(i, 1).Resize(1, 7).Interior.ColorIndex = 35
Next i
```

While running this code, VBA adds a light green shading to rows 2, 4, 6, and so on (see Figure 4.6).

Figure 4.6
The `Step` clause in the `For` statement of the loop causes the action to occur on every other row.

▲	A	B	C	D	E	
1	InvoiceDate	InvoiceNumber	SalesRepNumber	CustomerNumber	ProductRevenue	
2	6/7/2011	123829 S21		C8754	21000	
3	6/7/2011	123830 S45		C3390	188100	
4	6/7/2011	123831 S54		C2523	510600	
5	6/7/2011	123832 S21		C5519	86200	
6	6/7/2011	123833 S45		C3245	800100	
7	6/7/2011	123834 S54		C7796	339000	
8	6/7/2011	123835 S21		C1654	161000	

The Step clause can be any number. You might want to check every tenth row of a data set to extract a random sample. In this case, you would use Step 10:

```
FinalRow = Cells(Rows.Count, 1).End(xlUp).Row
NextRow = FinalRow + 5
Cells(NextRow-1, 1).Value = "Random Sample of Above Data"
For I = 2 to FinalRow Step 10
    Cells(I, 1).Resize(1, 8).Copy Destination:=Cells(NextRow, 1)
    NextRow = NextRow + 1
Next i
```

You can also have a For...Next loop run backward from high to low. This is particularly useful if you are selectively deleting rows. To do this, reverse the order of the For statement and have the Step clause specify a negative number:

```
' Delete all rows where column C is the Internal rep - S54
FinalRow = Cells(Rows.Count, 1).End(xlUp).Row
For I = FinalRow to 2 Step -1
    If Cells(I, 3).Value = "S54" Then
        Rows(I).Delete
    End If
Next i
```

> **NOTE** There is a faster way to delete the records, which is discussed in the "Replacing a Loop with AutoFilter" section of Chapter 11, "Data Mining with Advanced Filter."

Exiting a Loop Early After a Condition Is Met

Sometimes you don't need to execute a whole loop. Perhaps you just need to read through a data set until you find one record that meets a certain criteria. In this case, you want to find the first record and then stop the loop. A statement called Exit For does this.

The following sample macro looks for a row in the data set where service revenue in column F is positive and product revenue in column E is 0. If such a row is found, you might indicate a message that the file needs manual processing today and move the cell pointer to that row:

```
' Are there any special processing situations in the data?
FinalRow = Cells(Rows.Count, 1).End(xlUp).Row
ProblemFound = False
For I = 2 to FinalRow
    If Cells(I, 6).Value > 0 Then
        If cells(I, 5).Value = 0 Then
            Cells(I, 6).Select

            ProblemFound = True
            Exit For
        End If
    End If
Next I
If ProblemFound Then
```

4

```
        MsgBox "There is a problem at row " & I
        Exit Sub
    End If
End If
```

Nesting One Loop Inside Another Loop

It is okay to run a loop inside another loop. The following code has the first loop run through all the rows in a record set, while the second loop runs through all the columns:

```
' Loop through each row and column
' Add a checkerboard format
FinalRow = Cells(Rows.Count, 1).End(xlUp).Row
FinalCol = Cells(1, Columns.Count).End(xlToLeft).Column
For I = 2 to FinalRow
    ' For even numbered rows, start in column 1
    ' For odd numbered rows, start in column 2
    If I Mod 2 = 1 Then ' Divide I by 2 and keep remainder
        StartCol = 1
    Else
        StartCol = 2
    End If
    For J = StartCol to FinalCol Step 2
        Cells(I, J).Interior.ColorIndex = 35
    Next J
Next I
```

In this code, the outer loop is using the I counter variable to loop through all the rows in the data set. The inner loop is using the J counter variable to loop through all the columns in that row. Because Figure 4.7 has seven data rows, the code runs through the I loop seven times. Each time through the I loop, the code runs through the J loop six or seven times. This means that the line of code that is inside the J loop ends up being executed several times for each pass through the I loop. Figure 4.7 shows the result.

Figure 4.7
The result of nesting one loop inside the other; VBA can loop through each row and then each column.

	A	B	C	D	E
1	Item	January	February	March	April
2	Hardware Revenue	1,972,637	1,655,321	1,755,234	1,531,060
3	Software Revenue	236,716	198,639	210,628	183,727
4	Service Revenue	473,433	397,277	421,256	367,454
5	Cost of Good Sold	1,084,951	910,427	965,379	842,083
6	Selling Expense	394,527	331,064	351,047	306,212
7	G&A Expense	150,000	150,000	150,000	150,000
8	R&D	125,000	125,000	125,000	125,000

Do **Loops**

There are several variations of the Do loop. The most basic Do loop is useful for doing a bunch of mundane tasks. For example, suppose that someone sends you a list of addresses going down a column, as shown in Figure 4.8.

In this case, you might need to rearrange these addresses into a database with name in column B, street in column C, and city and state in column D. By setting relative recording (see Chapter 1, "Unleashing the Power of Excel with VBA") and using the hotkey Ctrl+A, you can record this bit of useful code:

```
Sub FixOneRecord()
' Keyboard Shortcut: Ctrl+Shift+A
    ActiveCell.Offset(1, 0).Range("A1").Select
    Selection.Cut
    ActiveCell.Offset(-1, 1).Range("A1").Select
    ActiveSheet.Paste
    ActiveCell.Offset(2, -1).Range("A1").Select
    Selection.Cut
    ActiveCell.Offset(-2, 2).Range("A1").Select
    ActiveSheet.Paste
    ActiveCell.Offset(1, -2).Range("A1:A3").Select
    Selection.EntireRow.Delete
    ActiveCell.Select
End Sub
```

Figure 4.8
It would be more useful to have these addresses in a database format to use in a mail merge.

This code is designed to copy one single address into database format. The code also navigates the cell pointer to the name of the next address in the list. Each time you press Ctrl+A, one address is reformatted.

> **NOTE** Do not assume that the preceding code is suitable for a professional application. Remember that you don't need to select something before acting on it. However, sometimes macros are written just to automate a one-time mundane task.

Without a macro, a lot of manual copying and pasting would be required. However, with the preceding recorded macro, you can simply place the cell pointer on a name in column A and press Ctrl+Shift+A. That one address is copied into three columns, and the cell pointer moves to the start of the next address (see Figure 4.9).

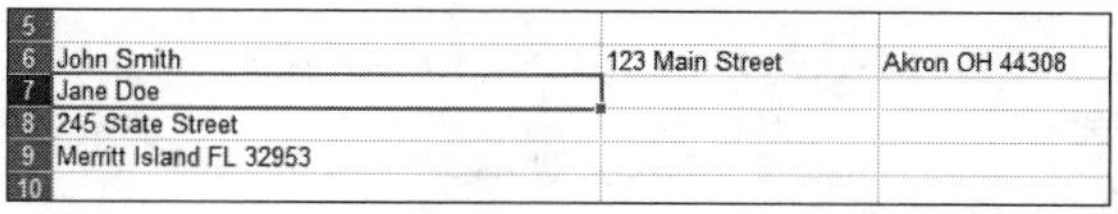

Figure 4.9
After the macro is run once, one address is moved into the proper format, and the cell pointer is positioned to run the macro again.

When you use this macro, you are able to process an address every second using the hotkey. However, when you need to process 5,000 addresses, you will not want to keep running the same macro over and over. In this case, you can use a `Do...Loop` to set up the macro to run continuously. You can have VBA run this code continuously by enclosing the recorded code with `Do` at the top and `Loop` at the end. Now you can sit back and watch the code perform this insanely boring task in minutes rather than hours.

Note that this particular `Do...Loop` will run forever because there is no mechanism to stop it. This works for the task at hand because you can watch the progress on the screen and press Ctrl+Break to stop execution when the program advances past the end of this database.

This code uses a `Do` loop to fix the addresses:

```
Sub FixAllRecords()
Do
    ActiveCell.Offset(1, 0).Range("A1").Select
    Selection.Cut
    ActiveCell.Offset(-1, 1).Range("A1").Select
    ActiveSheet.Paste
    ActiveCell.Offset(2, -1).Range("A1").Select
    Selection.Cut
    ActiveCell.Offset(-2, 2).Range("A1").Select
    ActiveSheet.Paste
    ActiveCell.Offset(1, -2).Range("A1:A3").Select
    Selection.EntireRow.Delete
    ActiveCell.Select
Loop
End Sub
```

These examples have shown quick-and-dirty loops that are great for when you need to accomplish a task quickly. The `Do...Loop` provides a number of options that enable you to have the program stop automatically when it accomplishes the end of the task.

The first option is to have a line in the `Do...Loop` that detects the end of the data set and exits the loop. In the current example, this could be accomplished by using the `Exit Do` command in an `If` statement. If the current cell is on a cell that is empty, you can assume that you have reached the end of the data and stopped processing the loop:

```
Sub LoopUntilDone
Do
    If Selection.Value = "" Then Exit Do
    ActiveCell.Offset(1, 0).Range("A1").Select
    Selection.Cut
    ActiveCell.Offset(-1, 1).Range("A1").Select
    ActiveSheet.Paste
    ActiveCell.Offset(2, -1).Range("A1").Select
    Selection.Cut
    ActiveCell.Offset(-2, 2).Range("A1").Select
    ActiveSheet.Paste
    ActiveCell.Offset(1, -2).Range("A1:A3").Select
    Selection.EntireRow.Delete
    ActiveCell.Select
Loop
End Sub
```

Using the `While` or `Until` **Clause in** `Do` **Loops**

There are four variations of using `While` or `Until`. These clauses can be added to either the `Do` statement or the `Loop` statement. In each case, the `While` or `Until` clause includes some test that evaluates to `True` or `False`.

With a `Do While <test expression>...Loop` construct, the loop is never executed if `<test expression>` is false. If you are reading records from a text file, you cannot assume that the file has one or more records. Instead, you need to test to see whether you are already at the end of file with the `EOF` function before you enter the loop:

```
' Read a text file, skipping the Total lines
   Open "C:\Invoice.txt" For Input As #1
   R = 1
   Do While Not EOF(1)
       Line Input #1, Data
       If Not Left (Data, 5) = "TOTAL" Then
           ' Import this row
           r = r + 1
           Cells(r, 1).Value = Data
       End If
   Loop
   Close #1
```

In this example, the `Not` keyword `EOF(1)` evaluates to `True` after there are no more records to be read from Invoice.txt. Some programmers think it is hard to read a program that contains a lot of instances of `Not`. To avoid the use of `Not`, use the `Do Until <test expression>...Loop` construct:

```
' Read a text file, skipping the Total lines
   Open "C:\Invoice.txt" For Input As #1
   R = 1
   Do Until EOF(1)
       Line Input #1, Data
       If Not Left(Data, 5) = "TOTAL" Then
           ' Import this row
           r = r + 1
           Cells(r, 1).Value = Data
       End If
   Loop
   Close #1
```

In other examples, you might always want the loop to be executed the first time. In these cases, move the `While` or `Until` instruction to the end of the loop. This code sample asks the user to enter sales amounts made that day; it continually asks for sales amounts until the user enters a zero:

```
TotalSales = 0
Do
    x = InputBox( _
        Prompt:="Enter Amount of Next Invoice. Enter 0 when done.", _
        Type:=1)
    TotalSales = TotalSales + x
Loop Until x = 0
MsgBox "The total for today is $" & TotalSales
```

4

In the following loop, a check amount is entered, and then it looks for open invoices to which the check can be applied. However, it is often the case that a single check is received that covers several invoices. The following program sequentially applies the check to the oldest invoices until 100% of the check has been applied:

```
' Ask for the amount of check received. Add zero to convert to numeric.
AmtToApply = InputBox("Enter Amount of Check") + 0
' Loop through the list of open invoices.
' Apply the check to the oldest open invoices and Decrement AmtToApply
NextRow = 2
Do While AmtToApply > 0
    OpenAmt = Cells(NextRow, 3)
    If OpenAmt > AmtToApply Then
        ' Apply total check to this invoice
        Cells(NextRow, 4).Value = AmtToApply
        AmtToApply = 0
    Else
        Cells(NextRow, 4).Value = OpenAmt
        AmtToApply = AmtToApply - OpenAmt
    End If
    NextRow = NextRow + 1
Loop
```

Because you can construct the Do...Loop with the While or Until qualifiers at the beginning or end, you have a great deal of subtle control over whether the loop is always executed once, even when the condition is true at the beginning.

While...Wend **Loops**

While...Wend loops are included in VBA for backward compatibility. In the VBA help file, Microsoft suggests that the Do...Loop construction is more flexible. However, because you might encounter While...Wend loops in code written by others, this chapter includes a quick example. In this loop, the first line is always While <condition>. The last line of the loop is always Wend. Note that there is no Exit While statement. In general, these loops are okay, but the Do...Loop construct is more robust and flexible. Because the Do loop offers either the While or Until qualifier, you can use this qualifier at the beginning or end of the loop, and there is the possibility to exit a Do loop early:

```
' Read a text file, adding the amounts
    Open "C:\Invoice.txt" For Input As #1
    TotalSales = 0
    While Not EOF(1)
        Line Input #1, Data
        TotalSales = TotalSales + Data
    Wend
    MsgBox "Total Sales=" & TotalSales
    Close #1
```

The VBA Loop: For Each

Even though the VBA loop is an excellent loop, the macro recorder never records this type of loop. VBA is an object-oriented language. It is common to have a collection of objects in Excel such as a collection of worksheets in a workbook, cells in a range, pivot tables on a worksheet, or data series on a chart.

This special type of loop is great for looping through all the items in a collection. However, before discussing this loop in detail, you need to understand a special kind of variable called object variables.

Object Variables

At this point, you have seen a variable that contains a single value. When you have a variable such as `TotalSales = 0`, `TotalSales` is a normal variable and generally contains only a single value. It is also possible to have a more powerful variable called an *object variable* that holds many values. In other words, any property associated with the object is also associated with the object variable.

Generally, developers do not take the time to declare variables. Many books implore you to use the `DIM` statement to identify all your variables at the top of the procedure. This enables you to specify that a certain variable must be of a certain type, such as `Integer` or `Double`. Although this saves a tiny bit of memory, it requires you to know up front which variables you plan on using. However, developers tend to whip up a new variable on the fly as the need arises. Even so, there are great benefits to declaring object variables. For example, the VBA AutoComplete feature turns on if you declare an object variable at the top of your procedure. The following lines of code declare three object variables—a worksheet, a range, and a pivot table:

```
Sub Test()
    Dim WSD as Worksheet
    Dim MyCell as Range
    Dim PT as PivotTable
    Set WSD = ThisWorkbook.Worksheets("Data")
    Set MyCell = WSD.Cells(Rows.Count, 1).End(xlUp).Offset(1, 0)
    Set PT = WSD.PivotTables(1)
    ...
```

In this code, you can see that more than an equals sign is used to assign object variables. You also need to use the `Set` statement to assign a specific object to the object variable.

There are many good reasons to use object variables, not the least of which is the fact that it can be a great shorthand notation. It is easier to have many lines of code refer to `WSD` than to `ThisWorkbook.Worksheets("Data")`. In addition, as mentioned earlier, the object variable inherits all the properties of the object to which it refers.

The `For Each...Loop` employs an object variable rather than a `Counter` variable. The following code loops through all the cells in column A:

```
For Each cell in Range("A1").CurrentRegion.Resize(, 1)
    If cell.Value = "Total" Then
        cell.resize(1,8).Font.Bold = True
    End If
Next cell
```

This code uses the `.CurrentRegion` property to define the current region and then uses the `.Resize` property to limit the selected range to a single column. The object variable is called `Cell`. Any name could be used for the object variable, but `Cell` seems more appropriate than something arbitrary like `Fred`.

The following code sample searches all open workbooks, looking for a workbook in which the first worksheet is called Menu:

```
For Each wb in Workbooks
    If wb.Worksheets(1).Name = "Menu" Then
    WBFound = True
    WBName = wb.Name
    Exit For
End If
Next wb
```

This code sample deletes all pivot tables on the current sheet:

```
For Each pt in ActiveSheet.PivotTables
    pt.TableRange2.Clear
Next pt
```

CASE STUDY: LOOPING THROUGH ALL FILES IN A DIRECTORY

This case study includes some useful procedures that make extensive use of loops.

The first procedure uses VBA's `Scripting.FileSystemObject` to find all .jpg picture files in a certain directory and then list the files down a column in Excel:

```
Sub FindJPGFilesInAFolder()
    Dim fso As Object
    Dim strName As String
    Dim strArr(1 To 1048576, 1 To 1) As String, i As Long

    ' Enter the folder name here
    Const strDir As String = "C:\Artwork\"

    strName = Dir$(strDir & "*.jpg")
    Do While strName <> vbNullString
        i = i + 1
        strArr(i, 1) = strDir & strName
        strName = Dir$()
    Loop
    Set fso = CreateObject("Scripting.FileSystemObject")
    Call recurseSubFolders(fso.GetFolder(strDir), strArr(), i)
    Set fso = Nothing
    If i > 0 Then
        Range("A1").Resize(i).Value = strArr
    End If

    ' Next, loop through all found files
    ' and break into path and filename
    FinalRow = Cells(Rows.Count, 1).End(xlUp).Row
    For i = 1 To FinalRow
```

```
          ThisEntry = Cells(i, 1)
          For j = Len(ThisEntry) To 1 Step -1
              If Mid(ThisEntry, j, 1) = Application.PathSeparator Then
                  Cells(i, 2) = Left(ThisEntry, j)
                  Cells(i, 3) = Mid(ThisEntry, j + 1)
                  Exit For
              End If
          Next j
      Next i

End Sub
Private Sub recurseSubFolders(ByRef Folder As Object, _
    ByRef strArr() As String, _
    ByRef i As Long)
Dim SubFolder As Object
Dim strName As String
For Each SubFolder In Folder.SubFolders
    strName = Dir$(SubFolder.Path & "*.jpg")
    Do While strName <> vbNullString
        i = i + 1
        strArr(i, 1) = SubFolder.Path & strName
        strName = Dir$()
    Loop
    Call recurseSubFolders(SubFolder, strArr(), i)
Next
End Sub
```

The idea in this situation is to organize the photos into new folders. In column D, if you want to move a picture to a new folder, type the path of that folder. The following `For...` `Each` loop takes care of copying the pictures. Each time through the loop, the object variable named `Cell` contains a reference to a cell in column A. This loop uses `Cell.Offset(0, 3)` to return the value from the cell three columns to the right of the range represented by the variable `Cell`:

```
Sub CopyToNewFolder()
    FinalRow = Cells(Rows.Count, 1).End(xlUp).Row
    For Each Cell In Range("A2:A" & FinalRow)
        OrigFile = Cell.Value
        NewFile = Cell.Offset(0, 3) & Application.PathSeparator & _
            Cell.Offset(0, 2)
        FileCopy OrigFile, NewFile
    Next Cell
End Sub
```

Note that `Application.PathSeparator` is a backslash on Windows computers but might be different if the code is running on a Macintosh.

Flow Control: Using `If...Then...Else` and `Select Case`

Another aspect of programming that will never be recorded by the macro recorder is the concept of flow control. Sometimes you do not want every line of a program to be executed every time you run a macro. VBA offers two excellent choices for flow control: the `If...Then...Else` construct and the `Select Case` construct.

Basic Flow Control: `If...Then...Else`

The most common device for program flow control is the `If` statement. For example, suppose you have a list of products, as shown in Figure 4.10. You want to loop through each product in the list and copy it to either a Fruits list or a Vegetables list. Beginning programmers might be tempted to loop through the rows twice—once to look for fruit and a second time to look for vegetables. However, there is no need to loop through twice because you can use an `If...Then...Else` construct on a single loop to copy each row to the correct place.

Figure 4.10
A single loop can look for fruits or vegetables.

	A	B	C
1	Class	Product	Quantity
2	Fruit	Apples	1
3	Fruit	Apricots	3
4	Vegetable	Asparagus	62
5	Fruit	Bananas	55
6	Fruit	Blueberry	17
7	Vegetable	Broccoli	56
8	Vegetable	Cabbage	35
9	Fruit	Cherries	59
10	Herbs	Dill	91
11	Vegetable	Eggplant	94
12	Fruit	Kiwi	86

Using Conditions

Any `If` statement needs a condition that is being tested. The condition should always evaluate to TRUE or FALSE. Here are some examples of simple and complex conditions:

- `If Range("A1").Value = "Title" Then`
- `If Not Range("A1").Value = "Title" Then`
- `If Range("A1").Value = "Title" And Range("B1").Value = "Fruit" Then`
- `If Range("A1").Value = "Title" Or Range("B1").Value = "Fruit" Then`

Using `If...Then...End If`

After the `If` statement, you can include one or more program lines that will be executed only if the condition is met. You should then close the `If` block with an `End If` line. Here is a simple example of an `If` statement:

```
Sub ColorFruitRedBold()
    FinalRow = Cells(Rows.Count, 1).End(xlUp).Row

    For i = 2 To FinalRow
        If Cells(i, 1).Value = "Fruit" Then
            Cells(i, 1).Resize(1, 3).Font.Bold = True
            Cells(i, 1).Resize(1, 3).Font.ColorIndex = 3
        End If
    Next i

    MsgBox "Fruit is now bold and red"
End Sub
```

Either/Or Decisions: If...Then...Else...End If

Sometimes you will want to do one set of statements if a condition is true and another set of statements if the condition is not true. To do this with VBA, the second set of conditions would be coded after the Else statement. There is still only one End If statement associated with this construct. For example, you could use the following code to color the fruit red and the vegetables green:

```
Sub FruitRedVegGreen()
    FinalRow = Cells(Rows.Count, 1).End(xlUp).Row

    For i = 2 To FinalRow
        If Cells(i, 1).Value = "Fruit" Then
            Cells(i, 1).Resize(1, 3).Font.ColorIndex = 3
        Else
            Cells(i, 1).Resize(1, 3).Font.ColorIndex = 50
        End If
    Next i

    MsgBox "Fruit is red / Veggies are green"
End Sub
```

Using If...ElseIf...End If for Multiple Conditions

Notice that the product list includes one item that is classified as an herb. Three conditions can be used to test items on the list. It is possible to build an If...End If structure with multiple conditions. First, test to see whether the record is a fruit. Next, use an Else If to test whether the record is a vegetable. Then test to see whether the record is an herb. Finally, if the record is none of those, highlight the record as an error. Here's the code that does all this:

```
Sub MultipleIf()
    FinalRow = Cells(Rows.Count, 1).End(xlUp).Row

    For i = 2 To FinalRow
        If Cells(i, 1).Value = "Fruit" Then
            Cells(i, 1).Resize(1, 3).Font.ColorIndex = 3
        ElseIf Cells(i, 1).Value = "Vegetable" Then
            Cells(i, 1).Resize(1, 3).Font.ColorIndex = 50
        ElseIf Cells(i, 1).Value = "Herbs" Then
            Cells(i, 1).Resize(1, 3).Font.ColorIndex = 5
        Else
            ' This must be a record in error
```

```
            Cells(i, 1).Resize(1, 3).Interior.ColorIndex = 6
        End If
    Next i

    MsgBox "Fruit is red / Veggies are green / Herbs are blue"
End Sub
```

Using `Select Case...End Select` for Multiple Conditions

When you have many different conditions, it becomes unwieldy to use many `ElseIf` statements. For this reason, VBA offers another construct, known as the `Select Case` construct. In your running example, always check the value of the class in column A. This value is called the *test expression*. The basic syntax of this construct starts with the words `Select Case` followed by the test expression:

```
Select Case Cells(i, 1).Value
```

Thinking about this problem in English, you might say, "In cases in which the record is fruit, color the record with red." VBA uses a shorthand version of this. You write the word `Case` followed by the literal `"Fruit"`. Any statements that follow `Case "Fruit"` are executed whenever the test expression is a fruit. After these statements, you have the next `Case` statement: `Case "Vegetables"`. You continue in this fashion, writing a `Case` statement followed by the program lines that are executed if that case is true.

After you have listed all the possible conditions you can think of, you can optionally include a `Case Else` section at the end. The `Case Else` section includes what the program should do if the test expression matches none of your cases. Below, the macro adds a note in column D if an unexpected value is found in A. Finally, you close the entire construct with the `End Select` statement.

The following program does the same operation as the previous macro but uses a `Select Case` statement:

```
Sub SelectCase()
    FinalRow = Cells(Rows.Count, 1).End(xlUp).Row

    For i = 2 To FinalRow
        Select Case Cells(i, 1).Value
            Case "Fruit"
                Cells(i, 1).Resize(1, 3).Font.ColorIndex = 3
            Case "Vegetable"
                Cells(i, 1).Resize(1, 3).Font.ColorIndex = 50
            Case "Herbs"
                Cells(i, 1).Resize(1, 3).Font.ColorIndex = 5
            Case Else
                Cells(i, 4).Value = "Unexpected value!"
        End Select
    Next i

    MsgBox "Fruit is red / Veggies are green / Herbs are blue"
End Sub
```

Complex Expressions in `Case` Statements

It is possible to have fairly complex expressions in `Case` statements. For example, say that you want to perform the same actions for all berry records:

```
Case "Strawberry", "Blueberry", "Raspberry"
     AdCode = 1
```

If it makes sense to do so, you might code a range of values in the `Case` statement:

```
Case 1 to 20
    Discount = 0.05
Case 21 to 100
    Discount = 0.1
```

You can include the keyword `Is` and a comparison operator, such as `>` or `<`:

```
Case Is < 10
    Discount = 0
Case Is > 100
    Discount = 0.2
Case Else
    Discount = 0.10
```

Nesting `If` Statements

It is not only possible but also common to nest an `If` statement inside another `If` statement. In this situation, it is important to use proper indentation. You will often find that you have several `End If` lines at the end of the construct. With proper indentation, it is easier to tell which `End If` is associated with a particular `If`.

The final macro in this chapter contains a lot of logic that handles the following discount rules:

- For fruit, quantities less than 5 cases get no discount.
- Quantities from 5 to 20 cases get a 10% discount.
- Quantities greater than 20 cases get a 15% discount.
- For herbs, quantities less than 10 cases get no discount.
- Quantities from 10 cases to 15 cases get a 3% discount.
- Quantities greater than 15 cases get a 6% discount.
- For vegetables except asparagus, quantities of 5 cases and greater earn a 12% discount.
- Asparagus requires 20 cases for a discount of 12%.
- None of the discounts applies if the product is on sale this week. The sale price is 25% off the normal price. This week's sale items are strawberries, lettuce, and tomatoes.

The code to execute this logic follows:

```
Sub ComplexIf()
    FinalRow = Cells(Rows.Count, 1).End(xlUp).Row

    For i = 2 To FinalRow
        ThisClass = Cells(i, 1).Value
```

```vba
ThisProduct = Cells(i, 2).Value
ThisQty = Cells(i, 3).Value

' First, figure out if the item is on sale
Select Case ThisProduct
    Case "Strawberry", "Lettuce", "Tomatoes"
        Sale = True
    Case Else
        Sale = False
End Select

' Figure out the discount
If Sale Then
    Discount = 0.25
Else
    If ThisClass = "Fruit" Then
        Select Case ThisQty
            Case Is < 5
                Discount = 0
            Case 5 To 20
                Discount = 0.1
            Case Is > 20
                Discount = 0.15
        End Select
    ElseIf ThisClass = "Herbs" Then
        Select Case ThisQty
            Case Is < 10
                Discount = 0
            Case 10 To 15
                Discount = 0.03
            Case Is > 15
                Discount = 0.06
        End Select
    ElseIf ThisClass = "Vegetables" Then
        ' There is a special condition for asparagus
        If ThisProduct = "Asparagus" Then
            If ThisQty < 20 Then
                Discount = 0
            Else
                Discount = 0.12
            End If
        Else
            If ThisQty < 5 Then
                Discount = 0
            Else
                Discount = 0.12
            End If
        End If ' Is the product asparagus or not?
    End If ' Is the product a vegetable?
End If ' Is the product on sale?

Cells(i, 4).Value = Discount

If Sale Then
    Cells(i, 4).Font.Bold = True
End If

Next i
```

```
    Range("D1").Value = "Discount"

    MsgBox "Discounts have been applied"

End Sub
```

Next Steps

Loops add a tremendous amount of power to your recorded macros. Any time you need to repeat a process over all worksheets or all rows in a worksheet, using a loop is the way to go. Excel VBA supports the traditional programming loops of `For...Next` and `Do...Loop` and the object-oriented loop `For Each...Next`. Chapter 5, "R1C1-Style Formulas," discusses the seemingly arcane R1C1 style of formulas and shows why it is important in Excel VBA.

4

R1C1-Style Formulas

Referring to Cells: A1 Versus R1C1 References

Understanding R1C1 formulas will make your job easier in VBA. You could skip this chapter, but if you do, your code will be harder to write. Taking 30 minutes to understand R1C1 will make every macro you write for the rest of your life easier to code.

We can trace the A1 style of referencing back to VisiCalc. Dan Bricklin and Bob Frankston used A1 to refer to the cell in the upper-left corner of the spreadsheet. Mitch Kapor used this same addressing scheme in Lotus 1-2-3. Upstart Multiplan from Microsoft attempted to buck the trend and used something called R1C1-style addressing. In R1C1 addressing, the cell known as A1 is referred to as R1C1 because it is in row 1, column 1.

With the dominance of Lotus 1-2-3 in the 1980s and early 1990s, the A1 style became the standard. Microsoft realized it was fighting a losing battle and eventually offered either R1C1-style addressing or A1-style addressing in Excel. When you open Excel today, the A1 style is used by default. Officially, however, Microsoft supports both styles of addressing.

You would think that this chapter would be a non-issue. Anyone who uses the Excel interface would agree that the R1C1 style is dead. However, we have what on the face of it seems to be an annoying problem: The macro recorder records formulas in the R1C1 style. So you might be thinking that you just need to learn R1C1 addressing so that you can read the recorded code and switch it back to the familiar A1 style.

I have to give Microsoft credit. R1C1-style formulas, you'll grow to understand, are actually more efficient, especially when you are dealing with writing formulas in VBA. Using R1C1-style addressing enables you to write more efficient code. Plus, there are some features such as setting up array formulas that require you to enter a formula in R1C1 style.

I can hear the collective groan from Excel users everywhere. You could skip these pages on this old-fashioned addressing style if it were only an annoyance or an efficiency issue. However, because it is necessary to understand R1C1 addressing to effectively use important features such as array formulas, you have to dive in and learn this style.

Toggling to R1C1-Style References

You don't need to switch to R1C1 style in order to use .FormulaR1C1 in your code. However, while you're learning about R1C1, it will help to temporarily switch to R1C1 style.

To switch to R1C1-style addressing, select Options from the File menu. In the Formulas category, select the R1C1 Reference Style check box (see Figure 5.1).

Figure 5.1
Selecting the R1C1 reference style in the Formulas category of the Excel Options dialog causes Excel to use R1C1 style in the Excel user interface.

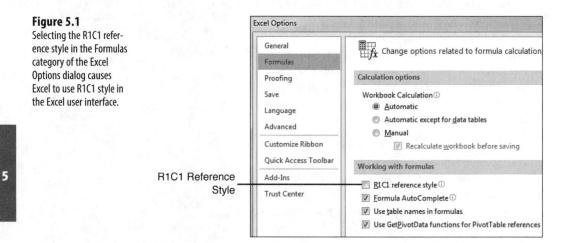

After you switch to R1C1 style, the column letters A, B, C across the top of the worksheet are replaced by numbers 1, 2, 3 (see Figure 5.2).

Figure 5.2
In R1C1 style, the column letters are replaced by numbers.

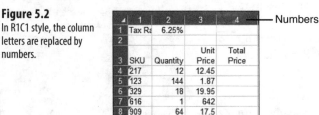

In this format, the cell that you know as B5 is called R5C2 because it is in row 5, column 2.

Every couple weeks, someone manages to accidentally turn on this option, and we get an urgent support request at MrExcel. This style is foreign to 99% of spreadsheet users.

Witnessing the Miracle of Excel Formulas

Automatically recalculating thousands of cells is the main benefit of electronic spreadsheets over the green ledger paper used up until 1979. However, a close second-prize award would be that you can enter one formula and copy that formula to thousands of cells.

Entering a Formula Once and Copying 1,000 Times

Switch back to A1 style referencing. Consider the worksheet shown in Figure 5.3. Enter a simple formula such as =C4*B4 in cell D4, double-click the AutoFill handle, and the formula intelligently changes as it is copied down the range.

Figure 5.3
Double-click the AutoFill handle, and Excel intelligently copies this relative-reference formula down the column.

	A	B	C	D	E
1	Tax Ra	6.25%			
2					
3	SKU	Quantity	Unit Price	Total Price	Taxable?
4	217	12	12.45	149.4	TRUE
5	123	144	1.87		TRUE
6	329	18	19.95		TRUE
7	616	1	642		FALSE
8	909	64	17.5		TRUE
9	527	822	0.12		TRUE
10	Total				

The formula is rewritten for each row, eventually becoming =C9*B9. It seems intimidating to consider having a macro enter all these different formulas. Figure 5.4 shows how the formulas change when you copy them down columns D, F, and G.

> **NOTE**
> Press Ctrl+' to switch to showing formulas rather than their results. Press it again to toggle back to seeing values.

Figure 5.4
Amazingly, Excel adjusts the cell references in each formula as you copy down the column.

	D	E	F	G
it	Total			
e	Price	Taxable?	Tax	Total
	=B4*C4	TRUE	=IF(E4,ROUND(D4*$B$1,2),0)	=F4+D4
	=B5*C5	TRUE	=IF(E5,ROUND(D5*$B$1,2),0)	=F5+D5
	=B6*C6	TRUE	=IF(E6,ROUND(D6*$B$1,2),0)	=F6+D6
	=B7*C7	FALSE	=IF(E7,ROUND(D7*$B$1,2),0)	=F7+D7
	=B8*C8	TRUE	=IF(E8,ROUND(D8*$B$1,2),0)	=F8+D8
	=B9*C9	TRUE	=IF(E9,ROUND(D9*$B$1,2),0)	=F9+D9
	=C10*B10		=SUM(G4:G9)	

5

The formula in cell F4 includes both relative and absolute formulas:
`=IF(E4,ROUND(D4*$B$1,2),0)`. Thanks to the dollar signs inserted in cell B1, you can copy down this formula, and it always multiplies the total price in this row by the tax rate in cell B1.

The Secret: It's Not That Amazing

Excel actually uses R1C1-style formulas behind the scenes. Excel shows addresses and formulas in A1 style merely because it needs to adhere to the standard made popular by VisiCalc and Lotus.

If you switch the worksheet in Figure 5.4 to use R1C1 notation, you will notice that the "different" formulas in D4:D9 are all actually identical formulas in R1C1 notation. The same is true of F4:F9 and G4:G9.

Use the Options dialog to change the sample worksheet to R1C1-style addresses. If you examine the formulas in Figure 5.5, you will see that in R1C1 language, every formula in column 4 is identical. Given that Excel is storing the formulas in R1C1 style, copying them, and then merely translating to A1 style for us to understand, it is no longer that amazing that Excel can easily manipulate A1-style formulas as it does.

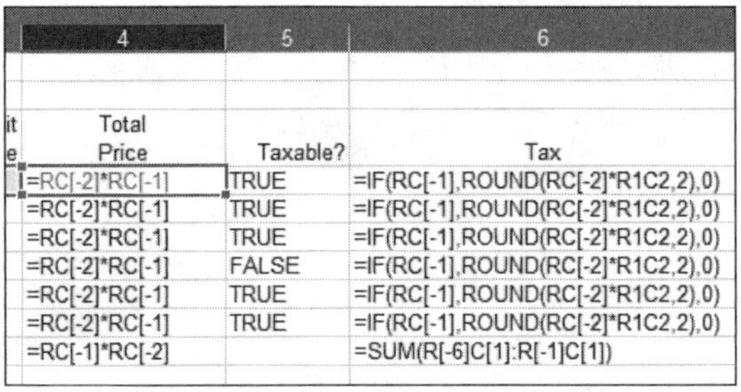

Figure 5.5
The same formulas in R1C1 style. Note that every formula in column 4 is the same, and every formula in column 6 is the same.

	4	5	6
it	Total		
e	Price	Taxable?	Tax
	=RC[-2]*RC[-1]	TRUE	=IF(RC[-1],ROUND(RC[-2]*R1C2,2),0)
	=RC[-2]*RC[-1]	TRUE	=IF(RC[-1],ROUND(RC[-2]*R1C2,2),0)
	=RC[-2]*RC[-1]	TRUE	=IF(RC[-1],ROUND(RC[-2]*R1C2,2),0)
	=RC[-2]*RC[-1]	FALSE	=IF(RC[-1],ROUND(RC[-2]*R1C2,2),0)
	=RC[-2]*RC[-1]	TRUE	=IF(RC[-1],ROUND(RC[-2]*R1C2,2),0)
	=RC[-2]*RC[-1]	TRUE	=IF(RC[-1],ROUND(RC[-2]*R1C2,2),0)
	=RC[-1]*RC[-2]		=SUM(R[-6]C[1]:R[-1]C[1])

This is one of the reasons R1C1-style formulas are more efficient than A1-style formulas in VBA. When you have the same formula being entered in an entire range, it is less confusing.

CASE STUDY: ENTERING A1 VERSUS R1C1 IN VBA

Think about how you would set up this spreadsheet in the Excel interface. First, you enter a formula in cells D4, F4, and G4. Next, you copy these cells and paste them the rest of the way down the column. By using R1C1-style formulas, you can enter the same formula in the entire column at once.

The equivalent code in R1C1 style allows the formulas to be entered for the entire column in a single statement. Remember, the advantage of R1C1-style formulas is that all the formulas in Columns D and F, and most of G, are identical:

```
Sub R1C1Style()
    ' Locate the FinalRow
```

```
        FinalRow = Cells(Rows.Count, 2).End(xlUp).Row
        ' Enter the first formula
        Range("D4:D" & FinalRow).FormulaR1C1 = "=RC[-1]*RC[-2]"
        Range("F4:F" & FinalRow).FormulaR1C1 = _
          "=IF(RC[-1],ROUND(RC[-2]*R1C2,2),0)"
        Range("G4:G" & FinalRow).FormulaR1C1 = "=RC[-1]+RC[-3]"
        ' Enter the Total Row
        Cells(FinalRow + 1, 1).Value = "Total"
        Cells(FinalRow + 1, 6).FormulaR1C1 = "=SUM(R4C:R[-1]C)"
    End Sub
```

> **NOTE**
> It seems counterintuitive, but when you specify an A1-style formula, Microsoft internally converts the formula to R1C1 and then enters that formula in the entire range. Thus, you can actually add the "same" A1-style formula to an entire range by using a single line of code:
>
> ```
> Range("D4:D" & FinalRow).Formula = "=B4*C4"
> ```

> **NOTE**
> Although you are asking for the formula =B4*C4 to be entered in D4:D1000, Excel enters this formula in row 4 and appropriately adjusts the formula for the additional rows.

Understanding the R1C1 Reference Style

An R1C1-style reference includes the letter R to refer to row and the letter C to refer to column. Because the most common reference in a formula is a relative reference, let's look at relative references in R1C1 style first.

Using R1C1 with Relative References

Imagine that you are entering a formula in a cell. To point to a cell in a formula, you use the letters R and C. After each letter, enter the number of rows or columns in square brackets.

The following list explains the "rules" for using R1C1 relative references:

- For columns, a positive number means to move to the right a certain number of columns, and a negative number means to move to the left a certain number of columns. For example, from cell E5, use RC[1] to refer to F5 and RC[-1] to refer to D5.

- For rows, a positive number means to move down the spreadsheet a certain number of rows. A negative number means to move toward the top of the spreadsheet a certain number of rows. For example, from cell E5, use R[1]C to refer to E6 and use cell R[-1]C to refer to E4.

- If you leave off the number for either the R or the C, it means that you are pointing to a cell in the same row or column as the cell with the formula. For example, the R in RC[3] means that you are pointing to the current row.

- If you enter =R[-1]C[-1] in cell E5, you are referring to a cell one row up and one column to the left. This would be cell D4.

- If you enter =RC[1] in cell E5, you are referring to a cell in the same row but one column to the right. This would be cell F5.

- If you enter =RC in cell E5, you are referring to a cell in the same row and column, which is cell E5 itself. You would generally not do this because it would create a circular reference.

Figure 5.6 shows how you would enter a reference in cell E5 to point to various cells around E5.

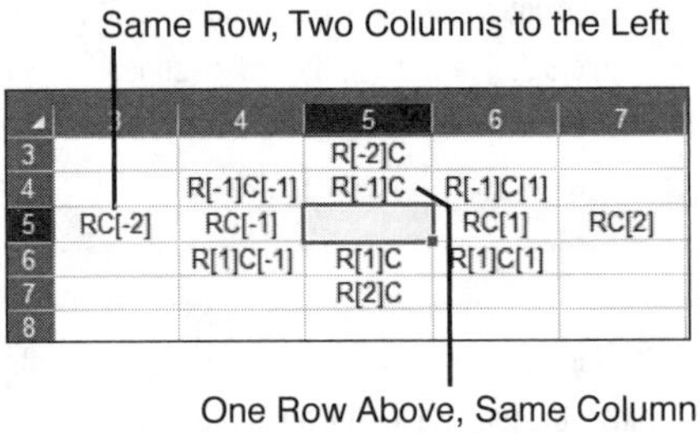

Figure 5.6
Here are various relative references. These would be entered in cell E5 to describe each cell around E5.

You can use R1C1 style to refer to a range of cells. If you want to add up the 12 cells to the left of the current cell, you use this formula:

```
=SUM(RC[-12]:RC[-1])
```

Using R1C1 with Absolute References

An *absolute reference* is a reference in which the row and column remain fixed when the formula is copied to a new location. In A1-style notation, Excel uses a $ before the row number or column letter to keep that row or column absolute as the formula is copied.

To always refer to an absolute row or column number, just leave off the square brackets. This reference refers to cell $B$3, no matter where it is entered:

```
=R3C2
```

Using R1C1 with Mixed References

A *mixed reference* is a reference in which the row is fixed and the column is allowed to be relative or in which the column is fixed and the row is allowed to be relative. This is useful in many situations.

Imagine that you have written a macro to import Invoice.txt into Excel. Using .End(xlUp), you find where the total row should go. As you are entering totals, you know that you want to sum from the row above the formula up to row 2. The following code would handle that:

```
Sub MixedReference()
```

```
        TotalRow = Cells(Rows.Count, 1).End(xlUp).Row + 1
        Cells(TotalRow, 1).Value = "Total"
        Cells(TotalRow, 5).Resize(1, 3).FormulaR1C1 = "=SUM(R2C:R[-1]C)"
    End Sub
```

In this code, the reference `R2C:R[-1]C` indicates that the formula should add from row 2 in the same column to the row just above the formula in the current column. Do you see the advantage to using R1C1 formulas in this case? You can use a single R1C1 formula with a mixed reference to easily enter a formula to handle an indeterminate number of rows of data (see Figure 5.7).

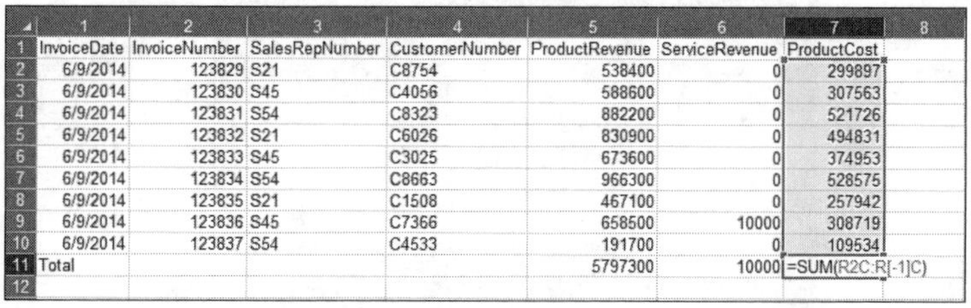

Figure 5.7
After the macro has run, the formulas in columns 5:7 of the total row will have a reference to a range that is locked to row 2, but all other aspects are relative.

	1	2	3	4	5	6	7	8
1	InvoiceDate	InvoiceNumber	SalesRepNumber	CustomerNumber	ProductRevenue	ServiceRevenue	ProductCost	
2	6/9/2014	123829	S21	C8754	538400	0	299897	
3	6/9/2014	123830	S45	C4056	588600	0	307563	
4	6/9/2014	123831	S54	C8323	882200	0	521726	
5	6/9/2014	123832	S21	C6026	830900	0	494831	
6	6/9/2014	123833	S45	C3025	673600	0	374953	
7	6/9/2014	123834	S54	C8663	966300	0	528575	
8	6/9/2014	123835	S21	C1508	467100	0	257942	
9	6/9/2014	123836	S45	C7366	658500	10000	308719	
10	6/9/2014	123837	S54	C4533	191700	0	109534	
11	Total				5797300	10000	=SUM(R2C:R[-1]C)	
12								

Referring to Entire Columns or Rows with R1C1 Style

You will occasionally write a formula that refers to an entire column. For example, you might want to know the maximum value in column G. If you don't know how many rows you will have in G, you can write `=MAX($G:$G)` in A1 style or `=MAX(C7)` in R1C1 style. To find the minimum value in row 1, use `=MIN($1:$1)` in A1 style or `=MIN(R1)` in R1C1 style. You can use relative reference for either rows or columns. To find the average of the row above the current cell, use `=AVERAGE(R[-1])`.

Replacing Many A1 Formulas with a Single R1C1 Formula

When you get used to R1C1-style formulas, they actually seem a lot more intuitive to build. One classic example to illustrate R1C1-style formulas is building a multiplication table. It is easy to build a multiplication table in Excel using a single mixed-reference formula.

Building the Table

Enter the numbers **1** through **12** going across B1:M1. Copy and transpose these so that the same numbers are going down A2:A13. Now the challenge is to build a single formula that works in all cells of B2:M13 and that shows the multiplication of the number in row 1 by the number in column 1. Using A1-style formulas, you must press the F4 key five times to get the dollar signs in the proper locations. The following is a far simpler formula in R1C1 style:

```
Sub MultiplicationTable()
    ' Build a multiplication table using a single formula
    Range("B1:M1").Value = Array(1, 2, 3, 4, 5, 6, 7, 8, 9, 10, 11, 12)
    Range("B1:M1").Font.Bold = True
    Range("B1:M1").Copy
```

5

```
        Range("A2:A13").PasteSpecial Transpose:=True
        Range("B2:M13").FormulaR1C1 = "=RC1*R1C"
        Cells.EntireColumn.AutoFit
    End Sub
```

The R1C1-style reference `=RC1*R1C` could not be simpler. In English, it is saying, “Take this row’s column 1 and multiply it by row 1 of this column.” It works perfectly to build the multiplication table shown in Figure 5.8.

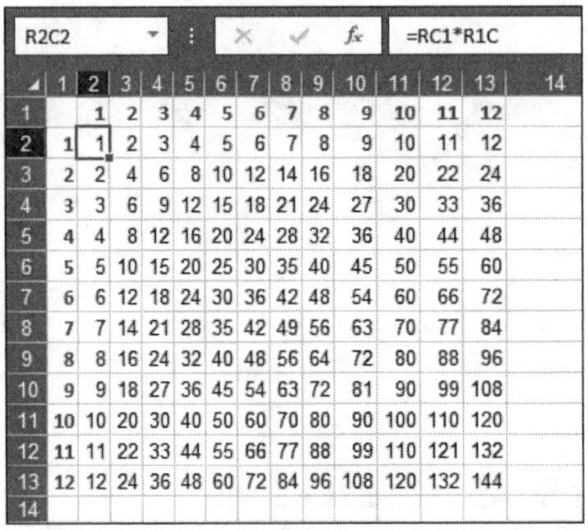

	1	2	3	4	5	6	7	8	9	10	11	12	13	14
1		1	2	3	4	5	6	7	8	9	10	11	12	
2	1	1	2	3	4	5	6	7	8	9	10	11	12	
3	2	2	4	6	8	10	12	14	16	18	20	22	24	
4	3	3	6	9	12	15	18	21	24	27	30	33	36	
5	4	4	8	12	16	20	24	28	32	36	40	44	48	
6	5	5	10	15	20	25	30	35	40	45	50	55	60	
7	6	6	12	18	24	30	36	42	48	54	60	66	72	
8	7	7	14	21	28	35	42	49	56	63	70	77	84	
9	8	8	16	24	32	40	48	56	64	72	80	88	96	
10	9	9	18	27	36	45	54	63	72	81	90	99	108	
11	10	10	20	30	40	50	60	70	80	90	100	110	120	
12	11	11	22	33	44	55	66	77	88	99	110	121	132	
13	12	12	24	36	48	60	72	84	96	108	120	132	144	
14														

Figure 5.8
The macro creates a multiplication table. The formula in B2 uses two mixed references: `=$A2*B$1`.

> **CAUTION**
>
> After running the macro and producing the multiplication table shown in Figure 5.8, note that Excel still has the copied range from line 2 of the macro as the active Clipboard item. If the user of this macro selects a cell and presses Enter, the contents of those cells copy to the new location. However, this is generally not desirable. To get Excel out of Cut/Copy mode, add this line of code before your program ends:
>
> ```
> Application.CutCopyMode = False
> ```

5

An Interesting Twist

Try this experiment: Move the cell pointer to F6. Turn on macro recording using the Record Macro button on the Developer tab. Click the Use Relative Reference button on the Developer tab. Enter the formula `=A1` and press Ctrl+Enter to stay in F6. Click the Stop Recording button on the floating toolbar. You get this single-line macro, which enters a formula that points to a cell five rows up and five columns to the left:

```
Sub Macro1()
    ActiveCell.FormulaR1C1 = "=R[-5]C[-5]"
End Sub
```

Now, move the cell pointer to cell A1 and run the macro that you just recorded. You might think that pointing to a cell five rows above A1 would lead to the ubiquitous Run Time Error 1004. But it doesn’t! When you run the macro, the formula in cell A1 is pointing to `=XFA1048572`, as shown in Figure 5.9, meaning that R1C1-style formulas actually wrap from the left side of the workbook to the right side. I cannot think of any instance in which this would actually be useful, but for those of you who rely on Excel to error out when you ask for something that does not make sense, be aware that your macro will happily provide a result and probably not the one that you expected!

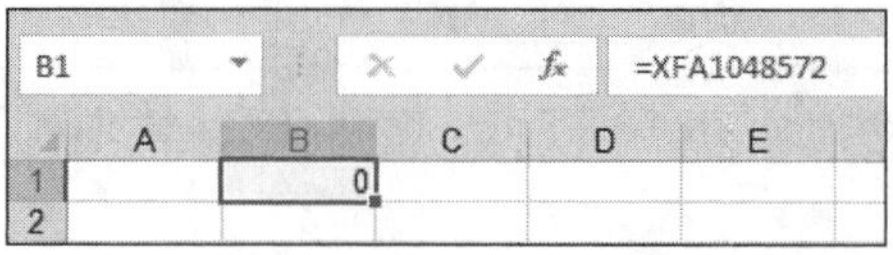

Figure 5.9
The formula to point to five rows above B1 wraps around to the bottom of the worksheet.

Remembering Column Numbers Associated with Column Letters

I like R1C1-style formulas enough to use them regularly in VBA. I don't like them enough to change my Excel interface over to R1C1-style numbers. So I routinely have to know that the cell known as U21, for example, is really R21C21.

Knowing that *U* is the twenty-first letter of the alphabet is not something that comes naturally. We have 26 letters, so *A* is 1 and *Z* is 26. *M* is the halfway point of the alphabet and is column 13. The rest of the letters are not particularly intuitive. A quick way to get the column number for any column is to enter =COLUMN() in any empty cell in that column. The result tells you that, for example, DGX is column 2910 (see Figure 5.10).

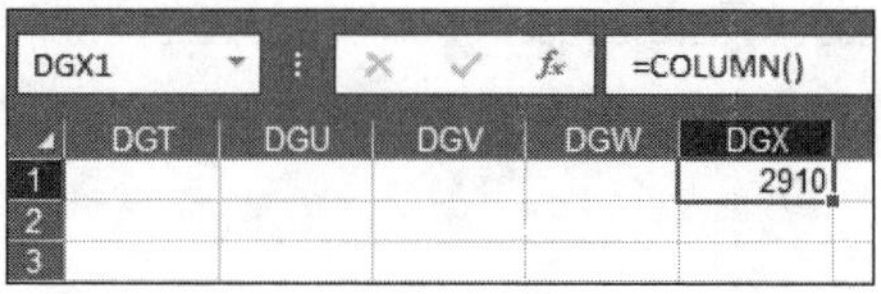

Figure 5.10
Use the temporary formula =COLUMN() to learn the column number of any cell.

You could also select any cell in DGX, switch to VBA, press Ctrl+G for the Immediate window, type **? ActiveCell.Column**, and press Enter.

Using R1C1 Formulas with Array Formulas

Array formulas are powerful "superformulas." At MrExcel.com, we call these CSE formulas because you have to use Ctrl+Shift+Enter to enter them. If you are not familiar with array formulas, you probably think they look as though they should not work.

The array formula in F4 in Figure 5.11 is a formula that does more than 19,000 multiplications and then sums the result. It looks as though this would be an illegal formula. In fact, if you happen to enter it without using Ctrl+Shift+Enter, you get the expected #VALUE! error. However, if you enter it with Ctrl+Shift+Enter, the formula miraculously pops out an array of 19,000 values and evaluates each one.

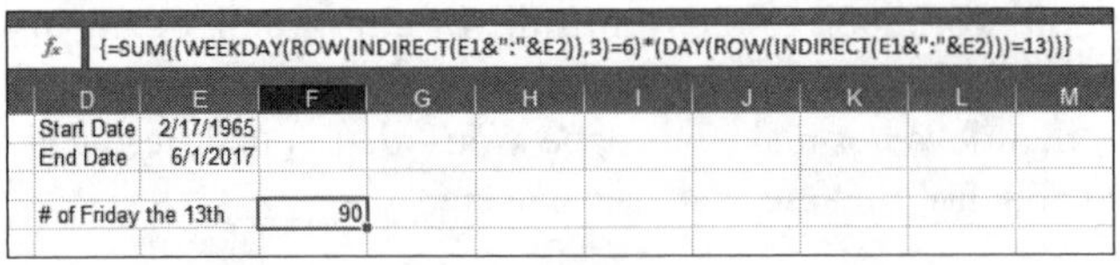

Figure 5.11
The array formula in F4 does 19,000 calculations. You must use Ctrl+Shift+Enter to enter this formula.

> **NOTE**
>
> You do not type the curly braces when entering the formula. Excel adds them for you when you press Ctrl+Shift+Enter.
>
> The code to enter these formulas follows:
>
> ```
> Sub EnterArrayFormulas()
> Cells(4, 6).FormulaArray = "=SUM((WEEKDAY(ROW(INDIRECT(" & _
>     "R[-3]C[-1]& "":""&R[-2]C[-1])),3)=6)*(DAY(ROW(INDIRECT(" & _
>     "(R[-3]C[-1]&"":""&R[-2]C[-1])))=13))"
> End Sub
> ```

Note that although the formulas appear in the user interface in A1-style notation, you must use R1C1-style notation for entering array formulas.

> **TIP**
>
> Use this trick to quickly find the R1C1 formula: Enter a regular A1-style formula or an array formula in any cell in Excel. Select that cell. Switch to the VB Editor. Press Ctrl+G to display the Immediate window. Type **Print ActiveCell.FormulaR1C1** and press Enter. Excel converts the formula in the formula bar to an R1C1-style formula. You also can use a question mark instead of `Print`.

Next Steps

Read Chapter 6, "Creating and Manipulating Names in VBA," to learn how to use named ranges in macros.

Creating and Manipulating Names in VBA

6

You've probably named ranges in a worksheet by highlighting a range and typing a name in the Name box to the left of the formula bar. You also might have created more complicated names containing formulas. For example, perhaps you created a name with a formula that finds the last row in a column. The ability to name a range makes it much easier to write formulas.

The ability to create and manipulate names is also available in VBA, and provides the same benefits as naming ranges in a worksheet. For example, you can store a new range in a name.

This chapter explains different types of names and the various ways you can use them.

Global Versus Local Names

Names that are *global* are available anywhere in a workbook. Names that are *local* are available only on a specific worksheet. With local names, you can have multiple references in the workbook with the same name. Global names must be unique to the workbook.

The Name Manager dialog box (accessed via the Formulas tab) lists all the names in a workbook, even a name that has been assigned to both the global and the local levels. The Scope column lists the scope of the name, whether it is the workbook or a specific sheet such as Sheet1.

For example, in Figure 6.1 the name Apples is assigned to Sheet1 and also to the workbook.

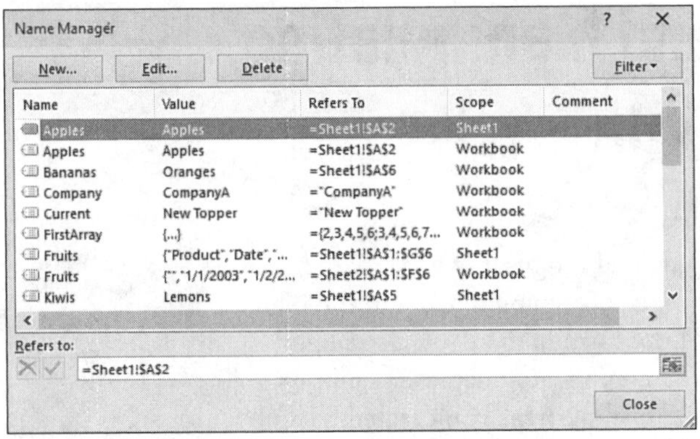

Figure 6.1
The Name Manager lists all local and global names.

Adding Names

If you record the creation of a named range and then view the code, you see something like this:

```
ActiveWorkbook.Names.Add Name:="Fruits", RefersToR1C1:="=Sheet2!R1C1:R6C6"
```

This creates a global name Fruits, which includes the range A1:F6 (R1C1:R6C6). The formula is enclosed in quotes, and the equal sign in the formula must be included. In addition, the range reference must be absolute (that is, it must include the $ sign) or in R1C1 notation. If the sheet on which the name is created is the active sheet, the sheet reference does not have to be included. However, including the sheet reference can make the code easier to understand.

> **NOTE** If a reference is not absolute, the name might be created, but it will not point to the correct range. For example, if you run the following line of code, the name is created in the workbook:
>
> ```
> ActiveWorkbook.Names.Add Name:="Citrus", _
>         RefersTo:="=Sheet1!A1"
> ```
>
> However, as you can see in Figure 6.2, the name hasn't actually been assigned to the range. The reference will change depending on which cell is the active cell when the name is viewed.

To create a local name, include the sheet name with the Name parameter:

```
ActiveWorkbook.Names.Add Name:="Sheet2!Fruits", _
        RefersToR1C1:="=Sheet2!R1C1:R6C6"
```

Alternatively, specify that the Names collection belongs to a worksheet:

```
Worksheets("Sheet2").Names.Add Name:="Fruits", _
    RefersToR1C1:="=Sheet2!R1C1:R6C6"
```

The preceding example shows what you would get from the macro recorder. There is simpler code to get the same result:

```
Range("A1:F6").Name = "Fruits"
```

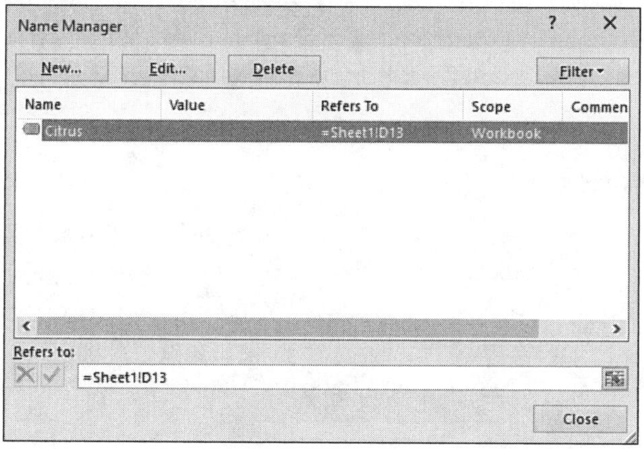

Figure 6.2
Despite what was coded, because absolute referencing was not used, Citrus refers to the active cell.

Alternatively, for a local variable only, you can use this:

```
Range("A1:F6").Name = "Sheet1!Fruits"
```

When creating names with these methods, absolute referencing is not required.

> **NOTE** You can use table names like defined names, but you don't create them the same way. See the "Tables" section later in this chapter for more information about creating table names.

Although this method is much easier and quicker than what the macro recorder creates, it is limited in that it works only for ranges. Formulas, strings, numbers, and arrays require the use of the Add method.

The name you create becomes an object when referenced like this:

```
Names("Fruits")
```

The object has many properties, including Name, which you can use to rename the existing name, like this:

```
Names("Fruits").Name = "Produce"
```

Fruits no longer exists; Produce is now the name of the range.

When you are renaming names in which a local reference and a global reference both carry the same name, the previous line renames the local reference first.

Deleting Names

Use the Delete method to delete a name:

```
Names("ProduceNum").Delete
```

An error occurs if you attempt to delete a name that does not exist.

6

Adding Comments

You can add comments about names, such as why a name was created or where it is used. To insert a comment for the local name `LocalOffice`, do this:

```
ActiveWorkbook.Worksheets("Sheet7").Names("LocalOffice").Comment = _
    "Holds the name of the current office"
```

The comments appear in a column in the Name Manager, as shown in Figure 6.3.

CAUTION

The name must exist before a comment can be added to it.

Figure 6.3
You can add comments about names to help remember their purpose.

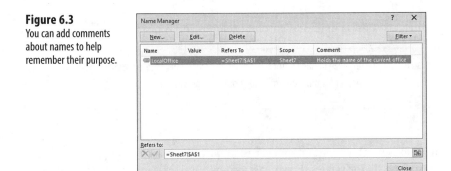

Types of Names

The most common use of names is for storing ranges; however, names can store more than just ranges. After all, names store information. Names make it simple to remember and use potentially complex or large amounts of information. In addition, unlike variables, names remember what they store beyond the life of the program.

You know how to create range names, but you can also assign names to name formulas, strings, numbers, and arrays, as described in the following pages.

Formulas

The syntax for storing a formula in a name is the same as for a range because the range is essentially a formula. The following code allows for a dynamic named column with the item listing starting in A2:

```
Names.Add Name:="ProductList", _
    RefersTo:="=OFFSET(Sheet2!$A$2,0,0,COUNTA(Sheet2!$A:$A))"
```

This code is useful for creating dynamic data sets or for referencing any dynamic listing on which calculations may be performed, as shown in Figure 6.4.

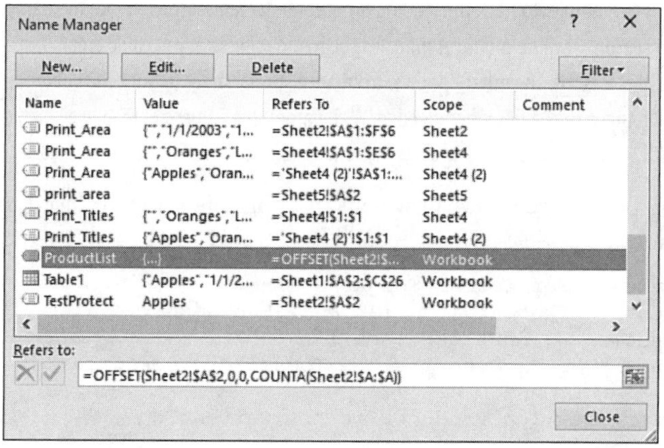

Figure 6.4
Dynamic formulas can be assigned to names.

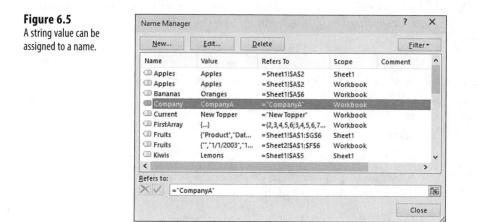

Strings

When using names to hold strings such as the name of the current fruit producer, enclose the string value in quotes. Because no formula is involved, an equal sign is not needed. If you were to include an equal sign, Excel would treat the value as a formula. Let Excel include the equal sign shown in the Name Manager.

```
Names.Add Name: = "Company", RefersTo:="CompanyA"
```

Figure 6.5 shows how the coded name appears in the Name Manager window.

Figure 6.5
A string value can be assigned to a name.

6

> **TIP** Because names do not lose their references between sessions, using names is a great way to store values as opposed to storing values in cells from which the information would have to be retrieved. For example, to track the leading producer between seasons, create the name `Leader`. If the new season's leading producer matches the name reference, you could create a special report comparing the seasons. The other option is to create a special sheet to track the values between sessions and then retrieve the values when needed. With names, the values are readily available.

The following procedure shows how cells in a variable sheet are used to retain information between sessions:

```
Sub NoNames(ByRef CurrentTop As String)
TopSeller = Worksheets("Variables").Range("A1").Value
If CurrentTop = TopSeller Then
    MsgBox "Top Producer is " & TopSeller & " again."
Else
    MsgBox "New Top Producer is " & CurrentTop
End If
End Sub
```

The following procedure shows how names are used to store information between sessions:

```
Sub WithNames()
If Evaluate("Current") = Evaluate("Previous") Then
    MsgBox "Top Producer is " & Evaluate("Previous") & " again."
Else
    MsgBox "New Top Producer is " & Evaluate("Current")
End If
End Sub
```

If `Current` and `Previous` are previously declared names, you access them directly rather than create variables in which to pass them. Note the use of the `Evaluate` method to extract the values in names. The string being stored cannot have more than 255 characters.

Numbers

You can use names to store numbers between sessions. Here's an example:

```
NumofSales = 5123
Names.Add Name:="TotalSales", RefersTo:=NumofSales
```

Alternatively, you can use this:

```
Names.Add Name:="TotalSales", RefersTo:=5123
```

Notice the lack of quotes and an equal sign in the `RefersTo` parameter. Using quotes changes the number to a string. With the addition of an equal sign in the quotes, the number changes to a formula.

To retrieve the value in the name, you have a longer and a shorter option:

```
NumofSales = Names("TotalSales").Value
```

or this:

```
NumofSales = [TotalSales]
```

NOTE Keep in mind that someone reading your code might not be familiar with the use of the `Evaluate` method (square brackets). If you know that someone else will be reading your code, avoid the use of the `Evaluate` method or add a comment explaining it.

Tables

Excel tables share some of the properties of defined names, but they also have their own unique methods. Unlike with the defined names you are used to dealing with, you cannot manually create tables. In other words, you cannot select a range on a sheet and type a name in the Name field. However, you can manually create them via VBA.

Tables are not created using the same method as defined names. Instead of `Range(xx).Add` or `Names.Add`, use `ListObjects.Add`.

To create a table from cells A1:C26, and assuming that the data table has column headers, as shown in Figure 6.6, use this:

```
ActiveSheet.ListObjects.Add(xlSrcRange, Range("$A$1:$C$26"), , xlYes)._
Name = "Table1"
```

Figure 6.6
You can turn a normal table into an Excel table by assigning a name to it using VBA.

`xlSrcRange` (the `SourceType`) tells Excel that the source of the data is an Excel range. You then need to specify the range (the source) of the table. If you have headers in the table, include that row when indicating the range. The next argument, which is not used in the preceding example, is `LinkSource`, a Boolean indicating whether there is an external data source that is not used if `SourceType` is `xlSrcRange`. `xlYes` lets Excel know that the data table has column headers; otherwise, Excel automatically generates them. The final argument, which is not shown in the preceding example, is the destination. This is used when `SourceType` is `xlSrcExternal`, indicating the upper-left cell where the table will begin.

Using Arrays in Names

A name can hold the data stored in an array. The array size is limited by available memory. See Chapter 8, "Arrays," for more information about arrays.

An array reference is stored in a name the same way as a numeric reference:

```
Sub NamedArray()
Dim myArray(10, 5)
Dim i As Integer, j As Integer
```

```
'The following For loops fill the array myArray
For i = 0 To 10 'by default arrays start at 0
    For j = 0 To 5
        myArray(i, j) = i + j
    Next j
Next i
'The following line takes our array and gives it a name
Names.Add Name:="FirstArray", RefersTo:=myArray
End Sub
```

Because the name references a variable, no quotes or equal signs are required.

Reserved Names

Excel uses local names of its own to keep track of information. These local names are considered reserved, and if you use them for your own references, they might cause problems.

Highlight an area on a sheet. Then from the Page Layout tab, select Print Area, Set Print Area.

As shown in Figure 6.7, a `Print_Area` listing is in the Name field. Deselect the area and look again in the Name field drop-down. The name is still listed there. Select it, and the print area that was previously set is now highlighted. If you save, close, and reopen the workbook, `Print_Area` is still set to the same range. `Print_Area` is a name reserved by Excel for its own use.

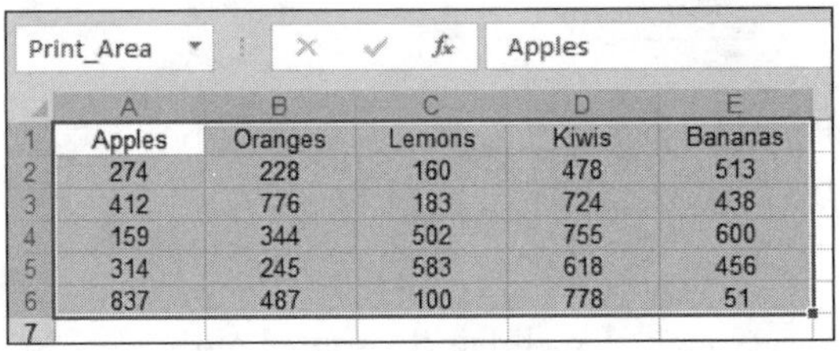

Figure 6.7
Excel creates its own names.

	A	B	C	D	E
1	Apples	Oranges	Lemons	Kiwis	Bananas
2	274	228	160	478	513
3	412	776	183	724	438
4	159	344	502	755	600
5	314	245	583	618	456
6	837	487	100	778	51
7					

NOTE   Each sheet has its own print area. In addition, setting a new print area on a sheet that has an existing print area overwrites the original print-area name.

Fortunately, Excel does not have a large list of reserved names:

```
Criteria
Database
Extract
Print_Area
Print_Titles
```

`Criteria` and `Extract` are used when Advanced Filter (on the Data tab, select Advanced from the Sort & Filter group) is configured to extract the results of the filter to a new location.

`Database` is no longer required in Excel. However, some features, such as Data Form, still recognize it. Legacy versions of Excel used it to identify the data you wanted to manipulate in certain functions.

`Print_Area` is used when a print area is set (from the Page Layout tab, select Print Area, Set Print Area) or when Page Setup options that designate the print area (from the Page Layout tab, Scale) are changed.

`Print_Titles` is used when print titles are set (select Page Layout, Print Titles).

You should avoid using these reserved names, and you should use variations on them with caution. For example, if you create the name `PrintTitles`, you might accidentally code this:

```
Worksheets("Sheet4").Names("Print_Titles").Delete
```

If you do this, you delete the Excel name rather than your custom name.

Hiding Names

Names are incredibly useful, but you don't necessarily want to see all the names you have created. Like many other objects, names have a `Visible` property. To hide a name, set the `Visible` property to `False`. To unhide a name, set the `Visible` property to `True`:

```
Names.Add Name:="ProduceNum", RefersTo:="=$A$1", Visible:=False
```

> **TIP** If a user creates a `Name` object with the same name as the hidden one, the hidden name is overwritten without any warning message. To prevent this, protect the worksheet.

Checking for the Existence of a Name

You can use the following function to check for the existence of a user-defined name, even a hidden one:

```
Function NameExists(FindName As String) As Boolean
Dim Rng As Range
Dim myName As String
On Error Resume Next 'skip the error if the name doesn't exist
myName = ActiveWorkbook.Names(FindName).Name
If Err.Number = 0 Then
    NameExists = True
Else
    NameExists = False
End If
On Error Goto 0
End Function
```

6

Keep in mind that this function does not return the existence of Excel's reserved names. Even so, this is a handy addition to your arsenal of "programmers' useful code." (See Chapter 14, "Sample User-Defined Functions," for more information on implementing custom functions.)

The preceding code is also an example of how to use errors to your advantage. If the name for which you are searching does not exist, an error message is generated. By adding the `On Error Resume Next` line at the beginning, you force the code to continue. Then you use `Err.Number` to find out whether it ran into an error. If it didn't, `Err.Number` is zero, which means the name exists. Otherwise, you had an error, and the name does not exist. Use `On Error Goto 0` to reset error trapping; otherwise, other errors may be skipped.

CASE STUDY: USING NAMED RANGES FOR VLOOKUP

Say that every day, you import a file of sales data from a chain of retail stores. The file includes the store number but not the store name. You obviously don't want to have to type store names every day, but you would like to have store names appear on all the reports that you run.

You have a table of store numbers and names on a back worksheet. You want to use VBA to help maintain the list of stores each day and then use the VLOOKUP function to get store names from the list into your data set.

The basic steps are listed here:

1. Import the data file.
2. Find all the unique store numbers in today's file.
3. See whether any of these store numbers are not in your current table of store names.
4. For any stores that are new, add them to the table, and ask the user for a store name.
5. The Store Names table is larger, but because tables automatically size themselves, you don't need to do anything.
6. Use a VLOOKUP function in the original data set to add a store name to all records. This VLOOKUP references the named range of the newly expanded Store Names data set.

The following code handles these six steps:

```
Sub ImportData()
'This routine imports sales.csv to the data sheet
'Check to see whether any stores in column A are new
'If any are new, then add them to the StoreList table
Dim WSD As Worksheet, WSM As Worksheet
Dim WB As Workbook
Dim tblStores As ListObject
Dim NewRow As ListRow

Set WB = ThisWorkbook
'Data is stored on the Data worksheet
Set WSD = WB.Worksheets("Data")
'StoreList is stored on a menu worksheet
Set WSM = WB.Worksheets("Menu")
Set tblStores = WSM.ListObjects("tblStoreLookup")

'Open the file. This makes the csv file active
Workbooks.Open Filename:="C:\Sales.csv"
'Copy the data to WSD and close
ActiveWorkbook.Range("A1").CurrentRegion.Copy _
    Destination:=WSD.Range("A1")
ActiveWorkbook.Close SaveChanges:=False
```

```vba
'Create a list of unique stores from column A and place in Z
FinalRow = WSD.Cells(WSD.Rows.Count, 1).End(xlUp).Row
WSD.Range("A1").Resize(FinalRow, 1).AdvancedFilter _
    Action:=xlFilterCopy, CopyToRange:=WSD.Range("Z1"), Unique:=True

'For all the unique stores, see whether they are in the
'current store list
'ISNA returns True for missing store because the VLOOKUP will
'return an error
FinalStore = WSD.Range("Z" & WSD.Rows.Count).End(xlUp).Row
WSD.Range("AA1").Value = "There?"
WSD.Range("AA2:AA" & FinalStore).FormulaR1C1 = _
    "=ISNA(VLOOKUP(RC[-1], tblStoreLookup[#All],1,False))"

'Loop through the list of today's stores. If they are shown
' as missing, then add them at the bottom of the StoreList
For i = 2 To FinalStore
    If WSD.Cells(i, 27).Value = True Then
        'get the next available row in the table
        Set NewRow = tblStores.ListRows.Add
        ThisStore = Cells(i, 26).Value
        With NewRow.Range
            .Columns(1) = ThisStore
            .Columns(2) = _
            InputBox(Prompt:="Enter name of store " _
            & ThisStore, Title:="New Store Found")
        End With
    End If
Next i

'Delete the temporary list of stores in Z & AA
WSD.Range("Z1:AA" & FinalStore).Clear

'Use VLOOKUP to add StoreName to column B of the data set
WSD.Range("B1").EntireColumn.Insert
WSD.Range("B1").Value = "StoreName"
WSD.Range("B2:B" & FinalRow).FormulaR1C1 = _
    "=VLOOKUP(RC1, tblStoreLookup[#All],2,False)"

'Change Formulas to Values
WSD.Range("B2:B" & FinalRow).Value = Range("B2:B" & FinalRow).Value

'Fix columnwidths
WSD.Range("A1").CurrentRegion.EntireColumn.AutoFit

'Release variables to free system memory
Set NewRow = Nothing
Set tblStores = Nothing
Set WB = Nothing
Set WSD = Nothing
Set WSM = Nothing
End Sub
```

6

Next Steps

In Chapter 7, "Event Programming," you'll find out how you can write code to run automatically based on users' actions such as activating a sheet or selecting a cell. This is done with events, which are actions in Excel that you can capture and use to your advantage.

6

Event Programming

In this book, you have read about workbook events, and you have seen examples of worksheet events. An *event* allows you to automatically trigger a procedure to run based on something a user or another procedure does in Excel. For example, if a user changes the contents of a cell, after he or she presses Enter or Tab, you can have code run automatically. The event that triggers the code is the changing of the contents of the cell.

7

Levels of Events

You can find events at the following levels:

- **Application level**—Control based on application actions, such as `Application_NewWorkbook`
- **Workbook level**—Control based on workbook actions, such as `Workbook_Open`
- **Worksheet level**—Control based on worksheet actions, such as `Worksheet_SelectionChange`
- **Chart sheet level**—Control based on chart actions, such as `Chart_Activate`

These are the places where you should put different types of events:

- Workbook events go into the ThisWorkbook module.
- Worksheet events go into the module of the sheet they affect, such as Sheet1.
- Chart sheet events go into the module of the chart sheet they affect, such as Chart1.
- Pivot table events go into the module of the sheet with the pivot table, or they can go into the ThisWorkbook module.
- Embedded chart and application events go into class modules.

The events can still make procedure or function calls outside their own modules. Therefore, if you want the same action to take place for two different sheets, you don't have to copy the code. Instead, place the code in a module and have each sheet event call the procedure.

This chapter explains different levels of events, where to find them, and how to use the events.

> **NOTE** Userform and control events are discussed in Chapter 10, "Userforms: An Introduction," and Chapter 22, "Advanced Userform Techniques."

Using Events

Each level consists of several types of events, and memorizing the syntax of them all would be a feat. Excel makes it easy to view and insert the available events in their proper modules right from the VB Editor.

When a ThisWorkbook, Sheet, Chart Sheet, or Class module is active, the corresponding events are available through the Object and Procedure drop-downs, as shown in Figure 7.1.

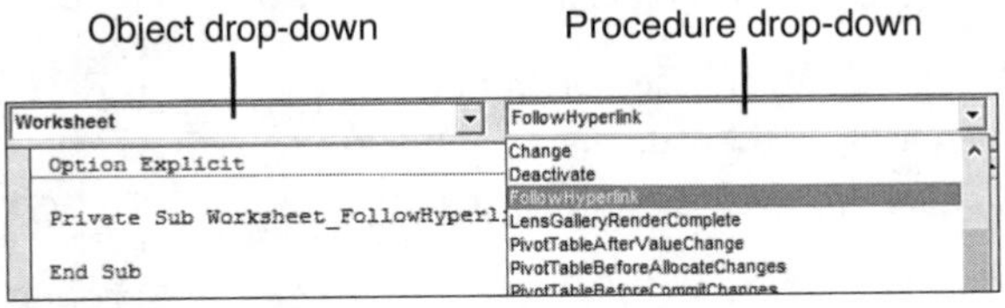

Figure 7.1
The different events are easy to access from the VB Editor Object and Procedure drop-downs.

After an object is selected, the Procedure drop-down updates to list the events available for that object. Selecting a procedure automatically places the procedure header (`Private Sub`) and footer (`End Sub`) in the editor, as shown in Figure 7.2.

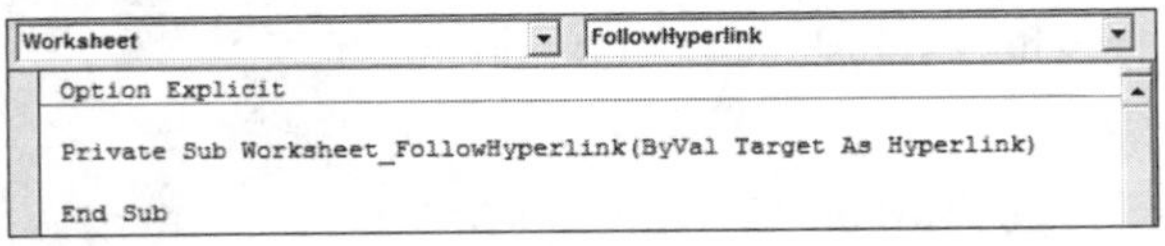

Figure 7.2
The procedure header and footer are automatically placed.

Event Parameters

Some events have parameters, such as `Target` or `Cancel`, that allow values to be passed into the procedure. For example, some procedures are triggered before the actual event, such as `BeforeRightClick`. Assigning `True` to the `Cancel` parameter prevents the default action from taking place. In this case, the shortcut menu is prevented from appearing:

```
Private Sub Worksheet_BeforeRightClick(ByVal Target As Range, _
    Cancel As Boolean)
Cancel = True
End Sub
```

Enabling Events

Some events can trigger other events, including themselves. For example, the `Worksheet_Change` event is triggered by a change in a cell. If the event is triggered and the procedure itself changes a cell, the event gets triggered again, which changes a cell, triggering the event, and so on. The procedure gets stuck in an endless loop.

To prevent an endless loop, disable the events and then reenable them at the end of the procedure:

```
Private Sub Worksheet_Change(ByVal Target As Range)
    Application.EnableEvents = False
    Range("A1").Value = Target.Value
    Application.EnableEvents = True
End Sub
```

> **TIP** To interrupt a macro, press Esc or Ctrl+Break. To restart it, use Run on the toolbar or press F5.

Workbook Events

Table 7.1 lists event procedures that are available at the workbook level. Some events, such as `Workbook_SheetActivate`, are sheet events that are available at the workbook level. This means you don't have to copy and paste the code in each sheet in which you want it to run.

Table 7.1   Workbook Events

Event Name	Description
`Workbook_Activate`	Occurs when the workbook containing this event becomes the active workbook.
`Workbook_Deactivate`	Occurs when the active workbook is switched from the workbook containing the event to another workbook.
`Workbook_Open`	The default workbook event; occurs when a workbook is opened; no user interface is required.
`Workbook_BeforeSave`	Occurs when the workbook is saved. `SaveAsUI` is set to `True` if the Save As dialog box is to be displayed. Setting `Cancel` to `True` prevents the workbook from being saved.
`Workbook_AfterSave`	Occurs after the workbook is saved. `Success` returns `True` if the file saved successfully and `False` if the save was not successful.
`Workbook_BeforePrint`	Occurs when any print command is used, whether it is in the ribbon, on the keyboard, or in a macro. Setting `Cancel` to `True` prevents the workbook from being printed.
`Workbook_BeforeClose`	Occurs when the user closes a workbook. Setting `Cancel` to `True` prevents the workbook from closing.

7

Event Name	Description
Workbook_NewSheet	Occurs when a new sheet is added to the active workbook. Sh is the new worksheet or chart sheet object.
Workbook_SheetBeforeDelete	Occurs before any worksheet in the workbook is deleted. Sh is the sheet being deleted.
Workbook_NewChart	Occurs when the user adds a new chart to the active workbook. Ch is the new chart object. The event is not triggered if a chart is moved from one location to another, unless it is moved between a chart sheet and a chart object. In that case, the event is triggered because a new chart sheet or object is being created.
Workbook_WindowResize	Occurs when the user resizes the active workbook's window. Wn is the window.
Workbook_WindowActivate	Occurs when the user activates any workbook window. Wn is the window. Only activating the workbook window starts this event.
Workbook_WindowDeactivate	Occurs when the user deactivates any workbook window. Wn is the window. Only deactivating the workbook window starts this event.
Workbook_AddInInstall	Occurs when the user installs the workbook as an add-in (by selecting File, Options, Add-ins). Double-clicking an .xlam file (an add-in) to open it does not activate the event.
Workbook_AddInUninstall	Occurs when the user uninstalls the workbook (add-in). The add-in is not automatically closed.
Workbook_Sync	Occurs when the user synchronizes the local copy of a sheet in a workbook that is part of a Document Workspace with the copy on the server. Synceventtype is the status of the synchronization.
Workbook_PivotTableCloseConnection	Occurs when a pivot table report closes its connection to its data source. Target is the pivot table that has closed the connection.
Workbook_PivotTableOpenConnection	Occurs when a pivot table report opens a connection to its data source. Target is the pivot table that has opened the connection.
Workbook_RowsetComplete	Occurs when the user drills through a record set or calls on the row set action on an OLAP pivot table. Description is a description of the event; Sheet is the name of the sheet on which the record set is created; Success indicates success or failure.
Workbook_BeforeXmlExport	Occurs when the user exports or saves XML data. Map is the map used to export or save the data; Url is the location of the XML file; setting Cancel to True cancels the export operation.
Workbook_AfterXmlExport	Occurs after the user exports or saves XML data. Map is the map used to export or save the data; Url is the location of the XML file; Result indicates success or failure.
Workbook_BeforeXmlImport	Occurs when the user imports or refreshes XML data. Map is the map used to import the data; Url is the location of the XML file; isrefresh returns True if the event was triggered by refreshing an existing connection and False if triggered by importing from a new data source; setting Cancel to True cancels the import or refresh operation.

Event Name	Description
`Workbook_AfterXmlImport`	Occurs when the user exports or saves XML data. `Map` is the map used to export or save the data; `isrefresh` returns `True` if the event was triggered by refreshing an existing connection and `False` if triggered by importing from a new data source; `Result` indicates success or failure.
`Workbook_ModelChange`	Occurs when the user changes the Data Model. `Changes` is the type of change, such as columns added, changed, or deleted, that was made to the Data Model.

Workbook-Level Sheet and Chart Events

Table 7.2 lists sheet and chart events that are available at the workbook level. These events affect all sheets in the workbook.

Table 7.2   Workbook-Level Sheet and Chart Events

Event Name	Description
`Workbook_SheetActivate`	Occurs when the user activates any chart sheet or worksheet in the workbook. `Sh` is the active sheet.
`Workbook_SheetBeforeDoubleClick`	Occurs when the user double-clicks any chart sheet or worksheet in the active workbook. `Sh` is the active sheet; `Target` is the object that's double-clicked; setting `Cancel` to `True` prevents the default action from taking place.
`Workbook_SheetBeforeRightClick`	Occurs when the user right-clicks any worksheet in the active workbook. `Sh` is the active worksheet; `Target` is the object that's right-clicked; setting `Cancel` to `True` prevents the default action from taking place.
`Workbook_SheetCalculate`	Occurs when any worksheet is recalculated or any updated data is plotted on a chart. `Sh` is the sheet that triggers the calculation.
`Workbook_SheetChange`	Occurs when the user changes any range in a worksheet. `Sh` is the worksheet; `Target` is the changed range.
`Workbook_SheetDeactivate`	Occurs when the user deactivates any chart sheet or worksheet in the workbook. `Sh` is the sheet being switched from.
`Workbook_SheetFollowHyperlink`	Occurs when the user clicks any hyperlink in Excel. `Sh` is the active worksheet; `Target` is the hyperlink.
`Workbook_SheetSelectionChange`	Occurs when the user selects a new range on any sheet. `Sh` is the active sheet; `Target` is the affected range.

7

Event Name	Description
Workbook_SheetTableUpdate	Occurs when the user changes a table object. Sh is the sheet with the table; Target is the table object that was updated.
Workbook_SheetLensGalleryRenderComplete	Occurs when the user selects the Quick Analysis tool. Sh is the active sheet.
Workbook_SheetPivotTableUpdate	Occurs when the user updates a pivot table. Sh is the sheet with the pivot table; Target is the updated pivot table.
Workbook_SheetPivotTableAfterValueChange	Occurs after the user edits cells inside a pivot table or the user recalculates them if they contain a formula. Sh is the sheet the pivot table is on; TargetPivotTable is the pivot table with the changed cells; TargetRange is the range that was changed.
Workbook_SheetPivotTableBeforeAllocateChanges	Occurs before a pivot table is updated from its OLAP data source. Sh is the sheet the pivot table is on; TargetPivotTable is the updated pivot table; ValueChangeStart is the index number of the first change; ValueChangeEnd is the index number of the last change; setting Cancel to True prevents the changes from being applied to the pivot table.
Workbook_SheetPivotTableBeforeCommitChanges	Occurs before an OLAP pivot table updates its data source. Sh is the sheet the pivot table is on; TargetPivotTable is the updated pivot table; ValueChangeStart is the index number of the first change; ValueChangeEnd is the index number of the last change; setting Cancel to True prevents the changes from being applied to the data source.
Workbook_SheetPivotTableBeforeDiscardChanges	Occurs before an OLAP pivot table discards changes from its data source. Sh is the sheet the pivot table is on; TargetPivotTable is the pivot table with changes to discard; ValueChangeStart is the index number of the first change; ValueChangeEnd is the index number of the last change.
Workbook_SheetPivotTableChangeSync	Occurs after the user changes a pivot table. Sh is the sheet the pivot table is on; Target is the pivot table that has been changed.

Worksheet Events

Table 7.3 lists event procedures that are available at the worksheet level.

Table 7.3 Worksheet Events

Event Name	Description
`Worksheet_Activate`	Occurs when the sheet on which the event is located becomes the active sheet.
`Worksheet_Deactivate`	Occurs when another sheet becomes the active sheet. If a `Deactivate` event is on the active sheet and you switch to a sheet with an `Activate` event, the `Deactivate` event runs first, followed by the `Activate` event.
`Worksheet_BeforeDoubleClick`	Allows control over what happens when the user double-clicks the sheet. `Target` is the selected range on the sheet; `Cancel` is set to `False` by default, but if set to `True`, it prevents the default action, such as entering a cell, from happening.
`Worksheet_BeforeRightClick`	Occurs when the user right-clicks a range. `Target` is the object that's right-clicked; setting `Cancel` to `True` prevents the default action from taking place.
`Worksheet_Calculate`	Occurs after a sheet is recalculated.
`Worksheet_Change`	Triggered by a change to a cell's value, such as when the user enters, edits, deletes or pastes text. Recalculation of a value does not trigger the event. `Target` is the cell that has been changed.
`Worksheet_SelectionChange`	Occurs when the user selects a new range. `Target` is the newly selected range.
`Worksheet_FollowHyperlink`	Occurs when the user clicks a hyperlink. `Target` is the hyperlink.
`Worksheet_LensGalleryRenderComplete`	Occurs when the user selects the Quick Analysis tool.
`Worksheet_PivotTableUpdate`	Occurs when the user updates a pivot table. `Target` is the updated pivot table.
`Worksheet_PivotTableAfterValueChange`	Occurs after the user edits cells inside a pivot table or the user recalculates them if they contain a formula. `TargetPivotTable` is the pivot table with the changed cells; `TargetRange` is the range that was changed.
`Worksheet_PivotTableBeforeAllocateChanges`	Occurs before a pivot table is updated from its OLAP data source. `Sh` is the sheet the pivot table is on; `TargetPivotTable` is the updated pivot table; `ValueChangeStart` is the index number of the first change; `ValueChangeEnd` is the index number of the last change; setting `Cancel` to `True` prevents the changes from being applied to the pivot table.
`Worksheet_PivotTableBeforeCommitChanges`	Occurs before an OLAP pivot table updates its data source. `TargetPivotTable` is the updated pivot table; `ValueChangeStart` is the index number of the first change; `ValueChangeEnd` is the index number of the last change; setting `Cancel` to `True` prevents the changes from being applied to the data source.

7

Event Name	Description
Worksheet_ PivotTableBeforeDiscardChanges	Occurs before an OLAP pivot table discards changes from its data source. `TargetPivotTable` is the pivot table with changes to discard; `ValueChangeStart` is the index number of the first change; `ValueChangeEnd` is the index number of the last change.
Worksheet_PivotTableChangeSync	Occurs after a pivot table has been changed. `Target` is the pivot table that has been changed.

CASE STUDY: QUICKLY ENTERING MILITARY TIME INTO A CELL

Say that you're entering arrival and departure times and want the times to be formatted with a 24-hour clock, also known as *military time*. You have tried formatting the cell, but no matter how you enter the times, they are displayed in the 0:00 hours and minutes format.

The only way to get the time to appear as military time, such as 23:45, is to have the time entered in the cell in that manner. Because typing the colon is time-consuming, it would be more efficient to enter the numbers and let Excel format the time for you.

The solution is to use a `Change` event to take what is in the cell and insert the colon for you:

```
Private Sub Worksheet_Change(ByVal Target As Range)
Dim ThisColumn As Integer
Dim UserInput As String, NewInput As String
ThisColumn = Target.Column
If ThisColumn < 3 Then
    If Target.Count > 1 Then Exit Sub 'check that only 1 cell is selected
    If Len(Target) = 1 Then Exit Sub 'check more than 1 character entered

    UserInput = Target.Value
        If UserInput > 1 Then
            NewInput = Left(UserInput, Len(UserInput) - 2) & ":" & _
            Right(UserInput, 2)
            Application.EnableEvents = False
            Target = NewInput
            Application.EnableEvents = True
        End If
End If
End Sub
```

An entry of 2345 displays as 23:45. Note that the code limits this format change to columns A and B (If ThisColumn < 3). Without this limitation, entering numbers anywhere on a sheet such as in a totals column would force the numbers to be reformatted.

> **NOTE** Use `Application.EnableEvents = False` to prevent the procedure from calling itself when the value in the target is updated.

Chart Events

Chart events occur when a chart is changed or activated. Embedded charts require the use of class modules to access the events. For more information about class modules, see Chapter 9, "Creating Classes and Collections."

Embedded Charts

Because embedded charts do not create chart sheets, the chart events are not as readily available as those of chart sheets. However, you can make them available by adding a class module, as described here:

1. Insert a class module.
2. Rename the module to something that will make sense to you, such as
   `cl_ChartEvents`.
3. Enter the following line of code in the class module:
   ```
   Public WithEvents myChartClass As Chart
   ```
   The chart events are now available to the chart, as shown in Figure 7.3. They are accessed in the class module rather than on a chart sheet.
4. Insert a standard module.
5. Enter the following lines of code in the standard module:

   ```
   Dim myClassModule As New cl_ChartEvents
   Sub InitializeChart()
       Set myClassModule.myChartClass = _
               Worksheets(1).ChartObjects(1).Chart
   End Sub
   ```

These lines initialize the embedded chart to be recognized as a chart object. The procedure must be run once per Excel session.

> **NOTE** You can use `Workbook_Open` to automatically run the `InitializeChart` procedure.

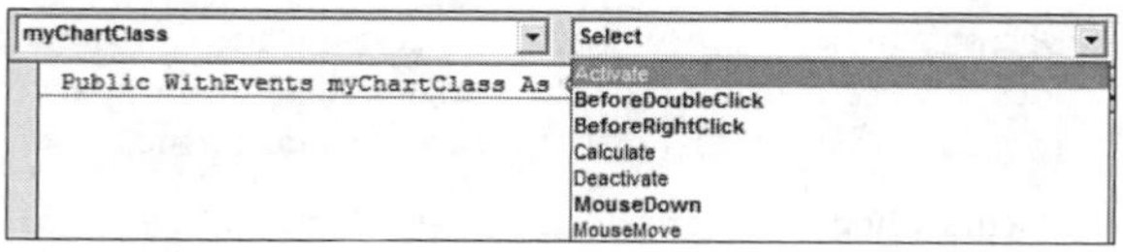

Figure 7.3
Embedded chart events are now available in the class module.

Embedded Chart and Chart Sheet Events

Whether a chart is embedded on a regular sheet or is its own chart sheet, the same events are available. The only difference will be that the procedure heading for an embedded chart replaces `Chart` with the class object you created. For example, to trigger the BeforeDoubleClick event on a chart sheet, the procedure header would be this:

`Chart_BeforeDoubleClick`

To trigger the BeforeDoubleClick event on an embedded chart (using the class object created in the previous section), the procedure header would be this:

`myChartClass_BeforeDoubleClick`

Table 7.4 lists the various chart events available to both embedded charts and chart sheets:

Table 7.4   Chart Events

Event Name	Description
`Chart_Activate`	Occurs when a chart sheet is activated or changed.
`Chart_BeforeDoubleClick`	Occurs when any part of a chart is double-clicked. `ElementID` is the part of the chart that is double-clicked, such as the legend. `Arg1` and `Arg2` are dependent on the `ElementID`; setting `Cancel` to `True` prevents the default double-click action from occurring.
`Chart_BeforeRightClick`	Occurs when the user right-clicks a chart. Setting `Cancel` to `True` prevents the default right-click action from occurring.
`Chart_Calculate`	Occurs when the user changes a chart's data.
`Chart_Deactivate`	Occurs when the user makes another sheet the active sheet.
`Chart_MouseDown`	Occurs when the cursor is over the chart and the user presses any mouse button. `Button` is the mouse button that was clicked; `Shift` is whether a Shift, Ctrl, or Alt key was pressed; `X` is the X coordinate of the cursor when the button is pressed; `Y` is the Y coordinate of the cursor when the button is pressed.
`Chart_MouseMove`	Occurs as the user moves the cursor over a chart. `Button` is the mouse button being held down, if any; `Shift` is whether a Shift, Ctrl, or Alt key was pressed; `X` is the X coordinate of the cursor on the chart; `Y` is the Y coordinate of the cursor on the chart.
`Chart_MouseUp`	Occurs when the user releases any mouse button while the cursor is on the chart. `Button` is the mouse button that was clicked; `Shift` is whether a Shift, Ctrl, or Alt key was pressed; `X` is the X coordinate of the cursor when the button is released; `Y` is the Y coordinate of the cursor when the button is released.
`Chart_Resize`	Occurs when the user resizes a chart using the resize handles. However, this does not occur when the size is changed using the size controls on the Chart Tools, Format tab or Format Chart Area task pane.
`Chart_Select`	Occurs when the user selects a chart element. `ElementID` is the part of the chart selected, such as the legend. `Arg1` and `Arg2` are dependent on the `ElementID`.
`Chart_SeriesChange`	Occurs when a chart data point is updated. `SeriesIndex` is the offset in the `Series` collection of updated series; `PointIndex` is the offset in the `Point` collection of updated points.

Application-Level Events

Application-level events, listed in Table 7.5, affect all open workbooks in an Excel session. You need a class module to access them. This is similar to the class module used to access events for embedded chart events. Follow these steps to create the class module:

1. Insert a class module.

2. Rename the module to something that will make sense to you, such as `cl_AppEvents`.

3. Enter the following line of code in the class module:

    ```
    Public WithEvents AppEvent As Application
    ```

    The application events are now available to the workbook, as shown in Figure 7.4. They are accessed in the class module rather than in a standard module.

4. Insert a standard module.

5. Enter the following lines of code in the standard module:

    ```
    Dim myAppEvent As New cl_AppEvents
    Sub InitializeAppEvent()
        Set myAppEvent.AppEvent = Application
    End Sub
    ```

These lines initialize the application to recognize application events. The procedure must be run once per session.

> **TIP**
>
> You can use `Workbook_Open` to automatically run the `InitializeAppEvent` procedure.

Figure 7.4
Application events are now available through the class module.

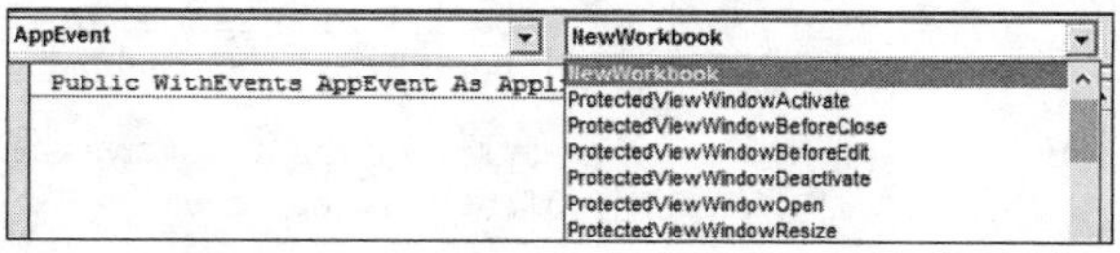

> **NOTE**
>
> The object in front of the event, such as `AppEvent`, is dependent on the name given in the class module.

7

Table 7.5 Application Events

Event Name	Description
`AppEvent_AfterCalculate`	Occurs after all calculations are complete, after `AfterRefresh`, and `SheetChange` events, and after `Application.CalculationState` is set to `xlDone`, and there aren't any outstanding queries or incomplete calculations.
`AppEvent_NewWorkbook`	Occurs when the user creates a new workbook. `Wb` is the new workbook.
`AppEvent_ProtectedViewWindowActivate`	Occurs when the user activates a workbook in Protected View mode. `Pvw` is the workbook being activated.
`AppEvent_ProtectedViewWindowBeforeClose`	Occurs when the user closes a workbook in Protected View mode. `Pvw` is the workbook being deactivated; `Reason` is why the workbook closed; setting `Cancel` to `True` prevents the workbook from closing.
`AppEvent_ProtectedViewWindowDeactivate`	Occurs when the user deactivates a workbook in Protected View mode. `Pvw` is the workbook being deactivated.
`AppEvent_ProtectedViewWindowOpen`	Occurs when a workbook is open in Protected View mode. `Pvw` is the workbook being opened.
`AppEvent_ProtectedViewWindowResize`	Occurs when the user resizes the window of the protected workbook. However, this does not occur in the application itself. `Pvw` is the workbook that's being resized.
`AppEvent_ProtectedViewWindowBeforeEdit`	Occurs when the user clicks the Enable Editing button of a protected workbook. `Pvw` is the protected workbook; setting `Cancel` to `True` prevents the workbook from being enabled.
`AppEvent_SheetActivate`	Occurs when the user activates a sheet. `Sh` is the worksheet or chart sheet.
`AppEvent_SheetBeforeDelete`	Occurs before any worksheet in a workbook is deleted. `Sh` is the sheet being deleted.
`AppEvent_SheetBeforeDoubleClick`	Occurs when the user double-clicks a worksheet. `Target` is the selected range on the sheet; `Cancel` is set to `False` by default. However, when set to `True`, it prevents the default action, such as entering a cell, from happening.
`AppEvent_SheetBeforeRightClick`	Occurs when the user right-clicks any worksheet. `Sh` is the active worksheet; `Target` is the object that's right-clicked; setting `Cancel` to `True` prevents the default action from taking place.
`AppEvent_SheetCalculate`	Occurs when the user recalculates any worksheet or plots any updated data on a chart. `Sh` is the active sheet.

Event Name	**Description**
AppEvent_SheetChange	Occurs when the user changes the value of any cell. Sh is the worksheet; Target is the changed range.
AppEvent_SheetDeactivate	Occurs when the user deactivates any chart sheet or worksheet in a workbook. Sh is the sheet being deactivated.
AppEvent_SheetFollowHyperlink	Occurs when the user clicks any hyperlink in Excel. Sh is the active worksheet; Target is the hyperlink.
AppEvent_SheetSelectionChange	Occurs when the user selects a new range on any sheet. Sh is the active sheet; Target is the selected range.
AppEvent_SheetTableUpdate	Occurs when the user changes a table object. Sh is the active sheet; Target is the table object that was updated.
AppEvent_SheetLensGalleryRenderComplete	Occurs when the user selects the Quick Analysis tool. Sh is the active sheet.
AppEvent_SheetPivotTableUpdate	Occurs when the user updates a pivot table. Sh is the active sheet; Target is the updated pivot table.
AppEvent_SheetPivotTableAfterValueChange	Occurs after the user edits cells inside a pivot table or, if the cells contain a formula, the user recalculates them. Sh is the sheet the pivot table is on; TargetPivotTable is the pivot table with the changed cells; TargetRange is the range that was changed.
AppEvent_SheetPivotTableBeforeAllocateChanges	Occurs before a pivot table is updated from its OLAP data source. Sh is the sheet the pivot table is on; TargetPivotTable is the updated pivot table; ValueChangeStart is the index number of the first change; ValueChangeEnd is the index number of the last change; setting Cancel to True prevents the changes from being applied to the pivot table.
AppEvent_SheetPivotTableBeforeCommitChanges	Occurs before an OLAP pivot table updates its data source. Sh is the sheet the pivot table is on; TargetPivotTable is the updated pivot table; ValueChangeStart is the index number of the first change; ValueChangeEnd is the index number of the last change; setting Cancel to True prevents the changes from being applied to the data source.
AppEvent_SheetPivotTableBeforeDiscardChanges	Occurs before an OLAP pivot table discards changes from its data source. Sh is the sheet the pivot table is on; TargetPivotTable is the pivot table with changes to discard; ValueChangeStart is the index number of the first change; ValueChangeEnd is the index number of the last change.
AppEvent_SheetPivotTableChangeSync	Occurs after the user changes a pivot table. Sh is the sheet the pivot table is on; Target is the pivot table that has been changed.

7

Event Name	Description
AppEvent_WindowActivate	Occurs when the user activates any workbook window. Wb is the workbook that's being deactivated; Wn is the window. This works only if there are multiple windows.
AppEvent_WindowDeactivate	Occurs when the user deactivates any workbook window. Wb is the active workbook; Wn is the window. This works only if there are multiple windows.
AppEvent_WindowResize	Occurs when the user resizes the active workbook. Wb is the active workbook; Wn is the window. This works only if there are multiple windows.
AppEvent_WorkbookActivate	Occurs when the user activates any workbook. Wb is the workbook being activated.
AppEvent_WorkbookDeactivate	Occurs when the user switches between workbooks. Wb is the workbook that's being switched away from.
AppEvent_WorkbookAddinInstall	Occurs when the user installs a workbook as an add-in (via File, Options, Add-ins). Double-clicking an .xlam file to open it does not activate the event. Wb is the workbook being installed.
AppEvent_WorkbookAddinUninstall	Occurs when the user uninstalls a workbook (add-in). The add-in is not automatically closed. Wb is the workbook being uninstalled.
AppEvent_WorkbookBeforeClose	Occurs when the user closes a workbook. Wb is the workbook; setting Cancel to True prevents the workbook from closing.
AppEvent_WorkbookBeforePrint	Occurs when the user uses any print command (via the ribbon, keyboard, or a macro). Wb is the workbook; setting Cancel to True prevents the workbook from being printed.
AppEvent_Workbook_BeforeSave	Occurs when the user saves the workbook. Wb is the workbook; SaveAsUI is set to True if the Save As dialog box is to be displayed; setting Cancel to True prevents the workbook from being saved.
AppEvent_WorkbookAfterSave	Occurs after the user has saved the workbook. Wb is the workbook; Success returns True if the file saved successfully and returns False if the save was not successful.
AppEvent_WorkbookNewSheet	Occurs when the user adds a new sheet to the active workbook. Wb is the workbook; Sh is the new worksheet.
AppEvent_WorkbookNewChart	Occurs when the user adds a new chart to the active workbook. Wb is the workbook; Ch is the new chart object. The event is not triggered if the user moves a chart from one location to another, unless the user moves it between a chart sheet and a chart object. In that case, the event is triggered because a new chart sheet or object is being created.

7

Event Name	Description
`AppEvent_WorkbookOpen`	Occurs when the user opens a workbook. `Wb` is the workbook that was just opened.
`AppEvent_WorkbookPivotTableCloseConnection`	Occurs when a pivot table report closes its connection to its data source. `Wb` is the workbook containing the pivot table that triggered the event; `Target` is the pivot table that has closed the connection.
`AppEvent_WorkbookPivotTableOpenConnection`	Occurs when a pivot table report opens a connection to its data source. `Wb` is the workbook containing the pivot table that triggered the event; `Target` is the pivot table that has opened the connection.
`AppEvent_WorkbookRowsetComplete`	Occurs when the user drills through a record set or calls upon the row set action on an OLAP pivot table. `Wb` is the workbook that triggered the event; `Description` is a description of the event; `Sheet` is the name of the sheet on which the record set is created; `Success` indicates success or failure.
`AppEvent_WorkbookSync`	Occurs when the user synchronizes the local copy of a sheet in a workbook that is part of a document workspace with the copy on the server. `Wb` is the workbook that triggered the event; `SyncEventType` is the status of the synchronization.
`AppEvent_WorkbookBeforeXmlExport`	Occurs when the user exports or saves XML data. `Wb` is the workbook that triggered the event; `Map` is the map used to export or save the data; `Url` is the location of the XML file; `Cancel` set to `True` cancels the export operation.
`AppEvent_WorkbookAfterXmlExport`	Occurs after the user exports or saves XML data. `Wb` is the workbook that triggered the event; `Map` is the map used to export or save the data; `Url` is the location of the XML file; `Result` indicates success or failure.
`AppEvent_WorkbookBeforeXmlImport`	Occurs when the user imports or refreshes XML data. `Wb` is the workbook that triggered the event; `Map` is the map used to import the data; `Url` is the location of the XML file; `IsRefresh` returns `True` if the event was triggered by refreshing an existing connection and `False` if triggered by importing from a new data source; setting `Cancel` to `True` cancels the import or refresh operation.
`AppEvent_WorkbookAfterXmlImport`	Occurs when the user exports or saves XML data. `Wb` is the workbook that triggered the event; `Map` is the map used to export or save the data; `IsRefresh` returns `True` if the event was triggered by refreshing an existing connection and `False` if triggered by importing from a new data source; `Result` indicates success or failure.

7

Event Name	Description
AppEvent_WorkbookModelChange	Occurs when the user changes the Data Model. Wb is the workbook that triggered the event; Changes is the type of change, such as columns added, changed, or deleted, that the user made to the Data Model.

Next Steps

In this chapter, you've learned more about interfacing with Excel. In Chapter 8, "Arrays," you'll find out how to use multidimensional arrays. Reading data into a multidimensional array, performing calculations on the array, and then writing the array back to a range can speed up your macros dramatically.

Arrays

An *array* is a type of variable that can be used to hold more than one piece of data. For example, if you have to work with the name and address of a client, your first thought might be to assign one variable for the name and another for the address of the client. Instead, consider using an array, which can hold both pieces of information—and not for just one client but for hundreds.

Declaring an Array

You declare an array by adding parentheses after the array name and specifying the number of array elements in the parentheses:

```
Dim myArray(2)
```

This creates an array, myArray, that contains three elements:

```
myArray(0) = 10
myArray(1) = 20
myArray(2) = 30
```

Three elements are included because, by default, the index count starts at 0. If the index count needs to start at 1, use Option Base 1 to force the count to start at 1. To do this, place the Option Base statement in the declarations section at the top of the module:

```
Option Base 1
Sub MyFirstArray()
Dim myArray(2)
```

This now forces the array to have only two elements.

You can also create an array independently of the Option Base statement by declaring its lower bound:

```
Dim myArray(1 to 10)
Dim BigArray(100 to 200)
```

Every array has a lower bound (LBound) and an upper bound (UBound). When you declare Dim myArray(2), you are declaring the upper bound and allowing the Option Base statement to declare the lower bound. By declaring Dim myArray(1 to 10), you declare the lower bound, 1, and the upper bound, 10.

Declaring a Multidimensional Array

The arrays just discussed are considered *one-dimensional arrays* because only one number designates the location of an element of the array. Such an array is like a single row of data, but because there can be only one row, you do not have to worry about the row number—only the column number. For example, to retrieve the second element (Option Base 0), use myArray(1).

In some cases, a single dimension is not enough. This is where multidimensional arrays come in. Whereas a one-dimensional array is a single row of data, a multidimensional array contains rows *and* columns.

> **NOTE** Another word for array is *matrix*, which is what a spreadsheet is. The Cells object refers to elements of a spreadsheet—and a cell consists of a row and a column. You have been using arrays all along!

To declare another dimension to an array, you add another argument. The following creates an array of 10 rows and 20 columns:

```
Dim myArray(1 to 10, 1 to 20)
```

The following code places values in the first two columns of the first row, as shown in Figure 8.1:

```
myArray(1,1) = 10
myArray(1,2) = 20
```

Figure 8.1
The VB Editor Watches window shows the first "row" of the array being filled from the previous lines of code.

The following code places values in the first two columns of the second row:

```
myArray(2,1) = 20
myArray(2,2) = 40
```

And so on. Of course, this is time-consuming and can require many lines of code. Other ways to fill an array are discussed in the next section.

> **NOTE** To get the upper or lower bounds of another dimension, you have to specify the dimension. For example, to retrieve the upper bound of the second dimension, use this: `UBound(MyArray,2)`.

Filling an Array

Now that you can declare an array, you need to fill it. One method discussed earlier is to enter a value for each element of the array individually. However, there is a quicker way, as shown in the following sample code and Figure 8.2:

```
Option Base 1

Sub ColumnHeaders()
Dim myArray As Variant 'Variants can hold any type of data, including arrays
Dim myCount As Integer

'Fill the variant with array data
myArray = Array("Name", "Address", "Phone", "Email")

'Empty the array by placing it in a range of the same size
'if not using Option Base 1, then add 1 to LBound
Worksheets("Sheet2").Range("A1").Resize(LBound(myArray), _
    UBound(myArray)).Value = myArray
End With
End Sub
```

Figure 8.2
Use an array to create column headers quickly.

⊿	A	B	C	D	E
1	Name	Address	Phone	Email	
2					

`Variant` variables can hold any type of information. Create a `Variant`-type variable that can be treated like an array. Use the `Array` function to shove the data into the variant and force the variant to take on the properties of an array. Notice that you don't declare the size of the array when you fill it, as shown in the previous example.

If the information needed in the array is on the sheet already, use the following to fill an array quickly. This code creates an array that is 16 rows by 2 columns:

```
Dim myArray As Variant
myArray = Worksheets("Sheet1").Range("B2:C17")
```

Although these two methods are quick and straightforward, they might not always suit the situation. For example, if you need every other row in an array, use the following code (see Figure 8.3):

```
Sub EveryOtherRow()
'there are 16 rows of data, but we are only filling every other row
'half the table size, so our array needs only 8 rows
Dim myArray(1 To 8, 1 To 2)
Dim i As Integer, j As Integer, myCount As Integer

'Fill the array with every other row
```

```
For i = 1 To 8
    For j = 1 To 2
'i*2 directs the program to retrieve every other row
        myArray(i, j) = Worksheets("Sheet1").Cells(i * 2, j + 1).Value
    Next j
Next i

'Calculate contents of array and transfer results to sheet
For myCount = LBound(myArray) To UBound(myArray)
    Worksheets("Sheet1").Cells(myCount * 2, 4).Value = _
    WorksheetFunction.Sum(myArray(myCount, 1), myArray(myCount, 2))
Next myCount
End Sub
```

Figure 8.3
Fill the array with only
the data needed.

	A	B	C	D
1		Dec '14	Jan '15	Sum
2	Apples	45	0	45
3	Oranges	12	10	
4	Grapefruit	86	12	98
5	Lemons	15	15	
6	Tomatoes	58	24	82

LBound finds the start location—the lower bound—of the array (myArray). UBound finds the end location—the upper bound—of the array. The program can then loop through the array and sum the information as it writes it to the sheet. How to empty an array is explained in the following section.

Retrieving Data from an Array

After an array is filled, the data needs to be retrieved. However, before you do that, you can manipulate the data or return information about it, such as the maximum integer, as shown in the following code (see Figure 8.4):

```
Sub QuickFillMax()
Dim myArray As Variant

myArray = Worksheets("Sheet1").Range("B2:C12").Value
MsgBox "Maximum Integer is: " & WorksheetFunction.Max(myArray)

End Sub
```

Figure 8.4
Return the Max variable
in an array.

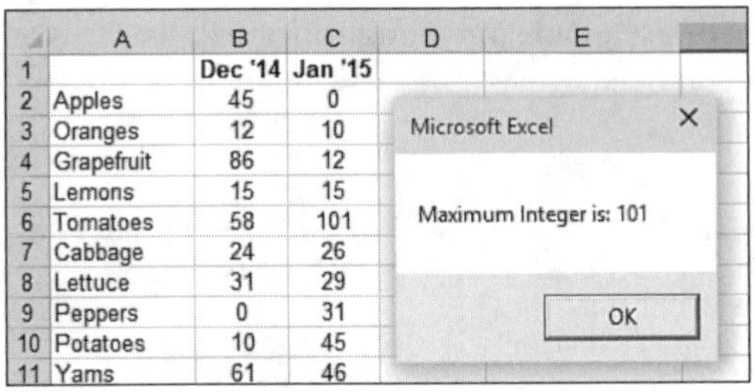

	A	B	C	D	E
1		Dec '14	Jan '15		
2	Apples	45	0		
3	Oranges	12	10	Microsoft Excel	×
4	Grapefruit	86	12		
5	Lemons	15	15		
6	Tomatoes	58	101	Maximum Integer is: 101	
7	Cabbage	24	26		
8	Lettuce	31	29		
9	Peppers	0	31		
10	Potatoes	10	45	OK	
11	Yams	61	46		

Data can also be manipulated before it is returned to the sheet. In the following example, LBound and UBound are used with a For loop to loop through the elements of the array and average each set:

NOTE MyCount + 1 is used to place the results back on the sheet because LBound is 1 and the data starts in row 2.

```
Sub QuickFillAverage()
Dim myArray As Variant
Dim myCount As Integer
'fill the array
myArray = Worksheets("Sheet1").Range("B2:C12")

'Average the data in the array just as it is placed on the sheet
For myCount = LBound(myArray) To UBound(myArray)
'calculate the average and place the result in column E
    Worksheets("Sheet1").Cells(myCount + 1, 5).Value = _
    WorksheetFunction.Average(myArray(myCount, 1), myArray(myCount, 2))
Next myCount
End Sub
```

The results are placed on the sheet in a new column (see Figure 8.5).

Figure 8.5
Calculations can be done on the data as it is returned to the sheet.

⊿	A	B	C	D	E
1		Dec '14	Jan '15	Sum	Average
2	Apples	45	0	45	22.5
3	Oranges	12	10		11
4	Grapefruit	86	12	98	49
5	Lemons	15	15		15
6	Tomatoes	58	101	159	79.5
7	Cabbage	24	26		25

Using Arrays to Speed Up Code

So far you have learned that arrays can make it easier to manipulate data and get information from it, but is that all they are good for? No, arrays are powerful because they can actually make the code run faster!

In the preceding example, each row was processed as it was placed on the sheet. Imagine doing that 10,000 times, 100,000 times, or more. Each time Excel has to write to the sheet, it slows down. You can minimize writing to the sheet by doing the processing in memory and then writing the data to the sheet one time.

In the following example, the calculated average is placed in a second array: MyAverage. First, you ReDim it so that it has enough room to hold all the calculated values. (See the section "Using Dynamic Arrays" later in this chapter for more information.) Then, after looping and filling it, you place the entire array on the sheet. Notice that the range you place it in is resized to fit the entire array. Also, because the array was created in code and is just a single element (row), you have to transpose it so it's in column form:

```
Sub QuickFillAverageFast()
'Writes the data to the sheet once
'Also more flexible with dynamic range
Dim myArray As Variant, MyAverage As Variant
Dim myCount As Long, LastRow As Long
Dim wksData As Worksheet
Set wksData = Worksheets("EveryOther")
With wksData
    LastRow = .Range("A" & .Rows.Count).End(xlUp).Row
    myArray = .Range("B2:C" & LastRow)

    ReDim MyAverage(UBound(myArray))
    For myCount = LBound(myArray) To UBound(myArray)
        MyAverage(myCount) = _
            WorksheetFunction.Average(myArray(myCount, 1), _
                myArray(myCount, 2))
    Next myCount
    .Range("E2").Resize(UBound(MyAverage)).Value = _
        Application.Transpose(MyAverage)
End With
End Sub
```

Using Dynamic Arrays

You don't always know how big an array needs to be. You could create an array based on how big it could ever need to be, but that's a waste of memory—and what if it turns out that it needs to be even bigger? To avoid this problem, you can use a *dynamic array*. A dynamic array is an array that does not have a set size. In other words, you declare the array but leave the parentheses empty, like this:

```
Dim myArray()
```

Later, as the program needs to use the array, ReDim is used to set the size of the array. The following program, which returns the names of all the sheets in the workbook, first creates a boundless array and then sets the upper bound after it knows how many sheets are in the workbook:

```
Sub MySheets()
Dim myArray() As String
Dim myCount As Integer, NumShts As Integer

NumShts = ActiveWorkbook.Worksheets.Count

'Size the array
ReDim myArray(1 To NumShts)

For myCount = 1 To NumShts
    myArray(myCount) = ActiveWorkbook.Sheets(myCount).Name
Next myCount

End Sub
```

Using ReDim reinitializes the array. Therefore, if you use it many times, such as in a loop, you lose all the data it holds. To prevent this from happening, use Preserve. The Preserve keyword enables you to resize the last array dimension, but you cannot use it to change the number of dimensions.

The following example looks for all the Excel files in a directory and puts the results in an array. Because you do not know how many files there will be until you actually look at them, you can't size the array before the program is run:

```
Sub XLFiles()
Dim FName As String
Dim arNames() As String
Dim myCount As Integer

FName = Dir("C:\Excel VBA 2016 by Jelen & Syrstad\*.xls*")
Do Until FName = ""
    myCount = myCount + 1
    ReDim Preserve arNames(1 To myCount)
    arNames(myCount) = FName
    FName = Dir
Loop
End Sub
```

> **NOTE** Using `Preserve` with large amounts of data in a loop can slow down the program. If possible, use code to figure out the maximum size of an array as soon as possible.

Passing an Array

Just like strings, integers, and other variables, arrays can be passed into other procedures. This makes for more efficient and easier-to-read code. The following sub, PassAnArray, passes the array myArray into the function RegionSales. The data in the array is summed for the specified region, and the result is returned to the sub:

```
Sub PassAnArray()
Dim myArray() As Variant
Dim myRegion As String

myArray = Range("mySalesData") 'named range containing all the data
myRegion = InputBox("Enter Region - Central, East, West")
MsgBox myRegion & " Sales are: " & Format(RegionSales(myArray, _
    myRegion), "$#,#00.00")
End Sub

Function RegionSales(ByRef BigArray As Variant, sRegion As String) As Long
Dim myCount As Integer

RegionSales = 0
For myCount = LBound(BigArray) To UBound(BigArray)
'The regions are listed in column 1 of the data,
'hence the 1st column of the array
    If BigArray(myCount, 1) = sRegion Then
        'The data to sum is the 6th column in the data
        RegionSales = BigArray(myCount, 6) + RegionSales
    End If
Next myCount
End Function
```

Refer to Chapter 14, "Sample User-Defined Functions," to learn more about using functions.

> **CAUTION**
>
> You can't assign the values of one array to be the values of another unless both arrays are the same size or the second array doesn't have specifically declared dimensions. To append values from one array to another or to pass values between arrays of differing sizes, you have to loop through the arrays.

Next Steps

Arrays are a type of variable used for holding more than one piece of data. In Chapter 9, "Creating Classes and Collections," you'll discover the powerful technique of setting up your own class module. With this technique, you can set up your own object with its own methods and properties.

Creating Classes and Collections

Excel already has many objects available, but there are times when the job at hand requires a custom object. You can create custom objects that you use in the same way as Excel's built-in objects. These special objects are created in *class modules*.

Class modules are used to create custom objects with custom properties and methods. They can also be used to trap application events, embedded chart events, ActiveX control events, and more.

Collections are a variable type that can hold groups of similar items, including custom objects. Each item in a collection has a unique key and you can use that unique key to retrieve a value, including all the properties of an object, from the collection.

Inserting a Class Module

From the VB Editor, select Insert, Class Module. A new module, Class1, is added to the VBAProject workbook and is visible in the Project Explorer window (see Figure 9.1). Here are two things to keep in mind concerning class modules:

- Each custom object must have its own module. (Event trapping can share a module.)
- The class module should be renamed to reflect the custom object.

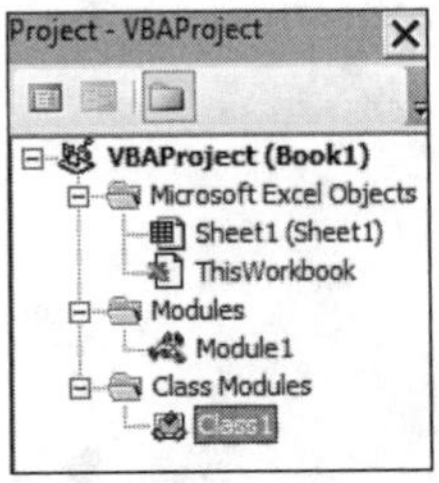

Figure 9.1
Custom objects are created in class modules.

Trapping Application and Embedded Chart Events

Chapter 7, "Event Programming," showed you how certain actions in workbooks, worksheets, and nonembedded charts can be trapped and used to activate code. It briefly reviewed how to set up a class module to trap application and chart events. The following text goes into more detail about what was shown in that chapter.

Application Events

The `Workbook_BeforePrint` event is triggered when the workbook in which it resides is printed. If you want to run the same code in every workbook available, you have to copy the code to each workbook. Alternatively, you can use an application event, `Workbook_BeforePrint`, which is triggered when any workbook is printed.

The application events already exist, but a class module must be set up first so that the events can be seen. To create a class module, follow these steps:

1. Insert a class module into the project. Select View, Properties Window and rename it something that makes sense to you, such as `cAppEvents`.

2. Enter the following into the class module:

   `Public WithEvents xlApp As Application`

   The name of the variable, `xlApp`, can be any variable name. The `WithEvents` keyword exposes the events associated with the `Application` object.

3. Select `xlApp` from the class module's Object drop-down list and then click the Procedure drop-down menu to its right to view the list of events that are available for the `xlApp`'s object type (`Application`), as shown in Figure 9.2.

➡ For a review of the various application events, **see** the "Application-Level Events" section in Chapter 7, **p. 125.**

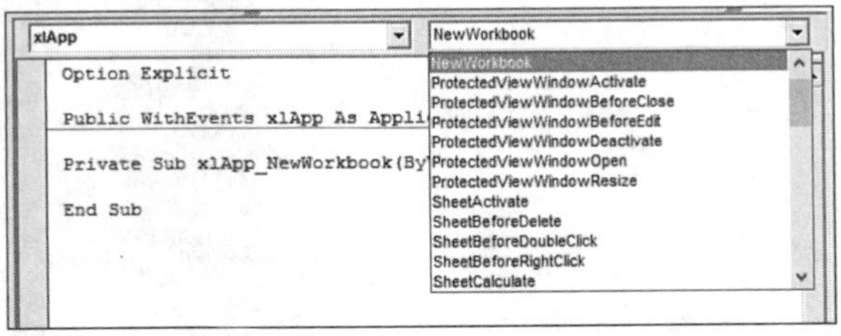

Figure 9.2
Events are made available after an object is created.

Any of the events listed can be captured, just as workbook and worksheet events were captured in Chapter 7. The following example uses the `NewWorkbook` event to set up footer information automatically. This code is placed in the class module, below the `xlApp` declaration line you just added:

```
Private Sub xlApp_NewWorkbook(ByVal Wb As Workbook)
Dim wks As Worksheet
With Wb
    For Each wks In .Worksheets
        wks.PageSetup.LeftFooter = "Created by: " & .Application.UserName
        wks.PageSetup.RightFooter = Now
    Next wks
End With
End Sub
```

The procedure placed in a class module does not run automatically, as events in workbook or worksheet modules would. An instance of the class module must be created, and the `Application` object must be assigned to the `xlApp` property. After that is complete, the `TrapAppEvent` procedure needs to run. As long as the procedure is running, the footer is created on each sheet every time a new workbook is added. Place the following in a standard module:

```
Public clsAppEvent As New cAppEvents

Sub TrapAppEvent()
    Set clsAppEvent.xlApp = Application
End Sub
```

> **NOTE** The application event trapping can be terminated by any action that resets the module level or public variables, including editing code in the VB Editor. To restart event trapping, run the procedure that creates the object (`TrapAppEvent`).

In this example, the public `myAppEvent` declaration was placed in a standard module with the `TrapAppEvent` procedure. To automate the running of the entire event trapping, all the modules could be transferred to the `Personal.xlsb` and the procedure transferred to a `Workbook_Open` event. In any case, the `Public` declaration of `myAppEvent` *must* remain in a standard module so that it can be shared among modules.

Embedded Chart Events

Preparing to trap embedded chart events is the same as preparing to trap application events. Create a class module, insert the public declaration for a chart type, create a procedure for the desired event, and then add a standard module procedure to initiate the trapping. The same class module used for the application event can be used for the embedded chart event.

Place the following line in the declaration section of the class module:

```
Public WithEvents xlChart As Chart
```

The available chart events are now viewable (see Figure 9.3).

➡ For a review of the various charts events, **see** "Chart Sheet Events" in Chapter 7 on **p. 123**.

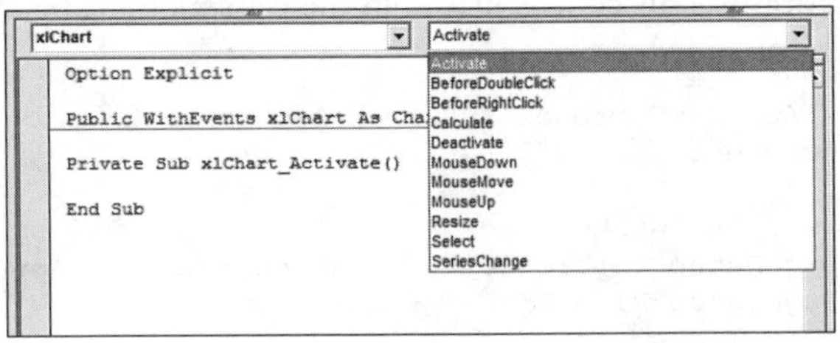

Figure 9.3
The chart events are available after the chart type variable has been declared.

Next you'll create a program to change the chart scale. You need to set up three events. The primary event, MouseDown, changes the chart scale with a right-click or double-click. Because these actions also have actions associated with them, you need two more events, BeforeRightClick and BeforeDoubleClick, which prevent the usual action from taking place.

The following BeforeDoubleClick event prevents the normal result of a double-click from taking place:

```
Private Sub xlChart_BeforeDoubleClick(ByVal ElementID As Long, _
    ByVal Arg1 As Long, ByVal Arg2 As Long, Cancel As Boolean)
    Cancel = True
End Sub
```

The following BeforeRightClick event prevents the normal result of a right-click from taking place:

```
Private Sub xlChart_BeforeRightClick(Cancel As Boolean)
    Cancel = True
End Sub
```

Now that the normal actions of the double-click and right-click have been controlled, ChartMouseDown rewrites the actions initiated by a right-click and double-click:

```
Private Sub xlChart_MouseDown(ByVal Button As Long, _
    ByVal Shift As Long, ByVal x As Long, ByVal y As Long)
    If Button = 1 Then 'left mouse button
        xlChart.Axes(xlValue).MaximumScale = _
            xlChart.Axes(xlValue).MaximumScale - 50
    End If

    If Button = 2 Then 'right mouse button
        xlChart.Axes(xlValue).MaximumScale = _
            xlChart.Axes(xlValue).MaximumScale + 50
    End If
End Sub
```

After the events are set in the class module, all that is left to do is declare the variable in a standard module, as follows:

```
Public myChartEvent As New clsEvents
```

Then create a procedure that captures the events on the embedded chart:

```
Sub TrapChartEvent()
    Set myChartEvent.xlChart = Worksheets("EmbedChart"). _
        ChartObjects("Chart 2").Chart
End Sub
```

Creating a Custom Object

Class modules are useful for trapping events, but they are also valuable because they can be used to create custom objects. When you are creating a custom object, the class module becomes a template of the object's properties and methods. To help you understand this better, in this section you'll create an employee object to track employee name, ID, hourly wage rate, and hours worked.

Insert a class module and rename it cEmployee. The cEmployee object has six properties and one method. *Properties* are variables in the object that you can assign a value to or read a value from. They can be private, in which case they are accessible only within the class module itself. Or they can be public, which means they're available from any module.

At the very top of the class module, place the following private variables. Notice that each line begins with the word Private. These variables will be used only within the class module itself. They receive their values from properties or functions within the class module:

```
Private m_employeename As String
Private m_employeeid As String
Private m_employeehourlyrate As String
Private m_employeeweeklyhours As String
Private m_normalhours As Double
Private m_overtimehours As Double
```

Property Let procedures are used to assign values to properties. By default, properties are public, so you don't actually have to state that:

```
Property Let EmployeeName(RHS As String)
    m_employeename = RHS
End Property

Property Let EmployeeID(RHS As String)
    m_employeeid = RHS
End Property

Property Let EmployeeHourlyRate(RHS As Double)
    m_employeehourlyrate = RHS
End Property

Property Let EmployeeWeeklyHours(RHS As Double)
    m_employeeweeklyhours = RHS
    m_normalhours = WorksheetFunction.Min(40, RHS)
    m_overtimehours = WorksheetFunction.Max(0, RHS - 40)
End Property
```

These four object's properties are writable. Place them after declaring the private variables. The argument, RHS, is the value being assigned to the property, which is then assigned to one of the private variables. I like to use RHS (Right Hand Side - easy to remember!) as a common argument name for consistency, but you can use what you want.

Property Get procedures are read-only properties of the class module:

```
Property Get EmployeeName() As String
    EmployeeName = m_employeename
End Property

Property Get EmployeeID() As String
    EmployeeID = m_employeeid
End Property

Property Get EmployeeWeeklyHours() As Double
    EmployeeWeeklyHours = m_employeeweeklyhours
End Property

Property Get EmployeeNormalHours() As Double
    EmployeeNormalHours = m_normalhours
End Property

Property Get EmployeeOverTimeHours() As Double
    EmployeeOverTimeHours = m_overtimehours
End Property
```

In addition to three of the properties you assign values to, two more are available to get values from: EmployeeNormalHours and EmployeeOverTimeHours. EmployeeHourlyRate is the one property that a value can be written to but not read from. Why? Imagine that you have another routine that reads all the values from a database into the program's memory. A programmer using your class module doesn't need to see this raw data. Using the Get property, you can control what data the programmer can access but still have the data available to the program.

> **NOTE**
>
> Property Set procedures are used to assign an object to a property. For example, if you want to create a worksheet property that gets passed a worksheet object, do this:
>
> ```
> Property Set DataWorksheets (RHS as Worksheet)
> ```
>
> You would use Get to retrieve, like this:
>
> ```
> Property Get DataWorksheets () As Worksheet
> ```

Finally, you have the function that becomes an object method:

```
Public Function EmployeeWeeklyPay() As Double
    EmployeeWeeklyPay = (m_normalhours * m_employeehourlyrate) + _
        (m_overtimehours * m_employeehourlyrate * 1.5)
End Function
```

Like a normal function, it can have arguments, but in this case, you've previously set all the variables it will need by using Let.

You can also use subs in class modules. In this case, a function is used because you want to return a value. But if you want to do an action, like Range.Cut, then you use a sub.

The object is now complete. The next step is to use the object in an actual program.

Using a Custom Object

When a custom object is properly configured in a class module, it can be referenced from other modules. To access the properties and functions of the object, first declare a variable as the class module and then set a new instance of the object. You can then write the code, referencing the custom object and taking advantage of IntelliSense to access its properties and methods, as shown in Figure 9.4.

The following example sets the values of the properties and then generates a message box, retrieving some of those values and also accessing the method you created:

```
Sub SingleEmployeePayTime()
'declare a variable as the class module/object
Dim clsEmployee As cEmployee
'set a new instance to the object
Set clsEmployee = New cEmployee
With clsEmployee
    .EmployeeName = "Tracy Syrstad"
    .EmployeeID = "1651"
    .EmployeeHourlyRate = 35.15
    .EmployeeWeeklyHours = 45
    MsgBox .EmployeeName & Chr(10) & Chr(9) & _
    "Normal Hours: " & .EmployeeNormalHours & Chr(10) & Chr(9) & _
    "OverTime Hours: " & .EmployeeOverTimeHours & Chr(10) & Chr(9) & _
    "Weekly Pay : $" & .EmployeeWeeklyPay
End With
End Sub
```

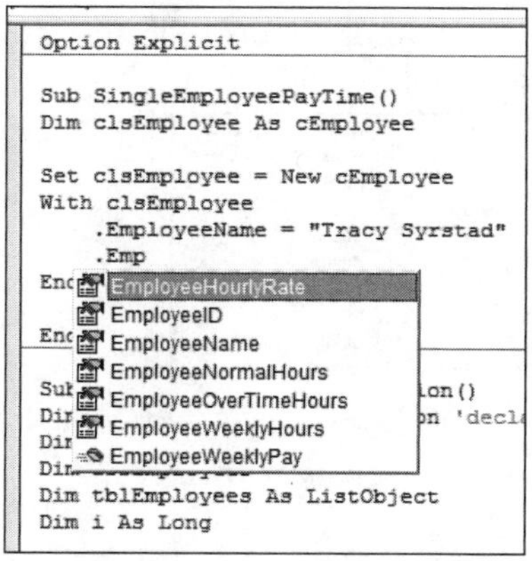

Figure 9.4
The properties and method of the custom object are just as easily accessible as they are for standard objects.

Using Collections

A *collection* holds a group of similar items. For example, `Worksheet` is a member of the `Worksheets` collection. You can add, remove, count, and refer to each worksheet in a workbook by its item number.

Creating a Collection

To use a collection, you first declare a variable as the collection and then set a new instance of the collection. You can then use the Add method to add items to it:

```
CollectionName.Add Item, Key, Before, After
```

The Add method has four arguments. Item is whatever information the collection holds. It can be anything from a string to an object such as a worksheet. The second value, which is optional, is Key. It is used to look up a member of the collection. It must be a unique string value. You can use Key to directly reference an item in a collection. If you don't know Key, then the only way to find an item in a collection is to loop through the collection.

Before and After are optional arguments you can use to position an item in a collection. You can refer to the key or position of the other item. The following example creates a collection with two items. The first item is added with a key; the second item is not.

```
Dim myFirstCollection as Collection
Set MyFirstCollection = New Collection
MyFirstCollection.Add Item1, "Key1" 'with a key
MyFirstCollection.Add Item2 'without a key
```

Notice that the key is a string. If you want to use numbers for the key, then force the number to be treated as a string, like this:

```
MyFirstCollection.Add Item3, CStr(1)
```

Creating a Collection in a Standard Module

By setting up a collection in a standard module, you can access the four default collection methods: Add, Remove, Count, and Item. The following example reads a list of employees from a sheet into an array. It then loops through the array, supplying each property of the custom object with a value, and places each record in the collection, as shown in Figure 9.5:

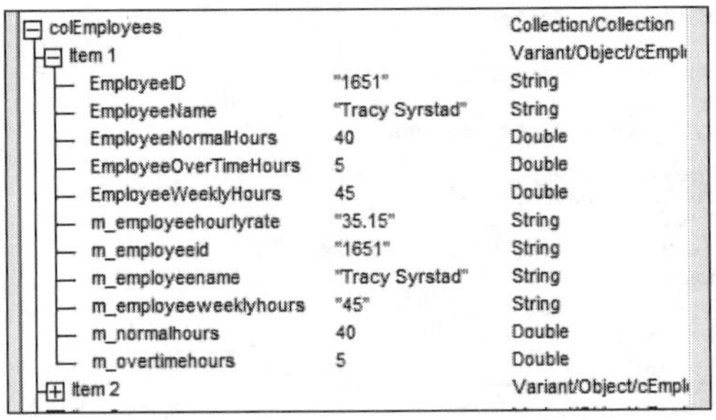

Figure 9.5

A collection can hold any type of variable, including a custom object's properties.

colEmployees		Collection/Collection
Item 1		Variant/Object/cEmpl
EmployeeID	"1651"	String
EmployeeName	"Tracy Syrstad"	String
EmployeeNormalHours	40	Double
EmployeeOverTimeHours	5	Double
EmployeeWeeklyHours	45	Double
m_employeehourlyrate	"35.15"	String
m_employeeid	"1651"	String
m_employeename	"Tracy Syrstad"	String
m_employeeweeklyhours	"45"	String
m_normalhours	40	Double
m_overtimehours	5	Double
Item 2		Variant/Object/cEmpl

NOTE This example stores a custom object in a collection. As I said earlier, the value a collection holds can be anything, including the multiple properties of a class module. Technically, a single record of the collection holds just one value: the custom object. But the custom object itself consists of multiple values.

```
Sub EmployeesPayUsingCollection()
Dim colEmployees As Collection 'declare a variable for the collection
Dim clsEmployee As cEmployee
Dim arrEmployees
Dim tblEmployees As ListObject
Dim i As Long

Set colEmployees = New Collection 'set a new instance of the collection
Set tblEmployees = Worksheets("Employee Info").ListObjects("tblEmployees")

arrEmployees = tblEmployees.DataBodyRange

'loop through each employee
'assign values to the custom object properties
'then place the custom object into the collection
'using the employee id as the unique key
For i = 1 To UBound(arrEmployees)
    Set clsEmployee = New cEmployee
    With clsEmployee
        .EmployeeName = arrEmployees(i, 1)
        .EmployeeID = arrEmployees(i, 2)
        .EmployeeHourlyRate = arrEmployees(i, 3)
        .EmployeeWeeklyHours = arrEmployees(i, 4)
        colEmployees.Add clsEmployee, CStr(.EmployeeID)
    End With
Next i

'retrieve information from the custom object in the collection
'specifically, the second member of the collection
Set clsEmployee = colEmployees(2)
MsgBox "Number of Employees: " & colEmployees.Count & Chr(10) & _
    "Employee(2) Name: " & clsEmployee.EmployeeName

'retrieve information using the key
MsgBox "Tracy's Weekly Pay: $" & colEmployees("1651").EmployeeWeeklyPay

Set colEmployees = Nothing
Set tblEmployees = Nothing
Set clsEmployee = Nothing
End Sub
```

The collection `colEmployees` is declared as a new collection, and the record `clsEmployee` is assigned as a new object of the class module `cEmployee`.

After the object's properties are given values, the record `clsEmployee` is added to the collection. The second parameter of the `Add` method applies a unique key to the record, which, in this case, is the employee ID number. This allows a specific record to be accessed quickly, as shown by the second message box (`colEmployees("1651").EmployeeWeeklyPay`) (see Figure 9.6).

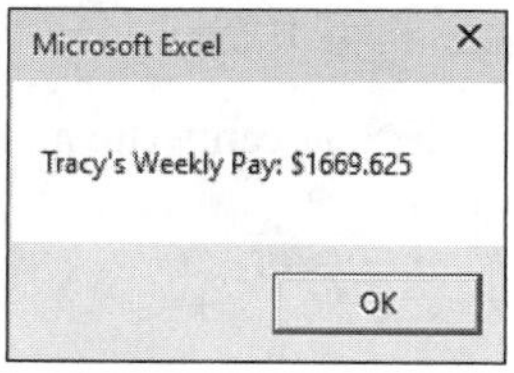

Figure 9.6
Individual records in a collection can be easily accessed.

Microsoft Excel ✕

Tracy's Weekly Pay: $1669.625

OK

Creating a Collection in a Class Module

When you create a collection in a class module, the innate methods of the collection (Add, Remove, Count, Item) are not available; they need to be created in the class module. These are the advantages of creating a collection in a class module:

- The entire code is in one module.
- You have more control over what is done with the collection.
- You can prevent access to the collection.

Insert a new class module for the collection and rename it cEmployees. Declare a private collection to be used within the class module:

```
Private AllEmployees As New Collection
```

Add the new properties and methods required to make the collection work. The innate methods of the collection are available within the class module and can be used to create the custom methods and properties.

Insert an Add method for adding new items to the collection:

```
Public Sub Add(recEmployee As clsEmployee)
AllEmployees.Add recEmployee, CStr(recEmployee.EmployeeID)
End Sub
```

Insert a Remove method to remove a specific item from the collection:

```
Public Sub Remove(myItem As Variant)
AllEmployees.Remove (myItem)
End Sub
```

Insert a Count property to return the number of items in the collection:

```
Public Property Get Count() As Long
Count = AllEmployees.Count
End Property
```

Insert an Items property to return the entire collection:

```
Public Property Get Items() As Collection
Set Items = AllEmployees
End Property
```

Insert an Item property to return a specific item from the collection:

```
Public Property Get Item(myItem As Variant) As cEmployee
Set Item = AllEmployees(myItem)
End Property
```

Property Get is used with Count, Item, and Items because these are read-only properties. Item returns a reference to a single member of the collection, whereas Items returns the entire collection so that it can be used in For Each Next loops.

After the collection is configured in the class module, you can write a procedure in a standard module to use it:

```
Sub EmployeesPayUsingCollection()
'using a collection in a class module
```

```
Dim colEmployees As cEmployees
Dim clsEmployee As cEmployee
Dim arrEmployees
Dim tblEmployees As ListObject
Dim i As Long

Set colEmployees = New cEmployees 'set a new instance of the collection
Set tblEmployees = Worksheets("Employee Info").ListObjects("tblEmployees")

arrEmployees = tblEmployees.DataBodyRange

'loop through each employee
'assign values to the custom object properties
'then place the custom object into the collection
'using the employee id as the unique key
For i = 1 To UBound(arrEmployees)
    Set clsEmployee = New cEmployee
    With clsEmployee
        .EmployeeName = arrEmployees(i, 1)
        .EmployeeID = arrEmployees(i, 2)
        .EmployeeHourlyRate = arrEmployees(i, 3)
        .EmployeeWeeklyHours = arrEmployees(i, 4)
        'the key is added by the class module Add method
        colEmployees.Add clsEmployee
    End With
Next i

'retrieve information from the custom object in the collection
'specifically, the second member of the collection
Set clsEmployee = colEmployees.Item(2)
MsgBox "Number of Employees: " & colEmployees.Count & Chr(10) & _
        "Employee(2) Name: " & clsEmployee.EmployeeName

'retrieve information using the key
MsgBox "Tracy's Weekly Pay: $" & colEmployees.Item("1651"). _
    EmployeeWeeklyPay

Set colEmployees = Nothing
Set tblEmployees = Nothing
Set clsEmployee = Nothing
End Sub
```

This program is not too different from the one used with the standard collection, but there are a few key differences:

■ Instead of declaring `colEmployees` as `Collection`, you declare it as type `cEmployees`, the new class module collection.

■ The array and collection are filled the same way, but the way the records in the collection are referenced has changed. When a member of the collection, such as employee record 2, is referenced, the `Item` property must be used.

Using Dictionaries

The ability to use a key to look up values in a collection is a major plus. I often parallel collections and arrays to help find information in an array. For example, I use the key in the collection to look up a value, which is the location of a record in the array.

But a major downside to collections is that after you add an item to a collection, you can't change it. So, if you need the advantages of a collection but also need to change the value, you should use a dictionary. A *dictionary* does everything a collection does and more, but it needs a little more setup because it's part of the Microsoft Scripting Runtime Library.

Some of the other differences between collections and dictionaries include the following:

- A dictionary requires a key.
- A dictionary key can be any variable type except for an array.
- A dictionary key can be changed.
- You have to use the key to retrieve a value. You can't use the item's position.
- You can change a value.
- You can check for the existence of a key.

In the following example, which declares the dictionary using late binding, data is placed into an array and processed, using the product name as the key. The summed quantities are then placed on the sheet, with the dictionary keys as labels, as shown in Figure 9.7:

Figure 9.7
Use a dictionary to hold changing data.

Region	Product	Date	Customer	Quantity
East	Tools	1/1/2015	Exclusive Shovel Trad	1000
Central	Accessories	1/2/2015	Bright Hairpin Compa	100
East	Jewelry	1/4/2015	Cool Jewelry Corpora	800
East	Food	1/4/2015	Tasty Kettle Inc.	400
East	Tools	1/7/2015	Remarkable Meter Cc	400
East	Jewelry	1/7/2015	Wonderful Jewelry In	1000
Central	Tools	1/9/2015	Remarkable Meter Cc	800
Central	Tools	1/10/2015	Safe Flagpole Supply	900
Central	Tools	1/12/2015	Reliable Tripod Comp	300
East	Tools	1/14/2015	Matchless Vise Inc.	100
East	Accessories	1/15/2015	Bright Hairpin Compa	500
East	Tools	1/16/2015	Appealing Calculator	600
West	Accessories	1/19/2015	Bright Hairpin Compa	100
East	Food	1/21/2015	Best Vegetable Comp	800
Electrical Tools	4100			
Accessories	700			
Jewelry	1800			
Food	1200			

➡ **See** Chapter 20, "Automating Word," for information on early versus late binding.

```
Sub UsingADictionary()
Dim dictData As Object
```

```
    Dim bItemExists As Boolean
    Dim tblSales As ListObject
    Dim arrData, arrReport, arrHeaders
    Dim i As Long
    Dim rng As Range

    'create the dictionary object
    Set dictData = CreateObject("Scripting.Dictionary")
    Set tblSales = Worksheets("Table").ListObjects("tblSales")

    'put the data into an array for faster processing
    arrData = tblSales.DataBodyRange

    'loop through the array
    For i = 1 To UBound(arrData)
        'if key exists, add to it
        'else create and add to it
        If dictData.Exists(arrData(i, 2)) Then
            dictData.Item(arrData(i, 2)) = dictData.Item(arrData(i, 2)) + _
                arrData(i, 5)
         Else
            dictData.Add arrData(i, 2), arrData(i, 5)
        End If
    Next i

    'rename a key, just for the heck of it
    'the only way to rename a key is to know the name of it
    dictData.Key("Tools") = "Electrical Tools"

    'the location 2 rows beneath the table
    Set rng = tblSales.Range.Offset(tblSales.Range.Rows.Count + 2).Resize(1, 1)

    'put the dictionary keys and values each into an array
    'then dump them on the sheet
    arrHeaders = dictData.Keys
    rng.Resize(dictData.Count, 1).Value = Application.Transpose(arrHeaders)
    arrReport = dictData.Items
    rng.Offset(, 1).Resize(dictData.Count, 1).Value = _
        Application.Transpose(arrReport)
    Set dictData = Nothing
    Set tblSales = Nothing
    Set rng = Nothing
    End Sub
```

CASE STUDY: HELP BUTTONS

Say that you have a complex sheet that requires a way for the user to get help. You can place the information in comment boxes, but they are not very obvious, especially to novice Excel users. Another option is to create help buttons.

To do this, create small ActiveX labels (not Form Control labels) with a question mark in each one on the worksheet. To get the button-like appearance shown in Figure 9.8, set the `SpecialEffect` property of the labels to `Raised` and darken the `BackColor`. Place one label per row. On another sheet, enter the help text you want to appear when the label is clicked. Ensure that the label name number matches the row in which the text is placed. For example, if the label name is `Label1`, place the corresponding text in cell A1; if the label name is `label151`, place the text in cell A51.

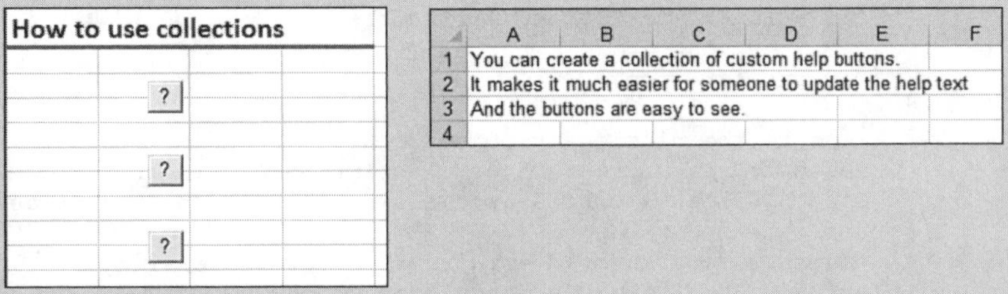

9

Figure 9.8
Attach help buttons to the sheet and enter help text on another sheet, which you can later hide.

How to use collections		
	?	
	?	
	?	

	A	B	C	D	E	F
1	You can create a collection of custom help buttons.					
2	It makes it much easier for someone to update the help text					
3	And the buttons are easy to see.					
4						

Create a simple userform with a label and a close button. (See Chapter 10, "Userforms—An Introduction" for more information on userforms.) Rename the form `HelpForm`, the button `CloseHelp`, and the label `HelpText`. Size the label large enough to hold the help text. Add the following macro, `CloseHelp_Click`, behind the form to hide it when the button is clicked:

```
Private Sub CloseHelp_Click()
Unload Me

End Sub
```

At this point, you could program each button separately. If you have many buttons, this would be tedious. And if you ever need to add more buttons, you will have to update the code. Or you could create a class module and a collection that will automatically include all the help buttons on the sheet, now and in the future.

Insert a class module named `cLabel`. You need a public variable, `HelpLabel`, to capture the control events:

```
Public WithEvents HelpLabel As MSForms.Label
```

In addition, you need a method of finding and displaying the corresponding help text. The following code extracts the number at the end of the label name and uses that to find the corresponding row on the sheet with the help text:

```
Private Sub HelpLabel_Click()
Dim RowNumber As Long

RowNumber = Right(HelpLabel.Name, Len(HelpLabel.Name) - 5)
If HelpLabel.Caption = "?" Then
    HelpForm.Caption = "Label in cell " & "A" & RowNumber
    HelpForm.HelpText.Caption = Worksheets("Help Text").
Cells(RowNumber, 1)
    HelpForm.Show
End If
End Sub
```

In the ThisWorkbook module declare a global collection at the top of the module. Then create a `Workbook_Open` procedure to create a collection of the labels in the workbook:

```
Dim colLabels As Collection

Sub Workbook_Open()
Dim wks As Worksheet
Dim clsLbl As cLabel
Dim OleObj As OLEObject
```

```
        Set colLabels= New Collection
        For Each wks In ThisWorkbook.Worksheets
            For Each OleObj In wks.OLEObjects
                If OleObj.OLEType = xlOLEControl Then
        'in case you have other controls on the sheet, include only the labels
                    If TypeName(OleObj.Object) = "Label" Then
                        Set clsLbl = New cLabel
                        Set clsLbl.HelpLabel = OleObj.Object
                        colLabels.Add clsLbl
                    End If
                End If
            Next OleObj
        Next wks
        End Sub
```

Run `Workbook_Open` to create the collection. Click a label on the worksheet. The corresponding help text appears in the help form, as shown in Figure 9.9.

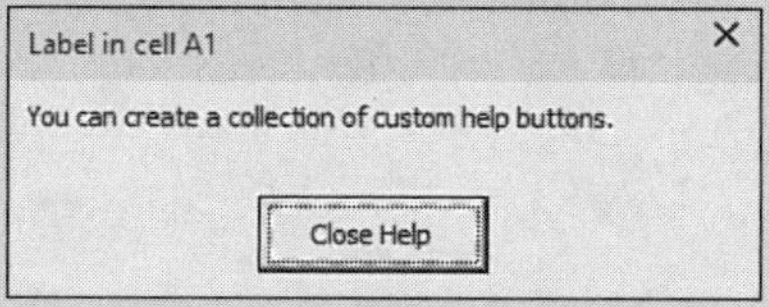

Figure 9.9
Help text is only a click away.

Label in cell A1   ✕

You can create a collection of custom help buttons.

                    Close Help

Using User-Defined Types to Create Custom Properties

User-defined types (UDTs) provide some of the power of a custom object, but without the need for a class module. A class module allows for the creation of custom properties and methods, whereas a UDT allows only custom properties. However, sometimes that is all you need.

A UDT is declared with a `Type...End Type` statement. It can be public or private. A name that is treated like an object is given to the UDT. Within `Type`, individual variables are declared that become the properties of the UDT.

Within a procedure, a variable of the custom type is defined. When that variable is used, the properties are available, just as they are in a custom object (see Figure 9.10).

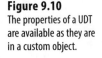

Figure 9.10
The properties of a UDT are available as they are in a custom object.

```
Option Explicit

Public Type Style
    StyleName As String
    Price As Single
    UnitsSold As Long
    UnitsOnHand As Long
End Type

Public Type Store
    ID As String
    Styles() As Style
End Type

Sub myUDT()
Dim mystyle As Style
mystyle.s
End Su
```
Price
StyleName
UnitsOnHand
UnitsSold

The following example uses two UDTs to summarize a report of product styles in various stores. The first UDT consists of properties for each product style:

```
Public Type Style
    StyleName As String
    Price As Single
    UnitsSold As Long
    UnitsOnHand As Long
End Type
```

The second UDT consists of the store name and an array whose type is the first UDT:

```
Public Type Store
    Name As String
    Styles() As Style
End Type
```

After the UDTs are established, the main program is written. Only a variable of the second UDT type, Store, is needed because that type contains the first type, Style (see Figure 9.11). However, all the properties of the UDTs are easily available. In addition, with the use of the UDT, the various variables are easy to remember—they are only a dot (.) away. Here is the main program:

```
Sub UDTMain()
Dim ThisStore As Long, ThisStyle As Long
Dim CurrRow As Long, i As Long
Dim TotalDollarsSold As Double, TotalDollarsOnHand As Double
Dim TotalUnitsSold As Long, TotalUnitsOnHand As Long
Dim StoreID As String
Dim tblStores As ListObject
Dim arrStores 'to hold the data from the table
ReDim Stores(0 To 0) As Store 'The UDT is declared as the outer array

Set tblStores = Worksheets("Sales Data").ListObjects("tblStores")
'ensure data is sorted by name
With tblStores
    .Sort.SortFields.Add .ListColumns(1).DataBodyRange, _
        xlSortOnValues, xlAscending
```

```
        .Sort.Apply
        .Sort.SortFields.Clear
    End With
    'put the data into an array so it's faster to process
    arrStores = tblStores.DataBodyRange

    'The following For loop fills both arrays.
    'The outer array is filled with the
    'store name and an inner array consisting of product details.
    'To accomplish this, the store name is tracked and when it changes,
    'the outer array is expanded.
    'The inner array for each outer array expands with each new product
    For i = LBound(arrStores) To UBound(arrStores)
        StoreID = arrStores(i, 1)
        'Checks whether this is the first entry in the outer array
        If LBound(Stores) = 0 Then
            ThisStore = 1
            ReDim Stores(1 To 1) As Store
            Stores(1).ID = StoreID
            ReDim Stores(1).Styles(0 To 0) As Style
        Else
        'if it's not the first entry, see if the Store has already been added
            For ThisStore = LBound(Stores) To UBound(Stores)
                'the store has already been added, no need to add again
                        If Stores(ThisStore).ID = StoreID Then Exit For
            Next ThisStore
            'the store hasn't been added, so add it now
            If ThisStore > UBound(Stores) Then
                ReDim Preserve Stores(LBound(Stores) To_
                    UBound(Stores) + 1) As Store
                Stores(ThisStore).ID = StoreID
                ReDim Stores(ThisStore).Styles(0 To 0) As Style
            End If
        End If
        'now add the store details
        With Stores(ThisStore)
            'check if the style already exists in the inner array
            If LBound(.Styles) = 0 Then
                ReDim .Styles(1 To 1) As Style
            Else
                ReDim Preserve .Styles(LBound(.Styles) To _
                    UBound(.Styles) + 1) As Style
            End If
            'add the rest of the details for the Style
            With .Styles(UBound(.Styles))
                .StyleName = arrStores(i, 2)
                .Price = arrStores(i, 3)
                .UnitsSold = arrStores(i, 4)
                .UnitsOnHand = arrStores(i, 5)
            End With
        End With
    Next i

    'Create a report on a new sheet
    Sheets.Add
    Range("A1").Resize(, 5).Value = Array("Store ID", "Units Sold", _
        "Dollars Sold", "Units On Hand", "Dollars On Hand")
    CurrRow = 2
```

```
'loop through the outer array
For ThisStore = LBound(Stores) To UBound(Stores)
    With Stores(ThisStore)
        TotalDollarsSold = 0
        TotalUnitsSold = 0
        TotalDollarsOnHand = 0
        TotalUnitsOnHand = 0
        'Go through the inner array of product styles within the array
        'of stores to summarize information
        For ThisStyle = LBound(.Styles) To UBound(.Styles)
            With .Styles(ThisStyle)
                TotalDollarsSold = TotalDollarsSold + .UnitsSold *.Price
                TotalUnitsSold = TotalUnitsSold + .UnitsSold
                TotalDollarsOnHand = TotalDollarsOnHand + .UnitsOnHand * _
                    .Price
                TotalUnitsOnHand = TotalUnitsOnHand + .UnitsOnHand
            End With
        Next ThisStyle
        Range("A" & CurrRow).Resize(, 5).Value = _
            Array(.ID, TotalUnitsSold, TotalDollarsSold, _
            TotalUnitsOnHand, TotalDollarsOnHand)
    End With
    CurrRow = CurrRow + 1
Next ThisStore
Set tblStores = Nothing
End Sub
```

Figure 9.11
The `Stores` variable is of type `Store`, which includes the `Styles` variable array. This allows you to organize multiple pieces of data in a couple variables.

Expression	Value	Type
Stores		Store(1 to 6)
Stores(1)		Store
ID	"Store 340001"	String
Styles		Style(1 to 500)
Styles(1)		Style
Price	8	Single
StyleName	"00012"	String
UnitsOnHand	1	Long
UnitsSold	0	Long
Styles(2)		Style
Styles(3)		Style

Next Steps

Chapter 10 introduces the tools you can use to interact with users. You'll find out how to prompt users for information to use in your code, warn them of illegal actions, or provide them with an interface to work with other than the spreadsheet.

Userforms:
An Introduction

10

Userforms enable you to display information and allow the user to input information. Using `InputBox` and `MsgBox` controls are simple ways of doing this. You can use the userform controls in the VB Editor to create forms that are more complex.

This chapter covers simple user interfaces using input boxes and message boxes and the basics of creating userforms in the VB Editor.

➡ To learn more about advanced userform programming, **see** Chapter 22, "Advanced Userform Techniques."

Input Boxes

The `InputBox` function is used to create a basic interface element that requests input from the user before the program can continue. You can configure the prompt, the title for the window, a default value, the window position, and user help files. The only two buttons provided are the OK and Cancel buttons. The returned value is a string.

The following code asks the user for the number of months to be averaged. Figure 10.1 shows the resulting `InputBox`.

```
AveMos = InputBox(Prompt:="Enter the number " & _
" of months to average", Title:="Enter Months", _
Default:="3")
```

Figure 10.1
A simple but effective input box.

Message Boxes

The `MsgBox` function creates a message box that displays information and waits for the user to click a button before continuing. Whereas `InputBox` has only OK and Cancel buttons, the `MsgBox` function enables you to choose from several configurations of buttons, including Yes, No, OK, and Cancel. You can also configure the prompt, the window title, and help files. The following code produces a prompt to find out whether the user wants to continue. A `Select Case` statement is then used to continue the program with the appropriate action:

```
myTitle = "Report Finalized"
MyMsg = "Do you want to save changes and close?"
Response = MsgBox(myMsg, vbExclamation + vbYesNoCancel, myTitle)
Select Case Response
    Case Is = vbYes
        ActiveWorkbook.Close SaveChanges:=False
    Case Is = vbNo
        ActiveWorkbook.Close SaveChanges:=True
    Case Is = vbCancel
        Exit Sub
End Select
```

Figure 10.2 shows the resulting customized message box.

Figure 10.2
The MsgBox function is used to display information and obtain a basic response from the user.

Creating a Userform

Userforms combine the capabilities of `InputBox` and `MsgBox` to create a more efficient way of interacting with the user. For example, rather than have the user fill out personal information on a sheet, you can create a userform that prompts for the required data (see Figure 10.3).

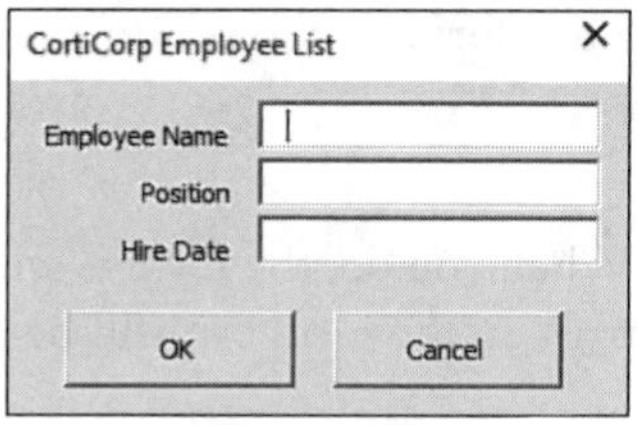

Figure 10.3
Create a custom userform to get more information from the user.

Insert a userform in the VB Editor by selecting Insert, UserForm from the main menu. When a UserForm module is added to the Project Explorer, a blank form appears in the window where your code usually is, and the Controls toolbox appears.

To change the codename of the userform, select the form and change the (Name) property. The codename of a userform is used to refer to the form, as shown in the following sections. You can resize a userform by grabbing and dragging the handles on its right side, bottom edge, or lower-right corner. To add controls to the form, click the desired control in the toolbox and draw it on the form. You can move and resize controls at any time.

> **NOTE**
> By default, the toolbox displays the most common controls. To access more controls, right-click the toolbox and select Additional Controls. However, be careful; other users might not have the same additional controls as you do. If you send users a form with a control they do not have installed, the program generates an error.

After you add a control to a form, you can change its properties from the Properties window. (Or, if you don't want to set the properties manually now, you can set them later programmatically.) If the Properties window is not visible, you can bring it up by selecting View, Properties Window. Figure 10.4 shows the Properties window for a text box.

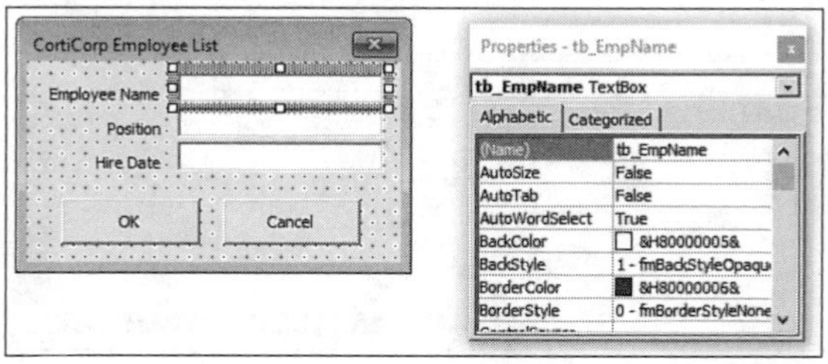

Figure 10.4
Use the Properties window to change the properties of a control.

Calling and Hiding a Userform

A userform can be called from any module. The syntax `FormName.Show` causes a form for the user to pop up:

```
frm_AddEmp.Show
```

The `Load` method can also be used to call a userform. It allows a form to be loaded but remain hidden:

```
Load frm_AddEmp
```

To hide a userform, use the `Hide` method. When you do, the form is still active but is hidden from the user. However, the controls on the form can still be accessed programmatically:

```
Frm_AddEmp.Hide
```

The `Unload` method unloads a form from memory and removes it from the user's view, which means the form cannot be accessed by the user or programmatically:

```
Unload Me
```

> **TIP**
>
> Me is a keyword that can be used to refer to the userform itself. It can be used in the code of any control to refer to itself.

Programming Userforms

The code for a control goes in the form's module. Unlike with the other modules, double-clicking the Form's module opens the form in Design view. To view the code, you can right-click either the module or the userform in Design view and select View Code.

Userform Events

Just like a worksheet, a userform has events that are triggered by actions. After the userform has been added to a project, the events are available in the properties drop-down list at the top right of the code window (see Figure 10.5); to access them, select UserForm from the objects drop-down on the left.

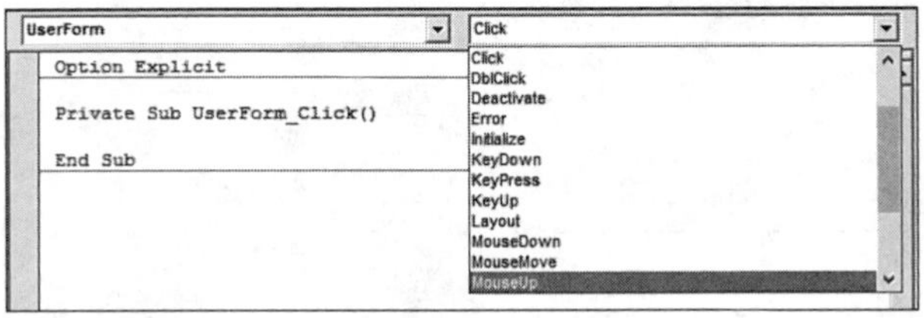

Figure 10.5
Various events for a user-form can be selected from the drop-down list at the top of the code window.

The available events for userforms are described in Table 10.1.

Table 10.1 Userform Events

Event	Description
Activate	Occurs when a userform is either loaded or shown. This event is triggered after the Initialize event.
AddControl	Occurs when a control is added to a userform at runtime. Does not run at design time or upon userform initialization.
BeforeDragOver	Occurs while the user does a drag and drop onto the userform.
BeforeDropOrPaste	Occurs right before the user is about to drop or paste data into the userform.
Click	Occurs when the user clicks the userform with the mouse.
DblClick	Occurs when the user double-clicks the userform with the mouse. If a click event is also in use, the double-click event will not work.
Deactivate	Occurs when a userform is deactivated.
Error	Occurs when the userform runs into an error and cannot return the error information.
Initialize	Occurs when the userform is first loaded, before the Activate event. If you hide and then show a form, Initialize will not trigger.
KeyDown	Occurs when the user presses a key on the keyboard.
KeyPress	Occurs when the user presses an ANSI key. An ANSI key is a typable character such as the letter *A*. An example of a nontypable character is the Tab key.
KeyUp	Occurs when the user releases a key on the keyboard.
Layout	Occurs when the control changes size.
MouseDown	Occurs when the user presses the mouse button within the borders of the userform.
MouseMove	Occurs when the user moves the mouse within the borders of the userform.
MouseUp	Occurs when the user releases the mouse button within the borders of the userform.
QueryClose	Occurs before a userform closes. It allows you to recognize the method used to close a form and have code respond accordingly.
RemoveControl	Occurs when a control is deleted from within the userform.
Resize	Occurs when the userform is resized.
Scroll	Occurs when a visible scrollbar box is repositioned.
Terminate	Occurs after the userform has been unloaded. This is triggered after QueryClose.
Zoom	Occurs when the zoom value is changed.

10

Programming Controls

To program a control, highlight the control and select View, Code. The footer, header, and default action for the control are entered in the programming field automatically. To see the other actions that are available for a control, select the control from the object drop-down and view the actions in the properties drop-down, as shown in Figure 10.6.

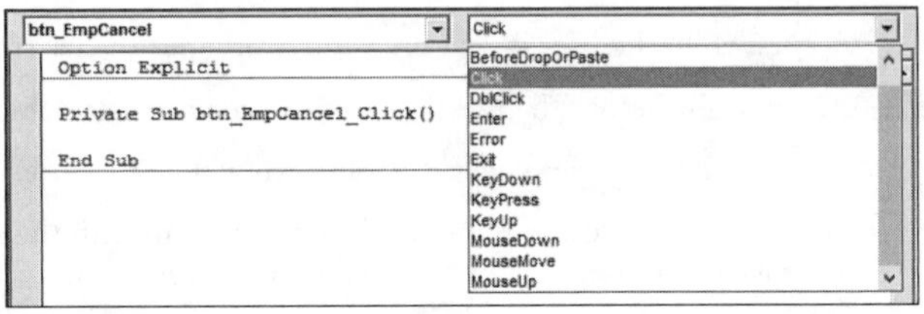

Figure 10.6
You can select various actions for a control from the VB Editor drop-downs.

The controls are objects, like `ActiveWorkbook`. They have properties and methods that depend on the type of control. Most of the programming for the controls is done in the form's module. However, if another module needs to refer to a control, the parent, which is the form, needs to be included with the object. Here's how this is done:

```
Private Sub btn_EmpCancel_Click()
Unload Me
End Sub
```

The preceding code can be broken down into three sections:

- `btn_EmpCancel`—Name given to the control
- `Click`—Action of the control
- `Unload Me`—Code behind the control, which, in this case, is unloading the form

> **TIP**
> Change the (Name) property in the control's Properties window to rename a control from the default assigned by the editor.

CASE STUDY: BUG FIX WHEN ADDING CONTROLS TO AN EXISTING FORM

If you have been using a userform for some time and later try to add a new control, you might find that Excel seems to get confused about the control. You will see that the control is added to the form, but when you right-click the control and select View Code, the code module does not seem to acknowledge that the control exists. The control name will not be available in the left drop-down at the top of the code module.

To work around this situation, follow these steps:

1. Add all the controls you need to add to the existing userform.

2. In the Project Explorer, right-click the userform and select Export File. Select Save to save the file in the default location.

3. In the Project Explorer, right-click the userform and select Remove. Because you just exported the userform, click No to the question about exporting.

4. Right-click anywhere in the Project Explorer and select Import File. Select the filename that you saved in step 2.

The new controls are now available in the code window of the userform.

Using Basic Form Controls

Each control has different events associated with it, so you can code what happens based on the user's actions. A table reviewing the control events is available at the end of each of the sections that follow.

A A label control is used to display text with information for the user.

 A text box control is used to get a manual entry from the user.

 A command button control is used to create a button a user can press to have the program perform an action.

Using Labels, Text Boxes, and Command Buttons

The basic form shown in Figure 10.7 consists of labels, text boxes, and command buttons. Using such a form is a simple yet effective method of requesting information from the user. After the text boxes have been filled in, the user clicks OK, and your code reformats the data if needed then adds the information to a sheet (see Figure 10.8), as shown in the following code:

Figure 10.7
A simple form to collect information from the user.

CortiCorp Employee List	✕
Employee Name	Cort Chilldon-Hoff
Position	CEO
Hire Date	8/6/03
OK	Cancel

Figure 10.8
The information is added to the sheet.

Add	View	
Name	**Position**	**Hire Date**
Tracy Syrstad	Developer	20-Jul-03
Cort Chilldon_Hoff	CEO	6-Aug-03

```
Private Sub btn_EmpOK_Click()
Dim LastRow As Long
LastRow = Worksheets("Employee").Cells(Worksheets("Employee").Rows.Count, 1) _
.End(xlUp).Row + 1
Cells(LastRow, 1).Value = tb_EmpName.Value
Cells(LastRow, 2).Value = tb_EmpPosition.Value
Cells(LastRow, 3).Value = Format(tb_EmpHireDate.Value, "d-mmm-yy")
End Sub
```

By changing the code as shown in the following sample, you can use the same form design to retrieve information. The following code retrieves the position and hire date after the employee's name is entered:

```
Private Sub btn_EmpOK_Click()
Dim EmpFound As Range
With Range("EmpList") 'a named range on a sheet listing the employee names
    Set EmpFound = .Find(tb_EmpName.Value)
    If EmpFound Is Nothing Then
        MsgBox "Employee not found!"
        tb_EmpName.Value = ""

    Else
        With Range(EmpFound.Address)
            tb_EmpPosition = .Offset(0, 1)
            tb_HireDate = Format(.Offset(0, 2), "d-mmm-yy")
        End With
    End If
End With
Set EmpFound = Nothing
End Sub
```

The available events for Label, TextBox, and CommandButton controls are described in Table 10.2.

Table 10.2 Label, TextBox, and CommandButton **Control Events**

Event	Description
AfterUpdate[1]	Occurs after the control's data has been changed by the user.
BeforeDragOver	Occurs while the user drags and drops data onto the control.
BeforeDropOrPaste	Occurs right before the user is about to drop or paste data into the control.
BeforeUpdate[1]	Occurs before the data in the control is changed.
Change[1]	Occurs when the value of the control is changed.
Click[2]	Occurs when the user clicks the control with the mouse.
DblClick	Occurs when the user double-clicks the control with the mouse.
DropButtonClick[1]	Occurs when the user presses F4 on the keyboard. This is similar to the drop-down control on the combo box, but there is no drop-down on a text box.
Enter[3]	Occurs right before the control receives the focus from another control on the same userform.
Error	Occurs when the control runs into an error and cannot return the error information.
Exit[3]	Occurs right after the control loses focus to another control on the same userform.
KeyDown[3]	Occurs when the user presses a key on the keyboard.

Event	Description
KeyPress[3]	Occurs when the user presses an ANSI key. An ANSI key is a typable character such as the letter *A*. An example of a nontypable character is the Tab key.
Key Up[3]	Occurs when the user releases a key on the keyboard.
MouseDown	Occurs when the user presses the mouse button within the borders of the control.
MouseMove	Occurs when the user moves the mouse within the borders of the control.
MouseUp	Occurs when the user releases the mouse button within the borders of the control.

[1] TextBox control only
[2] Label and CommandButton controls
[3] TextBox and CommandButton controls

Deciding Whether to Use List Boxes or Combo Boxes in Forms

You can let users type employee names to search for, but what if they misspell a name? You need a way to make sure that names are typed correctly. Which do you use for this, a list box or a combo box? As explained below, the two are similar, but the combobox has an additional feature that you may or may not need.

A list box displays a list of values from which the user can choose.

A combo box displays a list of values from which the user can choose and allows the user to enter a new value.

In this case, when you want to limit user options, you should use a list box to list the employee names, as shown in Figure 10.9.

Figure 10.9
Use a list box to control user input and selections.

In the RowSource property of the list box, enter the range from which the control should draw its data. Use a dynamic named range to keep the list updated if employees are added, as shown in the following code:

```
Private Sub btn_EmpOK_Click()
Dim EmpFound As Range
With Range("EmpList")
    Set EmpFound = .Find(lb_EmpName.Value)
    If EmpFound Is Nothing Then
        MsgBox ("Employee not found!")
        lb_EmpName.Value = ""
        Exit Sub
```

```
        Else
            With Range(EmpFound.Address)
                tb_EmpPosition = .Offset(0, 1)
                tb_HireDate = .Offset(0, 2)
            End With
        End If
    End With
    End Sub
```

Using the `MultiSelect` Property of a List Box

List boxes have a `MultiSelect` property, which enables the user to select multiple items from the choices in the list box, as shown in Figure 10.10:

- `fmMultiSelectSingle`—The default setting allows only a single item selection at a time.

- `fmMultiSelectMulti`—This allows an item to be deselected when it is clicked again; multiple items can also be selected.

- `fmMultiSelectExtended`—This allows the Ctrl and Shift keys to be used to select multiple items.

If multiple items are selected, the `Value` property cannot be used to retrieve the items. Instead, check to see whether the item is selected and then manipulate it as needed, using the following code:

```
Private Sub btn_EmpOK_Click()
Dim LastRow As Long, i As Integer
LastRow = Worksheets("Sheet2").Cells(Worksheets("Sheet2").Rows.Count, 1) _
.End(xlUp).Row + 1
Cells(LastRow, 1).Value = tb_EmpName.Value
'check the selection status of the items in the ListBox
For i = 0 To lb_EmpPosition.ListCount - 1
'if the item is selected, add it to the sheet
    If lb_EmpPosition.Selected(i) = True Then
        Cells(LastRow, 2).Value = Cells(LastRow, 2).Value & _
        lb_EmpPosition.List(i) & ","
    End If
Next i
Cells(LastRow, 2).Value = Left(Cells(LastRow, 2).Value, _
Len(Cells(LastRow, 2).Value) - 1) 'remove last comma from string
Cells(LastRow, 3).Value = tb_HireDate.Value
End Sub
```

Figure 10.10

`MultiSelect` enables the user to select multiple items from a list box.

CortiCorp Employee List

Employee Name	Eric Reynolds
Position	CEO
	Customer Service
	Programmer
	Project Consultant

| Hire Date | 5/1/15 |

OK   Cancel

The items in a list box start counting at zero. For this reason, if you use the `ListCount` property, you must subtract one from the result:

```
For i = 0 To lb_EmpPosition.ListCount - 1
```

The available events for `ListBox` controls and `ComboBox` controls are described in Table 10.3.

Table 10.3   `ListBox` **and** `ComboBox` **Control Events**

Event	Description
AfterUpdate	Occurs after the control's data has been changed by the user.
BeforeDragOver	Occurs while the user drags and drops data onto the control.
BeforeDropOrPaste	Occurs right before the user is about to drop or paste data into the control.
BeforeUpdate	Occurs before the data in the control is changed.
Change	Occurs when the value of the control is changed.
Click	Occurs when the user selects a value from the list box or combo box.
DblClick	Occurs when the user double-clicks the control with the mouse.
DropButtonClick[1]	Occurs when the drop-down list appears after the user clicks the drop-down arrow of the combo box or presses F4 on the keyboard.
Enter	Occurs right before the control receives the focus from another control on the same userform.
Error	Occurs when the control runs into an error and can't return the error information.
Exit	Occurs right after the control loses focus to another control on the same userform.
KeyDown	Occurs when the user presses a key on the keyboard.
KeyPress	Occurs when the user presses an ANSI key. An ANSI key is a typable character such as the letter *A*. An example of a nontypable character is the Tab key.
KeyUp	Occurs when the user releases a key on the keyboard.
MouseDown	Occurs when the user presses the mouse button within the borders of the control.
MouseMove	Occurs when the user moves the mouse within the borders of the control.
MouseUp	Occurs when the user releases the mouse button within the borders of the control.

[1] ComboBox control only

Adding Option Buttons to a Userform

 Option buttons are similar to check boxes in that they can be used to make selections. However, unlike check boxes, option buttons can be configured to allow only one selection out of a group.

Using the Frame tool, draw a frame to separate the next set of controls from the other controls on the userform. The frame is used to group option buttons together, as shown in Figure 10.11.

Figure 10.11
Use a frame to group option buttons together.

Option buttons have a `GroupName` property. If you assign the same group name, Buildings, to a set of option buttons, you force them to act collectively, as a toggle, so that only one button in the set can be selected. Selecting an option button automatically deselects the other buttons in the same group or frame. To prevent this behavior, either leave the `Group-Name` property blank or enter another name.

> **NOTE**
> For users who prefer to select the option button's label rather than the button itself, create a separate label and add code to the label, like this, to trigger the option button:
>
> ```
> Private Sub Lbl_Bldg1_Click()
>     Obtn_Bldg1.Value = True
> End Sub
> ```

The available events for `OptionButton` controls and `Frame` controls are described in Table 10.4.

Table 10.4 `OptionButton` **and** `Frame` **Control Events**

Event	Description
AfterUpdate[1]	Occurs after the control's data has been changed by the user.
AddControl[2]	Occurs when a control is added to a frame on a form at runtime. Does not run at design time or upon userform initialization.
BeforeDragOver	Occurs while the user does a drag and drop onto the control.
BeforeDropOrPaste	Occurs right before the user is about to drop or paste data into the control.
BeforeUpdate[1]	Occurs before the data in the control is changed.
Change[1]	Occurs when the value of the control is changed.
Click	Occurs when the user clicks the control with the mouse.
DblClick	Occurs when the user double-clicks the control with the mouse.
Enter	Occurs right before the control receives the focus from another control on the same userform.
Error	Occurs when the control runs into an error and cannot return the error information.

Event	Description
Exit	Occurs right after the control loses focus to another control on the same userform.
KeyDown	Occurs when the user presses a key on the keyboard.
KeyPress	Occurs when the user presses an ANSI key. An ANSI key is a typable character such as the letter A. An example of a nontypable character is the Tab key.
KeyUp	Occurs when the user releases a key on the keyboard.
Layout[2]	Occurs when the frame changes size.
MouseDown	Occurs when the user presses the mouse button within the borders of the control.
MouseMove	Occurs when the user moves the mouse within the borders of the control.
MouseUp	Occurs when the user releases the mouse button within the borders of the control.
RemoveControl[2]	Occurs when a control is deleted from within the frame control.
Scroll[2]	Occurs when the scrollbar box, if visible, is repositioned.
Zoom[2]	Occurs when the zoom value is changed.

[1] OptionButton control only

[2] Frame control only

Adding Graphics to a Userform

A list on a form can be even more helpful if a corresponding graphic is added to the form. The following code displays a photograph corresponding to the selected employee from the list box:

```
Private Sub lb_EmpName_Change()
Dim EmpFound As Range
With Range("EmpList")
    Set EmpFound = .Find(lb_EmpName.Value)
    If EmpFound Is Nothing Then
        MsgBox "Employee not found!"
        lb_EmpName.Value = ""
    Else
        With Range(EmpFound.Address)
            tb_EmpPosition = .Offset(0, 1)
            tb_HireDate = .Offset(0, 2)
            On Error Resume Next
            Img_Employee.Picture = LoadPicture _
    ("C:\Excel VBA 2016 by Jelen & Syrstad\" & EmpFound & ".bmp")
            On Error GoTo 0
        End With
    End If
End With
Set EmpFound = Nothing
Exit Sub
```

The available events for Graphic controls are described in Table 10.5.

Table 10.5 Graphic **Control Events**

Event	Description
BeforeDragOver	Occurs while the user drags and drops data onto the control.
BeforeDropOrPaste	Occurs right before the user is about to drop or paste data into the control.
Click	Occurs when the user clicks the image with the mouse.
DblClick	Occurs when the user double-clicks the image with the mouse.
Error	Occurs when the control runs into an error and can't return the error information.
MouseDown	Occurs when the user presses the mouse button within the borders of the image.
MouseMove	Occurs when the user moves the mouse within the borders of the image.
MouseUp	Occurs when the user releases the mouse button within the borders of the control.

Using a Spin Button on a Userform

 In the example we've been working with, the Hire Date field allows the user to enter the date in any format, such as 1/1/1 or January 1, 2001. This possible inconsistency can create problems later on, if you need to use or search for dates. The solution? Force users to enter dates in a unified manner.

Spin buttons allow the user to increment/decrement through a series of numbers. In this way, the user is forced to enter numbers rather than text. Draw a spin button for a Month entry on the form. In the Properties Window, set Min to 1 for January and Max to 12 for December. For the Value property, enter 1, the first month. Next, draw a text box next to the spin button. This text box reflects the value of the spin button. In addition, you can use labels. Place the code below behind the month's spin button control.

```
Private Sub SpBtn_Month_Change()
tb_Month.Value = SpBtn_Month.Value
End Sub
```

Finish building the form. Use a Min of 1 and Max of 31 for Day, or a Min of 1900 and a Max of 2100 for Year:

```
Private Sub btn_EmpOK_Click()
Dim LastRow As Long, i As Integer
LastRow = Worksheets("Sheet2").Cells(Worksheets("Sheet2").Rows.Count, 1)
_
.End(xlUp).Row + 1
Cells(LastRow, 1).Value = tb_EmpName.Value
For i = 0 To lb_EmpPosition.ListCount - 1
    If lb_EmpPosition.Selected(i) = True Then
        Cells(LastRow, 2).Value = Cells(LastRow, 2).Value & _
        lb_EmpPosition.List(i) & ","
    End If
Next i
'Concatenate the values from the textboxes to create the date
Cells(LastRow, 3).Value = tb_Month.Value & "/" & tb_Day.Value & _
    "/" & tb_Year.Value
```

```
Cells(LastRow, 2).Value = Left(Cells(LastRow, 2).Value, _
Len(Cells(LastRow, 2).Value) - 1) 'remove trailing comma
End Sub
```

The available events for `SpinButton` controls are described in Table 10.6.

Table 10.6 `SpinButton` **Control Events**

Event	Description
AfterUpdate	Occurs after the control's data has been changed by the user.
BeforeDragOver	Occurs while the user drags and drops data onto the control.
BeforeDropOrPaste	Occurs right before the user is about to drop or paste data into the control.
BeforeUpdate	Occurs before the data in the control is changed.
Change	Occurs when the value of the control is changed.
Enter	Occurs right before the control receives the focus from another control on the same userform.
Error	Occurs when the control runs into an error and cannot return the error information.
Exit	Occurs right after the control loses focus to another control on the same userform.
KeyDown	Occurs when the user presses a key on the keyboard.
KeyPress	Occurs when the user presses an ANSI key. An ANSI key is a typable character such as the letter *A*. An example of a nontypable character is the Tab key.
KeyUp	Occurs when the user releases a key on the keyboard.
SpinDown	Occurs when the user clicks the lower or left spin button, decreasing the value.
SpinUp	Occurs when the user clicks the upper or right spin button, increasing the value.

10

Using the `MultiPage` Control to Combine Forms

The `MultiPage` control provides a neat way of organizing multiple forms. Instead of having one form for personal employee information and one for on-the-job information, combine the information into one multipage form, as shown in Figures 10.12 and 10.13.

You can modify a page by right-clicking the tab of the page and then choosing from the following menu options: New Page, Delete Page, Rename, and Move.

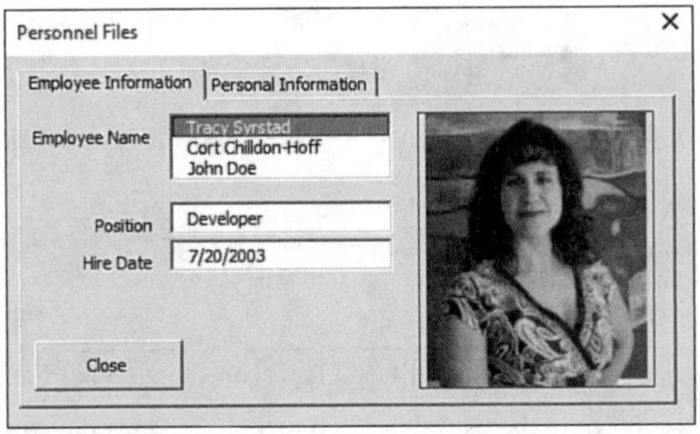

Figure 10.12
Use the `MultiPage`
control to combine
multiple forms. This is the
first page of the form.

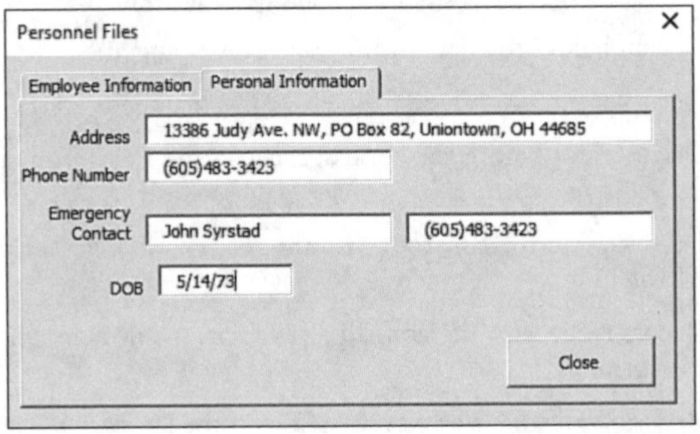

Figure 10.13
This is the second page of
the form.

TIP

Adding multipage forms after the rest of the form has been created is not an easy task. Therefore, plan
multipage forms from the beginning. If you decide later that you need a multipage form, insert a new
form, draw the `MultiPage`, and copy/paste the controls from the other forms to the new form.

NOTE

Do not right-click in the tab area to view the `MultiPage` code. Instead, right-click in the
`MultiPage`'s main area to get the View Code option.

Unlike many of the other controls in which the `Value` property holds a user-entered or
user-selected value, the `MultiPage` control uses the `Value` property to hold the number of
the active page, starting at zero. For example, if you have a five-page form and want to activate the fourth page, use this:

```
MultiPage1.Value = 3
```

If you have a control you want all the pages to share, such as a Save, Cancel, or Close button, place the control on the main userform rather than on the individual pages, as shown
in Figure 10.14.

The available events for `MultiPage` controls are described in Table 10.7.

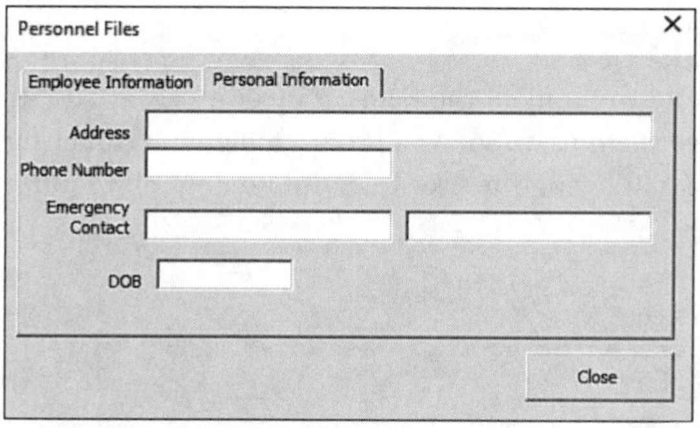

Figure 10.14
Place common controls
such as the Close button
on the main userform.

Table 10.7 `MultiPage` **Control Events**

Event	Description
AddControl	Occurs when a control is added to a page of the `MultiPage` control. Does not run at design time or upon userform initialization.
BeforeDragOver	Occurs while the user drags and drops data onto a page of the `MultiPage` control.
BeforeDropOrPaste	Occurs right before the user is about to drop or paste data onto a page of the `MultiPage` control.
Change	Occurs when the user changes pages of a `MultiPage` control.
Click	Occurs when the user clicks on a page of the `MultiPage` control.
DblClick	Occurs when the user double-clicks a page of the `MultiPage` control with the mouse.
Enter	Occurs right before the `MultiPage` control receives the focus from another control on the same userform.
Error	Occurs when the `MultiPage` control runs into an error and cannot return the error information.
Exit	Occurs right after the `MultiPage` control loses focus to another control on the same userform.
KeyDown	Occurs when the user presses a key on the keyboard.
KeyPress	Occurs when the user presses an ANSI key. An ANSI key is a typable character, such as the letter A. An example of a nontypable character is the Tab key.
KeyUp	Occurs when the user releases a key on the keyboard.
Layout	Occurs when the `MultiPage` control changes size.
MouseDown	Occurs when the user presses the mouse button within the borders of the control.
MouseMove	Occurs when the user moves the mouse within the borders of the control.
MouseUp	Occurs when the user releases the mouse button within the borders of the control.
RemoveControl	Occurs when a control is removed from a page of the `MultiPage` control.
Scroll	Occurs when the scrollbar box, if visible, is repositioned.
Zoom	Occurs when the zoom value is changed.

10

Verifying Field Entry

Even when users are told to fill in all the fields, they don't always do it. With a paper form, there is no way to force them to do so. As a programmer, you can ensure that all required fields are filled in by not allowing the user to continue until all requirements are met. Here's how to do this:

```
If tb_EmpName.Value = "" Then
    frm_AddEmp.Hide
    MsgBox "Please enter an Employee Name"
    frm_AddEmp.Show
    Exit Sub
End If
```

Illegal Window Closing

The userforms created in the VB Editor are not that different from normal dialog boxes; they also include the *X* close button in the upper-right corner. Although using the button is not wrong, it can cause problems, depending on the objective of the userform. In cases like this, you might want to control what happens if the user clicks the button. Use the QueryClose event of the userform to find out what method is used to close the form and code an appropriate action:

```
Private Sub UserForm_QueryClose(Cancel As Integer, CloseMode As Integer)
If CloseMode = vbFormControlMenu Then
    MsgBox "Please use the OK or Cancel buttons to close the form", _
        vbCritical
    Cancel = True 'prevent the form from closing
End If
End Sub
```

When you know which method the user used to try to close the form, you can create a message box similar to the one shown in Figure 10.15 to warn the user that the method was illegal.

Figure 10.15
Control what happens when the user clicks the *X* button.

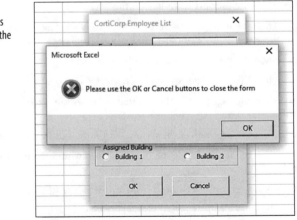

The `QueryClose` event can be triggered in four ways:

- `vbFormControlMenu`—The user either right-clicks on the form's title bar and selects the Close command or clicks the *X* in the upper-right corner of the form.
- `vbFormCode`—The `Unload` statement is used.
- `vbAppWindows`—Windows shuts down.
- `vbAppTaskManager`—The application is shut down by the Task Manager.

Getting a Filename

One of the most common client interactions occurs when you need the client to specify a path and filename. Excel VBA has a built-in function to display the File Open dialog box, as shown in Figure 10.16. The client browses to and selects a file. When the client clicks the Open button, instead of opening the file, Excel VBA returns the full path and filename to the code:

Figure 10.16
Use the File Open dialog box to allow the user to select a file.

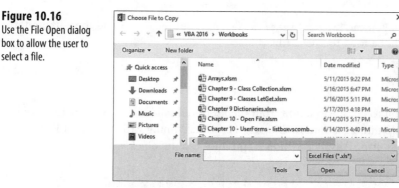

```
Sub SelectFile()
'Ask which file to copy
x = Application.GetOpenFilename( _
    FileFilter:="Excel Files (*.xls*), *.xls*", _
    Title:="Choose File to Copy", MultiSelect:=False)

'check in case no files were selected
If x = "False" Then Exit Sub

MsgBox "You selected " & x
End Sub
```

The preceding code allows the client to select one file. If you want the user to specify multiple files, use this code:

```
Sub ManyFiles()
Dim x As Variant

x = Application.GetOpenFilename( _
    FileFilter:="Excel Files (*.xls*), *.xls*", _
    Title:="Choose Files", MultiSelect:=True)

On Error Resume Next
If Ubound(x) > 0 Then
    For i = 1 To UBound(x)
        MsgBox "You selected " & x(i)
    Next i
ElseIf x = "False" Then
    Exit Sub
End If
On Error GoTo 0

End Sub
```

In a similar fashion, you can use `Application.GetSaveAsFileName` to find the path and filename that should be used to save a file.

Next Steps

Userforms allow you to get information from the users and guide them on how to provide the program with that information. In Chapter 11, "Data Mining with Advanced Filter," you'll find out about using Advanced Filter to produce reports quickly.

Data Mining with Advanced Filter

Read this chapter.

Although very few people use Advanced Filter in Excel, it is a workhorse in Excel VBA. I estimate that I end up using one of these filtering techniques as the core of a macro in 80% of the macros I develop for clients. Given that Advanced Filter is used in fewer than 1% of Excel sessions, this is a dramatic statistic.

So even if you hardly ever use Advanced Filter in regular Excel, you should study this chapter to learn some powerful VBA techniques.

Replacing a Loop with AutoFilter

In Chapter 4, "Looping and Flow Control," you read about several ways to loop through a data set to format records that match certain criteria. By using Filter (Microsoft's name for what was originally AutoFilter), you can achieve the same result much faster. While other examples in this chapter use the Advanced Filter, this example can be solved with the simpler Filter. Although Microsoft changed the name of AutoFilter to Filter in Excel 2007, the VBA code still refers to AutoFilter.

When AutoFilter was added to Excel, the team at Microsoft added extra care and attention to it. Items hidden because of AutoFilter are not simply treated like other hidden rows. AutoFilter gets special treatment. You've likely run into the frustrating situation in the past where you have applied formatting to visible rows and the formatting has gotten applied to the hidden rows. This is certainly a problem when you've hidden rows by clicking the #2 Group and

Outline button after using the Subtotal command. This is always a problem when you manually hide rows. But it is never a problem when the rows are hidden because of AutoFilter.

After you've applied AutoFilter to hide rows, any action performed on the `CurrentRegion` is applied only to the visible rows. You can apply bold. You can change the font to red. You can even use `CurrentRegion.EntireRow.Delete` to delete the visible rows and not impact the rows hidden by the filter.

Let's say that you have a data set like the one shown in Figure 11.1, and you want to perform some action on all the records that match a certain criteria, such as all Ford records.

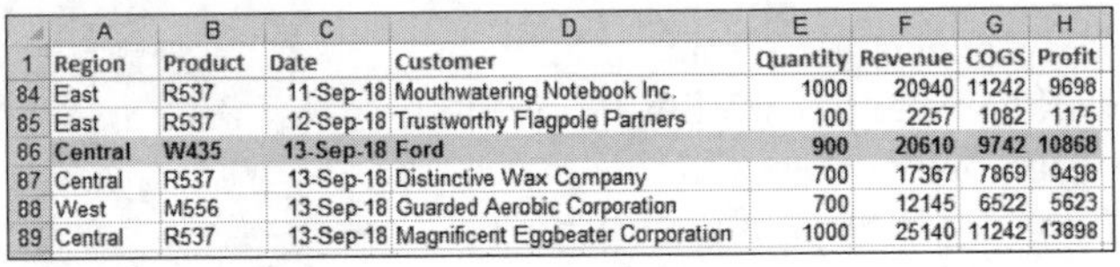

Figure 11.1
Find all Ford records and mark them.

	A	B	C	D	E	F	G	H
1	Region	Product	Date	Customer	Quantity	Revenue	COGS	Profit
84	East	R537	11-Sep-18	Mouthwatering Notebook Inc.	1000	20940	11242	9698
85	East	R537	12-Sep-18	Trustworthy Flagpole Partners	100	2257	1082	1175
86	Central	W435	13-Sep-18	Ford	900	20610	9742	10868
87	Central	R537	13-Sep-18	Distinctive Wax Company	700	17367	7869	9498
88	West	M556	13-Sep-18	Guarded Aerobic Corporation	700	12145	6522	5623
89	Central	R537	13-Sep-18	Magnificent Eggbeater Corporation	1000	25140	11242	13898

In Chapter 5, "R1C1-Style Formulas," you learned to write code like the following, which you could use to color all the Ford records green:

```
Sub OldLoop()
    FinalRow = Cells(Rows.Count, 1).End(xlUp).Row
    For i = 2 To FinalRow
        If Cells(i, 4) = "Ford" Then
            Cells(i, 1).Resize(1, 8).Interior.Color = RGB(0,255,0)
        End If
    Next i
End Sub
```

If you needed to delete records, you would need to be careful to run the loop from the bottom of the data set to the top, using code like this:

```
Sub OldLoopToDelete()
    FinalRow = Cells(Rows.Count, 1).End(xlUp).Row
    For i = FinalRow To 2 Step -1
        If Cells(i, 4) = "Ford" Then
            Rows(i).Delete
        End If
    Next i
End Sub
```

The `AutoFilter` method, however, enables you to isolate all the Ford records in a single line of code:

```
Range("A1").AutoFilter Field:=4, Criteria1:= "Ford"
```

After isolating the matching records, you do not need to use the `VisibleCellsOnly` setting to format the matching records. Instead, you can use the following line of code to make all the matching records green:

```
Range("A1").CurrentRegion.Interior.Color = RGB(0,255,00)
```

There are two problems with the current two-line macro. First, the program leaves the AutoFilter drop-downs in the data set. Second, the heading row is also formatted in green.

> **NOTE** Note that the `.CurrentRegion` property extends the A1 reference to include the entire data set.

This single line of code turns off the AutoFilter drop-downs and clears the filter:

```
Range("A1").AutoFilter
```

If you want to leave the AutoFilter drop-downs on but clear the column D drop-down from showing Ford, you can use this line of code:

```
ActiveSheet.ShowAllData
```

Addressing the second problem is a bit more difficult. After you apply the filter and select `Range("A1").CurrentRegion`, the selection automatically includes the headers in the selection. Any formatting is also applied to the header row.

If you do not care about the first blank row below the data, you can simply add OFFSET(1) to move the current region down to start in A2. This would be fine if your goal were to delete all the Ford records:

```
Sub DeleteFord()
    ' skips header, but also deletes blank row below
    Range("A1").AutoFilter Field:=4, Criteria1:="Ford"
    Range("A1").CurrentRegion.Offset(1).EntireRow.Delete
    Range("A1").AutoFilter

End Sub
```

> **NOTE** The OFFSET property usually requires the number of rows and the number of columns. Using `.OFFSET(-2, 5)` moves two rows up and five columns right. If you do not want to adjust by any columns, you can leave off the column parameter. Using `.OFFSET(1)` means one row down and zero columns over.

The preceding code works when you do not mind if the first blank row below the data is deleted. However, when you apply a green format to those rows, the code applies the green format to the blank row below the data set, and that would not look right.

If you will be doing some formatting, you can determine the height of the data set and use `.Resize` to reduce the height of the current region while you use OFFSET:

```
Sub ColorFord()
    DataHt = Range("A1").CurrentRegion.Rows.Count
    Range("A1").AutoFilter Field:=4, Criteria1:="Ford"
    With Range("A1").CurrentRegion.Offset(1).Resize(DataHt - 1)
    ' No need to use VisibleCellsOnly for formatting
        .Interior.Color = RGB(0,255,0)
        .Font.Bold = True
    End With
    ' Clear the AutoFilter & remove drop-downs
    Range("A1").AutoFilter
End Sub
```

Using AutoFilter Techniques

Excel 2007 introduced the possibility of selecting multiple items from a filter, filtering by color, filtering by icon, filtering by top 10, and filtering to virtual date filters. Excel 2010 introduced the search box in the filter drop-down. All these filters have VBA equivalents, although some of them are implemented in VBA using legacy filtering methods.

Selecting Multiple Items

Legacy versions of Excel allowed you to select two values, joined by AND or OR. In this case, you would specify xlAnd or xlOr as the operator:

```
Range("A1").AutoFilter Field:=4, _
    Criteria1:="Ford", _
    Operator:=xlOr, _
    Criteria2:="General Motors"
```

As the AutoFilter command became more flexible, Microsoft continued to use the same three parameters, even if they didn't quite make sense. For example, Excel still lets you filter a field by asking for the top five items or the bottom 8% of records. To use this type of filter, specify either "5" or "8" as the Criteria1 argument and then specify xlTop10Items, xlTop10Percent, xlBottom10Items, or xlBottom10Percent as the operator. For example, the following code produces the top 12 revenue records:

```
Sub Top10Filter()
    ' Top 12 Revenue Records
    Range("A1").AutoFilter Field:=6, _
        Criteria1:="12", _
        Operator:=xlTop10Items
End Sub
```

There are a lot of numbers (6, 12, 10) in the code for this AutoFilter. Field:=6 indicates that you are looking at the sixth column. xlTop10Items is the name of the filter, but the filter is not limited to 10 items. The criteria 12 indicates the number of items that you want the filter to return.

Excel offers several new filter options. It continues to force these filter options to fit in the old object model, where the filter command must fit in an operator and up to two criteria fields.

If you want to choose three or more items, change the operator to Operator: =xlFilterValues and specify the list of items as an array in the Criteria1 argument:

```
Range("A1").AutoFilter Field:=4, _
    Criteria1:=Array("General Motors", "Ford", "Fiat"), _
    Operator:=xlFilterValues
```

Selecting Using the Search Box

Excel 2010 introduced the Search box in the AutoFilter drop-down. After typing something in the Search box, you can use the Select All Search Results item.

The macro recorder does a poor job of recording the Search box. The macro recorder hard-codes a list of customers who matched the search at the time you ran the macro.

Think about the Search box. It is really a shortcut way of selecting Text Filters, Contains. Furthermore, the Contains filter is actually a shortcut way of specifying the search string surrounded by asterisks. Therefore, to filter to all the records that contain "at," use this:

```
Range("A1").AutoFilter, Field:=4, Criteria1:="*at*"
```

Filtering by Color

To find records that have a particular font color, use the operator `xlFilterFontColor` and specify a particular RGB value as the criteria. This code finds all cells with a red font in column F:

```
Sub FilterByFontColor()
    Range("A1").AutoFilter Field:=6, _
        Criteria1:=RGB(255, 0, 0), Operator:=xlFilterFontColor
End Sub
```

To find records that have no particular font color, use the operator `xlFilterAutomaticFillColor` and do not specify any criteria:

```
Sub FilterNoFontColor()
    Range("A1").AutoFilter Field:=6, _
        Operator:=xlFilterAutomaticFontColor
End Sub
```

To find records that have a particular fill color, use the operator `xlFilterCellColor` and specify a particular RGB value as the criteria. This code finds all red cells in column F:

```
Sub FilterByFillColor()
    Range("A1").AutoFilter Field:=6, _
        Criteria1:=RGB(255, 0, 0), Operator:=xlFilterCellColor
End Sub
```

To find records that have no fill color, use the operator `xlFilterNoFill` and do not specify any criteria.

Filtering by Icon

If you are expecting a data set to have an icon set applied, you can filter to show only records with one particular icon by using the `xlFilterIcon` operator.

For the criteria, you have to know which icon set has been applied, as well as which icon within the set you want to filter by. The icon sets are identified using the names shown in column A in Figure 11.2. The items range from 1 through 5. The following code filters the Revenue column to show the rows containing an upward-pointing arrow in the 5 Arrows Gray icon set:

```
Sub FilterByIcon()
    Range("A1").AutoFilter Field:=6, _
        Criteria1:=ActiveWorkbook.IconSets(xl5ArrowsGray).Item(5), _
        Operator:=xlFilterIcon
End Sub
```

To find records that have no conditional formatting icon, use the operator `xlFilterNoIcon` and do not specify any criteria.

11

Figure 11.2
To search for a particular icon, you need to know the icon set from column A and the item number from row 1.

Selecting a Dynamic Date Range Using AutoFilters

Perhaps the most powerful feature in the world of Excel filters is the dynamic filters. These filters enable you to choose records that are above average or with a date field to select virtual periods, such as next week or last year.

To use a dynamic filter, specify `xlFilterDynamic` as the operator and then use 1 of 34 values as `Criteria1`. The following code finds all dates that are in the next year:

```
Sub DynamicAutoFilter()
    Range("A1").AutoFilter Field:=3, _
        Criteria1:=xlFilterNextYear, _
        Operator:=xlFilterDynamic
End Sub
```

The following are all the dynamic filter criteria options, which you specify as `Criteria1` in the `AutoFilter` method:

- **Criteria for values**—Use `xlFilterAboveAverage` or `xlFilterBelowAverage` to find all the rows that are above or below average. Note that in Lake Wobegon, using `xlFilterBelowAverage` will likely return no records.

- **Criteria for future periods**—Use `xlFilterTomorrow, xlFilterNextWeek, xlFilterNextMonth, xlFilterNextQuarter,` or `xlFilterNextYear` to find rows that fall in a certain future period. Note that "next week" starts on Sunday and ends on Saturday.

- **Criteria for current periods**—Use `xlFilterToday, xlFilterThisWeek, xlFilterThisMonth, xlFilterThisQuarter,` or `xlFilterThisYear` to find rows that fall within the current period. Excel uses the system clock to find the current day.

- **Criteria for past periods**—Use `xlFilterYesterday, xlFilterLastWeek, xlFilterLastMonth, xlFilterLastQuarter, xlFilterLastYear,` or `xlFilterYearToDate` to find rows that fall within a previous period.

■ **Criteria for specific quarters**—Use `xlFilterDatesInPeriodQuarter1`, `xlFilterDatesInPeriodQuarter2`, `xlFilterDatesInPeriodQuarter3`, or `xlFilterDatesInPeriodQuarter4` to filter to rows that fall within a specific quarter. Note that these filters do not differentiate based on a year. If you ask for quarter 1, you might get records from this January, last February, and next March.

■ **Criteria for specific months**—Use `xlFilterDatesInPeriodJanuary` through `xlFilterDatesInPeriodDecember` to filter to records that fall during a certain month. As with quarters, the filter does not filter to any particular year.

Unfortunately, you cannot combine criteria. You might think that you can specify `xlFilterDatesInPeriodJanuary` as Criteria1 and `xlFilterDatesNextYear` as Criteria2. Even though this is a brilliant thought, Microsoft does not support this syntax (yet).

Selecting Visible Cells Only

After you apply a filter, most commands operate only on the visible rows in the selection. If you need to delete the records, format the records, or apply a conditional format to the records, you can simply refer to the `.CurrentRegion` of the first heading cell and perform the command.

However, if you have a data set in which the rows have been hidden using the Hide Rows command, any formatting applied to `.CurrentRegion` applies to the hidden rows, too. In these cases, you should use the Visible Cells Only option in the Go To Special dialog, as shown in Figure 11.3.

Figure 11.3
If rows have been manually hidden, use Visible Cells Only in the Go To Special dialog.

To use Visible Cells Only in code, use the `SpecialCells` property:

```
Range("A1").CurrentRegion.SpecialCells(xlCellTypeVisible)
```

CASE STUDY: USING GO TO SPECIAL INSTEAD OF LOOPING

The Go To Special dialog also plays a role in this case study.

At a Data Analyst Boot Camp, one of the attendees had a macro that was taking a long time to run. The workbook had a number of selection controls. A complex `IF()` function in cells H10:H750 was choosing which records should be included in a report. While that `IF()` statement had many nested conditions, the formula was inserting either KEEP or HIDE in each cell:

```
=IF(logical_test,"KEEP","HIDE")
```

The following section of code was hiding individual rows:

```
For Each cell In Range("H10:H750")
    If cell.Value = "HIDE" Then
        cell.EntireRow.Hidden = True
    End If
Next cell
```

The macro was taking several minutes to run. SUBTOTAL formulas that excluded hidden rows were recalculating after each pass through the loop. The first attempts to speed up the macro involved turning off screen updating and calculation:

```
Application.ScreenUpdating = False
Application.Calculation = xlCalculationManual
For Each cell In Range("H10:H750")
    If cell.Value = "HIDE" Then
        cell.EntireRow.Hidden = True
    End If
Next cell
Application.Calculation = xlCalculationAutomatic
Application.ScreenUpdating = True
```

For some reason, looping through all the records was still taking too long. We tried using AutoFilter to isolate the HIDE records and then hiding those rows, but we lost the manual row hiding after turning off AutoFilter.

The solution was to make use of the Go To Special dialog's ability to limit the selection to text results of formulas. First, the formula in column H was changed to return either HIDE or a number:

```
=IF(logical_test,"HIDE",1)
```

Then, the following single line of code was able to hide the rows that evaluated to a text value in column H:

```
Range("H10:H750") _
    .SpecialCells(xlCellTypeFormulas, xlTextValues) _
    .EntireRow.Hidden = True
```

Because all the rows were hidden in a single command, that section of the macro ran in seconds rather than minutes.

Advanced Filter—Easier in VBA Than in Excel

Using the arcane Advanced Filter command is so difficult in the Excel user interface that it is pretty rare to find someone who enjoys using it regularly.

However, in VBA, advanced filters are a joy to use. With a single line of code, you can rapidly extract a subset of records from a database or quickly get a unique list of values in any column. This is critical when you want to run reports for a specific region or customer. Two advanced filters are used most often in the same procedure—one to get a unique list of customers and a second to filter to each individual customer, as shown in Figure 11.4. The rest of this chapter builds toward such a routine.

Figure 11.4
A typical macro uses two advanced filters.

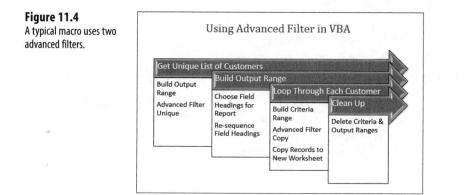

Using the Excel Interface to Build an Advanced Filter

Because not many people use the Advanced Filter feature, this section walks you through examples using the user interface to build an advanced filter and then shows you the analogous code. You will be amazed at how complex the user interface seems and yet how easy it is to program a powerful advanced filter to extract records.

One reason Advanced Filter is hard to use is that you can use it in several different ways. You must make three basic choices in the Advanced Filter dialog box. Because each choice has two options, there are eight (2 × 2 × 2) possible combinations of these choices. The three basic choices are shown in Figure 11.5 and described here:

- **Action**—You can select Filter the List, In-Place or you can select Copy to Another Location. If you choose to filter the records in place, the nonmatching rows are hidden. Choosing to copy to a new location copies the records that match the filter to a new range.
- **Criteria**—You can filter with or without criteria. Filtering with criteria is appropriate for getting a subset of rows. Filtering without criteria is still useful when you want a subset of columns or when you are using the Unique Records Only option.
- **Unique**—You can choose to request Unique Records Only or request all matching records. The Unique option makes using the Advanced Filter command one of the fastest ways to find a unique list of values in one field. By placing the Customer heading in the output range, you get a unique list of values for that one column.

Figure 11.5
The Advanced Filter dialog is complicated to use in the Excel user interface. Fortunately, it is much easier in VBA.

Using Advanced Filter to Extract a Unique List of Values

One of the simplest uses of Advanced Filter is to extract a unique list of a single field from a data set. In this example, you want to get a unique list of customers from a sales report. You know that Customer is in column D of the data set. You have an unknown number of records starting in cell A2, and row 1 is the header row. There is nothing located to the right of the data set.

Extracting a Unique List of Values with the User Interface

To extract a unique list of values, follow these steps:

1. With the cursor anywhere in the data range, select Advanced from the Sort & Filter group on the Data tab. The first time you use the Advanced Filter command on a worksheet, Excel automatically populates the List Range text box with the entire range of your data set. On subsequent uses of the Advanced Filter command, this dialog box remembers the settings from the prior advanced filter.

2. Select the Unique Records Only check box at the bottom of the dialog.

3. In the Action section, select Copy to Another Location.

4. Type J1 in the Copy To text box.

By default, Excel copies all the columns in the data set. You can filter just the Customer column either by limiting List Range to include only column D or by specifying one or more headings in the Copy To range. Each method has its own drawbacks.

Changing the List Range to a Single Column

Edit List Range to point to the Customer column. In this case, you need to change the default $A$1:$H$1127 to $D$1:$D$1127. The Advanced Filter dialog should appear.

> **NOTE** When you initially edit any range in the dialog box, Excel might be in Point mode. In this mode, pressing a left- or right-arrow key inserts a cell reference in the text box. If you see the word *Point* in the lower-left corner of your Excel window, press the F2 key to change from Point mode to Edit mode.

The drawback of this method is that Excel remembers the list range on subsequent uses of the Advanced Filter command. If you later want to get a unique list of regions, you will be constantly specifying the list range.

Copying the Customer Heading Before Filtering

With a little thought before invoking the Advanced Filter command, you can allow Excel to keep the default list range $A$1:$H$1127. In cell J1, type the Customer heading as shown in Figure 11.6. Leave the List Range field pointing to columns A through H. Because the Copy To range of J1 already contains a valid heading from the list range, Excel copies data only from the Customer column. This is the preferred method, particularly if you will be using multiple advanced filters. Because Excel remembers the settings from the preceding advanced filter, it is more convenient to always filter the entire columns of the list range and limit the columns by setting up headings in the Copy To range.

After you use either of these methods to perform the advanced filter, a concise list of the unique customers appears in column J (see Figure 11.6).

Figure 11.6
The advanced filter extracted a unique list of customers from the data set and copied it to column J.

J	K	L	M
Customer			
Trustworthy Flagpole Partners			
Amazing Shoe Company			
Mouthwatering Notebook Inc.			
Cool Saddle Traders			
Tasty Shovel Company			
Distinctive Wax Company			
Guarded Aerobic Corporation			
Tasty Yogurt Corporation			
Agile Aquarium Inc.			
Magnificent Eggbeater Corporation			
User-Friendly Luggage Corporation			
Guarded Umbrella Traders			

Extracting a Unique List of Values with VBA Code

In VBA, you use the `AdvancedFilter` method to carry out the Advanced Filter command. Again, you have three choices to make:

- **Action**—Choose to either filter in place with the parameter `Action:=xlFilterInPlace` or copy with `Action:=xlFilterCopy`. If you want to copy, you also have to specify the parameter `CopyToRange:=Range("J1")`.

- **Criteria**—To filter with criteria, include the parameter `CriteriaRange:=Range("L1:L2")`. To filter without criteria, omit this optional parameter.

- **Unique**—To return only unique records, specify the parameter `Unique:=True`.

The following code sets up a single-column output range two columns to the right of the last-used column in the data range:

```
Sub GetUniqueCustomers()
    Dim lRange As Range
```

```
    Dim ORange As Range

    ' Find the size of today's data set
    FinalRow = Cells(Rows.Count, 1).End(xlUp).Row
    NextCol = Cells(1, Columns.Count).End(xlToLeft).Column + 2

    ' Set up output range. Copy heading from D1 there
    Range("D1").Copy Destination:=Cells(1, NextCol)
    Set ORange = Cells(1, NextCol)

    ' Define the Input Range
    Set IRange = Range("A1").Resize(FinalRow, NextCol - 2)

    ' Do the Advanced Filter to get unique list of customers
    IRange.AdvancedFilter Action:=xlFilterCopy, CopyToRange:=ORange, _
      Unique:=True

End Sub
```

By default, an advanced filter copies all columns. If you just want one particular column, use that column heading as the heading in the output range.

The first bit of code finds the final row and column in the data set. Although it is not necessary to do so, you can define an object variable for the output range (ORange) and for the input range (IRange).

This code is generic enough that it will not have to be rewritten if new columns are added to the data set later. Setting up the object variables for the input and output range is done for readability rather than out of necessity. The previous code could be written just as easily like this shortened version:

```
Sub UniqueCustomerRedux()
    ' Copy a heading to create an output range
    Range("J1").Value = Range("D1").Value
    ' Do the Advanced Filter
    Range("A1").CurrentRegion.AdvancedFilter xlFilterCopy, _
        CopyToRange:=Range("J1"), Unique:=True
End Sub
```

When you run either of the previous blocks of code on the sample data set, you get a unique list of customers off to the right of the data. The key to getting a unique list of customers is copying the header from the Customer field to a blank cell and specifying this cell as the output range.

After you have the unique list of customers, you can sort the list and add a SUMIF formula to get total revenue by customer. The following code gets the unique list of customers, sorts it, and then builds a formula to total revenue by customer. Figure 11.7 shows the results:

```
Sub RevenueByCustomers()
    Dim IRange As Range
    Dim ORange As Range

    ' Find the size of today's data set
    FinalRow = Cells(Rows.Count, 1).End(xlUp).Row
    NextCol = Cells(1, Columns.Count).End(xlToLeft).Column + 2
```

```
' Set up output range. Copy heading from D1 there
Range("D1").Copy Destination:=Cells(1, NextCol)
Set ORange = Cells(1, NextCol)

' Define the Input Range
Set IRange = Range("A1").Resize(FinalRow, NextCol - 2)

' Do the Advanced Filter to get unique list of customers
IRange.AdvancedFilter Action:=xlFilterCopy, _
    CopyToRange:=ORange, Unique:=True

' Determine how many unique customers we have
LastRow = Cells(Rows.Count, NextCol).End(xlUp).Row

' Sort the data
Cells(1, NextCol).Resize(LastRow, 1).Sort Key1:=Cells(1, NextCol), _
    Order1:=xlAscending, Header:=xlYes

' Add a SUMIF formula to get totals
Cells(1, NextCol + 1).Value = "Revenue"
Cells(2, NextCol + 1).Resize(LastRow - 1).FormulaR1C1 = _
    "=SUMIF(R2C4:R" & FinalRow & _
    "C4,RC[-1],R2C6:R" & FinalRow & "C6)"

End Sub
```

Figure 11.7
This macro produced a summary report by customer from a lengthy data set. Using `AdvancedFilter` is the key to powerful macros such as these.

Another use of a unique list of values is to quickly populate a list box or a combo box on a userform. For example, suppose that you have a macro that can run a report for any one specific customer. To allow your clients to choose which customers to report, create a simple userform. Add a list box to the userform and set the list box's `MultiSelect` property to `1-fmMultiSelectMulti`. In this case, the form is named `frmReport`. In addition to the list box, there are four command buttons: OK, Cancel, Mark All, and Clear All. The code to run the form follows. Note that the `Userform_Initialize` procedure includes an advanced filter to get the unique list of customers from the data set:

```
Private Sub CancelButton_Click()
    Unload Me
End Sub

Private Sub cbSubAll_Click()
    For i = 0 To lbCust.ListCount - 1
        Me.lbCust.Selected(i) = True
```

```
        Next i
    End Sub

    Private Sub cbSubClear_Click()
        For i = 0 To lbCust.ListCount - 1
            Me.lbCust.Selected(i) = False
        Next i
    End Sub

    Private Sub OKButton_Click()
        For i = 0 To lbCust.ListCount - 1
            If Me.lbCust.Selected(i) = True Then
                ' Call a routine (discussed later) to produce this report
                RunCustReport WhichCust:=Me.lbCust.List(i)
            End If
        Next i
        Unload Me
    End Sub

    Private Sub UserForm_Initialize()
        Dim IRange As Range
        Dim ORange As Range

        ' Find the size of today's data set
        FinalRow = Cells(Rows.Count, 1).End(xlUp).Row
        NextCol = Cells(1, Columns.Count).End(xlToLeft).Column + 2

        ' Set up output range. Copy heading from D1 there
        Range("D1").Copy Destination:=Cells(1, NextCol)
        Set ORange = Cells(1, NextCol)

        ' Define the Input Range
        Set IRange = Range("A1").Resize(FinalRow, NextCol - 2)

        ' Do the Advanced Filter to get unique list of customers
        IRange.AdvancedFilter Action:=xlFilterCopy, _
            CopyToRange:=ORange, Unique:=True

        ' Determine how many unique customers we have
        LastRow = Cells(Rows.Count, NextCol).End(xlUp).Row

        ' Sort the data
        Cells(1, NextCol).Resize(LastRow, 1).Sort Key1:=Cells(1, NextCol), _
            Order1:=xlAscending, Header:=xlYes

With Me.lbCust
    .RowSource = ""
    .List = Cells(2, NextCol).Resize(LastRow - 1, 1).Value
End With

        ' Erase the temporary list of customers
        Cells(1, NextCol).Resize(LastRow, 1).Clear
    End Sub
```

Launch this form with a simple module, like this:

```
Sub ShowCustForm()
    frmReport.Show
End Sub
```

Your clients are presented with a list of all valid customers from the data set. Because the list box's MultiSelect property is set to allow it, they can select any number of customers.

Getting Unique Combinations of Two or More Fields

To get all unique combinations of two or more fields, build the output range to include the additional fields. This code sample builds a list of unique combinations of two fields: Customer and Product:

```
Sub UniqueCustomerProduct()
    Dim IRange As Range
    Dim ORange As Range

    ' Find the size of today's data set
    FinalRow = Cells(Rows.Count, 1).End(xlUp).Row
    NextCol = Cells(1, Columns.Count).End(xlToLeft).Column + 2

    ' Set up output range. Copy headings from D1 & B1
    Range("D1").Copy Destination:=Cells(1, NextCol)
    Range("B1").Copy Destination:=Cells(1, NextCol + 1)
    Set ORange = Cells(1, NextCol).Resize(1, 2)

    ' Define the Input Range
    Set IRange = Range("A1").Resize(FinalRow, NextCol - 2)

    ' Do the Advanced Filter to get unique list of customers & product
    IRange.AdvancedFilter Action:=xlFilterCopy, _
        CopyToRange:=ORange, Unique:=True

    ' Determine how many unique rows we have
    LastRow = Cells(Rows.Count, NextCol).End(xlUp).Row

    ' Sort the data
    Cells(1, NextCol).Resize(LastRow, 2).Sort Key1:=Cells(1, NextCol), _
        Order1:=xlAscending, Key2:=Cells(1, NextCol + 1), _
        Order2:=xlAscending, Header:=xlYes

End Sub
```

In the result shown in Figure 11.8, you can see that Enhanced Eggbeater buys only one product, and Distinctive Wax buys three products. This might be useful as a guide in running reports on either customer by product or product by customer.

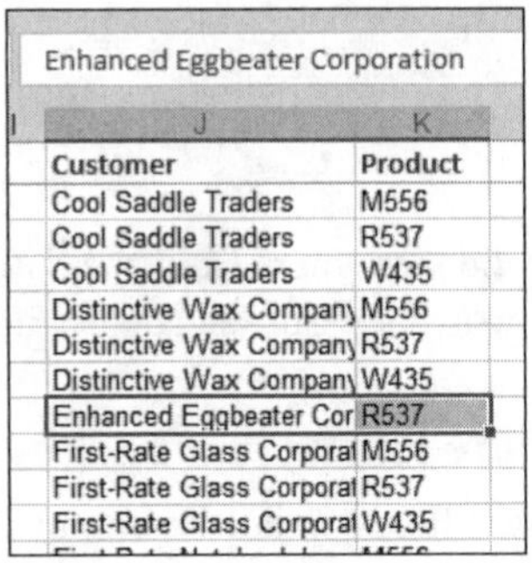

Figure 11.8
By including two columns in the output range on a Unique Values query, you get every combination of customer and product.

Enhanced Eggbeater Corporation	
J	K
Customer	Product
Cool Saddle Traders	M556
Cool Saddle Traders	R537
Cool Saddle Traders	W435
Distinctive Wax Company	M556
Distinctive Wax Company	R537
Distinctive Wax Company	W435
Enhanced Eggbeater Cor	R537
First-Rate Glass Corporal	M556
First-Rate Glass Corporal	R537
First-Rate Glass Corporal	W435

Using Advanced Filter with Criteria Ranges

As the name implies, Advanced Filter is usually used to filter records—in other words, to get a subset of data. You specify the subset by setting up a criteria range.

> **NOTE** Even if you are familiar with criteria, be sure to check out using the powerful Boolean formula in criteria ranges later in this chapter, in the section "The Most Complex Criteria: Replacing the List of Values with a Condition Created as the Result of a Formula."

Set up a criteria range in a blank area of a worksheet. A criteria range always includes two or more rows. The first row of the criteria range contains one or more field header values to match the one(s) in the data range you want to filter. The second row contains a value showing which records to extract. In Figure 11.9, J1:J2 is the criteria range, and L1 is the output range.

In the Excel user interface, to extract a unique list of products that were purchased by a particular customer, select Advanced Filter and set up the Advanced Filter dialog as shown in Figure 11.9. Figure 11.10 shows the results.

Figure 11.9
To learn a unique list of products purchased by Cool Saddle Traders, set up the criteria range in J1:J2.

Advanced Filter

Action
- ○ Filter the list, in-place
- ● Copy to another location

List range: $A$1:$H$1127
Criteria range: $J$1:$J$2
Copy to: $L$1

☑ Unique records only

OK   Cancel

Figure 11.10
The result of the advanced filter that uses a criteria range and asks for a unique list of products. Of course, more complex and interesting criteria can be built.

	J	K	L
	Customer		Product
	Cool Saddle Traders		R537
			M556
			W435

You can use the following VBA code to perform an equivalent advanced filter:

```
Sub UniqueProductsOneCustomer()
    Dim IRange As Range
    Dim ORange As Range
    Dim CRange As Range

    ' Find the size of today's data set
    FinalRow = Cells(Rows.Count, 1).End(xlUp).Row
    NextCol = Cells(1, Columns.Count).End(xlToLeft).Column + 2

    ' Set up the Output Range with one customer
    Cells(1, NextCol).Value = Range("D1").Value
    ' In reality, this value should be passed from the userform
    Cells(2, NextCol).Value = Range("D2").Value
    Set CRange = Cells(1, NextCol).Resize(2, 1)

    ' Set up output range. Copy heading from B1 there
    Range("B1").Copy Destination:=Cells(1, NextCol + 2)
    Set ORange = Cells(1, NextCol + 2)

    ' Define the Input Range
    Set IRange = Range("A1").Resize(FinalRow, NextCol - 2)

    ' Do the Advanced Filter to get unique list of customers & product
    IRange.AdvancedFilter Action:=xlFilterCopy, _
        CriteriaRange:=CRange, CopyToRange:=ORange, Unique:=True
    ' The above could also be written as:
    'IRange.AdvancedFilter xlFilterCopy, CRange, ORange, True

    ' Determine how many unique rows we have
    LastRow = Cells(Rows.Count, NextCol + 2).End(xlUp).Row

    ' Sort the data
    Cells(1, NextCol + 2).Resize(LastRow, 1).Sort Key1:=Cells(1, _
NextCol + 2), Order1:=xlAscending, Header:=xlYes

End Sub
```

Joining Multiple Criteria with a Logical OR

You might want to filter records that match one criteria or another. For example, you can extract customers who purchased either product M556 or product R537. This is called a *logical OR* criteria.

When your criteria should be joined by a logical OR, place the criteria on subsequent rows of the criteria range. For example, the criteria range shown in J1:J3 in Figure 11.11 tells you which customers order product M556 or product W435.

Figure 11.11
Place criteria on successive rows to join them with an OR. This criteria range gets customers who ordered either product M556 or W435.

Joining Two Criteria with a Logical AND

Sometimes, you will want to filter records that match one criteria *and* another criteria. For example, you might want to extract records in which the product sold was W435 and the region was the West region. This is called a *logical AND*.

To join two criteria with AND, put both criteria on the same row of the criteria range. For example, the criteria range shown in J1:K2 in Figure 11.12 gets the customers who ordered product W435 in the West region.

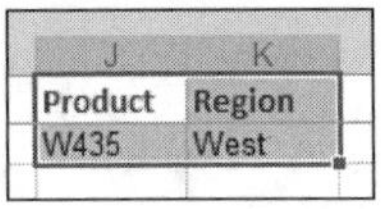

Figure 11.12
Place criteria on the same row to join them with an AND. The criteria range in J1:K2 gets customers from the West region who ordered product W435.

Product	Region
W435	West

Other Slightly Complex Criteria Ranges

The criteria range shown in Figure 11.13 is based on two different fields that are joined with an OR. The query finds all records that either are from the West region or in which the product is W435.

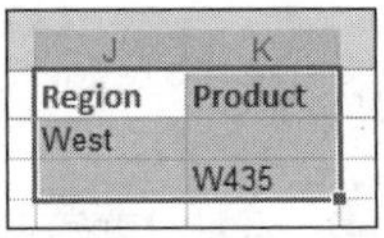

Figure 11.13
The criteria range in J1:K3 returns records in which either the region is West or the product is W435.

Region	Product
West	
	W435

The Most Complex Criteria: Replacing the List of Values with a Condition Created as the Result of a Formula

It is possible to have a criteria range with multiple logical AND and logical OR criteria joined together. Although this might work in some situations, in other scenarios it quickly gets out of hand. Fortunately, Excel allows for criteria in which the records are selected as the result of a formula to handle this situation.

CASE STUDY: WORKING WITH VERY COMPLEX CRITERIA

Your clients so loved the "Create a Customer" report that they hired you to write a new report. In this case, they could select any customer, any product, any region, or any combination of them. You can quickly adapt the `frmReport` userform to show three list boxes, as shown in Figure 11.14.

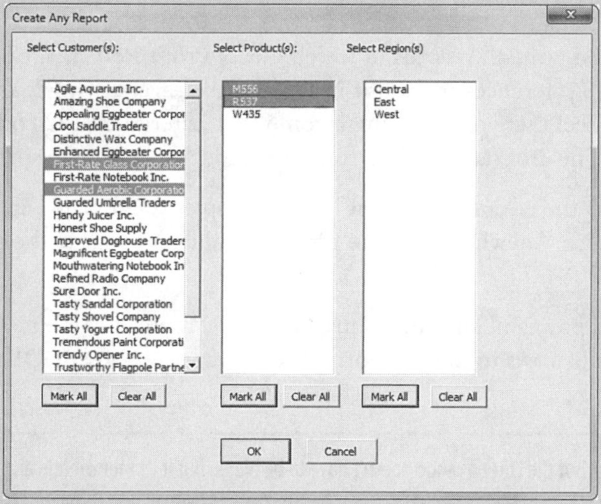

Figure 11.14
This super-flexible form lets clients run any types of reports that they can imagine. It creates some nightmarish criteria ranges, though, unless you know the way out.

In your first test, imagine that you select two customers and two products. In this case, your program has to build a five-row criteria range, as shown in Figure 11.15. This isn't too bad.

Figure 11.15
This criteria range returns any records for which the two selected customers ordered any of the two selected products.

Customer	Product
First-Rate Glass Corporation	R537
First-Rate Glass Corporation	M556
Guarded Aerobic Corporation	R537
Guarded Aerobic Corporation	M556

This gets crazy if someone selects 10 products, all regions except the house region, and all customers except the internal customer. Your criteria range would need unique combinations of the selected fields. This could easily be 10 products times 9 regions times 499 customers—or more than 44,000 rows of criteria range. You could quickly end up with a criteria range that spans thousands of rows and three columns. I was once foolish enough to actually try running an advanced filter with such a criteria range. It would still be trying to compute if I hadn't rebooted the computer.

The solution for this report is to replace the lists of values with a formula-based condition.

Setting Up a Condition as the Result of a Formula

Amazingly, there is an incredibly obscure version of Advanced Filter criteria that can replace the 44,000-row criteria range in the previous case study. In the alternative form of criteria range, the top row is left blank. There is no heading above the criteria. The criteria set up in row 2 is a formula that results in `True` or `False`. If the formula contains any relative references to row 2 of the data range, Excel compares that formula to every row of the data range, one by one.

For example, if you want all records in which Gross Profit Percentage is below 53%, the formula built in J2 references the profit in H2 and the revenue in F2. You need to leave J1 blank to tell Excel that you are using a computed criteria. Cell J2 contains the formula `=(H2/F2)<0.53`. The criteria range for the advanced filter would be specified as `J1:J2`.

As Excel performs the advanced filter, it logically copies the formula and applies it to all rows in the database. Anywhere that the formula evaluates to `True`, the record is included in the output range.

This is incredibly powerful and runs remarkably fast. You can combine multiple formulas in adjacent columns or rows to join the formula criteria with AND or OR, just as you do with regular criteria.

> **NOTE**
> Row 1 of the criteria range doesn't have to be blank, but it cannot contain any words that are headings in the data range. You could perhaps use that row to explain that someone should look to this page in this book for an explanation of these computed criteria.

CASE STUDY: USING FORMULA-BASED CONDITIONS IN THE EXCEL USER INTERFACE

You can use formula-based conditions to solve the report introduced in the previous case study. Figure 11.16 shows the flow involved in setting up a formula-based condition.

To illustrate, off to the right of the criteria range, set up a column of cells with the list of selected customers. Assign a name to the range, such as MyCust. In cell J2 of the criteria range, enter a formula such as

`=NOT(ISNA(Match(D2, MyCust,0)))`.

To the right of the MyCust range, set up a range with a list of selected products. Assign this range the name MyProd. In K2 of the criteria range, add this formula to check products:

`=NOT(ISNA(Match(B2,MyProd,0)))`.

To the right of the MyProd range, set up a range with a list of selected regions. Assign this range the name MyRegion. In L2 of the criteria range, add this formula to check for selected regions:

`=NOT(ISNA(Match(A2, MyRegion,0)))`.

Now, with a criteria range of J1:L2, you can effectively retrieve records that match any combination of selections from the userform.

Figure 11.16
Here are the logical steps in using formula-based conditions to solve the problem.

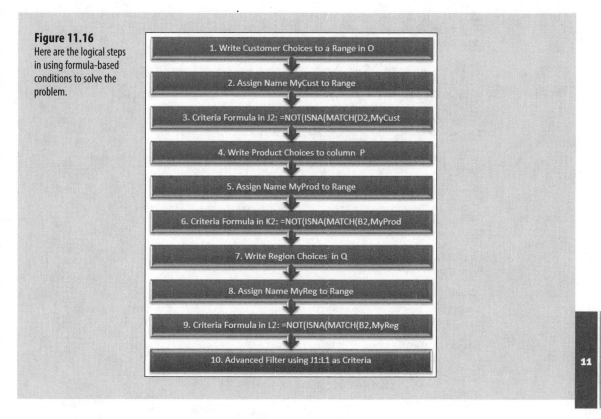

1. Write Customer Choices to a Range in O

2. Assign Name MyCust to Range

3. Criteria Formula in J2: =NOT(ISNA(MATCH(D2,MyCust

4. Write Product Choices to column P

5. Assign Name MyProd to Range

6. Criteria Formula in K2: =NOT(ISNA(MATCH(B2,MyProd

7. Write Region Choices in Q

8. Assign Name MyReg to Range

9. Criteria Formula in L2: =NOT(ISNA(MATCH(B2,MyReg

10. Advanced Filter using J1:L1 as Criteria

Using Formula-Based Conditions with VBA

Referring back to the userform shown in Figure 11.14, you can use formula-based conditions to filter the report using the userform. The following is the code for this userform. Note the logic in OKButton_Click that builds the formula. Figure 11.17 shows the Excel sheet just before the advanced filter is run.

Figure 11.17
The worksheet just before the macro runs the advanced filter.

	fx	=NOT(ISNA(MATCH($D2,$O$2:$O$11,FALSE)))							
H	I	J	K	L	M	N	O	P	Q
Profit									
11568		TRUE	FALSE	TRUE			Amazing Shoe Company	M556	Central
5586							Distinctive Wax Company	W435	East
1175							First-Rate Notebook Inc.		
5619							Handy Juicer Inc.		
4655							Improved Doghouse Traders		
9893							Refined Radio Company		
4707							Sure Door Inc.		
3133							Tasty Shovel Company		
4729							Tremendous Paint Corporation		
7061							Trustworthy Flagpole Partners		
10906									

The following code initializes the user form. Three advanced filters find the unique list of customers, products, and regions:

11

```vba
Private Sub UserForm_Initialize()
    Dim IRange As Range
    Dim ORange As Range

    ' Find the size of today's data set
    FinalRow = Cells(Rows.Count, 1).End(xlUp).Row
    NextCol = Cells(1, Columns.Count).End(xlToLeft).Column + 2

    ' Define the input range
    Set IRange = Range("A1").Resize(FinalRow, NextCol - 2)

    ' Set up output range for Customer. Copy heading from D1 there
    Range("D1").Copy Destination:=Cells(1, NextCol)
    Set ORange = Cells(1, NextCol)

    ' Do the Advanced Filter to get unique list of customers
    IRange.AdvancedFilter Action:=xlFilterCopy, CriteriaRange:="", _
        CopyToRange:=ORange, Unique:=True

    ' Determine how many unique customers we have
    LastRow = Cells(Rows.Count, NextCol).End(xlUp).Row

    ' Sort the data
    Cells(1, NextCol).Resize(LastRow, 1).Sort Key1:=Cells(1, NextCol), _
        Order1:=xlAscending, Header:=xlYes

    With Me.lbCust
        .RowSource = ""
        .List = Application.Transpose( _
            Cells(2,NextCol).Resize(LastRow-1,1))
    End With

    ' Erase the temporary list of customers
    Cells(1, NextCol).Resize(LastRow, 1).Clear

    ' Set up output range for product. Copy heading from D1 there
    Range("B1").Copy Destination:=Cells(1, NextCol)
    Set ORange = Cells(1, NextCol)

    ' Do the Advanced Filter to get unique list of customers
    IRange.AdvancedFilter Action:=xlFilterCopy, _
        CopyToRange:=ORange, Unique:=True

    ' Determine how many unique customers we have
    LastRow = Cells(Rows.Count, NextCol).End(xlUp).Row

    ' Sort the data
    Cells(1, NextCol).Resize(LastRow, 1).Sort Key1:=Cells(1, NextCol), _
        Order1:=xlAscending, Header:=xlYes

    With Me.lbProduct
        .RowSource = ""
        ' The list has to go across, so transpose the vertical data.
        .List = Application.Transpose( _
            Cells(2,NextCol).Resize(LastRow-1,1))
    End With

    ' Erase the temporary list of customers
```

```
    Cells(1, NextCol).Resize(LastRow, 1).Clear

    ' Set up output range for Region. Copy heading from A1 there
    Range("A1").Copy Destination:=Cells(1, NextCol)
    Set ORange = Cells(1, NextCol)

    ' Do the Advanced Filter to get unique list of customers
    IRange.AdvancedFilter Action:=xlFilterCopy, CopyToRange:=ORange, _
        Unique:=True

    ' Determine how many unique customers we have
    LastRow = Cells(Rows.Count, NextCol).End(xlUp).Row

    ' Sort the data
    Cells(1, NextCol).Resize(LastRow, 1).Sort Key1:=Cells(1, NextCol), _
        Order1:=xlAscending, Header:=xlYes

    With Me.lbRegion
        .RowSource = ""
        .List = Application.Transpose( _
            Cells(2,NextCol).Resize(LastRow-1,1))
    End With

    ' Erase the temporary list of customers
    Cells(1, NextCol).Resize(LastRow, 1).Clear
End Sub
```

These tiny procedures run when someone clicks Mark All or Clear All in the userform in Figure 11.14:

```
Private Sub CancelButton_Click()
    Unload Me
End Sub

Private Sub cbSubAll_Click()
    For i = 0 To lbCust.ListCount - 1
        Me.lbCust.Selected(i) = True
    Next i
End Sub

Private Sub cbSubClear_Click()
    For i = 0 To lbCust.ListCount - 1
        Me.lbCust.Selected(i) = False
    Next i
End Sub

Private Sub CommandButton1_Click()
    ' Clear all products
    For i = 0 To lbProduct.ListCount - 1
        Me.lbProduct.Selected(i) = False
    Next i
End Sub

Private Sub CommandButton2_Click()
    ' Mark all products
    For i = 0 To lbProduct.ListCount - 1
        Me.lbProduct.Selected(i) = True
    Next i
```

```
End Sub

Private Sub CommandButton3_Click()
    ' Clear all regions
    For i = 0 To lbRegion.ListCount - 1
        Me.lbRegion.Selected(i) = False
    Next i
End Sub

Private Sub CommandButton4_Click()
    ' Mark all regions
    For i = 0 To lbRegion.ListCount - 1
        Me.lbRegion.Selected(i) = True
    Next i
End Sub
```

The following code is attached to the OK button. This code builds three ranges in O, P, and Q that list the selected customers, products, and regions. The actual criteria range is composed of three blank cells in J1:L1 and then three formulas in J2:L2:

```
Private Sub OKButton_Click()
    Dim CRange As Range, IRange As Range, ORange As Range
    ' Build a complex criteria that ANDs all choices together
    NextCCol = 10
    NextTCol = 15

    For j = 1 To 3
        Select Case j
            Case 1
                MyControl = "lbCust"
                MyColumn = 4
            Case 2
                MyControl = "lbProduct"
                MyColumn = 2
            Case 3
                MyControl = "lbRegion"
                MyColumn = 1
        End Select
        NextRow = 2
        ' Check to see what was selected.
        For i = 0 To Me.Controls(MyControl).ListCount - 1
            If Me.Controls(MyControl).Selected(i) = True Then
                Cells(NextRow, NextTCol).Value = _
                    Me.Controls(MyControl).List(i)
                NextRow = NextRow + 1
            End If
        Next i
        ' If anything was selected, build a new criteria formula
        If NextRow > 2 Then
            ' the reference to Row 2 must be relative in order to work
            MyFormula = "=NOT(ISNA(MATCH(RC" & MyColumn & ",R2C" & _
                NextTCol & ":R" & NextRow - 1 & "C" & NextTCol & ",0)))"
            Cells(2, NextCCol).FormulaR1C1 = MyFormula
            NextTCol = NextTCol + 1
            NextCCol = NextCCol + 1
        End If
    Next j
    Unload Me
```

```
' Figure 11.19 shows the worksheet at this point
' If we built any criteria, define the criteria range
If NextCCol > 10 Then
    Set CRange = Range(Cells(1, 10), Cells(2, NextCCol - 1))
    Set IRange = Range("A1").CurrentRegion
    Set ORange = Cells(1, 20)
    IRange.AdvancedFilter xlFilterCopy, CRange, Orange

    ' Clear out the criteria
    Cells(1, 10).Resize(1, 10).EntireColumn.Clear
End If

' At this point, the matching records are in T1

End Sub
```

Figure 11.17 shows the worksheet just before the `AdvancedFilter` method is called. The user has selected customers, products, and regions. The macro has built temporary tables in columns O, P, and Q to show which values the user selected. The criteria range is J1:L2. The criteria formula in J2 looks to see whether the value in $D2 is in the list of selected customers in O. The formulas in K2 and L2 compare $B2 to column P and $A2 to column Q.

> **NOTE** Excel VBA Help says that if you do not specify a criteria range, no criteria are used. This is not true in Excel 2013 and 2016. If no criteria range is specified in Excel 2013 or 2016, the advanced filter inherits the criteria range from the prior advanced filter. You should include `CriteriaRange:=""` to clear the prior value.

Using Formula-Based Conditions to Return Above-Average Records

The formula-based conditions formula criteria are cool but are a rarely used feature in a rarely used function. Some interesting business applications use this technique. For example, this criteria formula would find all the above-average rows in the data set:

```
=$A2>Average($A$2:$A$1048576)
```

Using Filter in Place in Advanced Filter

It is possible to filter a large data set in place. In this case, you do not need an output range. You normally specify a criteria range; otherwise, you return 100% of the records, and there is no need to do the advanced filter!

In the user interface of Excel, running Filter in Place makes sense: You can easily peruse the filtered list, looking for something in particular.

Running a filter in place in VBA is a little less convenient. The only good way to programmatically peruse the filtered records is to use the `xlCellTypeVisible` option of the `SpecialCells` method. In the Excel user interface, the equivalent action is to select Home, Find & Select, Go to Special. In the Go to Special dialog, select Visible Cells Only.

To run a Filter in Place, use the constant `XLFilterInPlace` as the `Action` parameter in the `AdvancedFilter` command and remove the `CopyToRange` from the command:

```
IRange.AdvancedFilter Action:=xlFilterInPlace, CriteriaRange:=CRange, _
    Unique:=False
```

Then, you use this programmatic equivalent to looping by using Visible Cells Only:

```
For Each cell In Range("A2:A" & FinalRow).SpecialCells(xlCellTypeVisible)
    Ctr = Ctr + 1
Next cell
MsgBox Ctr & " cells match the criteria"
```

If you know that there will be no blanks in the visible cells, you can eliminate the loop with this:

```
Ctr = Application.Counta(Range("A2:A" & _
FinalRow).SpecialCells(xlCellTypeVisible))
```

Catching No Records When Using a Filter in Place

Just as when using `Copy`, you have to watch out for the possibility of having no records match the criteria. However, in this case, it is more difficult to realize that nothing is returned. You generally find out when the `.SpecialCells` method returns a runtime error 1004, which indicates that no cells were found.

To catch this condition, you have to set up an error trap to anticipate the 1004 error with the `SpecialCells` method:

```
On Error GoTo NoRecs
    For Each cell In _
        Range("A2:A" & FinalRow).SpecialCells(xlCellTypeVisible)
        Ctr = Ctr + 1
    Next cell
    On Error GoTo 0
    MsgBox Ctr & " cells match the criteria"
    Exit Sub
NoRecs:
    MsgBox "No records match the criteria"
End Sub
```

➡ **See** Chapter 24, "Handling Errors," for more information on catching errors.

This error trap works because it specifically excludes the header row from the `SpecialCells` range. The header row is always visible after an advanced filter. Including it in the range would prevent the 1004 error from being raised.

Showing All Records After Running a Filter in Place

After doing a filter in place, you can get all records to show again by using the `ShowAllData` method:

```
ActiveSheet.ShowAllData
```

The Real Workhorse: `xlFilterCopy` with All Records Rather Than Unique Records Only

The examples at the beginning of this chapter talk about using `xlFilterCopy` to get a unique list of values in a field. You used unique lists of customers, regions, and products to populate the list boxes in your report-specific userforms.

However, a more common scenario is to use an advanced filter to return all records that match the criteria. After the client selects which customer to report, an advanced filter can extract all records for that customer.

In all the examples in the following sections, you want to keep the Unique Records Only check box cleared. You do this in VBA by specifying `Unique:=False` as a parameter to the `AdvancedFilter` method. This is not difficult to do, and you have some powerful options. If you need only a subset of fields for a report, copy only those field headings to the output range. If you want to resequence the fields to appear exactly as you need them in the report, you can do this by changing the sequence of the headings in the output range.

The next sections walk you through three quick examples to show the options available.

Copying All Columns

To copy all columns, specify a single blank cell as the output range. You get all columns for those records that match the criteria, as shown in Figure 11.18:

```
Sub AllColumnsOneCustomer()
    Dim IRange As Range
    Dim ORange As Range
    Dim CRange As Range

    ' Find the size of today's data set
    FinalRow = Cells(Rows.Count, 1).End(xlUp).Row
    NextCol = Cells(1, Columns.Count).End(xlToLeft).Column + 2

    ' Set up the criteria range with one customer
    Cells(1, NextCol).Value = Range("D1").Value
    ' In reality, this value should be passed from the userform
    Cells(2, NextCol).Value = Range("D2").Value
    Set CRange = Cells(1, NextCol).Resize(2, 1)

    ' Set up output range. It is a single blank cell
    Set ORange = Cells(1, NextCol + 2)

    ' Define the Input Range
    Set IRange = Range("A1").Resize(FinalRow, NextCol - 2)

    ' Do the Advanced Filter to get unique list of customers & product
    IRange.AdvancedFilter Action:=xlFilterCopy, _
        CriteriaRange:=CRange, CopyToRange:=ORange

End Sub
```

Figure 11.18
When using
`xlFilterCopy` with
a blank output range,
you get all columns in
the same order as they
appear in the original list
range.

J	K	L	M	N
Customer		Region	Product	Date
Trustworthy	Flagpole	East	R537	19-Jul-18
		East	W435	3-Sep-18
		West	M556	7-Sep-18
		Central	W435	9-Sep-18

Copying a Subset of Columns and Reordering

If you are doing an advanced filter to send records to a report, it is likely that you might need only a subset of columns, and you might need them in a different sequence.

This example finishes the `frmReport` example that was presented earlier in this chapter. As you recall, `frmReport` allows the client to select a customer. The OK button then calls the `RunCustReport` routine, passing a parameter to identify for which customer to prepare a report.

Imagine that this is a report being sent to the customer. The customer really does not care about the surrounding region, and you do not want to reveal your cost of goods sold or profit. Assuming that you will put the customer's name in the title of the report, the fields that you need in order to produce the report are Date, Quantity, Product, and Revenue.

The following code copies those headings to the output range:

```
Sub RunCustReport(WhichCust As Variant)
    Dim IRange As Range
    Dim ORange As Range
    Dim CRange As Range
    Dim WBN As Workbook
    Dim WSN As Worksheet
    Dim WSO As Worksheet

    Set WSO = ActiveSheet
    ' Find the size of today's data set
    FinalRow = Cells(Rows.Count, 1).End(xlUp).Row
    NextCol = Cells(1, Columns.Count).End(xlToLeft).Column + 2

    ' Set up the criteria range with one customer
    Cells(1, NextCol).Value = Range("D1").Value
    Cells(2, NextCol).Value = WhichCust
    Set CRange = Cells(1, NextCol).Resize(2, 1)

    ' Set up output range. We want Date, Quantity, Product, Revenue
    ' These columns are in C, E, B, and F
    Cells(1, NextCol + 2).Resize(1, 4).Value = _
        Array(Cells(1, 3), Cells(1, 5), Cells(1, 2), Cells(1, 6))
    Set ORange = Cells(1, NextCol + 2).Resize(1, 4)

    ' Define the Input Range
    Set IRange = Range("A1").Resize(FinalRow, NextCol - 2)

    ' Do the Advanced Filter to get unique list of customers & products
```

```
IRange.AdvancedFilter Action:=xlFilterCopy, _
    CriteriaRange:=CRange, CopyToRange:=ORange

' Create a new workbook with one blank sheet to hold the output
' xlWBATWorksheet is the template name for a single worksheet
Set WBN = Workbooks.Add(xlWBATWorksheet)
Set WSN = WBN.Worksheets(1)

' Set up a title on WSN
WSN.Cells(1, 1).Value = "Report of Sales to " & WhichCust

' Copy data from WSO to WSN
WSO.Cells(1, NextCol + 2).CurrentRegion.Copy _
    Destination:=WSN.Cells(3, 1)
TotalRow = WSN.Cells(Rows.Count, 1).End(xlUp).Row + 1
WSN.Cells(TotalRow, 1).Value = "Total"
WSN.Cells(TotalRow, 2).FormulaR1C1 = "=SUM(R2C:R[-1]C)"
WSN.Cells(TotalRow, 4).FormulaR1C1 = "=SUM(R2C:R[-1]C)"

' Format the new report with bold
WSN.Cells(3, 1).Resize(1, 4).Font.Bold = True
WSN.Cells(TotalRow, 1).Resize(1, 4).Font.Bold = True
WSN.Cells(1, 1).Font.Size = 18

WBN.SaveAs ThisWorkbook.Path & Application.PathSeparator & _
    WhichCust & ".xlsx"
WBN.Close SaveChanges:=False

WSO.Select

' clear the output range, etc.
Range("J:Z").Clear

End Sub
```

The advanced filter produces data, as shown in Figure 11.19. The program then goes on to copy the matching records to a new workbook. A title and a total row are added, and the report is saved with the customer's name. Figure 11.20 shows the final report.

Figure 11.19
Immediately after the advanced filter, you have just the columns and records needed for the report.

J	K	L	M	N	O
Customer		Date	Quantity	Product	Revenue
Cool Saddle Traders		22-Jul-18	400	R537	9152
		25-Jul-18	600	R537	13806
		16-Aug-18	400	M556	7136
		23-Sep-18	100	R537	2358
		29-Sep-18	100	R537	1819
		21-Oct-18	100	R537	2484
		3-Mar-19	200	W435	4270
		18-Aug-19	700	W435	12145

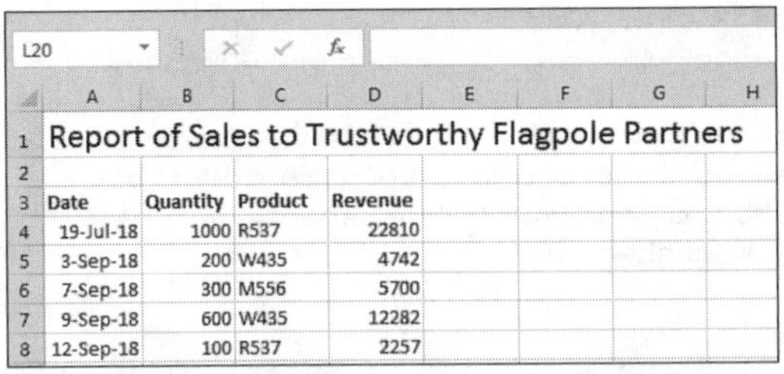

Figure 11.20
After copying the filtered data to a new sheet and applying some formatting, you have a good-looking report to send to each customer.

	A	B	C	D	E	F	G	H
1	Report of Sales to Trustworthy Flagpole Partners							
2								
3	Date	Quantity	Product	Revenue				
4	19-Jul-18	1000	R537	22810				
5	3-Sep-18	200	W435	4742				
6	7-Sep-18	300	M556	5700				
7	9-Sep-18	600	W435	12282				
8	12-Sep-18	100	R537	2257				

CASE STUDY: UTILIZING TWO KINDS OF ADVANCED FILTERS TO CREATE A REPORT FOR EACH CUSTOMER

The final advanced filter example for this chapter uses several advanced filter techniques. Let's say that after importing invoice records, you want to send a purchase summary to each customer. The process would be as follows:

1. Run an advanced filter, requesting unique values, to get a list of customers in column J. This `AdvancedFilter` specifies the `Unique:=True` parameter and uses a `CopyToRange` that includes a single heading, Customer:

```
' Set up output range. Copy heading from D1 there
Range("D1").Copy Destination:=Cells(1, NextCol)
Set ORange = Cells(1, NextCol)

' Define the Input Range
Set IRange = Range("A1").Resize(FinalRow, NextCol - 2)

' Do the Advanced Filter to get unique list of customers
IRange.AdvancedFilter Action:=xlFilterCopy, CriteriaRange:="", _
    CopyToRange:=ORange, Unique:=True
```

2. For each customer in the list of unique customers in column J, perform steps 3 through 7. Find the number of customers in the output range from step 1. Then use a `For Each Cell` loop to loop through the customers:

```
' Loop through each customer
FinalCust = Cells(Rows.Count, NextCol).End(xlUp).Row
For Each cell In Cells(2, NextCol).Resize(FinalCust - 1, 1)
    ThisCust = cell.Value
    ' ... Steps 3 through 7 here
Next Cell
```

3. Build a criteria range in L1:L2 to be used in a new advanced filter. The criteria range would include the heading Customer in L1 and the customer name from this iteration of the loop in cell L2:

```
' Set up the Criteria Range with one customer
Cells(1, NextCol + 2).Value = Range("D1").Value
Cells(2, NextCol + 2).Value = ThisCust
Set CRange = Cells(1, NextCol + 2).Resize(2, 1)
```

4. Do an advanced filter to copy matching records for this customer to column N. This `Advanced Filter` statement specifies the `Unique:=False` parameter. Because you want only the columns Date, Quantity, Product, and Revenue, the `CopyToRange` specifies a four-column range with those headings copied in the proper order:

```
' Set up output range. We want Date, Quantity, Product, Revenue
' These columns are in C, E, B, and F
Cells(1, NextCol + 4).Resize(1, 4).Value = _
    Array(Cells(1, 3), Cells(1, 5), Cells(1, 2), Cells(1, 6))
```

```
Set ORange = Cells(1, NextCol + 4).Resize(1, 4)

' Do the Advanced Filter to get unique list of customers & product
IRange.AdvancedFilter Action:=xlFilterCopy, CriteriaRange:=CRange, _
    CopyToRange:=Orange
```

5. Copy the customer records to a report sheet in a new workbook. The VBA code uses the `Workbooks.Add` method to create a new blank workbook. Using the template name xlWBATWorksheet is the way to specify that you want a workbook with a single worksheet. The extracted records from step 4 are copied to cell A3 of the new workbook:

```
' Create a new workbook with one blank sheet to hold the output
Set WBN = Workbooks.Add(xlWBATWorksheet)
Set WSN = WBN.Worksheets(1)
' Copy data from WSO to WSN
WSO.Cells(1, NextCol + 4).CurrentRegion.Copy _
    Destination:=WSN.Cells(3, 1)
```

6. Format the report with a title and totals. In VBA, add a title that reflects the customer's name in cell A1. Make the headings bold and add a total below the final row:

```
' Set up a title on WSN
WSN.Cells(1, 1).Value = "Report of Sales to " & ThisCust

TotalRow = WSN.Cells(Rows.Count, 1).End(xlUp).Row + 1
WSN.Cells(TotalRow, 1).Value = "Total"
WSN.Cells(TotalRow, 2).FormulaR1C1 = "=SUM(R2C:R[-1]C)"
WSN.Cells(TotalRow, 4).FormulaR1C1 = "=SUM(R2C:R[-1]C)"

' Format the new report with bold
WSN.Cells(3, 1).Resize(1, 4).Font.Bold = True
WSN.Cells(TotalRow, 1).Resize(1, 4).Font.Bold = True
WSN.Cells(1, 1).Font.Size = 18
```

7. Use SaveAs to save the workbook based on customer name. After the workbook is saved, close the new workbook. Return to the original workbook and clear the output range to prepare for the next pass through the loop:

```
WBN.SaveAs ThisWorkbook.Path & Application.PathSeparator & _
        WhichCust & ".xlsx"
WBN.Close SaveChanges:=False

WSO.Select
' Free up memory by setting object variables to nothing
Set WSN = Nothing
Set WBN = Nothing
' clear the output range, etc.
Cells(1, NextCol + 2).Resize(1, 10).EntireColumn.Clear
```

The complete code is as follows:

```
Sub RunReportForEachCustomer()
    Dim IRange As Range
    Dim ORange As Range
    Dim CRange As Range
    Dim WBN As Workbook
    Dim WSN As Worksheet
```

```
Dim WSO As Worksheet

Set WSO = ActiveSheet
' Find the size of today's data set
FinalRow = Cells(Rows.Count, 1).End(xlUp).Row
NextCol = Cells(1, Columns.Count).End(xlToLeft).Column + 2
' First - get a unique list of customers in J
' Set up output range. Copy heading from D1 there

Range("D1").Copy Destination:=Cells(1, NextCol)
Set ORange = Cells(1, NextCol)

' Define the Input Range
Set IRange = Range("A1").Resize(FinalRow, NextCol - 2)

' Do the Advanced Filter to get unique list of customers
 IRange.AdvancedFilter Action:=xlFilterCopy, CriteriaRange:="", _
    CopyToRange:=ORange, Unique:=True

' Loop through each customer
FinalCust = Cells(Rows.Count, NextCol).End(xlUp).Row
For Each cell In Cells(2, NextCol).Resize(FinalCust - 1, 1)
    ThisCust = cell.Value

    ' Set up the Criteria Range with one customer
    Cells(1, NextCol + 2).Value = Range("D1").Value
    Cells(2, NextCol + 2).Value = ThisCust
    Set CRange = Cells(1, NextCol + 2).Resize(2, 1)

    ' Set up output range. We want Date, Quantity, Product, Revenue
    ' These columns are in C, E, B, and F
    Cells(1, NextCol + 4).Resize(1, 4).Value = _
        Array(Cells(1, 3), Cells(1, 5), Cells(1, 2), Cells(1, 6))
    Set ORange = Cells(1, NextCol + 4).Resize(1, 4)

    ' Adv. Filter for unique customers & product
    IRange.AdvancedFilter Action:=xlFilterCopy, _
        CriteriaRange:=CRange, _
        CopyToRange:=Orange

    ' Create a new workbook with one blank sheet to hold the output
    Set WBN = Workbooks.Add(xlWBATWorksheet)
    Set WSN = WBN.Worksheets(1)
    ' Copy data from WSO to WSN
    WSO.Cells(1, NextCol + 4).CurrentRegion.Copy _
        Destination:=WSN.Cells(3, 1)

    ' Set up a title on WSN
    WSN.Cells(1, 1).Value = "Report of Sales to " & ThisCust

    TotalRow = WSN.Cells(Rows.Count, 1).End(xlUp).Row + 1
    WSN.Cells(TotalRow, 1).Value = "Total"
    WSN.Cells(TotalRow, 2).FormulaR1C1 = "=SUM(R2C:R[-1]C)"
    WSN.Cells(TotalRow, 4).FormulaR1C1 = "=SUM(R2C:R[-1]C)"
```

```
            ' Format the new report with bold
            WSN.Cells(3, 1).Resize(1, 4).Font.Bold = True
            WSN.Cells(TotalRow, 1).Resize(1, 4).Font.Bold = True
            WSN.Cells(1, 1).Font.Size = 18
            WBN.SaveAs ThisWorkbook.Path & Application.PathSeparator & _
                WhichCust & ".xlsx"
            WBN.Close SaveChanges:=False
            WSO.Select
            Set WSN = Nothing

            Set WBN = Nothing

            ' clear the output range, etc.
            Cells(1, NextCol + 2).Resize(1, 10).EntireColumn.Clear
        Next cell

        Cells(1, NextCol).EntireColumn.Clear
        MsgBox FinalCust - 1 & " Reports have been created!"
    End Sub
```

This is a remarkable 58 lines of code. By incorporating a couple of advanced filters and not much else, you have managed to produce a tool that created 27 reports in less than 1 minute. Even an Excel power user would normally take 2 to 3 minutes per report to create these manually. In less than 60 seconds, this code will save someone a few hours every time these reports need to be created. Imagine a real scenario in which there are hundreds of customers. Undoubtedly, there are people in every city who are manually creating these reports in Excel because they simply don't realize the power of Excel VBA.

11

Excel in Practice: Turning Off a Few Drop-downs in the AutoFilter

A really cool trick is possible only in Excel VBA. When you AutoFilter a list in the Excel user interface, every column in the data set gets a field drop-down in the heading row. Sometimes you have a field that does not make a lot of sense to AutoFilter. For example, in your current data set, you might want to provide AutoFilter drop-downs for Region, Product, and Customer but not the numeric or date fields. After setting up the AutoFilter, you need one line of code to turn off each drop-down that you do not want to appear. The following code turns off the drop-downs for columns C, E, F, G, and H:

```
    Sub AutoFilterCustom()
        Range("A1").AutoFilter Field:=3, VisibleDropDown:=False
        Range("A1").AutoFilter Field:=5, VisibleDropDown:=False
        Range("A1").AutoFilter Field:=6, VisibleDropDown:=False
        Range("A1").AutoFilter Field:=7, VisibleDropDown:=False
        Range("A1").AutoFilter Field:=8, VisibleDropDown:=False
    End Sub
```

Using this tool is a fairly rare treat. Most of the time, Excel VBA lets you do things that are possible in the user interface—and lets you do them very rapidly. The `VisibleDropDown` parameter actually enables you to do something in VBA that is generally not available in the Excel user interface. Your knowledgeable clients will be scratching their heads, trying to figure out how you set up the cool automatic filter with only a few filterable columns (see Figure 11.21).

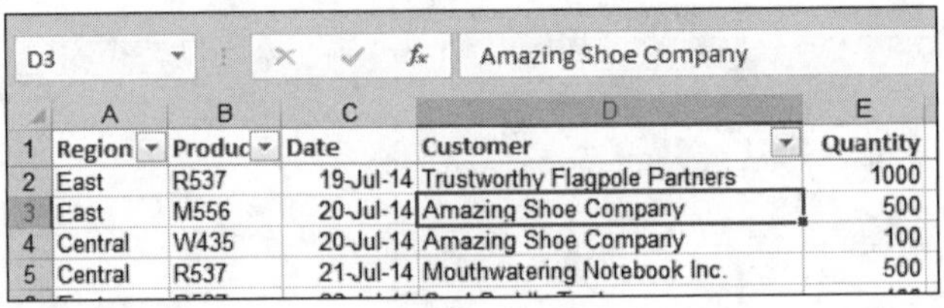

Figure 11.21

Using VBA, you can set up an automatic filter where only certain columns have the AutoFilter drop-down.

	A	B	C	D	E
1	Region ▾	Produc ▾	Date	Customer ▾	Quantity
2	East	R537	19-Jul-14	Trustworthy Flagpole Partners	1000
3	East	M556	20-Jul-14	Amazing Shoe Company	500
4	Central	W435	20-Jul-14	Amazing Shoe Company	100
5	Central	R537	21-Jul-14	Mouthwatering Notebook Inc.	500

D3 · ✕ ✓ ƒx Amazing Shoe Company

To clear the filter from the customer column, use this code:

```
Sub SimpleFilter()
    Worksheets("SalesReport").Select
    Range("A1").AutoFilter
    Range("A1").AutoFilter Field:=4
End Sub
```

Next Steps

The techniques from this chapter give you many reporting techniques available via the arcane Advanced Filter tool. Chapter 12, "Using VBA to Create Pivot Tables," introduces the most powerful feature in Excel: the pivot table. The combination of advanced filters and pivot tables can help you create reporting tools that enable amazing applications.

Using VBA to Create Pivot Tables

12

Pivot tables are the most powerful tools that Excel has to offer. The concept was first put into practice by Lotus, with its Improv product.

I love pivot tables because they help you very quickly summarize massive amounts of data. The name *pivot table* comes from the ability you have to drag fields in the PivotTable Fields list and have them recalculate. You can use a basic vanilla pivot table to produce a concise summary in seconds. However, pivot tables come in so many flavors that they can be the tools of choice for many different uses. You can build pivot tables to act as the calculation engine to produce reports by store or by style or to quickly find the top 5 or bottom 10 of anything.

I don't suggest that you use VBA to build pivot tables for a user; rather, I suggest that you use pivot tables as a means to an end—to extract a summary of data that you can then take on to better uses.

Understanding How Pivot Tables Evolved Over Various Excel Versions

As Microsoft invests in making Excel the premier choice in business intelligence, pivot tables continue to evolve. They were introduced in Excel 5 and perfected in Excel 97. In Excel 2000, pivot table creation in VBA was dramatically altered. Some new parameters were added in Excel 2002. A few new properties, such as `PivotFilters` and `TableStyle2`, were added in Excel 2007. These are some of the changes Microsoft has made in the most recent three versions:

- Excel 2010 introduced slicers, Repeat All Item Labels, Named Sets, and several new calculation options: `xlPercentOfParentColumn`, `xlPercentOfParentRow`, `xlPercentRunningTotal`, `xlRankAscending`, and `xlRankDescending`. These do not work in Excel 2007.

■ Excel 2013 introduced timelines, the `xlDistinctCount` function, and the Power Pivot Data Model. You can add tables to the Data Model, create a relationship, and produce a pivot table, but this code does not run in Excel 2010 or earlier.

■ Excel 2016 introduced AutoGrouping for dates. Although this is automatic, it does not affect pivot tables built with VBA.

Because of all the changes from version to version, you need to be extremely careful when writing code in Excel 2016 that might be run in other versions.

> **NOTE**   Much of the code in this chapter works with Excel 2010 and newer. Although this book does not include code for Excel 2007, one Excel 2007 example has been included in the sample file for this chapter. The code listings from this chapter are available for download at http://www.MrExcel.com/getcode2016.html.

While Building a Pivot Table in Excel VBA

As I mentioned earlier, this chapter does not mean to imply that you should use VBA to build pivot tables to give to your clients. Instead, the purpose of this chapter is to remind you that you can use pivot tables as a means to an end: You can use a pivot table to extract a summary of data and then use that summary elsewhere.

> **NOTE**   Although the Excel user interface has names for the various sections of a pivot table, VBA code continues to refer to the old names. Microsoft made this choice because otherwise, millions of lines of code would stop working in Excel 2007 because they would refer to, say, a *page field* rather than a *filter field*. Today the four sections of a pivot table in the Excel user interface are Filter, Columns, Rows, and Values, but VBA continues to use the old terms: Page fields, Column fields, Row fields, and Data fields.

Defining the Pivot Cache

In this first part of this chapter, the data set is an eight-column by 5,000-row data set, as shown in Figure 12.1. The macros create a regular pivot table from the worksheet data. Near the end of the chapter, an example shows how to build a pivot table based on the Data Model and Power Pivot.

Figure 12.1
Create summary reports from this data set.

	A	B	C	D	E	F	G	H
1	Region	Product	Date	Customer	Quantity	Revenue	COGS	Profit
2	West	D625	1/4/2018	Guarded Kettle Corporatic	430	10937	6248	4689
3	Central	A292	1/4/2018	Mouthwatering Jewelry C	400	8517	4564	3953
4	West	B722	1/4/2018	Agile Glass Supply	940	23188	11703	11485
5	Central	E438	1/4/2018	Persuasive Kettle Inc.	190	5520	2958	2562
6	East	E438	1/4/2018	Safe Saddle Corporation	130	3933	2024	1909
7	West	C409	1/4/2018	Agile Glass Supply	440	11304	5936	5368
8	West	C409	1/4/2018	Guarded Kettle Corporatic	770	20382	10387	9995
9	Central	E438	1/4/2018	Matchless Yardstick Inc.	570	17584	8875	8709
10	East	D625	1/4/2018	Unique Marble Company	380	10196	5521	4675

In Excel 2010 and later, you first create a pivot cache object to describe the input area of the data:

```
Dim WSD As Worksheet
Dim PTCache As PivotCache
Dim PT As PivotTable
Dim PRange As Range
Dim FinalRow As Long
Dim FinalCol As Long
Set WSD = Worksheets("PivotTable")

' Delete any prior pivot tables
For Each PT In WSD.PivotTables
    PT.TableRange2.Clear
Next PT

' Define input area and set up a Pivot Cache
FinalRow = WSD.Cells(Rows.Count, 1).End(xlUp).Row
FinalCol = WSD.Cells(1, Columns.Count).End(xlToLeft).Column
Set PRange = WSD.Cells(1, 1).Resize(FinalRow, FinalCol)
Set PTCache = ActiveWorkbook.PivotCaches.Create( _
][ ][ ][  SourceType:=xlDatabase, _
    SourceData:=PRange, _
][ ][ ][  Version:=xlPivotTableVersion14)
```

Creating and Configuring the Pivot Table

After defining the pivot cache, use the CreatePivotTable method to create a blank pivot table based on the defined pivot cache:

```
Set PT = PTCache.CreatePivotTable(TableDestination:=WSD.Cells(2, _
    FinalCol + 2), TableName:="PivotTable1", Version:=xlPivotTableVersion14)
```

In the CreatePivotTable method, you specify the output location and optionally give the table a name. After running the preceding code, you have a strange-looking blank pivot table like the one shown in Figure 12.2. You need to use code to drop fields onto the table.

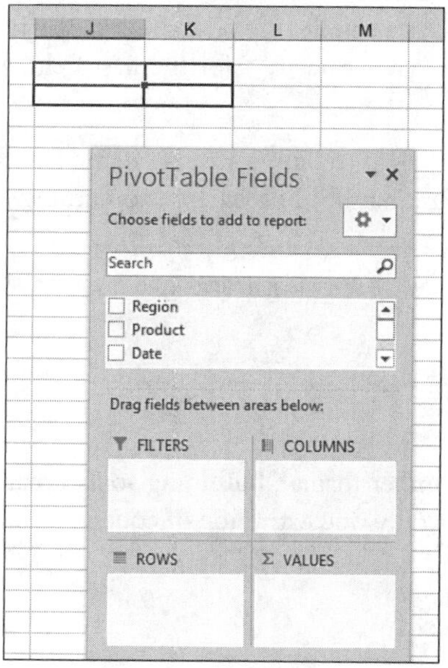

Figure 12.2
When you use the CreatePivotTable method, Excel gives you a four-cell blank pivot table that is not very useful.

12

You can now run through the steps needed to lay out the pivot table. In the `.AddFields` method, you can specify one or more fields that should be in the row, column, or filter area of the pivot table.

The `RowFields` parameter enables you to define fields that appear in the Rows area of the PivotTable Fields list. The `ColumnFields` parameter corresponds to the Columns area. The `PageFields` parameter corresponds to the Filter area.

The following line of code populates a pivot table with two fields in the row area and one field in the column area:

```
' Set up the row & column fields
PT.AddFields RowFields:=Array("Region", "Customer"), _
    ColumnFields:="Product"
```

To add a field such as Revenue to the values area of the table, you change the `Orientation` property of the field to be `xlDataField`.

Adding Fields to the Data Area

When you are adding fields to the data area of a pivot table, there are many settings you should control instead of letting Excel's IntelliSense decide. For example, say that you are building a report with revenue in which you will likely want to sum the revenue. If you don't explicitly specify the calculation, Excel scans through the values in the underlying data. If 100% of the revenue columns are numeric, Excel sums those columns. If one cell is blank or contains text, Excel decides on that day to count the revenue, which produces confusing results. Because of this possible variability, you should never use the `DataFields` argument in the `AddFields` method. Instead, change the property of the field to `xlDataField`. You can then specify the `Function` to be `xlSum`.

Although you are setting up the Data field, you can change several other properties within the same `With...End With` block. For example, the `Position` property is useful when you are adding multiple fields to the data area. Specify `1` for the first field, `2` for the second field, and so on.

By default, Excel renames a Revenue field to have a strange name like Sum of Revenue. You can use the `.Name` property to change that heading back to something normal.

> **NOTE**
> Note that you cannot reuse the word Revenue as a name. Instead, you should add a trailing space after the word Revenue.

You are not required to specify a number format, but doing so can make the resulting pivot table easier to understand and takes only one extra line of code:

```
' Set up the data fields
With PT.PivotFields("Revenue")
    .Orientation = xlDataField
```

```
            .Function = xlSum
            .Position = 1
            .NumberFormat = "#,##0"
            .Name = "Revenue "
        End With
```

Your pivot table inherits the table style settings selected as the default on whatever computer happens to run the code. If you want control over the final format, you can explicitly choose a table style. The following code applies banded rows and a medium table style:

```
    ' Format the pivot table
    PT.ShowTableStyleRowStripes = True
    PT.TableStyle2 = "PivotStyleMedium10"
```

If you want to reuse the data from the pivot table, turn off the grand totals and subtotals and fill in the labels along the left column. The fastest way to suppress the 11 possible subtotals is to set `Subtotals(1)` to `True` and then to `False`, like this:

```
    With PT
        .ColumnGrand = False
        .RowGrand = False
        .RepeatAllLabels xlRepeatLabels ' New in Excel 2010
    End With
    PT.PivotFields("Region").Subtotals(1) = True
    PT.PivotFields("Region").Subtotals(1) = False
```

At this point, you have a complete pivot table like the one shown in Figure 12.3.

Figure 12.3
Running fewer than 50 lines of code created this pivot table in less than a second.

Revenue		Product				
Region	Customer	A292	B722	C409	D625	E438
Central	Enhanced Toothpick Corporation	293,017	403,764	364,357	602,380	635,402
Central	Inventive Clipboard Corporation	410,968	440,937	422,647	292,109	346,605
Central	Matchless Yardstick Inc.	476,223	352,550	260,833	392,890	578,970
Central	Mouthwatering Jewelry Company	374,000	446,290	471,812	291,793	522,434
Central	Persuasive Kettle Inc.	1,565,368	1,385,296	1,443,434	1,584,759	2,030,578
Central	Remarkable Umbrella Company	362,851	425,325	469,054	653,531	645,140
Central	Tremendous Bobsled Corporation	560,759	711,826	877,247	802,303	1,095,329
East	Excellent Glass Traders	447,771	386,804	723,888	522,227	454,540
East	Magnificent Patio Traders	395,186	483,856	484,067	430,971	539,616
East	Mouthwatering Tripod Corporation	337,100	310,841	422,036	511,184	519,701
East	Safe Saddle Corporation	646,559	857,573	730,463	1,038,371	1,053,369
East	Unique Marble Company	1,600,347	1,581,665	1,765,305	1,707,140	2,179,242
East	Unique Saddle Inc.	408,114	311,970	543,737	458,428	460,826
East	Vibrant Tripod Corporation	317,953	368,601	313,807	499,055	519,112
West	Agile Glass Supply	628,204	652,845	905,059	712,285	978,745
West	Functional Shingle Corporation	504,818	289,670	408,567	505,071	484,777
West	Guarded Kettle Corporation	1,450,110	1,404,742	1,889,149	1,842,751	2,302,023
West	Innovative Oven Corporation	452,320	364,200	420,624	539,300	582,773
West	Persuasive Yardstick Corporation	268,394	426,882	441,914	257,998	402,987
West	Tremendous Flagpole Traders	446,799	557,376	237,439	554,595	564,562
West	Trouble-Free Eggbeater Inc.	390,917	520,048	506,324	370,819	515,235

12

Listing 12.1 shows the complete code used to generate this pivot table.

Listing 12.1   Code to Generate the Pivot Table Shown in Figure 12.3

```
    Sub CreatePivot()
        Dim WSD As Worksheet
        Dim PTCache As PivotCache
        Dim PT As PivotTable
        Dim PRange As Range
        Dim FinalRow As Long
```

```
Set WSD = Worksheets("PivotTable")

' Delete any prior pivot tables
For Each PT In WSD.PivotTables
    PT.TableRange2.Clear
Next PT

' Define input area and set up a Pivot Cache
FinalRow = WSD.Cells(Application.Rows.Count, 1).End(xlUp).Row
FinalCol = WSD.Cells(1, Application.Columns.Count). _
    End(xlToLeft).Column
Set PRange = WSD.Cells(1, 1).Resize(FinalRow, FinalCol)
Set PTCache = ActiveWorkbook.PivotCaches.Create( _
    SourceType:= xlDatabase, _
    SourceData:=PRange.Address, _
    Version:=xlPivotTableVersion14)

' Create the Pivot Table from the Pivot Cache
Set PT = PTCache.CreatePivotTable(TableDestination:=WSD. _
    Cells(2, FinalCol + 2), TableName:="PivotTable1")

' Set up the row & column fields
PT.AddFields RowFields:=Array("Region", "Customer"), _
    ColumnFields:="Product"

' Set up the data fields
With PT.PivotFields("Revenue")
    .Orientation = xlDataField
    .Function = xlSum
    .Position = 1
    .NumberFormat = "#,##0"
    .Name = "Revenue "
End With

'Format the pivot table
PT.ShowTableStyleRowStripes = True
PT.TableStyle2 = "PivotStyleMedium10"
With PT
    .ColumnGrand = False
    .RowGrand = False
    .RepeatAllLabels xlRepeatLabels
End With
PT.PivotFields("Region").Subtotals(1) = True
PT.PivotFields("Region").Subtotals(1) = False
WSD.Activate
Range("J2").Select

End Sub
```

Learning Why You Cannot Move or Change Part of a Pivot Report

Although pivot tables are incredible, they have annoying limitations; for example, you cannot move or change just part of a pivot table. Try to run a macro that clears row 2. The macro comes to a screeching halt with the error 1004, as shown in Figure 12.4. To get around this limitation, you can copy the pivot table and paste as values.

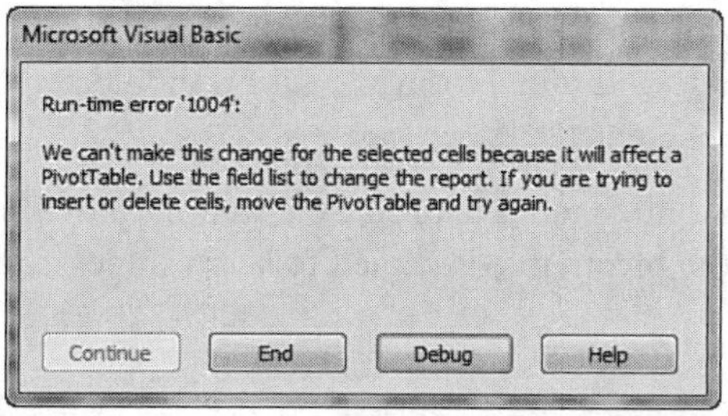

Figure 12.4
You cannot delete just part of a pivot table.

Microsoft Visual Basic

Run-time error '1004':

We can't make this change for the selected cells because it will affect a PivotTable. Use the field list to change the report. If you are trying to insert or delete cells, move the PivotTable and try again.

| Continue | End | Debug | Help |

Determining the Size of a Finished Pivot Table to Convert the Pivot Table to Values

Knowing the size of a pivot table in advance is difficult. If you run a report of transactional data on one day, you might or might not have sales from the West region, for example. This could cause your table to be either six or seven columns wide. Therefore, you should use the special property `TableRange2` to refer to the entire pivot table.

`PT.TableRange2` includes the entire pivot table. In Figure 12.5, `TableRange2` includes the extra row at the top with the field heading Revenue. To eliminate that row, the code copies `PT.TableRange2` but offsets this selection by one row by using `.Offset(1, 0)`. Depending on the nature of your pivot table, you might need to use an offset of two or more rows to get rid of extraneous information at the top of the pivot table.

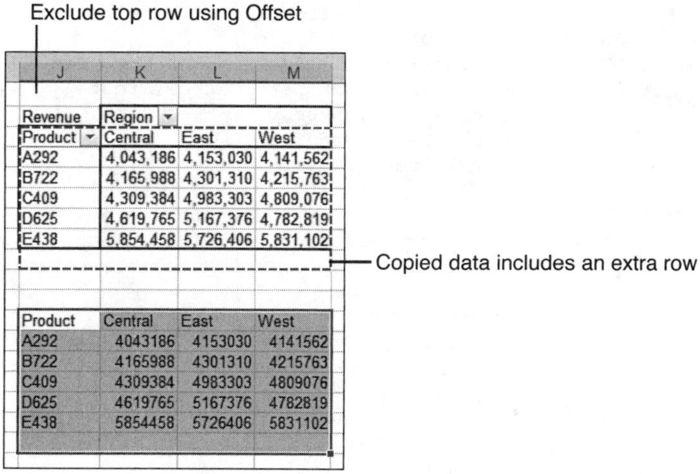

Figure 12.5
This figure shows an intermediate result of the macro. Only the summary in J12:M17 will remain after the macro finishes.

Exclude top row using Offset

Revenue	Region ▾		
Product ▾	Central	East	West
A292	4,043,186	4,153,030	4,141,562
B722	4,165,988	4,301,310	4,215,763
C409	4,309,384	4,983,303	4,809,076
D625	4,619,765	5,167,376	4,782,819
E438	5,854,458	5,726,406	5,831,102

Copied data includes an extra row

Product	Central	East	West
A292	4043186	4153030	4141562
B722	4165988	4301310	4215763
C409	4309384	4983303	4809076
D625	4619765	5167376	4782819
E438	5854458	5726406	5831102

The code copies `PT.TableRange2` and uses `PasteSpecial` on a cell five rows below the current pivot table. At that point in the code, your worksheet looks as shown in Figure 12.5. The table in J2 is a live pivot table, and the table in J12 is the copied results.

You can then eliminate the pivot table by applying the `Clear` method to the entire table. If your code is then going on to do additional formatting, you should remove the pivot cache from memory by setting `PTCache` equal to `Nothing`.

The code in Listing 12.2 uses a pivot table to produce a summary from the underlying data. At the end of the code, the pivot table is copied to static values, and the pivot table is cleared.

Listing 12.2   Code to Produce a Static Summary from a Pivot Table

```
Sub CreateSummaryReportUsingPivot()
    ' Use a Pivot Table to create a static summary report
    ' with product going down the rows and regions across
    Dim WSD As Worksheet
    Dim PTCache As PivotCache
    Dim PT As PivotTable
    Dim PRange As Range
    Dim FinalRow As Long
    Set WSD = Worksheets("PivotTable")

    ' Delete any prior pivot tables
    For Each PT In WSD.PivotTables
        PT.TableRange2.Clear
    Next PT
    WSD.Range("J1:Z1").EntireColumn.Clear

    ' Define input area and set up a Pivot Cache
    FinalRow = WSD.Cells(Application.Rows.Count, 1).End(xlUp).Row
    FinalCol = WSD.Cells(1, Application.Columns.Count). _
        End(xlToLeft).Column
    Set PRange = WSD.Cells(1, 1).Resize(FinalRow, FinalCol)
    Set PTCache = ActiveWorkbook.PivotCaches.Create( _
            SourceType:= xlDatabase, _
            SourceData:=PRange.Address, _
            Version:=xlPivotTableVersion14)

    ' Create the Pivot Table from the Pivot Cache
    Set PT = PTCache.CreatePivotTable(TableDestination:=WSD. _
            Cells(2, FinalCol + 2), TableName:="PivotTable1")

    ' Set up the row fields
    PT.AddFields RowFields:="Product", ColumnFields:="Region"

    ' Set up the data fields
    With PT.PivotFields("Revenue")
        .Orientation = xlDataField
        .Function = xlSum
        .Position = 1
        .NumberFormat = "#,##0"
        .Name = "Revenue "
    End With

    With PT
        .ColumnGrand = False
        .RowGrand = False
        .NullString = "0"
```

```
        End With

         ' PT.TableRange2 contains the results. Move these to J12
         ' as just values and not a real pivot table.
        PT.TableRange2.Offset(1, 0).Copy
        WSD.Cells(5 + PT.TableRange2.Rows.Count, FinalCol + 2). _
            PasteSpecial xlPasteValues

         ' At this point, the worksheet looks like Figure 12.5
         ' Stop

         ' Delete the original Pivot Table & the Pivot Cache
        PT.TableRange2.Clear
        Set PTCache = Nothing

        WSD.Activate
        Range("J12").Select
    End Sub
```

The code in Listing 12.2 creates the pivot table. It then copies the results and pastes them as values in J12:M13. Figure 12.5, which was shown previously, includes an intermediate result just before the original pivot table is cleared.

So far, this chapter has walked you through building very simple pivot table reports. Pivot tables offer far more flexibility, though. The sections that follow present more complex reporting examples.

Using Advanced Pivot Table Features

In this section, you'll use the detailed transactional data to produce a series of reports for each product line manager. This section covers the following advanced pivot table steps that are required in these reports:

1. Group the daily dates up to yearly dates.
2. Add multiple fields to the values area.
3. Control the sort order so the largest customers are listed first.
4. Use the ShowPages feature to replicate the report for each product line manager.
5. After producing the pivot tables, convert the pivot table to values and do some basic formatting.

Figure 12.6 shows the report for one product line manager to give you an idea of the final goal.

Figure 12.6
Using pivot tables simplifies the creation of the report.

	A	B	C	D	E
1	Product report for A292				
2					
3					
4		2018			2019
5	Customer	# of Orders	Revenue	% of Total	# of Orders
6	Unique Marble Company	59	716,631	12.4%	70
7	Persuasive Kettle Inc.	64	860,540	14.9%	53
8	Guarded Kettle Corporation	63	710,732	12.3%	54
9	Safe Saddle Corporation	15	184,144	3.2%	36

Using Multiple Value Fields

The report has three fields in the values area: Count of Orders, Revenue, and % of Total Revenue. Anytime you have two or more fields in the values area, a new virtual field named Data becomes available in your pivot table. In Excel 2016, the Data field appears as Σ Values in the PivotTable Fields list. When creating your pivot table, you can specify Data as one of the column fields or row fields. The position of the Data field is important: It usually works best as the innermost column field.

When you define a pivot table in VBA, you have two column fields: the Date field and the Data field. To specify two or more fields in the AddFields method, you wrap those fields in an array function.

Use this code to define the pivot table:

```
' Set up the row fields
PT.AddFields RowFields:="Customer", _
    ColumnFields:=Array("Date", "Data"), _
    PageFields:="Product"
```

This is the first time you have seen the PageFields parameter in this chapter. When you are creating a pivot table for someone to use, you should know that the fields in PageFields allow for easy ad hoc analysis. In this case, the value in PageFields is going to make it easy to replicate the report for every product line manager.

Counting the Number of Records

So far, the .Function property of the Data fields has always been xlSum. A total of 11 functions are available: xlSum, xlCount, xlAverage, xlStdDev, xlMin, xlMax, and so on.

Count is the only function that works for text fields. To count the number of records, and hence the number of orders, add a text field to the data area and choose xlCount as the function:

```
With PT.PivotFields("Region")
    .Orientation = xlDataField
    .Function = xlCount
    .Position = 1
    .NumberFormat = "#,##0"
    .Name = "# of Orders "
End With
```

> **NOTE** This is a count of the number of records. It is not a count of the distinct values in a field. This kind of count was previously difficult to do in a pivot table. It is now possible using the Data Model. See the "Using the Data Model in Excel 2016" section later in this chapter for details.

Grouping Daily Dates to Months, Quarters, or Years

Pivot tables have the amazing capability to group daily dates up to months, quarters, and/or years. In VBA, this feature is a bit annoying because you must select a date cell before issuing the grouping command.

> **NOTE** I used to go through all sorts of gyrations to figure out where the first date field was. In fact, you can simply refer to `PT.PivotFields("Date").LabelRange` to point to the Date heading.

There are seven choices for group times or dates: Seconds, Minutes, Hours, Days, Months, Quarters, and Years. Note that you can group a field by multiple items. To do so, you specify a series of `True/False` values corresponding to Seconds, Minutes, and so on.

For example, to group by Months, Quarters, and Years, you would use the following:

```
PT.PivotFields("Date").LabelRange.Group , Periods:= _
    Array(False, False, False, False, True, True, True)
```

> **NOTE** Never choose to group by only months without including years. If you do this, Excel combines January from all years in the data into a single item called January. Although this is great for seasonality analyses, it is rarely what you want in a summary. Always choose Years and Months in the Grouping dialog.

If you want to group by week, you group only by day and use 7 as the value for the `By` parameter:

```
PT.PivotFields("Date").LabelRange.Group _
    Start:=True, End:=True, By:=7, _
    Periods:=Array(False, False, False, True, False, False, False)
```

Specifying `True` for `Start` and `End` starts the first week at the earliest date in the data. If you want to show only the weeks from Monday, December 30, 2013, to Sunday, January 3, 2016, use this code:

```
With PT.PivotFields("Date")
    .LabelRange.Group _
        Start:=DateSerial(2013, 12, 30), _
        End:=DateSerial(2016, 1, 3), _
        By:=7, _
        Periods:=Array(False, False, False, True, False, False, False)
    On Error Resume Next
    .PivotItems("<12/30/2013").Visible = False
    .PivotItems(">1/3/2016").Visible = False
    On Error Goto 0
End With
```

> **NOTE** There is one limitation to grouping by week. When you group by week, you cannot also group by any other measure. For example, grouping by both week and quarter is not valid.

Excel 2016 introduced the concept of AutoGrouping for dates. Excel 2016 has built-in rules that analyze the span of dates in and decide whether dates should be grouped by month or by month, quarter, and year. This does not happen in VBA, but you can force it by using this:

```
PT.AutoGroup
```

For this report, you need to group only by year, so the code is as follows:

```
' Group daily dates up to years
PT.PivotFields("Date").LabelRange.Group , Periods:= _
    Array(False, False, False, False, False, False, True)
```

> **TIP** Before grouping the daily dates up to years, you had about 500 date columns across this report. After grouping, you have two date columns plus a total. I prefer to group the dates as soon as possible in the macro. If you added the other two data fields to the report before grouping, your report would be 1,500 columns wide. Although this is not a problem since Excel 2007 increased the column limit from 256 to 16,384, it still creates an unusually large report when you ultimately need only a few columns. Allowing the pivot table to grow to 1,500 columns, even for a few lines of code, would make the worksheet's last cell be column BER.

After you group daily dates to years, the new Year field is still called Date. This might not always be the case. If you roll daily dates up to months and to years, the Date field contains months, and a new Year field is added to the PivotTable Fields list to hold years.

Changing the Calculation to Show Percentages

Excel 2016 offers 15 choices on the Show Values As tab of the Value Field Settings dialog. These calculations enable you to change how a field is displayed in the report. Instead of showing sales, you could show sales as a percentage of total sales. You could show a running total. You could show each day's sales as a percentage of the previous day's sales.

All these settings are controlled through the `.Calculation` property of the pivot field. Each calculation has its own unique set of rules. Some, such as % of Column, work without any further settings. Others, such as Running Total In, require a base field. Others, such as Running Total, require a base field and a base item.

To get the percentage of the total, specify `xlPercentOfTotal` as the `.Calculation` property for the page field:

```
.Calculation = xlPercentOfTotal
```

To set up a running total, you have to specify a `BaseField`. If you need a running total along a date column, use this:

```
' Set up Running Total
    .Calculation = xlRunningTotal
    .BaseField = "Date"
```

With ship months going down the columns, you might want to see the percentage of revenue growth from month to month. You can set up this arrangement with the `xlPercentDifferenceFrom` setting. In this case, you must specify that the `BaseField` is `"Date"` and that the `BaseItem` is something called `(previous)`:

```
' Set up % change from prior month
With PT.PivotFields("Revenue")
    .Orientation = xlDataField
    .Function = xlSum
    .Caption = "%Change"
    .Calculation = xlPercentDifferenceFrom
    .BaseField = "Date"
    .BaseItem = "(previous)"
    .NumberFormat = "#0.0%"
End With
```

Note that with positional calculations, you cannot use the `AutoShow` or `AutoSort` methods. This is too bad; it would be interesting to sort the customers from high to low and see their sizes in relation to each other.

You can use the `xlPercentDifferenceFrom` setting to express revenues as a percentage of the West region sales:

```
' Show revenue as a percentage of California
With PT.PivotFields("Revenue")
    .Orientation = xlDataField
    .Function = xlSum
    .Caption = "% of West"
    .Calculation = xlPercentDifferenceFrom
    .BaseField = "State"
    .BaseItem = "California"
    .Position = 3
    .NumberFormat = "#0.0%"
End With
```

Table 12.1 shows the complete list of `.Calculation` options. The second column indicates the compatibility of the calculation with earlier versions of Excel. The third column indicates whether you need a base field and/or base item.

Table 12.1 Complete List of `.Calculation` Options

Calculation	Version Compatibility	BaseField/BaseItem
xlDifferenceFrom	All	Both required
xlIndex	All	Neither
xlNoAdditionalCalculation	All	Neither
xlPercentDifferenceFrom	All	Both required
xlPercentOf	All	Both required

Calculation	Version Compatibility	BaseField/BaseItem
xlPercentOfColumn	All	Neither
xlPercentOfParent	2010+	BaseField only
xlPercentOfParentColumn	2010+	Both required
xlPercentOfParentRow	2010+	Both required
xlPercentOfRow	All	Neither
xlPercentOfTotal	All	Neither
xlPercentRunningTotal	2010+	BaseField only
xlRankAscending	2010+	BaseField only
xlRankDescending	2010+	BaseField only
xlRunningTotal	All	BaseField only

After that long explanation of the .Calculation property, you can build the other two pivot table fields for the product line report.

Add Revenue to the report twice. The first time, there is no calculation. The second time, calculate the percentage of total:

```
' Set up the data fields - Revenue
With PT.PivotFields("Revenue")
    .Orientation = xlDataField
    .Function = xlSum
    .Position = 2
    .NumberFormat = "#,##0"
    .Name = "Revenue "
End With

' Set up the data fields - % of total Revenue
With PT.PivotFields("Revenue")
    .Orientation = xlDataField
    .Function = xlSum
    .Position = 3
    .NumberFormat = "0.0%"
    .Name = "% of Total "
    .Calculation = xlPercentOfColumn
End With
```

> **NOTE**
>
> Take careful note of the name of the first field in the preceding code. By default, Excel would use Sum of Revenue. If you think this is a goofy title (as I do), you can change it. However, you cannot change it to Revenue because there is already a field in the PivotTable Fields list with that name.
>
> In the preceding code, I use the name Revenue with a trailing space. This works fine, and no one notices the extra space. However, in the rest of the macro, when you refer to this field, remember to refer to it as Revenue with a trailing space.

Eliminating Blank Cells in the Values Area

If you have some customers who were new in year 2, their sales will appear blank in year 1. Anyone using Excel 97 or later can replace blank cells with zeros. In the Excel interface, you can find the setting for this on the Layout & Format tab of the PivotTable Options dialog box. Select the For Empty Cells, Show option and type 0 in the box.

The equivalent operation in VBA is to set the `NullString` property for the pivot table to `"0"`:

```
PT.NullString = "0"
```

> **NOTE**
> Although the proper code is to set this value to a text zero, Excel actually puts a real zero in the empty cells.

Controlling the Sort Order with AutoSort

The Excel interface offers an AutoSort option that enables you to show customers in descending order, based on revenue. The equivalent code in VBA to sort the product field by descending revenue uses the `AutoSort` method:

```
PT.PivotFields("Customer").AutoSort Order:=xlDescending, _
    Field:="Revenue "
```

After applying some formatting in the macro, you now have one report with totals for all products, as shown in Figure 12.7.

Figure 12.7
The Product drop-down in column K enables you to filter the report to certain products.

	J	K	L	M	N
Product		(All)			
		Date	Data		
		2018			2019
Customer		# of Orders	Revenue	% of Total	# of Orders
Guarded Kettle Corporation		316	4,501,310	13.2%	283
Unique Marble Company		307	4,418,324	13.0%	314
Persuasive Kettle Inc.		268	3,870,414	11.4%	288
Safe Saddle Corporation		135	1,979,144	5.8%	158

Replicating the Report for Every Product

As long as your pivot table was not built on an OLAP data source, you now have access to one of the most powerful, but least-well-known, features in pivot tables. The command is called Show Report Filter Pages, and it replicates your pivot table for every item in one of the fields in the Filters area.

Because you built the report in this example with Product as a filter field, it takes only the following code to replicate the pivot table for every product:

```
' Replicate the pivot table for each product
PT.ShowPages PageField:="Product"
```

After running this code, you have a new worksheet for every product in the data set. From there, you have some simple formatting and calculations to do. Check the end of the macro, shown in Listing 12.3, for these techniques, which should be second nature by this point in the book.

Listing 12.3   Code to Produce One Report per Product

```
Sub CustomerByProductReport()
    ' Use a Pivot Table to create a report for each product
    ' with customers in rows and years in columns
    Dim WSD As Worksheet
    Dim PTCache As PivotCache
    Dim PT As PivotTable
    Dim PT2 As PivotTable
    Dim WS As Worksheet
    Dim WSF As Worksheet
    Dim PRange As Range
    Dim FinalRow As Long
    Set WSD = Worksheets("PivotTable")

    ' Delete any prior pivot tables
    For Each PT In WSD.PivotTables
        PT.TableRange2.Clear
    Next PT
    WSD.Range("J1:Z1").EntireColumn.Clear

    ' Define input area and set up a Pivot Cache
    FinalRow = WSD.Cells(Application.Rows.Count, 1).End(xlUp).Row
    FinalCol = WSD.Cells(1, Application.Columns.Count). _
        End(xlToLeft).Column
    Set PRange = WSD.Cells(1, 1).Resize(FinalRow, FinalCol)
    Set PTCache = ActiveWorkbook.PivotCaches.Create( _
        SourceType:= xlDatabase, _
        SourceData:=PRange.Address, _
        Version:=xlPivotTableVersion14)

    ' Create the Pivot Table from the Pivot Cache
    Set PT = PTCache.CreatePivotTable(TableDestination:=WSD. _
        Cells(2, FinalCol + 2), TableName:="PivotTable1")

    ' Set up the row fields
    PT.AddFields RowFields:="Customer", _
        ColumnFields:=Array("Date", "Data"), _
        PageFields:="Product"

    ' Set up the data fields - count of orders
    With PT.PivotFields("Region")
        .Orientation = xlDataField
        .Function = xlCount
        .Position = 1
        .NumberFormat = "#,##0"
        .Name = "# of Orders "
    End With

    ' Group daily dates up to years
    PT.PivotFields("Date").LabelRange.Group , Periods:= _
        Array(False, False, False, False, False, False, True)
```

```vba
' Set up the data fields - Revenue
With PT.PivotFields("Revenue")
    .Orientation = xlDataField
    .Function = xlSum
    .Position = 2
    .NumberFormat = "#,##0"
    .Name = "Revenue "
End With

' Set up the data fields - % of total Revenue
With PT.PivotFields("Revenue")
    .Orientation = xlDataField
    .Function = xlSum
    .Position = 3
    .NumberFormat = "0.0%"
    .Name = "% of Total "
    .Calculation = xlPercentOfColumn
End With

' Sort the customers so the largest is at the top
PT.PivotFields("Customer").AutoSort Order:=xlDescending, _
    Field:="Revenue "

With PT
    .ShowTableStyleColumnStripes = True
    .ShowTableStyleRowStripes = True
    .TableStyle2 = "PivotStyleMedium10"
    .NullString = "0"
End With

 ' Replicate the pivot table for each product
PT.ShowPages PageField:="Product"

Ctr = 0
For Each WS In ActiveWorkbook.Worksheets
    If WS.PivotTables.Count > 0 Then
        If WS.Cells(1, 1).Value = "Product" Then
            ' Save some info
            WS.Select
            ThisProduct = Cells(1, 2).Value
            Ctr = Ctr + 1
            If Ctr = 1 Then
                Set WSF = ActiveSheet
            End If
            Set PT2 = WS.PivotTables(1)
            CalcRows = PT2.TableRange1.Rows.Count - 3

            PT2.TableRange2.Copy
            PT2.TableRange2.PasteSpecial xlPasteValues

            Range("A1:C3").ClearContents
            Range("A1:B2").Clear
            Range("A1").Value = "Product report for " & ThisProduct
            Range("A1").Style = "Title"

            ' Fix some headings
            Range("b5:d5").Copy Destination:=Range("H5:J5")
            Range("H4").Value = "Total"
```

```
            Range("I4:J4").Clear

            ' Copy the format
            Range("J1").Resize(CalcRows + 5, 1).Copy
            Range("K1").Resize(CalcRows + 5, 1). _
                PasteSpecial xlPasteFormats
            Range("K5").Value = "% Rev Growth"
            Range("K6").Resize(CalcRows, 1).FormulaR1C1 = _
                "=IFERROR(RC6/RC3-1,1)"

            Range("A2:K5").Style = "Heading 4"
            Range("A2").Resize(CalcRows + 10, 11).Columns.AutoFit

        End If
    End If
Next WS

WSD.Select
PT.TableRange2.Clear
Set PTCache = Nothing

WSF.Select
MsgBox Ctr & " product reports created."

End Sub
```

Filtering a Data Set

There are many ways to filter a pivot table, from using the new slicers, to the conceptual filters, to simply selecting and clearing items from one of the many field drop-downs.

Manually Filtering Two or More Items in a Pivot Field

When you open a field heading drop-down and select or clear items from the list, you are applying a manual filter (see Figure 12.8).

For example, say that you have one client who sells shoes. In the report showing sales of sandals, he wants to see just the stores that are in warm-weather states. The code to hide a particular store is as follows:

```
PT.PivotFields("Store").PivotItems("Minneapolis").Visible = False
```

Figure 12.8
This filter drop-down offers manual filters, a search box, and conceptual filters.

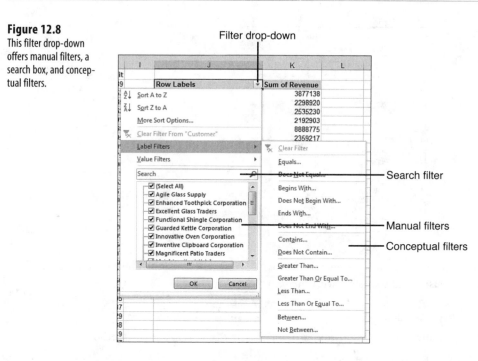

This process is easy in VBA. After building the table with Product in the page field, loop through to change the Visible property to show only the total of certain products:

```
' Make sure all PivotItems along line are visible
For Each PivItem In _
    PT.PivotFields("Product").PivotItems
    PivItem.Visible = True
Next PivItem

' Now - loop through and keep only certain items visible
For Each PivItem In _
    PT.PivotFields("Product").PivotItems
    Select Case PivItem.Name
        Case "Landscaping/Grounds Care", _
            "Green Plants and Foliage Care"
            PivItem.Visible = True
        Case Else
            PivItem.Visible = False
    End Select
Next PivItem
```

Using the Conceptual Filters

Excel 2007 introduced conceptual filters for date fields, numeric fields, and text fields. Open the drop-down for any field label in the pivot table, and you can choose Label Filters, Date Filters, or Value Filters. The date filters offer the capability to filter to a conceptual period such as last month or next year (see Figure 12.9).

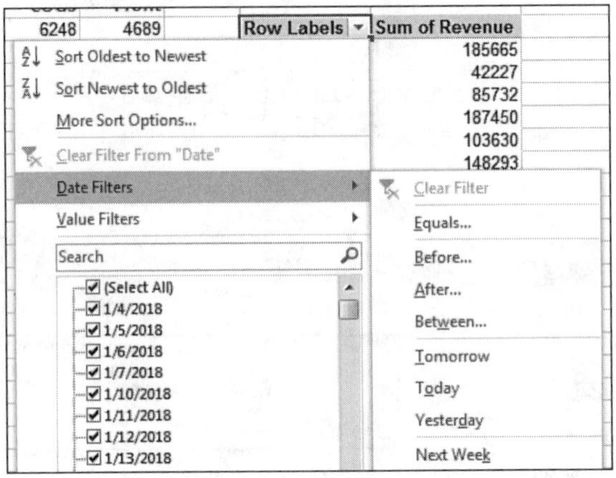

Figure 12.9
These date filters were
introduced in Excel 2007.

To apply a label filter in VBA, use the `PivotFilters.Add` method. The following code filters to the customers that start with the letter *E*:

```
PT.PivotFields("Customer").PivotFilters.Add _
    Type:=xlCaptionBeginsWith, Value1:="E"
```

To clear the filter from the Customer field, use the `ClearAllFilters` method:

```
PT.PivotFields("Customer").ClearAllFilters
```

To apply a date filter to the date field to find records from this week, use this code:

```
PT.PivotFields("Date").PivotFilters.Add Type:=xlThisWeek
```

The value filters enable you to filter one field based on the value of another field. For example, to find all the markets where the total revenue is more than $100,000, use this code:

```
PT.PivotFields("Market").PivotFilters.Add _
    Type:=xlValueIsGreaterThan, _
    DataField:=PT.PivotFields("Sum of Revenue"), _
    Value1:=100000
```

Other value filters might enable you to specify, for example, that you want branches where the revenue is between $50,000 and $100,000. In this case, you specify one limit as `Value1` and the second limit as `Value2`:

```
PT.PivotFields("Market").PivotFilters.Add _
    Type:=xlValueIsBetween, _
    DataField:=PT.PivotFields("Sum of Revenue"), _
    Value1:=50000, Value2:=100000
```

Table 12.2 lists all the possible filter types.

Table 12.2 Filter Types	
Filter Type	**Description**
xlBefore	Filters for all dates before a specified date.
xlBeforeOrEqualTo	Filters for all dates on or before a specified date.

Filter Type	Description
xlAfter	Filters for all dates after a specified date.
xlAfterOrEqualTo	Filters for all dates on or after a specified date.
xlAllDatesInPeriodJanuary	Filters for all dates in January.
xlAllDatesInPeriodFebruary	Filters for all dates in February.
xlAllDatesInPeriodMarch	Filters for all dates in March.
xlAllDatesInPeriodApril	Filters for all dates in April.
xlAllDatesInPeriodMay	Filters for all dates in May.
xlAllDatesInPeriodJune	Filters for all dates in June.
xlAllDatesInPeriodJuly	Filters for all dates in July.
xlAllDatesInPeriodAugust	Filters for all dates in August.
xlAllDatesInPeriodSeptember	Filters for all dates in September.
xlAllDatesInPeriodOctober	Filters for all dates in October.
xlAllDatesInPeriodNovember	Filters for all dates in November.
xlAllDatesInPeriodDecember	Filters for all dates in December.
xlAllDatesInPeriodQuarter1	Filters for all dates in Quarter 1.
xlAllDatesInPeriodQuarter2	Filters for all dates in Quarter 2.
xlAllDatesInPeriodQuarter3	Filters for all dates in Quarter 3.
xlAllDatesInPeriodQuarter4	Filters for all dates in Quarter 4.
xlBottomCount	Filters for the specified number of values from the bottom of a list.
xlBottomPercent	Filters for the specified percentage of values from the bottom of a list.
xlBottomSum	Sums the values from the bottom of the list.
xlCaptionBeginsWith	Filters for all captions, beginning with the specified string.
xlCaptionContains	Filters for all captions that contain the specified string.
xlCaptionDoesNotBeginWith	Filters for all captions that do not begin with the specified string.
xlCaptionDoesNotContain	Filters for all captions that do not contain the specified string.
xlCaptionDoesNotEndWith	Filters for all captions that do not end with the specified string.
xlCaptionDoesNotEqual	Filters for all captions that do not match the specified string.
xlCaptionEndsWith	Filters for all captions that end with the specified string.
xlCaptionEquals	Filters for all captions that match the specified string.
xlCaptionIsBetween	Filters for all captions that are within a specified range of values.
xlCaptionIsGreaterThan	Filters for all captions that are greater than the specified value.
xlCaptionIsGreater ThanOrEqualTo	Filters for all captions that are greater than or match the specified value.
xlCaptionIsLessThan	Filters for all captions that are less than the specified value.

12

Filter Type	Description
xlCaptionIsLessThanOrEqualTo	Filters for all captions that are less than or match the specified value.
xlCaptionIsNotBetween	Filters for all captions that are not within a specified range of values.
xlDateBetween	Filters for all dates that are within a specified range of dates.
xlDateLastMonth	Filters for all dates that apply to the previous month.
xlDateLastQuarter	Filters for all dates that apply to the previous quarter.
xlDateLastWeek	Filters for all dates that apply to the previous week.
xlDateLastYear	Filters for all dates that apply to the previous year.
xlDateNextMonth	Filters for all dates that apply to the next month.
xlDateNextQuarter	Filters for all dates that apply to the next quarter.
xlDateNextWeek	Filters for all dates that apply to the next week.
xlDateNextYear	Filters for all dates that apply to the next year.
xlDateThisMonth	Filters for all dates that apply to the current month.
xlDateThisQuarter	Filters for all dates that apply to the current quarter.
xlDateThisWeek	Filters for all dates that apply to the current week.
xlDateThisYear	Filters for all dates that apply to the current year.
xlDateToday	Filters for all dates that apply to the current date.
xlDateTomorrow	Filters for all dates that apply to the next day.
xlDateYesterday	Filters for all dates that apply to the previous day.
xlNotSpecificDate	Filters for all dates that do not match a specified date.
xlSpecificDate	Filters for all dates that match a specified date.
xlTopCount	Filters for the specified number of values from the top of a list.
xlTopPercent	Filters for the specified percentage of values from the top of a list.
xlTopSum	Sums the values from the top of the list.
xlValueDoesNotEqual	Filters for all values that do not match the specified value.
xlValueEquals	Filters for all values that match the specified value.
xlValueIsBetween	Filters for all values that are within a specified range of values.
xlValueIsGreaterThan	Filters for all values that are greater than the specified value.
xlValueIsGreaterThanOrEqualTo	Filters for all values that are greater than or match the specified value.
xlValueIsLessThan	Filters for all values that are less than the specified value.
xlValueIsLessThanOrEqualTo	Filters for all values that are less than or match the specified value.
xlValueIsNotBetween	Filters for all values that are not within a specified range of values.
xlYearToDate	Filters for all values that are within one year of a specified date.

12

Using the Search Filter

Excel 2010 added a Search box to the filter drop-down. Although this is a slick feature in the Excel interface, there is no equivalent magic in VBA. Whereas the drop-down offers the Select All Search Results check box, the equivalent VBA just lists all the items that match the selection. To achieve the same results in VBA, use the xlCaptionContains filter described in the code that precedes Table 12.2.

CASE STUDY FILTERING TO THE TOP 5 OR TOP 10 BY USING A FILTER

If you are designing an executive dashboard utility, you might want to spotlight the top 5 customers. As with the AutoSort option, you could be a pivot table pro and never have stumbled across the Top 10 AutoShow feature in Excel. This setting enables you to select either the top or the bottom *n* records, based on any Data field in the report.

The code to use AutoShow in VBA involves the .AutoShow method:

```
' Show only the top 5 Customers
PT.PivotFields("Customer").AutoShow Top:=xlAutomatic, Range:=xlTop, _
    Count:=5, Field:= "Sum of Revenue"
```

When you create a report using the .AutoShow method, it is often helpful to copy the data and then go back to the original pivot report to get the totals for all markets. In the code, this is achieved by removing the Customer field from the pivot table and copying the grand total to the report. The code that follows produces the report shown in Figure 12.10:

```
Sub Top5Customers()
    ' Produce a report of the top 5 customers
    Dim WSD As Worksheet
    Dim WSR As Worksheet
    Dim WBN As Workbook
    Dim PTCache As PivotCache
    Dim PT As PivotTable
    Dim PRange As Range
    Dim FinalRow As Long
    Set WSD = Worksheets("PivotTable")

    ' Delete any prior pivot tables
    For Each PT In WSD.PivotTables
        PT.TableRange2.Clear
    Next PT
    WSD.Range("J1:Z1").EntireColumn.Clear

    ' Define input area and set up a Pivot Cache
    FinalRow = WSD.Cells(Application.Rows.Count, 1).End(xlUp).Row

    FinalCol = WSD.Cells(1, Application.Columns.Count). _
        End(xlToLeft).Column
    Set PRange = WSD.Cells(1, 1).Resize(FinalRow, FinalCol)
    Set PTCache = ActiveWorkbook.PivotCaches.Create( _
        SourceType:= xlDatabase, _
        SourceData:=PRange.Address, _
        Version:=xlPivotTableVersion14)
```

12

```vba
' Create the Pivot Table from the Pivot Cache
Set PT = PTCache.CreatePivotTable(TableDestination:=WSD. _
    Cells(2, FinalCol + 2), TableName:="PivotTable1")

' Set up the row fields
PT.AddFields RowFields:="Customer", ColumnFields:="Product"

' Set up the data fields
With PT.PivotFields("Revenue")
    .Orientation = xlDataField
    .Function = xlSum
    .Position = 1
    .NumberFormat = "#,##0"
    .Name = "Total Revenue"
End With

' Ensure that we get zeros instead of blanks in the data area
PT.NullString = "0"

' Sort customers descending by sum of revenue
PT.PivotFields("Customer").AutoSort Order:=xlDescending, _
    Field:="Total Revenue"

' Show only the top 5 customers
PT.PivotFields("Customer").AutoShow _
    Type:=xlAutomatic, Range:=xlTop, _
    Count:=5, Field:="Total Revenue"

' Create a new blank workbook with one worksheet
Set WBN = Workbooks.Add(xlWBATWorksheet)
Set WSR = WBN.Worksheets(1)
WSR.Name = "Report"
' Set up title for report
With WSR.[A1]
    .Value = "Top 5 Customers"
    .Font.Size = 14
End With

' Copy the pivot table data to row 3 of the report sheet
' Use offset to eliminate the title row of the pivot table

PT.TableRange2.Offset(1, 0).Copy
WSR.[A3].PasteSpecial Paste:=xlPasteValuesAndNumberFormats
LastRow = WSR.Cells(Rows.Count, 1).End(xlUp).Row
WSR.Cells(LastRow, 1).Value = "Top 5 Total"

' Go back to the pivot table to get totals without the AutoShow
PT.PivotFields("Customer").Orientation = xlHidden
PT.ManualUpdate = False
PT.ManualUpdate = True
PT.TableRange2.Offset(2, 0).Copy
WSR.Cells(LastRow + 2, 1).PasteSpecial Paste:= _
    xlPasteValuesAndNumberFormats
WSR.Cells(LastRow + 2, 1).Value = "Total Company"
```

```
        ' Clear the pivot table
        PT.TableRange2.Clear
        Set PTCache = Nothing

        ' Do some basic formatting

        ' Autofit columns, bold the headings, right-align
        WSR.Range(WSR.Range("A3"), WSR.Cells(LastRow + 2, 6)).Columns.AutoFit
        Range("A3").EntireRow.Font.Bold = True
        Range("A3").EntireRow.HorizontalAlignment = xlRight
        Range("A3").HorizontalAlignment = xlLeft

        Range("A2").Select
        MsgBox "CEO Report has been Created"
    End Sub
```

Figure 12.10
The Top 5 Customers report contains two pivot tables.

	A	B	C	D	E	F	G
1	Top 5 Customers						
2							
3	Customer	A292	B722	C409	D625	E438	Grand Total
4	Guarded Kettle Corporation	1,450,110	1,404,742	1,889,149	1,842,751	2,302,023	8,888,775
5	Unique Marble Company	1,600,347	1,581,665	1,765,305	1,707,140	2,179,242	8,833,699
6	Persuasive Kettle Inc.	1,565,368	1,385,296	1,443,434	1,584,759	2,030,578	8,009,435
7	Safe Saddle Corporation	646,559	857,573	730,463	1,038,371	1,053,369	4,326,335
8	Tremendous Bobsled Corporation	560,759	711,826	877,247	802,303	1,095,329	4,047,464
9	Top 5 Total	5,823,143	5,941,102	6,705,598	6,975,324	8,660,541	34,105,708
10							
11	Total Company	12,337,778	12,683,061	14,101,763	14,569,960	17,411,966	71,104,528
12							

The Top 5 Customers report actually contains two snapshots of a pivot table. After using the AutoShow feature to grab the top five markets with their totals, the macro went back to the pivot table, removed the AutoShow option, and grabbed the total of all customers to produce the Total Company row.

Setting Up Slicers to Filter a Pivot Table

Excel 2010 introduced the concept of slicers for filtering pivot tables. A *slicer* is a visual filter that you can resize and reposition. You can control the color of a slicer and control the number of columns in it. You can also select or unselect items from a slicer by using VBA.

Figure 12.11 shows a pivot table with two slicers. Both of the slicers have been modified to show multiple columns.

Figure 12.11
Slicers provide a visual filter of several fields.

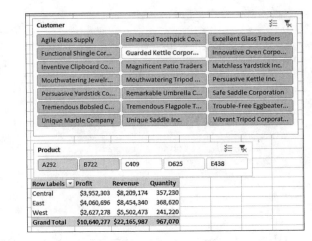

Slicers were new in Excel 2010 and work only with pivot tables designed to be used by Excel 2010 or newer. A slicer consists of a slicer cache and a slicer. To define a slicer cache, you need to specify a pivot table as the source and a field name as the `SourceField`. The slicer cache is defined at the workbook level. The following code would enable you to have a slicer on a different worksheet than the pivot table:

```
Dim SCP as SlicerCache
Dim SCR as SlicerCache
Set SCP = ActiveWorkbook.SlicerCaches.Add(Source:=PT,
SourceField:="Product")
Set SCR = ActiveWorkbook.SlicerCaches.Add(Source:=PT,
SourceField:="Region")
```

After you have defined the slicer cache, you can add the slicer. The slicer is defined as an object of the slicer cache. Specify a worksheet as the destination. The `name` argument controls the internal name for the slicer. The `Caption` argument is the heading that is visible in the slicer. This might be useful if you would like to show the name Region, but the IT department defined the field as IDKRegn. Specify the size of the slicer by using height and width in points. Specify the location by using top and left in points.

In the following code, the values for top, left, height, and width are assigned to be equal to the location or size of certain cell ranges:

```
Dim SLP as Slicer
Set SLP = SCP.Slicers.Add(SlicerDestination:=WSD, Name:="Product", _
    Caption:="Product", _
    Top:=WSD.Range("A12").Top, _
    Left:=WSD.Range("A12").Left + 10, _
    Width:=WSR.Range("A12:C12").Width, _
    Height:=WSD.Range("A12:A16").Height)
```

Every slicer starts out as one column. You can change the style and number of columns code like this:

```
' Format the color and number of columns
With SLP
    .Style = "SlicerStyleLight6"
    .NumberOfColumns = 5
End With
```

After the slicer is defined, you can use VBA to choose which items are activated in the slicer. It seems counterintuitive, but to choose items in the slicer, you have to change `SlicerItem`, which is a member of the `SlicerCache`, not a member of the `Slicer`:

```
With SCP
    .SlicerItems("A292").Selected = True
    .SlicerItems("B722").Selected = True
    .SlicerItems("C409").Selected = False
    .SlicerItems("D625").Selected = False
    .SlicerItems("E438").Selected = False
End With
```

Listing 12.4 shows how to build a pivot table with two slicers.

Listing 12.4   Code to Build a Pivot with Two Slicers

```
Sub PivotWithTwoSlicers()
    Dim SCP As SlicerCache ' For Product Slicer
    Dim SCC As SlicerCache ' For Customer Slicer
    Dim SLP As Slicer
    Dim SLC As Slicer
    Dim WSD As Worksheet
    Dim WSR As Worksheet
    Dim WBD As Workbook
    Dim PT As PivotTable
    Dim PTCache As PivotCache
    Dim PRange As Range
    Dim FinalRow As Long
    Set WBD = ActiveWorkbook
    Set WSD = Worksheets("Data")

    ' Delete any prior pivot tables
    For Each PT In WSD.PivotTables
        PT.TableRange2.Clear
    Next PT

    ' Delete any prior slicer cache
    For Each SC In ActiveWorkbook.SlicerCaches
        SC.Delete
    Next SC

    ' Define input area and set up a Pivot Cache
    WSD.Select
    FinalRow = WSD.Cells(Rows.Count, 1).End(xlUp).Row
    FinalCol = WSD.Cells(1, Columns.Count). _
        End(xlToLeft).Column
    Set PRange = WSD.Cells(1, 1).Resize(FinalRow, FinalCol)

    ' Define the pivot table cache
    Set PTCache = ActiveWorkbook.PivotCaches.Create( _
        SourceType:=xlDatabase, _
        SourceData:=PRange.Address, _
```

```
                        Version:=xlPivotTableVersion15)

    ' Create the Pivot Table from the Pivot Cache
    Set PT = PTCache.CreatePivotTable( _
        TableDestination:=Cells(18, FinalCol + 2), _
        TableName:="PivotTable1", _
        DefaultVersion:=xlPivotTableVersion15)

    ' Set up the row & column fields
    PT.AddFields RowFields:=Array("Region")

    ' Set up the data fields
    With PT.PivotFields("Quantity")
        .Orientation = xlDataField
        .Function = xlSum
        .Position = 1
        .NumberFormat = "#,##0"
        .Name = "Quantity "
    End With

    With PT.PivotFields("Revenue")
        .Orientation = xlDataField
        .Function = xlSum
        .Position = 1
        .NumberFormat = "$#,##0"
        .Name = "Revenue "
    End With

    With PT.PivotFields("Profit")
        .Orientation = xlDataField
        .Function = xlSum
        .Position = 1
        .NumberFormat = "$#,##0"
        .Name = "Profit "
    End With

    ' Define the Slicer Caches
    Set SCC = WBD.SlicerCaches.Add(PT, "Customer")
    Set SCP = WBD.SlicerCaches.Add(PT, "Product")

    ' Define Product as a slicer
    Set SLP = SCP.Slicers.Add(WSD, , _
        Name:="Product", _
        Caption:="Product", _
        Top:=WSD.Range("J14").Top + 5, _
        Left:=WSD.Range("J14").Left + 5, _
        Width:=343, Height:=54)
    SLP.Style = "SlicerStyleLight4"
    SLP.NumberOfColumns = 5

    ' Define Customer as a slicer
    Set SLC = SCC.Slicers.Add(WSD, , _
        Name:="Customer", _
        Caption:="Customer", _
        Top:=WSD.Range("J1").Top + 5, _
        Left:=WSD.Range("J1").Left + 5, _
        Width:=415, Height:=184)
    SLC.Style = "SlicerStyleLight2"
```

```
    SLC.NumberOfColumns = 3

    ' Unselect some products
    With SCP
        .SlicerItems("C409").Selected = False
        .SlicerItems("D625").Selected = False
        .SlicerItems("E438").Selected = False
    End With

    ' Unselect One Customer
    With SCC
        .SlicerItems("Guarded Kettle Corporation").Selected = False
    End With

End Sub
```

The preceding code assigned the newly created slicer to an object variable so you could easily format the slicer. What if a slicer was created before your macro starts running? You can easily figure out the name of the slicer. If a slicer is created for the Product field, for example, the name of the SlicerCache is "Slicer_Product". The following code formats existing slicers:

```
Sub MoveAndFormatSlicer()
    Dim SCP As SlicerCache
    Dim SLP as Slicer
    Dim WSD As Worksheet
    Set WSD = ActiveSheet
    Set SCP = ActiveWorkbook.SlicerCaches("Slicer_Product")
    Set SLP = SCS.Slicers("Product")
    With SLP
        .Style = "SlicerStyleLight6"
        .NumberOfColumns = 5
        .Top = WSD.Range("A1").Top + 5
        .Left = WSD.Range("A1").Left + 5
        .Width = WSD.Range("A1:B14").Width - 60
        .Height = WSD.Range("A1:B14").Height
    End With
End Sub
```

Setting Up a Timeline to Filter an Excel 2016 Pivot Table

Microsoft introduced the Timeline slicer in Excel 2013. This is a special type of slicer that is not compatible with Excel 2010 or earlier. The marketing name of Excel 2013 was Version 15, and VBA still uses that name, so if you plan on using a Timeline slicer, you have to specify xlPivotTableVersion15 (or higher) in two places in the code:

```
' Define the pivot table cache
Set PTCache = ActiveWorkbook.PivotCaches.Create( _
    SourceType:=xlDatabase, _
    SourceData:=PRange.Address, _
    Version:=xlPivotTableVersion15)

' Create the Pivot Table from the Pivot Cache
Set PT = PTCache.CreatePivotTable( _
    TableDestination:=Cells(10, FinalCol + 2), _
    TableName:="PivotTable1", _
    DefaultVersion:=xlPivotTableVersion15)
```

12

Later, after adding fields to your pivot table, you define a slicer cache and specify the type as `xlTimeLine`:

```
' Define the Slicer Cache
' First two arguments are Source and SourceField
' Third argument, Name should be skipped
Set SC = WBD.SlicerCaches.Add2(PT, "ShipDate", , _
    SlicerCacheType:=xlTimeline)
```

Then you add the slicer to the slicer cache:

```
' Define the timeline as a slicer
Set SL = SC.Slicers.Add(WSD, , _
    Name:="ShipDate", _
    Caption:="Year", _
    Top:=WSD.Range("J1").Top, _
    Left:=WSD.Range("J1").Left, _
    Width:=262.5, Height:=108)
```

Timelines can exist at the day, month, quarter, or year level. To change the level of a timeline, use the `TimelineViewState.Level` property:

```
SL.TimelineViewState.Level = xlTimelineLevelYears
```

To filter a timeline to certain dates, you have to use the `Timeline State.SetFilterDataRange` property, which applies to the slicer cache:

```
SC.TimelineState.SetFilterDateRange "1/1/2014", "12/31/2015"
```

Listing 12.5 shows the complete macro to build a version 15 pivot table and add a Timeline slicer.

Listing 12.5   Code to Build a Pivot with a Timeline

```
Sub PivotWithYearSlicer()
    Dim SC As SlicerCache
    Dim SL As Slicer
    Dim WSD As Worksheet
    Dim WSR As Worksheet
    Dim WBD As Workbook
    Dim PT As PivotTable
    Dim PTCache As PivotCache
    Dim PRange As Range
    Dim FinalRow As Long
    Set WBD = ActiveWorkbook
    Set WSD = Worksheets("Data")

    ' Delete any prior pivot tables
    For Each PT In WSD.PivotTables
        PT.TableRange2.Clear
    Next PT

    ' Delete any prior slicer cache
    For Each SC In ActiveWorkbook.SlicerCaches
        SC.Delete
    Next SC

    ' Define input area and set up a Pivot Cache
    WSD.Select
```

12

```
        FinalRow = WSD.Cells(Rows.Count, 1).End(xlUp).Row
        FinalCol = WSD.Cells(1, Columns.Count). _
            End(xlToLeft).Column
        Set PRange = WSD.Cells(1, 1).Resize(FinalRow, FinalCol)

        ' Define the pivot table cache
        Set PTCache = ActiveWorkbook.PivotCaches.Create( _
            SourceType:=xlDatabase, _
            SourceData:=PRange.Address, _
            Version:=xlPivotTableVersion15)

        ' Create the Pivot Table from the Pivot Cache
        Set PT = PTCache.CreatePivotTable( _
            TableDestination:=Cells(10, FinalCol + 2), _
            TableName:="PivotTable1", _
            DefaultVersion:=xlPivotTableVersion15)

        ' Set up the row & column fields
        PT.AddFields RowFields:=Array("Customer")

        ' Set up the data fields
        With PT.PivotFields("Revenue")
            .Orientation = xlDataField
            .Function = xlSum
            .Position = 1
            .NumberFormat = "#,##0"
            .Name = "Revenue "
        End With

        ' Define the Slicer Cache
        ' First two arguments are Source and SourceField
        ' Third argument, Name should be skipped
        Set SC = WBD.SlicerCaches.Add2(PT, "ShipDate", , _
            SlicerCacheType:=xlTimeline)

        ' Define the timeline as a slicer
        Set SL = SC.Slicers.Add(WSD, , _
            Name:="ShipDate", _
            Caption:="Year", _
            Top:=WSD.Range("J1").Top, _
            Left:=WSD.Range("J1").Left, _
            Width:=262.5, Height:=108)

        ' Set the timeline to show years
        SL.TimelineViewState.Level = xlTimelineLevelYears

        ' Set the dates for the timeline
        SC.TimelineState.SetFilterDateRange "1/1/2018", "12/31/2018"
    End Sub
```

Figure 12.12 shows the Timeline slicer built by the code in Listing 12.5.

12

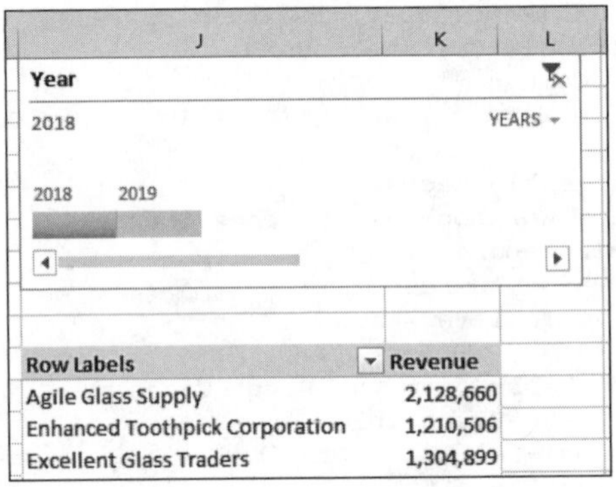

Figure 12.12
Timelines were intro-
duced in Excel 2013.

Using the Data Model in Excel 2016

Excel 2016 incorporates parts of Power Pivot into the core Excel product. Items in the Excel ribbon are incorporated into the Data Model. Items in the Power Pivot ribbon are not. This means you can add two tables to the Data Model, create a relationship, and then build a pivot table from the Data Model.

To follow along with this example, open the 12-BeforeDataModel.xlsm file from the sample download files. This workbook has two tables: Sales and Sector. Sector is a lookup table that is related to the Sales table via a customer field. To build the pivot table, follow these general steps:

1. Add the main table to the Data Model.
2. Add the lookup table to the Data Model.
3. Link the two tables with a relationship.
4. Create a pivot cache from `ThisWorkbookDataModel`.
5. Create a pivot table from the cache.
6. Add row fields.
7. Define a measure. Add the measure to the pivot table.

Adding Both Tables to the Data Model

You should already have a data set in the workbook that has been converted to a table using the Ctrl+T shortcut. On the Table Tools Design tab, change the table name to Sales. To link this table to the Data Model, use this code:

```
' Build Connection to the main Sales table
Set WBT = ActiveWorkbook
TableName = "Sales"
WBT.Connections.Add Name:="LinkedTable_" & TableName, _
    Description:="", _
    ConnectionString:="WORKSHEET;" & WBT.FullName, _
    CommandText:=WBT.Name & "!" & TableName, _
    lCmdType:=7, _
```

```
        CreateModelConnection:=True, _
        ImportRelationships:=False
```

There are several variables in this code that use the table name, the workbook path, and/or the workbook name. By storing the table name in a variable at the top of the code, you can use the variables to build the connection name, connection string, and command text.

Adapting the preceding code to link to the lookup table then requires only changing the `TableName` variable:

```
    TableName = "Sector"
    WBT.Connections.Add Name:="LinkedTable_" & TableName, _
        Description:="", _
        ConnectionString:="WORKSHEET;" & WBT.FullName, _
        CommandText:=WBT.Name & "!" & TableName, _
        lCmdType:=7, _
        CreateModelConnection:=True, _
        ImportRelationships:=False
```

Creating a Relationship Between the Two Tables

When you create a relationship in the Excel interface, you specify four items in the Create Relationship dialog box. The code to create the relationship is more streamlined. There can be only one Data Model per workbook. Set an object variable MO to refer to the model in this workbook. Use the `ModelRelationships.Add` method, specifying the two fields that are linked:

```
    ' Relate the two tables
    Dim MO As Model
    Set MO = ActiveWorkbook.Model
    MO.ModelRelationships.Add _
        ForeignKeyColumn:= _
            MO.ModelTables("Sales").ModelTableColumns("Customer"), _
            PrimaryKeyColumn:= _
            MO.ModelTables("Sector").ModelTableColumns("Customer")
```

Defining the PivotCache and Building the Pivot Table

The code to define the pivot cache specifies that the data is external. Even though the linked tables are in your workbook, and even though the Data Model is stored as a binary large object within the workbook, this is still considered an external data connection. The connection is always called `ThisWorkbookDataModel`. To set up the pivot cache, use this code::

```
    ' Define the PivotCache
    Set PTCache = WBT.PivotCaches.Create(SourceType:=xlExternal, _
        SourceData:=WBT.Connections("ThisWorkbookDataModel"), _
        Version:=xlPivotTableVersion15)

    ' Create the Pivot Table from the Pivot Cache
    Set PT = PTCache.CreatePivotTable( _
        TableDestination:=WSD.Cells(1, 1), TableName:="PivotTable1")
```

12

Adding Model Fields to the Pivot Table

There are two types of fields you need to add to the pivot table. Text fields such as Customer, Sector, or Product are simply fields that can be added to the row or column area of the pivot table. No calculation has to happen to these fields. The code for adding text fields is shown in this section. When you add a numeric field to the values area in the Excel interface, you are actually implicitly defining a new calculated field. To do this in VBA, you have to explicitly define the field and then add it.

First, let's look at the simpler example of adding a text field to the row area. The VBA code generically looks like this:

```
With PT.CubeFields("[TableName].[FieldName]")
    .Orientation = xlRowField
    .Position = 1
End With
```

In the current example, add the Sector field from the Sector table by using this code:

```
With PT.CubeFields("[Sector].[Sector]")
    .Orientation = xlRowField
    .Position = 1
End With
```

Adding Numeric Fields to the Values Area

If you have a Data Model pivot table and you check the Revenue field, you see the Revenue field move to the Values area. Behind the scenes, though, Excel is implicitly defining a new measure called Sum of Revenue. (You can see the implicit measures in the Power Pivot window if you have Excel 2016 Pro Plus.) In VBA, you need to define a new measure for Sum of Revenue. To make it easier to refer to this measure later, assign the new measure to an object variable:

```
' Before you can add Revenue to the pivot table,
' you have to define the measure.
' This happens using the GetMeasure method.
' Assign the cube field to CFRevenue object
Dim CFRevenue As CubeField
Set CFRevenue = PT.CubeFields.GetMeasure( _
    AttributeHierarchy:="[Sales].[Revenue]", _
    Function:=xlSum, _
    Caption:="Sum of Revenue")
' Add the newly created cube field to the pivot table
PT.AddDataField Field:=CFRevenue, _
    Caption:="Total Revenue"
PT.PivotFields("Total Revenue").NumberFormat = "$#,##0,K"
```

You can use the preceding code to create a new measure. The following measure uses the new `xlDistinctCount` function to count the number of unique customers in each sector:

```
' Add Distinct Count of Customer as a Cube Field
Dim CFCustCount As CubeField
Set CFCustCount = PT.CubeFields.GetMeasure( _
    AttributeHierarchy:="[Sales].[Customer]", _
    Function:=xlDistinctCount, _
    Caption:="Customer Count")
```

```
' Add the newly created cube field to the pivot table
PT.AddDataField Field:=CFCustCount, _
    Caption:="Customer Count"
```

> **CAUTION**
>
> Before you get too excited, you should know that the Excel team drew an interesting line in the sand with regard to what parts of Power Pivot are available via VBA. Any functionality that is available in Office 2016 Standard is available in VBA. If you try to define a new calculated field that uses the Power Pivot DAX formula language, it will not work in VBA.

Putting It All Together

Figure 12.13 shows the Data Model pivot table created using the code in Listing 12.6.

Figure 12.13
Two tables linked with a pivot table and two measures via a macro.

	A	B	C
1	Row Labels ▾	Total Revenue	Customer Count
2	Apparel	$758K	2
3	Chemical	$569K	1
4	Consumer	$2,195K	7
5	Electronics	$222K	4
6	Food	$750K	1
7	Hardware	$2,179K	11
8	Textiles	$35K	1
9	Grand Total	$6,708K	27
10			

Listing 12.6   Code to Create a Data Model Pivot Table

```
Sub BuildModelPivotTable()
    Dim WBT As Workbook
    Dim WC As WorkbookConnection
    Dim MO As Model
    Dim PTCache As PivotCache
    Dim PT As PivotTable
    Dim WSD As Worksheet
    Dim CFRevenue As CubeField
    Dim CFCustCount As CubeField

    Set WBT = ActiveWorkbook
    Set WSD = WBT.Worksheets("Report")

    ' Build Connection to the main Sales table
    TableName = "Sales"
    WBT.Connections.Add2 Name:="LinkedTable_" & TableName, _
        Description:="MainTable", _
        ConnectionString:="WORKSHEET;" & WBT.FullName, _
        CommandText:=WBT.Name & "!" & TableName, _
        lCmdType:=7, _
        CreateModelConnection:=True, _
        ImportRelationships:=False
```

```
' Build Connection to the Sector lookup table
TableName = "Sector"
WBT.Connections.Add2 Name:="LinkedTable_" & TableName, _
    Description:="LookupTable", _
    ConnectionString:="WORKSHEET;" & WBT.FullName, _
    CommandText:=WBT.Name & "!" & TableName, _
    lCmdType:=7, _
    CreateModelConnection:=True, _
    ImportRelationships:=False

' Relate the two tables
Set MO = ActiveWorkbook.Model
MO.ModelRelationships.Add _
    ForeignKeyColumn:=MO.ModelTables("Sales") _
        .ModelTableColumns("Customer"), _
    PrimaryKeyColumn:=MO.ModelTables("Sector") _
        .ModelTableColumns("Customer")

' Delete any prior pivot tables
For Each PT In WSD.PivotTables
    PT.TableRange2.Clear
Next PT

' Define the PivotCache
Set PTCache = WBT.PivotCaches.Create(SourceType:=xlExternal, _
    SourceData:=WBT.Connections("ThisWorkbookDataModel"), _
    Version:=xlPivotTableVersion15)

' Create the Pivot Table from the Pivot Cache
Set PT = PTCache.CreatePivotTable( _
    TableDestination:=WSD.Cells(1, 1), TableName:="PivotTable1")

' Add the Sector field from the Sector table to the Row areas
With PT.CubeFields("[Sector].[Sector]")
    .Orientation = xlRowField
    .Position = 1
End With

' Before you can add Revenue to the pivot table,
' you have to define the measure.
' This happens using the GetMeasure method
' Assign the cube field to CFRevenue object
Set CFRevenue = PT.CubeFields.GetMeasure( _
    AttributeHierarchy:="[Sales].[Revenue]", _
    Function:=xlSum, _
    Caption:="Sum of Revenue")
' Add the newly created cube field to the pivot table
PT.AddDataField Field:=CFRevenue, _
    Caption:="Total Revenue"
 PT.PivotFields("[Measures].[Sum of Revenue]") _
    .NumberFormat = "$#,##0,K"

' Add Distinct Count of Customer as a Cube Field
Set CFCustCount = PT.CubeFields.GetMeasure( _
    AttributeHierarchy:="[Sales].[Customer]", _
    Function:=xlDistinctCount, _
    Caption:="Customer Count")
' Add the newly created cube field to the pivot table
```

```
    PT.AddDataField Field:=CFCustCount, _
        Caption:="Customer Count"

End Sub
```

Using Other Pivot Table Features

This section covers a few additional features in pivot tables that you might need to code with VBA.

Calculated Data Fields

Pivot tables offer two types of formulas. The most useful type creates a calculated field. This adds a new field to the pivot table. Calculations for calculated fields are always done at the summary level. If you define a calculated field for average price as revenue divided by units sold, Excel first adds the total revenue and total quantity, and then it does the division of these totals to get the result. In many cases, this is exactly what you need. If your calculation does not follow the associative law of mathematics, it might not work as you expect.

To set up a calculated field, use the `Add` method with the `CalculatedFields` object. You have to specify a field name and a formula, as shown here:

> **NOTE**
>
> Note that if you create a field called Profit Percent, the default pivot table produces a field called Sum of Profit Percent. This title is misleading and downright silly. To prevent this, use the `Name` property when defining the Data field to replace Sum of Profit Percent with something such as GP Pct. Keep in mind that this name must differ from the name for the calculated field.

```
' Define Calculated Fields
    PT.CalculatedFields.Add Name:="ProfitPercent", _
        Formula:="=Profit/Revenue"
    With PT.PivotFields("ProfitPercent")
        .Orientation = xlDataField
        .Function = xlSum
        .Position = 3
        .NumberFormat = "#0.0%"
        .Name = "GP Pct"
    End With
```

Calculated Items

Suppose you have a Measure field with two items: Budget and Actual. You would like to add a new position to calculate Variance as Actual minus Budget. You can do this with a calculated item by using this code:

```
' Define calculated item along the product dimension
PT.PivotFields("Measure").CalculatedItems _
    .Add "Variance", "='Actual'-'Budget'"
```

12

Using `ShowDetail` to Filter a Record Set

When you double-click any number in any pivot table in the Excel user interface, Excel inserts a new sheet in the workbook and copies all the source records that represent that number. In the Excel user interface, this is a great way to perform a drill-down query into a data set.

The equivalent VBA property is `ShowDetail`. By setting this property to `True` for any cell in the pivot table, you generate a new worksheet with all the records that make up that cell:

```
PT.TableRange2.Offset(2, 1).Resize(1, 1).ShowDetail = True
```

Changing the Layout from the Design Tab

The Layout group on the Design tab contains four drop-downs that control the following:

- Location of subtotals (top or bottom)
- Presence of grand totals
- Report layout, including whether outer row labels are repeated
- Presence of blank rows

Subtotals can appear either at the top or at the bottom of a group of pivot items. The `SubtotalLocation` property applies to the entire pivot table; valid values are `xlAtBottom` or `xlAtTop`:

```
PT.SubtotalLocation:=xlAtTop
```

Grand totals can be turned on or off for rows or columns. Because these two settings can be confusing, remember that at the bottom of a report, there is a total line that most people would call the grand total row. To turn off that row, you have to use the following:

```
PT.ColumnGrand = False
```

You need to turn off `ColumnGrand` when you want to suppress the total row because Microsoft calls that row the "grand total for columns." Get it? In other words, Microsoft is saying that the row at the bottom contains the total of the columns above it. It is one of the more awkward phrases in the Excel ribbon. It confuses me every time.

To suppress what you would call the grand total column along the right side of the report, you have to suppress what Microsoft calls the "total for rows" by using the following code:

```
PT.RowGrand = False
```

Settings for the Report Layout

There are three settings for the report layout:

- **Tabular layout**—Similar to the default layout in Excel 2003
- **Outline layout**—Optionally available in Excel 2003
- **Compact layout**—Introduced in Excel 2007

When you create a pivot table in the Excel interface, you get the Compact layout. When you build a pivot table in VBA, you get the Tabular layout. You can change to one of the other layouts with one of these lines:

```
PT.RowAxisLayout xlTabularRow
PT.RowAxisLayout xlOutlineRow
PT.RowAxisLayout xlCompactRow
```

Starting in Excel 2007, you can add a blank line to the layout after each group of pivot items. Although the Design tab offers a single setting to affect the entire pivot table, the setting is actually applied individually to each pivot field. The macro recorder responds by recording a dozen lines of code for a pivot table with 12 fields. You can intelligently add a single line of code for the outer row fields:

```
PT.PivotFields("Region").LayoutBlankLine = True
```

Suppressing Subtotals for Multiple Row Fields

As soon as you have more than one row field, Excel automatically adds subtotals for all but the innermost row field. That extra row field can get in the way if you plan to reuse the results of the pivot table as a new data set for some other purpose. Although accomplishing this task manually can be relatively simple, the VBA code to suppress subtotals is surprisingly complex.

Most people do not realize that it is possible to show multiple types of subtotals. For example, you can choose to show Total, Average, Min, and Max in the same pivot table.

To suppress subtotals for a field, you must set the Subtotals property equal to an array of 12 False values. The first False turns off automatic subtotals, the second False turns off the Sum subtotal, the third False turns off the Count subtotal, and so on. This code suppresses the Region subtotal:

```
PT.PivotFields("Region").Subtotals = Array(False, False, False, False, _
    False, False, False, False, False, False, False, False)
```

A different technique is to turn on the first subtotal. This method automatically turns off the other 11 subtotals. You can then turn off the first subtotal to make sure that all subtotals are suppressed:

```
PT.PivotFields("Region").Subtotals(1) = True
PT.PivotFields("Region").Subtotals(1) = False
```

12

CASE STUDY APPLYING A DATA VISUALIZATION

Beginning with Excel 2007, fantastic data visualizations such as icon sets, color gradients, and in-cell data bars are offered. When you apply a visualization to a pivot table, you should exclude the total rows from the visualization.

If you have 20 customers that average $3 million in revenue each, the total for the 20 customers is $60 million. If you include the total in the data visualization, the total gets the largest bar, and all the customer records have tiny bars.

In the Excel user interface, you always want to use the Add Rule or Edit Rule choice to select the option All Cells Showing "Sum of Revenue" for "Customer."

The code to add a data bar to the Revenue field is as follows:

```
' Apply a Databar
PT.TableRange2.Cells(3, 2).Select
Selection.FormatConditions.AddDatabar
Selection.FormatConditions(1).ShowValue = True
Selection.FormatConditions(1).SetFirstPriority
With Selection.FormatConditions(1)
    .MinPoint.Modify newtype:=xlConditionValueLowestValue
    .MaxPoint.Modify newtype:=xlConditionValueHighestValue
End With
With Selection.FormatConditions(1).BarColor
    .ThemeColor = xlThemeColorAccent3
    .TintAndShade = -0.5
End With
Selection.FormatConditions(1).ScopeType = xlFieldsScope
```

Next Steps

You may be able to tell that pivot tables are my favorite feature in Excel. They are incredibly powerful and flexible. Combined with VBA, they provide an excellent calculation engine and power many of the reports I build for clients. Chapter 13, "Excel Power," offers multiple techniques for handling various tasks in VBA.

Excel Power

13

A major secret of successful programmers is to never waste time writing the same code twice. They all have little bits—or even big bits—of code that they use over and over again. Another big secret is to never take 8 hours doing something that can be done in 10 minutes—which is what this book is about!

This chapter contains programs donated by several Excel power programmers. These are programs they have found useful and that they hope will help you, too. Not only can these programs save you time, but they also can teach you new ways of solving common problems.

Different programmers have different programming styles, and we did not rewrite the submissions. As you review the code in this chapter, you will notice different ways of doing the same task, such as referring to ranges.

File Operations

The utilities shown in the following sections deal with handling files in folders. Being able to loop through a list of files in a folder is a useful task.

Listing Files in a Directory

This utility was submitted by our good friend Nathan P. Oliver of Minneapolis, Minnesota.

This program returns the filename, size, and date modified of all specified file types in the selected directory and its subfolders:

```
Sub ExcelFileSearch()
Dim srchExt As Variant, srchDir As Variant
Dim i As Long, j As Long, strName As String
Dim varArr(1 To 1048576, 1 To 3) As Variant
Dim strFileFullName As String
Dim ws As Worksheet
Dim fso As Object

Let srchExt = Application.InputBox("Please Enter File Extension", _
    "Info Request")
If srchExt = False And Not TypeName(srchExt) = "String" Then
    Exit Sub
End If

Let srchDir = BrowseForFolderShell
If srchDir = False And Not TypeName(srchDir) = "String" Then
    Exit Sub
End If

Application.ScreenUpdating = False

Set ws = ThisWorkbook.Worksheets.Add(Sheets(1))
On Error Resume Next
Application.DisplayAlerts = False
ThisWorkbook.Worksheets("FileSearch Results").Delete
Application.DisplayAlerts = True
On Error GoTo 0
ws.Name = "FileSearch Results"

Let strName = Dir$(srchDir & "\*" & srchExt)
Do While strName <> vbNullString
    Let i = i + 1
    Let strFileFullName = srchDir & strName
    Let varArr(i, 1) = strFileFullName
    Let varArr(i, 2) = FileLen(strFileFullName) \ 1024
    Let varArr(i, 3) = FileDateTime(strFileFullName)
    Let strName = Dir$()
Loop

Set fso = CreateObject("Scripting.FileSystemObject")
Call recurseSubFolders(fso.GetFolder(srchDir), varArr(), i, CStr(srchExt))
Set fso = Nothing

ThisWorkbook.Windows(1).DisplayHeadings = False
With ws
    If i > 0 Then
        .Range("A2").Resize(i, UBound(varArr, 2)).Value = varArr
        For j = 1 To i
            .Hyperlinks.Add anchor:=.Cells(j + 1, 1), Address:=varArr(j, 1)
        Next
    End If
    .Range(.Cells(1, 4), .Cells(1, .Columns.Count)).EntireColumn.Hidden = _
        True
    .Range(.Cells(.Rows.Count, 1).End(xlUp)(2), _
        .Cells(.Rows.Count, 1)).EntireRow.Hidden = True
    With .Range("A1:C1")
```

```
            .Value = Array("Full Name", "Kilobytes", "Last Modified")
            .Font.Underline = xlUnderlineStyleSingle
            .EntireColumn.AutoFit
            .HorizontalAlignment = xlCenter
        End With
    End With
Application.ScreenUpdating = True
End Sub


Private Sub recurseSubFolders(ByRef Folder As Object, _
    ByRef varArr() As Variant, _
    ByRef i As Long, _
    ByRef srchExt As String)
Dim SubFolder As Object
Dim strName As String, strFileFullName As String
For Each SubFolder In Folder.SubFolders
    Let strName = Dir$(SubFolder.Path & "\*" & srchExt)
    Do While strName <> vbNullString
        Let i = i + 1
        Let strFileFullName = SubFolder.Path & "\" & strName
        Let varArr(i, 1) = strFileFullName
        Let varArr(i, 2) = FileLen(strFileFullName) \ 1024
        Let varArr(i, 3) = FileDateTime(strFileFullName)
        Let strName = Dir$()
    Loop
    If i > 1048576 Then Exit Sub
    Call recurseSubFolders(SubFolder, varArr(), i, srchExt)
Next
End Sub


Private Function BrowseForFolderShell() As Variant
Dim objShell As Object, objFolder As Object
Set objShell = CreateObject("Shell.Application")
Set objFolder = objShell.BrowseForFolder(0, "Please select a folder", _
    0, "C:\")
If Not objFolder Is Nothing Then
    On Error Resume Next
    If IsError(objFolder.Items.Item.Path) Then
        BrowseForFolderShell = CStr(objFolder)
    Else
        On Error GoTo 0
        If Len(objFolder.Items.Item.Path) > 3 Then
            BrowseForFolderShell = objFolder.Items.Item.Path & _
            Application.PathSeparator
        Else
            BrowseForFolderShell = objFolder.Items.Item.Path
        End If
    End If
Else
    BrowseForFolderShell = False
End If
Set objFolder = Nothing: Set objShell = Nothing
End Function
```

13

Importing and Deleting a CSV File

This utility was submitted by Masaru Kaji of Kobe, Japan. Masaru is a computer systems administrator. He maintains an Excel VBA tip site, Cell Masters, at cellmasters.net/vbatips.htm.

If you find yourself importing a lot of comma-separated value (CSV) files and then having to go back and delete them, this program is for you. It quickly opens a CSV file in Excel and permanently deletes the original file:

```
Option Base 1

Sub OpenLargeCSVFast()
Dim buf(1 To 16384) As Variant
Dim i As Long
'Change the file location and name here
Const strFilePath As String = "C:\temp\Sales.CSV"

Dim strRenamedPath As String
strRenamedPath = Split(strFilePath, ".")(0) & "txt"

With Application
    .ScreenUpdating = False
    .DisplayAlerts = False
End With
'Setting an array for FieldInfo to open CSV
For i = 1 To 16384
    buf(i) = Array(i, 2)
Next
Name strFilePath As strRenamedPath
Workbooks.OpenText Filename:=strRenamedPath, DataType:=xlDelimited, _
    Comma:=True, FieldInfo:=buf
Erase buf
ActiveSheet.UsedRange.Copy ThisWorkbook.Sheets(1).Range("A1")
ActiveWorkbook.Close False
Kill strRenamedPath
With Application
    .ScreenUpdating = True
    .DisplayAlerts = True
End With
End Sub
```

Reading a Text File into Memory and Parsing

This utility was submitted by Rory Archibald, a reinsurance analyst residing in East Sussex, United Kingdom. A self-admitted geek by inclination, he also maintains the website ExcelMatters.com.

This utility takes a different approach to reading a text file than you might have used in the past. Instead of reading one record at a time, the macro loads the entire text file into memory in a single string variable. The macro then parses the string into individual records, all still in memory. It then places all the records on the sheet at one time (what I like to call "dumping" the data on the sheet). The advantage of this method is that you access the file on disk only one time. All subsequent processing occurs in memory and is very fast. Without further ado, here's the utility:

```
Sub LoadLinesFromCSV()
Dim sht                 As Worksheet
Dim strtxt              As String
Dim textArray()         As String

' Add new sheet for output
Set sht = Sheets.Add

' open the csv file
With CreateObject("Scripting.FileSystemObject") _
    .GetFile("c:\temp\sales.csv").OpenAsTextStream(1)
    'read the contents into a variable
    strtxt = .ReadAll
    ' close it!
    .Close
End With

'split the text into an array using carriage return and line feed
'separator
textArray = VBA.Split(strtxt, vbCrLf)

sht.Range("A1").Resize(UBound(textArray) + 1).Value = _
Application.Transpose(textArray)
End Sub
```

Combining and Separating Workbooks

The utilities in the following sections demonstrate how to combine worksheets into a single workbook or separate a single workbook into individual worksheets or export data on a sheet to an XML file.

Separating Worksheets into Workbooks

This utility was submitted by Tommy Miles of Houston, Texas.

This sample goes through the active workbook and saves each sheet as its own workbook in the same path as the original workbook. It names the new workbooks based on the sheet name, and it overwrites files without prompting. Notice that you need to choose whether you save the file as .xlsm (macro-enabled) or .xlsx (with macros stripped). In the following code, both lines are included—xlsm and xlsx—but the xlsx lines are commented out to make them inactive:

```
Sub SplitWorkbook()
Dim ws As Worksheet
Dim DisplayStatusBar As Boolean

DisplayStatusBar = Application.DisplayStatusBar
Application.DisplayStatusBar = True
Application.ScreenUpdating = False
Application.DisplayAlerts = False

For Each ws In ThisWorkbook.Sheets
    Dim NewFileName As String
    Application.StatusBar = ThisWorkbook.Sheets.Count & _
        " Remaining Sheets"
    If ThisWorkbook.Sheets.Count <> 1 Then
```

13

```
                NewFileName = ThisWorkbook.Path & "\" & ws.Name & ".xlsm" _
                    'Macro-Enabled
'                NewFileName = ThisWorkbook.Path & "\" & ws.Name & ".xlsx" _
                    'Not Macro-Enabled
                ws.Copy
                ActiveWorkbook.Sheets(1).Name = "Sheet1"
                ActiveWorkbook.SaveAs Filename:=NewFileName, _
                    FileFormat:=xlOpenXMLWorkbookMacroEnabled
'                ActiveWorkbook.SaveAs Filename:=NewFileName, _
                    FileFormat:=xlOpenXMLWorkbook
                ActiveWorkbook.Close SaveChanges:=False
            Else
                NewFileName = ThisWorkbook.Path & "\" & ws.Name & ".xlsm"
'                NewFileName = ThisWorkbook.Path & "\" & ws.Name & ".xlsx"
                ws.Name = "Sheet1"
        End If
    Next

    Application.DisplayAlerts = True
    Application.StatusBar = False
    Application.DisplayStatusBar = DisplayStatusBar
    Application.ScreenUpdating = True
    End Sub
```

Combining Workbooks

This utility was submitted by Tommy Miles.

This sample goes through all the Excel files in a specified directory and combines them into a single workbook. It renames the sheets based on the name of the original workbook:

```
Sub CombineWorkbooks()
Dim CurFile As String, DirLoc As String
Dim DestWB As Workbook
Dim ws As Object 'allows for different sheet types

DirLoc = ThisWorkbook.Path & "\tst\" 'location of files
CurFile = Dir(DirLoc & "*.xls*")

Application.ScreenUpdating = False
Application.EnableEvents = False

Set DestWB = Workbooks.Add(xlWorksheet)

Do While CurFile <> vbNullString
    Dim OrigWB As Workbook
    Set OrigWB = Workbooks.Open(Filename:=DirLoc & CurFile, _
        ReadOnly:=True)

    ' Limit to valid sheet names and removes .xls*
    CurFile = Left(Left(CurFile, Len(CurFile) - 5), 29)

    For Each ws In OrigWB.Sheets
        ws.Copy After:=DestWB.Sheets(DestWB.Sheets.Count)

        If OrigWB.Sheets.Count > 1 Then
            DestWB.Sheets(DestWB.Sheets.Count).Name = CurFile & ws.Index
        Else
```

```
                DestWB.Sheets(DestWB.Sheets.Count).Name = CurFile
            End If
        Next

        OrigWB.Close SaveChanges:=False
        CurFile = Dir
    Loop

    Application.DisplayAlerts = False
    DestWB.Sheets(1).Delete
    Application.DisplayAlerts = True

    Application.ScreenUpdating = True
    Application.EnableEvents = True

    Set DestWB = Nothing
End Sub
```

Filtering and Copying Data to Separate Worksheets

This utility was submitted by Dennis Wallentin of Ostersund, Sweden. Dennis provides
Excel tips and tricks at http://xldennis.wordpress.com.

This sample uses a specified column to filter data and copies the results to new worksheets
in the active workbook:

```
Sub Filter_NewSheet()
Dim wbBook As Workbook
Dim wsSheet As Worksheet
Dim rnStart As Range, rnData As Range
Dim i As Long

Set wbBook = ThisWorkbook
Set wsSheet = wbBook.Worksheets("Sheet1")

With wsSheet
    'Make sure that the first row contains headings.
    Set rnStart = .Range("A2")
    Set rnData = .Range(.Range("A2"), .Cells(.Rows.Count, 3).End(xlUp))
End With

Application.ScreenUpdating = True

For i = 1 To 5
    'Here we filter the data with the first criterion.
    rnStart.AutoFilter Field:=1, Criteria1:="AA" & i
    'Copy the filtered list
    rnData.SpecialCells(xlCellTypeVisible).Copy
    'Add a new worksheet to the active workbook.
    Worksheets.Add Before:=wsSheet
    'Name the added new worksheets.
    ActiveSheet.Name = "AA" & i
    'Paste the filtered list.
    Range("A2").PasteSpecial xlPasteValues
Next i

'Reset the list to its original status.
```

13

```
rnStart.AutoFilter Field:=1

With Application
    'Reset the clipboard.
    .CutCopyMode = False
    .ScreenUpdating = False
End With
End Sub
```

Copying Data to Separate Worksheets Without Using Filter

This utility was submitted by Zack Barresse from Boardman, Oregon. Zack is an Excel ninja and VBA nut, and he's a former firefighter and paramedic who owns/operates exceltables.com and wrote *Excel Tables: A Complete Guide for Creating, Using, and Automating Lists and Tables* (Holy Macro! Books, 2014) with Kevin Jones.

The previous example uses Filter to get the desired records. Although that method works great in many cases, if you are dealing with a lot of data or have formulas in the data set, it can take a while to run. Instead of using Filter, consider using a formula to mark the desired records and then sort by that column to group the desired records together. Combine this with `SpecialCells`, and you could have a procedure that runs up to 10 times faster than the code using Filter. Here's how it looks:

```
Sub CriteriaRange_Copy()
Dim Table As ListObject
Dim SortColumn As ListColumn
Dim CriteriaColumn As ListColumn
Dim FoundRange As Range
Dim TargetSheet As Worksheet
Dim HeaderVisible As Boolean

Set Table = ActiveSheet.ListObjects(1) ' Set as desired
HeaderVisible = Table.ShowHeaders
Table.ShowHeaders = True

On Error GoTo RemoveColumns
Set SortColumn = Table.ListColumns.Add(Table.ListColumns.Count + 1)
Set CriteriaColumn = Table.ListColumns.Add _
    (Table.ListColumns.Count + 1)
On Error GoTo 0

'Add a column to keep track of the original order of the records
SortColumn.Name = " Sort"
CriteriaColumn.Name = " Criteria"
SortColumn.DataBodyRange.Formula = "=ROW(A1)"
SortColumn.DataBodyRange.Value = SortColumn.DataBodyRange.Value

'add the formula to mark the desired records
'the records not wanted will have errors
CriteriaColumn.DataBodyRange.Formula = "=1/(([@Units]<10)*([@Cost]<5))"
CriteriaColumn.DataBodyRange.Value = CriteriaColumn.DataBodyRange.Value

Table.Range.Sort Key1:=CriteriaColumn.Range(1, 1), _
    Order1:=xlAscending, Header:=xlYes
On Error Resume Next
```

```
    Set FoundRange = Intersect(Table.Range, CriteriaColumn.DataBodyRange. _
        SpecialCells(xlCellTypeConstants, xlNumbers).EntireRow)
    On Error GoTo 0

    If Not FoundRange Is Nothing Then
        Set TargetSheet = ThisWorkbook.Worksheets.Add(After:=ActiveSheet)
        FoundRange(1, 1).Offset(-1, 0).Resize(FoundRange.Rows.Count + 1, _
            FoundRange.Columns.Count - 2).Copy
        TargetSheet.Range("A1").PasteSpecial xlPasteValuesAndNumberFormats
        Application.CutCopyMode = False
    End If
    Table.Range.Sort Key1:=SortColumn.Range(1, 1), Order1:=xlAscending, _
        Header:=xlYes

RemoveColumns:
    If Not SortColumn Is Nothing Then SortColumn.Delete
    If Not CriteriaColumn Is Nothing Then CriteriaColumn.Delete
    Table.ShowHeaders = HeaderVisible
End Sub
```

Exporting Data to an XML File

This utility was submitted by Livio Lanzo. Livio is currently working as a business analyst in finance in Luxembourg. His main task is to develop Excel/Access tools for a bank. Livio is also active on the MrExcel.com forums under the handle VBA Geek.

This program exports the data from a table to an XML file. It uses early binding, so a reference must be established in the VB Editor using Tools, References to the Microsoft XML, v6.0 library:

```
    Const ROOT_ELEMENT_NAME = "SAMPLEDATA"
    Const GROUPS_NAME = "EMPLOYEES"
    Const XML_EXPORT_PATH = "C:\temp\myXMLFile.xml"

    Sub CreateXML()
    Dim xml_DOM As MSXML2.DOMDocument60
    Dim xml_El  As MSXML2.IXMLDOMElement
    Dim xRow    As Long
    Dim xCol    As Long
    Set xml_DOM = CreateObject("MSXML2.DOMDocument.6.0")
    xml_DOM.appendChild xml_DOM.createElement(ROOT_ELEMENT_NAME)
    With Sheet1.ListObjects("TableEmployees")
        For xRow = 1 To .ListRows.Count
            CREATE_APPEND_ELEMENT xml_DOM, ROOT_ELEMENT_NAME, GROUPS_NAME, _
                0, NODE_ELEMENT
            For xCol = 1 To .ListColumns.Count
                CREATE_APPEND_ELEMENT xml_DOM, GROUPS_NAME, _
                    .HeaderRowRange(1, xCol).Text, (xRow - 1), NODE_ELEMENT
                CREATE_APPEND_ELEMENT xml_DOM, .HeaderRowRange(1, xCol).Text, _
                    .DataBodyRange(xRow, xCol).Text, (xRow - 1), NODE_TEXT
            Next xCol
        Next xRow
    End With
    xml_DOM.Save XML_EXPORT_PATH
    MsgBox "File Created: " & XML_EXPORT_PATH, vbInformation
    End Sub
```

13

```
Private Sub CREATE_APPEND_ELEMENT(xmlDOM As MSXML2.DOMDocument60, _
                                  ParentElName As String, _
                                  NewElName As String, _
                                  ParentElIndex As Long, _
                                  ELType As MSXML2.tagDOMNodeType)
Dim xml_ELEMENT As Object
If ELType = NODE_ELEMENT Then
    Set xml_ELEMENT = xmlDOM.createElement(NewElName)
ElseIf ELType = NODE_TEXT Then
    Set xml_ELEMENT = xmlDOM.createTextNode(NewElName)
End If
xmlDOM.getElementsByTagName(ParentElName)(ParentElIndex).appendChild _
    xml_ELEMENT
End Sub
```

Working with Cell Comments

Cell comments are an often-underused feature in Excel. The following two utilities help you get the most out of cell comments.

Resizing Comments

This utility was submitted by Tom Urtis of San Francisco, California. Tom is the principal owner of Atlas Programming Management, an Excel consulting firm in the Bay Area.

Excel doesn't automatically resize cell comments. In addition, if you have several of them on a sheet, as shown in Figure 13.1, resizing them one at a time can be a hassle. The following utility resizes all the comment boxes on a sheet so that, when selected, the entire comment is easily viewable, as shown in Figure 13.2:

Figure 13.1
By default, Excel doesn't size the comment boxes to show all the entered text.

Figure 13.2
Resize the comment boxes to fit all the text.

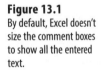

```
Sub CommentFitter()
Application.ScreenUpdating = False
Dim x As Range, y As Long

For Each x In Cells.SpecialCells(xlCellTypeComments)
    Select Case True
        Case Len(x.NoteText) <> 0
            With x.Comment
                .Shape.TextFrame.AutoSize = True
            If .Shape.Width > 250 Then
                y = .Shape.Width * .Shape.Height
                .Shape.Width = 150
                .Shape.Height = (y / 200) * 1.3
            End If
        End With
    End Select
Next x
Application.ScreenUpdating = True
End Sub
```

Placing a Chart in a Comment

This is another utility submitted by Tom Urtis.

A live chart cannot exist in a shape, but you can take a picture of a chart and load it into the comment shape, as shown in Figure 13.3.

Figure 13.3
Place a chart in a cell comment.

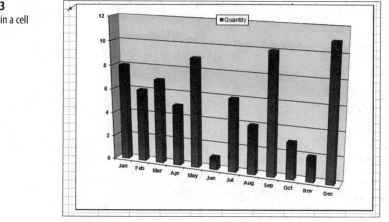

These are the steps to do this manually:

1. Create and save the picture image you want the comment to display.

2. If you have not already done so, create the comment and select the cell in which the comment is located.

3. From the Review tab, select Edit Comment or right-click the cell and select Edit Comment.

13

4. Right-click the comment border and select Format Comment.

5. Select the Colors and Lines tab and click the down arrow belonging to the Color field of the Fill section.

6. Select Fill Effects, select the Picture tab, and then click the Select Picture button.

7. Navigate to your desired image, select the image, and click OK twice.

The effect of having a "live chart" in a comment can be achieved if, for example, the code is part of a SheetChange event when the chart's source data is being changed. In addition, business charts are updated often, so you might want a macro to keep the comment updated and to avoid repeating the same steps.

The following utility does just that—and you can use it by simply modifying the file pathname, chart name, destination sheet, cell, and size of comment shape, depending on the size of the chart:

```
Sub PlaceGraph()
Dim x As String, z As Range

Application.ScreenUpdating = False

'assign a temporary location to hold the image
x = "C:\temp\XWMJGraph.gif"

'assign the cell to hold the comment
Set z = Worksheets("ChartInComment").Range("A3")

'delete any existing comment in the cell
On Error Resume Next
z.Comment.Delete
On Error GoTo 0

'select and export the chart
ActiveSheet.ChartObjects("Chart 1").Activate
ActiveChart.Export x

'add a new comment to the cell, set the size and insert the chart
With z.AddComment
    With .Shape
        .Height = 322
        .Width = 465
        .Fill.UserPicture x
    End With
End With

'delete the temporary image
Kill x

Range("A1").Activate
Application.ScreenUpdating = True

Set z = Nothing
End Sub
```

Selecting Cells

Selecting cells is a vital part of Excel, but the tools to help the user in this process are limited. The following sections include two ways you can help users more easily locate the selected cell by also highlighting the row and column. Also included is a method to help make noncontiguous cell selection a little less frustrating, especially when you select the wrong cell. Finally, you'll find an example of using the Change event to create a hidden log file of user changes.

Using Conditional Formatting to Highlight the Selected Cell

This utility was submitted by Ivan F. Moala of Auckland, New Zealand. Ivan is the site author of The XcelFiles (excelplaza.com/ep_ivan/default.php), where you can find out how to do things you thought you could not do in Excel.

In this utility, conditional formatting is used to highlight the row and column of the active cell to help you visually locate it, as shown in Figure 13.4:

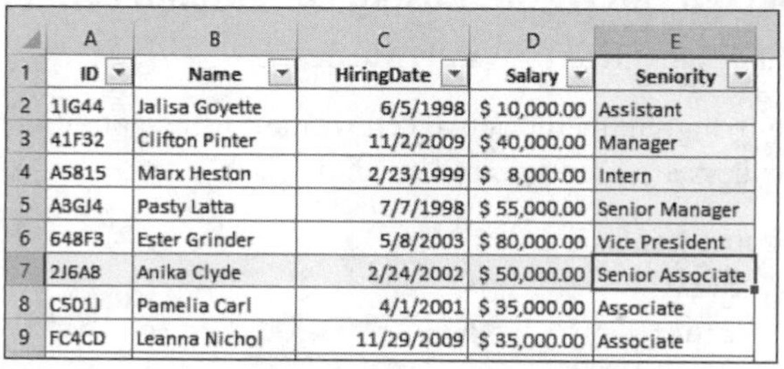

Figure 13.4
Use conditional formatting to highlight the row and column of the selected cell in a table.

	A	B	C	D	E
1	ID	Name	HiringDate	Salary	Seniority
2	1IG44	Jalisa Goyette	6/5/1998	$ 10,000.00	Assistant
3	41F32	Clifton Pinter	11/2/2009	$ 40,000.00	Manager
4	A5815	Marx Heston	2/23/1999	$ 8,000.00	Intern
5	A3GJ4	Pasty Latta	7/7/1998	$ 55,000.00	Senior Manager
6	648F3	Ester Grinder	5/8/2003	$ 80,000.00	Vice President
7	2J6A8	Anika Clyde	2/24/2002	$ 50,000.00	Senior Associate
8	C501J	Pamelia Carl	4/1/2001	$ 35,000.00	Associate
9	FC4CD	Leanna Nichol	11/29/2009	$ 35,000.00	Associate

> **NOTE** Do *not* use this method if you already have conditional formats on the worksheet. Any existing conditional formats will be overwritten. In addition, this program clears the Clipboard. Therefore, it is not possible to use this method while doing copy, cut, or paste.

```
Const iInternational As Integer = Not (0)

Private Sub Worksheet_SelectionChange(ByVal Target As Range)
Dim iColor As Integer
'// On error resume in case
'// user selects a range of cells
On Error Resume Next
iColor = Target.Interior.ColorIndex
'// Leave On Error ON for Row offset errors

If iColor < 0 Then
    iColor = 36
Else
    iColor = iColor + 1
End If

'// Need this test in case font color is the same
```

```
If iColor = Target.Font.ColorIndex Then iColor = iColor + 1

Cells.FormatConditions.Delete

'// Horizontal color banding
With Range("A" & Target.Row, Target.Address) 'Rows(Target.Row)
    .FormatConditions.Add Type:=2, Formula1:=iInternational 'Or just 1
        '"TRUE"
    .FormatConditions(1).Interior.ColorIndex = iColor
End With

'// Vertical color banding
With Range(Target.Offset(1 - Target.Row, 0).Address & ":" & _
    Target.Offset(-1, 0).Address)
    .FormatConditions.Add Type:=2, Formula1:=iInternational 'Or just 1
        '"TRUE"
    .FormatConditions(1).Interior.ColorIndex = iColor
End With

End Sub
```

Highlighting the Selected Cell Without Using Conditional Formatting

Here is another utility submitted by Ivan F. Moala.

This example visually highlights the active cell without using conditional formatting when the keyboard arrow keys are used to move around the sheet.

Place the following in a standard module:

```
Dim strCol As String
Dim iCol As Integer
Dim dblRow As Double

Sub HighlightRight()
    HighLight 0, 1
End Sub

Sub HighlightLeft()
    HighLight 0, -1
End Sub

Sub HighlightUp()
    HighLight -1, 0, -1
End Sub

Sub HighlightDown()
    HighLight 1, 0, 1
End Sub

Sub HighLight(dblxRow As Double, iyCol As Integer, _
    Optional dblZ As Double = 0)
On Error GoTo NoGo
strCol = Mid(ActiveCell.Offset(dblxRow, iyCol).Address, _
        InStr(ActiveCell.Offset(dblxRow, iyCol).Address, "$") + 1, _
        InStr(2, ActiveCell.Offset(dblxRow, iyCol).Address, "$") - 2)
iCol = ActiveCell.Column
dblRow = ActiveCell.Row
```

```
    Application.ScreenUpdating = False

With Range(strCol & ":" & strCol & "," & dblRow + dblZ & ":" & _
    dblRow + dblZ)
        .Select
        Application.ScreenUpdating = True
        .Item(dblRow + dblxRow).Activate
End With

NoGo:
End Sub

Sub ReSet() 'manual reset
    Application.OnKey "{RIGHT}"
    Application.OnKey "{LEFT}"
    Application.OnKey "{UP}"
    Application.OnKey "{DOWN}"
End Sub
```

Place the following in the `ThisWorkbook` module:

```
Private Sub Workbook_Open()
    Application.OnKey "{RIGHT}", "HighlightRight"
    Application.OnKey "{LEFT}", "HighlightLeft"
    Application.OnKey "{UP}", "HighlightUp"
    Application.OnKey "{DOWN}", "HighlightDown"
    Application.OnKey "{DEL}", "DisableDelete"
End Sub

Private Sub Workbook_BeforeClose(Cancel As Boolean)
    Application.OnKey "{RIGHT}"
    Application.OnKey "{LEFT}"
    Application.OnKey "{UP}"
    Application.OnKey "{DOWN}"
    Application.OnKey "{DEL}"
End Sub
```

Selecting/Deselecting Noncontiguous Cells

This is another utility submitted by Tom Urtis.

Ordinarily, to deselect a single cell or range on a sheet, you must click an unselected cell to deselect all cells and then start over by reselecting all the correct cells. This is inconvenient if you need to reselect a lot of noncontiguous cells.

This utility adds two new options to the context menu of a selection: Deselect ActiveCell and Deselect ActiveArea. With the noncontiguous cells selected, hold down the Ctrl key, click the cell you want to deselect to make it active, release the Ctrl key, and then right-click the cell you want to deselect. The context menu shown in Figure 13.5 appears. Click the menu item that deselects either that one active cell or the contiguously selected area of which it is a part.

13

Figure 13.5
The `ModifyRightClick` procedure provides a custom context menu for deselecting noncontiguous cells.

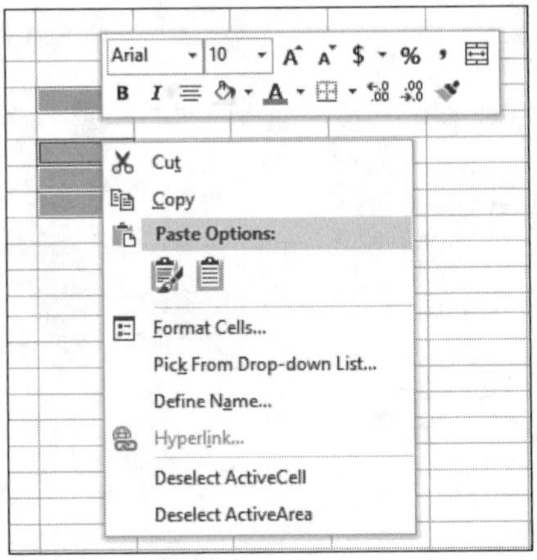

Enter the following procedures in a standard module:

```
Sub ModifyRightClick()
'add the new options to the right-click menu
Dim O1 As Object, O2 As Object

'delete the options if they exist already
On Error Resume Next
With CommandBars("Cell")
    .Controls("Deselect ActiveCell").Delete
    .Controls("Deselect ActiveArea").Delete
End With
On Error GoTo 0

'add the new options
Set O1 = CommandBars("Cell").Controls.Add

With O1
    .Caption = "Deselect ActiveCell"
    .OnAction = "DeselectActiveCell"
End With

Set O2 = CommandBars("Cell").Controls.Add

With O2
    .Caption = "Deselect ActiveArea"
    .OnAction = "DeselectActiveArea"
End With
End Sub

Sub DeselectActiveCell()
Dim x As Range, y As Range

If Selection.Cells.Count > 1 Then
    For Each y In Selection.Cells
        If y.Address <> ActiveCell.Address Then
            If x Is Nothing Then
                Set x = y
            Else
```

```
                Set x = Application.Union(x, y)
            End If
        End If
    Next y
    If x.Cells.Count > 0 Then
        x.Select
    End If
End If
End Sub

Sub DeselectActiveArea()
Dim x As Range, y As Range

If Selection.Areas.Count > 1 Then
    For Each y In Selection.Areas
        If Application.Intersect(ActiveCell, y) Is Nothing Then
            If x Is Nothing Then
                Set x = y
            Else
                Set x = Application.Union(x, y)
            End If
        End If
    Next y
    x.Select
End If
End Sub
```

Add the following procedures to the ThisWorkbook module:

```
Private Sub Workbook_Activate()
ModifyRightClick
End Sub

Private Sub Workbook_Deactivate()
Application.CommandBars("Cell").Reset
End Sub
```

Creating a Hidden Log File

This utility was submitted by Chris "Smitty" Smith of Crested Butte, Colorado. Smitty is a professional Office developer, leveraging past corporate experience across a host of different corporate clientele. When he's not busy at work, he is an avid rock and ice climber and occasional mountaineer.

The Change event is a code solution posted often at Excel forums, primarily because it fills a void that formulas alone can't manage (for example, inserting a date and time stamp when a user changes a specific range.). This utility takes advantage of the Change event in order to create a log file that tracks the cell address, new value, date, time, and username for changes made to column A of the sheet in which the code is placed:

```
Private Sub Worksheet_Change(ByVal Target As Range)
'Code goes in the Worksheet specific module
Dim ws As Worksheet
Dim lr As Long
Dim rng As Range
'Set the Destination worksheet
```

13

```
Set ws = Sheets("Log Sheet")
'Get the first unused row on the Log sheet
lr = ws.Cells(Rows.Count, "A").End(xlUp).Row
'Set Target Range, i.e. Range("A1, B2, C3"), or Range("A1:B3")
Set rng = Target.Parent.Range("A:A")
'Only look at single cell changes
If Target.Count > 1 Then Exit Sub
'Only look at that range
If Intersect(Target, rng) Is Nothing Then Exit Sub
'Action if Condition(s) are met (do your thing here...)
'Put the Target cell's Address in Column A
ws.Cells(lr + 1, "A").Value = Target.Address
'Put the Target cell's value in Column B
ws.Cells(lr + 1, "B").Value = Target.Value
'Put the Date in Column C
ws.Cells(lr + 1, "C").Value = Date
'Put the Time in Column D
ws.Cells(lr + 1, "D").Value = Format(Now, "HH:MM:SS AM/PM")
'Put the Date in Column E
ws.Cells(lr + 1, "E").Value = Environ("UserName")
End Sub
```

Techniques for VBA Pros

The utilities provided in the following sections amaze me. In the various message board communities on the Internet, VBA programmers are constantly coming up with new ways to do things faster and better. When someone posts some new code that obviously runs circles around the prior generally accepted best code, everyone benefits.

Creating an Excel State Class Module

This utility was submitted by Juan Pablo Gonzàlez Ruiz of Bogotà, Colombia. Juan Pablo is an Excel consultant who runs his photography business at www.juanpg.com.

The following class module is one of my favorites, and I use it in almost every project I create. Before Juan shared the module with me, I used to enter the four lines of code to turn off and back on screen updating, events, alerts, and calculations. At the beginning of a sub I would turn them off, and at the end I would turn them back on. That was quite a bit of typing. Now I just place the class module in a new workbook I create and call it as needed.

Insert a class module named CAppState and place the following code in it:

```
Private m_su As Boolean
Private m_ee As Boolean
Private m_da As Boolean
Private m_calc As Long
Private m_cursor As Long

Private m_except As StateEnum

Public Enum StateEnum
    None = 0
    ScreenUpdating = 1
    EnableEvents = 2
```

```vba
        DisplayAlerts = 4
        Calculation = 8
        Cursor = 16
End Enum

Public Sub SetState(Optional ByVal except As StateEnum = StateEnum.None)
        m_except = except
With Application
    If Not m_except And StateEnum.ScreenUpdating Then
        .ScreenUpdating = False
    End If

    If Not m_except And StateEnum.EnableEvents Then
      .EnableEvents = False
    End If

    If Not m_except And StateEnum.DisplayAlerts Then
        .DisplayAlerts = False
    End If

    If Not m_except And StateEnum.Calculation Then
        .Calculation = xlCalculationManual
    End If

    If Not m_except And StateEnum.Cursor Then
        .Cursor = xlWait
    End If
End With
End Sub

Private Sub Class_Initialize()
With Application
    m_su = .ScreenUpdating
    m_ee = .EnableEvents
    m_da = .DisplayAlerts
    m_calc = .Calculation
    m_cursor = .Cursor
End With
End Sub

Private Sub Class_Terminate()
With Application
    If Not m_except And StateEnum.ScreenUpdating Then
        .ScreenUpdating = m_su
    End If

    If Not m_except And StateEnum.EnableEvents Then
        .EnableEvents = m_ee
    End If

    If Not m_except And StateEnum.DisplayAlerts Then
        .DisplayAlerts = m_da
    End If

    If Not m_except And StateEnum.Calculation Then
        .Calculation = m_calc
    End If
```

13

```
        If Not m_except And StateEnum.Cursor Then
            .Cursor = m_cursor
        End If
    End With
End Sub
```

The following code is an example of calling the class module to turn off the various states, running your code, and then setting the states back:

```
Sub RunFasterCode
Dim appState As CAppState
Set appState = New CAppState
appState.SetState None
'run your code
'if you have any formulas that need to update, use
'Application.Calculate
'to force the workbook to calculate
Set appState = Nothing
End Sub
```

Drilling-Down a Pivot Table

This is yet another utility submitted by Tom Urtis.

When you are double-clicking the data section, a pivot table's default behavior is to insert a new worksheet and display that drill-down information on the new sheet. This utility serves as an option for convenience, to keep the drilled-down record sets on the same sheet as the pivot table (see Figure 13.6) so that you can delete them as you want.

Figure 13.6
Show the drill-down record set on the same sheet as the pivot table.

27	⊟Zelda	Q4		86	1803	5037	
28	Zelda Total			86	1803	5037	
29	Grand Total			48780	20396	38672	11738
30							
31	**Name**	**Region**	**Quarter**	**Item**	**Color**	**Sales**	
32	Jim	East	Q3	Hats	Black	4525	
33	Jim	South	Q3	Hats	Yellow	1941	
34	Jim	South	Q3	Hats	Yellow	7400	
35	Jim	West	Q3	Hats	Red	191	
36							

To use this macro, double-click the data section or the totals section to create stacked drill-down record sets in the next available row of the sheet. To delete any drill-down record sets you have created, double-click anywhere in their respective current region.

Here's the utility:

```
Private Sub Worksheet_BeforeDoubleClick(ByVal Target As Range, _
    Cancel As Boolean)
Application.ScreenUpdating = False
Dim LPTR&

With ActiveSheet.PivotTables(1).DataBodyRange
    LPTR = .Rows.Count + .Row - 1
End With

Dim PTT As Integer
On Error Resume Next
```

```
        PTT = Target.PivotCell.PivotCellType
    If Err.Number = 1004 Then
        Err.Clear
        If Not IsEmpty(Target) Then
            If Target.Row > Range("A1").CurrentRegion.Rows.Count + 1 Then
                Cancel = True
                With Target.CurrentRegion
                    .Resize(.Rows.Count + 1).EntireRow.Delete
                End With
            End If
        Else
            Cancel = True
        End If
    Else
        CS = ActiveSheet.Name
    End If
    Application.ScreenUpdating = True
    End Sub
```

Filtering an OLAP Pivot Table by a List of Items

This utility was submitted by Jerry Sullivan of San Diego, California. Jerry is an operations manager for exp (www.exp.com), a building engineering consulting firm.

This procedure filters an OLAP pivot table to show items in a separate list, whether or not an item in that list has a matching record.

The code converts user-friendly items into MDX member references—for example, from "banana" to "[tblSales].[product_name].&[banana]"]":

```
Sub FilterOLAP_PT()
'example showing call to function sOLAP_FilterByItemList

Dim pvt As PivotTable
Dim sErrMsg As String, sTemplate As String
Dim vItemsToBeVisible As Variant

On Error GoTo ErrProc
With Application
    .EnableCancelKey = xlErrorHandler
    .ScreenUpdating = False
    .DisplayStatusBar = False
    .EnableEvents = False
End With

'read filter items from worksheet table
vItemsToBeVisible = Application.Transpose( _
        wksPivots.ListObjects("tblVisibleItemsList").DataBodyRange.Value)

Set pvt = wksPivots.PivotTables("PivotTable1")
'call function
sErrMsg = sOLAP_FilterByItemList( _
    pvf:=pvt.PivotFields("[tblSales].[product_name].[product_name]"), _
    vItemsToBeVisible:=vItemsToBeVisible, _
    sItemPattern:="[tblSales].[product_name].&[ThisItem]")

ExitProc:
```

```
On Error Resume Next
With Application
    .EnableEvents = True
    .DisplayStatusBar = True
    .ScreenUpdating = True
End With
If Len(sErrMsg) > 0 Then MsgBox sErrMsg
Exit Sub


ErrProc:
sErrMsg = Err.Number & " - " & Err.Description
Resume ExitProc
End Sub


Private Function sOLAP_FilterByItemList(ByVal pvf As PivotField, _
    ByVal vItemsToBeVisible As Variant, _
    ByVal sItemPattern As String) As String

'filters an OLAP pivot table to display a list of items,
'    where some of the items might not exist
'works by testing whether each pivotitem exists, then building an
'    array of existing items to be used with the VisibleItemsList
' property

'Input Parameters:
'pvf - pivotfield object to be filtered
'vItemsToBeVisible - 1-D array of strings representing items to be
' visible
'sItemPattern - string that has MDX pattern of pivotItem reference
'                where the text "ThisItem" will be replaced by each
'                item in vItemsToBeVisible to make pivotItem references.
'                e.g.: "[tblSales].[product_name].&[ThisItem]"

Dim lFilterItemCount As Long, lNdx As Long
Dim vFilterArray As Variant
Dim vSaveVisibleItemsList As Variant
Dim sReturnMsg As String, sPivotItemName As String

'store existing visible items
vSaveVisibleItemsList = pvf.VisibleItemsList

If Not (IsArray(vItemsToBeVisible)) Then _
    vItemsToBeVisible = Array(vItemsToBeVisible)
ReDim vFilterArray(1 To _
    UBound(vItemsToBeVisible) - LBound(vItemsToBeVisible) + 1)
pvf.Parent.ManualUpdate = True

'check if pivotitem exists then build array of items that exist
For lNdx = LBound(vItemsToBeVisible) To UBound(vItemsToBeVisible)
    'create MDX format pivotItem reference by substituting item into
    'pattern
    sPivotItemName = Replace(sItemPattern, "ThisItem", _
                            vItemsToBeVisible(lNdx))

    'attempt to make specified item the only visible item
    On Error Resume Next
    pvf.VisibleItemsList = Array(sPivotItemName)
    On Error GoTo 0
```

```
        'if item doesn't exist in field, this will be false
        If LCase$(sPivotItemName) = LCase$(pvf.VisibleItemsList(1)) Then
            lFilterItemCount = lFilterItemCount + 1
            vFilterArray(lFilterItemCount) = sPivotItemName
        End If
    Next lNdx

    'if at least one existing item found, filter pivot using array
    If lFilterItemCount > 0 Then
        ReDim Preserve vFilterArray(1 To lFilterItemCount)
        pvf.VisibleItemsList = vFilterArray
    Else
        sReturnMsg = "No matching items found."
        pvf.VisibleItemsList = vSaveVisibleItemsList
    End If
    pvf.Parent.ManualUpdate = False

    sOLAP_FilterByItemList = sReturnMsg
End Function
```

Creating a Custom Sort Order

This utility was submitted by Wei Jiang of Wuhan City, China. Jiang is a consultant for MrExcel.com.

By default, Excel enables you to sort lists numerically or alphabetically, but sometimes that is not what is needed. For example, a client might need each day's sales data sorted by the default division order of belts, handbags, watches, wallets, and everything else. Although you can manually set up a custom series and sort using it, if you're creating an automated workbook for other users, that might not be an option. This utility uses a custom sort order list to sort a range of data into default division order and then deletes the custom sort order, and Figure 13.7 shows the results:

Figure 13.7

When you use the macro, the list in A:C is sorted first by date and then by the custom sort list in Column I.

Date	Category	# sold				
1/1/2015	Belts	15				Belts
1/1/2015	Handbags	23				Handbags
1/1/2015	Watches	42				Watches
1/1/2015	Wallets	17				Wallets
1/1/2015	Everything Else	36				Everything Else
1/2/2015	Belts	17				
1/2/2015	Handbags	21				

13

```
Sub CustomSort()
' add the custom list to Custom Lists
Application.AddCustomList ListArray:=Range("I1:I5")

' get the list number
nIndex = Application.GetCustomListNum(Range("I1:I5").Value)

' Now, we could sort a range with the custom list.
' Note, we should use nIndex + 1 as the custom list number here,
' for the first one is Normal order
```

```
Range("A2:C16").Sort Key1:=Range("B2"), Order1:=xlAscending, _
    Header:=xlNo, Orientation:=xlSortColumns, _
    OrderCustom:=nIndex + 1
Range("A2:C16").Sort Key1:=Range("A2"), Order1:=xlAscending, _
    Header:=xlNo, Orientation:=xlSortColumns

' At the end, we should remove this custom list...
Application.DeleteCustomList nIndex
End Sub
```

Creating a Cell Progress Indicator

Here is another utility submitted by the prolific Tom Urtis.

I have to admit, the conditional formatting options in Excel, such as data bars, are fantastic. However, there still isn't an option for a visual like the examples shown in Figure 13.8. The following utility builds a progress indicator in column C, based on entries in columns A and B:

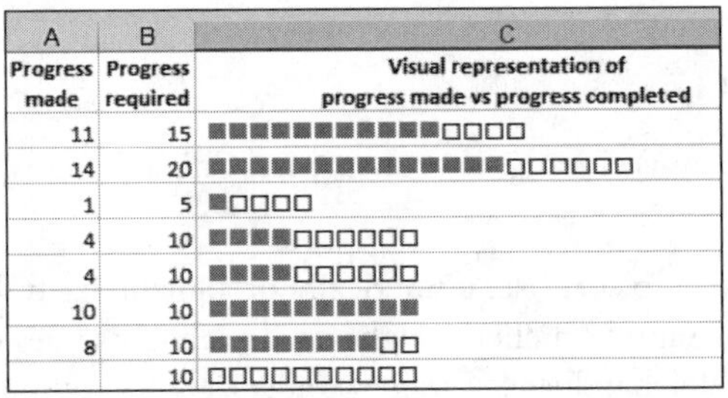

A	B	C
Progress made	Progress required	Visual representation of progress made vs progress completed
11	15	■■■■■■■■■■■□□□□
14	20	■■■■■■■■■■■■■■□□□□□□
1	5	■□□□□
4	10	■■■■□□□□□□
4	10	■■■■□□□□□□
10	10	■■■■■■■■■■
8	10	■■■■■■■■□□
	10	□□□□□□□□□□

Figure 13.8
Use indicators in cells to show progress.

```
Private Sub Worksheet_Change(ByVal Target As Range)
If Target.Column > 2 Or Target.Cells.Count > 1 Then Exit Sub
If Application.IsNumber(Target.Value) = False Then
    Application.EnableEvents = False
    Application.Undo
    Application.EnableEvents = True
    MsgBox "Numbers only please."
    Exit Sub
End If
Select Case Target.Column
    Case 1
        If Target.Value > Target.Offset(0, 1).Value Then
            Application.EnableEvents = False
            Application.Undo
            Application.EnableEvents = True
            MsgBox "Value in column A may not be larger than value " & _
                "in column B."
            Exit Sub
        End If
    Case 2
        If Target.Value < Target.Offset(0, -1).Value Then
            Application.EnableEvents = False
            Application.Undo
            Application.EnableEvents = True
            MsgBox "Value in column B may not be smaller " & _
```

```
                              "than value in column A."
                    Exit Sub
              End If
       End Select
       Dim x As Long
       x = Target.Row
       Dim z As String
       z = Range("B" & x).Value - Range("A" & x).Value
       With Range("C" & x)
            .Formula = "=IF(RC[-1]<=RC[-2],REPT(""n"",RC[-1])&" & _
                "REPT(""n"",RC[-2]-RC[-1]),REPT(""n"",RC[-2])&" & _
                "REPT(""o"",RC[-1]-RC[-2]))"
            .Value = .Value
            .Font.Name = "Wingdings"
            .Font.ColorIndex = 1
            .Font.Size = 10
            If Len(Range("A" & x)) <> 0 Then
                .Characters(1, (.Characters.Count - z)).Font.ColorIndex = 3
                .Characters(1, (.Characters.Count - z)).Font.Size = 12
            End If
       End With
       End Sub
```

Using a Protected Password Box

This utility was submitted by Daniel Klann of Sydney, Australia. Daniel works mainly with VBA in Excel and Access but dabbles in all sorts of languages.

Using an input box for password protection has a major security flaw: The characters being entered are easily viewable. This program changes the characters to asterisks as they are entered—just like a real password field (see Figure 13.9). Note that the code that follows does not work in 64-bit Excel. Refer to Chapter 23, "The Windows Application Programming Interface (API)," for information on modifying the code for 64-bit Excel.

Figure 13.9
Use an input box as a secure password field.

Password Required	✕
Please enter password	OK
	Cancel
************	

Here is the utility:

```
Private Declare Function CallNextHookEx Lib "user32" _
(ByVal hHook As Long, _
ByVal ncode As Long, ByVal wParam As Long, lParam As Any) As Long

Private Declare Function GetModuleHandle Lib "kernel32" _
    Alias "GetModuleHandleA" (ByVal lpModuleName As String) As Long

Private Declare Function SetWindowsHookEx Lib "user32" _
    Alias "SetWindowsHookExA" _
```

```
    (ByVal idHook As Long, ByVal lpfn As Long, _
    ByVal hmod As Long,ByVal dwThreadId As Long) As Long

Private Declare Function UnhookWindowsHookEx Lib "user32" _
    (ByVal hHook As Long) As Long

Private Declare Function SendDlgItemMessage Lib "user32" _
    Alias "SendDlgItemMessageA" _
    (ByVal hDlg As Long, _
    ByVal nIDDlgItem As Long, ByVal wMsg As Long, _
    ByVal wParam As Long, ByVal lParam As Long) As Long

Private Declare Function GetClassName Lib "user32" _
    Alias "GetClassNameA" (ByVal hwnd As Long, _
    ByVal lpClassName As String, _
    ByVal nMaxCount As Long) As Long

Private Declare Function GetCurrentThreadId _
    Lib "kernel32" () As Long

'Constants to be used in our API functions
Private Const EM_SETPASSWORDCHAR = &HCC
Private Const WH_CBT = 5
Private Const HCBT_ACTIVATE = 5
Private Const HC_ACTION = 0

Private hHook As Long

Public Function NewProc(ByVal lngCode As Long, _
    ByVal wParam As Long, ByVal lParam As Long) As Long
Dim RetVal
Dim strClassName As String, lngBuffer As Long

If lngCode < HC_ACTION Then
    NewProc = CallNextHookEx(hHook, lngCode, wParam, lParam)
    Exit Function
End If

strClassName = String$(256, " ")
lngBuffer = 255

If lngCode = HCBT_ACTIVATE Then      'A window has been activated

    RetVal = GetClassName(wParam, strClassName, lngBuffer)

    'Check for class name of the Inputbox
    If Left$(strClassName, RetVal) = "#32770" Then
        'Change the edit control to display the password character *.
        'You can change the Asc("*") as you please.
        SendDlgItemMessage wParam, &H1324, EM_SETPASSWORDCHAR, Asc("*"), &H0
    End If

End If

'This line will ensure that any other hooks that may be in place are
'called correctly.
CallNextHookEx hHook, lngCode, wParam, lParam
End Function
```

```
Public Function InputBoxDK(Prompt, Optional Title, _
    Optional Default, Optional XPos, _
    Optional YPos, Optional HelpFile, Optional Context) As String
    Dim lngModHwnd As Long, lngThreadID As Long

    lngThreadID = GetCurrentThreadId
    lngModHwnd = GetModuleHandle(vbNullString)

    hHook = SetWindowsHookEx(WH_CBT, AddressOf NewProc, lngModHwnd, _
        lngThreadID)
    On Error Resume Next
    InputBoxDK = InputBox(Prompt, Title, Default, XPos, YPos, HelpFile, _
        Context)
    UnhookWindowsHookEx hHook
End Function

Sub PasswordBox()
If InputBoxDK("Please enter password", "Password Required") <> _
    "password" Then
        MsgBox "Sorry, that was not a correct password."
    Else
        MsgBox "Correct Password!  Come on in."
    End If
End Sub
```

Changing Case

This is another utility submitted by Ivan F. Moala.

Word can change the case of selected text, but that capability is notably lacking in Excel. This program enables an Excel user to change the case of text in any selected range, as shown in Figure 13.10:

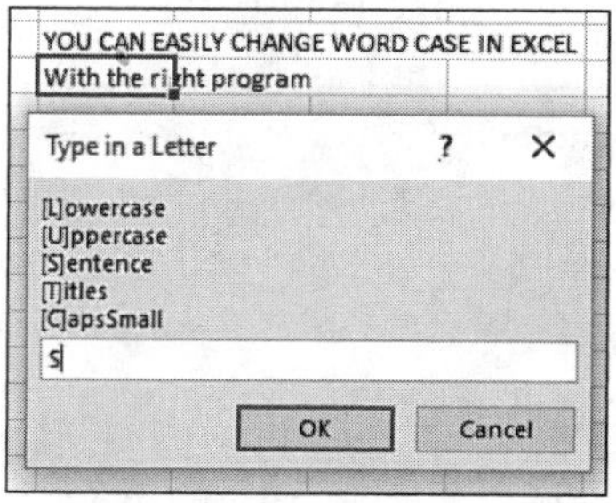

Figure 13.10
You can now change the case of words, just like in Word.

```
Sub TextCaseChange()
Dim RgText As Range
Dim oCell As Range
Dim Ans As String
Dim strTest As String
Dim sCap As Integer, _
    lCap As Integer, _
    i As Integer
```

```
'// You need to select a range to alter first!

Again:
Ans = Application.InputBox("[L]owercase" & vbCr & "[U]ppercase" & vbCr & _
        "[S]entence" & vbCr & "[T]itles" & vbCr & "[C]apsSmall", _
        "Type in a Letter", Type:=2)

If Ans = "False" Then Exit Sub
If InStr(1, "LUSTC", UCase(Ans), vbTextCompare) = 0 _
    Or Len(Ans) > 1 Then GoTo Again

On Error GoTo NoText
If Selection.Count = 1 Then
    Set RgText = Selection
Else
    Set RgText = Selection.SpecialCells(xlCellTypeConstants, 2)
End If
On Error GoTo 0

For Each oCell In RgText
    Select Case UCase(Ans)
        Case "L": oCell = LCase(oCell.Text)
        Case "U": oCell = UCase(oCell.Text)
        Case "S": oCell = UCase(Left(oCell.Text, 1)) & _
            LCase(Right(oCell.Text, Len(oCell.Text) - 1))
        Case "T": oCell = Application.WorksheetFunction.Proper(oCell.Text)
        Case "C"
            lCap = oCell.Characters(1, 1).Font.Size
            sCap = Int(lCap * 0.85)
            'Small caps for everything.
            oCell.Font.Size = sCap
            oCell.Value = UCase(oCell.Text)
            strTest = oCell.Value
            'Large caps for 1st letter of words.
            strTest = Application.Proper(strTest)
            For i = 1 To Len(strTest)
                If Mid(strTest, i, 1) = UCase(Mid(strTest, i, 1)) Then
                    oCell.Characters(i, 1).Font.Size = lCap
                End If
            Next i
    End Select
Next

Exit Sub
NoText:
MsgBox "No text in your selection @ " & Selection.Address

End Sub
```

Selecting with SpecialCells

Ivan F. Moala submitted this handy utility.

Typically, when you want to find certain values, text, or formulas in a range, the range is selected, and each cell is tested. The following utility shows how `SpecialCells` can be used to select only the desired cells. Having fewer cells to check speeds up your code.

The following code ran in the blink of an eye on my machine. However, the version that checked each cell in the range (A1:Z20000) took 14 seconds—an eternity in the automation world!

```
Sub SpecialRange()
Dim TheRange As Range
Dim oCell As Range

Set TheRange = Range("A1:Z20000").SpecialCells(__
    xlCellTypeConstants, xlTextValues)

For Each oCell In TheRange
    If oCell.Text = "Your Text" Then
      MsgBox oCell.Address
      MsgBox TheRange.Cells.Count
    End If
Next oCell
End Sub
```

Resetting a Table's Format

Here's another utility submitted by Zack Barresse.

Tables are great tools to use, but they're not perfect. One issue you'll eventually run into is a table's formatting acting up. For example, formatting might suddenly no longer be applied to new rows. The following procedure resets a table's format so it functions properly:

```
Sub ResetFormat(ByVal Table As ListObject, _
    Optional ByVal RetainNumberFormats As Boolean = True)
Dim Formats() As Variant
Dim ColumnStep As Long

If Table.Parent.ProtectContents = True Then
    MsgBox "The worksheet is protected.", vbExclamation, "Whoops!"
    Exit Sub
End If

If RetainNumberFormats Then
    ReDim Formats(Table.ListColumns.Count - 1)
    For ColumnStep = 1 To Table.ListColumns.Count
        On Error Resume Next
        Formats(ColumnStep - 1) = Table.ListColumns(ColumnStep). _
            DataBodyRange.NumberFormat
        On Error GoTo 0
        If IsEmpty(Formats(ColumnStep - 1)) Then
            Formats(ColumnStep - 1) = "General"
        End If
    Next ColumnStep
```

13

```
      End If

      Table.Range.Style = "Normal"

      If RetainNumberFormats Then
          For ColumnStep = 1 To Table.ListColumns.Count
              On Error Resume Next
              Table.ListColumns(ColumnStep).DataBodyRange.NumberFormat = _
                  Formats(ColumnStep - 1)
              On Error GoTo 0
              If Err.Number <> 0 Then
                  Table.ListColumns(ColumnStep).DataBodyRange.NumberFormat = _
                      "General"
                  Err.Clear
              End If
          Next ColumnStep
      End If
  End Sub
```

Cool Applications

These last samples are interesting applications that you might be able to incorporate into your own projects.

Getting Historical Stock/Fund Quotes

This is another utility submitted by Nathan P. Oliver.

The following code retrieves the average of a valid stock ticker or the close of a fund for the specified date:

```
Private Sub GetQuote()
Dim ie As Object, lCharPos As Long, sHTML As String
Dim HistDate As Date, HighVal As String, LowVal As String
Dim cl As Range

Set cl = ActiveCell
HistDate = cl(, 0)

If Intersect(cl, Range("C2:C" & Cells.Rows.Count)) Is Nothing Then
    MsgBox "You must select a cell in column C."
    Exit Sub
End If

If Not CBool(Len(cl(, -1))) Or Not CBool(Len(cl(, 0))) Then
    MsgBox "You must enter a symbol and date."
    Exit Sub
End If

Set ie = CreateObject("InternetExplorer.Application")

With ie
    .Navigate _
        "http://bigcharts.marketwatch.com/historical" & _
        "/default.asp?detect=1&symb=" _
        & cl(, -1) & "&closedate=" & Month(HistDate) & "%2F" & _
```

```
            Day(HistDate) & "%2F" & Year(HistDate) & "&x=0&y=0"
        Do While .Busy And .ReadyState <> 4
            DoEvents
        Loop
        sHTML = .Document.body.innertext
        .Quit
    End With

    Set ie = Nothing

    lCharPos = InStr(1, sHTML, "High:", vbTextCompare)
    If lCharPos Then HighVal = Mid$(sHTML, lCharPos + 5, 15)

    If Not Left$(HighVal, 3) = "n/a" Then
        lCharPos = InStr(1, sHTML, "Low:", vbTextCompare)
        If lCharPos Then LowVal = Mid$(sHTML, lCharPos + 4, 15)
        cl.Value = (Val(LowVal) + Val(HighVal)) / 2
    Else: lCharPos = InStr(1, sHTML, "Closing Price:", vbTextCompare)
        cl.Value = Val(Mid$(sHTML, lCharPos + 14, 15))
    End If

    Set cl = Nothing
    End Sub
```

Using VBA Extensibility to Add Code to New Workbooks

Say that you have a macro that moves data to a new workbook for the regional managers. What if you need to also copy macros to the new workbook? You can use VBA Extensibility to import modules to a workbook or to actually write lines of code to the workbook.

To use any of the following examples, you must first open VB Editor, select References from the Tools menu, and select the reference for Microsoft Visual Basic for Applications Extensibility 5.3. You must also trust access to VBA by going to the Developer tab, choosing Macro Security, and checking Trust Access to the VBA Project Object Model.

The easiest way to use VBA Extensibility is to export a complete module or userform from the current project and import it to the new workbook. Perhaps you have an application with thousands of lines of code, and you want to create a new workbook with data for the regional manager and give her three macros to enable custom formatting and printing. Place all of these macros in a module called modToRegion. Macros in this module also call the frmRegion userform. The following code transfers this code from the current workbook to the new workbook:

```
Sub MoveDataAndMacro()
Dim WSD as worksheet
Set WSD = Worksheets("Report")
' Copy Report to a new workbook
WSD.Copy
' The active workbook is now the new workbook
' Delete any old copy of the module from C
On Error Resume Next
' Delete any stray copies from hard drive
Kill ("C:\temp\ModToRegion.bas")
Kill ("C:\temp\frmRegion.frm")
```

13

```
On Error GoTo 0
' Export module & form from this workbook
ThisWorkbook.VBProject.VBComponents("ModToRegion").Export _
    ("C:\temp\ModToRegion.bas")
ThisWorkbook.VBProject.VBComponents("frmRegion").Export _
    ("C:\temp\frmRegion. frm")
' Import to new workbook
ActiveWorkbook.VBProject.VBComponents.Import ("C:\temp\ModToRegion.bas")
ActiveWorkbook.VBProject.VBComponents.Import ("C:\temp\frmRegion.frm")
On Error Resume Next
Kill ("C:\temp\ModToRegion.bas")
Kill ("C:\temp\frmRegion.bas")
On Error GoTo 0
End Sub
```

This method works if you need to move modules or userforms to a new workbook. However, what if you need to write some code to the Workbook_Open macro in the ThisWorkbook module? There are two tools to use. The Lines method enables you to return a particular set of code lines from a given module. The InsertLines method enables you to insert code lines to a new module.

> **NOTE** With each call to InsertLines, you must insert a complete macro. Excel attempts to compile the code after each call to InsertLines. If you insert lines that do not completely compile, Excel might crash with a general protection fault (GPF).

```
Sub MoveDataAndMacro()
Dim WSD as worksheet
Dim WBN as Workbook
Dim WBCodeMod1 As Object, WBCodeMod2 As Object
Set WSD = Worksheets("Report")
' Copy Report to a new workbook
WSD.Copy
' The active workbook is now the new workbook
Set WBN = ActiveWorkbook
' Copy the Workbook level Event handlers
Set WBCodeMod1 = ThisWorkbook.VBProject.VBComponents("ThisWorkbook") _
    .CodeModule
Set WBCodeMod2 = WBN.VBProject.VBComponents("ThisWorkbook").CodeModule
WBCodeMod2.insertlines 1, WBCodeMod1.Lines(1, WBCodeMod1.countoflines)
End Sub
```

Next Steps

The utilities in this chapter aren't Excel's only source of programming power. User-defined functions (UDFs) enable you to create complex custom formulas to cover what Excel's functions don't. In Chapter 14, "Sample User-Defined Functions," you'll find out how to create and share your own functions.

Sample User-Defined Functions

14

Excel provides many built-in functions. However, sometimes you need a complex custom function that Excel doesn't offer, such as a function that sums a range of cells based on their interior color.

So, what do you do? You could go down your list and copy the colored cells to another section. Or perhaps you have a calculator next to you as you work your way down your list—but be careful not to enter the same number twice! Both methods are time-consuming and prone to accidents. What to do?

You could write a procedure to solve this problem—after all, that's what this book is about. However, you have another option: *user-defined functions* (UDFs).

Creating User-Defined Functions

You can create your own functions in VBA and then use them just like you use Excel's built-in functions, such as SUM. After the custom function is created, a user needs to know only the function name and its arguments.

NOTE You can enter UDFs only into standard modules. Sheet and ThisWorkbook modules are a special type of module. If you enter a UDF in either of those modules, Excel does not recognize that you are creating a UDF.

CASE STUDY: CUSTOM FUNCTIONS: EXAMPLE AND EXPLANATION

In this case study, you'll build a custom function to add two values. After you have created it, you will use it on a worksheet.

Insert a new module in the VB Editor. Type the following function into the module. It is a function called ADD that totals two numbers in different cells. The function has two arguments:

```
Add(Number1,Number2)
```

Number1 is the first number to add; Number2 is the second number to add:

```
Function Add(Number1 As Integer, Number2 As Integer) As Integer
Add = Number1 + Number2
End Function
```

Let's break this down:

- The function name is ADD.
- Arguments are placed in parentheses after the name of the function. This example has two arguments: Number1 and Number2.
- As Integer defines the variable type of the result as a whole number.
- ADD = Number1 + Number2 is the result of the function that is returned.

Here is how to use the function on a worksheet:

1. Type numbers into cells A1 and A2.
2. Select cell A3.
3. Press Shift+F3 to open the Insert Function dialog box, or choose Formulas, Insert Function.
4. In the Insert Function dialog, select the User Defined category (see Figure 14.1).
5. Select the Add function.
6. In the first argument box, select cell A1 (see Figure 14.2).
7. In the second argument box, select cell A2.
8. Click OK.

Congratulations! You have created your first custom function.

14

Figure 14.1
You can find your UDFs under the User Defined category of the Insert Function dialog box.

Figure 14.2
Use the Function Arguments dialog to enter your arguments.

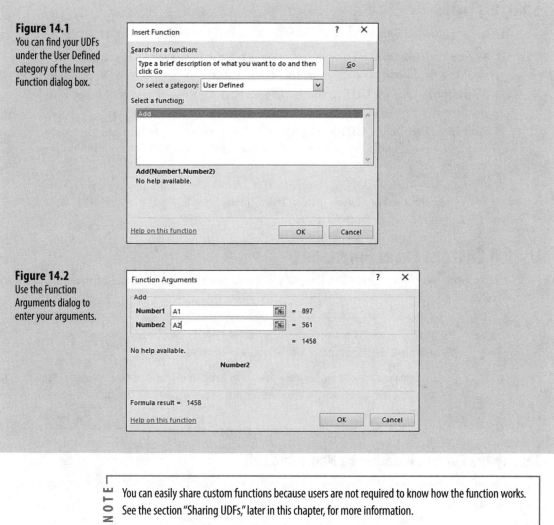

> **NOTE**
> You can easily share custom functions because users are not required to know how the function works.
> See the section "Sharing UDFs," later in this chapter, for more information.

Most of the functions used on sheets can also be used in VBA and vice versa. However, in VBA you call the UDF (ADD) from a procedure (Addition), like this:

```
Sub Addition ()
Dim Total as Integer
Total = Add (1,10) 'we use a user-defined function Add
MsgBox "The answer is: " & Total
End Sub
```

14

Sharing UDFs

Where you store a UDF affects how you can share it:

■ **Personal.xlsb**—Store a UDF in `Personal.xlsb` if it is just for your use and won't be used in a workbook opened on another computer.

■ **Workbook**—Store a UDF in the workbook in which it is being used if it needs to be distributed to many people.

■ **Add-in**—Distribute a UDF via an add-in if the workbook is to be shared among a select group of people. See Chapter 26, "Creating Add-ins," for information on how to create an add-in.

■ **Template**—Store a UDF in a template if it needs to be used to create several workbooks and the workbooks are distributed to many people.

Useful Custom Excel Functions

The sections that follow include a sampling of functions that can be useful in the everyday Excel world.

> **NOTE**
> This chapter shows functions donated by several Excel programmers. These are functions that they have found useful and that they hope will also be of help to you.
>
> Different programmers have different programming styles. We did not rewrite the submissions. As you review the lines of code, you might notice different ways of doing the same task, such as referring to ranges.

Setting the Current Workbook's Name in a Cell

The following function sets the name of the active workbook in a cell, as shown in Figure 14.3:

```
MyName()
```

Figure 14.3
Use a UDF to show the filename or the filename with the directory path.

| ProjectFilesChapter14.xlsm | =MyName() |
| C:\VBA 2016\Workbooks\ProjectFilesChapter14.xlsm | =MyFullname() |

No arguments are used with this function:

```
Function MyName() As String
    MyName = ThisWorkbook.Name
End Function
```

Setting the Current Workbook's Name and File Path in a Cell

A variation of the preceding function, the following function sets the file path and name of the active workbook in a cell, as shown previously in Figure 14.3:

```
MyFullName()
```

No arguments are used with this function:

```
Function MyFullName() As String
    MyFullName = ThisWorkbook.FullName
End Function
```

Checking Whether a Workbook Is Open

There might be times when you need to check whether a workbook is open. The following function returns True if a workbook is open and False if it is not:

```
BookOpen(Bk)
```

The argument is Bk, which is the name of the workbook being checked:

```
Function BookOpen(Bk As String) As Boolean
Dim T As Excel.Workbook
Err.Clear 'clears any errors
On Error Resume Next 'if the code runs into an error, it skips it and
'continues
Set T = Application.Workbooks(Bk)
BookOpen = Not T Is Nothing
'If the workbook is open, then T will hold the workbook object and
'therefore will NOT be Nothing
Err.Clear
On Error GoTo 0
End Function
```

Here is an example of using the function:

```
Sub OpenAWorkbook()
Dim IsOpen As Boolean
Dim BookName As String
BookName = "ProjectFilesChapter14.xlsm"
IsOpen = BookOpen(BookName) 'calling our function - don't forget the
'parameter
If IsOpen Then
    MsgBox BookName & " is already open!"
Else
    Workbooks.Open (BookName)
End If
End Sub
```

Checking Whether a Sheet in an Open Workbook Exists

This function requires that the workbook(s) it checks be open. It returns True if the sheet is found and False if it is not:

```
SheetExists(SName, WBName)
```

14

These are the arguments:

- SName—The name of the sheet being searched
- WBName—(Optional) The name of the workbook that contains the sheet

Here is the function. If the workbook argument is not provided, it uses the active workbook:

```
Function SheetExists(SName As String, Optional WB As Workbook) As Boolean
    Dim WS As Worksheet

    ' Use active workbook by default
    If WB Is Nothing Then
        Set WB = ActiveWorkbook
    End If

    On Error Resume Next
        SheetExists = CBool(Not WB.Sheets(SName) Is Nothing)
    On Error GoTo 0

End Function
```

> **NOTE**
> CBool is a function that converts the expression between the parentheses to a Boolean value.

Here is an example of using this function:

```
Sub CheckForSheet()
Dim ShtExists As Boolean
ShtExists = SheetExists("Sheet9")
'notice that only one parameter was passed; the workbook name is optional
If ShtExists Then
    MsgBox "The worksheet exists!"
Else
    MsgBox "The worksheet does NOT exist!"
End If
End Sub
```

Counting the Number of Workbooks in a Directory

This function searches the current directory, and its subfolders if you want, counting all Excel macro workbook files (.xlsm), including hidden files, or just the ones starting with a string of letters:

```
NumFilesInCurDir (LikeText, Subfolders)
```

These are the arguments:

- LikeText—(Optional) A string value to search for; must include an asterisk (*), such as Mr*
- Subfolders—(Optional) True to search subfolders, False (default) not to

NOTE `FileSystemObject` requires the Microsoft Scripting Runtime reference library. To enable this setting, go to Tools, References and check Microsoft Scripting Runtime.

This function is a recursive function, which means it calls itself until a specific condition is met—in this case, until all subfolders are processed. Here is the function:

```
Function NumFilesInCurDir(Optional strInclude As String = "", _
    Optional blnSubDirs As Boolean = False)
Dim fso As FileSystemObject
Dim fld As Folder
Dim fil As File
Dim subfld As Folder
Dim intFileCount As Integer
Dim strExtension As String
  strExtension = "XLSM"
  Set fso = New FileSystemObject
  Set fld = fso.GetFolder(ThisWorkbook.Path)
  For Each fil In fld.Files
    If UCase(fil.Name) Like "*" & UCase(strInclude) & "*." & _
        UCase(strExtension) Then
      intFileCount = intFileCount + 1
    End If
  Next fil
  If blnSubDirs Then
    For Each subfld In fld.Subfolders
      intFileCount = intFileCount + NumFilesInCurDir(strInclude, True)
    Next subfld
  End If
  NumFilesInCurDir = intFileCount
  Set fso = Nothing
End Function
```

Here is an example of using this function:

```
Sub CountMyWkbks()
Dim MyFiles As Integer
MyFiles = NumFilesInCurDir("MrE*", True)
MsgBox MyFiles & " file(s) found"
End Sub
```

Retrieving the User ID

Ever need to keep a record of who saves changes to a workbook? With the USERID function, you can retrieve the name of the user who is logged in to a computer. Combine it with the function discussed in the "Retrieving Permanent Date and Time" section, later in this chapter, and you have a nice log file. You can also use the USERID function to set up user rights to a workbook.

```
WinUserName ()
```

No arguments are used with this function.

> **NOTE** The USERID function is an advanced function that uses the *application programming interface* (API), which is reviewed in Chapter 23, "The Windows Application Programming Interface (API)." The code is specific to 32-bit Excel. If you are running 64-bit Excel, refer to Chapter 23 for changes to make it work.

This first section (Private declarations) must be at the top of the module:

```
Private Declare Function WNetGetUser Lib "mpr.dll" Alias "WNetGetUserA" _
    (ByVal lpName As String, ByVal lpUserName As String, _
    lpnLength As Long) As Long
Private Const NO_ERROR = 0
Private Const ERROR_NOT_CONNECTED = 2250&
Private Const ERROR_MORE_DATA = 234
Private Const ERROR_NO_NETWORK = 1222&
Private Const ERROR_EXTENDED_ERROR = 1208&
Private Const ERROR_NO_NET_OR_BAD_PATH = 1203&
```

You can place the following section of code anywhere in the module, as long as it is below the preceding section:

```
Function WinUsername() As String
    'variables
    Dim strBuf As String, lngUser As Long, strUn As String
    'clear buffer for user name from api func
    strBuf = Space$(255)
    'use api func WNetGetUser to assign user value to lngUser
    'will have lots of blank space
    lngUser = WNetGetUser("", strBuf, 255)
    'if no error from function call
    If lngUser = NO_ERROR Then
        'clear out blank space in strBuf and assign val to function
        strUn = Left(strBuf, InStr(strBuf, vbNullChar) - 1)
        WinUsername = strUn
    Else
    'error, give up
        WinUsername = "Error :" & lngUser
    End If
End Function
```

Here's an example of using this function:

```
Sub CheckUserRights()
Dim UserName As String
UserName = WinUsername
Select Case UserName
    Case "Administrator"
        MsgBox "Full Rights"
    Case "Guest"
        MsgBox "You cannot make changes"
    Case Else
        MsgBox "Limited Rights"
End Select
End Sub
```

Retrieving Date and Time of Last Save

This function retrieves the saved date and time of any workbook, including the current one:

```
LastSaved(FullPath)
```

> **NOTE**
> The cell must be formatted for date and time to display the date/time correctly.

The argument is `FullPath`, a string showing the full path and filename of the file in question:

```
Function LastSaved(FullPath As String) As Date
LastSaved = FileDateTime(FullPath)
End Function
```

Retrieving Permanent Date and Time

Because of the volatility of the NOW function, it isn't very useful for stamping a worksheet with the creation or editing date. Every time the workbook is opened or recalculated, the result of the NOW function is updated. The following UDF uses the NOW function. However, because you need to reenter the cell to update the function, it is much less volatile (see Figure 14.4):

```
DateTime()
```

Figure 14.4
Even after forcing a recalculation, the `DateTime()` cell shows the time when it was originally placed in the cell, whereas NOW() shows the current system time.

| 6/15/15 10:56 AM | =NOW() |
| 6/15/15 10:51 AM | =DateTime() |

No arguments are used with this function:

```
DateTime()
```

> **NOTE**
> The cell must be formatted properly to display the date/time.

Here's is the function:

```
Function DateTime()
    DateTime = Now
End Function
```

Validating an Email Address

If you manage an email subscription list, you might receive invalid email addresses, such as addresses with a space before the "at" symbol (@). The ISEMAILVALID function can check addresses and confirm that they are proper email addresses (see Figure 14.5):

```
IsEmailValid (strEmail)
```

Figure 14.5
Validating email addresses.

Tracy@ MrExcel.com	FALSE	<-a space after the @
ExcelGGirl@gmail.com	TRUE	
consult$@MrExcel.com	FALSE	<-invalid characters

> **NOTE**
> This function cannot verify that an email address is an existing one. It only checks the syntax to verify that the address might be legitimate.

The function's only argument is strEmail, an email address:

```
Function IsEmailValid(strEmail As String) As Boolean
Dim strArray As Variant
Dim strItem As Variant
Dim i As Long
Dim c As String
Dim blnIsItValid As Boolean
blnIsItValid = True
'count the @ in the string
i = Len(strEmail) - Len(Application.Substitute(strEmail, "@", ""))
'if there is more than one @, invalid email
If i <> 1 Then IsEmailValid = False: Exit Function
ReDim strArray(1 To 2)
'the following two lines place the text to the left and right
'of the @ in their own variables
strArray(1) = Left(strEmail, InStr(1, strEmail, "@", 1) - 1)
strArray(2) = Application.Substitute(Right(strEmail, Len(strEmail) - _
    Len(strArray(1))), "@", "")

For Each strItem In strArray
    'verify there is something in the variable.
    'If there isn't, then part of the email is missing
    If Len(strItem) <= 0 Then
        blnIsItValid = False
        IsEmailValid = blnIsItValid
        Exit Function
    End If
    'verify only valid characters in the email
    For i = 1 To Len(strItem)
        'lowercases all letters for easier checking
        c = LCase(Mid(strItem, i, 1))
        If InStr("abcdefghijklmnopqrstuvwxyz_-.", c) <= 0 _
            And Not IsNumeric(c) Then
            blnIsItValid = False
            IsEmailValid = blnIsItValid
```

14

```
                    Exit Function
                End If
        Next i
    'verify that the first character of the left and right aren't periods
        If Left(strItem, 1) = "." Or Right(strItem, 1) = "." Then
            blnIsItValid = False
            IsEmailValid = blnIsItValid
            Exit Function
        End If
    Next strItem
    'verify there is a period in the right half of the address
    If InStr(strArray(2), ".") <= 0 Then
        blnIsItValid = False
        IsEmailValid = blnIsItValid
        Exit Function
    End If
    i = Len(strArray(2)) - InStrRev(strArray(2), ".") 'locate the period
    'verify that the number of letters corresponds to a valid domain
    'extension
    If i <> 2 And i <> 3 And i <> 4 Then
        blnIsItValid = False
        IsEmailValid = blnIsItValid
        Exit Function
    End If
    'verify that there aren't two periods together in the email
    If InStr(strEmail, "..") > 0 Then
        blnIsItValid = False
        IsEmailValid = blnIsItValid
        Exit Function
    End If
    IsEmailValid = blnIsItValid
End Function
```

Summing Cells Based on Interior Color

Let's say you have created a list of how much each of your clients owes. From this list, you want to sum just the cells to which you have applied a cell fill to indicate clients who are 30 days past due. This function sums cells based on their fill color.

```
SumColor(CellColor, SumRange)
```

> NOTE
>
> Cells colored by conditional formatting will not work; the cells must have an interior color.

These are the arguments:

- CellColor—The address of a cell with the target color
- SumRange—The range of cells to be searched

14

Here is the function's code:

```
Function SumByColor(CellColor As Range, SumRange As Range)
Dim myCell As Range
Dim iCol As Integer
Dim myTotal
iCol = CellColor.Interior.ColorIndex 'get the target color
For Each myCell In SumRange 'look at each cell in the designated range
    'if the cell color matches the target color
    If myCell.Interior.ColorIndex = iCol Then
        'add the value in the cell to the total
        myTotal = WorksheetFunction.Sum(myCell) + myTotal
    End If
Next myCell
SumByColor = myTotal
End Function
```

Figure 14.6 shows a sample worksheet using this function.

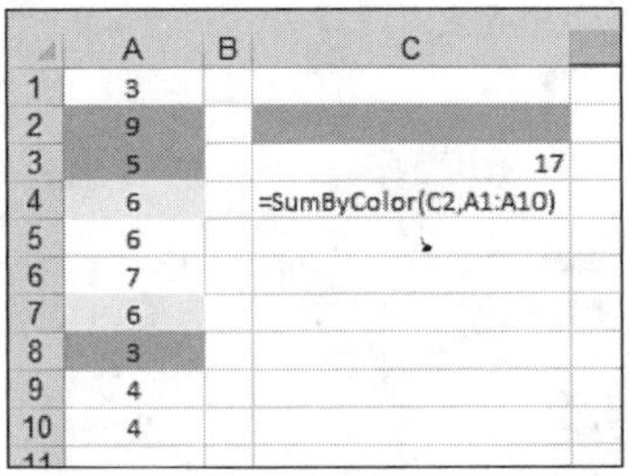

Figure 14.6
Sum cells based on interior color.

Counting Unique Values

How many times have you had a long list of values and needed to know how many were unique values? This function goes through a range and provides that information, as shown in Figure 14.7:

```
NumUniqueValues(Rng)
```

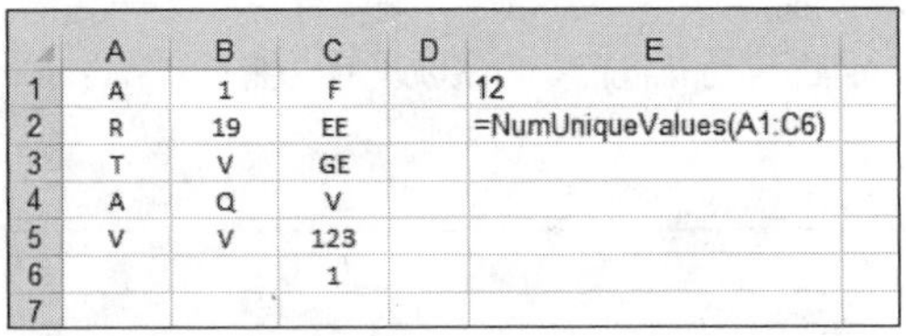

Figure 14.7
Count the number of unique values in a range.

The argument is Rng, the range to search unique values.

Here is the function's code:

```
Function NumUniqueValues(Rng As Range) As Long
Dim myCell As Range
Dim UniqueVals As New Collection
```

```
        Application.Volatile 'forces the function to recalculate when the range
        'changes
    On Error Resume Next
    'the following places each value from the range into a collection
    'because a collection, with a key parameter, can contain only unique
    'values,there will be no duplicates. The error statements force the
    'program to continue when the error messages appear for duplicate
    'items in the collection
    For Each myCell In Rng
        UniqueVals.Add myCell.Value, CStr(myCell.Value)
    Next myCell
    On Error GoTo 0
    'returns the number of items in the collection
    NumUniqueValues = UniqueVals.Count
    End Function
```

Removing Duplicates from a Range

No doubt you have also had a list of items and needed to list only the unique values. The following function goes through a range and stores only the unique values:

```
UniqueValues (OrigArray)
```

The argument is `OrigArray`, an array from which the duplicates will be removed.

This first section (`Const` declarations) must be at the top of the module:

```
Const ERR_BAD_PARAMETER = "Array parameter required"
Const ERR_BAD_TYPE = "Invalid Type"
Const ERR_BP_NUMBER = 20000
Const ERR_BT_NUMBER = 20001
```

You can place the following section of code anywhere in the module, as long as it is below the code just shown:

```
Public Function UniqueValues(ByVal OrigArray As Variant) As Variant
    Dim vAns() As Variant
    Dim lStartPoint As Long
    Dim lEndPoint As Long
    Dim lCtr As Long, lCount As Long
    Dim iCtr As Integer
    Dim col As New Collection
    Dim sIndex As String
    Dim vTest As Variant, vItem As Variant
    Dim iBadVarTypes(4) As Integer
    'Function does not work if array element is one of the
    'following types
    iBadVarTypes(0) = vbObject
    iBadVarTypes(1) = vbError
    iBadVarTypes(2) = vbDataObject
    iBadVarTypes(3) = vbUserDefinedType
    iBadVarTypes(4) = vbArray
    'Check to see whether the parameter is an array
    If Not IsArray(OrigArray) Then
        Err.Raise ERR_BP_NUMBER, , ERR_BAD_PARAMETER
        Exit Function
    End If
    lStartPoint = LBound(OrigArray)
    lEndPoint = UBound(OrigArray)
```

14

```
        For lCtr = lStartPoint To lEndPoint
            vItem = OrigArray(lCtr)
            'First check to see whether variable type is acceptable
            For iCtr = 0 To UBound(iBadVarTypes)
                If VarType(vItem) = iBadVarTypes(iCtr) Or _
                    VarType(vItem) = iBadVarTypes(iCtr) + vbVariant Then
                        Err.Raise ERR_BT_NUMBER, , ERR_BAD_TYPE
                        Exit Function
                End If
            Next iCtr
            'Add element to a collection, using it as the index
            'if an error occurs, the element already exists
            sIndex = CStr(vItem)
            'first element, add automatically
            If lCtr = lStartPoint Then
                col.Add vItem, sIndex
                ReDim vAns(lStartPoint To lStartPoint) As Variant
                vAns(lStartPoint) = vItem
            Else
                On Error Resume Next
                col.Add vItem, sIndex
                If Err.Number = 0 Then
                    lCount = UBound(vAns) + 1
                    ReDim Preserve vAns(lStartPoint To lCount)
                    vAns(lCount) = vItem
                End If
            End If
            Err.Clear
        Next lCtr
        UniqueValues = vAns
End Function
```

Here is an example of using this function:

```
Function nodupsArray(rng As Range) As Variant
    Dim arr1() As Variant
    If rng.Columns.Count > 1 Then Exit Function
    arr1 = Application.Transpose(rng)
    arr1 = UniqueValues(arr1)
    nodupsArray = Application.Transpose(arr1)
End Function
```

Finding the First Nonzero-Length Cell in a Range

Suppose you have imported a large list of data with many empty cells. Here is a function that evaluates a range of cells and returns the value of the first nonzero-length cell:

```
FirstNonZeroLength(Rng)
```

The argument is Rng, the range to search.

Here's the function:

```
Function FirstNonZeroLength(Rng As Range)
Dim myCell As Range
FirstNonZeroLength = 0#
For Each myCell In Rng
    If Not IsNull(myCell) And myCell <> "" Then
```

```
        FirstNonZeroLength = myCell.Value
        Exit Function
    End If
Next myCell
FirstNonZeroLength = myCell.Value
End Function
```

Figure 14.8 shows the function on a sample worksheet.

Figure 14.8
Find the value of the first nonzero-length cell in a range.

⊿	A	B	C	D
1		2		
2		=FirstNonZeroLength(A1:A7)		
3	2			
4				
5	7			
6	8			
7	9			
8				

Substituting Multiple Characters

Excel has a substitute function, but it is a value-for-value substitution. What if you have several characters you need to substitute? Figure 14.9 shows several examples of how this function works.

```
MSubstitute(trStr, frStr, toStr)
```

Figure 14.9
Substitute multiple characters in a cell.

⊿	A	B	C
1	1 Introduction	Introduction	=msubstitute(A1,"1","")
2	This wam a test	This was a test	=msubstitute(A2,"wam", "was")
3	123abc456	abc	=msubstitute(A3,"1234567890","")
4	Adnothyer Tuiest	Another Test	=msubstitute(A4,"dyui","")
5			

These are the arguments:

- trStr—The string to be searched
- frStr—The text being searched for
- toStr—The replacement text

Here's the function's code:

```
Function MSubsitute(ByVal trStr As Variant, frStr As String, _
    toStr As String) As Variant
Dim iCol As Integer
Dim j As Integer
Dim Ar As Variant
Dim vfr() As String
Dim vto() As String
ReDim vfr(1 To Len(frStr))
ReDim vto(1 To Len(frStr))
'place the strings into an array
```

14

```
For j = 1 To Len(frStr)
    vfr(j) = Mid(frStr, j, 1)
    If Mid(toStr, j, 1) <> "" Then
        vto(j) = Mid(toStr, j, 1)
    Else
        vto(j) = ""
    End If
Next j
'compare each character and substitute if needed
If IsArray(trStr) Then
    Ar = trStr
    For iRow = LBound(Ar, 1) To UBound(Ar, 1)
        For iCol = LBound(Ar, 2) To UBound(Ar, 2)
            For j = 1 To Len(frStr)
                Ar(iRow, iCol) = Application.Substitute(Ar(iRow, iCol), _
                    vfr(j), vto(j))
            Next j
        Next iCol
    Next iRow
Else
    Ar = trStr
    For j = 1 To Len(frStr)
        Ar = Application.Substitute(Ar, vfr(j), vto(j))
    Next j
End If
MSUBSTITUTE = Ar
End Function
```

> **NOTE**
> The `toStr` argument is assumed to be the same length as `frStr`. If it isn't, the remaining characters are considered null (" "). The function is case sensitive. To replace all instances of `a`, use `a` and `A`. You cannot replace one character with two characters. For example, this:
>
> ```
> =MSUBSTITUTE("This is a test","i","$@")
> ```
>
> results in this:
>
> ```
> "Th$s $s a test"
> ```

Retrieving Numbers from Mixed Text

This function extracts and returns numbers from text that is a mixture of numbers and letters:

```
RetrieveNumbers (myString)
```

The argument is `myString`, the text containing the numbers to be extracted.

Here's the function's code:

```
Function RetrieveNumbers(myString As String)
Dim i As Integer, j As Integer
Dim OnlyNums As String
'starting at the END of the string and moving backwards (Step -1)
For i = Len(myString) To 1 Step -1
'IsNumeric is a VBA function that returns True if a variable is a number
```

```
'When a number is found, it is added to the OnlyNums string
    If IsNumeric(Mid(myString, i, 1)) Then
        j = j + 1
        OnlyNums = Mid(myString, i, 1) & OnlyNums
    End If
    If j = 1 Then OnlyNums = CInt(Mid(OnlyNums, 1, 1))
Next i
RetrieveNumbers = CLng(OnlyNums)
End Function
```

Converting Week Number into Date

Have you ever received a spreadsheet report in which all the headers showed the week number? This can be confusing because you probably wouldn't know what Week 15 actually is. You would have to get out your calendar and count the weeks. This problem is exacerbated if you need to count weeks in a previous year. In this case, you need a nice little function that converts Week ## Year into the date of a particular day in a given week, as shown in Figure 14.10:

```
Weekday(Str)
```

Figure 14.10
Convert a week number into a date more easily referenced.

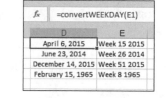

	D	E
	April 6, 2015	Week 15 2015
	June 23, 2014	Week 26 2014
	December 14, 2015	Week 51 2015
	February 15, 1965	Week 8 1965

f_x =convertWEEKDAY(E1)

> **NOTE** The result must be formatted as a date.

The argument is Str, the week to be converted, in "Week ## YYYY" format.

Here's the function's code:

```
Function ConvertWeekDay(Str As String) As Date
Dim Week As Long
Dim FirstMon As Date
Dim TStr As String
FirstMon = DateSerial(Right(Str, 4), 1, 1)
FirstMon = FirstMon - FirstMon Mod 7 + 2
TStr = Right(Str, Len(Str) - 5)
Week = Left(TStr, InStr(1, TStr, " ", 1)) + 0
ConvertWeekDay = FirstMon + (Week - 1) * 7
End Function
```

14

Extracting a Single Element from a Delimited String

Say that you need to paste a column of delimited data. You could use Excel's Text to Columns feature, but you need only an element or two from each cell. Text to Columns parses the entire thing. In this case, you need a function that lets you specify the number of the element in a string that you need, as shown in Figure 14.11:

```
StringElement(str,chr,ind)
```

Figure 14.11
Extracting a single element from delimited text.

⊿	A	B	C	D	E	F	G	H
1					ind			
2	str	chr	1	2	3	4	5	6
3	A|B|C|D|E|F			A	B	C	D	E	F
4			=StringElement($A$3,$B$3,C2)					
5								

These are the arguments:

- `str`—The string to be parsed
- `chr`—The delimiter
- `ind`—The position of the element to be returned

Here's the function's code:

```
Function StringElement(str As String, chr As String, ind As Integer)
Dim arr_str As Variant
arr_str = Split(str, chr) 'Not compatible with XL97
StringElement = arr_str(ind - 1)
End Function
```

Sorting and Concatenating

The following function enables you to take a column of data, sort it by numbers and then by letters, and concatenate it using a comma (,) as the delimiter (see Figure 14.12). Note that since the numbers are treated as strings, they are sorted lexicographically (all numbers that start with 1, then numbers that start with 2, etc.). For example, if sorting 1,2,10, you would actually get 1,10,2 since 10 starts with a 1, which comes before 2:

```
SortConcat(Rng)
```

Figure 14.12
Sort and concatenate a range of variables.

⊿	A	B
1	Unsorted List	Sorted String
2	q	1,14,50,9,a,f,gg,q,r,rrrrr
3	r	=sortConcat(A2:A11)
4	f	
5	a	
6	gg	
7	1	
8	9	
9	50	
10	14	
11	rrrrr	
12		

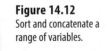

The argument is `Rng`, the range of data to be sorted and concatenated. `SortConcat` calls another procedure, `BubbleSort`, that must be included.

Here's the main function:

```
Function SortConcat(Rng As Range) As Variant
Dim MySum As String, arr1() As String
Dim j As Integer, i As Integer
Dim cl As Range
Dim concat As Variant
On Error GoTo FuncFail:
'initialize output
SortConcat = 0#
'avoid user issues
If Rng.Count = 0 Then Exit Function
'get range into variant variable holding array
ReDim arr1(1 To Rng.Count)
'fill array
i = 1
For Each cl In Rng
    arr1(i) = cl.Value
    i = i + 1
Next
'sort array elements
Call BubbleSort(arr1)
'create string from array elements
For j = UBound(arr1) To 1 Step -1
    If Not IsEmpty(arr1(j)) Then
        MySum = arr1(j) & ", " & MySum
    End If
Next j
'assign value to function
SortConcat = Left(MySum, Len(MySum) - 1)
'exit point
concat_exit:
Exit Function
'display error in cell
FuncFail:
SortConcat = Err.Number & " - " & Err.Description
Resume concat_exit
End Function
```

The following function is the ever-popular `BubbleSort`. Many developers use this program to do a simple sort of data.

```
Sub BubbleSort(List() As String)
'    Sorts the List array in ascending order
Dim First As Integer, Last As Integer
Dim i As Integer, j As Integer
Dim Temp
First = LBound(List)
Last = UBound(List)
For i = First To Last - 1
    For j = i + 1 To Last
        If List(i) > List(j) Then
            Temp = List(j)
            List(j) = List(i)
            List(i) = Temp
```

```
            End If
        Next j
    Next i
    End Sub
```

Sorting Numeric and Alpha Characters

This function takes a mixed range of numeric and alpha characters and sorts them—first numerically and then alphabetically:

```
sorter(Rng)
```

The result is placed in an array that can be displayed on a worksheet by using an array formula, as shown in Figure 14.13.

Figure 14.13
Sort a mixed alphanumeric list.

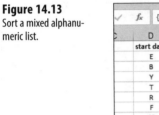

The argument is Rng, the range to be sorted.

The function uses the following two procedures to sort the data in the range:

```
Public Sub QuickSort(ByRef vntArr As Variant, _
    Optional ByVal lngLeft As Long = -2, _
    Optional ByVal lngRight As Long = -2)
Dim i, j, lngMid As Long
Dim vntTestVal As Variant
If lngLeft = -2 Then lngLeft = LBound(vntArr)
If lngRight = -2 Then lngRight = UBound(vntArr)
If lngLeft < lngRight Then
    lngMid = (lngLeft + lngRight) \ 2
    vntTestVal = vntArr(lngMid)
    i = lngLeft
    j = lngRight
    Do
        Do While vntArr(i) < vntTestVal
            i = i + 1
        Loop
        Do While vntArr(j) > vntTestVal
            j = j - 1
        Loop
        If i <= j Then
            Call SwapElements(vntArr, i, j)
```

```
            i = i + 1
            j = j - 1
        End If
    Loop Until i > j
    If j <= lngMid Then
        Call QuickSort(vntArr, lngLeft, j)
        Call QuickSort(vntArr, i, lngRight)
    Else
        Call QuickSort(vntArr, i, lngRight)
        Call QuickSort(vntArr, lngLeft, j)
    End If
End If
End Sub

Private Sub SwapElements(ByRef vntItems As Variant, _
    ByVal lngItem1 As Long, _
    ByVal lngItem2 As Long)
Dim vntTemp As Variant
vntTemp = vntItems(lngItem2)
vntItems(lngItem2) = vntItems(lngItem1)
vntItems(lngItem1) = vntTemp
End Sub
```

Here's an example of using this function:

```
Function sorter(Rng As Range) As Variant
'returns an array
Dim arr1() As Variant
If Rng.Columns.Count > 1 Then Exit Function
arr1 = Application.Transpose(Rng)
QuickSort arr1
sorter = Application.Transpose(arr1)
End Function
```

Searching for a String Within Text

Ever needed to find out which cells contain a specific string of text? This function can search strings in a range, looking for specified text:

```
ContainsText(Rng,Text)
```

It returns a result that identifies which cells contain the text, as shown in Figure 14.14.

Figure 14.14
Return a result that identifies which cells contain a specified string.

	A	B	C	D
1	This is an apple		A3	=ContainsText(A1:A3,"banana")
2	This is an orange		A1,A2	=ContainsText(A1:A3,"This is")
3	Here is a banana			
4				

These are the arguments:

- Rng—The range in which to search
- Text—The text for which to search

Here's the function's code:

```
Function ContainsText(Rng As Range, Text As String) As String
Dim T As String
Dim myCell As Range
For Each myCell In Rng 'look in each cell
    If InStr(myCell.Text, Text) > 0 Then 'look in the string for the text
        If Len(T) = 0 Then
            'if the text is found, add the address to my result
            T = myCell.Address(False, False)
        Else
            T = T & "," & myCell.Address(False, False)
        End If
    End If
Next myCell
ContainsText = T
End Function
```

Reversing the Contents of a Cell

This function is mostly fun, but you might find it useful—it reverses the contents of a cell:

```
ReverseContents(myCell, IsText)
```

These are the arguments:

- myCell—The specified cell

- IsText—(Optional) Whether the cell value should be treated as text (default) or a number

Here's the function's code:

```
Function ReverseContents(myCell As Range, _
    Optional IsText As Boolean = True)
Dim i As Integer
Dim OrigString As String, NewString As String
OrigString = Trim(myCell) 'remove leading and trailing spaces
For i = 1 To Len(OrigString)
'by adding the variable NewString to the character,
'instead of adding the character to NewString the string is reversed
    NewString = Mid(OrigString, i, 1) & NewString
Next i
If IsText = False Then
    ReverseContents = CLng(NewString)
Else
    ReverseContents = NewString
End If
End Function
```

Returning the Addresses of Duplicate Max Values

MAX finds and returns the maximum value in a range, but it doesn't tell you whether there is more than one maximum value. This function returns the addresses of the maximum values in a range, as shown in Figure 14.15:

```
ReturnMaxs(Rng)
```

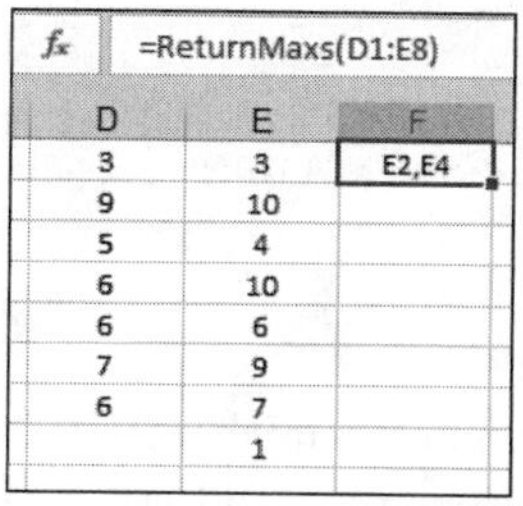

fx =ReturnMaxs(D1:E8)

D	E	F
3	3	E2,E4
9	10	
5	4	
6	10	
6	6	
7	9	
6	7	
	1	

Figure 14.15
Return the addresses of all maximum values in a range.

The argument is `Rng`, the range to search for the maximum values.

Here's the function's code:

```
Function ReturnMaxs(Rng As Range) As String
Dim Mx As Double
Dim myCell As Range
'if there is only one cell in the range, then exit
If Rng.Count = 1 Then ReturnMaxs = Rng.Address(False, False): _
    Exit Function
Mx = Application.Max(Rng) 'uses Excel's Max to find the max in the range
'Because you now know what the max value is,
'search the range to find matches and return the address
For Each myCell In Rng
    If myCell = Mx Then
        If Len(ReturnMaxs) = 0 Then
            ReturnMaxs = myCell.Address(False, False)
        Else
            ReturnMaxs = ReturnMaxs & ", " & myCell.Address(False, False)
        End If
    End If
Next myCell
End Function
```

Returning a Hyperlink Address

Let's say that you've received a spreadsheet containing a list of hyperlinked information. You want to see the actual links, not the descriptive text. You could just right-click a hyperlink and select Edit Hyperlink, but you want something more permanent. This function extracts the hyperlink address, as shown in Figure 14.16:

```
GetAddress(HyperlinkCell)
```

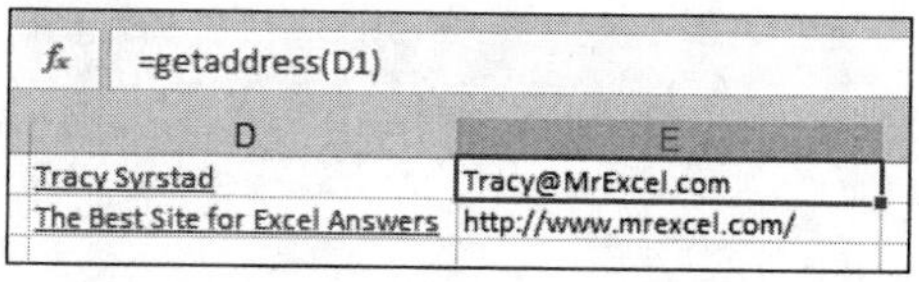

fx =getaddress(D1)

D	E
Tracy Syrstad	Tracy@MrExcel.com
The Best Site for Excel Answers	http://www.mrexcel.com/

Figure 14.16
Extract the hyperlink address from behind a hyperlink.

14

The argument is `HyperlinkCell`, the hyperlinked cell from which you want the address extracted.

Here's the function's code:

```
Function GetAddress(HyperlinkCell As Range)
    GetAddress = Replace(HyperlinkCell.Hyperlinks(1).Address, "mailto:", "")
End Function
```

Returning the Column Letter of a Cell Address

You can use CELL("Col") to return a column number; but what if you need the column letter? This function extracts the column letter from a cell address, as shown in Figure 14.17:

```
ColName(Rng)
```

Figure 14.17
Return the column letter of a cell address.

| A | =ColName(A1) |
| XL | =ColName(XL20) |

The argument is Rng, the cell for which you want the column letter.

Here's the function's code:

```
Function ColName(Rng As Range) As String
ColName = Left(Rng.Range("A1").Address(True, False), _
    InStr(1, Rng.Range("A1").Address(True, False), "$", 1) - 1)
End Function
```

Using Static Random

The function =RAND() can be very useful for creating random numbers, but it constantly recalculates. What if you need random numbers but don't want them to change constantly? The following function places a random number, but the number changes only if you force the cell to recalculate, as shown in Figure 14.18:

```
StaticRAND()
```

Figure 14.18
Produce random numbers that are not quite so volatile.

	A	B
1	0.143182	=StaticRAND()
2	99.67826	=StaticRAND()*100
3	58.00789	=SUM(A1:A2)*StaticRAND()
4		

There are no arguments for this function.

Here's the function's code:

```
Function StaticRAND() As Double
Randomize
STATICRAND = Rnd
End Function
```

Using `Select Case` on a Worksheet

At some point, you have probably nested an `If...Then...Else` on a worksheet to return a value. The `Select...Case` statement available in VBA makes this a lot easier, but you can't use `Select...Case` statements in a worksheet formula. Instead, you can create a UDF (see Figure 14.19).

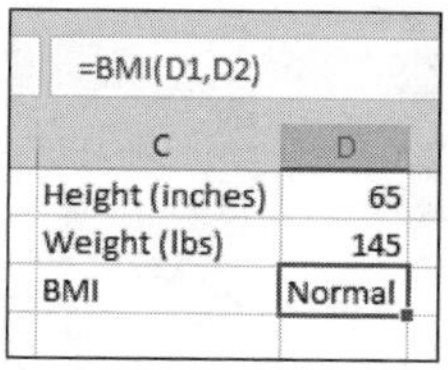

Figure 14.19
Example of using the `Select...Case` structure in a UDF rather than nested `If...Then` statements.

This example takes the user input, calculates the BMI (body mass index), and then compares that calculated value to various ranges to return a BMI descriptive, as shown in Figure 14.19. When creating a UDF, think of the formula in the same way you would write it down, because this is very similar to how you enter it in the UDF. The formula for calculating BMI is as follows:

BMI=(weight in pounds*703)/height in inches(squared)

The table for returning the BMI descriptive is as follows:

Below 18.5 = underweight

18.5–24.9 = normal

25–29.9 = overweight

30 & above = obese

The following code calculates the BMI and then returns the descriptive:

```
Function BMI(Height As Long, Weight As Long) As String
'Do the initial BMI calculation to get the numerical value
calcBMI = (Weight / (Height ^ 2)) * 703
Select Case calcBMI 'evaluate the calculated BMI to get a string value
    Case Is <=18.5 'if the calcBMI is less than 18.5
        BMI = "Underweight"
    Case 18.5 To 24.9 'if the calcBMI is a value between 18.5 and 24.9
        BMI = "Normal"
    Case 24.9 To 29.9
        BMI = "Overweight"
    Case Is >= 30 'if the calcBMI is greater than 30
        BMI = "Obese"
End Select
End Function
```

14

Next Steps

In Chapter 15, "Creating Charts," you'll find out how spreadsheet charting has become highly customizable and capable of handling large amounts of data.

Creating Charts

15

Charting in Excel 2016 picks up six new chart types and also moves to a modern charting engine. While this sounds like a good thing, the transition is going to introduce chaos to your charting macros over the next several years. Here's why: You have 73 old-style charts where the macro recorder works and you can create charts using VBA code that has worked reliably. The 6 new-style charts are not supported by the macro recorder. The VBA code is buggy. In order to work around the code, you need to use poor VBA practices, such as selecting the chart data before you create the chart.

Microsoft promises to slowly convert the 73 old-style charts to the modern charting engine over time. If Microsoft doesn't fix the VBA bugs before it starts moving charts to the new chart engine, with each monthly update, more of your working VBA code will stop working, and you will have to convert to the bad coding style. A preemptive move would be to assume that the Excel team won't bother to fix the VBA bugs and start creating all your code using the bad coding style.

Contrasting the Good and Bad VBA to Create Charts

Traditionally, the goal of VBA is to never select anything in the worksheet. Thus, you first create a chart by using the `.AddChart2` method and then assign the data to the chart by using the `.SetSource` method. Here is the macro recorder code to create an old-style clustered column chart using VBA:

15

```
ActiveSheet.Shapes.AddChart2(-1, xlColumnClustered).Select
ActiveChart.SetSourceData Source:=Range("Sheet1!$A$1:$B$7")
```

To prevent selecting the chart, you can assign the shape and the chart to an object variable, like this:

```
Dim WS as Worksheet
Dim CH as Chart
Set WS = ActiveSheet
Set CH = WS.Shapes.AddChart2(-1, xlColumnClustered).Chart
CH.SetSourceData Source:=Range("Sheet1!$A$1:$B$7")
```

The previous code works for all the old-style charts. But when used with a new-style chart as in the following code that attempts to create a waterfall chart, you get an empty chart. Microsoft confirms that this is a bug. You cannot turn to the macro recorder to learn how to successfully create new-style charts because the macro recorder is recording nothing when you use the new-style charts.

```
Dim WS as Worksheet
Dim CH as Chart
Set WS = ActiveSheet
Set CH = WS.Shapes.AddChart2(-1, xlWaterfall).Chart
CH.SetSourceData Source:=Range("Sheet1!$A$1:$B$7")
```

However, the bad sign is that the Excel team views the following workaround as a viable solution:

```
.Range("A1:B7").Select
ActiveSheet.Shapes.AddChart2(-1, xlWaterfall).Select
```

Thus, they may never get around to fixing the bug. In this code, you have to first select the data that will be used in the chart. Then you use the `.AddChart2` method without ever using `.SetSourceData` to change the data source.

Planning for More Charts to Break

You might be tempted to keep using the good code for the 73 existing chart types and use the bad code only for the 6 new chart types:

- `xlBoxWhisker`
- `xlHistogram`
- `xlPareto`
- `xlSunburst`
- `xlTreeMap`
- `xlWaterfall`

But then what happens when the Excel team migrates the pie chart over to the new engine? Your code will suddenly stop working. Thus, although the rest of this book teaches you that selecting data is not necessary, the examples in this chapter select the data before creating the chart.

The following code creates an old-style clustered column chart by selecting the data before using the .AddChart2 method. It uses a CH object variable that references the newly created chart:

```
Sub SafeWayToCreateAChart()
' Create a clustered column chart from A1:E7
Dim WS as Worksheet
Dim CH as Chart
Set WS = Worksheets("Sheet1")
WS.Select
Range("A1:E7").Select
Set CH = WS.Shapes.AddChart2(-1, xlColumnClustered)
End Sub
```

You can use that object variable later, when you format the chart. For example, the following code creates a new-style waterfall chart and marks the sixth column as a total:

```
Sub SafeWayToCreateAChart()
' Create a waterfall chart from A1:B7
Dim WS as Worksheet
Dim CH as Chart
Set WS = Worksheets("Sheet1")
WS.Select
Range("A1:B7").Select
Set CH = WS.Shapes.AddChart2(-1, xlWaterfall)
CH.FullSeriesCollection(1).Points(6).IsTotal = True
End Sub
```

Using .AddChart2 to Create a Chart

Excel 2013 introduced a streamlined .AddChart2 method. With this method, you can specify a chart style, type, size, and location, as well as a property introduced in Excel 2013: NewLayout:=True. When you choose NewLayout, you can avoid having a legend in a single-series chart.

The .AddChart2 method enables you to specify the chart style, chart type, left, top, width, height, and new layout. This code takes the data from A3:G7 and creates a chart to fill B8:G15:

```
Sub CreateChartUsingAddChart2()
'Create a Clustered Column Chart in B8:G15 from data in A3:G6
Dim CH As Chart
Range("A3:G6").Select
Set CH = ActiveSheet.Shapes.AddChart2( _
    Style:=201, _
    XlChartType:=xlColumnClustered, _
    Left:=Range("B8").Left, _
    Top:=Range("B8").Top, _
    Width:=Range("B8:G15").Width, _
    Height:=Range("B8:G15").Height, _
    NewLayout:=True).Chart
End Sub
```

The values for `Left`, `Top`, `Width`, and `Height` are in pixels. Here you don't have to try to guess that column B is 27.34 pixels from the left edge of the worksheet because the preceding code finds the `.Left` property of cell B8 and uses that as the `Left` of the chart.

Figure 15.1 shows the resulting chart.

Figure 15.1
Create a chart to fill a specific range.

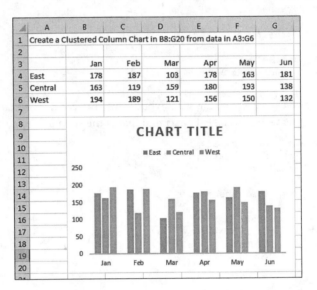

Understanding Chart Styles

Excel 2013 introduced professionally designed chart styles that are shown in the Chart Styles gallery on the Design tab of the ribbon. These innovative designs use combinations of properties that have been in Excel for years, but they allow you to apply a group of properties in a single command. Figure 15.2 shows the Chart Styles gallery for a clustered column chart.

Figure 15.2
Apply a chart style to quickly format a chart.

The styles for the old chart types run from 201 to 353. Styles 354 to 418 are for the six new chart types. Follow these steps to learn the style number associated with your favorite style:

1. Create a chart in the Excel user interface.
2. Open the Chart Styles gallery on the Design tab and choose the Chart style you want to use. Keep the chart selected before moving to Step 3.

> **CAUTION**
>
> You might have a tendency to click away from the chart in order to admire the newly selected style. If you do unselect the chart, be certain to re-select the chart before continuing with the following steps.

3. Switch to VBA by pressing Alt+F11.

4. Open the Immediate window by pressing Ctrl+G.

5. Type `? ActiveChart.ChartStyle` in the Immediate window and press Enter. The resulting number shows you the value to use for the `.Style` argument in the `.AddChart2` method.

6. If you don't care what chart style you will get, specify `-1` as the `.Style` argument. This gives you the default style for that chart type.

It is strange that the `.AddChart2` method uses an argument called `Style:=201`, but if you want to change the chart style later, you have to use the `.ChartStyle` property. Both `Style` and `ChartStyle` refer to the chart styles introduced in Excel 2013.

Table 15.1 lists the `ChartType` argument values.

Table 15.1 Chart Types for Use in VBA

Chart Type	Enumerated Constant
Clustered column	`xlColumnClustered`
Stacked column	`xlColumnStacked`
100% stacked column	`xlColumnStacked100`
3-D clustered column	`xl3DColumnClustered`
Stacked column in 3-D	`xl3DColumnStacked`
100% stacked column in 3-D	`xl3DColumnStacked100`
3-D column	`xl3DColumn`
Waterfall	`xlWaterfall`
Tree map	`xlTreeMap`
Sunburst	`xlSunburst`
Histogram	`xlHistogram`
Pareto	`xlPareto`
Box and whisker	`xlBoxWhisker`
Line	`xlLine`
Stacked line	`xlLineStacked`
100% stacked line	`xlLineStacked100`
Line with markers	`xlLineMarkers`

Chart Type	Enumerated Constant
Stacked line with markers	xlLineMarkersStacked
100% stacked line with markers	xlLineMarkersStacked100
Pie	xlPie
Pie in 3-D	xl3DPie
Pie of pie	xlPieOfPie
Exploded pie	xlPieExploded
Exploded pie in 3-D	xl3DPieExploded
Bar of pie	xlBarOfPie
Clustered bar	xlBarClustered
Stacked bar	xlBarStacked
100% stacked bar	xlBarStacked100
Clustered bar in 3-D	xl3DBarClustered
Stacked bar in 3-D	xl3DBarStacked
100% stacked bar in 3-D	xl3DBarStacked100
Area	xlArea
Stacked area	xlAreaStacked
100% stacked area	xlAreaStacked100
3-D area	xl3DArea
Stacked area in 3-D	xl3DAreaStacked
100% stacked area in 3-D	xl3DAreaStacked100
Scatter with only markers	xlXYScatter
Scatter with smooth lines and markers	xlXYScatterSmooth
Scatter with smooth lines	xlXYScatterSmoothNoMarkers
Scatter with straight lines and markers	xlXYScatterLines
Scatter with straight lines	xlXYScatterLinesNoMarkers
High-low-close	xlStockHLC
Open-high-low-close	xlStockOHLC
Volume-high-low-close	xlStockVHLC
Volume-open-high-low-close	xlStockVOHLC
3-D surface	xlSurface
Wireframe 3-D surface	xlSurfaceWireframe
Contour	xlSurfaceTopView
Wireframe contour	xlSurfaceTopViewWireframe
Doughnut	xlDoughnut

Chart Type	Enumerated Constant
Exploded doughnut	`xlDoughnutExploded`
Bubble	`xlBubble`
Bubble with a 3-D effect	`xlBubble3DEffect`
Radar	`xlRadar`
Radar with markers	`xlRadarMarkers`
Filled radar	`xlRadarFilled`

Excel supports a few other chart types that misrepresent your data, such as the cone and pyramid charts. For backward compatibility, these are still in VBA, but they are omitted from Table 15.1. If your manager forces you to create those old chart types, you can find them by searching for *xlChartType enumeration* in your favorite search engine.

Formatting a Chart

After creating a chart, you will often want to add or move elements of the chart. The following sections describe code to control the myriad chart elements.

Referring to a Specific Chart

The macro recorder has an unsatisfactory way of writing code for chart creation. The macro recorder uses the `.AddChart2` method and adds a `.Select` to the end of the line in order to select the chart. The rest of the chart settings then apply to the `ActiveChart` object. This approach is a bit frustrating because you are required to do all the chart formatting before you select anything else in the worksheet. The macro recorder does this because chart names are unpredictable. The first time you run a macro, the chart might be called Chart 1. But if you run the macro on another day or on a different worksheet, the chart might be called Chart 3 or Chart 5.

For the most flexibility, you should assign each new chart to a `Chart` object. Since Excel 2007, the `Chart` object has existed inside a `Shape` object.

Ignoring the specifics of the `AddChart2` method for a moment, you could use this coding approach, which captures the `Shape` object in the `SH` object variable and then assigns `SH.Chart` to the `CH` object variable:

```
Dim WS as Worksheet
Dim SH as Shape
Dim CH as Chart
Set WS = ActiveSheet
Set SH = WS.Shapes.AddChart2(...)
Set CH = SH.Chart
```

You can simplify the preceding code by appending `.Chart` to the end of the `AddChart2` method. The following code has one object variable fewer:

```
Dim WS as Worksheet
Dim CH as Chart
Set WS = ActiveSheet
Set CH = WS.Shapes.AddChart2(...).Chart
```

If you need to modify a preexisting chart—such as a chart that you did not create—and there is only one shape on the worksheet, you can use this line of code:

```
WS.Shapes(1).Chart.Interior.Color = RGB(0,0,255)
```

If there are many charts, and you need to find the one with the upper-left corner located in cell A4, you can loop through all the Shape objects until you find one in the correct location, like this:

```
For each Sh in ActiveSheet.Shapes
If Sh.TopLeftCell.Address = "$A$4" then
Sh.Chart.Interior.Color = RGB(0,255,0)
End If
Next Sh
```

Specifying a Chart Title

Every chart created with NewLayout:=True has a chart title. When the chart has two or more series, that title is "Chart Title." You should plan on changing the chart title to something useful.

To specify a chart title in VBA, use this code:

```
ActiveChart.ChartTitle.Caption = "Sales by Region"
```

If you are changing the chart title of a newly created chart that is assigned to the CH object variable, you can use this:

```
CH.ChartTitle.Caption = "Sales by Region"
```

This code works if your chart already has a title. If you are not sure that the selected chart style has a title, you can ensure that the title is present first with this:

```
CH.SetElement msoElementChartTitleAboveChart
```

Although it is relatively easy to add a chart title and specify the words in the title, it becomes increasingly complex to change the formatting of the chart title. The following code changes the font, size, and color of the title:

```
With CH.ChartTitle.Format.TextFrame2.TextRange.Font
.Name = "Rockwell"
.Fill.ForeColor.ObjectThemeColor = msoThemeColorAccent2
.Size = 14
End With
```

The two axis titles operate the same as the chart title. To change the words, use the .Caption property. To format the words, use the Format property. Similarly, you can specify the axis titles by using the Caption property. The following code changes the axis title along the category axis:

```
CH.SetElement msoElementPrimaryCategoryAxisTitleHorizontal
CH.Axes(xlCategory, xlPrimary).AxisTitle.Caption = "Months"
CH.Axes(xlCategory, xlPrimary).AxisTitle. _
Format.TextFrame2.TextRange.Font.Fill. _
ForeColor.ObjectThemeColor = msoThemeColorAccent2
```

Applying a Chart Color

Excel 2013 introduced a `ch.ChartColor` property that assigns 1 of 26 color themes to a chart. Assign a value from `1` to `26`, but be aware that the order of the colors in the Chart Styles fly-out menu (see Figure 15.3) has nothing to do with the 26 values.

Figure 15.3
Color schemes in the menu are called Color 1, Color 2, and so on but have nothing to do with the VBA settings.

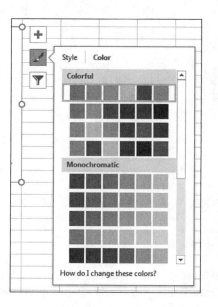

To understand the `ChartColor` values, consider the color drop-down shown in Figure 15.4. This drop-down offers 10 columns of colors: Background 1, Text 1, Background 2, Text 2, and then Theme 1 through Theme 6.

Here is a synopsis of the 26 values you can use for `ChartColor`:

- `ChartColor` 1, 9, and 20 use grayscale colors from column 3. A `ChartColor` value of `1` starts with a dark gray, then a light gray, then a medium gray. A `ChartColor` value of `9` starts with a light gray and moves to darker grays. A `ChartColor` value of `20` starts with three medium grays, then black, then very light gray, then medium gray.

- Value `2` uses the six theme colors in the top row, from left to right.

- Values `3` through `8` use a single column of colors. For example, `ChartColor = 3` uses the six colors in Theme 1, from dark to light. `ChartColor` values of `4` through `8` correspond to Themes 2 through 6.

- Value `10` repeats value `2` but adds a light border around the chart element.

- Values `11` through `13` are the most inventive. They use three theme colors from the top row combined with the same three theme colors from the bottom row. This produces light and dark versions of three different colors. `ChartColor` `11` uses the odd-numbered themes (1, 3, and 5). `ChartColor` `12` uses the even-numbered themes. `ChartColor` `13` uses Themes 6, 5, and 4.

■ Values 14 through 19 repeat values 3 through 8 but add a light border.

■ Values 21 through 26 are similar to values 3 through 8, but the colors progress from light to dark.

Figure 15.4
`ChartColor` combinations include a mix of colors from the current theme.

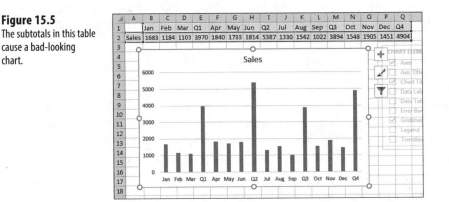

The following code changes the chart to use varying shades of Themes 6, 5, and 4:

```
ch.ChartColor = 13
```

Filtering a Chart

In real life, creating charts from tables of data is not always simple. Tables frequently have totals or subtotals. The table in Figure 15.5 has quarterly total columns intermixed with monthly values. When you create a chart from this data, the total columns create a bad chart.

Figure 15.5
The subtotals in this table cause a bad-looking chart.

To filter a row or column in VBA, you set the new `.IsFiltered` property to `True`. The following code removes the total columns:

```
CH.ChartGroups(1).FullCategoryCollection(4).IsFiltered = True
CH.ChartGroups(1).FullCategoryCollection(8).IsFiltered = True
CH.ChartGroups(1).FullCategoryCollection(12).IsFiltered = True
CH.ChartGroups(1).FullCategoryCollection(16).IsFiltered = True
```

Using `SetElement` **to Emulate Changes from the Plus Icon**

When you select a chart, three icons appear to the right of the chart. The top icon is a plus sign. All the choices in the first- and second-level fly-out menus use the `SetElement` method in VBA. Note that the Add Chart Element drop-down on the Design tab includes all of these settings, plus Lines and Up/Down Bars.

> **NOTE**
>
> `SetElement` does not cover all of the choices in the Format task pane that often appears. See the "Using the `Format` Method to Micromanage Formatting Options" section later in this chapter to change those settings.

If you do not feel like looking up the proper constant in this book, you can always quickly record a macro. Provided you are not using one of the six new chart types introduced in Excel 2016, the macro recorder should show you the correct `SetElement` constant.

The `SetElement` method is followed by a constant that specifies which menu item to select. For example, if you want to choose Show Legend at Left, you can use this code:

```
ActiveChart.SetElement msoElementLegendLeft
```

Table 15.2 shows all the available constants you can use with the `SetElement` method. These constants are in roughly the same order in which they appear in the Add Chart Element drop-down.

Table 15.2   Constants Available with `SetElement`

Element Group	`SetElement` Constant
Axes	msoElementPrimaryCategoryAxisNone
Axes	msoElementPrimaryCategoryAxisShow
Axes	msoElementPrimaryCategoryAxisWithoutLabels
Axes	msoElementPrimaryCategoryAxisReverse
Axes	msoElementPrimaryCategoryAxisThousands
Axes	msoElementPrimaryCategoryAxisMillions
Axes	msoElementPrimaryCategoryAxisBillions
Axes	msoElementPrimaryCategoryAxisLogScale
Axes	msoElementSecondaryCategoryAxisNone
Axes	msoElementSecondaryCategoryAxisShow
Axes	msoElementSecondaryCategoryAxisWithoutLabels
Axes	msoElementSecondaryCategoryAxisReverse
Axes	msoElementSecondaryCategoryAxisThousands
Axes	msoElementSecondaryCategoryAxisMillions

Element Group	`SetElement` **Constant**
Axes	`msoElementSecondaryCategoryAxisBillions`
Axes	`msoElementSecondaryCategoryAxisLogScaIe`
Axes	`msoElementPrimaryValueAxisNone`
Axes	`msoElementPrimaryValueAxisShow`
Axes	`msoElementPrimaryValueAxisThousands`
Axes	`msoElementPrimaryValueAxisMillions`
Axes	`msoElementPrimaryValueAxisBillions`
Axes	`msoElementPrimaryValueAxisLogScale`
Axes	`msoElementSecondaryValueAxisNone`
Axes	`msoElementSecondaryValueAxisShow`
Axes	`msoElementSecondaryValueAxisThousands`
Axes	`msoElementSecondaryValueAxisMillions`
Axes	`msoElementSecondaryValueAxisBillions`
Axes	`msoElementSecondaryValueAxisLogScale`
Axes	`msoElementSeriesAxisNone`
Axes	`msoElementSeriesAxisShow`
Axes	`msoElementSeriesAxisReverse`
Axes	`msoElementSeriesAxisWithoutLabeling`
Axis Titles	`msoElementPrimaryCategoryAxisTitleNone`
Axis Titles	`msoElementPrimaryCategoryAxisTitleBelowAxis`
Axis Titles	`msoElementPrimaryCategoryAxisTitleAdjacentToAxis`
Axis Titles	`msoElementPrimaryCategoryAxisTitleHorizontal`
Axis Titles	`msoEIementPrimaryCategoryAxisTitleVertical`
Axis Titles	`msoElementPrimaryCategoryAxisTitleRotated`
Axis Titles	`msoElementSecondaryCategoryAxisTitleAdjacentToAxis`
Axis Titles	`msoElementSecondaryCategoryAxisTitleBelowAxis`
Axis Titles	`msoElementSecondaryCategoryAxisTitleHorizontal`
Axis Titles	`msoElementSecondaryCategoryAxisTitleNone`
Axis Titles	`msoElementSecondaryCategoryAxisTitleRotated`
Axis Titles	`msoElementSecondaryCategoryAxisTitleVertical`
Axis Titles	`msoElementPrimaryValueAxisTitleAdjacentToAxis`
Axis Titles	`msoElementPrimaryValueAxisTitleBelowAxis`
Axis Titles	`msoElementPrimaryValueAxisTitleHorizontal`
Axis Titles	`msoElementPrimaryValueAxisTitleNone`

Element Group	SetElement Constant
Axis Titles	msoElementPrimaryValueAxisTitleRotated
Axis Titles	msoElementPrimaryValueAxisTitleVertical
Axis Titles	msoElementSecondaryValueAxisTitleBelowAxis
Axis Titles	msoElementSecondaryValueAxisTitleHorizontal
Axis Titles	msoElementSecondaryValueAxisTitleNone
Axis Titles	msoElementSecondaryValueAxisTitleRotated
Axis Titles	msoElementSecondaryValueAxisTitleVertical
Axis Titles	msoElementSeriesAxisTitleHorizontal
Axis Titles	msoElementSeriesAxisTitleNone
Axis Titles	msoElementSeriesAxisTitleRotated
Axis Titles	msoElementSeriesAxisTitleVertical
Axis Titles	msoElementSecondaryValueAxisTitleAdjacentToAxis
Chart Title	msoElementChartTitleNone
Chart Title	msoElementChartTitleCenteredOverlay
Chart Title	msoElementChartTitleAboveChart
Data Labels	msoElementDataLabelCallout (new in Excel 2016)
Data Labels	msoElementDataLabelCenter
Data Labels	msoElementDataLabelInsideEnd
Data Labels	msoElementDataLabelNone
Data Labels	msoElementDataLabelInsideBase
Data Labels	msoElementDataLabelOutSideEnd
Data Labels	msoElementDataLabelTop
Data Labels	msoElementDataLabelBottom
Data Labels	msoElementDataLabelRight
Data Labels	msoElementDataLabelLeft
Data Labels	msoElementDataLabelShow
Data Labels	msoElementDataLabelBestFit
Data Table	msoElementDataTableNone
Data Table	msoElementDataTableShow
Data Table	msoElementDataTableWithLegendKeys
Error Bars	msoElementErrorBarNone
Error Bars	msoElementErrorBarStandardError
Error Bars	msoElementErrorBarPercentage
Error Bars	msoElementErrorBarStandardDeviation

15

Element Group	SetElement Constant
GridLines	msoElementPrimaryCategoryGridLinesNone
GridLines	msoElementPrimaryCategoryGridLinesMajor
GridLines	msoElementPrimaryCategoryGridLinesMinor
GridLines	msoElementPrimaryCategoryGridLinesMinorMajor
GridLines	msoElementSecondaryCategoryGridLinesNone
GridLines	msoElementSecondaryCategoryGridLinesMajor
GridLines	msoElementSecondaryCategoryGridLinesMinor
GridLines	msoElementSecondaryCategoryGridLinesMinorMajor
GridLines	msoElementPrimaryValueGridLinesNone
GridLines	msoElementPrimaryValueGridLinesMajor
GridLines	msoElementPrimaryValueGridLinesMinor
GridLines	msoElementPrimaryValueGridLinesMinorMajor
GridLines	msoElementSecondaryValueGridLinesNone
GridLines	msoElementSecondaryValueGridLinesMajor
GridLines	msoElementSecondaryValueGridLinesMinor
GridLines	msoElementSecondaryValueGridLinesMinorMajor
GridLines	msoElementSeriesAxisGridLinesNone
GridLines	msoElementSeriesAxisGridLinesMajor
GridLines	msoElementSeriesAxisGridLinesMinor
GridLines	msoElementSeriesAxisGridLinesMinorMajor
Legend	msoElementLegendNone
Legend	msoElementLegendRight
Legend	msoElementLegendTop
Legend	msoElementLegendLeft
Legend	msoElementLegendBottom
Legend	msoElementLegendRightOverlay
Legend	msoElementLegendLeftOverlay
Lines	msoElementLineNone
Lines	msoElementLineDropLine
Lines	msoElementLineHiLoLine
Lines	msoElementLineDropHiLoLine
Lines	msoElementLineSeriesLine
Trendline	msoElementTrendlineNone
Trendline	msoElementTrendlineAddLinear

Element Group	SetElement **Constant**
Trendline	`msoElementTrendlineAddExponential`
Trendline	`msoElementTrendlineAddLinearForecast`
Trendline	`msoElementTrendlineAddTwoPeriodMovingAverage`
Up/Down Bars	`msoElementUpDownBarsNone`
Up/Down Bars	`msoElementUpDownBarsShow`
Plot Area	`msoElementPlotAreaNone`
Plot Area	`msoElementPlotAreaShow`
Chart Wall	`msoElementChartWallNone`
Chart Wall	`msoElementChartWallShow`
Chart Floor	`msoElementChartFloorNone`
Chart Floor	`msoElementChartFloorShow`

> **NOTE** If you attempt to format an element that is not present, Excel returns a `-2147467259 Method Failed` error.

Using `SetElement` enables you to change chart elements quickly. As an example, charting gurus say that the legend should always appear to the left or above the chart. Few of the built-in styles show the legend above the chart. I also prefer to show the values along the axis in thousands or millions, when appropriate. This is better than displaying three or six zeros on every line.

The following code handles these settings after you create the chart:

```
Sub UseSetElement()
Dim WS As Worksheet
Dim CH As Chart

Set WS = ActiveSheet
Range("A1:M4").Select
Set CH = WS.Shapes.AddChart2(Style:=201, _
XlChartType:=xlColumnClustered, _
Left:=[B6].Left, _
Top:=[B6].Top, _
NewLayout:=False).Chart

' Set value axis to display thousands
CH.SetElement msoElementPrimaryValueAxisThousands

' move the legend to the top
CH.SetElement msoElementLegendTop
End Sub
```

15

Using the `Format` Method to Micromanage Formatting Options

The Format tab offers icons for changing colors and effects for individual chart elements. Although many people call the Shadow, Glow, Bevel, and Material settings "chart junk," there are ways in VBA to apply these formats.

Excel 2016 includes an object called the `ChartFormat` object that contains the settings for `Fill`, `Glow`, `Line`, `PictureFormat`, `Shadow`, `SoftEdge`, `TextFrame2`, and `ThreeD`. You can access the `ChartFormat` object by using the `Format` method on many chart elements. Table 15.3 lists a sampling of chart elements you can format using the `Format` method.

Table 15.3 Chart3 Chart Elements to Which Formatting Applies

Chart Element	VBA to Refer to This Chart Element
Chart Title	`ChartTitle`
Axis Title–Category	`Axes(xlCategory, xlPrimary).AxisTitle`
Axis Title–Value	`Axes(xlValue, xlPrimary).AxisTitle`
Legend	`Legend`
Data Labels for Series 1	`SeriesCollection(1).DataLabels`
Data Labels for Point 2	`SeriesCollection(1).DataLabels(2)` or `SeriesCollection(1).Points(2).DataLabel`
Data Table	`DataTable`
Axes–Horizontal	`Axes(xlCategory, xlPrimary)`
Axes–Vertical	`Axes(xlValue, xlPrimary)`
Axis–Series (Surface Charts Only)	`Axes(xlSeries, xlPrimary)`
Major Gridlines	`Axes(xlValue, xlPrimary).MajorGridlines`
Minor Gridlines	`Axes(xlValue, xlPrimary).MinorGridlines`
Plot Area	`PlotArea`
Chart Area	`ChartArea`
Chart Wall	`Walls`
Chart Back Wall	`BackWall`
Chart Side Wall	`SideWall`
Chart Floor	`Floor`
Trendline for Series 1	`SeriesCollection(1).TrendLines(1)`
Droplines	`ChartGroups(1).DropLines`
Up/Down Bars	`ChartGroups(1).UpBars`
Error Bars	`SeriesCollection(1).ErrorBars`
Series(1)	`SeriesCollection(1)`
Series(1) DataPoint	`SeriesCollection(1).Points(3)`

The `Format` method is the gateway to settings for `Fill`, `Glow`, and so on. Each of those objects has different options. The following sections provide examples of how to set up each type of format.

Changing an Object's Fill

The Shape Fill drop-down on the Format tab enables you to choose a single color, a gradient, a picture, or a texture for the fill.

To apply a specific color, you can use the RGB (red, green, blue) setting. To create a color, you specify a value from `0` to `255` for levels of red, green, and blue. The following code applies a simple blue fill:

```
Dim cht As Chart
Dim upb As UpBars
Set cht = ActiveChart
Set upb = cht.ChartGroups(1).UpBars
upb.Format.Fill.ForeColor.RGB = RGB(0, 0, 255)
```

If you would like an object to pick up the color from a specific theme accent color, you use the `ObjectThemeColor` property. The following code changes the bar color of the first series to accent color 6, which is an orange color in the Office theme (but might be another color if the workbook is using a different theme):

```
Sub ApplyThemeColor()
Dim cht As Chart
Dim ser As Series
Set cht = ActiveChart
Set ser = cht.SeriesCollection(1)
ser.Format.Fill.ForeColor.ObjectThemeColor = msoThemeColorAccent6
End Sub
```

To apply a built-in texture, you use the `PresetTextured` method. The following code applies a green marble texture to the second series. However, you can apply any of the 20 textures:

```
Sub ApplyTexture()
Dim cht As Chart
Dim ser As Series
Set cht = ActiveChart
Set ser = cht.SeriesCollection(2)
ser.Format.Fill.PresetTextured msoTextureGreenMarble
End Sub
```

> **NOTE** When you type `PresetTextured` followed by a space, the VB Editor offers a complete list of possible texture values.

To fill the bars of a data series with a picture, you use the `UserPicture` method and specify the path and filename of an image on the computer, as in the following example:

```
Sub FormatWithPicture()
Dim cht As Chart
Dim ser As Series
Set cht = ActiveChart
Set ser = cht.SeriesCollection(1)
MyPic = "C:\PodCastTitle1.jpg"
ser.Format.Fill.UserPicture MyPic
End Sub
```

In Excel 2016, you can apply a pattern by using the `.Patterned` method. Patterns have a type such as `msoPatternPlain`, as well as foreground and background colors. The following code creates dark red vertical lines on a white background:

```
Sub FormatWithPicture()
Dim cht As Chart
Dim ser As Series
Set cht = ActiveChart
Set ser = cht.SeriesCollection(1)
With ser.Format.Fill
.Patterned msoPatternDarkVertical
.BackColor.RGB = RGB(255,255,255)
.ForeColor.RGB = RGB(255,0,0)
End With
End Sub
```

> **CAUTION**
>
> Code that uses patterns does not work with Excel 2007. Patterns were removed from Excel 2007, but they were restored in Excel 2010 due to outcry from fans of patterns.

Gradients are more difficult to specify than fills. Excel 2016 provides three methods that help you set up the common gradients. The `OneColorGradient` and `TwoColorGradient` methods require that you specify a gradient direction such as `msoGradientFromCorner`. You can then specify one of four styles, numbered 1 through 4, depending on whether you want the gradient to start at the top left, top right, bottom left, or bottom right. After using a gradient method, you need to specify the `ForeColor` and the `BackColor` settings for the object. The following macro sets up a two-color gradient using two theme colors:

```
Sub TwoColorGradient()
Dim cht As Chart
Dim ser As Series
Set cht = ActiveChart
Set ser = cht.SeriesCollection(1)
ser.Format.Fill.TwoColorGradient msoGradientFromCorner, 3
ser.Format.Fill.ForeColor.ObjectThemeColor = msoThemeColorAccent6
ser.Format.Fill.BackColor.ObjectThemeColor = msoThemeColorAccent2
End Sub
```

When using the `OneColorGradient` method, you specify a direction, a style (1 through 4), and a darkness value between 0 and 1 (0 for darker gradients to 1 for lighter gradients).

When using the `PresetGradient` method, you specify a direction, a style (1 through 4), and the type of gradient, such as `msoGradientBrass`, `msoGradientLateSunset`, or `msoGradient-Rainbow`. Again, as you are typing this code in the VB Editor, the AutoComplete tool provides a complete list of the available preset gradient types.

Formatting Line Settings

The `LineFormat` object formats either a line or the border around an object. You can change numerous properties of a line, such as the color, arrows, and dash style.

The following macro formats the trendline for the first series in a chart:

```
Sub FormatLineOrBorders()
Dim cht As Chart
Set cht = ActiveChart
With cht.SeriesCollection(1).Trendlines(1).Format.Line
.DashStyle = msoLineLongDashDotDot
.ForeColor.RGB = RGB(50, 0, 128)
.BeginArrowheadLength = msoArrowheadShort
.BeginArrowheadStyle = msoArrowheadOval
.BeginArrowheadWidth = msoArrowheadNarrow
.EndArrowheadLength = msoArrowheadLong
.EndArrowheadStyle = msoArrowheadTriangle
.EndArrowheadWidth = msoArrowheadWide
End With
End Sub
```

When you are formatting a border, the arrow settings are not relevant, so the code is shorter than the code for formatting a line. The following macro formats the border around a chart:

```
Sub FormatBorder()
Dim cht As Chart
Set cht = ActiveChart
With cht.ChartArea.Format.Line
.DashStyle = msoLineLongDashDotDot
.ForeColor.RGB = RGB(50, 0, 128)
End With
End Sub
```

Creating a Combo Chart

Sometimes you need to chart series of data that are of differing orders of magnitude. Normal charts do a lousy job of showing smaller series. Combo charts can save the day.

Consider the data and chart in Figure 15.6. Here you want to plot the number of sales per month and also show two quality ratings. Perhaps this is a fictitious car dealer that sells 80 to 100 cars a month, and the customer satisfaction usually runs in the 80% to 90% range. When you try to plot this data on a regular line chart, the column for 90 cars sold dwarfs the column for 80% customer satisfaction.

Figure 15.6
The two small series are moved to a secondary axis.

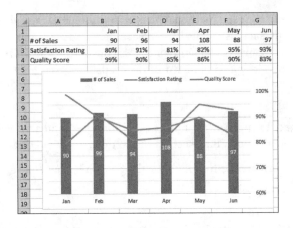

The following case study shows you the VBA needed to create a combo chart.

CASE STUDY CREATING A COMBO CHART

You want to create a chart that shows the number of sales and also two percentage measurements. In this process, you have to format each of the three series. At the top of the macro, declare object variables for the worksheet, the chart, and each of the series:

```
Dim WS As Worksheet
Dim CH As Chart
Dim Ser1 As Series
Dim Ser2 As Series
Dim Ser3 As Series
```

Create the chart as a regular clustered column chart.

```
Set WS = ActiveSheet
Range("A1:G4").Select
Set CH = WS.Shapes.AddChart2(Style:=201, _
XlChartType:=xlColumnClustered, _
Left:=[B6].Left, _
Top:=[B6].Top, _
NewLayout:=False).Chart
```

To work with a series, assign `FullSeriesCollection` to an object variable such as `Ser2`. You could get away with a single object variable called `Ser` that you use over and over. This code enables you to come back later in the macro to refer to any of the three series. After you have the `Ser2` object variable defined, assign the series to the secondary axis group and change the chart type of just that series to a line; then repeat the code for Series 3:

```
' Move Series 2 to secondary axis as line
Set Ser2 = CH.FullSeriesCollection(2)
With Ser2
.AxisGroup = xlSecondary
.ChartType = xlLine
End With
```

```
' Move Series 3 to secondary axis as line
Set Ser3 = CH.FullSeriesCollection(3)
With Ser3
.AxisGroup = xlSecondary
.ChartType = xlLine
End With
```

Note that so far you have not had to touch Series 1. Series 1 is fine as a column chart on the primary axis. You'll come back to Series 1 later in the macro.Because too many of the data points in Series 3 were close to 100%, the Excel charting engine decided to make the right axis span all the way up to 120%. This is silly because no one can get a rating higher than 100%. You can override the automatic settings and choose a scale for the right axis. The following code uses 0.6 (for 60%) as the minimum and 1 (for 100%) as the maximum:

```
' Set the secondary axis to go from 60% to 100%
CH.Axes(xlValue, xlSecondary).MinimumScale = 0.6
CH.Axes(xlValue, xlSecondary).MaximumScale = 1
```

When you override the scale values, Excel automatically guesses where you want the gridlines and axis labels. Rather than leave this to chance, you can use MajorUnit and MinorUnit:

```
' Labels every 10%, secondary gridline at 5%
CH.Axes(xlValue, xlSecondary).MajorUnit = 0.1
CH.Axes(xlValue, xlSecondary).MinorUnit = 0.05
CH.Axes(xlValue, xlSecondary).TickLabels.NumberFormat = "0%"
```

Axis labels and major gridlines appear at the increment specified by MajorUnit. MinorUnit, and that is important only if you plan on showing minor gridlines.

At this point, there are numbers on the left axis and numbers on the right axis. I instantly went to the percentages on the right side and tried to follow the gridlines across. But this doesn't work because the gridlines don't line up with the numbers on the right side. They line up with the numbers on the left side. You can't really tell this for sure, though, because the gridlines coincidentally happen to line up with 100%, 80%, and 60%.

At this point, you might decide to get creative. You could use the following code to delete the gridlines for the left axis, add major and minor gridlines for the right axis, delete the numbers along the left axis, and replace the numbers on the axis with a data label in the center of each column:

```
' Turn off the gridlines for left axis
CH.Axes(xlValue).HasMajorGridlines = False
' Add gridlines for right axis
CH.SetElement (msoElementSecondaryValueGridLinesMajor)
CH.SetElement (msoElementSecondaryValueGridLinesMinorMajor)

' Hide the labels on the primary axis
CH.Axes(xlValue).TickLabelPosition = xlNone
' Replace axis labels with a data label on the column
Set Ser1 = CH.FullSeriesCollection(1)
Ser1.ApplyDataLabels

Ser1.DataLabels.Position = xlLabelPositionCenter
```

Now you almost have it. Because the book is printed in monochrome, change the color of the Series 1 data label to white:

15

```
' Data Labels in white
With Ser1.DataLabels.Format.TextFrame2.TextRange.Font.Fill
.Visible = msoTrue
.ForeColor.ObjectThemeColor = msoThemeColorBackground1
.Solid
End With
```

And because my charting mentors drilled it into my head, the legend has to be at the top or the left. Here's how you move it to the top:

```
' Legend at the top, per Gene Z.
CH.SetElement msoElementLegendTop
```

The resulting chart is shown in Figure 15.7. Thanks to the minor gridlines, you can easily tell if each rating was in the 80%–85%, 85%–90%, or 90%–95% range. The columns show the sales, and the labels stay out of the way, but they are still readable.

Figure 15.7
The gridlines and the two series represented by a line correspond to the axis labels on the right side.

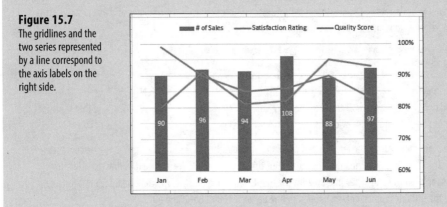

Exporting a Chart as a Graphic

You can export any chart to an image file on your hard drive. The `ExportChart` method requires you to specify a filename and a graphic type. The available graphic types depend on graphic file filters installed in your Registry. It is a safe bet that JPG, BMP, PNG, and GIF work on most computers.

For example, the following code exports the active chart as a GIF file:

```
Sub ExportChart()
Dim cht As Chart
Set cht = ActiveChart
cht.Export Filename:="C:\Chart.gif", Filtername:="GIF"
End Sub
```

Considering Backward Compatibility

The `.AddChart2` method works in Excel 2013 and Excel 2016. For Excel 2007 and 2010, you have to revert to using the `.AddChart` method, as shown here:

```
Sub CreateChartIn20072010()
'Create a Clustered Column Chart in B8:G15 from data in A3:G6
Dim CH As Chart
Range("A3:G6").Select
Set CH = ActiveSheet.Shapes.AddChart( _
    XlChartType:=xlColumnClustered, _
    Left:=Range("B8").Left, _
    Top:=Range("B8").Top, _
    Width:=Range("B8:G15").Width, _
    Height:=Range("B8:G15").Height).Chart
End Sub
```

With this method, you can specify neither a `Style` nor a `NewLayout`.

Next Steps

In Chapter 16, "Data Visualizations and Conditional Formatting," you'll find out how to automate data visualization tools such as icon sets, color scales, and data bars.

Data Visualizations and Conditional Formatting

16

Data visualization tools were introduced in Excel 2007 and improved in Excel 2010. Data visualizations appear on a drawing layer that can hold icon sets, data bars, color scales, and sparklines. Unlike with SmartArt graphics, Microsoft exposed the entire object model for the data visualization tools, so you can use VBA to add data visualizations to your reports.

➡ **See** Chapter 17, "Dashboarding with Sparklines in Excel 2016," for more information about sparklines.

Excel 2016 provides a variety of data visualizations, as described here and shown in Figure 16.1:

- **Data bars**—A data bar adds an in-cell bar chart to each cell in a range. The largest numbers have the largest bars, and the smallest numbers have the smallest bars. You can control the bar color as well as the values that should receive the smallest and largest bars. Data bars can be solid or a gradient. The gradient bars can have borders.

- **Color scales**—Excel applies a color to each cell from among a two- or three-color gradient. The two-color gradients are best for reports that are presented in monochrome. The three-color gradients require a presentation in color but can represent a report in a traditional traffic light color combination of red–yellow–green. You can control the points along the continuum where each color begins, and you can choose the two or three colors.

- **Icon sets**—Excel assigns an icon to each number. Icon sets can contain three icons, such as the red–yellow–green traffic lights; four icons; or five icons (as with cell phone signal bars). With icon sets, you can control the numeric limits for each icon, reverse the order of the icons, or choose to show only the icons.

- **Above/below average**—Found under the top/bottom rules fly-out menu, these rules make it easy to highlight all the cells that are above or below average. You can choose the formatting to apply to the cells. Note in column G of Figure 16.1 that only 30% of the cells are above average. Contrast this with the top 50% in column K.
- **Duplicate values**—Excel highlights any values that are repeated within a data set. Because the Delete Duplicates command on the Data tab of the ribbon is so destructive, you might prefer to highlight the duplicates and then intelligently decide which records to delete.
- **Top/bottom rules**—Excel highlights the top or bottom *n* percent of cells or highlights the top or bottom *n* cells in a range.
- **Highlight cells**—The legacy conditional formatting rules such as greater than, less than, between, and text that contains are still available in Excel 2016. The powerful `Formula` conditions are also available, although you might need to use these less frequently now that you have the average and top/bottom rules.

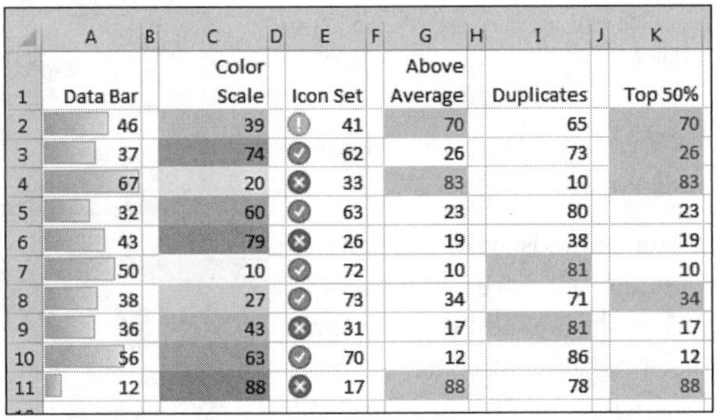

	A	C	E	G	I	K
1	Data Bar	Color Scale	Icon Set	Above Average	Duplicates	Top 50%
2	46	39	41	70	65	70
3	37	74	62	26	73	26
4	67	20	33	83	10	83
5	32	60	63	23	80	23
6	43	79	26	19	38	19
7	50	10	72	10	81	10
8	38	27	73	34	71	34
9	36	43	31	17	81	17
10	56	63	70	12	86	12
11	12	88	17	88	78	88

Figure 16.1 Visualizations such as data bars, color scales, icon sets, and top/bottom rules are controlled in the Excel user interface from the Conditional Formatting drop-down on the Home tab of the ribbon.

VBA Methods and Properties for Data Visualizations

All the data visualization settings are managed in VBA with the `FormatConditions` collection. Conditional formatting has been in Excel since Excel 97. In Excel 2007, Microsoft expanded the `FormatConditions` object to handle the new visualizations. Whereas legacy versions of Excel would use the `FormatConditions.Add` method, Excel 2007–2016 offer additional methods, such as `AddDataBar`, `AddIconSetCondition`, `AddColorScale`, `AddTop10`, `AddAboveAverage`, and `AddUniqueValues`.

It is possible to apply several different conditional formatting conditions to the same range. For example, you can apply a two-color color scale, an icon set, and a data bar to the same range. Excel includes a `Priority` property to specify which conditions should be calculated first. Methods such as `SetFirstPriority` and `SetLastPriority` ensure that a new format condition is executed before or after all others.

The `StopIfTrue` property works in conjunction with the `Priority` property. Say that you are highlighting duplicates but want to check only text cells. Create a new formula-based condition that uses `=ISNUMBER()` to find numeric values. Give the `ISNUMBER` condition a higher priority and apply `StopIfTrue` to prevent Excel from ever reaching the duplicates condition for numeric cells.

Beginning with Excel 2007, the `Type` property was expanded dramatically. This property was formerly a toggle between `CellValue` and `Expression`, but 13 new types were added in Excel 2007. Table 16.1 shows the valid values for the `Type` property. Items 3 and above were introduced in Excel 2007. The Excel team must have had plans for more conditions; items 7, 14, and 15 do not exist, so they must have been on the drawing board at one time but then removed from the final version of Excel 2007. One of these was likely the ill-fated "highlight entire table row" feature that was in the Excel 2007 beta but removed in the final version.

Table 16.1   Valid Types for a Format Condition

Value	Description	VBA Constant
1	Cell value	xlCellValue
2	Expression	xlExpression
3	Color scale	xlColorScale
4	Data bar	xlDatabar
5	Top 10 values	xlTop10
6	Icon set	xlIconSet
8	Unique values	xlUniqueValues
9	Text string	xlTextString
10	Blanks condition	xlBlanksCondition
11	Time period	xlTimePeriod
12	Above average condition	xlAboveAverageCondition
13	No blanks condition	xlNoBlanksCondition
16	Errors condition	xlErrorsCondition
17	No errors condition	xlNoErrorsCondition

Adding Data Bars to a Range

The Data Bar command adds an in-cell bar chart to each cell in a range. Many charting experts complained to Microsoft about problems in the Excel 2007 data bars. For this reason, Microsoft changed the data bars in Excel 2010 to address these problems.

In Figure 16.2, cell C37 reflects changes introduced in Excel 2010. Notice that this cell, which has a value of 0, has no data bar at all. In Excel 2007, the smallest value receives a 4-pixel data bar, even if that smallest value is 0. In addition, in Excel 2016 the largest bar in the data set typically takes up the entire width of the cell.

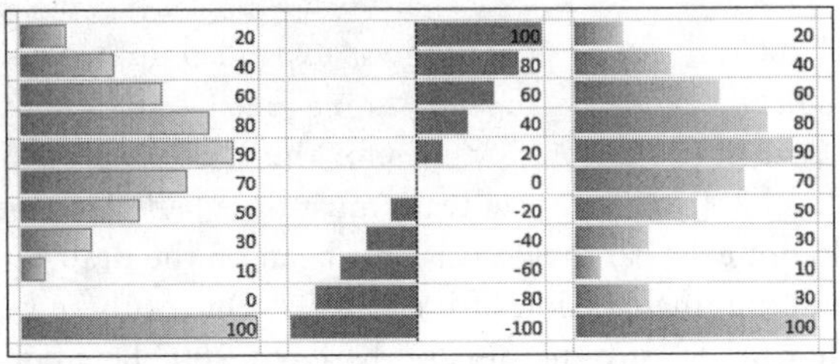

Figure 16.2
Excel 2016 offers many variations on data bars.

In Excel 2007, the data bars would end in a gradient that made it difficult to tell where the bar ended. Excel 2010–2016 offer a border around the bar. You can choose to change the color of the border or even to remove the border, as shown in column K of the figure.

Excel 2010–2016 also offer support for negative data bars, as shown in column G and the data bars that run right to left, as shown in cells C43:C45 in Figure 16.2. These allow comparative histograms.

To add a data bar, you apply the `.FormatConditions.AddDataBar` method to a range that contains your numbers. This method requires no arguments, and it returns an object of the `DataBar` type.

After you add the data bar, you will most likely need to change some of its properties. One method of referring to the data bar is to assume that the recently added data bar is the last item in the collection of format conditions. This code would add a data bar, identify the data bar by counting the conditions, and then change the color:

```
Range("A2:A11").FormatConditions.AddDatabar
ThisCond = Range("A2:A11").FormatConditions.Count
With Range("A2:A11").FormatConditions(ThisCond).BarColor
    .Color = RGB(255, 0, 0) ' Red
    .TintAndShade = -0.5 ' Darker than normal
End With
```

A safer way to go is to define an object variable of type `DataBar`. You can then assign the newly created data bar to the variable:

```
Dim DB As Databar
' Add the data bars
Set DB = Range("A2:A11").FormatConditions.AddDatabar
' Use a red that is 25% darker
With DB.BarColor
    .Color = RGB(255, 0, 0)
    .TintAndShade = -0.25
End With
```

When specifying colors for the data bar or the border, you should use the RGB function to assign a color. You can modify the color by making it darker or lighter, using the `TintAndShade` property. Valid values are from `-1` to `1`. Negative values make the color darker, a value of `0` means no modification, and positive values make the color lighter.

By default, Excel assigns the shortest data bar to the minimum value and the longest data bar to the maximum value. If you want to override the defaults, use the `Modify` method for either the `MinPoint` or `MaxPoint` properties. Specify a type from those shown in Table 16.2. Types `0`, `3`, `4`, and `5` require a value. Table 16.2 shows valid types.

Table 16.2 `MinPoint` and `MaxPoint` Types

Value	Description	VBA Constant
0	Number is used	`xlConditionNumber`
1	Lowest value from the list of values	`xlConditionValueLowestValue`
2	Highest value from the list of values	`xlConditionValueHighestValue`
3	Percentage is used	`xlConditionValuePercent`
4	Formula is used	`xlConditionValueFormula`
5	Percentile is used	`xlConditionValuePercentile`
-1	No conditional value	`xlConditionValueNone`

Use the following code to have the smallest bar assigned to values of `0` and below:

```
DB.MinPoint.Modify _
    Newtype:=xlConditionValueNumber, NewValue:=0
```

To give the top 20% of the bars the largest bar, use this code:

```
DB.MaxPoint.Modify _
    Newtype:=xlConditionValuePercent, NewValue:=80
```

An interesting alternative is to show only the data bars and not the value. To do this, use this code:

```
DB.ShowValue = False
```

To show negative data bars in Excel 2016, use this line:

```
DB.AxisPosition = xlDataBarAxisAutomatic
```

When you allow negative data bars, you can specify an axis color, a negative bar color, and a negative bar border color. Samples of how to change the various colors are shown in the following code, which creates the data bars shown in column C in Figure 16.3:

```
Sub DataBar2()
' Add a Data bar
' Include negative data bars
' Control the min and max point
'
    Dim DB As Databar
```

```
With Range("C2:C11")
    .FormatConditions.Delete
    ' Add the data bars
    Set DB = .FormatConditions.AddDatabar()
End With

' Set the lower limit
DB.MinPoint.Modify newtype:=xlConditionFormula, NewValue:="-600"
DB.MaxPoint.Modify newtype:=xlConditionValueFormula, NewValue:="600"

' Change the data bar to Green
With DB.BarColor
    .Color = RGB(0, 255, 0)
    .TintAndShade = -0.15
End With

' All of this is new in Excel 2010
With DB
    ' Use a gradient
    .BarFillType = xlDataBarFillGradient
    ' Left to Right for direction of bars
    .Direction = xlLTR
    ' Assign a different color to negative bars
    .NegativeBarFormat.ColorType = xlDataBarColor
    ' Use a border around the bars
    .BarBorder.Type = xlDataBarBorderSolid
    ' Assign a different border color to negative
    .NegativeBarFormat.BorderColorType = xlDataBarSameAsPositive
    ' All borders are solid black
    With .BarBorder.Color
        .Color = RGB(0, 0, 0)
    End With
    ' Axis where it naturally would fall, in black
    .AxisPosition = xlDataBarAxisAutomatic
    With .AxisColor
        .Color = 0
        .TintAndShade = 0
    End With
    ' Negative bars in red
    With .NegativeBarFormat.Color
        .Color = 255
        .TintAndShade = 0
    End With
    ' Negative borders in red
End With

End Sub
```

In Excel 2016, you have a choice of showing a gradient or a solid bar. To show a solid bar, use the following:

```
DB.BarFillType = xlDataBarFillSolid
```

The following code sample produces the solid bars shown in column E in Figure 16.3:

```
Sub DataBar3()
' Add a Data bar
' Show solid bars
' Allow negative bars
```

```
' hide the numbers, show only the data bars
'
    Dim DB As Databar
    With Range("E2:E11")
        .FormatConditions.Delete
        ' Add the data bars
        Set DB = .FormatConditions.AddDatabar()
    End With

    With DB.BarColor
        .Color = RGB(0, 0, 255)
        .TintAndShade = 0.1
    End With
    ' Hide the numbers
    DB.ShowValue = False

    ' New in Excel 2010
    DB.BarFillType = xlDataBarFillSolid
    DB.NegativeBarFormat.ColorType = xlDataBarColor
    With DB.NegativeBarFormat.Color
        .Color = 255
        .TintAndShade = 0
    End With
    ' Allow negatives
    DB.AxisPosition = xlDataBarAxisAutomatic
    ' Negative border color is different
    DB.NegativeBarFormat.BorderColorType = xlDataBarColor
    With DB.NegativeBarFormat.BorderColor
        .Color = RGB(127, 127, 0)
        .TintAndShade = 0
    End With

End Sub
```

To allow the bars to go right to left, use this code:

```
DB.Direction = xlRTL ' Right to Left
```

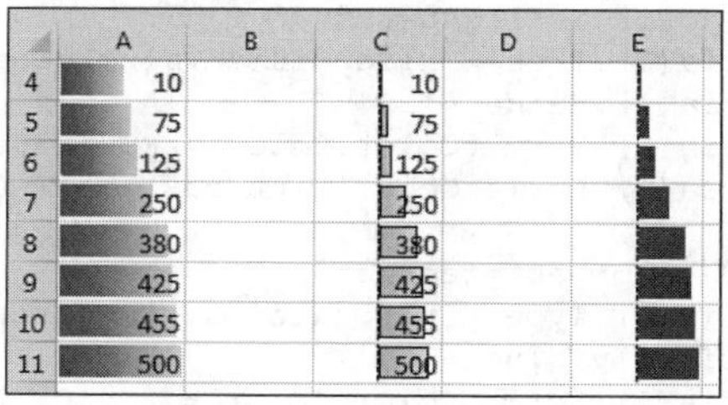

Figure 16.3
Data bars created by the macros in this section.

Adding Color Scales to a Range

You can add color scales in either two-color or three-color scale varieties. Figure 16.4 shows the available settings in the Excel user interface for a color scale using three colors.

Figure 16.4
Color scales enable you
to show hot spots in your
data set.

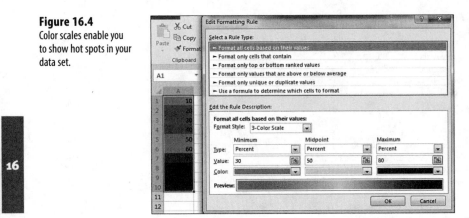

As with data bars, you apply a color scale to a range object by using the `AddColorScale` method. You should specify a `ColorScaleType` of either 2 or 3 as the only argument of the `AddColorScale` method.

Next, you can indicate a color and tint for both or all three of the color scale criteria. Using the values shown previously in Table 16.2, you can also specify whether the shade is applied to the lowest value, the highest value, a particular value, or a percentage or at a percentile.

The following code generates a three-color color scale in the range A1:A10:

```
Sub Add3ColorScale()
    Dim CS As ColorScale

    With Range("A1:A10")
        .FormatConditions.Delete
        ' Add the Color Scale as a 3-color scale
        Set CS = .FormatConditions.AddColorScale(ColorScaleType:=3)
    End With

    ' Format the first color as light red
    CS.ColorScaleCriteria(1).Type = xlConditionValuePercent
    CS.ColorScaleCriteria(1).Value = 30
    CS.ColorScaleCriteria(1).FormatColor.Color = RGB(255, 0, 0)
    CS.ColorScaleCriteria(1).FormatColor.TintAndShade = 0.25

    ' Format the second color as green at 50%
    CS.ColorScaleCriteria(2).Type = xlConditionValuePercent
    CS.ColorScaleCriteria(2).Value = 50
    CS.ColorScaleCriteria(2).FormatColor.Color = RGB(0, 255, 0)
    CS.ColorScaleCriteria(2).FormatColor.TintAndShade = 0

    ' Format the third color as dark blue
    CS.ColorScaleCriteria(3).Type = xlConditionValuePercent
    CS.ColorScaleCriteria(3).Value = 80
    CS.ColorScaleCriteria(3).FormatColor.Color = RGB(0, 0, 255)
    CS.ColorScaleCriteria(3).FormatColor.TintAndShade = -0.25
End Sub
```

Adding Icon Sets to a Range

Icon sets in Excel come with three, four, or five different icons in the set. Figure 16.5 shows the settings for an icon set with five different icons.

To add an icon set to a range, use the `AddIconSet` method. No arguments are required. You can adjust three properties that apply to the icon set, and you can use several additional lines of code to specify the icon set in use and the limits for each icon.

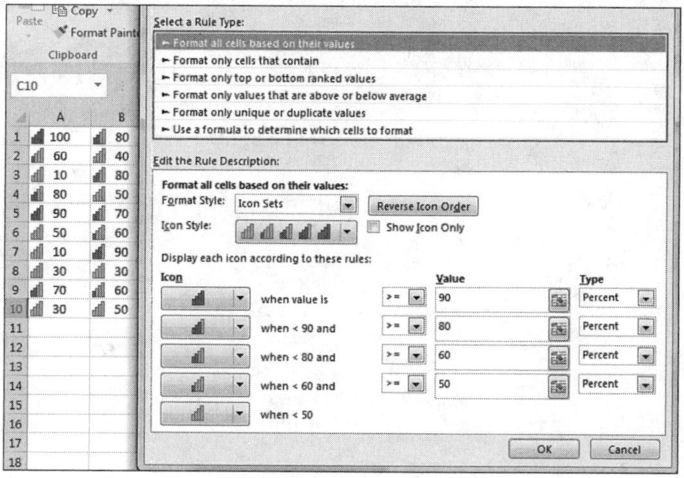

Figure 16.5
With additional icons, the complexity of the code increases.

Specifying an Icon Set

After adding an icon set, you can control whether the icon order is reversed and whether Excel shows only the icons, and you can also specify 1 of the 20 built-in icon sets, like this:

```
Dim ICS As IconSetCondition
With Range("A1:C10")
    .FormatConditions.Delete
    Set ICS = .FormatConditions.AddIconSetCondition()
End With

' Global settings for the icon set
With ICS
    .ReverseOrder = False
    .ShowIconOnly = False
    .IconSet = ActiveWorkbook.IconSets(xl5CRV)
End With
```

> **NOTE** It is somewhat curious that the `IconSets` collection is a property of the active workbook. This seems to indicate that in future versions of Excel, new icon sets might be available.

Table 16.3 shows the complete list of icon sets.

Table 16.3   **Available Icon Sets and Their VBA Constants**

Icon Set	Value	Description	Constant
	1	3 arrows	xl3Arrows
	2	3 arrows gray	xl3ArrowsGray
	3	3 flags	xl3Flags
	4	3 traffic lights 1	xl3TrafficLights1
	5	3 traffic lights 2	xl3TrafficLights2
	6	3 signs	xl3Signs
	7	3 symbols	xl3Symbols
	8	3 symbols 2	xl3Symbols2
	9	4 arrows	xl4Arrows
	10	4 arrows gray	xl4ArrowsGray
	11	4 red to black	xl4RedToBlack
	12	4 power bars	xl4CRV
	13	4 traffic lights	xl4TrafficLights
	14	5 arrows	xl5Arrows
	15	5 arrows gray	xl5ArrowsGray
	16	5 power bars	xl5CRV
	17	5 quarters	xl5Quarters
	18	3 stars	xl3Stars

Icon Set	Value	Description	Constant
▲ ━ ▼	19	3 triangles	xl3Triangles
▦ ▦ ▦ ▦ ▦	20	5 boxes	xl5Boxes

Specifying Ranges for Each Icon

After specifying the type of icon set, you can specify ranges for each icon within the set. By default, the first icon starts at the lowest value. You can adjust the settings for each of the additional icons in the set, as shown here:

```
' The first icon always starts at 0

' Settings for the second icon - start at 50%
With ICS.IconCriteria(2)
    .Type = xlConditionValuePercent
    .Value = 50
    .Operator = xlGreaterEqual
End With
With ICS.IconCriteria(3)
    .Type = xlConditionValuePercent
    .Value = 60
    .Operator = xlGreaterEqual
End With
With ICS.IconCriteria(4)
    .Type = xlConditionValuePercent
    .Value = 80
    .Operator = xlGreaterEqual
End With
With ICS.IconCriteria(5)
    .Type = xlConditionValuePercent
    .Value = 90
    .Operator = xlGreaterEqual
End With
```

Valid values for the `Operator` property are `XlGreater` or `xlGreaterEqual`.

> **CAUTION**
>
> With VBA, it is easy to create overlapping ranges such as icon 1 from 0 to 50 and icon 2 from 30 to 90. Even though the Edit Formatting Rule dialog box prevents overlapping ranges, VBA allows them. However, keep in mind that your icon set will display unpredictably if you create invalid ranges.

Using Visualization Tricks

If you use an icon set or a color scale, Excel applies a color to all cells in the data set. Two tricks in this section enable you to apply an icon set to only a subset of the cells or to apply two different colors of data bars to the same range. The first trick is available in the user interface, but the second trick is available only in VBA.

Creating an Icon Set for a Subset of a Range

Sometimes, you might want to apply a red *X* only to the bad cells in a range. This is tricky to do in the Excel user interface.

In the user interface, follow these steps to apply a red *X* to values greater than or equal to 66:

1. Add a three-symbols icon set to the range.
2. Choose Home, Conditional Formatting, Manage Rules, and edit the rule. You will see the default settings that appear in Figure 16.6.
3. Specify no cell icon for the first two groups.
4. Specify that the top group has a Type of Number and >=80.
5. Specify that the second group has a type of Number and > 66. Excel will default the Red X group to be used for <=66 (see Figure 16.7).

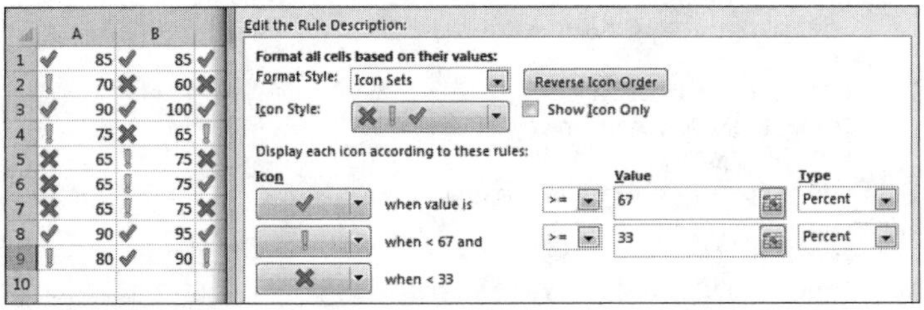

Figure 16.6
These default rules appear when you add a three-icon set.

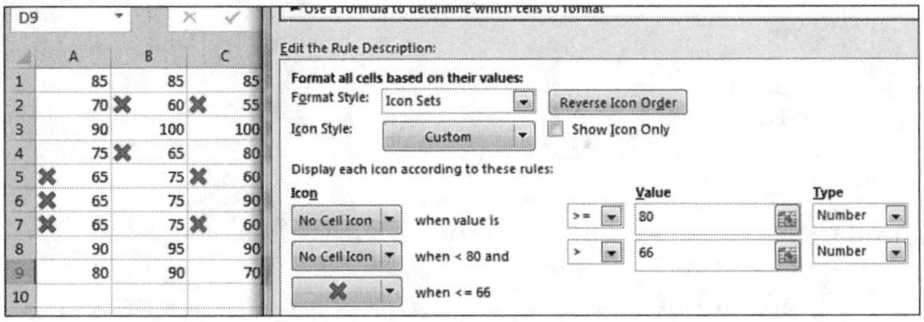

Figure 16.7
Although the first two ranges have no cell icon, use the number values to force the red X to before <=66.

The code to create this effect in VBA is straightforward. A great deal of the code makes sure that the icon set has the red *X* symbols on the cells greater than or equal to 80. To hide the icons for rules 2 and 3, set the .Icon property to xlIconNoCellIcon.

The code to highlight values greater than or equal to 80 with a red *X* is shown here:

```
Sub TrickyFormatting()
    ' mark the bad cells
    Dim ICS As IconSetCondition
    Dim FC As FormatCondition
    With Range("A1:D9")
```

```
            .FormatConditions.Delete
            Set ICS = .FormatConditions.AddIconSetCondition()
    End With
    With ICS
            .ShowIconOnly = False
            .IconSet = ActiveWorkbook.IconSets(xl3Symbols2)
    End With
    With ICS.IconCriteria(1)
            .Type = xlConditionValue
            .Value = 80
            .Operator = xlGreater
            .Icon = xlIconNoCellIcon
    End With
    ' The threshold for this icon doesn't really matter,
    ' but you have to make sure that it does not overlap the 3rd icon
    With ICS.IconCriteria(2)
            .Type = xlConditionValue
            .Value = 66
            .Operator = xlGreater
            .Icon = xlIconNoCellIcon
    End With
End Sub
```

Using Two Colors of Data Bars in a Range

This trick is particularly cool because it can be achieved only with VBA. Say that values greater than 90 are acceptable and those 90 and below indicate trouble. You would like acceptable values to have a green bar and others to have a red bar.

Using VBA, you first add the green data bars. Then, without deleting the format condition, you add red data bars.

In VBA, every format condition has a Formula property that defines whether the condition is displayed for a given cell. Therefore, the trick is to write a formula that defines when the green bars are displayed. When the formula is not True, the red bars are allowed to show through.

In Figure 16.8, the effect is applied to the range A1:D10. You need to write the formula in A1 style, as if it applies to the top-left corner of the selection. The formula needs to evaluate to True or False. Excel automatically copies the formula to all the cells in the range. The formula for this condition is =IF(A1>90,True,False).

> **NOTE** The formula is evaluated relative to the current cell pointer location. Even though it is not usually necessary to select cells before adding a FormatCondition, in this case, selecting the range ensures that the formula will work.

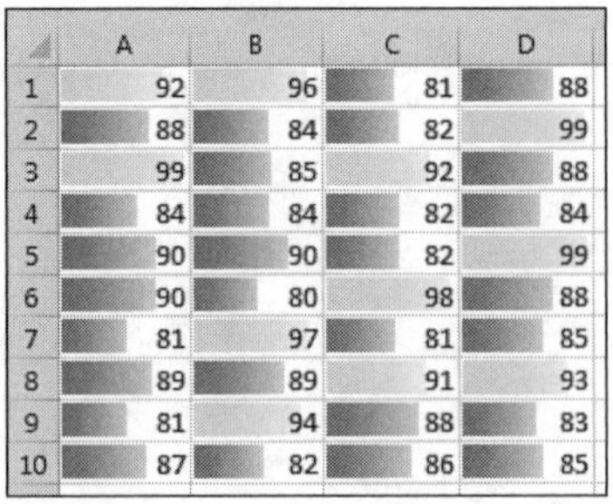

	A	B	C	D
1	92	96	81	88
2	88	84	82	99
3	99	85	92	88
4	84	84	82	84
5	90	90	82	99
6	90	80	98	88
7	81	97	81	85
8	89	89	91	93
9	81	94	88	83
10	87	82	86	85

Figure 16.8
The dark bars are red, and the lighter bars are green. VBA was used to create two overlapping data bars, and then the `Formula` property hid the top bars for cells 90 and below.

The following code creates the two-color data bars:

```
Sub AddTwoDataBars()
    ' passing values in green, failing in red
    Dim DB As Databar
    Dim DB2 As Databar
    With Range("A1:D10")
        .FormatConditions.Delete
        ' Add a Light Green Data Bar
        Set DB = .FormatConditions.AddDatabar()

        DB.BarColor.Color = RGB(0, 255, 0)
        DB.BarColor.TintAndShade = 0.25
        ' Add a Red Data Bar
        Set DB2 = .FormatConditions.AddDatabar()
        DB2.BarColor.Color = RGB(255, 0, 0)
        ' Make the green bars only
        .Select ' Required to make the next line work
        .FormatConditions(1).Formula = "=IF(A1>90,True,False)"
        DB.Formula = "=IF(A1>90,True,False)"
        DB.MinPoint.Modify newtype:=xlConditionFormula, NewValue:="60"
        DB.MaxPoint.Modify newtype:=xlConditionValueFormula, _
            NewValue:="100"
        DB2.MinPoint.Modify newtype:=xlConditionFormula, NewValue:="60"
        DB2.MaxPoint.Modify newtype:=xlConditionValueFormula, _
            NewValue:="100"
    End With
End Sub
```

The `Formula` property works for all the conditional formats, which means you could potentially create some obnoxious combinations of data visualizations. In Figure 16.9, five different icon sets are combined in a single range. No one will be able to figure out whether a red flag is worse than a gray down arrow. Even so, this ability opens interesting combinations for those with a little creativity.

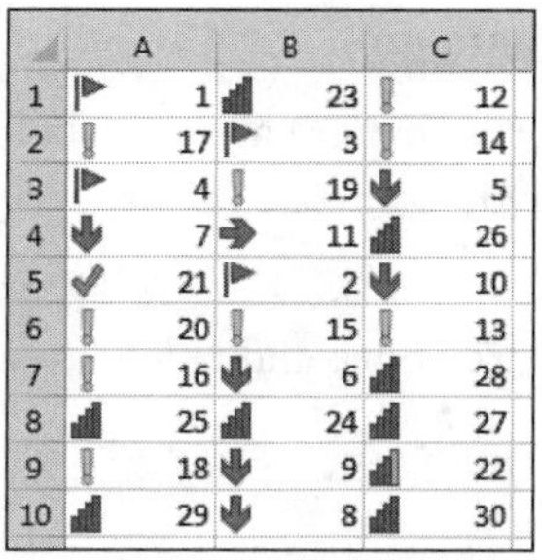

Figure 16.9
VBA created this mixture of five different icon sets in a single range. The `Formula` property in VBA is the key to combining icon sets.

Use the following code to create the crazy icon set shown in Figure 16.9:

```
Sub AddCrazyIcons()
    With Range("A1:C10")
        .Select ' The .Formula lines below require .Select here
        .FormatConditions.Delete

        ' First icon set
        .FormatConditions.AddIconSetCondition
        .FormatConditions(1).IconSet = ActiveWorkbook.IconSets(xl3Flags)
        .FormatConditions(1).Formula = "=IF(A1<5,TRUE,FALSE)"

        ' Next icon set
        .FormatConditions.AddIconSetCondition
        .FormatConditions(2).IconSet = _
            ActiveWorkbook.IconSets(xl3ArrowsGray)
        .FormatConditions(2).Formula = "=IF(A1<12,TRUE,FALSE)"

        ' Next icon set
        .FormatConditions.AddIconSetCondition
        .FormatConditions(3).IconSet = _
            ActiveWorkbook.IconSets(xl3Symbols2)
        .FormatConditions(3).Formula = "=IF(A1<22,TRUE,FALSE)"

        ' Next icon set
        .FormatConditions.AddIconSetCondition
        .FormatConditions(4).IconSet = ActiveWorkbook.IconSets(xl4CRV)
        .FormatConditions(4).Formula = "=IF(A1<27,TRUE,FALSE)"

        ' Next icon set
        .FormatConditions.AddIconSetCondition
        .FormatConditions(5).IconSet = ActiveWorkbook.IconSets(xl5CRV)
    End With
End Sub
```

Using Other Conditional Formatting Methods

Although the icon sets, data bars, and color scales get most of the attention, there are still plenty of other uses for conditional formatting.

The remaining examples in this chapter show some of the other conditional formatting rules and methods available.

Formatting Cells That Are Above or Below Average

Use the `AddAboveAverage` method to format cells that are above or below average. After adding the conditional format, specify whether the `AboveBelow` property is `xlAboveAverage` or `xlBelowAverage`.

The following two macros highlight cells that are above and below average:

```
Sub FormatAboveAverage()
    With Selection
        .FormatConditions.Delete
        .FormatConditions.AddAboveAverage
        .FormatConditions(1).AboveBelow = xlAboveAverage
        .FormatConditions(1).Interior.Color = RGB(255, 0, 0)
    End With
End Sub

Sub FormatBelowAverage()
    With Selection
        .FormatConditions.Delete
        .FormatConditions.AddAboveAverage
        .FormatConditions(1).AboveBelow = xlBelowAverage
        .FormatConditions(1).Interior.Color = RGB(255, 0, 0)
    End With
End Sub
```

Formatting Cells in the Top 10 or Bottom 5

Four of the choices on the Top/Bottom Rules fly-out menu are controlled with the `AddTop10` method. After you add the format condition, you need to set three properties that control how the condition is calculated:

■ `TopBottom`—Set this to either `xlTop10Top` or `xlTop10Bottom`.

■ `Rank`—Set this to 5 for the top 5, 6 for the top 6, and so on.

■ `Percent`—Set this to `False` if you want the top 10 items. Set this to `True` if you want the top 10% of the items.

The following code highlights the top or bottom cells:

```
Sub FormatTop10Items()
    With Selection
        .FormatConditions.Delete
        .FormatConditions.AddTop10
        .FormatConditions(1).TopBottom = xlTop10Top
        .FormatConditions(1).Rank = 10
        .FormatConditions(1).Percent = False
        .FormatConditions(1).Interior.Color = RGB(255, 0, 0)
    End With
End Sub

Sub FormatBottom5Items()
    With Selection
        .FormatConditions.Delete
        .FormatConditions.AddTop10
        .FormatConditions(1).TopBottom = xlTop10Bottom
```

```
            .FormatConditions(1).Rank = 5
            .FormatConditions(1).Percent = False
            .FormatConditions(1).Interior.Color = RGB(255, 0, 0)
        End With
    End Sub

    Sub FormatTop12Percent()
        With Selection
            .FormatConditions.Delete
            .FormatConditions.AddTop10
            .FormatConditions(1).TopBottom = xlTop10Top
            .FormatConditions(1).Rank = 12
            .FormatConditions(1).Percent = True
            .FormatConditions(1).Interior.Color = RGB(255, 0, 0)
        End With
    End Sub
```

Formatting Unique or Duplicate Cells

The Remove Duplicates command on the Data tab of the ribbon is a destructive command. Instead of using it, you might want to mark the duplicates without removing them. If so, you can use the `AddUniqueValues` method to mark the duplicate or unique cells. After you call this method, set the `DupeUnique` property to either `xlUnique` or `xlDuplicate`.

I do not really like either of these options. Choosing duplicate values marks both cells that contain the duplicate, as shown in column A in Figure 16.10. For example, both A2 and A8 are marked, when A8 is really the only duplicate value.

Choosing unique values marks only the cells that do not have duplicates, as shown in column C in Figure 16.10. This leaves several cells unmarked. For example, none of the cells containing 17 is marked.

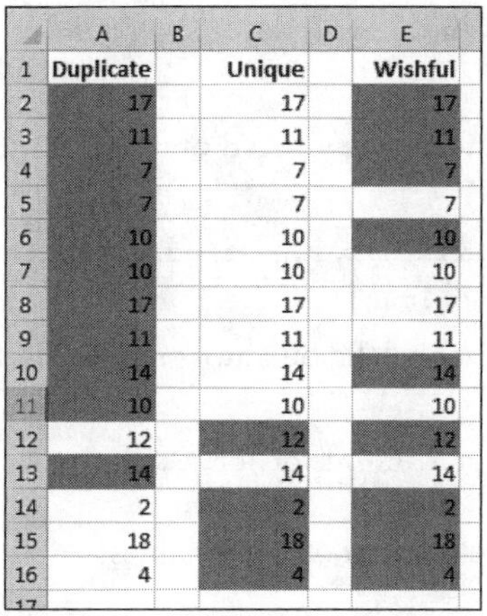

	A	B	C	D	E
1	Duplicate		Unique		Wishful
2	17		17		17
3	11		11		11
4	7		7		7
5	7		7		7
6	10		10		10
7	10		10		10
8	17		17		17
9	11		11		11
10	14		14		14
11	10		10		10
12	12		12		12
13	14		14		14
14	2		2		2
15	18		18		18
16	4		4		4

Figure 16.10
The `AddUniqueValues` method can mark cells such as those in columns A and C. Unfortunately, it cannot mark the truly useful pattern in column E.

As any data analyst knows, the truly useful option would be to mark the first unique value. In this wishful state, Excel would mark one instance of each unique value. In this case, the

17 in E2 would be marked, but any subsequent cells that contain 17, such as E8, would remain unmarked.

The code to mark duplicates or unique values is shown here:

```
Sub FormatDuplicate()
    With Selection
        .FormatConditions.Delete
        .FormatConditions.AddUniqueValues
        .FormatConditions(1).DupeUnique = xlDuplicate
        .FormatConditions(1).Interior.Color = RGB(255, 0, 0)
    End With
End Sub

Sub FormatUnique()
    With Selection
        .FormatConditions.Delete
        .FormatConditions.AddUniqueValues
        .FormatConditions(1).DupeUnique = xlUnique
        .FormatConditions(1).Interior.Color = RGB(255, 0, 0)
    End With
End Sub

Sub HighlightFirstUnique()
    With Range("E2:E16")
        .Select
        .FormatConditions.Delete
        .FormatConditions.Add Type:=xlExpression, _
            Formula1:="=COUNTIF(E$2:E2,E2)=1"
        .FormatConditions(1).Interior.Color = RGB(255, 0, 0)
    End With
End Sub
```

Formatting Cells Based on Their Value

The value conditional formats have been around for several versions of Excel. Use the Add method with the following arguments:

- ■ Type—Since this section deals with formatting based on the cell value, the type is xlCellValue.

- ■ Operator—This can be xlBetween, xlEqual, xlGreater, xlGreaterEqual, xlLess, xlLessEqual, xlNotBetween, or xlNotEqual.

- ■ Formula1—Formula1 is used with each of the operators specified to provide a numeric value.

- ■ Formula2—This is used for xlBetween and xlNotBetween.

The following code sample highlights cells based on their values:

```
Sub FormatBetween10And20()
    With Selection
        .FormatConditions.Delete
        .FormatConditions.Add Type:=xlCellValue, Operator:=xlBetween, _
            Formula1:="=10", Formula2:="=20"
        .FormatConditions(1).Interior.Color = RGB(255, 0, 0)
```

```
        End With
    End Sub

    Sub FormatLessThan15()
        With Selection
            .FormatConditions.Delete
            .FormatConditions.Add Type:=xlCellValue, Operator:=xlLess, _
                Formula1:="=15"
            .FormatConditions(1).Interior.Color = RGB(255, 0, 0)
        End With
    End Sub
```

Formatting Cells That Contain Text

When you are trying to highlight cells that contain a certain bit of text, you use the `Add` method, the `xlTextString` type, and an operator of `xlBeginsWith`, `xlContains`, `xlDoesNotContain`, or `xlEndsWith`.

The following code highlights all cells that contain an upper- or lowercase letter *A*:

```
    Sub FormatContainsA()
        With Selection
            .FormatConditions.Delete
            .FormatConditions.Add Type:=xlTextString, String:="A", _
                TextOperator:=xlContains
            ' other choices: xlBeginsWith, xlDoesNotContain, xlEndsWith
            .FormatConditions(1).Interior.Color = RGB(255, 0, 0)
        End With
    End Sub
```

Formatting Cells That Contain Dates

Conditional formatting allows you to filter to a virtual date filter. The list of available date operators is a subset of the date operators available in the pivot table filters. Use the `Add` method, the `xlTimePeriod` type, and one of these `DateOperator` values: `xlYesterday`, `xlToday`, `xlTomorrow`, `xlLastWeek`, `xlLast7Days`, `xlThisWeek`, `xlNextWeek`, `xlLastMonth`, `xlThisMonth`, or `xlNextMonth`.

The following code highlights all dates in the past week:

```
    Sub FormatDatesLastWeek()
        With Selection
            .FormatConditions.Delete
            ' DateOperator choices include xlYesterday, xlToday, xlTomorrow,
            ' xlLastWeek, xlThisWeek, xlNextWeek, xlLast7Days
            ' xlLastMonth, xlThisMonth, xlNextMonth,
            .FormatConditions.Add Type:=xlTimePeriod, _
                DateOperator:=xlLastWeek
            .FormatConditions(1).Interior.Color = RGB(255, 0, 0)
        End With
    End Sub
```

Formatting Cells That Contain Blanks or Errors

Buried deep within the Excel interface are options to format cells that contain blanks, that contain errors, that do not contain blanks, or that do not contain errors. If you use the macro recorder, Excel uses the complicated `xlExpression` version of conditional formatting. For example, to look for a blank, Excel tests to see whether `=LEN(TRIM(A1))=0`. Instead, you can use any of these four self-explanatory types:

```
.FormatConditions.Add Type:=xlBlanksCondition
.FormatConditions.Add Type:=xlErrorsCondition
.FormatConditions.Add Type:=xlNoBlanksCondition
.FormatConditions.Add Type:=xlNoErrorsCondition
```

You are not required to use any other arguments with these types.

Using a Formula to Determine Which Cells to Format

The most powerful conditional format is the `xlExpression` type. With this type, you provide a formula for the active cell that evaluates to `True` or `False`. Make sure to write the formula with relative or absolute references so that the formula is correct when Excel copies it to the remaining cells in the selection.

An infinite number of conditions can be identified with a formula. Two popular conditions are shown here.

Highlighting the First Unique Occurrence of Each Value in a Range

Say that in column A in Figure 16.11, you would like to highlight the first occurrence of each value in the column. The highlighted cells will then contain a complete list of the unique numbers found in the column.

Figure 16.11
A formula-based condition can mark the first unique occurrence of each value, as shown in column A, or the entire row with the largest sales, as shown in D:F.

	A	B	C	D	E	F
1	17			Region	Invoice	Sales
2	11			West	1001	112
3	7			East	1002	321
4	7	7 is duplicate of A3		Central	1003	332
5	10			West	1004	596
6	10	10 is duplicate of A5		East	1005	642
7	17	17 appears in A1		West	1006	700
8	11	11 appears in A2		West	1007	253
9	14			Central	1008	529
10	10	10 is duplicate		East	1009	122
11	12			West	1010	601
12	14	Duplicate of A9		Central	1011	460
13	2			East	1012	878
14	18			West	1013	763
15	4			Central	1014	193

The macro should select cells A1:A15. The formula should be written to return a `True` or `False` value for cell A1. Because Excel logically copies this formula to the entire range, you should use a careful combination of relative and absolute references.

The formula can use the `COUNTIF` function. Check to see how many times the range from A$1 to A1 contains the value A1. If the result is equal to `1`, the condition is `True`, and the cell is highlighted. The first formula is `=COUNTIF(A$1:A1,A1)=1`. As the formula is copied down to, say A12, the formula changes to `=COUNTIF(A$1:A12,A12)=1`.

The following macro creates the formatting shown in column A in Figure 16.11:

```
Sub HighlightFirstUnique()
    With Range("A1:A15")
        .Select
        .FormatConditions.Delete
        .FormatConditions.Add Type:=xlExpression, _
            Formula1:="=COUNTIF(A$1:A1,A1)=1"
        .FormatConditions(1).Interior.Color = RGB(255, 0, 0)
    End With
End Sub
```

Highlighting the Entire Row for the Largest Sales Value

Another example of a formula-based condition involves highlighting the entire row of a data set in response to a value in one column. Consider the data set in cells D2:F15 of Figure 16.11. If you want to highlight the entire row that contains the largest sale, you select cells D2:F15 and write a formula that works for cell D2: `=$F2=MAX($F$2:$F$15)`. The code required to format the row with the largest sales value is as follows:

```
Sub HighlightWholeRow()
    With Range("D2:F15")
        .Select
        .FormatConditions.Delete
        .FormatConditions.Add Type:=xlExpression, _
            Formula1:="=$F2=MAX($F$2:$F$15)"
        .FormatConditions(1).Interior.Color = RGB(255, 0, 0)
    End With
End Sub
```

Using the New `NumberFormat` Property

In legacy versions of Excel, a cell that matched a conditional format could have a particular font, font color, border, or fill pattern. Since Excel 2007, you have also been able to specify a number format. This can be useful for selectively changing the number format used to display the values.

For example, you might want to display numbers greater than 999 in thousands, numbers greater than 999,999 in hundred thousands, and numbers greater than 9,000,000 in millions.

If you turn on the macro recorder and attempt to record setting the conditional format to a custom number format, the Excel 2016 VBA macro recorder actually records the action of executing an XL4 macro! You can skip the recorded code and use the `NumberFormat` property as shown here:

```
Sub NumberFormat()
    With Range("E1:G26")
        .FormatConditions.Delete
        .FormatConditions.Add Type:=xlCellValue, Operator:=xlGreater, _
            Formula1:="=9999999"
```

```
        .FormatConditions(1).NumberFormat = "$#,##0,""M"""
        .FormatConditions.Add Type:=xlCellValue, Operator:=xlGreater,
            Formula1:="=999999"
        .FormatConditions(2).NumberFormat = "$#,##0.0,""M"""
        .FormatConditions.Add Type:=xlCellValue, Operator:=xlGreater,
            Formula1:="=999"
        .FormatConditions(3).NumberFormat = "$#,##0,K"
    End With
End Sub
```

Figure 16.12 shows the original numbers in columns A:C. The results of running the macro are shown in columns E:G. The dialog box shows the conditional format rules that are applied.

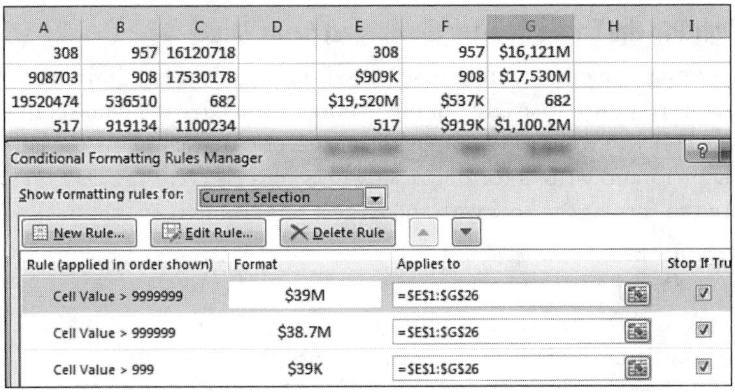

Figure 16.12
Since Excel 2007, conditional formats have been able to specify a specific number format.

	A	B	C	D	E	F	G	H	I
	308	957	16120718		308	957	$16,121M		
	908703	908	17530178		$909K	908	$17,530M		
	19520474	536510	682		$19,520M	$537K	682		
	517	919134	1100234		517	$919K	$1,100.2M		

Conditional Formatting Rules Manager

Show formatting rules for: Current Selection

New Rule... | Edit Rule... | ✕ Delete Rule

Rule (applied in order shown)	Format	Applies to		Stop If Tru
Cell Value > 9999999	$39M	=$E$1:$G$26		✓
Cell Value > 999999	$38.7M	=$E$1:$G$26		✓
Cell Value > 999	$39K	=$E$1:$G$26		✓

Next Steps

Chapter 17 shows you how to create dashboards from tiny charts called sparklines.

Dashboarding with Sparklines in Excel 2016

17

A feature that's been around since Excel 2010 is the ability to create tiny, word-size charts called sparklines. If you are creating dashboards, you will want to leverage these charts.

The concept of sparklines was first introduced by Professor Edward Tufte, who promoted sparklines as a way to show a maximum amount of information with a minimal amount of ink.

Microsoft supports three types of sparklines:

- **Line**—A sparkline shows a single series on a line chart within a single cell. On a sparkline, you can add markers for the highest point, the lowest point, the first point, and the last point. Each of those points can have a different color. You can also choose to mark all the negative points or even all points.

- **Column**—A spark column shows a single series on a column chart. You can choose to show a different color for the first bar, the last bar, the lowest bar, the highest bar, and/or all negative points.

- **Win/loss**—This is a special type of column chart in which every positive point is plotted at 100% height and every negative point is plotted at –100% height. The theory is that positive columns represent wins and negative columns represent losses. With these charts, you always want to change the color of the negative columns. It is possible to highlight the highest/lowest point based on the underlying data.

Creating Sparklines

Microsoft figures that you will usually be creating a group of sparklines. The main VBA object for sparklines is `SparklineGroup`. To create sparklines, you apply the `SparklineGroups.Add` method to the range where you want the sparklines to appear.

In the `Add` method, you specify a type for the sparkline and the location of the source data.

Say that you apply the `Add` method to the three-cell range B2:D2. Then the source must be a range that is either three columns wide or three rows tall.

The `Type` parameter can be `xlSparkLine` for a line, `xlSparkColumn` for a column, or `xlSparkColumn100` for win/loss.

If the `SourceData` parameter is referring to ranges on the current worksheet, it can be as simple as `"D3:F100"`. If it is pointing to another worksheet, use `"Data!D3:F100"` or `"'My Data'!D3:F100"`. If you've defined a named range, you can specify the name of the range as the source data.

Figure 17.1 shows a table of S&P 500 closing prices for three years. Notice that the actual data for the sparklines is in three contiguous columns, D, E, and F.

Figure 17.1
Arrange the data for the sparklines in a contiguous range.

	A	B	C	D	E	F
1	Date 2012	Date 2013	Date 2014	Close 2012	Close 2013	Close 2014
2	1/3/2012	1/2/2013	1/2/2014	1277.06	1462.42	1831.98
3	1/4/2012	1/3/2013	1/3/2014	1277.30	1459.37	1831.37
4	1/5/2012	1/4/2013	1/6/2014	1281.06	1466.47	1826.77
5	1/6/2012	1/7/2013	1/7/2014	1277.81	1461.89	1837.88
6	1/9/2012	1/8/2013	1/8/2014	1280.70	1457.15	1837.49
7	1/10/2012	1/9/2013	1/9/2014	1292.08	1461.02	1838.13
8	1/11/2012	1/10/2013	1/10/2014	1292.48	1472.12	1842.37

In this example, the data is on the Data worksheet, and the sparklines are created on the Dashboard worksheet. The `WSD` object variable is used for the Data worksheet. `WSL` is used for the Dashboard worksheet.

Because each column might have one or two extra points, the code to find the final row is slightly different than usual:

```
FinalRow = WSD.[A1].CurrentRegion.Rows.Count
```

The `.CurrentRegion` property starts from cell A1 and extends in all directions until it hits the edge of the worksheet or the edge of the data. In this case, the `CurrentRegion` reports that row 253 is the final row.

For this example, the sparklines are created in a row of three cells. Because each cell is showing 252 points, I am going with fairly large sparklines. The sparkline grows to the size of the cell, so this code makes each cell fairly wide and tall:

```
With WSL.Range("B1:D1")
    .Value = array(2012,2013,2014)
```

```
    .HorizontalAlignment = xlCenter
    .Style = "Title"
    .ColumnWidth = 39
    .Offset(1, 0).RowHeight = 100
End With
```

The following code creates three default sparklines:

```
Dim SG as SparklineGroup
Set SG = WSL.Range("B2:D2").SparklineGroups.Add( _
    Type:=xlSparkLine, _
    SourceData:="Data!D2:F" & FinalRow)
```

As shown in Figure 17.2, these sparklines aren't perfect (but the next section shows how to format them). There are a number of problems with the default sparklines. Think about the vertical axis of a chart. Sparklines always default to have the scale automatically selected. Because you never really get to see what the scale is, you cannot tell the range of the chart.

Figure 17.2
Three default sparklines.

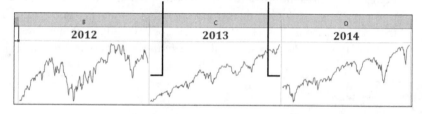

Figure 17.3 shows the minimum and maximum for each year. From this data, you can guess that the sparkline for 2012 probably goes from about 1275 to 1470. The sparkline for 2013 probably goes from 1455 to 1850. The sparkline for 2013 probably goes from 1740 to 2095.

Figure 17.3
Each sparkline assigns the minimum and maximum scales to be just outside these limits.

D255			fx	=MIN(D2:D253)	
	A	B	C	D	E	F
1	Date 2012	Date 2013	Date 2014	Close 2012	Close 2013	Close 2014
250	12/28/2012	12/26/2013	12/26/2014	1402.43	1842.02	2088.77
251	12/31/2012	12/27/2013	12/29/2014	1426.19	1841.40	2090.57
252		12/30/2013	12/30/2014		1841.06995	2080.3501
253		12/31/2013	12/31/2014		1848.35999	2058.8999
254						
255			Min	1277	1457	1742
256			Max	1466	1848	2091
257						

Scaling Sparklines

The default choice for the sparkline vertical axis is that each sparkline has a different minimum and maximum. There are two other choices available.

One choice is to group all the sparklines together but to continue to allow Excel to choose the minimum and maximum scales. You still won't know exactly what values are chosen for the minimum and maximum.

To force the sparklines to have the same automatic scale, use this code:

```
' Allow automatic axis scale, but all three of them the same
With SG.Axes.Vertical
     .MinScaleType = xlSparkScaleGroup
     .MaxScaleType = xlSparkScaleGroup
End With
```

Note that `.Axes` belongs to the sparkline group, not to the individual sparklines themselves. In fact, almost all the good properties are applied at the `SparklineGroup` level. This has some interesting ramifications. If you want one sparkline to have an automatic scale and another sparkline to have a fixed scale, you have to create each of those sparklines separately, or at least ungroup them.

Figure 17.4 shows the sparklines when both the minimum and the maximum scales are set to act as a group. All three lines nearly meet now, which is a good sign. You can guess that the scale runs from about 1270 up to perhaps 2100. Again, though, there is no way to tell. The solution is to use a custom value for both the minimum and maximum axes.

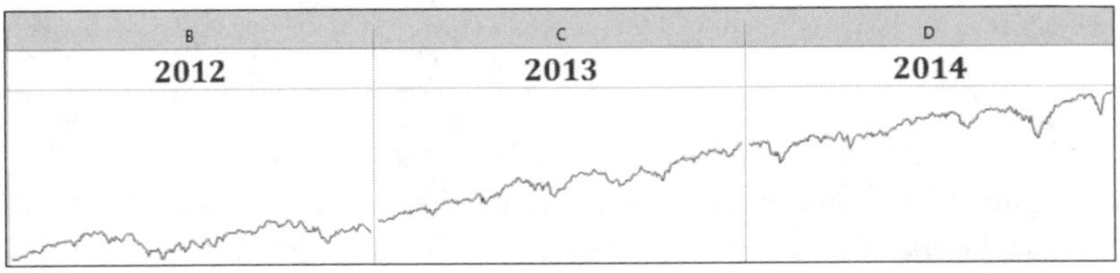

Figure 17.4
All three sparklines have the same minimum and maximum scales, but you don't know what it is.

Another choice is to take absolute control and assign a minimum and a maximum for the vertical axis scale. The following code forces the sparklines to run from a minimum of 0 up to a maximum that rounds up to the next 100 above the largest value:

```
Set AF = Application.WorksheetFunction
AllMin = AF.Min(WSD.Range("D2:F" & FinalRow))
AllMax = AF.Max(WSD.Range("D2:F" & FinalRow))
AllMin = Int(AllMin)
AllMax = Int(AllMax + 0.9)
With SG.Axes.Vertical
     .MinScaleType = xlSparkScaleCustom
     .MaxScaleType = xlSparkScaleCustom
     .CustomMinScaleValue = AllMin
     .CustomMaxScaleValue = AllMax
End With
```

Figure 17.5 shows the resulting sparklines. Now *you* know the minimum and the maximum, but you need a way to communicate it to the reader.

Figure 17.5
You've manually assigned a min and max scale, but it does not appear on the chart.

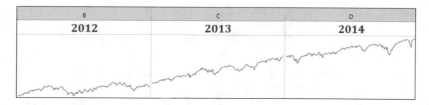

One method is to put the minimum and maximum values in A2. With 8-point bold Calibri, a row height of 113 allows 10 rows of wrapped text in the cell. So you could put the max value, then vbLf eight times, then the min value. (Using vbLf is the equivalent of pressing Alt+Enter when you are entering values in a cell.)

On the right side, you can put the final point's value and attempt to position it within the cell so that it falls roughly at the same height as the final point. Figure 17.6 shows this option.

Figure 17.6
Labels on the left show the min and max. Labels on the right show the final value.

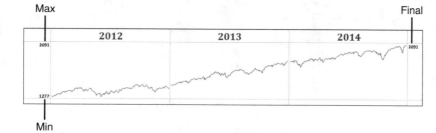

The following code produces the sparklines in Figure 17.6:

```
Sub NASDAQMacro()
' NASDAQMacro Macro
'
Dim SG As SparklineGroup
Dim SL As Sparkline
Dim WSD As Worksheet ' Data worksheet
Dim WSL As Worksheet ' Dashboard

    On Error Resume Next
    Application.DisplayAlerts = False
    Worksheets("Dashboard").Delete
    On Error GoTo 0

    Set WSD = Worksheets("Data")
    Set WSL = ActiveWorkbook.Worksheets.Add
    WSL.Name = "Dashboard"

    FinalRow = WSD.Cells(1, 1).CurrentRegion.Rows.Count
    WSD.Cells(2, 4).Resize(FinalRow - 1, 3).Name = "MyData"

    WSL.Select
    ' Set up Headings
    With WSL.Range("B1:D1")
        .Value = Array(2009, 2010, 2011)
        .HorizontalAlignment = xlCenter
```

```
        .Style = "Title"
        .ColumnWidth = 39
        .Offset(1, 0).RowHeight = 100
End With

Set SG = WSL.Range("B2:D2").SparklineGroups.Add( _
        Type:=xlSparkLine, _
        SourceData:="Data!D2:F250")

Set SL = SG.Item(1)

Set AF = Application.WorksheetFunction
AllMin = AF.Min(WSD.Range("D2:F" & FinalRow))
AllMax = AF.Max(WSD.Range("D2:F" & FinalRow))
AllMin = Int(AllMin)
AllMax = Int(AllMax + 0.9)


' Allow automatic axis scale, but all three of them the same
With SG.Axes.Vertical
        .MinScaleType = xlSparkScaleCustom
        .MaxScaleType = xlSparkScaleCustom
        .CustomMinScaleValue = AllMin
        .CustomMaxScaleValue = AllMax
End With

' Add two labels to show minimum and maximum
With WSL.Range("A2")
        .Value = AllMax & vbLf & vbLf & vbLf & vbLf _
            & vbLf & vbLf & vbLf & vbLf & AllMin
        .HorizontalAlignment = xlRight
        .VerticalAlignment = xlTop
        .Font.Size = 8
        .Font.Bold = True
        .WrapText = True
End With

' Put the final value on the right
FinalVal = Round(WSD.Cells(Rows.Count, 6).End(xlUp).Value, 0)
Rg = AllMax - AllMin
RgTenth = Rg / 10
FromTop = AllMax - FinalVal
FromTop = Round(FromTop / RgTenth, 0) - 1
If FromTop < 0 Then FromTop = 0

Select Case FromTop
    Case 0
        RtLabel = FinalVal
    Case Is > 0
        RtLabel = Application.WorksheetFunction. _
            Rept(vbLf, FromTop) & FinalVal
End Select

With WSL.Range("E2")
        .Value = RtLabel
        .HorizontalAlignment = xlLeft
        .VerticalAlignment = xlTop
        .Font.Size = 8
```

```
        .Font.Bold = True
    End With
End Sub
```

Formatting Sparklines

Most of the formatting available with sparklines involves setting the color of various elements of the sparkline.

There are a few methods for assigning colors in Excel 2016. Before diving into the sparkline properties, you can read about the two methods of assigning colors in Excel VBA.

Using Theme Colors

Excel 2007 introduced the concept of a theme for a workbook. A theme is composed of a body font, a headline font, a series of effects, and then a series of colors.

The first four colors are used for text and backgrounds. The next six colors are the accent colors. The 20-plus built-in themes include colors that work well together. There are also two colors used for hyperlinks and followed hyperlinks. For now, focus on the accent colors.

Go to Page Layout, Themes and choose a theme. Next to the theme drop-down is a Colors drop-down. Open that drop-down and select Create New Theme Colors from the bottom of the drop-down. Excel shows the Create New Theme Colors dialog (see Figure 17.7). This dialog gives you a good picture of the 12 colors associated with the theme.

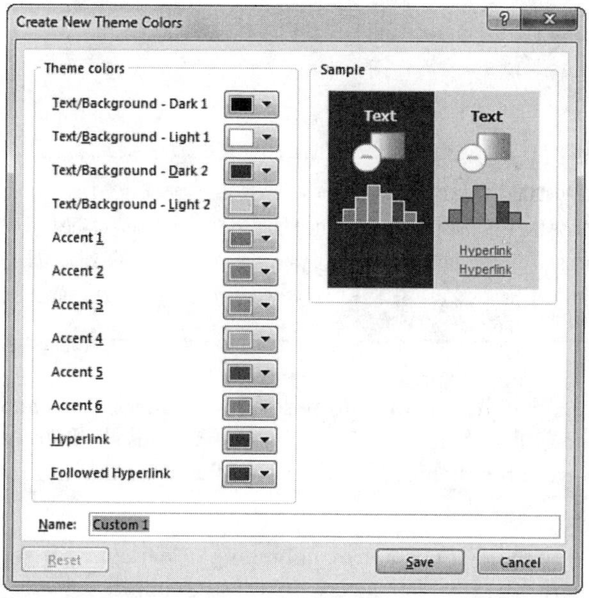

Figure 17.7
The current theme includes 12 colors.

Throughout Excel, there are many color chooser drop-downs. As shown in Figure 17.8, a section of each color chooser drop-down is called Theme Colors. The top row under Theme Colors shows the four font and six accent colors.

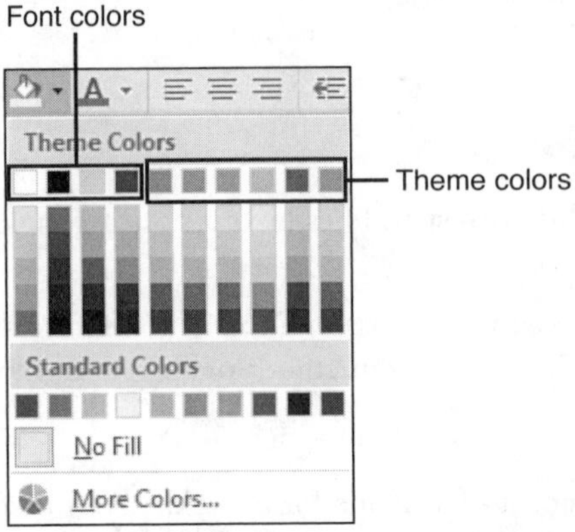

Figure 17.8
All but the hyperlink colors from the theme appear across the top row. The decimal numbers indicated in the figure are explained in a minute.

Font colors

Theme colors

If you want to choose the last color in the first row, the VBA is as follows:

```
ActiveCell.Font.ThemeColor = xlThemeColorAccent6
```

Going across that top row of Figure 17.8, these are the 10 colors:

```
xlThemeColorDark1
xlThemeColorLight1
xlThemeColorDark2
xlThemeColorLight2
xlThemeColorAccent1
xlThemeColorAccent2
xlThemeColorAccent3
xlThemeColorAccent4
xlThemeColorAccent5
xlThemeColorAccent6
```

> **CAUTION**
>
> Note that the first four colors seem to be reversed. `xlThemeColorDark1` is a white color. This is because the VBA constants were written from the point of view of the font color to use when the cell contains a dark or light background. If you have a cell filled with a dark color, you want to display a white font. Hence, `xlThemeColorDark1` is white, and `xlThemeColorLight1` is black.

On your computer, open the fill color drop-down on the Home tab and look at it in color. If you are using the Office theme, the last column is various shades of green. The top row is the actual color from the theme. Then there are five rows that go from a light green to a very dark green.

Excel lets you modify the theme color by lightening or darkening it. The values range from –1, which is very dark, to +1, which is very light. For example, the very light green in row 2 of Figure 17.8 has a tint and shade value of 0.8, which is almost completely light. The next row has a tint and shade level of 0.6. The next row has a tint and shade level of 0.4. That gives you three choices that are lighter than the theme color. The next two rows are darker than the theme color. These two darker rows have values of –.25 and –.5.

If you turn on the macro recorder and choose one of these colors, you see a confusing bunch of code:

```
.Pattern = xlSolid
.PatternColorIndex = xlAutomatic
.ThemeColor = xlThemeColorAccent6
.TintAndShade = 0.799981688894314
.PatternTintAndShade = 0
```

If you are using a solid fill, you can leave out the first, second, and fifth lines of code.

The .TintAndShade line looks confusing because computers cannot round decimal tenths very well. Remember that computers store numbers in binary. In binary, a simple number like 0.1 is a repeating decimal. As the macro recorder tries to convert 0.8 from binary to decimal, it "misses" by a bit and comes up with a very close number: 0.7998168894314. This is really saying that it should be 80% lighter than the base number.

If you are writing code by hand, you only have to assign two values to use a theme color. Assign the .ThemeColor property to one of the six xlThemeColorAccent1 through xlThemeColorAccent6 values. If you want to use a theme color from the top row of the drop-down, the .TintAndShade should be 0 and can be omitted. If you want to lighten the color, use a positive decimal for .TintAndShade. If you want to darken the color, use a negative decimal.

> **TIP**
>
> Note that the five shades in the color palette drop-downs are not the complete set of variations. In VBA, you can assign any two-digit decimal value from −1.00 to +1.00. Figure 17.9 shows 201 variations of one theme color created using the .TintAndShade property in VBA.

Figure 17.9
Shades of one theme color.

	B	C	D	E	F	G	H	I	J	K
1	Darker (Negative Tint & Shade)									
3	-1.00	-0.99	-0.98	-0.97	-0.96	-0.95	-0.94	-0.93	-0.92	-0.91
4	-0.90	-0.89	-0.88	-0.87	-0.86	-0.85	-0.84	-0.83	-0.82	-0.81
5	-0.80	-0.79	-0.78	-0.77	-0.76	-0.75	-0.74	-0.73	-0.72	-0.71
6	-0.70	-0.69	-0.68	-0.67	-0.66	-0.65	-0.64	-0.63	-0.62	-0.61
7	-0.60	-0.59	-0.58	-0.57	-0.56	-0.55	-0.54	-0.53	-0.52	-0.51
8	-0.50	-0.49	-0.48	-0.47	-0.46	-0.45	-0.44	-0.43	-0.42	-0.41
9	-0.40	-0.39	-0.38	-0.37	-0.36	-0.35	-0.34	-0.33	-0.32	-0.31
10	-0.30	-0.29	-0.28	-0.27	-0.26	-0.25	-0.24	-0.23	-0.22	-0.21
11	-0.20	-0.19	-0.18	-0.17	-0.16	-0.15	-0.14	-0.13	-0.12	-0.11
12	-0.10	-0.09	-0.08	-0.07	-0.06	-0.05	-0.04	-0.03	-0.02	-0.01
14	Zero	0								
16	Lighter (Positive Tint & Shade)									
18	+0.01	+0.02	+0.03	+0.04	+0.05	+0.06	+0.07	+0.08	+0.09	+0.10
19	+0.11	+0.12	+0.13	+0.14	+0.15	+0.16	+0.17	+0.18	+0.19	+0.20
20	+0.21	+0.22	+0.23	+0.24	+0.25	+0.26	+0.27	+0.28	+0.29	+0.30
21	+0.31	+0.32	+0.33	+0.34	+0.35	+0.36	+0.37	+0.38	+0.39	+0.40
22	+0.41	+0.42	+0.43	+0.44	+0.45	+0.46	+0.47	+0.48	+0.49	+0.50
23	+0.51	+0.52	+0.53	+0.54	+0.55	+0.56	+0.57	+0.58	+0.59	+0.60
24	+0.61	+0.62	+0.63	+0.64	+0.65	+0.66	+0.67	+0.68	+0.69	+0.70
25	+0.71	+0.72	+0.73	+0.74	+0.75	+0.76	+0.77	+0.78	+0.79	+0.80
26	+0.81	+0.82	+0.83	+0.84	+0.85	+0.86	+0.87	+0.88	+0.89	+0.90
27	+0.91	+0.92	+0.93	+0.94	+0.95	+0.96	+0.97	+0.98	+0.99	+1.00

To recap, if you want to work with theme colors, you generally change two properties: the theme color, in order to choose one of the six accent colors, and the tint and shade, to lighten or darken the base color, like this:

```
.ThemeColor = xlThemeColorAccent6
.TintAndShade = 0.4
```

> **NOTE** One advantage of using theme colors is that your sparklines change color based on the theme. If you later decide to switch from the Office theme to the Metro theme, the colors change to match the theme.

Using RGB Colors

For the past decade, computers have offered a palette of 16 million colors. These colors derive from adjusting the amount of red, green, and blue light in a cell.

Do you remember art class in elementary school? You probably learned that the three primary colors are red, yellow, and blue. You could make green by mixing some yellow and blue paint. You could make purple by mixing some red and blue paint. You could make orange by mixing some yellow and red paint. As all of my male classmates and I soon discovered, you could make black by mixing all the paint colors. Those rules all work with pigments in paint, but they don't work with light.

Those pixels on your computer screen are made up of light. In the light spectrum, the three primary colors are red, green, and blue. You can make the 16 million colors of the RGB color palette by mixing various amounts of red, green, and blue light. Each of the three colors is assigned an intensity from 0 (no light) to 255 (full light).

You will often see a color described using the RGB function. In this function, the first value is the amount of red, the second value is the amount of green, and the third value is the amount of blue:

- To make red, you use =RGB(255,0,0).
- To make green, use =RGB(0,255,0).
- To make blue, use =RGB(0,0,255).
- What happens if you mix 100% of all three colors of light? You get white! To make white, use =RGB(255,255,255).
- What if you shine no light in a pixel? You get black: =RGB(0,0,0).
- To make purple, you use some red, a little green, and some blue: RGB(139,65,123).
- To make yellow, use full red and green and no blue: =RGB(255,255,0).
- To make orange, use less green than for yellow: =RGB(255,153,0).

In VBA, you can use the RGB function just as it is shown here. The macro recorder is not a big fan of using the RGB function, though. It instead shows the result of the RGB function. Here is how you convert from the three arguments of the RGB function to the color value:

- Take the red value times 1.
- Add the green value times 256.
- Add the blue value times 65,536.

> **NOTE**
>
> Why 65,536? It is 256 raised to the second power.

If you choose a red for your sparkline, you frequently see the macro recorder assign `.Color = 255`. This is because `=RGB(255,0,0)` is `255`.

When the macro recorder assigns a value of `5287936`, what color does this mean? Here are the steps you follow to find out:

1. In Excel, enter `=Dec2Hex(5287936)`. You get the answer `50B000`. This is the color that web designers refer to as #50B000.

2. Go to your favorite search engine and search for "color chooser." Choose one of the many utilities that allow you to type in the hex color code and see the color. Type `50B000`. You will see that #50B000 is RGB(80,176,0).

While at the color chooser web page, you will be offered additional colors that complement the original color. Click around to find other shades of colors and see the RGB values for those.

To recap, to skip theme colors and use RGB colors, you set the `.Color` property to the result of an `RGB` function.

Formatting Sparkline Elements

Figure 17.10 shows a plain sparkline. The data is created from 12 points that show performance versus a budget. You really have no idea about the scale from this sparkline.

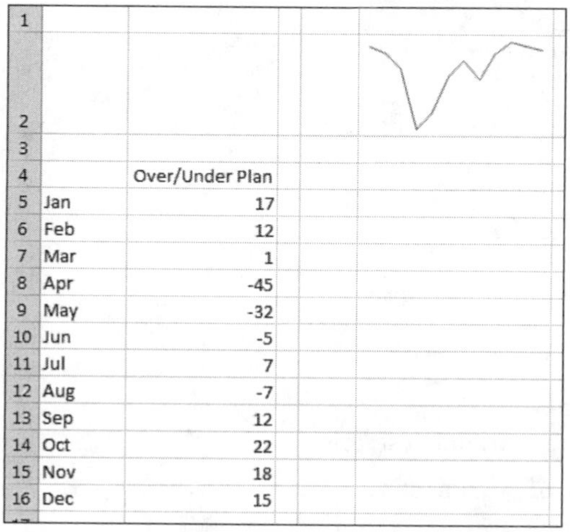

Figure 17.10
A default sparkline.

		Over/Under Plan	
	Jan	17	
	Feb	12	
	Mar	1	
	Apr	-45	
	May	-32	
	Jun	-5	
	Jul	7	
	Aug	-7	
	Sep	12	
	Oct	22	
	Nov	18	
	Dec	15	

If your sparkline includes both positive and negative numbers, it helps to show the horizontal axis so that you can figure out which points are above budget and which points are below budget.

To show the axis, use the following:

```
SG.Axes.Horizontal.Axis.Visible = True
```

Figure 17.11 shows the horizontal axis. This helps to show which months were above or below budget.

Figure 17.11
Add the horizontal axis to show which months were above or below budget.

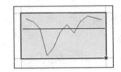

Using code from the section "Scaling Sparklines" earlier in this chapter, you can add high and low labels to the cell to the left of the sparkline:

```
Set AF = Application.WorksheetFunction
MyMax = AF.Max(Range("B5:B16"))
MyMin = AF.Min(Range("B5:B16"))
LabelStr = MyMax & vbLf & vbLf & vbLf & vbLf & MyMin

With SG.Axes.Vertical
    .MinScaleType = xlSparkScaleCustom
    .MaxScaleType = xlSparkScaleCustom
    .CustomMinScaleValue = MyMin
    .CustomMaxScaleValue = MyMax
End With

With Range("D2")
    .WrapText = True
    .Font.Size = 8
    .HorizontalAlignment = xlRight
    .VerticalAlignment = xlTop
    .Value = LabelStr
    .RowHeight = 56.25
End With
```

The result of this macro is shown in Figure 17.12.

Figure 17.12
Use a nonsparkline feature to label the vertical axis.

To change the color of the sparkline, use this:

```
SG.SeriesColor.Color = RGB(255, 191, 0)
```

The Show group of the Sparkline Tools Design tab offers six options. You can further modify those elements by using the Marker Color drop-down. You can choose to turn on a marker for every point in the dataset, as shown in Figure 17.13.

Figure 17.13
Show All Markers.

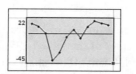

This code shows a black marker at every point:

```
With SG.Points
    .Markers.Color.Color = RGB(0, 0, 0) ' black
    .Markers.Visible = True
End With
```

Instead, you can use markers to show only the minimum, maximum, first, and last points. The following code shows the minimum in red, maximum in green, and first and last points in blue:

```
With SG.Points
    .Lowpoint.Color.Color = RGB(255, 0, 0) ' red
    .Highpoint.Color.Color = RGB(51, 204, 77) ' Green
    .Firstpoint.Color.Color = RGB(0, 0, 255) ' Blue
    .Lastpoint.Color.Color = RGB(0, 0, 255) ' blue
    .Negative.Color.Color = RGB(127, 0, 0) ' pink
    .Markers.Color.Color = RGB(0, 0, 0) ' black
    ' Choose Which points to Show
    .Highpoint.Visible = True
    .Lowpoint.Visible = True
    .Firstpoint.Visible = True
    .Lowpoint.Visible = True
    .Negative.Visible = False
    .Markers.Visible = False
End With
```

Figure 17.14 shows the sparkline with the only the high, low, first, and last points marked.

Figure 17.14
Show only key markers.

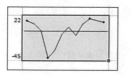

> **NOTE**
> Negative markers are particularly handy when you are formatting win/loss charts, as discussed in the next section.

17

Formatting Win/Loss Charts

Win/loss charts are a special type of sparkline for tracking binary events. A win/loss chart shows an upward-facing marker for a positive value and a downward-facing marker for any negative value. For a zero, no marker is shown.

You can use these charts to track proposal wins versus losses. In Figure 17.15, a win/loss chart shows the last 25 regular-season baseball games of the famed 1951 pennant race between the Brooklyn Dodgers and the New York Giants. This chart shows that the Giants went on a seven-game winning streak to finish the regular season. The Dodgers went 3–4 during this period and ended in a tie with the Giants, forcing a three-game playoff. The Giants won the first game, lost the second, and then advanced to the World Series by winning the third playoff game. The Giants leapt out to a 2–1 lead over the Yankees but then lost three straight.

Figure 17.15
This win/loss chart documents the most famous pennant race in history.

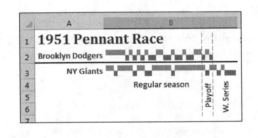

> **NOTE**
> The words *Regular season*, *Playoff*, and *W. Series*, as well as the two dotted lines, are not part of the sparkline. The lines are drawing objects manually added with Insert, Shapes.

To create the chart, you use `SparklineGroups.Add` with the type `xlSparkColumnStacked100`, like this:

```
Set SG = Range("B2:B3").SparklineGroups.Add( _
    Type:=xlSparkColumnStacked100, _
    SourceData:="C2:AD3")
```

You generally show the wins and losses using different colors. One obvious color scheme is red for losses and green for wins.

There is no specific way to change only the "up" markers, so change the color of all markers to be green:

```
' Show all points as green
SG.SeriesColor.Color = 5287936
```

Then change the color of the negative markers to red:

```
'Show losses as red
With SG.Points.Negative
    .Visible = True
    .Color.Color = 255
End With
```

It is easier to create the up/down charts. You don't have to worry about setting the line color, and the vertical axis is always fixed.

Creating a Dashboard

Sparklines provide the benefit of communicating a lot of information in a very tiny space. In this section, you'll see how to fit 130 charts on one page.

Figure 17.16 shows a dataset that summarizes a 1.8-million-row data set. I used the Power Pivot add-in for Excel to import the records and then calculated three new measures:

- YTD sales by month by store
- YTD sales by month for the previous year
- % increase of YTD sales versus the previous year

A key statistic in retail stores is how you are doing now compared to the same time last year. Also, this analysis has the benefit of being cumulative. The final number for December represents whether the store was up or down compared to the previous year.

Figure 17.16
This summary of 1.8 million records is a sea of numbers.

	A	B	C	D	E	F	G	H	I	J	K	L	M
1	**YTD Sales - % Change from Previous Year**												
2													
3	Store	Jan	Feb	Mar	Apr	May	Jun	Jul	Aug	Sep	Oct	Nov	Dec
4	Sherman (	1.9%	-1.3%	-0.8%	-0.2%	-0.1%	-0.1%	0.2%	-0.1%	0.0%	0.7%	0.4%	1.1%
5	Brea Mall	6.3%	-0.5%	-0.2%	0.1%	0.1%	-0.8%	-0.1%	-0.7%	-0.5%	-0.3%	-0.5%	0.1%
6	Park Place	4.4%	-0.8%	-0.4%	-0.5%	-0.4%	-0.4%	-0.3%	-0.8%	-0.9%	-0.6%	-1.1%	-1.5%
7	Galleria at	-0.3%	-3.5%	-3.2%	-1.8%	-1.0%	-0.8%	-0.5%	-0.4%	-0.5%	-0.2%	-0.8%	-1.4%
8	Mission V	7.3%	-0.1%	-1.2%	-0.8%	-0.2%	-0.3%	0.0%	0.0%	-0.2%	-0.3%	0.1%	0.1%
9	Corona De	5.2%	-0.2%	-1.0%	-0.1%	0.4%	0.6%	0.4%	0.1%	0.5%	0.8%	0.4%	0.4%
10	San Franci	0.6%	-1.8%	-2.0%	-0.9%	-0.6%	-0.9%	-0.5%	-1.1%	-0.7%	-0.6%	-0.4%	-0.5%

Observations About Sparklines

After working with sparklines for a while, some observations come to mind:

- Sparklines are transparent. You can see through them to the underlying cell. This means that the fill color of the underlying cell shows through, and the text in the underlying cell shows through.
- If you make the font really small and align the text with the edge of the cell, you can make the text look like a title or a legend.
- If you turn on text wrapping and make the cell tall enough for 5 or 10 lines of text in the cell, you can control the position of the text in the cell by using vbLf characters in VBA.
- Sparklines work best when they are bigger than a typical cell. For all the examples in this chapter I made the column wider, the height taller, or both.

- Sparklines created together are grouped. Changes made to one sparkline are made to all sparklines.

- Sparklines can be created on a worksheet separate from the data.

- Sparklines look better when there is some white space around the cells. This would be tough to do manually because you would have to create the sparklines one at a time. It is easy to do here because you can leverage VBA.

Creating Hundreds of Individual Sparklines in a Dashboard

You address all the issues just listed as you are creating this dashboard. The plan is to create each store's sparkline individually. This way, a blank row and column appear between the sparklines.

After inserting a new worksheet for the dashboard, you can format the cells with this code:

```
' Set up the dashboard as alternating cells for sparkline then blank
For c = 1 To 11 Step 2
    WSL.Cells(1, c).ColumnWidth = 15
    WSL.Cells(1, c + 1).ColumnWidth = 0.6
Next c
For r = 1 To 45 Step 2
    WSL.Cells(r, 1).RowHeight = 38
    WSL.Cells(r + 1, 1).RowHeight = 3
Next r
```

Keep track of which cell contains the next sparkline with two variables:

```
NextRow = 1
NextCol = 1
```

Figure out how many rows of data there are on the Data worksheet. Loop from row 4 to the final row. For each row, you make a sparkline.

Build a text string that points back to the correct row on the Data sheet, using this code, and use that as the source data argument when defining the sparkline:

```
ThisSource = "Data!B" & i & ":M" & i
Set SG = WSL.Cells(NextRow, NextCol).SparklineGroups.Add( _
    Type:=xlSparkColumn, _
    SourceData:=ThisSource)
```

In this case you want to show a horizontal axis at the zero location. The range of values for all stores was –5% to +10%. The maximum scale value here is being set to 0.15 (which is equivalent to 15%) to allow extra room for the "title" in the cell:

```
SG.Axes.Horizontal.Axis.Visible = True
With SG.Axes.Vertical
    .MinScaleType = xlSparkScaleCustom
    .MaxScaleType = xlSparkScaleCustom
    .CustomMinScaleValue = -0.05
    .CustomMaxScaleValue = 0.15
End With
```

As in the previous example with the win/loss chart, you want the positive columns to be green and the negative columns to be red:

```
' All columns green
SG.SeriesColor.Color = RGB(0, 176, 80)
' Negative columns red
SG.Points.Negative.Visible = True
SG.Points.Negative.Color.Color = RGB(255, 0, 0)
```

Remember that the sparkline has a transparent background. Thus, you can write really small text to the cell, and it behaves almost like chart labels.

The following code joins the store name and the final percentage change for the year into a title for the chart. The program writes this title to the cell but makes it small, centered, and vertically aligned:

```
ThisStore = WSD.Cells(i, 1).Value & " " & _
    Format(WSD.Cells(i, 13), "+0.0%;-0.0%;0%")
' Add a label
With WSL.Cells(NextRow, NextCol)
    .Value = ThisStore
    .HorizontalAlignment = xlCenter
    .VerticalAlignment = xlTop
    .Font.Size = 8
    .WrapText = True
End With
```

The final element is to change the background color of the cell based on the final percentage so that if it is up, the background is light green, and if it is down, the background is light red:

```
FinalVal = WSD.Cells(i, 13)
' Color the cell light red for negative, light green for positive
With WSL.Cells(NextRow, NextCol).Interior
    If FinalVal <= 0 Then
        .Color = 255
        .TintAndShade = 0.9
    Else
        .Color = 14743493
        .TintAndShade = 0.7
    End If
End With
```

After that sparkline is done, the column and/or row positions are incremented to prepare for the next chart:

```
NextCol = NextCol + 2
If NextCol > 11 Then
    NextCol = 1
    NextRow = NextRow + 2
End If
```

After this, the loop continues with the next store.

The complete code is shown here:

```
Sub StoreDashboard()
Dim SG As SparklineGroup
Dim SL As Sparkline
Dim WSD As Worksheet ' Data worksheet
Dim WSL As Worksheet ' Dashboard
```

17

```
On Error Resume Next
Application.DisplayAlerts = False
Worksheets("Dashboard").Delete
On Error GoTo 0

Set WSD = Worksheets("Data")
Set WSL = ActiveWorkbook.Worksheets.Add
WSL.Name = "Dashboard"

' Set up the dashboard as alternating cells for sparkline then blank
For c = 1 To 11 Step 2
    WSL.Cells(1, c).ColumnWidth = 15
    WSL.Cells(1, c + 1).ColumnWidth = 0.6
Next c
For r = 1 To 45 Step 2
    WSL.Cells(r, 1).RowHeight = 38
    WSL.Cells(r + 1, 1).RowHeight = 3
Next r

NextRow = 1
NextCol = 1

FinalRow = WSD.Cells(Rows.Count, 1).End(xlUp).Row

For i = 4 To FinalRow
    ThisStore = WSD.Cells(i, 1).Value & " " & _
        Format(WSD.Cells(i, 13), "+0.0%;-0.0%;0%")
    ThisSource = "Data!B" & i & ":M" & i
    FinalVal = WSD.Cells(i, 13)

    Set SG = WSL.Cells(NextRow, NextCol).SparklineGroups.Add( _
        Type:=xlSparkColumn, _
        SourceData:=ThisSource)

    SG.Axes.Horizontal.Axis.Visible = True
    With SG.Axes.Vertical
        .MinScaleType = xlSparkScaleCustom
        .MaxScaleType = xlSparkScaleCustom
        .CustomMinScaleValue = -0.05
        .CustomMaxScaleValue = 0.15
    End With

    ' All columns green
    SG.SeriesColor.Color = RGB(0, 176, 80)
    ' Negative columns red
    SG.Points.Negative.Visible = True
    SG.Points.Negative.Color.Color = RGB(255, 0, 0)

    ' Add a label
    With WSL.Cells(NextRow, NextCol)
        .Value = ThisStore
        .HorizontalAlignment = xlCenter
        .VerticalAlignment = xlTop
        .Font.Size = 8
        .WrapText = True
    End With

    ' Color the cell light red for negative, light green for positive
```

```
With WSL.Cells(NextRow, NextCol).Interior
    If FinalVal <= 0 Then
        .Color = 255
        .TintAndShade = 0.9
    Else
        .Color = 14743493
        .TintAndShade = 0.7
    End If
End With

NextCol = NextCol + 2
If NextCol > 11 Then
    NextCol = 1
    NextRow = NextRow + 2
End If
Next i
End Sub
```

Figure 17.17 shows the final dashboard, which prints on a single page and summarizes 1.8 million rows of data.

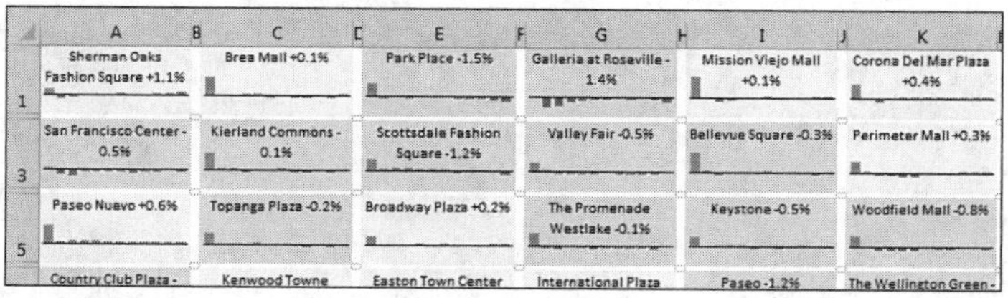

Figure 17.17
One page summarizes the sales from hundreds of stores.

If you zoom in, you can see that every cell tells a story. In Figure 17.18, Park Meadows in cell I33 had a great January, managed to stay ahead of last year through the entire year, and finished up 0.8%. Lakeside in cell I35 also had a positive January, but then it had a bad February and a worse March. Lakeside struggled back toward 0% for the rest of the year but ended up down seven-tenths of a percent.

> **NOTE**
> The report is addictive. I find myself studying all sorts of trends, but then I have to remind myself that I created the 1.8-million-row data set using `RandBetween` just a few weeks ago! The report is so compelling that I am getting drawn into studying fictional data.

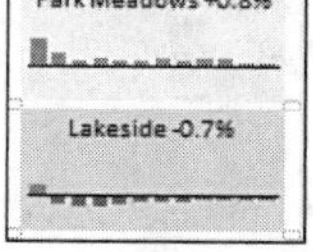

Figure 17.18
Detail of two sparkline charts.

Next Steps

In Chapter 18, "Reading from and Writing to the Web," you find out how to use web queries to automatically import data from the Internet to your Excel applications.

Reading from and Writing to the Web

18

The Internet has become pervasive and has changed our lives. From your desktop, millions of answers are available at your fingertips. In addition, publishing a report on the Web enables millions of others to instantly access your information.

This chapter discusses automated ways to pull data from the Web into spreadsheets, using new features from the former Power Query add-in. You'll find out how to use VBA to call a website repeatedly to gather information for many data points. This chapter also shows how to save data from a spreadsheet directly to the Web.

Getting Data from the Web

There is an endless variety of data on the Internet. You have two options when it comes to getting data from the Web: You can use the Excel interface to build a query and then use VBA to refresh the query, or you can attempt to write the query in the M language. The Power Query add-in that Microsoft introduced for Excel 2010/2013 is now built in to Excel 2016. When you use New Query in the Get & Transform group on the Data tab, you are using the former Power Query add-in to build your query in the M language.

The code for the query you would need to write to get date from the Web is lengthy and difficult:

```
Sub CreatePowerQuery()
    ActiveWorkbook.Queries.Add Name:="Table 1", _
        Formula:="let" & Chr(13) & "" & Chr(10) & _
        "    Source = Web.Page(Web.Contents(" & _
        """http://www.flightstats.com/go/FlightStatus/" & _
        "flightStatusByFlightPositionDetails.do?id=" & _
        "562694389&airlineCode=AA&flightNumber=5370""))," _
        & Chr(13) & "" & Chr(10) & "    Data1 = Source{1}[Data]," _
        & Chr(13) & "" & Chr(10) & "    #""Changed Type"" = " & _
        "Table.TransformColumnTypes(Data1,{{""UTC Time""," & _
        "type text}, {""Time At Departure"", type text}, " & _
        "{""Time At Arrival"", type text}, {""Spee" & _
        "d"", type text}, {""Altitude"", type text}, " & _
        "{""Latitude"", type number}, {""Longitude"", " & _
        "type number}})," & Chr(13) & "" & Chr(10) & "    " & _
        "#""Removed Columns"" = Table.RemoveColumns" & _
        "(#""Changed Type"",{""UTC Time"", ""Time At " & _
        "Departure""})," & Chr(13) & "" & Chr(10) & _
        "    #""Split Column by Position"" = Table.Split" & _
        "Column(#""Removed Columns"",""Time At Arrival""," & _
        "Splitter.SplitTextByPositions({0, 6}, false)," & _
        Formula = Formula & _
        "{""Time At Arrival.1"", ""Time At Arrival.2""})," & Chr(13) & _
        "" & Chr(10) & "    #""Changed Type1"" = " & _
        "Table.TransformColumnTypes(#""Split Column by " & _
        "Position"",{{""Time At Arrival.1"", type date}," & _
        "{""Time At Arrival.2"", type time}})," & Chr(13) & _
        "" & Chr(10) & "    #""Removed Columns1"" = " & _
        "Table.RemoveColumns(#""Changed Type1"",{""Time At Arrival.1" _
        "})," & _
        Chr(13) & "" & Chr(10) & "    #""Split Column by Delimiter"" = " & _
        "Table.SplitColumn(#""Removed Columns1"",""Spe" & _
        "ed"",Splitter.SplitTextByEachDelimiter({"" ""}, " & _
        "null, false),{""Speed.1"", ""Speed.2""})," & Chr(13) & _
        "" & Chr(10) & "    #""Changed Type2"" = " & _
        "Table.TransformColumnTypes(#""Split Column by Delimiter""," & _
        "{{""Speed.1"", Int64.Type}, {""Speed.2"", type text}})," & _
        Chr(13) & "" & Chr(10) & "    #""Removed Columns2"" = " & _
        "Table.RemoveColumns(#""Changed Type2"",{""Speed.2""})," & _
        Chr(13) & "" & Chr(10) & "    #""Split Column by Delimiter1"" " & _
        "= Table.SplitColumn(#""Removed Columns2""," & _
        """Altitude"",Splitter.SplitTextByEachDelimiter({"" ""}, " & _
        "null, false),{""Altitude.1"", ""Altitude.2""})," & _
        Chr(13) & "" & Chr(10) & "    #""Changed Type3"" = " & _
        Formula = Formula & "Table.TransformColumnTypes(#""Split " & _
        "Column by Delimiter1""," & _
        "{{""Altitude.1"", Int64.Type}, {""Altitude.2"", type text}})," & _
        Chr(13) & "" & Chr(10) & "    #""Removed Columns3"" = " & _
        "Table.RemoveColumns(#""Changed Type3"",{""Altitude.2""})" & _
        Chr(13) & "" & Chr(10) & "in" & Chr(13) & "" & Chr(10) & "    " & _
        "    #""Removed Columns3"""
    Sheets.Add After:=ActiveSheet
    With ActiveSheet.ListObjects.Add(SourceType:=0, Source:= _
        "OLEDB;Provider=Microsoft.Mashup.OleDb.1;" _
        "Data Source=$Workbook$;Location=""Table 1""" _
```

```
    , Destination:=Range("$A$1")).QueryTable
    .CommandType = xlCmdSql
    .CommandText = Array("SELECT * FROM [Table 1]")
    .RowNumbers = False
    .FillAdjacentFormulas = False
    .PreserveFormatting = True
    .RefreshOnFileOpen = False
    .BackgroundQuery = True
    .RefreshStyle = xlInsertDeleteCells
    .SavePassword = False
    .SaveData = True
    .AdjustColumnWidth = True
    .RefreshPeriod = 0
    .PreserveColumnInfo = False
    .ListObject.DisplayName = "Table_1"
    .Refresh BackgroundQuery:=False
End With
Selection.ListObject.QueryTable.Refresh BackgroundQuery:=False
End Sub
```

The easier solution is to build the query in the Power Query interface and then refresh the query with this code:

```
Sub RefreshPowerQuery()
ActiveWorkbook.RefreshAll
End Sub
```

Building Multiple Queries with VBA

Say that you want to collect data from a web site, such as historical weather statistics. Hourly weather statistics are available from http://www.wunderground.com/history/airport/ KCAK/2015/6/17/DailyHistory.html. In this URL, KCAK is the location code for the Akron Canton airport (CAK). The 2015/6/17 refers to June 17, 2015. You can imagine how you can iterate through multiple cities or multiple dates.

The strategy would be to build the Power Query from scratch, refresh, copy the data to a new sheet, and then delete the Power Query and move on to the next city or date.

To gather weather data for 24 months, you have to repeat the web query process more than 700 times. Doing this manually would be tedious.

The first part can be hard-coded because it never changes:

```
"URL;http://www.wunderground.com/history/airport/K"
```

The next part is the three-letter airport code. If you are retrieving data for many cities, this part will change:

```
CAK
```

The third part is a slash, the date in YYYY/M/D format, and a slash:

```
/2015/6/17/
```

The final part can be hard-coded:

```
"DailyHistory.html"
```

Insert a new worksheet and build an output table. In cell A2, enter the first date for which you have sales history. Use the fill handle to drag the dates down to the current date.

The formula in B2 is `="/"&Text(A2,"YYYY/M/D")&"/"`.

Add friendly headings across row 1 for the statistics you will collect.

Finding Results from Retrieved Data

Next, you have a decision to make. It looks as though the Weather Underground website is fairly static. The snow statistic even shows up if I ask for JHM airport in Maui. If you are positive that rainfall is always going to appear in cell B28 of your results sheet, you could write the macro to get data from there. However, to be safe, you can build some lookup formulas at the top of the worksheet to look for certain row labels and to pull that data. In Figure 18.1, eight INDEX and MATCH formulas find the statistics for high, low, rain, and snow from the web query.

Figure 18.1

VLOOKUPs at the top of the web worksheet find and pull the relevant data from a web page.

A	B	C	D	E	F
	High	Low	Rain	Snow	
Words in web page results:	Max Temperature	Min Temperature	Precipitation	Snow	
Row number below:	117	118	132	136	
Result:	68 °F	42 °F	0.00 in	0.00 in	
Formula:	=INDEX($B:$B,B3)	=INDEX($B:$B,C3)	=INDEX($B:$B	=INDEX($B:$B,E3+1)	

> **NOTE**
> The variable web location of the web data happens more often than you might think. If you are pulling name and address information, some addresses have three lines, and some have four lines. Anything that appears after that address might be off by a row. Some stock quote sites show a different version of the data, depending on whether the market is open or closed. If you kick off a series of web queries at 3:45 p.m., the macro might work until 4:00 p.m. and then stop working. For these reasons, it is often safer to take the extra steps of retrieving the correct data from the web query by using VLOOKUP statements.

To build the macro, you add some code before the recorded code:

```
Dim WSD as worksheet
Dim WSW as worksheet
Set WSD = Worksheets("Data")
Set WSW = Worksheets("Web")
FinalRow = WSD.Cells(Rows.Count, 1).End(xlUp).Row
```

Then add a loop to go through all the dates in the data worksheet:

```
For I = 2 to FinalRow
    ThisDate = WSD.Cells(I, 2).value
    ' Build the ConnectString
    CS = "URL: URL;http://www.wunderground.com/history/airport/KCAK"
    CS = CS & ThisDate & "DailyHistory.html"
```

If a web query is about to overwrite existing data on the worksheet, it moves that data to the right. You want to clear the previous web query and all the contents:

```
For Each qt In WSD.QueryTables
    qt.Delete
Next qt
WSD.Range("A10:A300").EntireRow.Clear
```

You can now go into the recorded code and change the `QueryTables.Add` line to the following:

```
With WSD.QueryTables.Add(Connection:= CS, Destination:=WSW.Range("A10"))
```

After the recorded code, add some lines to calculate the VLOOKUPs, copy the results, and finish the loop:

```
WSW.Calculate
WSD.Cells(i, 3).Resize(1, 4).Value = WSW.Range("B4:E4").Value
Next i
```

Step through the code as it goes through the first loop to make sure that everything is working. You should notice that the actual `.Refresh` line takes about 5 to 10 seconds. Gathering two or three years' worth of web pages requires more than an hour of processing time. Run the macro, head to lunch, and then come back to a good data set.

Putting It All Together

In the final macro here, I turned off screen updating and showed the row number that the macro is processing in the status bar. I also deleted some unnecessary properties from the recorded code:

```
Sub GetData()
    Dim WSD As Worksheet
    Dim WSW As Worksheet
    Set WSD = Worksheets("Data")
    Set WSW = Worksheets("Web")
    FinalRow = WSD.Cells(Rows.Count, 1).End(xlUp).Row

    For i = 1 To FinalRow
        ThisDate = WSD.Cells(i, 2).Value
        ' Build the ConnectString
        CS = "URL;http://www.wunderground.com/history/airport/KCAK/"
        CS = CS & ThisDate
        CS = CS & "DailyHistory.html"
        ' Clear results of last web query
        For Each qt In WSW.QueryTables
            qt.Delete
        Next qt
        WSD.Range("A10:A300").EntireRow.Clear

        With WSW.QueryTables.Add(Connection:=CS, _
            Destination:=Range("$A$10"))
            .Name = "DailyHistory"
            .FieldNames = True
            .RowNumbers = False
            .FillAdjacentFormulas = False
            .PreserveFormatting = True
```

18

```
        .RefreshOnFileOpen = False
        .BackgroundQuery = True
        .RefreshStyle = xlInsertDeleteCells
        .SavePassword = False
        .SaveData = True
        .AdjustColumnWidth = True
        .RefreshPeriod = 0
        .WebSelectionType = xlEntirePage
        .WebFormatting = xlWebFormattingNone
        .WebPreFormattedTextToColumns = True
        .WebConsecutiveDelimitersAsOne = True
        .WebSingleBlockTextImport = False
        .WebDisableDateRecognition = False
        .WebDisableRedirections = False
        .Refresh BackgroundQuery:=False
    End With

    WSW.Calculate
    WSD.Cells(i, 3).Resize(1, 4).Value = WSW.Range("B4:E4").Value
Next i

End Sub
```

After an hour, you have data retrieved from hundreds of web pages (see Figure 18.2).

Figure 18.2
The results of running
the web query hundreds
of times.

	A	B	C	D	E	F
1	Date	Format	High	Low	Rain	Snow
2	10/7/2012	/2012/10/7/	48 °F	36 °F	0.02 in	0.00 in
3	10/6/2012	/2012/10/6/	55 °F	41 °F	0.34 in	0.00 in
4	10/5/2012	/2012/10/5/	70 °F	49 °F	0.28 in	0.00 in
5	10/4/2012	/2012/10/4/	73 °F	55 °F	0.00 in	0.00 in
6	10/3/2012	/2012/10/3/	72 °F	58 °F	0.00 in	0.00 in
7	10/2/2012	/2012/10/2/	72 °F	54 °F	0.17 in	0.00 in
8	10/1/2012	/2012/10/1/	63 °F	42 °F	0.15 in	0.00 in
9	9/30/2012	/2012/9/30/	65 °F	45 °F	T in	0.00 in
10	9/29/2012	/2012/9/29/	68 °F	42 °F	0.00 in	0.00 in

Examples of Scraping Websites Using Web Queries

Over the years, I have used the web query trick many times. Examples include the following:

- I used a web query to get names and company addresses for all Fortune 1000 CFOs so that I could pitch my Power Excel seminars to them.

- I used a web query to find the complete membership roster for a publishing association of which I am a member. (I already had the printed roster, but with an electronic database, I could filter to find publishers in certain cities.)

- I used a web query to get a mailing address for every public library in the United States.

- I used a web query to get a complete list of Chipotle restaurants (which later ended up in my GPS, but that is a story for the [yet unwritten] Microsoft MapPoint book).

Using `Application.OnTime` to Periodically Analyze Data

VBA offers the `OnTime` method for running any VBA procedure at a specific time of day or after a specific amount of time has passed.

You can write a macro to capture data every hour throughout the day. This macro would have times hard-coded. The following code will, theoretically, capture data from a website every hour throughout the day:

```
Sub ScheduleTheDay()
    Application.OnTime EarliestTime:=TimeValue("8:00 AM"), _
        Procedure:= "CaptureData"
    Application.OnTime EarliestTime:=TimeValue("9:00 AM"), _
        Procedure:= "CaptureData"
    Application.OnTime EarliestTime:=TimeValue("10:00 AM"), _
        Procedure:= "CaptureData"
    Application.OnTime EarliestTime:=TimeValue("11:00 AM"), _
        Procedure:= "CaptureData"
    Application.OnTime EarliestTime:=TimeValue("12:00 AM"), _
        Procedure:= "CaptureData"
    Application.OnTime EarliestTime:=TimeValue("1:00 PM"), _
        Procedure:= "CaptureData"
    Application.OnTime EarliestTime:=TimeValue("2:00 PM"), _
        Procedure:= "CaptureData"
    Application.OnTime EarliestTime:=TimeValue("3:00 PM"), _
        Procedure:= "CaptureData"
    Application.OnTime EarliestTime:=TimeValue("4:00 PM"), _
        Procedure:= "CaptureData"
    Application.OnTime EarliestTime:=TimeValue("5:00 PM"), _
        Procedure:= "CaptureData"
End Sub

Sub CaptureData()
    Dim WSQ As Worksheet
    Dim NextRow As Long
    Set WSQ = Worksheets("MyQuery")
    ' Refresh the web query
    WSQ.Range("A2").QueryTable.Refresh BackgroundQuery:=False
    ' Make sure the data is updated
    Application.Wait (Now + TimeValue("0:00:10"))
    ' Copy the web query results to a new row
    NextRow = WSQ.Cells(Rows.Count, 1).End(xlUp).Row + 1
    WSQ.Range("A2:B2").Copy WSQ.Cells(NextRow, 1)
End Sub
```

Using Ready Mode for Scheduled Procedures

The `OnTime` method runs only when Excel is in Ready, Copy, Cut, or Find mode at the prescribed time. If you start to edit a cell at 7:59:55 a.m. and keep that cell in Edit mode, Excel cannot run the `CaptureData` macro at 8:00 a.m., as directed.

In the preceding code example, I specified only the start time for the procedure to run. Excel waits anxiously until the spreadsheet is returned to Ready mode and then runs the scheduled program as soon as it can.

18

The classic example is that you start to edit a cell at 7:59 a.m., and then your manager walks in and asks you to attend a surprise staff meeting down the hall. If you leave your spreadsheet in Edit mode and attend the staff meeting until 10:30 a.m., the program cannot run the first three scheduled hours of updates. As soon as you return to your desk and press Enter to exit Edit mode, the program runs all previously scheduled tasks. In the preceding code, you find that the first three scheduled updates of the program all happen between 10:30 and 10:31 a.m.

Specifying a Window of Time for an Update

You can provide Excel with a window of time within which to make an update. The following code tells Excel to run an update at any time between 8:00 a.m. and 8:05 a.m.:

```
Application.OnTime EarliestTime:=TimeValue("8:00 AM"), _
    Procedure:= "CaptureData ", _
  LatestTime:=TimeValue("8:05 AM")
```

If the Excel session remains in Edit mode for the entire five minutes, the scheduled task is skipped.

Canceling a Previously Scheduled Macro

It is fairly difficult to cancel a previously scheduled macro. You must know the exact time that the macro is scheduled to run. To cancel a pending operation, call the `OnTime` method and use the `Schedule:=False` parameter to unschedule the event. The following code cancels the 11:00 a.m. run of `CaptureData`:

```
Sub CancelEleven()
Application.OnTime EarliestTime:=TimeValue("11:00 AM"), _
    Procedure:= "CaptureData", Schedule:=False
End Sub
```

It is interesting to note that the `OnTime` schedules are remembered by a running instance of Excel. If you keep Excel open but close the workbook with the scheduled procedure, it still runs. Consider this hypothetical series of events:

1. Open Excel at 7:30 a.m.

2. Open Schedule.xlsm and run a macro to schedule a procedure at 8:00 a.m.

3. Close Schedule.xlsm but keep Excel open.

4. Open a new workbook and begin entering data.

At 8:00 a.m., Excel reopens Schedule.xlsm and runs the scheduled macro. Excel doesn't close Schedule.xlsm. As you can imagine, this is fairly annoying and alarming if you are not expecting it. If you are going to make extensive use of `Application.Ontime`, you might want to have it running in one instance of Excel while you work in a second instance of Excel.

> **NOTE**
> If you are using a macro to schedule a macro a certain amount of time later, you could remember the time in an out-of-the way cell to be able to cancel the update. See an example in the "Scheduling a Macro to Run *x* Minutes in the Future" section of this chapter.

Closing Excel Cancels All Pending Scheduled Macros

If you close Excel with File, Exit, all future scheduled macros are automatically canceled. When you have a macro that has scheduled a bunch of macros at indeterminate times, closing Excel is the only way to prevent the macros from running.

Scheduling a Macro to Run *x* Minutes in the Future

You can schedule a macro to run at a certain time in the future. The following macro uses the TIME function to return the current time and adds 2 minutes and 30 seconds to the time. The following macro runs something 2 minutes and 30 seconds from now:

```
Sub ScheduleAnything()
    ' This macro can be used to schedule anything
    WaitHours = 0
    WaitMin = 2
    WaitSec = 30
    NameOfScheduledProc = "CaptureData"
    ' --- End of Input Section -------

    ' Determine the next time this should run
    NextTime = Time + TimeSerial(WaitHours, WaitMin, WaitSec)

    ' Schedule ThisProcedure to run then
    Application.OnTime EarliestTime:=NextTime,
Procedure:=NameOfScheduledProc

End Sub
```

Later, canceling this scheduled event would be nearly impossible. You won't know the exact time that the macro grabbed the TIME function. You might try to save this value in an out-of-the-way cell:

```
Sub ScheduleWithCancelOption
    NameOfScheduledProc = "CaptureData"

    ' Determine the next time this should run
    NextTime = Time + TimeSerial(0,2,30)
    Range("ZZ1").Value = NextTime

    ' Schedule ThisProcedure to run then
    Application.OnTime EarliestTime:=NextTime, _
        Procedure:=NameOfScheduledProc

End Sub

Sub CancelLater()
    NextTime = Range("ZZ1").value
    Application.OnTime EarliestTime:=NextTime, _
    Procedure:=CaptureData, Schedule:=False
End Sub
```

Scheduling a Verbal Reminder

The text-to-speech tools in Excel can be fun. The following macro sets up a schedule that reminds you when it is time to go to a staff meeting:

```
Sub ScheduleSpeak()
    Application.OnTime EarliestTime:=TimeValue("9:14 AM"), _
        Procedure:="RemindMe"
End Sub

Sub RemindMe()
    Application.Speech.Speak _
        Text:="Bill. It is time for the staff meeting."
End Sub
```

If you want to pull a prank on your manager, you can schedule Excel to automatically turn on the Speak on Enter feature. Follow this scenario:

1. Tell your manager that you are taking him out to lunch to celebrate April 1.

2. At some point in the morning, while your manager is getting coffee, run the ScheduleSpeech macro. Design the macro to run 15 minutes after your lunch starts.

3. Take your manager to lunch.

4. While the manager is away, the scheduled macro will run.

5. When the manager returns and starts typing data in Excel, the computer will repeat the cells as they are entered. This is slightly reminiscent of the computer on *Star Trek* that repeated everything Lieutenant Uhura said.

After this starts happening, you can pretend to be innocent; after all, you have a strong alibi for when the prank began to happen. Here's the code you use to do it:

```
Sub ScheduleSpeech()
    Application.OnTime EarliestTime:=TimeValue("12:15 PM"), _
        Procedure:="SetUpSpeech"
End Sub

Sub SetupSpeech())
    Application.Speech.SpeakCellOnEnter = True
End Sub
```

> **NOTE** To turn off Speak on Enter, you can either dig out the button from the QAT Customization panel (look in the category called Commands Not on the Ribbon) or, if you can run some VBA, change the SetupSpeech macro to change the True to False.

Scheduling a Macro to Run Every Two Minutes

Say that you want to ask Excel to run a certain macro every two minutes. However, you realize that if a macro gets delayed because you accidentally left the workbook in Edit mode while going to the staff meeting, you don't want dozens of updates to happen in a matter of seconds.

The easy solution is to have the ScheduleAnything procedure recursively schedule itself to run again in two minutes. The following code schedules a run in two minutes and then performs CaptureData:

```
Sub ScheduleAnything()
    ' This macro can be used to schedule anything
    ' Enter how often you want to run the macro in hours and minutes
    WaitHours = 0
    WaitMin = 2
    WaitSec = 0
    NameOfThisProcedure = "ScheduleAnything"
    NameOfScheduledProc = "CaptureData"
    ' --- End of Input Section -------

    ' Determine the next time this should run
    NextTime = Time + TimeSerial(WaitHours, WaitMin, WaitSec)

    ' Schedule ThisProcedure to run then
    Application.OnTime EarliestTime:=NextTime, _
        Procedure:=NameOfThisProcedure

    ' Get the Data
    Application.Run NameOfScheduledProc

End Sub
```

This method has some advantages. It doesn't schedule a million updates in the future. You have only one future update scheduled at any given time. Therefore, if you decide that you are tired of seeing the national debt every 15 seconds, you only need to comment out the `Application.OnTime` line of code and wait 15 seconds for the last update to happen.

Publishing Data to a Web Page

This chapter has highlighted many ways to capture data from the Web. But you can also publish Excel data back to the Web. That's what this section is about.

The `RunReportForEachCustomer` macro shown in Chapter 11, "Data Mining with Advanced Filter," produces reports for each customer in a company. Instead of printing and faxing a report, it would be cool to save the Excel file as HTML and post the results on a company intranet so that the customer service reps can instantly access the latest version of the report.

With the Excel user interface, it is easy to save the report as a web page to create an HTML view of the data.

In Excel 2016, use File, Save As. Select Web Page (*.htm, *html) in the Save as Type drop-down. You have control over the title that appears in the window title bar. This title also gets written to the top center of your web page. Click the Change Title button to change the `<Title>` tag for the web page. Type a name that ends in either .htm or .html and click Publish.

The result is a file that can be viewed in any web browser. The web page accurately shows the number formats and font sizes (see Figure 18.3).

Whereas the macro from Chapter 11 did `WBN.SaveAs`, the current macro uses this code to write out each web page:

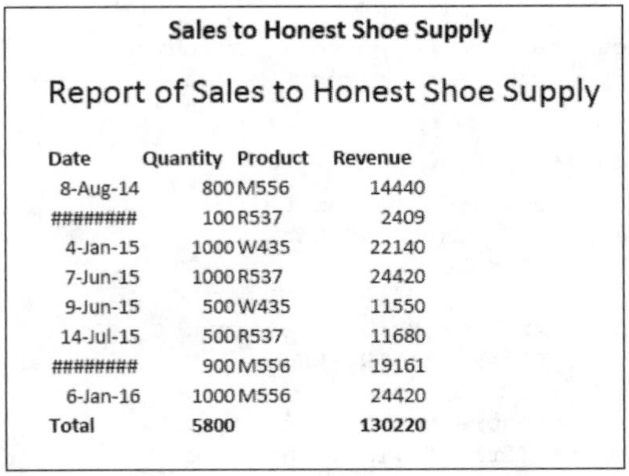

Figure 18.3
The formatting is close
to that of the original
worksheet.

Sales to Honest Shoe Supply

Report of Sales to Honest Shoe Supply

Date	Quantity	Product	Revenue
8-Aug-14	800	M556	14440
########	100	R537	2409
4-Jan-15	1000	W435	22140
7-Jun-15	1000	R537	24420
9-Jun-15	500	W435	11550
14-Jul-15	500	R537	11680
########	900	M556	19161
6-Jan-16	1000	M556	24420
Total	5800		130220

```
HTMLFN = "C:\Intranet\" & ThisCust & ".html"
On Error Resume Next
Kill HTMLFN
On Error GoTo 0
With WBN.PublishObjects.Add( _
    SourceType:=xlSourceSheet, _
    Filename:=HTMLFN, _
    Sheet:="Sheet1", _
    Source:="", _
    HtmlType:=xlHtmlStatic, _
    DivID:="A", _
    Title:="Sales to " & ThisCust)
    .Publish True
    .AutoRepublish = False
End With
```

Although the data is accurately presented in Figure 18.3, it is not extremely fancy. For example, you don't have a company logo or navigation bar to examine other reports.

Using VBA to Create Custom Web Pages

Long before Microsoft introduced the Save as Web Page functionality, people had been using VBA to publish Excel data as HTML. The advantage of using VBA for this is that you can write out specific HTML statements to display company logos and navigation bars.

Consider a typical web page template:

- There is code to display a logo and navigation bar at the top/side.
- There is content for the page.
- There is some HTML code to finish the page.

The following macro reads the code behind a web page and writes it to Excel:

```
Sub ImportHTML()
    ThisFile = "C:\Intranet\schedule.html"
    Open ThisFile For Input As #1
    Ctr = 2
    Do
```

```
            Line Input #1, Data
            Worksheets("HTML").Cells(Ctr, 2).Value = Data
            Ctr = Ctr + 1
        Loop While EOF(1) = False
        Close #1
    End Sub
```

If you import the text of a web page into Excel, even if you don't understand the HTML involved, you can probably find the first lines that contain the page content.

Examine the HTML code in Excel. Copy the lines needed to draw the top part of the web page to a worksheet called Top. Copy the lines of code needed to close the web page to a worksheet called Bottom.

You can use VBA to write out the top, generate content from your worksheet, and then write out the bottom.

Using Excel as a Content Management System

Half a billion people are proficient in Excel. Companies everywhere have data in Excel and many staffers who are comfortable maintaining that data. Rather than force these people to learn how to create HTML pages, why not build a content management system to take their Excel data and write out custom web pages?

You probably already have data for a web page in Excel. Using the ImportHTML routine to read the HTML into Excel, you know the top and bottom portions of the HTML needed to render the web page. Building a content management system with these tools is simple, and I'll show you an example. To the existing Excel data, I added two worksheets. In the worksheet called Top, I copied the HTML needed to generate the navigation bar of the website. To the worksheet called Bottom, I copied the HTML needed to generate the end of the HTML page. Figure 18.4 shows the simple Bottom worksheet.

Figure 18.4

Companies everywhere are maintaining all sorts of data in Excel and are comfortable updating the data in Excel. Why not marry Excel with a simple bit of VBA so that custom HTML can be produced from Excel?

	A	B	C	D	E	F	G	H	I	J	K
1	Sequence	Content									
2	1	</UL></p>									
3	2										
4	3										
5	4	Contact: Bill Jelen P.O. Box 82, Uniontown, OH 44685; 									
6	5	online at: www.mrexcel.com ; and by email at Bill@mrexcel.com 									
7	6	</p>									
8	7	.									
9	8	<center>###</center> 									
10	9										
11	10										
12	11										
13	12	</p>									
14	13	<font>									
15	14	<p></td>									
16	15	</tr>									
17	16	</table>									
18	17	<td>									
19	18	</tr>									
20	19	</table>									
21	20										
22	21	<p align="center"><font size="1" color="#1E2463">Excel is a registered trademark									
23	22	of the Microsoft® Corporation. MrExcel is a registered trademark of Tickling Keys,Inc.</font></p>									
24	23	<p align="center"><font size="1" color="#1E2463">All contents Copyright									
25	24										
26	25	1998-2015 by MrExcel Consulting.</font></p>									
27	26	</font></p>									
28	27										
29	28	</body>									
30	29										
31	30	</html>									

The macro code opens a text file called `directory.html` for output. First, all the HTML code from the Top worksheet is written to the file. Then the macro loops through each row in the membership directory, writing data to the file. After completing this loop, the following macro writes out the HTML code from the Bottom worksheet to finish the file:

```
Sub WriteMembershipHTML()
    ' Write web pages
    Dim WST As Worksheet
    Dim WSB As Worksheet
    Dim WSM As Worksheet
    Set WSB = Worksheets("Bottom")
    Set WST = Worksheets("Top")
    Set WSM = Worksheets("Membership")

    ' Figure out the path
    MyPath = ThisWorkbook.Path

    LineCtr = 0

    FinalT = WST.Cells(Rows.Count, 1).End(xlUp).Row
    FinalB = WSB.Cells(Rows.Count, 1).End(xlUp).Row
    FinalM = WSM.Cells(Rows.Count, 1).End(xlUp).Row

    MyFile = "sampleschedule.html"

    ThisFile = MyPath & Application.PathSeparator & MyFile
    ThisHostFile = MyFile

    ' Delete the old HTML page
    On Error Resume Next
    Kill (ThisFile)
    On Error GoTo 0

    ' Build the title
    ThisTitle = "<Title>LTCC Membership Directory</Title>"
    WST.Cells(3, 2).Value = ThisTitle

    ' Open the file for output
    Open ThisFile For Output As #1

    ' Write out the top part of the HTML
    For j = 2 To FinalT
        Print #1, WST.Cells(j, 2).Value
    Next j

    ' For each row in Membership, write out lines of data to HTML file
    For j = 2 To FinalM
        ' Surround Member name with bold tags
        Print #1, "<li>" & WSM.Cells(j, 1).Value
    Next j

    ' Close old file
    Print #1, "This page current as of " & Format(Date, "mmmm dd, yyyy") & _
        " " & Format(Time, "h:mm AM/PM")

    ' Write out HTML code from Bottom worksheet
```

```
        For j = 2 To FinalB
            Print #1, WSB.Cells(j, 2).Value
        Next j
        Close #1

        Application.StatusBar = False
        Application.CutCopyMode = False
        MsgBox "web pages updated"

    End Sub
```

Figure 18.5 shows the finished web page. This web page looks a lot better than the generic page created by Excel's Save as Web Page option, and it maintains the look and feel of the rest of the site.

Using this approach has many advantages. The person who maintains the schedule data is comfortable working in Excel. She has already been maintaining the data in Excel on a regular basis. Now, after updating some records, she clicks a button to produce a new version of the web page.

Of course, the web designer is clueless about Excel. However, if he ever wants to change the web design, it is a simple matter of opening his new sample.html file in Notepad and copying the new code to the Top and Bottom worksheets.

Figure 18.5
A simple content management system in Excel was used to generate this web page. The look and feel match the look and feel of the rest of the website. Excel achieved it without any expensive web database coding.

The resulting web page has a small file size—about one-sixth the size of an equivalent page created by Excel's Save as Web Page.

> **NOTE**
> In real life, the content management system in this example was extended to allow easy maintenance of the organization's calendar, board members, and so on. The resulting workbook made it possible to maintain 41 web pages at the click of a button.

Bonus: FTP from Excel

Even when you are able to update web pages from Excel, you still have the hassle of using an FTP program to upload the pages from your hard drive to the Internet. Again, many people are proficient in Excel, but not so many are comfortable with using an FTP client.

Ken Anderson has written a cool command-line FTP freeware utility. Download WCL_ FTP from http://www.softlookup.com/display.asp?id=20483. Save WCL_FTP.exe to the root directory of your hard drive and then use this code to automatically upload your recently created HTML files to your web server:

```
Sub DoFTP(fname, pathfname)
' To have this work, copy wcl_ftp.exe to the C:\ root directory
' Download from http://www.softlookup.com/display.asp?id=20483

' Build a string to FTP. The syntax is
' WCL_FTP.exe "Caption" hostname username password host-directory _
' host-filename local-filename get-or-put 0Ascii1Binanry 0NoLog _
' 0Background 1CloseWhenDone 1PassiveMode  1ErrorsText

If Not Worksheets("Menu").Range("I1").Value = True Then Exit Sub

s = """c:\wcl_ftp.exe "" " _
    & """Upload File to website"" " _
    & "ftp.MySite.com FTPUser FTPPassword www " _
    & fname & " " _
    & """" & pathfname & """ " _
    & "put " _
    & "0 0 0 1 1 1"

Shell s, vbMinimizedNoFocus
End Sub
```

Next Steps

Chapter 19, "Text File Processing," covers importing from a text file and writing to a text file. Being able to write to a text file is useful when you need to write out data for another system to read.

Text File Processing

VBA simplifies both reading and writing from text files. This chapter covers importing from a text file and writing to a text file. Being able to write to a text file is useful when you need to write out data for another system to read or even when you need to produce HTML files.

Importing from Text Files

There are two basic scenarios when reading from text files. If a file contains fewer than 1,048,576 records, it is not difficult to import the file using the `Workbooks.OpenText` method. If the file contains more than 1,048,576 records, you have to read the file one record at a time.

Importing Text Files with Fewer Than 1,048,576 Rows

Text files typically come in one of two formats. In one format, the fields in each record are separated by some delimiter, such as a comma, pipe, or tab. In the second format, each field takes a particular number of character positions. This is called a *fixed-width file*, and this format was very popular in the days of COBOL.

Excel can import either type of file. You can also open both types by using the `OpenText` method. In both cases, it is best to record the process of opening the file and then use the recorded snippet of code.

Opening a Fixed-Width File

Figure 19.1 shows a text file in which each field takes up a certain amount of space in the record. Writing the code to open this type of file is slightly arduous because you need to specify the length of each field. In my collection of antiques, I still have a metal ruler used by COBOL programmers to measure the number of characters in a field printed on a green-bar printer. In theory, you could change the font of your file to a monospace font and use this same method. However, using the macro recorder is a slightly more up-to-date method.

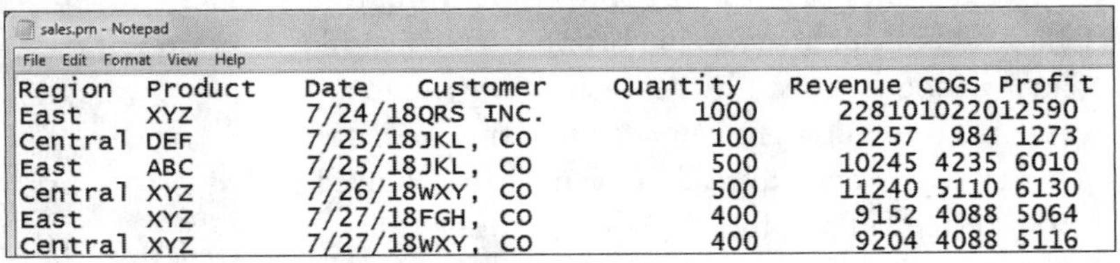

Figure 19.1
This file is fixed width. Because you must specify the exact length of each field in the file, opening this file is quite involved.

Turn on the macro recorder by selecting Record Macro from the Developer tab. Use the default macro name. From the File menu, select Open. Change the Files of Type to All Files and find your text file.

In the Text Import Wizard's step 1, specify that the data is Fixed Width and click Next. Excel looks at your data and attempts to figure out where each field begins and ends. Figure 19.2 shows Excel's guess on this particular file. Because the Date field is too close to the Customer field, Excel missed drawing that line.

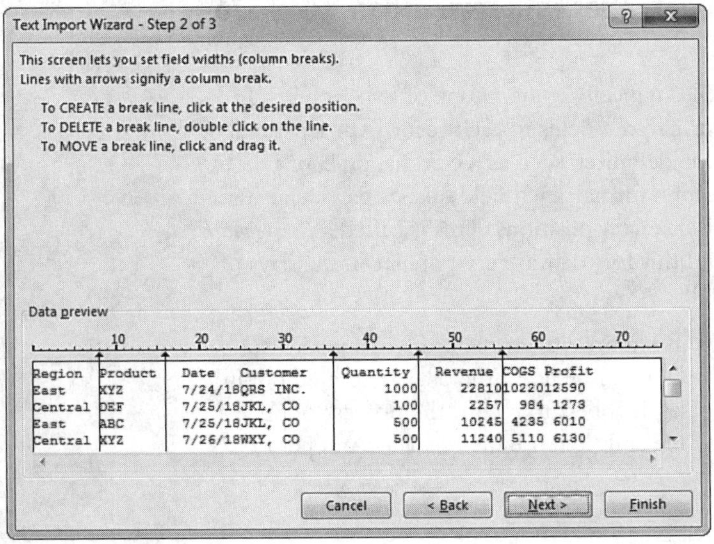

Figure 19.2
Excel guesses at where each field starts and ends. In this case, it guessed incorrectly for two of the fields.

To add a new field indicator in step 2 of the wizard, click in the appropriate place in the Data Preview window. If you click in the wrong column, click the line and drag it to the right place. If Excel inadvertently put in an extra field line, double-click the line to remove it. Figure 19.3 shows the Data Preview window after the appropriate changes have been made. Note the little ruler above the data. When you click to add a field marker, Excel is actually handling the tedious work of figuring out that the Customer field starts in position 25 and has a length of 11.

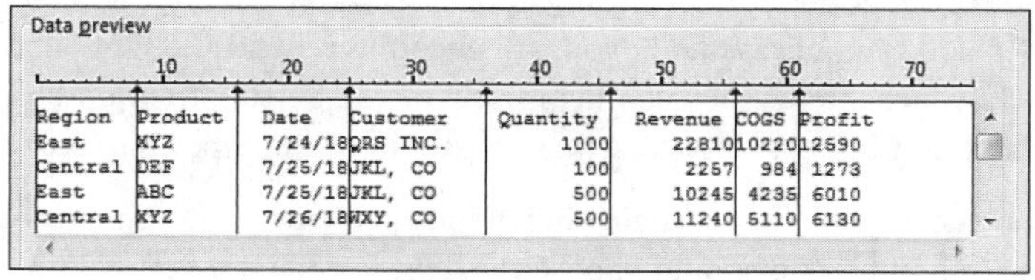

Figure 19.3
After you add a new field marker and adjust the marker between Customer and Quantity to the right place, Excel can build the code that gives you an idea of the start position and length of each field.

In step 3 of the wizard, Excel assumes that every field is in General format. Change the format of any fields that require special handling. Click the third column and choose the appropriate format from the Column Data Format section of the dialog box. Figure 19.4 shows the selections for this file.

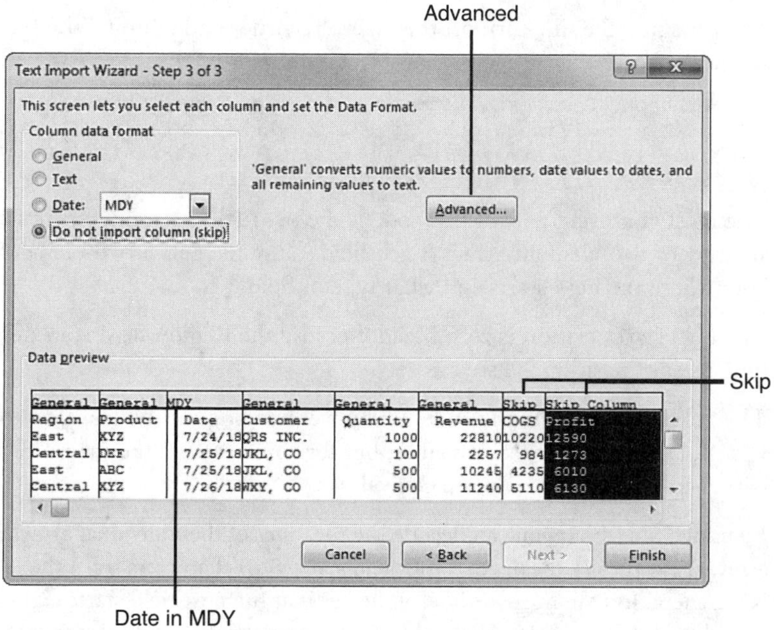

Figure 19.4
The third column is a date, and you do not want to import the Cost and Profit columns.

If you have date fields, click the heading above that column and change the column data format choice to a Date format. If you have a file with dates in year-month-day format or day-month-year format, select the drop-down next to Date and choose the appropriate date sequence.

If you prefer to skip some fields, click those columns and select Do Not Import Column (Skip) from the Column Data Format selection. This is useful in a couple instances. If the file includes sensitive data that you do not want to show to a client, you can leave it out of the import. For example, perhaps this report is for a customer to whom you do not want to show the cost of goods sold or profit. In this case, you can choose to skip these fields in the import. In addition, occasionally you will encounter a text file that is both fixed width and delimited by a character such as the pipe character. Setting the one-character-wide pipe columns as "do not import" is a great way to get rid of the pipe characters.

If you have text fields that contain alphabetic characters, you can choose the General format. The only time you should choose the Text format is if you have a numeric field that you explicitly need imported as text. One example of this is an account number with leading zeros or a column of ZIP Codes. In this case, change the field to Text format to ensure that ZIP Code 01234 does not lose the leading zero.

> **NOTE** After you import a text file and specify that one field is text, that field exhibits seemingly bizarre behavior. Try inserting a new row and entering a formula in the middle of a column imported as text. Instead of getting the results of the formula, Excel enters the formula as text. The solution is to delete the formula, format the entire column as General, and then enter the formula again.

After opening the file, turn off the macro recorder and examine the recorded code, which should look like this:

```
Workbooks.OpenText Filename:="C:\sales.prn", Origin:=437, StartRow:=1, _
DataType:=xlFixedWidth, FieldInfo:=Array(Array(0, 1), Array(8, 1), _
Array(17, 3), Array(27, 1), Array(54, 1), Array(62, 1), Array(71, 9), _
Array(79, 9)), TrailingMinusNumbers:=True
```

The most confusing part of this code is the `FieldInfo` parameter. You are supposed to code an array of two-element arrays. Each field in the file gets a two-element array to identify both where the field starts and what type of field it is.

The field start position is zero based. Because the Region field is in the first character position, its start position is listed as zero.

The field type is a numeric code. If you were coding this by hand, you would use the `xlColumnDataType` constant names; but for some reason, the macro recorder uses the harder-to-understand numeric equivalents.

By using Table 19.1, you can decode the meaning of the individual arrays in the `FieldInfo` array. `Array(0, 1)` means that this field starts zero characters from the left edge of the file and is a General format. `Array(8, 1)` indicates that the next field starts eight characters from the left edge of the file and is General format. `Array(17, 3)` indicates that the next field starts 17 characters from the left edge of the file and is a Date format in month-day-year sequence.

Table 19.1	`xlColumnDataType` **Values**	
Value	**Constant**	**Used For**
1	`xlGeneralFormat`	General
2	`xlTextFormat`	Text
3	`xlMDYFormat`	MDY date
4	`xlDMYFormat`	DMY date
5	`xlYMDFormat`	YMD date
6	`xlMYDFormat`	MYD date
7	`xlDYMFormat`	DYM date
8	`xlYDMFormat`	YDM date
9	`xlSkipColumn`	Skip Column
10	`xlEMDFormat`	EMD date (for use in Taiwan)

As you can see, the `FieldInfo` parameter for fixed-width files is arduous to code and confusing to look at. This is one situation in which it is easier to record the macro and copy the code snippet.

> **NOTE**
> The `xlTrailingMinusNumbers` parameter was new in Excel 2002. If you have any clients who might be using Excel 97 or Excel 2000, take out the recorded parameter. The code runs fine without the parameter in newer versions. However, if left in, it leads to a compile error on older versions. In my experience, this is the number-one reason code crashes on earlier versions of Excel.

19

Opening a Delimited File

Figure 19.5 shows a text file in which the fields are comma separated. The main task in opening such a file is to tell Excel that the delimiter in the file is a comma and then identify any special processing for each field. In this case, you definitely want to identify the third column as being a date in MDY format.

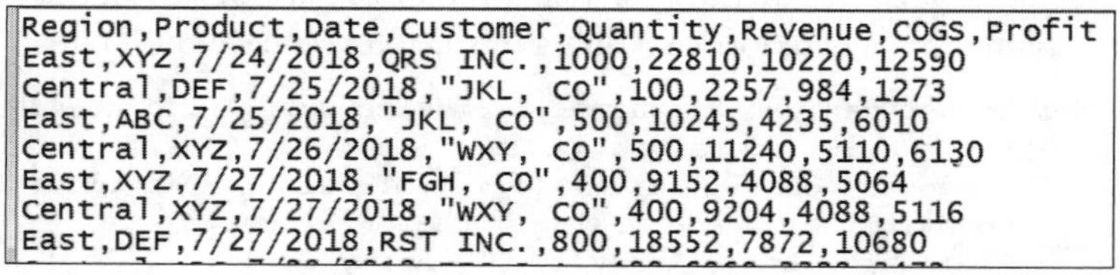

Figure 19.5
This file is comma delimited. Opening this file involves telling Excel to look for a comma as the delimiter and then identifying any special handling, such as treating the third column as a date. This is much easier than handling fixed-width files.

```
Region,Product,Date,Customer,Quantity,Revenue,COGS,Profit
East,XYZ,7/24/2018,QRS INC.,1000,22810,10220,12590
Central,DEF,7/25/2018,"JKL, CO",100,2257,984,1273
East,ABC,7/25/2018,"JKL, CO",500,10245,4235,6010
Central,XYZ,7/26/2018,"WXY, CO",500,11240,5110,6130
East,XYZ,7/27/2018,"FGH, CO",400,9152,4088,5064
Central,XYZ,7/27/2018,"WXY, CO",400,9204,4088,5116
East,DEF,7/27/2018,RST INC.,800,18552,7872,10680
```

> **NOTE**
> If you try to record the process of opening a comma-delimited file whose filename ends in .csv, Excel records the `Workbooks.Open` method rather than `Workbooks.OpenText`. If you need to control the formatting of certain columns, rename the file to have a .txt extension before recording the macro. You can then edit the recorded macro to change the filename back to a .csv extension.

Turn on the macro recorder and record the process of opening the text file. In step 1 of the wizard, specify that the file is delimited.

In the Text Import Wizard's step 2, the Data Preview window might initially look horrible. This is because Excel defaults to assuming that the fields are separated by tab characters (see Figure 19.6).

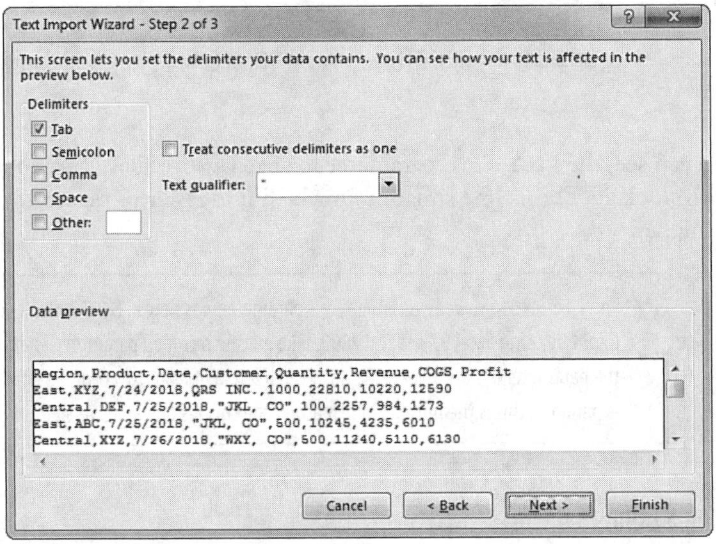

Figure 19.6
Before you import a delimited text file, the initial Data Preview window is a confusing mess of data because Excel is looking for tab characters between fields when a comma is actually the delimiter in this file.

After you've cleared the Tab check box and selected the proper delimiter choice, which in this case is a comma, the Data Preview window in step 2 looks perfect, as shown in Figure 19.7.

Step 3 of the wizard is identical to step 3 for a fixed-width file. In this case, specify that the third column has a date format. Click Finish, and you have this code in the macro recorder:

```
Workbooks.OpenText Filename:="C:\sales.txt", Origin:=437, _
    StartRow:=1, DataType:=xlDelimited, TextQualifier:=xlDoubleQuote, _
    ConsecutiveDelimiter:=False, Tab:=False, Semicolon:=False, _
    Comma:=True, Space:=False, Other:=False, _
    FieldInfo:=Array(Array(1, 1), Array(2, 1), _
    Array(3, 3), Array(4, 1), Array(5, 1), Array(6, 1), _
    Array(7, 1), Array(8, 1)), TrailingMinusNumbers:=True
```

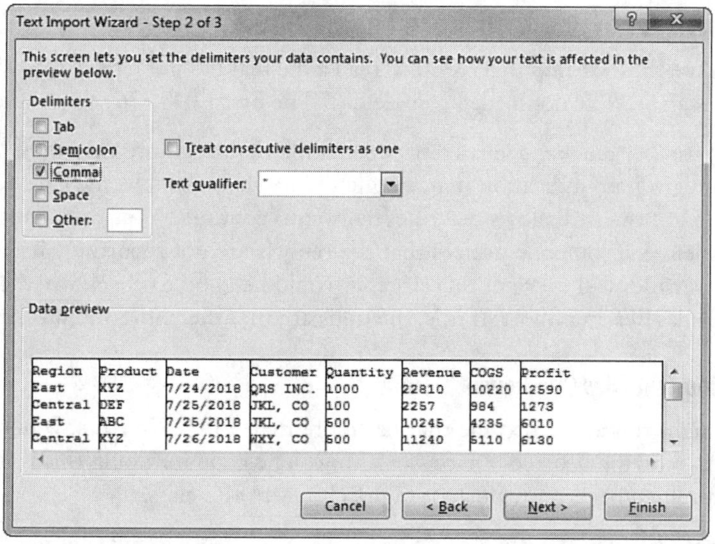

Figure 19.7
After the delimiter field has been changed from a tab to a comma, the Data Preview window looks perfect. This is certainly easier than the cumbersome process in step 2 for a fixed-width file. Note that Excel ignores the commas in the Customer field when there are quotation marks around the customer.

Although this code appears longer than the earlier code, it is actually simpler. In the `FieldInfo` parameter, the two element arrays consist of a sequence number, starting at 1 for the first field, and then an `xlColumnDataType` from Table 19.1. In this example, `Array(2, 1)` is saying "the second field is of general type." `Array(3, 3)` is saying "the third field is a date in MDY format." The code is longer because it explicitly specifies that each possible delimiter is set to `False`. Because `False` is the default for all delimiters, you really need only the one you will use. The following code is equivalent:

```
Workbooks.OpenText Filename:= "C:\sales.txt", _
    DataType:=xlDelimited, Comma:=True, _
    FieldInfo:=Array(Array(1, 1), Array(2, 1), Array(3, 3), _
    Array(4, 1), Array(5, 1), Array(6, 1), _
    Array(7, 1), Array(8, 1))
```

Finally, to make the code more readable, you can use the constant names rather than the code numbers:

```
Workbooks.OpenText Filename:="C:\sales.txt", _
    DataType:=xlDelimited, _Comma:=True, _
    FieldInfo:=Array(Array(1, xlGeneralFormat), _
    Array(2, xlGeneralFormat), _
    Array(3, xlMDYFormat), Array(4, xlGeneralFormat), _
    Array(5, xlGeneralFormat), Array(6, xlGeneralFormat), _
    Array(7, xlGeneralFormat), Array(8, xlGeneralFormat))
```

Excel has built-in options to read files in which fields are delimited by tabs, semicolons, commas, or spaces. Excel can actually handle anything as a delimiter. If someone sends pipe-delimited text, you set the `Other` parameter to `True` and specify an `OtherChar` parameter:

```
Workbooks.OpenText Filename:= "C:\sales.txt", Origin:=437, _
    DataType:=xlDelimited, Other:=True, OtherChar:= "|", FieldInfo:=...
```

19

Dealing with Text Files with More Than 1,048,576 Rows

If you use the Text Import Wizard to read a file that has more than 1,048,576 rows of data, you get this error: "File not loaded completely." The first 1,048,576 rows of the file load correctly.

If you use `Workbooks.OpenText` to open a file that has more than 1,048,576 rows of data, you are given no indication that the file did not load completely. Excel 2016 loads the first 1,048,576 rows and allows macro execution to continue. Your only indication that there is a problem is if someone notices that the reports are not reporting all the sales. If you think that your files will ever get this large, it would be good to check whether cell A1048576 is nonblank after an import. If it is, the odds are that the entire file was not loaded.

Reading Text Files One Row at a Time

You might run into a text file that has more than 1,048,576 rows. When this happens, you have to read the text file one row at a time. The code for doing this is the same code you might remember from your first high-school BASIC class.

You need to open the file for `INPUT` as `#1`. You use `#1` to indicate that this is the first file you are opening. If you had to open two files, you could open the second file as `#2`. You can then use the `Line Input #1` statement to read a line of the file into a variable. The following code opens sales.txt, reads 10 lines of the file into the first 10 cells of the worksheet, and closes the file:

```
Sub Import10()
    ThisFile = "C\sales.txt"
    Open ThisFile For Input As #1
    For i = 1 To 10
        Line Input #1, Data
        Cells(i, 1).Value = Data
    Next i
    Close #1
End Sub
```

Rather than read only 10 records, you want to read until you get to the end of the file. Excel automatically updates a variable called `EOF`. If you open a file for input as `#1`, checking `EOF(1)` tells you whether you have read the last record.

Use a `Do...While` loop to keep reading records until you have reached the end of the file:

```
Sub ImportAll()
    ThisFile = "C:\sales.txt"
    Open ThisFile For Input As #1
    Ctr = 0
    Do
        Line Input #1, Data
        Ctr = Ctr + 1
        Cells(Ctr, 1).Value = Data
    Loop While EOF(1) = False
    Close #1
End Sub
```

After reading records with code such as this, note in Figure 19.8 that the data is not parsed into columns. All the fields are in column A of the file.

Use the `TextToColumns` method to parse the records into columns. The parameters for `TextToColumns` are nearly identical to those for the `OpenText` method:

```
Cells(1, 1).Resize(Ctr, 1).TextToColumns Destination:=Range("A1"), _
DataType:=xlDelimited, Comma:=True, FieldInfo:=Array(Array(1, _
xlGeneralFormat), Array(2, xlMDYFormat), Array(3, xlGeneralFormat), _
Array(4, xlGeneralFormat), Array(5, xlGeneralFormat), Array(6, _
xlGeneralFormat), Array(7,xlGeneralFormat), Array(8, xlGeneralFormat), _
Array(9, xlGeneralFormat), Array(10,xlGeneralFormat), Array(11, _
xlGeneralFormat))
```

Figure 19.8
When you are reading a text file one row at a time, all the data fields end up in one long entry in column A.

Cell A1 contains data for eight columns

For the remainder of your Excel session, Excel remembers the delimiter settings. There is an annoying bug (feature?) in Excel. After Excel remembers that you are using a comma or a tab as a delimiter, any time that you attempt to paste data from the Clipboard to Excel, the data is parsed automatically by the delimiters specified in the `OpenText` method. Therefore, if you attempt to paste some text that includes the customer ABC, Inc., the text is parsed automatically into two columns, with text up to ABC in one column and Inc. in the next column.

Rather than hard-code that you are using the #1 designator to open the text file, it is safer to use the `FreeFile` function. This returns an integer representing the next file number available for use by the `Open` statement. The complete code to read a text file smaller than 1,048,576 rows is as follows:

```
Sub ImportAll()
    ThisFile = "C:\sales.txt"
    FileNumber = FreeFile
    Open ThisFile For Input As #FileNumber
    Ctr = 0
    Do
        Line Input #FileNumber, Data
        Ctr = Ctr + 1
        Cells(Ctr, 1).Value = Data
    Loop While EOF(FileNumber) = False
    Close #FileNumber
    Cells(1, 1).Resize(Ctr, 1).TextToColumns Destination:=Range("A1"), _
        DataType:=xlDelimited, Comma:=True, _
        FieldInfo:=Array(Array(1, xlGeneralFormat), _
        Array(2, xlMDYFormat), Array(3, xlGeneralFormat), _
```

19

```
          Array(4, xlGeneralFormat), Array(5, xlGeneralFormat), _
          Array(5, xlGeneralFormat), Array(6, xlGeneralFormat), _
          Array(7, xlGeneralFormat), Array(8, xlGeneralFormat), _
          Array(9, xlGeneralFormat), Array(10, xlGeneralFormat), _
          Array(10, xlGeneralFormat), Array(11, xlGeneralFormat))
End Sub
```

Reading Text Files with More Than 1,048,576 Rows

You can use the `Line Input` method to read a large text file. A good strategy is to read rows into cells A1:A1048575 and then begin reading additional rows into cell AA2. You can start in row 2 on the second set so that the headings can be copied from row 1 of the first data set. If the file is large enough that it fills up column AA, move to BA2, CA2, and so on.

Also, you should stop writing columns when you get to row 1048574 and leave two blank rows at the bottom. This ensures that the code `Cells(Rows.Count, 1).End(xlup).Row` finds the final row. The following code reads a large text file into several sets of columns:

```
Sub ReadLargeFile()
    ThisFile = "C:\sales.txt"
    FileNumber = FreeFile
    Open ThisFile For Input As #FileNumber

    NextRow = 1
    NextCol = 1
    Do While Not EOF(1)
        Line Input #FileNumber, Data
        Cells(NextRow, NextCol).Value = Data
        NextRow = NextRow + 1
        If NextRow = (Rows.Count -2)  Then
            ' Parse these records
            Range(Cells(1, NextCol), Cells(Rows.Count, NextCol)) _
                TextToColumns _
                Destination:=Cells(1, NextCol), DataType:=xlDelimited, _
                Comma:=True, FieldInfo:=Array(Array(1, xlGeneralFormat), _
                Array(2, xlMDYFormat), Array(3, xlGeneralFormat), _
                Array(4, xlGeneralFormat), Array(5, xlGeneralFormat), _
                Array(6, xlGeneralFormat), Array(7, xlGeneralFormat), _
                Array(8, xlGeneralFormat), Array(9, xlGeneralFormat), _
                Array(10, xlGeneralFormat), Array(11, xlGeneralFormat))
            ' Copy the headings from section 1
            If NextCol > 1 Then
                Range("A1:K1").Copy Destination:=Cells(1, NextCol)
            End If
            ' Set up the next section
            NextCol = NextCol + 26
            NextRow = 2
        End If
    Loop
    Close #FileNumber
    ' Parse the final Section of records
    FinalRow = NextRow - 1
    If FinalRow = 1 Then
        ' Handle if the file coincidentally had 1048574 rows exactly
        NextCol = NextCol - 26
    Else
```

```
        Range(Cells(2, NextCol), Cells(FinalRow, NextCol)).TextToColumns _
                Destination:=Cells(1, NextCol), DataType:=xlDelimited, _
                Comma:=True, FieldInfo:=Array(Array(1, xlGeneralFormat), _
                Array(2, xlMDYFormat), Array(3, xlGeneralFormat), _
                Array(4, xlGeneralFormat), Array(5, xlGeneralFormat), _
                Array(6, xlGeneralFormat), Array(7, xlGeneralFormat), _
                Array(8, xlGeneralFormat), Array(9, xlGeneralFormat), _
                Array(10, xlGeneralFormat), Array(11, xlGeneralFormat))
        If NextCol > 1 Then
            Range("A1:K1").Copy Destination:=Cells(1, NextCol)
        End If
    End If

    DataSets = (NextCol - 1) / 26 + 1

End Sub
```

Usually you should write the DataSets variable to a named cell somewhere in the workbook so that later you know how many data sets you have in the worksheet.

As you can imagine, using this method, it is possible to read 660,601,620 rows of data into a single worksheet. The code you formerly used to filter and report the data now becomes more complex. You might find yourself creating pivot tables from each set of columns to create a data set summary and then summarizing all the summary tables with a final pivot table. At some point, you need to consider whether the application really belongs in Access. You can also consider whether the data should be stored in Access with an Excel front end, which is discussed in Chapter 21, "Using Access as a Back End to Enhance Multiuser Access to Data."

Using Power Query to Load Large Files to the Data Model

If your goal is to create a pivot table from the text file, you can bypass the worksheet grid and load millions of rows directly into the Data Model. Now that Power Query is built in to Excel 2016, the macro recorder will record the process of importing data to the Data Model with Power Query. Use the following steps:

1. On the Data tab, in the Power Query group, select New Query, From File, From Text File.

2. Browse to the text file.

3. In the Power Query Home tab, open the Close and Load drop-down and choose Close and Load To.

4. In the Load To dialog, choose Only Create Connection and Add This Data to the Data Model, as shown in Figure 19.9. Click OK. The data is loaded to the Power Pivot engine.

If you use the macro recorder during this process, your recorded code includes the M language statements required to define the query:

```
Sub ImportToDataModel()
'
' ImportToDataModel Macro
```

19

```
ActiveWorkbook.Queries.Add Name:="demo", Formula:= _
    "let" & Chr(13) & "" & Chr(10) & _
    "    Source = Csv.Document(File.Contents(""C:\demo.txt""), " & _
    "[Delimiter="","",Encoding=1252]]," & Chr(13) & "" & Chr(10) & _
    "    #""First Row as Header"" = Table.PromoteHeaders(Source)," & _
    Chr(13) & "" & Chr(10) & _
    "    #""Changed Type"" = Table.TransformColumnTypes(" & _
    "#""First Row as Header""," & _
    "{{""StoreID"", Int64.Type}, {""Date"", type date}," & _
    "{""Division"", type text}, {""Units"", Int64.Type}," & _
    "{""Revenue"", Int64.Type}})" & Chr(13) & "" & Chr(10) & "i" & _
    """Changed Type"""
Workbooks("Book4").Connections.Add2 "Power Query - demo", _
    "Connection to the 'demo' query in the workbook.", _
    "OLEDB;Provider=Microsoft.Mashup.OleDb.1;" & _
    "Data Source=$Workbook$;Location=demo", _
    """demo""", 6, True, False
End Sub
```

You can now use Insert, Pivot Table and specify This Workbook Data Model as the source for the pivot table.

Writing Text Files

The code for writing text files is similar to the code for reading text files. You need to open a specific file for output as #1. Then, as you loop through various records, you write them to the file by using the Print #1 statement.

Before you open a file for output, make sure that any prior examples of the file have been deleted. You can use the Kill statement to delete a file. Kill returns an error if the file was not there in the first place. In this case, you use On Error Resume Next to prevent an error.

The following code writes out a text file for use by another application:

```
Sub WriteFile()
    ThisFile = "C:\Results.txt"

    ' Delete yesterday's copy of the file
    On Error Resume Next
    Kill ThisFile
    On Error GoTo 0

    ' Open the file
    Open ThisFile For Output As #1
    FinalRow = Cells(Rows.Count, 1).End(xlUp).Row
    ' Write out the file
    For j = 1 To FinalRow
        Print #1, Cells(j, 1).Value
    Next j
End Sub
```

This is a somewhat trivial example. You can use this method to write out any type of text-based file. The code at the end of Chapter 18, "Reading from and Writing to the Web," uses the same concept to write out HTML files.

Next Steps

The next chapter steps outside the world of Excel and talks about how to transfer Excel data into Microsoft Word documents. Chapter 20, "Automating Word," looks at using Excel VBA to automate and control Microsoft Word.

19

Automating Word

20

Word, Excel, PowerPoint, Outlook, and Access all use the same VBA language. The only difference is their object models. For example, Excel has a Workbooks object, and Word has Documents. Any one of these applications can access the object model of another of the applications, as long as the second application is installed.

To access Word's object library, Excel must establish a link to it by using either early binding or late binding. With *early binding*, the reference to the application object is created when the program is compiled. With *late binding*, the reference is created when the program is run.

This chapter provides an introduction to accessing Word from Excel.

> **NOTE**
> This chapter does not review Word's entire object model or the object models of other applications. Refer to the VBA Object Browser in the appropriate application to learn about other object models.

Using Early Binding to Reference a Word Object

Code written with early binding executes faster than code with late binding. A reference is made to Word's object library before the code is written so that Word's objects, properties, and methods are available in the Object Browser. Tips such as a list of members of an object also appear, as shown in Figure 20.1.

The disadvantage of early binding is that the referenced object library must exist on the system. For example, if you write a macro referencing Word 2016's object library and someone with Word 2010 attempts to run the code, the program fails because it cannot find the Word 2016 object library.

Figure 20.1
Early binding allows access to a Word object's syntax.

```
Sub WordEarlyBinding()
Dim wdApp As Word.Application
Dim wdDoc As Document

Set wdApp = New Word.Application
Set wdDoc = wdApp.Do
        Documents
        DontResetInsertionPointProperties
        EmailOptions
        EmailTemplate
        EnableCancelKey
        FeatureInstall
        FileConverters
```

You add the object library through the VB Editor, as described here:

1. Select Tools, References.
2. Check Microsoft Word 16.0 Object Library in the Available References list (see Figure 20.2). If the object library is not found, Word is not installed. If another version is found in the list, such as 12.0, another version of Word is installed, and you should check that.
3. Click OK.

20

Figure 20.2
Select the object library from the Available References list.

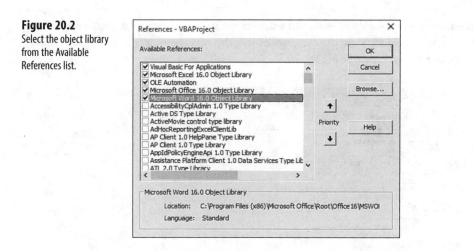

After the reference is set, Word variables can be declared with the correct Word variable type, such as `Document`. However, if the object variable is declared `As Object`, this forces the program to use late binding. The following example creates a new instance of Word and opens an existing Word document from Excel:

```
Sub WordEarlyBinding()
Dim wdApp As Word.Application
Dim wdDoc As Document
Set wdApp = New Word.Application
wdApp.Visible = True 'make Word visible
Set wdDoc = wdApp.Documents.Open(ThisWorkbook.Path & _
    "\Automating Word.docx")
Set wdApp = Nothing
Set wdDoc = Nothing
End Sub
```

The declared variables, `wdApp` and `wdDoc`, are Word object types. `wdApp` is used to create a reference to the Word application in the same way the `Application` object is used in Excel. `New Word.Application` is used to create a new instance of Word. If you are opening a document in a new instance of Word, Word is not visible. If the application needs to be shown, it must be unhidden (`wdApp.Visible = True`). When the program is done, release the connection to Word by setting the object, `wdApp`, to `Nothing`.

> **TIP**
> Excel searches through the selected libraries to find the reference for the object type. If the type is found in more than one library, the first reference is selected. You can influence which library is chosen by changing the priority of the reference in the list of selected libraries.

When the process is finished, it's a good idea to set the object variables to `Nothing` and release the memory being used by the application, as shown here:

```
Set wdApp = Nothing
Set wdDoc = Nothing
```

20

If the referenced version of Word does not exist on the system, an error message appears when the code is compiled. View the References list; the missing object is highlighted with the word *MISSING*, as shown in Figure 20.3.

Figure 20.3
Excel won't find the expected Word 2016 object library if the workbook is opened in Excel 2010.

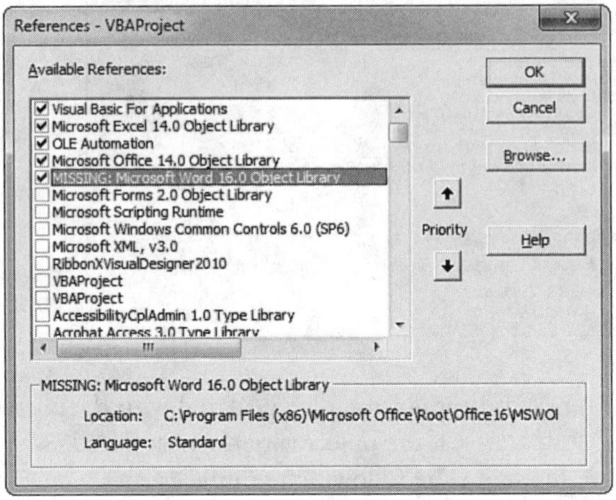

If a previous version of Word is available, you can try running the program with that version referenced. Many objects are the same between versions.

Using Late Binding to Reference a Word Object

When using late binding, you create an object that refers to the Word application before linking to the Word library. Because you do not set up a reference beforehand, the only constraint on the Word version is that the objects, properties, and methods must exist. In the case where there are differences between versions of Word, the version can be verified and the correct object used accordingly.

The disadvantage of late binding is that because Excel does not know what is going on, it does not understand that you are referring to Word. This prevents the tips from appearing when referencing Word objects. In addition, built-in constants are not available. This means that when Excel is compiling, it cannot verify that the references to Word are correct. After the program is executed, the links to Word begin to build, and any coding errors are detected at that point.

The following example creates a new instance of Word and then opens and makes visible an existing Word document:

```
Sub WordLateBinding()
Dim wdApp As Object, wdDoc As Object
Set wdApp = CreateObject("Word.Application")
Set wdDoc = wdApp.Documents.Open(ThisWorkbook.Path & _
    "\Automating Word.docx")
wdApp.Visible = True
```

```
    Set wdApp = Nothing
    Set wdDoc = Nothing
    End Sub
```

An object variable (`wdApp`) is declared and set to reference the application (`CreateObject("Word.Application")`). Other required variables are then declared (`wdDoc`), and the application object is used to refer these variables to Word's object model. Declaring `wdApp` and `wdDoc` as objects forces the use of late binding. The program cannot create the required links to the Word object model until it executes the `CreateObject` function.

Using the `New` Keyword to Reference a Word Application

In the early-binding example, the keyword `New` was used to reference the Word application. The `New` keyword can be used only with early binding; it does not work with late binding. `CreateObject` or `GetObject` would also work, but `New` is best for this example. If an instance of the application is running and you want to use it, use the `GetObject` function instead.

CAUTION

If your code to open Word runs smoothly but you don't see an instance of Word (and should because you code it to be `Visible`), open your Task Manager and look for the process WinWord.exe. If it exists, from the Immediate window in Excel's VB Editor, type the following (which uses early binding):

```
Word.Application.Visible = True
```

If multiple instances of WinWord.exe are found, you need to make each instance visible and close the extra instance(s) of WinWord.exe.

Using the `CreateObject` Function to Create a New Instance of an Object

The earlier late-binding example uses the `CreateObject` function. However, you can also use this function in early binding. You use it to create a new instance of an object, in this case the Word application. `CreateObject` has a `class` parameter, which consists of the name and type of the object to be created (`Name.Type`). For example, the examples in this chapter have used (`Word.Application`), in which `Word` is the `Name` and `Application` is the `Type`.

20

Using the `GetObject` Function to Reference an Existing Instance of Word

You can use the `GetObject` function to reference an instance of Word that is already running. An error is generated if no instance of the application can be found. You can use the existence of the error to include code that creates an instance of the application.

`GetObject`'s two parameters are optional. The first parameter specifies the full path and filename to open, and the second parameter specifies the application program. The following example leaves off the application and allows the default program, which is Word, to open the document:

```
Sub UseGetObject()
Dim wdDoc As Object
Set wdDoc = GetObject(ThisWorkbook.Path & "\Automating Word.docx")
wdDoc.Application.Visible = True
'more code interacting with the Word document
Set wdDoc = Nothing
End Sub
```

This example opens a document in an existing instance of Word, if there is one; otherwise, it creates one. It ensures that the Word application's `Visible` property is set to `True`. Note that to make the document visible, you have to refer to the application object (`wdDoc.Application.Visible`) because `wdDoc` is referencing a document rather than the application.

> **NOTE** Although the Word application's `Visible` property is set to `True`, this code does not make the Word application the active application. In most cases, the Word application icon stays in the taskbar, and Excel remains the active application on the user's screen.

The following example uses errors to learn whether Word is already open before pasting the selected chart at the end of a document. If Word is not open, it opens Word and creates a new document:

```
Sub IsWordOpen()
Dim wdApp As Word.Application 'early binding

ActiveChart.ChartArea.Copy

On Error Resume Next 'returns Nothing if Word isn't open
Set wdApp = GetObject(, "Word.Application")
If wdApp Is Nothing Then
    'since Word isn't open, open it
    Set wdApp = GetObject("", "Word.Application")
    With wdApp
        .Documents.Add
        .Visible = True
    End With
End If
On Error GoTo 0
```

20

```
With wdApp.Selection
    .EndKey Unit:=wdStory
    .TypeParagraph
    .PasteSpecial Link:=False, DataType:=wdPasteOLEObject, _
        Placement:=wdInLine, DisplayAsIcon:=False
End With

Set wdApp = Nothing
End Sub
```

Using On Error Resume Next forces the program to continue even if it runs into an error. In this case, an error occurs when you attempt to link wdApp to an object that does not exist. wdApp will have no value. The next line, If wdApp Is Nothing Then, takes advantage of this and opens an instance of Word, adds an empty document, and makes the application visible. Use On Error Goto 0 to return to normal VBA error-handling behavior.

> **TIP**
> Note the use of empty quotes for the first parameter in GetObject("", "Word. Application"). This is how you use the GetObject function to open a new instance of Word.

Using Constant Values

The preceding example used constants, such as wdPasteOLEObject and wdInLine, that are specific to Word. When you are programming using early binding, Excel helps by showing these constants in the ScreenTip.

With late binding, these tips do not appear. So what can you do? You might write your program using early binding and then change it to late binding after you compile and test the program. The problem with this method is that the program will not compile because Excel does not recognize the Word constants.

The words wdPasteOLEObject and wdInLine are just terms for your convenience as a programmer. Behind each of these text constants is the real value that VBA understands. The solution to this is to retrieve and use these real values with your late-binding program.

Using the Watches Window to Retrieve the Real Value of a Constant

One way to retrieve the value of a constant is to add a watch for constants. Then you step through your code and check the value of the constant as it appears in the Watches window, as shown in Figure 20.4.

20

Figure 20.4
Use the Watches window to get the real value behind a Word constant.

Watches	
Expression	Value
6ó wdStory	6

NOTE

See "Querying by Using a Watches Window" in Chapter 2, "This Sounds Like BASIC, so Why Doesn't It Look Familiar?" for more information on using the Watches window.

Using the Object Browser to Retrieve the Real Value of a Constant

Another way to retrieve the value of a constant is to look up the constant in the Object Browser. However, you need the Word library set up as a reference in order to use this method. Once it is set up, right-click the constant and select Definition. The Object Browser opens to the constant and shows the value in the bottom window, as shown in Figure 20.5.

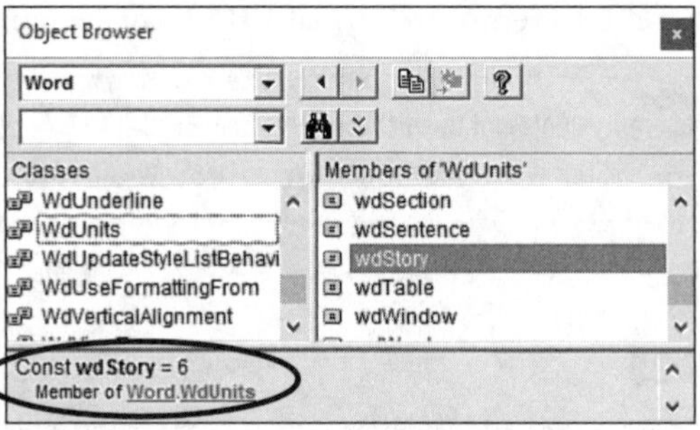

Figure 20.5
Use the Object Browser to get the real value of a Word constant.

TIP

You can set up the Word reference library to be accessed from the Object Browser. However, you do not have to set up your code with early binding. When you do this, the reference is at your fingertips, but your code is still late binding. Turning off the reference library is just a few clicks away.

Replacing the constants in the earlier code example with their real values would look like this:

```
With wdApp.Selection
    .EndKey Unit:=6
    .TypeParagraph
    .PasteSpecial Link:=False, DataType:=0, Placement:=0, _
        DisplayAsIcon:=False
End With
```

However, what happens a month from now, when you return to the code and you try to remember what those numbers mean? The solution is up to you. Some programmers add comments to the code, referencing the Word constant. Other programmers create their own variables to hold the real value and use those variables in place of the constants, like this:

```
Const xwdStory As Long = 6
Const xwdPasteOLEObject As Long = 0
Const xwdInLine As Long = 0

With wdApp.Selection
    .EndKey Unit:=xwdStory
```

```
        .TypeParagraph
        .PasteSpecial Link:=False, DataType:=xwdPasteOLEObject, _
            Placement:=xwdInLine, DisplayAsIcon:=False
    End With
```

Understanding Word's Objects

You can use Word's macro recorder to get a preliminary understanding of the Word object model. However, much as with Excel's macro recorder, the results will be long-winded. Keep this in mind and use the recorder to lead you toward the objects, properties, and methods in Word.

> **CAUTION**
>
> The macro recorder is limited in what it allows you to record. While the mouse can be used to move the cursor or select objects, it doesn't record those movements. But there are no limits on what it records from keyboard movements..

This is what the Word macro recorder produces when you add a new, blank document by selecting File, New, Blank Document:

```
    Documents.Add Template:="Normal", NewTemplate:=False, DocumentType:=0
```

You can make this more efficient in Word by using this:

```
    Documents.Add
```

`Template`, `NewTemplate`, and `DocumentType` are all optional properties that the recorder includes but that are not required unless you need to change a default property or ensure that a property is what you require.

To use the same line of code in Excel, a link to the Word object library is required, as you learned earlier. After that link is established, an understanding of Word's objects is all you need. The next section provides a review of *some* of Word's objects—enough to get you off the ground. For a more detailed listing, refer to the object model in Word's VB Editor.

The Document Object

Word's `Document` object is equivalent to Excel's `Workbook` object. It consists of characters, words, sentences, paragraphs, sections, and headers/footers. It is through the `Document` object that methods and properties affecting the entire document—such as printing, closing, searching, and reviewing—are accomplished.

Creating a New Blank Document

To create a blank document in an existing instance of Word, use the `Add` method, as shown here:

```
    Sub NewDocument()
    Dim wdApp As Word.Application
```

```
Set wdApp = GetObject(, "Word.Application")

wdApp.Documents.Add
'any other Word code you need here

Set wdApp = Nothing
End Sub
```

This example opens a new, blank document that uses the default template.

> **NOTE** You already learned how to create a new document when Word is closed: Refer to `GetObject` and `CreateObject`.

To create a new document that uses a specific template, use this:

```
wdApp.Documents.Add Template:="Memo (Contemporary design).dotx"
```

This creates a new document that uses the Memo (Contemporary design) template. `Template` can be either the name of a template from the default template location or the file path and name.

Opening an Existing Document

To open an existing document, use the `Open` method. Several parameters are available, including `Read Only` and `AddtoRecentFiles`. The following example opens an existing document as `Read Only` and prevents the file from being added to the Recent File List under the File menu:

```
wdApp.Documents.Open _
    Filename:="C:\Excel VBA 2016 by Jelen & Syrstad\" & _
    "Chapter 8 - Arrays.docx", ReadOnly:=True, AddtoRecentFiles:=False
```

Saving Changes to a Document

After you have made changes to a document, most likely you will want to save it. To save a document with its existing name, use this:

```
wdApp.Documents.Save
```

If you use the `Save` command with a new document without a name, nothing happens. To save a document with a new name, you must use the `SaveAs2` method instead:

```
wdApp.ActiveDocument.SaveAs2 _
    "C:\Excel VBA 2016 by Jelen & Syrstad\MemoTest.docx"
```

`SaveAs2` requires the use of members of the `Document` object, such as `ActiveDocument`.

> **NOTE** `SaveAs` still works, but it isn't an IntelliSense option. `SaveAs2` offers a compatibility mode argument. If you don't need it, you can still use `SaveAs`.

Closing an Open Document

Use the `Close` method to close a specified document or all open documents. By default, a Save dialog appears for any documents that have unsaved changes. You can use the `SaveChanges` argument to change this. To close all open documents without saving changes, use this code:

```
wdApp.Documents.Close SaveChanges:=wdDoNotSaveChanges
```

To close a specific document, you can close the active document, like this:

```
wdApp.ActiveDocument.Close
```

or you can specify a document name, like this:

```
wdApp.Documents("Chapter 8 - Arrays.docx").Close
```

Printing a Document

Use the `PrintOut` method to print part or all of a document. To print a document with all the default print settings, use this:

```
wdApp.ActiveDocument.PrintOut
```

By default, the print range is the entire document, but you can change this by setting the `Range` and `Pages` arguments of the `PrintOut` method. For example, to print only page 2 of the active document, use this:

```
wdApp.ActiveDocument.PrintOut Range:=wdPrintRangeOfPages, Pages:="2"
```

The `Selection` Object

The `Selection` object represents what is selected in the document, such as a word, a sentence, or the insertion point. It also has a `Type` property that returns the type that is selected, such as `wdSelectionIP`, `wdSelectionColumn`, or `wdSelectionShape`.

Navigating with `HomeKey` and `EndKey`

The `HomeKey` and `EndKey` methods are used to change the selection; they correspond to using the Home and End keys, respectively, on the keyboard. They have two parameters: `Unit` and `Extend`. `Unit` is the range of movement to make, to either the beginning (`Home`) or end (`End`) of a line (`wdLine`), document (`wdStory`), column (`wdColumn`), or row (`wdRow`). `Extend` is the type of movement: `wdMove` moves the selection, and `wdExtend` extends the selection from the original insertion point to the new insertion point.

To move the cursor to the beginning of the document, use this code:

```
wdApp.Selection.HomeKey Unit:=wdStory, Extend:=wdMove
```

To select the document from the insertion point to the end of the document, use this code:

```
wdApp.Selection.EndKey Unit:=wdStory, Extend:=wdExtend
```

Inserting Text with `TypeText`

The `TypeText` method is used to insert text into a Word document. User settings, such as the `ReplaceSelection` setting, can affect what happens when text is typed into the

20

document when text is selected. The following example first makes sure that the setting for overwriting selected text is turned on. Then it selects the second paragraph (using the Range object, described in the next section) and overwrites it:

```
Sub InsertText()
Dim wdApp As Word.Application
Dim wdDoc As Document
Dim wdSln As Selection

Set wdApp = GetObject(, "Word.Application")
Set wdDoc = wdApp.ActiveDocument

wdDoc.Application.Options.ReplaceSelection = True
wdDoc.Paragraphs(2).Range.Select
wdApp.Selection.TypeText "Overwriting the selected paragraph."

Set wdApp = Nothing
Set wdDoc = Nothing
End Sub
```

The Range Object

The Range object uses the following syntax:

```
Range(StartPosition, EndPosition)
```

The Range object represents a contiguous area or areas in a document. It has a starting character position and an ending character position. The object can be the insertion point, a range of text, or the entire document, including nonprinting characters such as spaces or paragraph marks.

The Range object is similar to the Selection object, but in some ways it is better. For example, the Range object requires less code to accomplish the same tasks, and it has more capabilities. In addition, it saves time and memory because the Range object does not require Word to move the cursor or highlight objects in the document to manipulate them.

Defining a Range

To define a range, enter a starting position and an ending position, as shown in this code segment:

```
Sub RangeText()
Dim wdApp As Word.Application
Dim wdDoc As Document
Dim wdRng As Word.Range

Set wdApp = GetObject(, "Word.Application")
Set wdDoc = wdApp.ActiveDocument

Set wdRng = wdDoc.Range(0, 50)
wdRng.Select

Set wdApp = Nothing
Set wdDoc = Nothing
Set wdRng = Nothing
End Sub
```

Figure 20.6 shows the results of running this code. The first 50 characters are selected, including nonprinting characters such as paragraph returns.

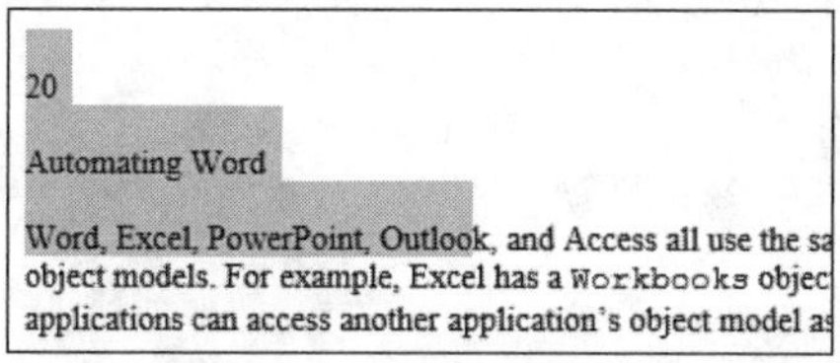

Figure 20.6
The `Range` object selects everything in its path.

> **NOTE**
> In Figure 20.6 the range was selected (`wdRng.Select`) for easier viewing. It is not required that the range be selected in order to be manipulated. For example, to delete the range, do this:
>
> ```
> wdRng.Delete
> ```

The first character position in a document is always zero, and the last is equivalent to the number of characters in the document.

The `Range` object also selects paragraphs. The following example copies the third paragraph in the active document and pastes it into Excel. Depending on how the paste is done, the text can be pasted into a text box (see Figure 20.7) or into a cell:

```
Sub SelectSentence()
Dim wdApp As Word.Application
Dim wdRng As Word.Range

Set wdApp = GetObject(, "Word.Application")

With wdApp.ActiveDocument
    If .Paragraphs.Count >= 3 Then
        Set wdRng = .Paragraphs(3).Range
        wdRng.Copy
    End If
End With

'This line pastes the copied text into a text box
'because that is the default PasteSpecial method for Word text
Worksheets("Sheet2").PasteSpecial

'This line pastes the copied text in cell A1
Worksheets("Sheet2").Paste Destination:=Worksheets("Sheet2").Range("A1")

Set wdApp = Nothing
Set wdRng = Nothing
End Sub
```


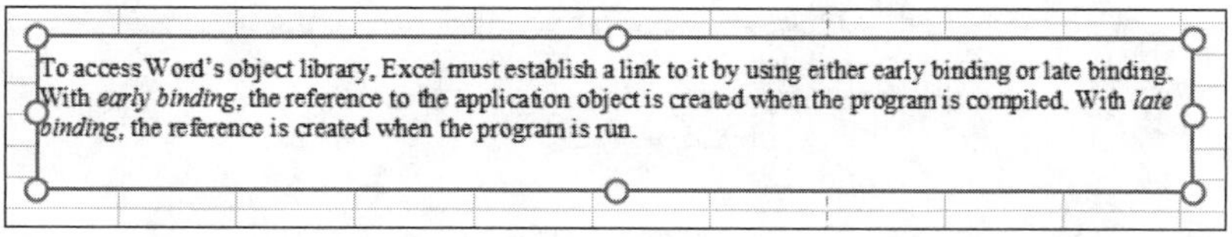

Figure 20.7
Paste Word text into an Excel text box.

Formatting a Range

After a range is selected, formatting can be applied to it (see Figure 20.8). The following program loops through all the paragraphs of the active document and applies bold to the first word of each paragraph:

```
Sub ChangeFormat()
Dim wdApp As Word.Application
Dim wdRng As Word.Range
Dim count As Integer

Set wdApp = GetObject(, "Word.Application")

With wdApp.ActiveDocument
    For count = 1 To .Paragraphs.Count
        Set wdRng = .Paragraphs(count).Range
        With wdRng
            .Words(1).Font.Bold = True
            .Collapse 'unselects the text
        End With
    Next count
End With

Set wdApp = Nothing
Set wdRng = Nothing
End Sub
```

Figure 20.8
Format the first word of each paragraph in a document.

This chapter is an introduction to accessing Word from Excel.

Word, Excel, PowerPoint, Outlook, and Access all use the same VBA object models. For example, Excel has a Workbooks object and Wor applications can access another application's object model as long as t

To access Word's object library, Excel must establish a link to it by us With *early binding*, the reference to the application object is created w *binding*, the reference is created when the program is run.

A quick way to change the formatting of entire paragraphs is to change the style (see Figures 20.9 and 20.10). The following program finds a paragraph with the Normal style and changes it to H3:

```
Sub ChangeStyle()
Dim wdApp As Word.Application
Dim wdRng As Word.Range
Dim count As Integer

Set wdApp = GetObject(, "Word.Application")

With wdApp.ActiveDocument
    For count = 1 To .Paragraphs.Count
        Set wdRng = .Paragraphs(count).Range
        With wdRng
            If .Style = "Normal" Then
                .Style = "H3"
            End If
        End With
```

```
        Next count
    End With

    Set wdApp = Nothing
    Set wdRng = Nothing
    End Sub
```

Figure 20.9
Before: A paragraph with the Normal style needs to be changed to the H3 style.

Word, Excel, PowerPoint, Outlook, and Access all use the same VBA language. The only difference is their object models. For example, Excel has a Workbooks object and Word has Documents. Any one of these applications can access another application's object model as long as the second application is installed.

a. NL1_FIRST	¶
Normal	¶
PD	¶ª
SF DPGM ONLY	¶

Figure 20.10
After: Apply styles with code to change paragraph formatting quickly.

Word, Excel, PowerPoint, Outlook, and Access all use the same VBA language. The only difference is their object models. For example, Excel has a Workbooks object and Word has Documents. Any one of these applications can access another application's object model as long as the second application is installed.

H2	¶
H3	¶
HEADFIRST	¶
1. NL_FIRST	¶

Bookmarks

Bookmarks are members of the Document, Selection, and Range objects. They can help make it easier to navigate around Word. Instead of having to choose words, sentences, or paragraphs, use bookmarks to manipulate sections of a document swiftly.

> **NOTE** You are not limited to using only existing bookmarks. Instead, you can create bookmarks using code.

Bookmarks appear as gray I-bars in Word documents. In Word, go to File, Options, Advanced, Show Document Content and select Show Bookmarks to turn on bookmarks.

After you have set up bookmarks in a document, you can use the bookmarks to move quickly to a range to insert text or other items, such as charts. The following code automatically inserts text and a chart after bookmarks that were previously set up in the document. Figure 20.11 shows the results.

```
Sub FillInMemo()
Dim myArray()
Dim wdBkmk As String

Dim wdApp As Word.Application
Dim wdRng As Word.Range

myArray = Array("To", "CC", "From", "Subject", "Chart")
Set wdApp = GetObject(, "Word.Application")
```

20

```
'insert text
Set wdRng = wdApp.ActiveDocument.Bookmarks(myArray(0)).Range
wdRng.InsertBefore ("Bill Jelen")
Set wdRng = wdApp.ActiveDocument.Bookmarks(myArray(1)).Range
wdRng.InsertBefore ("Tracy Syrstad")
Set wdRng = wdApp.ActiveDocument.Bookmarks(myArray(2)).Range
wdRng.InsertBefore ("MrExcel")
Set wdRng = wdApp.ActiveDocument.Bookmarks(myArray(3)).Range
wdRng.InsertBefore ("Fruit & Vegetable Sales")

'insert chart
Set wdRng = wdApp.ActiveDocument.Bookmarks(myArray(4)).Range
Worksheets("Fruit Sales").ChartObjects("Chart 1").Copy
wdRng.PasteAndFormat Type:=wdPasteOLEObject

wdApp.Activate
Set wdApp = Nothing
Set wdRng = Nothing

End Sub
```

Figure 20.11
Use bookmarks to enter text or charts into a Word document.

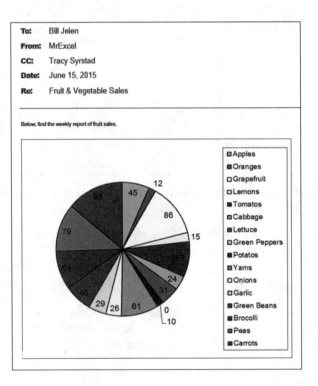

Controlling Form Fields in Word

You have seen how to modify a document by inserting charts and text, modifying formatting, and deleting text. However, a document might contain other items, such as controls, that you can modify.

For the following example, a template named `New Client.dotx` was created, consisting of text and bookmarks. The bookmarks are placed after the Name and Date fields. Form field check boxes were also added. The controls are found under Legacy Forms in the Controls section of the Developer tab in Word, as shown in Figure 20.12. Notice in the code sample that follows that the check boxes have all been renamed so they make more sense. For example, one bookmark was renamed `chk401k` from `Checkbox5`. To rename a bookmark, right-click the check box, select Properties, and type a new name in the Bookmark field.

Figure 20.12
You can use the form fields found under the Legacy Tools to add check boxes to a document.

The questionnaire was set up in Excel, and it allows the user to enter free text in B1 and B2 but select from data validation in B3 and B5:B8, as shown in Figure 20.13.

Figure 20.13
Create an Excel sheet to collect your data.

Name	Mary Beth Jacobson
Date	6/15/2015
Are you a new customer?	Yes
Are you interested in the following options:	
401K	Yes
Roth	No
Stocks	Yes
Bonds	Yes
	Yes
	No

The following code goes into a standard module, and the name and date go straight into the document:

```
Sub FillOutWordForm()
Dim TemplatePath As String
Dim wdApp As Object
Dim wdDoc As Object

'Open the template in a new instance of Word
TemplatePath = ThisWorkbook.Path & "\New Client.dotx"
Set wdApp = CreateObject("Word.Application")
Set wdDoc = wdApp.documents.Add(Template:=TemplatePath)

'Place our text values in document
With wdApp.ActiveDocument
    .Bookmarks("Name").Range.InsertBefore Range("B1").Text
    .Bookmarks("Date").Range.InsertBefore Range("B2").Text
End With
```

20

```
'Using basic logic, select the correct form object
If Range("B3").Value = "Yes" Then
    wdDoc.formfields("chkCustYes").CheckBox.Value = True
Else
    wdDoc.formfields("chkCustNo").CheckBox.Value = True
End If

With wdDoc
    If Range("B5").Value = "Yes" Then .Formfields("chk401k"). _
        CheckBox.Value = True
    If Range("B6").Value = "Yes" Then .Formfields("chkRoth"). _
        CheckBox.Value = True
    If Range("B7").Value = "Yes" Then .Formfields("chkStocks"). _
        CheckBox.Value = True
    If Range("B8").Value = "Yes" Then .Formfields("chkBonds"). _
        CheckBox.Value = True
End With

wdApp.Visible = True

ExitSub:

    Set wdDoc = Nothing
    Set wdApp = Nothing

End Sub
```

The check boxes use logic to verify whether the user selected Yes or No to confirm if the corresponding check box should be checked. Figure 20.14 shows a sample document that has been completed.

Figure 20.14
Excel can control Word's form fields and help automate filling out documents.

| Name: Mary Beth Jacobson |
| Date: 6/15/2015 |
| New Customer: ☒Yes ☐No |
| Interested in the following: |

| ☒ 401k | ☐ Roth | ☒ Stocks | ☒ Bonds |

Next Steps

Chapter 19, "Text File Processing," showed you how to read from a text file to import data from another system. In this chapter, you learned how to connect to another Office program and access its object module. In Chapter 21, "Using Access as a Back End to Enhance Multiuser Access to Data," you'll connect to an Access database and learn about writing to Access multidimensional database (MDB) files. Compared to text files, Access files are faster; in addition Access file are indexable and allow multiuser access to data.

Using Access as a Back End to Enhance Multiuser Access to Data

21

The example near the end of Chapter 19, "Text File Processing," propose a method for storing 660,601,620 records in an Excel worksheet. At some point, you need to admit that even though Excel is the greatest product in the world, there is a time to move to Access and take advantage of Access multi-dimensional database (MDB) files.

Even before you have more than 1 million rows, another compelling reason to use MDB data files is to allow multiuser access to data without the headaches associated with shared workbooks.

Microsoft Excel offers an option to share a workbook, but you automatically lose a number of important Excel features when you do this type of sharing. After you share a workbook, you cannot use automatic subtotals, pivot tables, Group and Outline mode, scenarios, protection, or the Styles, Pictures, Add Charts, and Insert Worksheets options.

By using an Excel VBA front end and storing data in an MDB database, you have the best of both worlds. You have the power and flexibility of Excel and the multiuser access capability available in Access.

> **TIP**
>
> MDB is the official file format of both Microsoft Access and Microsoft Visual Basic. This means you can deploy an Excel solution that reads and writes from an MDB to customers who do not have Microsoft Access. Of course, it helps if you as the developer have a copy of Access because you can use the Access front end to set up tables and queries.

> **TIP**
>
> The examples in this chapter make use of the Microsoft Jet Database Engine for reading from and writing to an Access database. The Jet engine works with Access data stored in Access 97 through 2013. If you are sure that all the people running the macro will have Office 2007 or newer, you could instead use the ACE engine. Microsoft now offers a 64-bit version of the ACE engine but not the Jet engine.

ADO Versus DAOs

For several years, Microsoft recommended using data access objects (DAOs) for accessing data in an external database. DAOs became very popular, and a great deal of code was written for them. When Microsoft released Excel 2000, it started pushing ActiveX Data Objects (ADO). The concepts are similar, and the syntax differs only slightly. I use ADO in this chapter. Realize that if you start going through code written a decade ago, you might run into DAO code. Other than a few syntax changes, the code for both ADO and DAO looks similar.

If you discover that you have to debug some old code that includes DAOs, check out the Microsoft Knowledge Base articles that discuss the differences between ADO and DAOs. You can find them at http://support.microsoft.com/kb/225048.

The following two articles provide a Rosetta Stone between DAO and ADO. The DAO code is shown at http://support.microsoft.com/kb/q146607. The equivalent ADO code is shown at http://support.microsoft.com/kb/q142938.

To use any code in this chapter, open the VB Editor. Select Tools, References from the main menu and then select Microsoft ActiveX Data Objects Library from the Available References list, as shown in Figure 21.1.

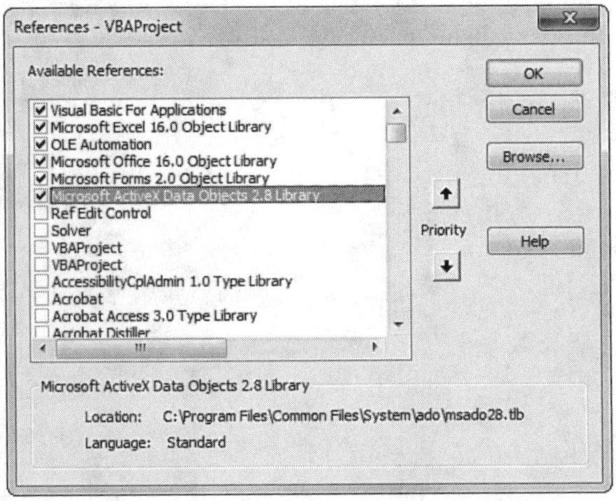

Figure 21.1
To read or write from an Access MDB file, add the reference for Microsoft ActiveX Data Objects Library 2.8 or higher.

CASE STUDY: CREATING A SHARED ACCESS DATABASE

Linda and Janine are two buyers for a retail chain of stores. Each morning, they import data from the cash registers to get current information on sales and inventory for 2,000 styles. Throughout the day, either buyer may enter transfers of inventory from one store to another. It would be ideal if Linda could see the pending transfers entered by Janine and vice versa.

Each buyer has an Excel application with VBA running on her desktop. They each import the cash register data and have VBA routines that facilitate the creation of pivot table reports to help them make buying decisions.

Attempting to store the transfer data in a common Excel file causes problems. When either buyer attempts to write to the Excel file, the entire file becomes read-only for the other buyer. With a shared workbook, Excel turns off the capability to create pivot tables, and this is required in their application.

Neither Linda nor Janine has the professional version of Office, so they do not have Access running on their desktop PCs. The solution is to produce an Access database on a network drive that both Linda and Janine can see. These are the steps:

1. Using Access on another PC, produce a new database called transfers.mdb and add a table called `tblTransfer`, as shown in Figure 21.2.

Figure 21.2
Multiple people using their own Excel workbooks will read and write to this table inside an MDB file on a network drive.

Field Name	Data Type
ID	AutoNumber
Style	Short Text
FromStore	Number
ToStore	Number
Qty	Number
TDate	Date/Time
Sent	Yes/No
Receive	Yes/No

2. Move the Transfers.mdb file to a network drive. You might find that this common folder uses different drive-letter mappings on each machine. It might be H:\Common\ on Linda's machine and I:\Common\ on Janine's machine.

3. On both machines, go to the VB Editor and under Tools, References, add a reference to ActiveX Data Objects Library.

4. In both of their applications, find an out-of-the-way cell in which to store the path to transfers.mdb. Name this cell `TPath`.

The application provides nearly seamless multiuser access to both buyers. Both Linda and Janine can read or write to the table at the same time. The only time a conflict occurs is when they both happen to try to update the same record at the same time.

Other than the out-of-the-way cell reference to the path to transfers.mdb, neither buyer is aware that her data is being stored in a shared Access table, and neither computer needs to have Access installed.

21

The remainder of this chapter gives you the code necessary to allow the application included in the preceding case study to read or write data from the `tblTransfer` table.

The Tools of ADO

You encounter several terms when using ADO to connect to an external data source:

- **Record set**—When connecting to an Access database, the record set is either a table in the database or a query in the database. Most of the ADO methods reference the record set. You might also want to create your own query on the fly. In this case, write a SQL statement to extract only a subset of records from a table.

- **Connection**—The connection defines the path to the database and the type of database. In the case of Access databases, you specify that the connection is using the Microsoft Jet Engine.

- **Cursor**—Think of the cursor as a pointer that keeps track of which record you are using in the database. There are several types of cursors and two places for the cursor to be located (described in the following bullets).

- **Cursor type**—A dynamic cursor is the most flexible cursor. If you define a record set and someone else updates a row in the table while a dynamic cursor is active, the dynamic cursor knows about the updated record. Although this is the most flexible, it requires the most overhead. If your database doesn't have a lot of transactions, you might specify a static cursor; this type of cursor returns a snapshot of the data at the time the cursor is established.

- **Cursor location**—The cursor can be located either on the client or on the server. For an Access database residing on your hard drive, a server location for the cursor means that the Access Jet Engine on your computer is controlling the cursor. When you specify a client location for the cursor, your Excel session is controlling the cursor. On a very large external data set, it would be better to allow the server to control the cursor. For small data sets, a client cursor is faster.

- **Lock type**—The point of this chapter is to allow multiple people to access a data set at the same time. The lock type defines how ADO will prevent crashes when two people try to update a record at the same time. With an optimistic lock type, an individual record is locked only when you attempt to update the record. If your application will be doing 90% reads and only occasionally updating, then an optimistic lock is perfect. However, if you know that every time you read a record, you will soon update the record, you should use a pessimistic lock type. With pessimistic locks, a record is locked as soon as you read it. If you know that you will never write back to the database, you can use a read-only lock. This enables you to read the records without preventing others from writing to them.

The primary objects needed to access data in an MDB file are an ADO connection and an ADO record set.

The ADO connection defines the path to the database and specifies that the connection is based on the Microsoft Jet Engine.

After you have established the connection to the database, you usually use that connection to define a record set. A record set can be a table or a subset of records in the table or a pre-defined query in the Access database. To open a record set, you have to specify the connection and the values for the `CursorType`, `CursorLocation`, `LockType`, and `Options` parameters.

Assuming that you have only two users trying to access the table at a time, you should use a dynamic cursor and an optimistic lock type. For large data sets, the `adUseServer` value of the `CursorLocation` property allows the database server to process records without using up RAM on the client machine. If you have a small data set, it might be faster to use `adUseClient` for the `CursorLocation`. When the record set is opened, all the records are transferred to memory of the client machine. This allows faster navigation from record to record.

Reading data from the Access database is easy, provided that you have fewer than 1048576 records. You can use the `CopyFromRecordset` method to copy all selected records from the record set to a blank area of the worksheet.

To add a record to an Access table, use the `AddNew` method for the record set. You then specify the value for each field in the table and use the `Update` method to commit the changes to the database.

To delete a record from the table, you can use a pass-through query to delete records that match a certain criteria.

> **NOTE** If you ever find yourself frustrated with ADO and think, "If I could just open Access, I could knock out a quick SQL statement to do exactly what I need," then the pass-through query is for you. Rather than use ADO to read through the records, the pass-through query sends a request to the database to run the SQL statement that your program builds. This effectively enables you to handle any tasks that your database might support but that are not handled by ADO. The types of SQL statements handled by the pass-through query are dependent on which database type you are connecting to.

Other tools are available that let you make sure that a table exists or that a particular field exists in a table. You can also use VBA to add new fields to a table definition on the fly.

Adding a Record to a Database

Going back to the case study earlier in the chapter, the application you are creating has a userform where buyers can enter transfers. To make the calls to the Access database as simple as possible, a series of utility modules handle the ADO connection to the database. This way, the userform code can simply call `AddTransfer(Style, FromStore, ToStore, Qty)`.

Here's how you add records after the connection is defined:

1. Open a record set that points to the table. In the code that follows, see the sections commented `' Open the Connection,' Define the Recordset`, and `' Open the Table`.

2. Use `AddNew` to add a new record.

21

3. Update each field in the new record.

4. Use Update to update the record set.

5. Close the record set and then close the connection.

The following code adds a new record to the tblTransfer table:

```
Sub AddTransfer(Style As Variant, FromStore As Variant, _
    ToStore As Variant, Qty As Integer)
    Dim cnn As ADODB.Connection
    Dim rst As ADODB.Recordset

    MyConn = "J:\transfers.mdb"

    ' Open the Connection
    Set cnn = New ADODB.Connection
    With cnn
        .Provider = "Microsoft.Jet.OLEDB.4.0"
        .Open MyConn
    End With

    ' Define the Recordset
    Set rst = New ADODB.Recordset
    rst.CursorLocation = adUseServer

    ' Open the Table
    rst.Open Source:="tblTransfer", _
        ActiveConnection:=cnn, _
        CursorType:=adOpenDynamic, _
        LockType:=adLockOptimistic, _
        Options:=adCmdTable

    ' Add a record
    rst.AddNew

    ' Set up the values for the fields. The first four fields
    ' are passed from the calling userform. The date field
    ' is filled with the current date.
    rst("Style") = Style
    rst("FromStore") = FromStore
    rst("ToStore") = ToStore
    rst("Qty") = Qty
    rst("tDate") = Date
    rst("Sent") = False
    rst("Receive") = False

    ' Write the values to this record
    rst.Update

    ' Close
    rst.Close
    cnn.Close

End Sub
```

21

Retrieving Records from a Database

Reading records from an Access database is easy. As you define a record set, you pass a SQL string to return the records you are interested in.

> **NOTE** A great way to generate the SQL is to design a query in Access that retrieves the records. While viewing the query in Access, select SQL View from the View drop-down on the Query Tools Design tab of the ribbon. Access shows you the SQL statement required to execute that query. You can use that SQL statement as a model for building the SQL string in your VBA code.

After the record set is defined, use the `CopyFromRecordSet` method to copy all the matching records from Access to a specific area of the worksheet.

The following routine queries the `Transfer` table to find all records in which the `Sent` flag is not yet set to `True`:

```vba
Sub GetUnsentTransfers()
    Dim cnn As ADODB.Connection
    Dim rst As ADODB.Recordset
    Dim WSOrig As Worksheet
    Dim WSTemp As Worksheet
    Dim sSQL as String
    Dim FinalRow as Long

    Set WSOrig = ActiveSheet

    'Build a SQL String to get all fields for unsent transfers
    sSQL = "SELECT ID, Style, FromStore, ToStore, Qty, tDate" _
    & "FROM tblTransfer"
    sSQL = sSQL & " WHERE Sent=FALSE"

    ' Path to Transfers.mdb
    MyConn = "J:\transfers.mdb"

    Set cnn = New ADODB.Connection
    With cnn
        .Provider = "Microsoft.Jet.OLEDB.4.0"
        .Open MyConn
    End With

    Set rst = New ADODB.Recordset
    rst.CursorLocation = adUseServer
    rst.Open Source:=sSQL, ActiveConnection:=cnn, _
        CursorType:=AdForwardOnly, LockType:=adLockOptimistic, _
            Options:=adCmdText

    ' Create the report in a new worksheet
    Set WSTemp = Worksheets.Add

    ' Add Headings
    Range("A1:F1").Value = Array("ID", "Style", "From", "To", "Qty",
"Date")
```

21

```
' Copy from the record set to row 2
Range("A2").CopyFromRecordset rst

' Close the connection
rst.Close
cnn.Close

' Format the report
FinalRow = Range("A65536").End(xlUp).Row

' If there were no records, then stop
If FinalRow = 1 Then
    Application.DisplayAlerts = False
    WSTemp.Delete
    Application.DisplayAlerts = True
    WSOrig.Activate
    MsgBox "There are no transfers to confirm"
    Exit Sub
End If

' Format column F as a date
Range("F2:F" & FinalRow).NumberFormat = "m/d/y"

' Show the userform -- used in next section
frmTransConf.Show

' Delete the temporary sheet
Application.DisplayAlerts = False
WSTemp.Delete
Application.DisplayAlerts = True

End Sub
```

The results are placed on a blank worksheet. The final few lines display the results in a userform to illustrate how to update a record in the next section.

The CopyFromRecordSet method copies records that match the SQL query to a range on the worksheet. Note that you receive only the data rows. The headings do not come along automatically. You must use code to write the headings to row 1. Figure 21.3 shows the results.

Figure 21.3

Range("A2"). CopyFromRecord Set brought matching records from the Access database to the worksheet.

	A	B	C	D	E	F
1	ID	Style	From	To	Qty	Date
2	1935	B11275	340000	340000	8	6/9/04
3	1936	B10133	340000	340000	4	6/9/04
4	1937	B15422	340000	340000	5	6/9/04
5	1938	B10894	340000	340000	9	6/9/04
6	1939	B10049	340000	340000	3	6/9/04
7	1941	B18722	340000	340000	10	6/9/04
8	1944	B12886	340000	340000	10	6/9/04
9	1947	B17947	340000	340000	7	6/9/04
10	1950	B16431	340000	340000	9	6/9/04
11	1953	B19857	340000	340000	7	6/9/04
12	1954	B11562	340000	340000	1	6/9/04
13	1955	B19413	340000	340000	2	6/9/04

Updating an Existing Record

To update an existing record, you need to build a record set with exactly one record. This requires that the user select some sort of unique key when identifying the records. After you have opened the record set, use the `Fields` property to change the field in question and then the `Update` method to commit the changes to the database.

The earlier example returned a record set to a blank worksheet and then called the user-form `frmTransConf`. This form uses a simple `Userform_Initialize` to display the range in a large list box:

```
Private Sub UserForm_Initialize()

    ' Determine how many records we have
    FinalRow = Cells(Rows.Count, 1).End(xlUp).Row
    If FinalRow > 1 Then
        Me.lbXlt.RowSource = "A2:F" & FinalRow
    End If

End Sub
```

The list box's properties have the `MultiSelect` property set to `True`.

After the `Userform_Initialize` procedure is run, the unconfirmed records are displayed in a list box. The logistics planner can mark all the records that have actually been sent, as shown in Figure 21.4.

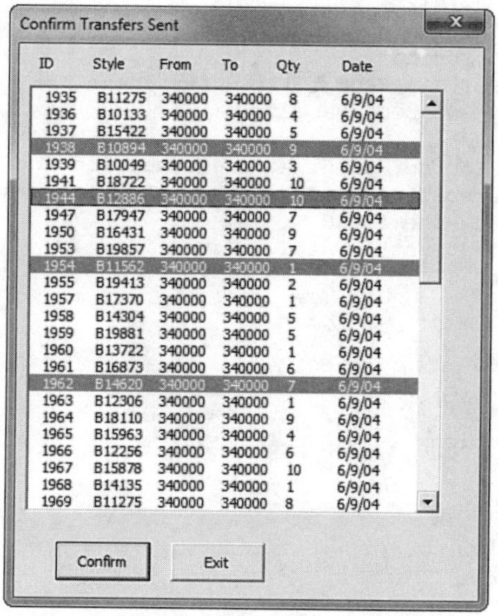

Figure 21.4

This userform displays particular records from the Access record set. When the buyer selects certain records and then clicks the Confirm button, you have to use ADO's Update method to update the Sent field on the selected records.

The code attached to the Confirm button follows:

```
Private Sub cbConfirm_Click()
    Dim cnn As ADODB.Connection
    Dim rst As ADODB.Recordset
```

```
' If nothing is selected, warn them
CountSelect = 0
For x = 0 To Me.lbXlt.ListCount - 1
    If Me.lbXlt.Selected(x) Then
        CountSelect = CountSelect + 1
    End If
Next x

If CountSelect = 0 Then
    MsgBox "There were no transfers selected. " & _
        "To exit without confirming any transfers, use Cancel."
    Exit Sub
End If

' Establish a connection to transfers.mdb
' Path to Transfers.mdb is on Menu
MyConn = "J:\transfers.mdb"

Set cnn = New ADODB.Connection

With cnn
    .Provider = "Microsoft.Jet.OLEDB.4.0"
    .Open MyConn
End With

' Mark as complete
For x = 0 To Me.lbXlt.ListCount - 1
    If Me.lbXlt.Selected(x) Then
        ThisID = Cells(2 + x, 1).Value
        ' Mark ThisID as complete
        'Build SQL String
        sSQL = "SELECT * FROM tblTransfer Where ID=" & ThisID
        Set rst = New ADODB.Recordset
        With rst
            .Open Source:=sSQL, ActiveConnection:=cnn, _
                CursorType:=adOpenKeyset, LockType:=adLockOptimistic
            ' Update the field
            .Fields("Sent").Value = True
            .Update
            .Close
        End With
    End If
Next x

' Close the connection
cnn.Close
Set rst = Nothing
Set cnn = Nothing

' Close the userform
Unload Me

End Sub
```

Including the ID field in the fields returned in the prior example is important if you want to narrow the information down to a single record.

Deleting Records via ADO

As with updating a record, the key to deleting records is being able to write a bit of SQL to uniquely identify the records to be deleted. The following code uses the `Execute` method to pass the `Delete` command through to Access:

```
Public Sub ADOWipeOutAttribute(RecID)
    ' Establish a connection to transfers.mdb
    MyConn = "J:\transfers.mdb"

    With New ADODB.Connection
        .Provider = "Microsoft.Jet.OLEDB.4.0"
        .Open MyConn
        .Execute "Delete From tblTransfer Where ID = " & RecID
        .Close
    End With
End Sub
```

Summarizing Records via ADO

One of Access's strengths is running summary queries that group by a particular field. If you build a summary query in Access and examine the SQL view, you'll see that complex queries can be written. Similar SQL can be built in Excel VBA and passed to Access via ADO.

The following code uses a fairly complex query to get a net total by store:

```
Sub NetTransfers(Style As Variant)
    ' This builds a table of net open transfers
    ' on Styles AI1
    Dim cnn As ADODB.Connection
    Dim rst As ADODB.Recordset

    ' Build the large SQL query
    ' Basic Logic:  Get all open Incoming Transfers by store,
    ' union with -1* outgoing transfers by store
    ' Sum that union by store, and give us min date as well
    ' A single call to this macro will replace 60
    ' calls to GetTransferIn, GetTransferOut, TransferAge
    sSQL = "Select Store, Sum(Quantity), Min(mDate) From " & _
        "(SELECT ToStore AS Store, Sum(Qty) AS Quantity, " & _
        "Min(TDate) AS mDate FROM tblTransfer where Style='" & Style & _
        "& "' AND Receive=FALSE GROUP BY ToStore "
    sSQL = sSQL & " Union All SELECT FromStore AS Store, " & _
        "Sum(-1*Qty) AS Quantity, Min(TDate) AS mDate " & _
        "FROM tblTransfer where Style='" & Style & "' AND " & _
        "Sent=FALSE GROUP BY FromStore)"
    sSQL = sSQL & " Group by Store"

    MyConn = "J:\transfers.mdb"

    ' open the connection.
    Set cnn = New ADODB.Connection
    With cnn
        .Provider = "Microsoft.Jet.OLEDB.4.0"
        .Open MyConn
    End With
```

```
        Set rst = New ADODB.Recordset

        rst.CursorLocation = adUseServer

        ' open the first query
        rst.Open Source:=sSQL, _
            ActiveConnection:=cnn, _
            CursorType:=AdForwardOnly, _
            LockType:=adLockOptimistic, _
            Options:=adCmdText

        Range("A1:C1").Value = Array("Store", "Qty", "Date")
        ' Return Query Results
        Range("A2").CopyFromRecordset rst
        rst.Close
        cnn.Close

    End Sub
```

Other Utilities via ADO

Consider the application you created for this chapter's case study: The buyers now have an Access database located on their network but possibly no copy of Access. It would be ideal if you could deliver changes to the Access database on the fly as their application opens.

> **NOTE** If you are wondering how you would ever coax the person using the application to run these queries, consider using an update macro hidden in the `Workbook_Open` routine of the client application. Such a routine might first check to see whether a field exists and then add the field if it is missing.

➡ For details on the mechanics of hiding the update query in the `Workbook_Open` routine, **see** the case study "Using a Hidden Code Workbook to Hold All Macros and Forms" in Chapter 26, "Creating Add-ins," **p. 509**.

Checking for the Existence of Tables

If the application in this chapter's example needs a new table in the database, you can use the code in the next section. However, because you have a multiuser application, only the first person who opens the application has to add the table on the fly. When the next buyer shows up, the table might have already been added by the first buyer's application. Because this code is a function instead of a sub, it returns either `True` or `False` to the calling routine.

This code uses the `OpenSchema` method to query the database schema:

```
Function TableExists(WhichTable)
    Dim cnn As ADODB.Connection
    Dim rst As ADODB.Recordset
    Dim fld As ADODB.Field
    TableExists = False
```

21

```
                     ' Path to Transfers.mdb is on Menu
                     MyConn = "J:\transfers.mdb"

                     Set cnn = New ADODB.Connection

                     With cnn
                         .Provider = "Microsoft.Jet.OLEDB.4.0"
                         .Open MyConn
                     End With

                     Set rst = cnn.OpenSchema(adSchemaTables)

                     Do Until rst.EOF
                         If LCase(rst!Table_Name) = LCase(WhichTable) Then
                             TableExists = True
                             GoTo ExitMe
                         End If
                         rst.MoveNext
                     Loop

                 ExitMe:
                     rst.Close
                     Set rst = Nothing
                     ' Close the connection
                     cnn.Close

                 End Function
```

Checking for the Existence of a Field

Sometimes you want to add a new field to an existing table. The following code does this, and it uses the OpenSchema method but this time looks at the columns in the tables:

```
                 Function ColumnExists(WhichColumn, WhichTable)
                     Dim cnn As ADODB.Connection
                     Dim rst As ADODB.Recordset
                     Dim WSOrig As Worksheet
                     Dim WSTemp As Worksheet
                     Dim fld As ADODB.Field
                     ColumnExists = False

                     ' Path to Transfers.mdb is on menu
                     MyConn = ActiveWorkbook.Worksheets("Menu").Range("TPath").Value
                     If Right(MyConn, 1) = "\" Then
                         MyConn = MyConn & "transfers.mdb"
                     Else
                         MyConn = MyConn & "\transfers.mdb"
                     End If

                     Set cnn = New ADODB.Connection

                     With cnn
                         .Provider = "Microsoft.Jet.OLEDB.4.0"
                         .Open MyConn
                     End With

                     Set rst = cnn.OpenSchema(adSchemaColumns)
```

21

```
        Do Until rst.EOF
            If LCase(rst!Column_Name) = LCase(WhichColumn) And _
                LCase(rst!Table_Name) = LCase(WhichTable) Then
                ColumnExists = True
                GoTo ExitMe
            End If
            rst.MoveNext
        Loop

    ExitMe:
        rst.Close
        Set rst = Nothing
        ' Close the connection
        cnn.Close

    End Function
```

Adding a Table On the Fly

The following code uses a pass-through query to tell Access to run a `Create Table` command:

```
Sub ADOCreateReplenish()
    ' This creates tblReplenish
    ' There are five fields:
    ' Style
    ' A = Auto replenishment for A
    ' B = Auto replenishment level for B stores
    ' C = Auto replenishment level for C stores
    ' RecActive = Yes/No field
    Dim cnn As ADODB.Connection
    Dim cmd As ADODB.Command

    ' Define the connection
    MyConn = "J:\transfers.mdb"

    ' open the connection
    Set cnn = New ADODB.Connection
    With cnn
        .Provider = "Microsoft.Jet.OLEDB.4.0"
        .Open MyConn
    End With

    Set cmd = New ADODB.Command
    Set cmd.ActiveConnection = cnn
    'create table
    cmd.CommandText = "CREATE TABLE tblReplenish " & _
        "(Style Char(10) Primary Key, " & _
        "A int, B  int, C Int, RecActive YesNo)"
    cmd.Execute , , adCmdText
    Set cmd = Nothing
    Set cnn = Nothing
    Exit Sub
End Sub
```

Adding a Field On the Fly

If you determine that a field does not exist, you can use a pass-through query to add a field to the table, like this:

```
Sub ADOAddField()
    ' This adds a grp field to tblReplenish
    Dim cnn As ADODB.Connection
    Dim cmd As ADODB.Command

    ' Define the connection
    MyConn = "J:\transfers.mdb"

    ' open the connection
    Set cnn = New ADODB.Connection
    With cnn
        .Provider = "Microsoft.Jet.OLEDB.4.0"
        .Open MyConn
    End With


    Set cmd = New ADODB.Command
    Set cmd.ActiveConnection = cnn
    'create table
    cmd.CommandText = "ALTER TABLE tblReplenish Add Column Grp Char(25)"
    cmd.Execute , , adCmdText
    Set cmd = Nothing
    Set cnn = Nothing

End Sub
```

SQL Server Examples

If you have 64-bit versions of Office and if Microsoft does not provide the 64-bit Microsoft.Jet. OLEDB.4.0 drivers, you have to switch over to using SQL Server or another database technology:

```
Sub DataExtract()

Application.DisplayAlerts = False

'clear out all previous data
Sheet1.Cells.Clear

' Create a connection object.
Dim cnPubs As ADODB.Connection
Set cnPubs = New ADODB.Connection

' Provide the connection string.
Dim strConn As String

'Use the SQL Server OLE DB Provider.
strConn = "PROVIDER=SQLOLEDB;"

'Connect to the Pubs database on the local server.
strConn = strConn & "DATA SOURCE=a_sql_server;INITIAL CATALOG=a_database;"

'Use an integrated login.
strConn = strConn & " INTEGRATED SECURITY=sspi;"

'Now open the connection.
cnPubs.Open strConn
```

21

```vba
' Create a record set object.
Dim rsPubs As ADODB.Recordset
Set rsPubs = New ADODB.Recordset

With rsPubs
    ' Assign the Connection object.
    .ActiveConnection = cnPubs
    ' Extract the required records.
    .Open "exec a_database..a_stored_procedure"
    ' Copy the records into cell A1 on Sheet1.
    Sheet1.Range("A2").CopyFromRecordset rsPubs


Dim myColumn As Range
'Dim title_string As String
Dim K As Integer
For K = 0 To rsPubs.Fields.Count - 1
   'Sheet1.Columns(K).Value = rsPubs.Fields(K).Name
   'title_string = title_string & rsPubs.Fields(K).Name & Chr(9)
   'Sheet1.Columns(K).Cells(1).Name = rsPubs.Fields(K).Name
   'Sheet1.Columns.Column(K) = rsPubs.Fields(K).Name
   'Set myColumn = Sheet1.Columns(K)
   'myColumn.Cells(1, K).Value = rsPubs.Fields(K).Name
   'Sheet1.Cells(1, K) = rsPubs.Fields(K).Name
   Sheet1.Cells(1, K + 1) = rsPubs.Fields(K).Name
   Sheet1.Cells(1, K + 1).Font.Bold = "TRUE"
Next K
'Sheet1.Range("A1").Value = title_string


    ' Tidy up
    .Close
End With

cnPubs.Close
Set rsPubs = Nothing
Set cnPubs = Nothing

'clear out errors
Dim cellval As Range
Dim myRng As Range
Set myRng = ActiveSheet.UsedRange
For Each cellval In myRng
   cellval.Value = cellval.Value
   'cellval.NumberFormat = "@" 'this works as well as setting
   'HorizontalAlignment
   cellval.HorizontalAlignment = xlRight
Next

End Sub
```

Next Steps

In Chapter 22, "Advanced Userform Techniques," you'll discover more controls and techniques you can use in building userforms.

Advanced Userform Techniques

22

Chapter 10, "Userforms: An Introduction," covered the basics of adding controls to userforms. This chapter continues the topic, looking at more advanced controls and methods for making the most out of userforms.

Using the UserForm Toolbar in the Design of Controls on Userforms

In the VB Editor, under View, Toolbars, you'll find a few toolbars that do not appear unless the user selects them. One of these is the UserForm toolbar, shown in Figure 22.1. It has functionality useful for organizing the controls you add to a userform; for example, you can use it to make all the controls you select the same size.

Figure 22.1
The UserForm toolbar has tools for organizing the controls on a userform.

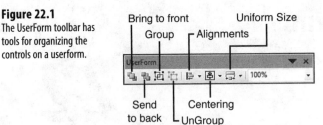

More Userform Controls

The following sections cover more userform controls you can use to help obtain information from users. At the end of each of the following subsections is a table that lists that control's events.

Checkbox **Controls**

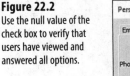

Check boxes allow the user to select one or more options on a userform. Unlike with the option buttons discussed in Chapter 10, a user can select one or more check boxes at a time.

The value of a checked box is `True`; the value of an unchecked box is `False`. If you clear the value of a check box (`Checkbox1.Value = ""`), when the userform runs, the check box will have a grayed-out check in it, as shown in Figure 22.2. This can be useful for verifying that users have viewed all options and made a selection.

Figure 22.2
Use the null value of the check box to verify that users have viewed and answered all options.

You can use code like the following to review all the check boxes in the Languages group of the dialog shown in Figure 22.2. If a value is null, the user is prompted to review the selections:

```
Private Sub btnClose_Click()
Dim Msg As String
Dim Chk As Control

Set Chk = Nothing

'narrow down the search to just the 2nd page's controls
```

```
    For Each Chk In frm_Multipage.MultiPage1.Pages(1).Controls
        'only need to verify checkbox controls
        If TypeName(Chk) = "CheckBox" Then
            'and just in case we add more check box controls,
            'just check the ones in the group
            If Chk.GroupName = "Languages" Then
                'if the value is null (the property value is empty)
                If IsNull(Chk.Object.Value) Then
                    'add the caption to a string
                    Msg = Msg & vbNewLine & Chk.Caption
                End If
            End If
        End If
    Next Chk

    If Msg <> "" Then
        Msg = "The following check boxes were not verified:" & vbNewLine & Msg
        MsgBox Msg, vbInformation, "Additional Information Required"
    End If
    Unload Me
End Sub
```

Table 22.1 lists the events for `CheckBox` controls.

Table 22.1   `CheckBox` **Control Events**

Event	Description
AfterUpdate	Occurs after a check box has been selected/cleared.
BeforeDragOver	Occurs while the user drags and drops data onto the check box.
BeforeDropOrPaste	Occurs right before the user is about to drop or paste data onto the check box.
BeforeUpdate	Occurs before the check box is selected/cleared.
Change	Occurs when the value of the check box is changed.
Click	Occurs when the user clicks the control with the mouse.
DblClick	Occurs when the user double-clicks the check box with the mouse.
Enter	Occurs right before the check box receives the focus from another control on the same userform.
Error	Occurs when the check box runs into an error and cannot return the error information.
Exit	Occurs right after the check box loses focus to another control on the same userform.
KeyDown	Occurs when the user presses a key on the keyboard.
KeyPress	Occurs when the user presses an ANSI key. An ANSI key is a typable character such as the letter *A*.
KeyUp	Occurs when the user releases a key on the keyboard.
MouseDown	Occurs when the user presses the mouse button within the borders of the check box.
MouseMove	Occurs when the user moves the mouse within the borders of the check box.
MouseUp	Occurs when the user releases the mouse button within the borders of the check box.

TabStrip **Controls**

The MultiPage control allows a userform to have several pages. Each page of the form can have its own set of controls, unrelated to any other control on the form. A TabStrip control also allows a userform to have many pages, but the controls on a tab strip are identical; they are drawn only once. Yet when the form is run, the information changes depending on which tab strip is active (see Figure 22.3).

➡ To learn more about MultiPage controls, **see** "Using the MultiPage Control to Combine Forms" on **p. 171**.

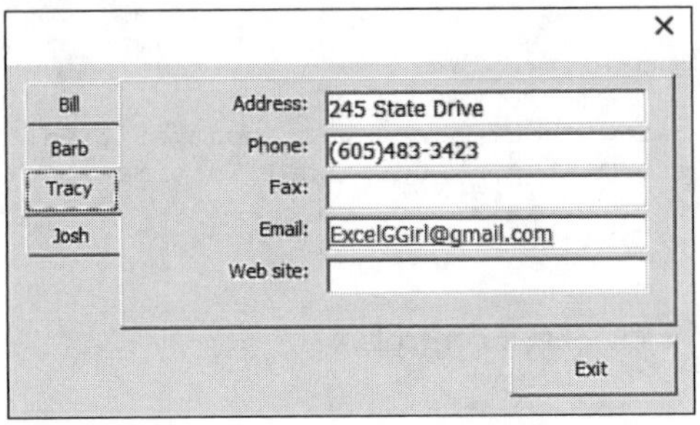

Figure 22.3
A tab strip allows a user-form with multiple pages to share controls but not information.

By default, a tab strip is thin, with two tabs at the top. Right-clicking a tab enables you to add, remove, rename, or move that tab. Size the tab strip to hold all the controls. Outside the tab strip area, draw a button for closing the form.

You can move the tabs around the strip, as shown in Figure 22.3. This is done by changing the TabOrientation property. The tabs can be at the top, bottom, left, or right side of the userform.

The following lines of code were used to create the tab strip form shown in Figure 22.3. The Initialize sub calls the sub SetValuesToTabStrip, which sets the value for the first tab:

```
Private Sub UserForm_Initialize()
SetValuesToTabStrip 1 'As default
End Sub
```

These lines of code handle what happens when a new tab is selected:

```
Private Sub TabStrip1_Change()
Dim lngRow As Long

lngRow = TabStrip1.Value + 1
SetValuesToTabStrip lngRow
End Sub
```

This sub provides the data shown on each tab. A sheet was set up, with each row corresponding to a tab:

```
Private Sub SetValuesToTabStrip(ByVal lngRow As Long)
With frm_Staff
```

```
            .lbl_Address.Caption = Cells(lngRow, 2).Value
            .lbl_Phone.Caption = Cells(lngRow, 3).Value
            .lbl_Fax.Caption = Cells(lngRow, 4).Value
            .lbl_Email.Caption = Cells(lngRow, 5).Value
            .lbl_Website.Caption = Cells(lngRow, 6).Value
            .Show
        End With
    End Sub
```

The tab strip's values are automatically filled in. They correspond to the tab's position in the strip; moving a tab changes its value. The value of the first tab of a tab strip is 0, which is why, in the preceding code, we add 1 to the tab strip value when the form is initialized to get it to correspond with the row on the sheet.

> **TIP**
>
> If you want a single tab to have an extra control, the control could be added at runtime, when the tab is activated, and removed when the tab is deactivated.

Table 22.2 lists the events for the TabStrip control.

Table 22.2   TabStrip Control Events

Event	Description
BeforeDragOver	Occurs while the user drags and drops data onto the control.
BeforeDropOrPaste	Occurs right before the user drops or pastes data into the control.
Change	Occurs when the value of the control is changed.
Click	Occurs when the user clicks the control with the mouse.
DblClick	Occurs when the user double-clicks the control with the mouse.
Enter	Occurs right before the control receives the focus from another control on the same userform.
Error	Occurs when the control runs into an error and cannot return the error information.
Exit	Occurs right after the control loses focus to another control on the same userform.
KeyDown	Occurs when the user presses a key on the keyboard.
KeyPress	Occurs when the user presses an ANSI key. An ANSI key is a typable character, such as the letter A.
KeyUp	Occurs when the user releases a key on the keyboard.
MouseDown	Occurs when the user presses the mouse button within the borders of the control.
MouseMove	Occurs when the user moves the mouse within the borders of the control.
MouseUp	Occurs when the user releases the mouse button within the borders of the control.

RefEdit **Controls**

The RefEdit control allows the user to select a range on a sheet; the range is returned as the value of the control. You can add it to any form. When you click the button on the right side of the field, the userform disappears and is replaced with the range selection form that is used for selecting ranges with Excel's many wizard tools, as shown in Figure 22.4. Click the button on the right of the field to show the userform once again.

Figure 22.4
Use RefEdit to enable the user to select a range on a sheet.

⊿	A	B	C	D
1	Store #	Store Name		
2	340001	Santa Ana		
3	34000...	...		
4	3400	Select Range to Format	?	×
5	3400	RefEdit!$A$1:$B$1		
6	34000...	Roseville		

The following code used with a RefEdit control allows the user to select a range, which is then made bold:

```
Private Sub cb1_Click()
Range(RefEdit1.Value).Font.Bold = True
Unload Me
End Sub
```

Table 22.3 lists the events for RefEdit controls.

CAUTION

RefEdit control events are notorious for not working properly. If you run into this problem, use a different control's event to trigger code.

Table 22.3 RefEdit **Control Events**

Event	Description
AfterUpdate	Occurs after the control's data has been changed by the user.
BeforeDragOver	Occurs while the user drags and drops data onto the control.
BeforeDropOrPaste	Occurs right before the user drops or pastes data into the control.
BeforeUpdate	Occurs before the data in the control is changed.
Change	Occurs when the value of the control is changed.
Click	Occurs when the user clicks the control with the mouse.
DblClick	Occurs when the user double-clicks the control with the mouse.
DropButtonClick	Occurs when the user clicks the drop button on the right side of the field.
Enter	Occurs right before the control receives the focus from another control on the same userform.
Error	Occurs when the control runs into an error and cannot return the error information.

Event	Description
Exit	Occurs right after the control loses focus to another control on the same userform.
KeyDown	Occurs when the user presses a key on the keyboard.
KeyPress	Occurs when the user presses an ANSI key. An ANSI key is a typable character, such as the letter *A*.
KeyUp	Occurs when the user releases a key on the keyboard.
MouseDown	Occurs when the user presses the mouse button within the borders of the control.
MouseMove	Occurs when the user moves the mouse within the borders of the control.
MouseUp	Occurs when the user releases the mouse button within the borders of the control.

ToggleButton Controls

A toggle button looks like a normal command button, but when the user presses it, it stays pressed until it is clicked again. This allows a True or False value to be returned based on the status of the button. Table 22.4 lists the events for the ToggleButton controls.

Table 22.4 ToggleButton **Control Events**

Event	Description
AfterUpdate	Occurs after the control's data has been changed by the user.
BeforeDragOver	Occurs while the user drags and drops data onto the control.
BeforeDropOrPaste	Occurs right before the user drops or pastes data into the control.
BeforeUpdate	Occurs before the data in the control is changed.
Change	Occurs when the value of the control is changed.
Click	Occurs when the user clicks the control with the mouse.
DblClick	Occurs when the user double-clicks the control with the mouse.
Enter	Occurs right before the control receives the focus from another control on the same userform.
Error	Occurs when the control runs into an error and cannot return the error information.
Exit	Occurs right after the control loses focus to another control on the same userform.
KeyDown	Occurs when the user presses a key on the keyboard.
KeyPress	Occurs when the user presses an ANSI key. An ANSI key is a typable character, such as the letter *A*.
KeyUp	Occurs when the user releases a key on the keyboard.
MouseDown	Occurs when the user presses the mouse button within the borders of the control.
MouseMove	Occurs when the user moves the mouse within the borders of the control.
MouseUp	Occurs when the user releases the mouse button within the borders of the control.

Using a Scrollbar as a Slider to Select Values

Chapter 10 discusses using a SpinButton control to enable someone to choose a date. A spin button is useful, but it allows users to adjust up or down by only one unit at a time. An alternative method is to draw a horizontal or vertical scrollbar in the middle of the userform and use it as a slider. Users can use arrows on the ends of the scrollbar as they would the spin button arrows, but they can also grab the scrollbar and instantly drag it to a certain value.

The userform shown in Figure 22.5 includes a label named Label1 and a scrollbar called ScrollBar1.

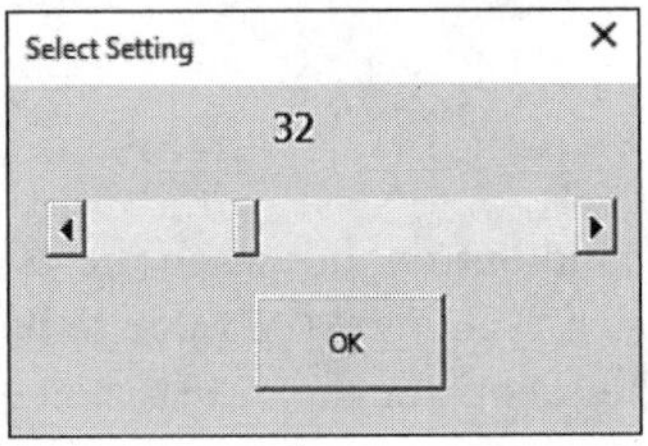

Figure 22.5
Using a scrollbar control allows the user to drag to a particular numeric or data value.

The userform's Initialize code sets up the Min and Max values for the scrollbar. It initializes the scrollbar to a value from cell A1 and updates the Label1.Caption:

```
Private Sub UserForm_Initialize()
    Me.ScrollBar1.Min = 0
    Me.ScrollBar1.Max = 100
    Me.ScrollBar1.Value = Worksheets("Scrollbar").Range("A1").Value
    Me.Label1.Caption = Me.ScrollBar1.Value
End Sub
```

Two event handlers are needed for the scrollbar. The Change event triggers when users click the arrows at the ends of the scrollbar. The Scroll event triggers when they drag the slider to a new value:

```
Private Sub ScrollBar1_Change()
    ' This event triggers when they touch
    ' the arrows on the end of the scrollbar
    Me.Label1.Caption = Me.ScrollBar1.Value
End Sub

Private Sub ScrollBar1_Scroll()
    ' This event triggers when they drag the slider
    Me.Label1.Caption = Me.ScrollBar1.Value
End Sub
```

Finally, the event attached to the button writes the scrollbar value out to the worksheet:

```
Private Sub btnClose_Click()
    Worksheets("Scrollbar").Range("A1").Value = Me.ScrollBar1.Value
    Unload Me
End Sub
```

Table 22.5 lists the events for Scrollbar controls.

Table 22.5 `Scrollbar` **Control Events**

Event	Description
AfterUpdate	Occurs after the control's data has been changed by the user.
BeforeDragOver	Occurs while the user drags and drops data onto the control.
BeforeDropOrPaste	Occurs right before the user drops or pastes data into the control.
BeforeUpdate	Occurs before the data in the control is changed.
Change	Occurs when the value of the control is changed.
Enter	Occurs right before the control receives the focus from another control on the same userform.
Error	Occurs when the control runs into an error and cannot return the error information.
Exit	Occurs right after the control loses focus to another control on the same userform.
KeyDown	Occurs when the user presses a key on the keyboard.
KeyPress	Occurs when the user presses an ANSI key. An ANSI key is a typable character, such as the letter *A*.
KeyUp	Occurs when the user releases a key on the keyboard.
Scroll	Occurs when the slider is moved.

Controls and Collections

In Chapter 9, "Creating Classes and Collections," several labels on a sheet were grouped together into a collection. With a little more code, these labels were turned into help screens for the users. Userform controls can also be grouped into collections to take advantage of class modules. The following example selects or clears all the check boxes on the userform, depending on which label the user chooses.

Place the following code in the class module, `clsFormCtl`. It consists of one property, `chb`, and two methods, `SelectAll` and `UnselectAll`.

The `SelectAll` method selects a check box by setting its value to `True`:

```
Public WithEvents chb As MSForms.CheckBox

Public Sub SelectAll()
chb.Value = True
End Sub
```

The `UnselectAll` method clears the check box:

```
Public Sub UnselectAll()
chb.Value = False
End Sub
```

That sets up the class module. Next, the controls need to be placed in a collection. The following code, placed behind the form `frm_Movies`, places the check boxes into a collection. The check boxes are part of the frame `frm_Selection`, which makes it easier to create the collection because it narrows the number of controls that need to be checked from the entire userform to just those controls within the frame:

```
Dim col_Selection As New Collection

Private Sub UserForm_Initialize()
Dim ctl As MSForms.CheckBox
Dim chb_ctl As clsFormCtl

'Go through the members of the frame and add them to the collection
For Each ctl In frm_Selection.Controls
    Set chb_ctl = New clsFormCtl
    Set chb_ctl.chb = ctl
    col_Selection.Add chb_ctl
Next ctl
End Sub
```

When the form is opened, the controls are placed into the collection. All that's left now is to add the code for labels to select and clear the check boxes:

```
Private Sub lbl_SelectAll_Click()
Dim ctl As clsFormCtl

For Each ctl In col_Selection
    ctl.SelectAll
Next ctl
End Sub
```

The following code clears the check boxes in the collection:

```
Private Sub lbl_unSelectAll_Click()
Dim ctl As clsFormCtl

For Each ctl In col_Selection
    ctl.Unselectall
Next ctl
End Sub
```

All the check boxes can be selected and cleared with a single click of the mouse, as shown in Figure 22.6.

Figure 22.6
Use frames, collections, and class modules together to create quick and efficient userforms.

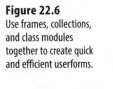

> **TIP**
>
> If your controls cannot be placed in a frame, you can use the `Tag` property to create an improvised grouping. `Tag` is a property that holds more information about a control. Its value is of type `String`, so it can hold any type of information. For example, it can be used to create an informal group of controls from different groupings.

Modeless Userforms

Have you ever had a userform active but needed to manipulate something on the active sheet or switch to another sheet? Forms can be *modeless*, in which case they don't have to interfere with the functionality of Excel. The user can type in a cell, switch to another sheet, copy/paste data, and use the ribbon—as if the userform were not there.

By default, a userform is modal, which means that there can be no interaction with Excel other than with the form. To make the form modeless, change the `ShowModal` property to `False`. After it is modeless, the user can select a cell on the sheet while the form is active, as shown in Figure 22.7.

Figure 22.7
A modeless form enables the user to enter a cell while the form is still active.

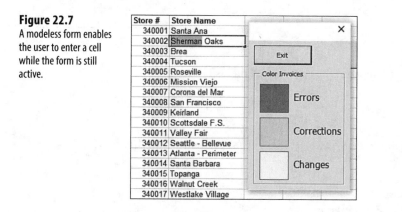

Using Hyperlinks in Userforms

In the userform example shown in Figure 22.3, there is a field for email and a field for website address. It would be nice to click these and have a blank email message or web page appear automatically. You can do this by using the following program, which creates a new message or opens a web browser when the corresponding label is clicked:

```
Private Declare PtrSafe Function ShellExecute Lib "shell32.dll" Alias _
    "ShellExecuteA"(ByVal hWnd As Long, ByVal lpOperation As String, _
    ByVal lpFile As String, ByVal lpParameters As String, _
    ByVal lpDirectory As String, ByVal nShowCmd As Long) As LongPtr

Const SWNormal = 1
```

The application programming interface (API) declaration and any other constants go at the very top of the module.

This sub controls what happens when the email label is clicked, as shown in Figure 22.8:

```
Private Sub lbl_Email_Click()
Dim lngRow As Long

lngRow = TabStrip1.Value + 1
ShellExecute 0&, "open", "mailto:" & Cells(lngRow, 5).Value, _
    vbNullString, vbNullString, SWNormal
End Sub
```

Figure 22.8
Turn email addresses and websites into clickable links by using a few lines of code.

This sub controls what happens when a website label is clicked:

```
Private Sub lbl_Website_Click()
Dim lngRow As Long

lngRow = TabStrip1.Value + 1
ShellExecute 0&, "open", Cells(lngRow, 6).Value, vbNullString, _
    vbNullString, SWNormal
End Sub
```

Adding Controls at Runtime

It is possible to add controls to a userform at runtime. This is convenient if you are not sure how many items you will be adding to a form.

Figure 22.9 shows a plain form with only one button. This plain form is used to display any number of pictures from a product catalog. The pictures and accompanying labels appear at runtime, as the form is being displayed.

A sales rep making a sales presentation uses this form to display a product catalog. He can select any number of SKUs from an Excel worksheet and press a hotkey to display the form. If he selects six items on the worksheet, the form displays with a small version of each picture, as shown in Figure 22.10.

If the sales rep selects fewer items, the images are displayed larger, as shown in Figure 22.11.

A number of techniques are used to create this userform on the fly. The initial form contains only one button, cbClose. Everything else is added on the fly.

Figure 22.9
Flexible forms can be created if you add most controls at runtime.

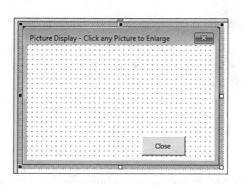

Figure 22.10
The sales rep asked to see photos of six SKUs. The `UserForm_ Initialize` procedure adds each picture and label on the fly.

Figure 22.11
The logic in `Userform_ Initialize` decides how many pictures are being displayed and adds the appropriately sized image controls.

Resizing the Userform On the Fly

Giving the best view of the images in the product catalog involves having the form appear as large as possible. The following code uses the form's `Height` and `Width` properties to make sure the form fills almost the entire screen:

```
'resize the form
Me.Height = Int(0.98 * ActiveWindow.Height)
Me.Width = Int(0.98 * ActiveWindow.Width)
```

Adding a Control On the Fly

For a normal control added at design time, such as a button called `cbClose`, it is easy to refer to the control by using its name:

```
Me.cbClose.Left = 100
```

However, for a control that is added at runtime, you have to use the `Controls` collection to set any properties for the control. For this reason, it is important to set up a variable, such as `LC`, to hold the name of the control. Controls are added with the `.Add` method. The important parameter is `bstrProgId`. This property dictates whether the added control is a label, a text box, a command button, or something else.

The following code adds a new label to the form. `PicCount` is a counter variable used to ensure that each label has a unique name. After the form is added, specify a position for the control by setting the `Top` and `Left` properties. You should also set `Height` and `Width` properties for the control:

```
LC = "LabelA" & PicCount
Me.Controls.Add bstrProgId:="forms.label.1", Name:=LC, Visible:=True
Me.Controls(LC).Top = 25
Me.Controls(LC).Left = 50
Me.Controls(LC).Height = 18
Me.Controls(LC).Width = 60
Me.Controls(LC).Caption = Cell.Value
```

> **CAUTION**
>
> You lose some of the AutoComplete options with this method. Normally, if you would start to type `Me.cbClose.`, the AutoComplete options would present the valid choices for a command button. However, when you use the `Me.Controls(LC)` collection to add controls on the fly, VBA does not know what type of control is referenced. In this case, it is helpful to know you need to set the `Caption` property rather than the `Value` property for a label.

Sizing On the Fly

In reality, you need to be able to calculate values for `Top`, `Left`, `Height`, and `Width` on the fly. You do this based on the actual height and width of a form and based on how many controls are needed.

Adding Other Controls

To add other types of controls, change the `ProgId` used with the `Add` method. Table 22.6 shows the `ProgIds` for various types of controls.

Table 22.6   Userform Controls and Corresponding `ProgIds`

Control	ProgId
CheckBox	Forms.CheckBox.1
ComboBox	Forms.ComboBox.1
CommandButton	Forms.CommandButton.1
Frame	Forms.Frame.1
Image	Forms.Image.1
Label	Forms.Label.1
ListBox	Forms.ListBox.1
MultiPage	Forms.MultiPage.1
OptionButton	Forms.OptionButton.1
ScrollBar	Forms.ScrollBar.1
SpinButton	Forms.SpinButton.1
TabStrip	Forms.TabStrip.1
TextBox	Forms.TextBox.1
ToggleButton	Forms.ToggleButton.1

Adding an Image On the Fly

There is some unpredictability in adding images to a userform. Any given image might be shaped either landscape or portrait. An image might be small or huge. The strategy you might want to use is to let an image load at full size by setting the `.AutoSize` parameter to `True` before loading it:

```
TC = "Image" & PicCount
Me.Controls.Add bstrProgId:="forms.image.1", Name:=TC, Visible:=True
Me.Controls(TC).Top = LastTop
Me.Controls(TC).Left = LastLeft
Me.Controls(TC).AutoSize = True
On Error Resume Next
Me.Controls(TC).Picture = LoadPicture(fname)
On Error GoTo 0
```

After the image has loaded, you can read the control's `Height` and `Width` properties to determine whether the image is landscape or portrait and whether the image is constrained by available width or available height:

```
'The picture resized the control to full size
```

```
'determine the size of the picture
Wid = Me.Controls(TC).Width
Ht = Me.Controls(TC).Height
'CellWid and CellHt are calculated in the full code sample below
WidRedux = CellWid / Wid
HtRedux = CellHt / Ht
If WidRedux < HtRedux Then
    Redux = WidRedux
Else
    Redux = HtRedux
End If
NewHt = Int(Ht * Redux)
NewWid = Int(Wid * Redux)
```

After you find the proper size for the image so that it draws without distortion, set the AutoSize property to False and use the correct height and width to have the image not appear distorted:

```
'Now resize the control
Me.Controls(TC).AutoSize = False
Me.Controls(TC).Height = NewHt
Me.Controls(TC).Width = NewWid
Me.Controls(TC).PictureSizeMode = fmPictureSizeModeStretch
```

Putting It All Together

This is the complete code for the picture catalog userform:

```
Private Sub UserForm_Initialize()
    'Display pictures of each SKU selected on the worksheet
    'This may be anywhere from 1 to 36 pictures
    PicPath = "C:\qimage\qi"

    'resize the form
    Me.Height = Int(0.98 * ActiveWindow.Height)
    Me.Width = Int(0.98 * ActiveWindow.Width)

    'determine how many cells are selected
    'We need one picture and label for each cell
    CellCount = Selection.Cells.Count
    ReDim Preserve Pics(1 To CellCount)

    'Figure out the size of the resized form
    TempHt = Me.Height
    TempWid = Me.Width

    'The number of columns is a roundup of SQRT(CellCount)
    'This will ensure 4 rows of 5 pictures for 20, etc.
    NumCol = Int(0.99 + Sqr(CellCount))
    NumRow = Int(0.99 + CellCount / NumCol)

    'Figure out the height and width of each square
    'Each column will have 2 points to left & right of pics
    CellWid = Application.WorksheetFunction.Max(Int(TempWid / NumCol) - 4, 1)
    'each row needs to have 33 points below it for the label
    CellHt = Application.WorksheetFunction.Max(Int(TempHt / NumRow) - 33, 1)
```

```
PicCount = 0 'Counter variable
LastTop = 2
MaxBottom = 1
'Build each row on the form
For x = 1 To NumRow
    LastLeft = 3
    'Build each column in this row
    For Y = 1 To NumCol
        PicCount = PicCount + 1
        If PicCount > CellCount Then
            'There is not an even number of pictures to fill
            'out the last row
            Me.Height = MaxBottom + 100
            Me.cbClose.Top = MaxBottom + 25
            Me.cbClose.Left = Me.Width - 70
            Repaint 'redraws the form
            Exit Sub
        End If
        ThisStyle = Selection.Cells(PicCount).Value
        ThisDesc = Selection.Cells(PicCount).Offset(0, 1).Value
        fname = PicPath & ThisStyle & ".jpg"
        TC = "Image" & PicCount
        Me.Controls.Add bstrProgId:="forms.image.1", Name:=TC, _
          Visible:=True
        Me.Controls(TC).Top = LastTop
        Me.Controls(TC).Left = LastLeft
        Me.Controls(TC).AutoSize = True
        On Error Resume Next
        Me.Controls(TC).Picture = LoadPicture(fname)
        On Error GoTo 0

        'The picture resized the control to full size
        'determine the size of the picture
        Wid = Me.Controls(TC).Width
        Ht = Me.Controls(TC).Height
        WidRedux = CellWid / Wid
        HtRedux = CellHt / Ht
        If WidRedux < HtRedux Then
            Redux = WidRedux
        Else
            Redux = HtRedux
        End If
        NewHt = Int(Ht * Redux)
        NewWid = Int(Wid * Redux)

        'Now resize the control
        Me.Controls(TC).AutoSize = False
        Me.Controls(TC).Height = NewHt
        Me.Controls(TC).Width = NewWid
        Me.Controls(TC).PictureSizeMode = fmPictureSizeModeStretch
        Me.Controls(TC).ControlTipText = "Style " & _
                ThisStyle & " " & ThisDesc

        'Keep track of the bottommost & rightmost picture
        ThisRight = Me.Controls(TC).Left + Me.Controls(TC).Width
        ThisBottom = Me.Controls(TC).Top + Me.Controls(TC).Height
        If ThisBottom > MaxBottom Then MaxBottom = ThisBottom
```

```
                    'Add a label below the picture
                    LC = "LabelA" & PicCount
                    Me.Controls.Add bstrProgId:="forms.label.1", Name:=LC, _
                      Visible:=True
                    Me.Controls(LC).Top = ThisBottom + 1
                    Me.Controls(LC).Left = LastLeft
                    Me.Controls(LC).Height = 18
                    Me.Controls(LC).Width = CellWid
                    Me.Controls(LC).Caption = ThisDesc

                    'Keep track of where the next picture should display
                    LastLeft = LastLeft + CellWid + 4
            Next Y ' end of this row
            LastTop = MaxBottom + 21 + 16
        Next x

        Me.Height = MaxBottom + 100
        Me.cbClose.Top = MaxBottom + 25
        Me.cbClose.Left = Me.Width - 70
        Repaint
    End Sub
```

Adding Help to a Userform

You have already designed a great userform in this chapter, but there is one thing missing: guidance for users. The following sections show four ways you can help users fill out the form properly.

Showing Accelerator Keys

Built-in forms often have keyboard shortcuts that allow actions to be triggered or fields selected with a few keystrokes. These shortcuts are identified by an underlined letter on a button or label.

You can add this same capability to custom userforms by entering a value in the `Accelerator` property of the control. Pressing Alt + the accelerator key selects the control. For example, in Figure 22.12, Alt+T selects the Streaming check box. Repeating the combination clears the box.

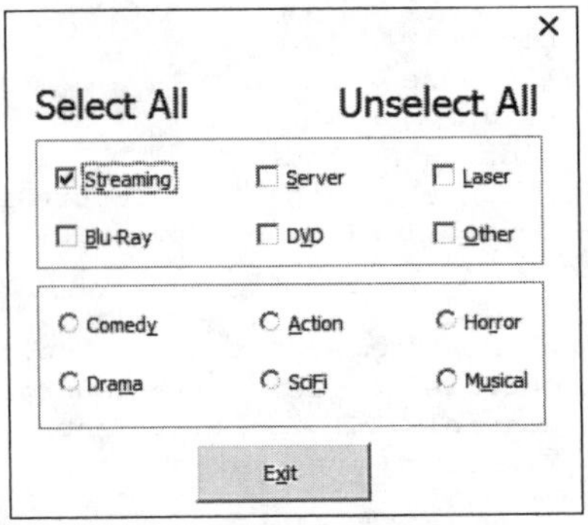

Figure 22.12
Use accelerator key combinations, like ALT+T to select Streaming, in order to give userforms the power of keyboard shortcuts.

Adding Control Tip Text

When a cursor passes over a ribbon control, tip text appears, hinting at what the control does. You can also add tip text to userforms by entering a value in the `ControlTipText` property of a control. In Figure 22.13, tip text has been added to the frame surrounding the various categories.

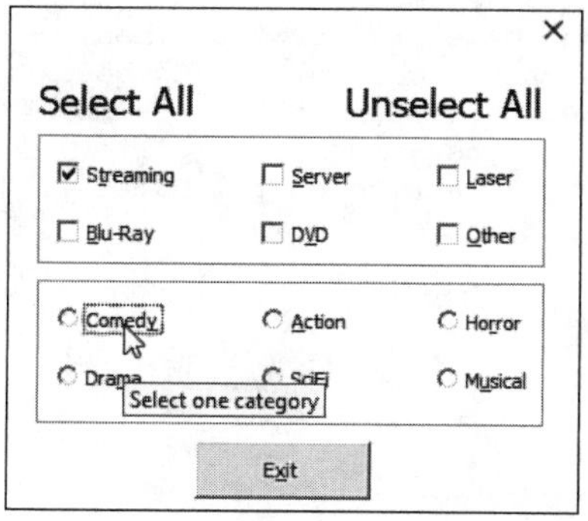

Figure 22.13
Add tips to controls to provide help to users.

Creating the Tab Order

Users can tab from one field to another. This is an automatic feature in a form. To control which field the next tab brings a user to, you can set the `TapStop` property value for each control.

The first tab stop is `0`, and the last tab stop is equal to the number of controls in a group. Remember that a group can be created with a frame. Excel does not allow multiple controls within a group to have the same tab stop. After tab stops are set, the user can use the Tab key and spacebar to select/deselect various options.

> **TIP**
> If you right-click a userform (not one of its controls) and select Tab Order, a form appears, listing all the controls. You can reorder the controls on this form to set the tab order.

Coloring the Active Control

Another method for helping a user fill out a form is to color the active field. The following example changes the color of a text box or combo box when it is active. `RaiseEvent` is used to call the events declared at the top of the class module. The code for the events is part of the userform.

Place the following code in a class module called `clsCtlColor`:

```
Public Event GetFocus()
Public Event LostFocus(ByVal strCtrl As String)
Private strPreCtr As String
```

```
Public Sub CheckActiveCtrl(objForm As MSForms.UserForm)
With objForm
    If TypeName(.ActiveControl) = "ComboBox" Or _
        TypeName(.ActiveControl) = "TextBox" Then
        strPreCtr = .ActiveControl.Name
        On Error GoTo Terminate
        Do
            DoEvents
            If .ActiveControl.Name <> strPreCtr Then
                If TypeName(.ActiveControl) = "ComboBox" Or _
                    TypeName(.ActiveControl) = "TextBox" Then
                    RaiseEvent LostFocus(strPreCtr)
                    strPreCtr = .ActiveControl.Name
                    RaiseEvent GetFocus
                End If
            End If
        Loop
    End If
End With

Terminate:
    Exit Sub

End Sub
```

Place the following code behind the userform:

```
Private WithEvents objForm As clsCtlColor

Private Sub UserForm_Initialize()
Set objForm = New clsCtlColor
End Sub
```

This sub changes the BackColor of the active control when the form is activated:

```
Private Sub UserForm_Activate()
If TypeName(ActiveControl) = "ComboBox" Or _
    TypeName(ActiveControl) = "TextBox" Then
    ActiveControl.BackColor = &HC0E0FF
End If
objForm.CheckActiveCtrl Me
End Sub
```

This sub changes the BackColor of the active control when it gets the focus:

```
Private Sub objForm_GetFocus()
ActiveControl.BackColor = &HC0E0FF
End Sub
```

This sub changes the BackColor back to white when the control loses the focus:

```
Private Sub objForm_LostFocus(ByVal strCtrl As String)
Me.Controls(strCtrl).BackColor = &HFFFFFF
End Sub
```

This sub clears the objForm when the form is closed:

```
Private Sub UserForm_QueryClose(Cancel As Integer, CloseMode As Integer)
Set objForm = Nothing
End Sub
```

CASE STUDY: MULTICOLUMN LIST BOXES

You have created several spreadsheets containing store data. The primary key of each set is the store number. The workbook is used by several people, but not everyone memorizes stores by store numbers. You need some way of letting a user select a store by its name. At the same time, you need to return the store number to be used in the code. You could use VLOOKUP or MATCH, but there is another way.

A list box can have more than one column, but not all the columns need to be visible to the user. In addition, the user can select an item from the visible list, but the list box can return the corresponding value from another column.

Draw a list box and set the ColumnCount property to 2. Set the RowSource to a two-column range called Stores. The first column of the range is the store number; the second column is the store name. At this point, the list box is displaying both columns of data. To change this, set the ColumnWidths to 0, 100—and the text automatically updates to 0 pt;100 pt. The first column is now hidden. Figure 22.14 shows the list box properties as they need to be.

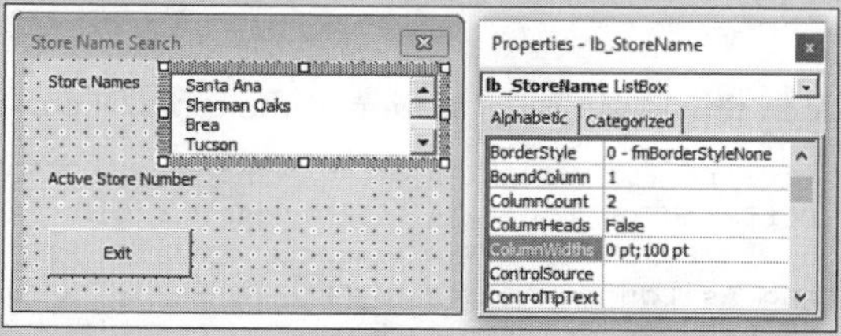

Figure 22.14
Setting the list box properties creates a two-column list box that appears to be a single column of data.

The appearance of the list box has now been set. When the user activates the list box, she sees only the store names. To return the value of the first column, set the BoundColumn property to 1. You can do this through the Properties window or through code. This example uses code to maintain the flexibility of returning the store number (see Figure 22.15):

```
Private Sub UserForm_Initialize()
    lb_StoreName.BoundColumn = 1
End Sub

Private Sub lb_StoreName_Click()
lbl_StoreNum.Caption = lb_StoreName.Value

End Sub
```

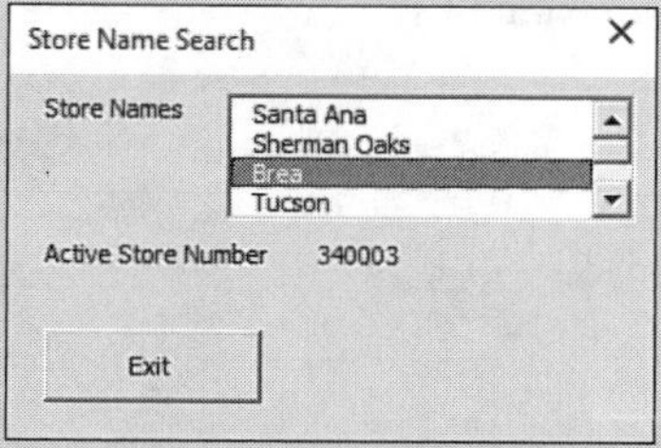

Figure 22.15
Use a two-column list box to allow the user to select a store name but return the store number.

Creating Transparent Forms

Have you ever had a form that you had to keep moving out of the way so you could see the data behind it? The following code sets the userform at a 50% transparency (see Figure 22.16) so that you can see the data behind it without moving the form somewhere else on the screen (and blocking more data).

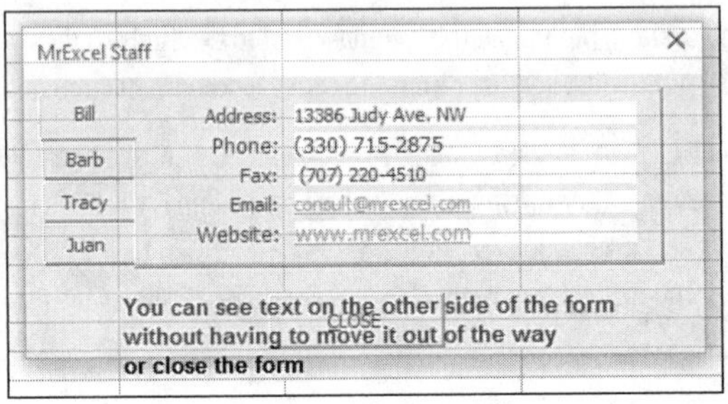

Figure 22.16
Create a 50% transparent form to view the data on the sheet behind it.

Place the following code in the declarations section at the top of the userform:

```
Private Declare PtrSafe Function GetActiveWindow Lib "USER32" () As LongPtr
Private Declare PtrSafe Function SetWindowLongPtr Lib "USER32" Alias _
    "SetWindowLongA" (ByVal hWnd As LongPtr, ByVal nIndex As Long, _
    ByVal dwNewLong As LongPtr) As LongPtr
Private Declare PtrSafe Function GetWindowLongPtr Lib "USER32" Alias _
    "GetWindowLongA" (ByVal hWnd As LongPtr, ByVal nIndex As Long) As Long
Private Declare PtrSafe Function SetLayeredWindowAttributes Lib "USER32" _
    (ByVal hWnd As LongPtr, ByVal crKey As Integer, _
    ByVal bAlpha As Integer, ByVal dwFlags As LongPtr) As LongPtr
Private Const WS_EX_LAYERED = &H80000
Private Const LWA_COLORKEY = &H1
Private Const LWA_ALPHA = &H2
Private Const GWL_EXSTYLE = &HFFEC
Dim hWnd As Long
```

Place the following code behind a toggle button. When the button is pressed in, the transparency is reduced 50%. When the user toggles the button back up, the transparency is set to 0.

```
Private Sub ToggleButton1_Click()
If ToggleButton1.Value = True Then
    '127 sets the 50% semitransparent
    SetTransparency 127
Else
    'a value of 255 is opaque and 0 is transparent
    SetTransparency 255
End If
End Sub
```

```
Private Sub SetTransparency(TRate As Integer)
Dim nIndex As Long
hWnd = GetActiveWindow
nIndex = GetWindowLong(hWnd, GWL_EXSTYLE)
SetWindowLong hWnd, GWL_EXSTYLE, nIndex Or WS_EX_LAYERED
SetLayeredWindowAttributes hWnd, 0, TRate, LWA_ALPHA
End Sub
```

Next Steps

This chapter showed you how to take advantage of API calls to perform functions that Excel can't normally do. In Chapter 23, "The Windows Application Programming Interface (API)," you'll discover more about how to access these functions and procedures that are hidden in files on your computer.

The Windows Application Programming Interface (API)

23

With all the wonderful things you can do in Excel VBA, there are some things that are out of VBA's reach or that are just too difficult to do, such as finding out what the user's screen resolution setting is. This is where the Windows application programming interface (API) can help.

If you look in the Windows System directory \ Windows\System32 (Windows NT systems), you will see many files with the extension .dll. These files, which are dynamic link libraries (DLLs), contain various functions and procedures that other programs, including VBA, can access. They give the user access to functionality used by the Windows operating system and many other programs.

> **CAUTION**
>
> Keep in mind that Windows API declarations are accessible only on computers running the Microsoft Windows operating system.

This chapter does not teach you how to write API declarations, but it does teach you the basics of interpreting and using them. Several useful examples are also included. You can find more online by searching for terms like "Windows API List."

Understanding an API Declaration

The following is an example of an API function:

```
Private Declare PtrSafe Function GetUserName _
    Lib "advapi32.dll" Alias "GetUserNameA"  _
    (ByVal lpBuffer As String, nSize As Long) _
    As LongPtr
```

There are two types of API declarations, which are structured similarly:

- **Functions**—Return information
- **Procedures**—Do something to the system

Basically, this is what you can tell about the API function above:

- It is `Private`; therefore, it can be used only in the module in which it is declared. Declare it `Public` in a standard module if you want to share it among several modules.

> **CAUTION**
>
> API declarations in standard modules can be public or private. API declarations in class modules must be private.

- It will be referred to as `GetUserName` in a program. This is the variable name assigned in the code.
- The function being used is found in `advapi32.dll`.
- The alias, `GetUserNameA`, is what the function is referred to in the DLL. This name is case sensitive and cannot be changed; it is specific to the DLL. There are often two versions of each API function. One version uses the ANSI character set and has aliases that end with the letter *A*. The other version uses the Unicode character set and has aliases that end with the letter *W*. When specifying the alias, you are telling VBA which version of the function to use.
- There are two parameters: `lpBuffer` and `nSize`. These are two arguments that the DLL function accepts.

> **CAUTION**
>
> The downside of using APIs is that there may be no errors when your code compiles or runs. This means that an incorrectly configured API call can cause your computer to crash or lock up. For this reason, it is a good idea to save often.

Using an API Declaration

Using an API is no different from calling a function or procedure you created in VBA. The following example uses the GetUserName declaration in a function to return the UserName in Excel:

```
Public Function UserName() As String
Dim sName As String * 256
Dim cChars As Long
cChars = 256
If GetUserName(sName, cChars) Then
    UserName = Left$(sName, cChars - 1)
End If
End Function

Sub ProgramRights()
Dim NameofUser As String
NameofUser = UserName
Select Case NameofUser
    Case Is = "Administrator"
        MsgBox "You have full rights to this computer"
    Case Else
        MsgBox "You have limited rights to this computer"
End Select
End Sub
```

Run the ProgramRights macro, and you learn whether you are currently signed on as administrator. The result shown in Figure 23.1 indicates that Administrator is the current username.

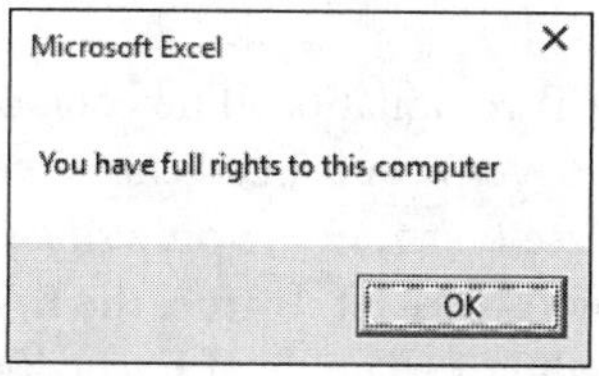

Figure 23.1
The GetUserName API function can be used to get a user's Windows login name—which is more difficult to edit than the Excel username. You can then control what rights a user has with your program.

Making 32-Bit- and 64-Bit-Compatible API Declarations

With Excel 2010, Microsoft increased the compatibility between 32-bit and 64-bit API calls by allowing 64-bit calls to work on 32-bit systems but not vice versa. This is not the case with Excel 2007, so if you're writing code that might be used in Excel 2007, you need to check the bit version and adjust accordingly.

The examples in this chapter are 64-bit API declarations and might not work in older versions of 32-bit Excel. For example, say that in a 64-bit version you have this declaration:

```
Private Declare PtrSafe Function GetWindowLongptr Lib _
"USER32" Alias _
"GetWindowLongA" (ByVal hWnd As LongPtr, ByVal nIndex As _
Long) As LongPtr
```

It will need to be changed to the following to work in the 32-bit version:

```
Private Declare Function GetWindowLongptr Lib "USER32" Alias _
"GetWindowLongA" (ByVal hWnd As Long, ByVal nIndex As _
Long) As LongPtr
```

The difference is that `PtrSafe` needs to be removed from the declaration. You might also notice that there is a new variable type in use: `LongPtr`. Actually, `LongPtr` isn't a true data type; it is `LongLong` for 64-bit environments and `Long` in 32-bit environments. This does *not* mean that you should use it throughout your code; it has a specific use, such as in API calls. But you might find yourself using it in your code for API variables. For example, if you return an API variable of `LongPtr` to another variable in your code, that variable must also be `LongPtr`.

If you need to distribute a workbook to Excel 2007 32-bit and 64-bit users, you don't need to create two workbooks. You can create an `If...Then...Else` statement in the declarations area and set up the API calls for both versions. So, for the preceding two examples, you could declare them like so:

```
#If VBA7 Or Win64 Then
Private Declare PtrSafe Function GetUserName Lib "advapi32.dll" _
    Alias "GetUserNameA" (ByVal lpBuffer As String, nSize As Long) _
    As LongPtr
#Else
Private Declare Function GetUserName Lib "advapi32.dll" _
    Alias "GetUserNameA" (ByVal lpBuffer As String, nSize As Long) _
    As LongPtr
#End If
```

The pound sign (#) is used to mark conditional compilation. The code compiles only the line(s) of code that satisfy the logic check. `#If VBA7 Or Win64` checks to see whether the current environment is using the new code base (`VBA7`, in use only since Office 2010) or whether the environment (Excel, not Windows) is 64-bit. If true, the first API declaration is processed; otherwise, the second one is used. For example, if Excel 2007 64-bit or Excel 2010 or newer is running, the first API declaration is processed, but if the environment is 32-bit Excel 2007, the second one is used. Note that in 64-bit environments, the second API declaration will be colored as an error but will compile just fine.

The change to 64-bit API calls is still novel, and there is some confusion as Microsoft continues to make changes. To help make sense of it all, Jan Karel Pieterse of JKP Application Development Services (www.jkp-ads.com) is working on an ever-growing web page that lists the proper syntax for the 64-bit declarations. You can find it at www.jkp-ads.com/articles/apideclarations.asp.

API Function Examples

The following sections provide more examples of helpful API declarations you can use in your Excel programs. Each example starts with a short description of what the function can do, followed by the actual declarations, and an example of its use.

Retrieving the Computer Name

This API function returns the computer name (that is, the name of the computer found under Computer, Computer Name):

```
Private Declare PtrSafe Function GetComputerName Lib "kernel32" Alias _
    "GetComputerNameA" (ByVal lpBuffer As String, ByRef nSize As Long) _
    As LongPtr

Private Function ComputerName() As String
Dim stBuff As String * 255, lAPIResult As LongPtr
Dim lBuffLen As Long

lBuffLen = 255
lAPIResult = GetComputerName(stBuff, lBuffLen)
If lBuffLen > 0 Then ComputerName = Left(stBuff, lBuffLen)
End Function

Sub ComputerCheck()
Dim CompName As String

CompName = ComputerName

If CompName <> "BillJelenPC" Then
    MsgBox _
    "This application does not have the right to run on this computer."
    ActiveWorkbook.Close SaveChanges:=False
End If
End Sub
```

The `ComputerCheck` macro uses an API call to get the name of the computer. In this example, the workbook refuses to open on any computer except the hard-coded computer name of the owner.

Checking Whether an Excel File Is Open on a Network

You can check whether you have a file open in Excel by trying to set the workbook to an object. If the object is `Nothing` (empty), you know that the file is not open. However, what if you want to see whether someone else on a network has the file open? The following API function returns that information:

```
Private Declare PtrSafe Function lOpen Lib "kernel32" Alias "_lopen" _
    (ByVal lpPathName As String, ByVal iReadWrite As Long) As LongPtr
Private Declare PtrSafe Function lClose Lib "kernel32" _
    Alias "_lclose" (ByVal hFile As LongPtr) As LongPtr
Private Const OF_SHARE_EXCLUSIVE = &H10

Private Function FileIsOpen(strFullPath_FileName As String) As Boolean
Dim hdlFile As LongPtr
```

23

```
Dim lastErr As Long

hdlFile = -1
hdlFile = lOpen(strFullPath_FileName, OF_SHARE_EXCLUSIVE)

If hdlFile = -1 Then
    lastErr = Err.LastDllError
Else
    lClose (hdlFile)
End If
FileIsOpen = (hdlFile = -1) And (lastErr = 32)
End Function

Sub CheckFileOpen()
If FileIsOpen("C:\XYZ Corp.xlsx") Then
    MsgBox "File is open"
Else
    MsgBox "File is not open"
End If
End Sub
```

You can call the `FileIsOpen` function with a particular path and filename as the parameter to find out whether someone has the file open.

Retrieving Display-Resolution Information

The following API function retrieves the computer's display size:

```
Declare PtrSafe Function DisplaySize Lib "user32" Alias _
    "GetSystemMetrics" (ByVal nIndex As Long) As LongPtr

Public Const SM_CXSCREEN = 0
Public Const SM_CYSCREEN = 1

Function VideoRes() As String
Dim vidWidth
Dim vidHeight

vidWidth = DisplaySize(SM_CXSCREEN)
vidHeight = DisplaySize(SM_CYSCREEN)

Select Case (vidWidth * vidHeight)
    Case 307200
        VideoRes = "640 x 480"
    Case 480000
        VideoRes = "800 x 600"
    Case 786432
        VideoRes = "1024 x 768"
    Case Else
        VideoRes = "Something else"
End Select
End Function

Sub CheckDisplayRes()
Dim VideoInfo As String
Dim Msg1 As String, Msg2 As String, Msg3 As String

VideoInfo = VideoRes
```

```
Msg1 = "Current resolution is set at " & VideoInfo & Chr(10)
Msg2 = "Optimal resolution for this application is 1024 x 768" & Chr(10)
Msg3 = "Please adjust resolution"

Select Case VideoInfo
    Case Is = "640 x 480"
        MsgBox Msg1 & Msg2 & Msg3
    Case Is = "800 x 600"
        MsgBox Msg1 & Msg2
    Case Is = "1024 x 768"
        MsgBox Msg1
    Case Else
        MsgBox Msg2 & Msg3
End Select
End Sub
```

The CheckDisplayRes macro warns the client that the display setting is not optimal for the application.

Customizing the About Dialog

If you go to Help, About Windows in File Explorer, you get a nice little About dialog with information about the File Explorer and a few system details. With the following code, you can get that window to pop up in your own program and customize a few items, as shown in Figure 23.2.

Figure 23.2
You can customize the About dialog used by Windows for your own program.

```
Declare PtrSafe Function ShellAbout Lib "shell32.dll" Alias "ShellAboutA" _
    (ByVal hwnd As LongPtr, ByVal szApp As String, ByVal szOtherStuff As _
    String, ByVal hIcon As Long) As LongPtr
Declare PtrSafe Function GetActiveWindow Lib "user32" () As LongPtr

Sub AboutMrExcel()
Dim hwnd As LongPtr
On Error Resume Next
hwnd = GetActiveWindow()
ShellAbout hwnd, Nm, "Developed by Tracy Syrstad" + vbCrLf + _
    Chr(169) + "" & " MrExcel.com Consulting" + vbCrLf + vbCrLf, 0
On Error GoTo 0
End Sub
```

Disabling the *X* for Closing a Userform

The *X* button located in the upper-right corner of a userform can be used to shut down the
form. You can capture the close event with `QueryClose`, but to prevent the button from being
active and working at all, you need an API call. The following API declarations work together
to disable that *X* and force the user to use the Close button. When the form is initialized, the
X button is disabled. After the form is closed, the *X* button is reset to normal:

```
Private Declare PtrSafe Function FindWindow Lib "user32" Alias _
    "FindWindowA" (ByVal lpClassName As String, ByVal lpWindowName _
    As String) As LongPtr
Private Declare PtrSafe Function GetSystemMenu Lib "user32" _
    (ByVal hWnd As LongPtr, ByVal bRevert As Long) As LongPtr
Private Declare PtrSafe Function DeleteMenu Lib "user32" _
    (ByVal hMenu As LongPtr, ByVal nPosition As Long, _
    ByVal wFlags As Long) As LongPtr
Private Const SC_CLOSE As Long = &HF060

Private Sub UserForm_Initialize()
Dim hWndForm As LongPtr
Dim hMenu As LongPtr
'ThunderDFrame is the class name of all userforms
hWndForm = FindWindow("ThunderDFrame", Me.Caption)
hMenu = GetSystemMenu(hWndForm, 0)
DeleteMenu hMenu, SC_CLOSE, 0&
End Sub
```

The `DeleteMenu` macro in the `UserForm_Initialize` procedure causes the *X* in the corner of
the userform to be grayed out, as shown in Figure 23.3. The client must therefore use your
programmed Close button.

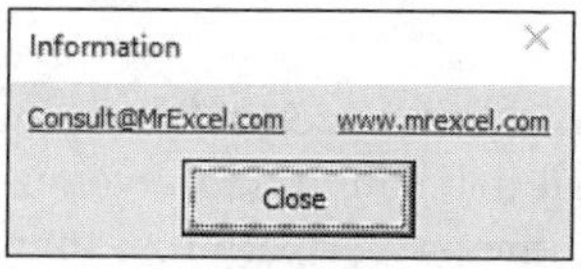

Figure 23.3
Disable the X button on a userform to force users to use the Close button to shut down the form properly and prevent them from bypassing any code attached to the Close button.

Creating a Running Timer

You can use the NOW function to get the time, but what if you need a running timer that displays the exact time as the seconds tick by? The following API declarations work together to provide this functionality. The timer is placed in cell A1 of Sheet1:

```
Public Declare PtrSafe Function SetTimer Lib "user32" _
    (ByVal hWnd As Long, ByVal nIDEvent As Long, _
    ByVal uElapse As Long, ByVal lpTimerFunc As LongPtr) As LongPtr
Public Declare PtrSafe Function KillTimer Lib "user32" _
    (ByVal hWnd As Long, ByVal nIDEvent As Long) As LongPtr
Public Declare PtrSafe Function FindWindow Lib "user32" _
    Alias "FindWindowA" (ByVal lpClassName As String, _
    ByVal lpWindowName As String) As LongPtr
Private lngTimerID As Long
Private datStartingTime As Date

Public Sub StartTimer()
StopTimer 'stop previous timer
lngTimerID = SetTimer(0, 1, 10, AddressOf RunTimer)
End Sub

Public Sub StopTimer()
Dim lRet As LongPtr, lngTID As Long

If IsEmpty(lngTimerID) Then Exit Sub

lngTID = lngTimerID
lRet = KillTimer(0, lngTID)
lngTimerID = Empty
End Sub

Private Sub RunTimer(ByVal hWnd As Long, _
    ByVal uint1 As Long, ByVal nEventId As Long, _
    ByVal dwParam As Long)
On Error Resume Next
Sheet1.Range("A1").Value = Format(Now - datStartingTime, "hh:mm:ss")
End Sub
```

Run the StartTimer macro to have the current date and time constantly updated in cell A1.

Playing Sounds

Have you ever wanted to play a sound to warn users or congratulate them? To do this, you can add a sound object to a sheet and then call that sound. However, it would be easier to use the following API declaration and specify the proper path to a sound file:

```
Public Declare PtrSafe Function PlayWavSound Lib "winmm.dll" _
    Alias "sndPlaySoundA" (ByVal LpszSoundName As String, _
    ByVal uFlags As Long) As LongPtr

Public Sub PlaySound()
Dim SoundName As String

SoundName = "C:\Windows\Media\Chimes.wav"
PlayWavSound SoundName, 0

End Sub
```

Next Steps

In Chapter 24, "Handling Errors," you'll find out about error handling. In a perfect world, you want to be able to hand off your applications to a co-worker, leave for vacation, and not have to worry about an unhandled error appearing while you are on the beach. Chapter 24 discusses how to handle obvious and not-so-obvious errors.

Handling Errors

24

Errors are bound to happen. Even when you test and retest your code, after a report is put into daily production and used for hundreds of days, something unexpected will eventually happen. Your goal should be to try to head off obscure errors as you code. For this reason, you should always be thinking of what unexpected things could happen someday that could make your code not work.

What Happens When an Error Occurs?

When VBA encounters an error and you have no error-checking code in place, the program stops and presents you or your client with the 1004 runtime error message, as shown in Figure 24.1.

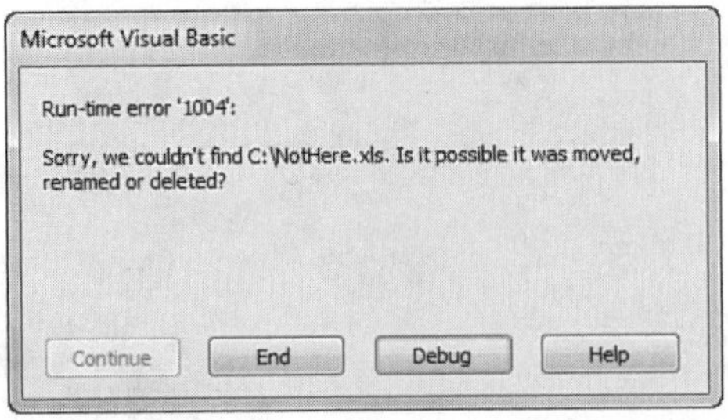

Figure 24.1
With an unhandled error in an unprotected module, you get a choice to end or debug.

Microsoft Visual Basic

Run-time error '1004':

Sorry, we couldn't find C:\NotHere.xls. Is it possible it was moved, renamed or deleted?

| Continue | End | Debug | Help |

When presented with the choice to end or debug, you should click Debug. (If Debug is grayed out, then someone has protected the VBA code, and you will have to call the developer.) The VB Editor highlights in yellow the line that caused the error. When you hover the cursor over any variable, you see the current value of the variable, which provides a lot of information about what could have caused the error (see Figure 24.2).

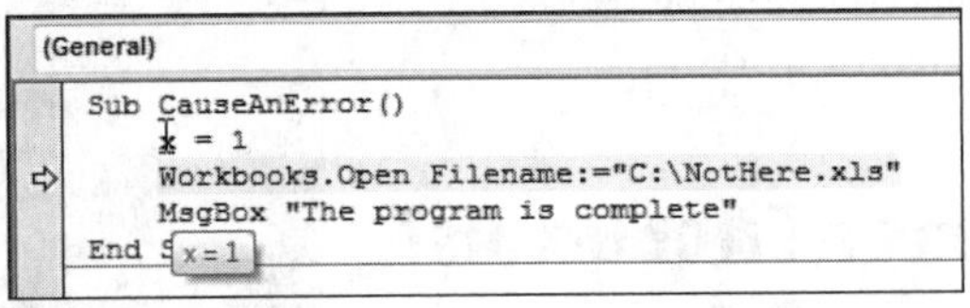

Figure 24.2
After clicking Debug, the macro is in break mode. Hover the cursor over a variable; after a few seconds, the current value of the variable is shown.

```
(General)

    Sub CauseAnError()
        x = 1
        Workbooks.Open Filename:="C:\NotHere.xls"
        MsgBox "The program is complete"
    End S x = 1
```

Especially in older versions, Excel has been notorious for returning error messages that are not very meaningful. For example, dozens of situations can cause a 1004 error. Seeing the offending line highlighted in yellow and examining the current value of any variables helps you discover the real cause of an error. However, many error messages in Excel 2016— including the VBA error messages—are more meaningful than the equivalent message in Excel 2010.

After examining the line in error, click the Reset button to stop execution of the macro. The Reset button is the square button under the Run item in the main menu, as shown in Figure 24.3.

Figure 24.3
The Reset button looks like the Stop button in the set of three buttons that resembles a DVD control panel.

If you fail to click Reset to end the macro and then attempt to run another macro, you are presented with the annoying error message shown in Figure 24.4. The message is annoying because you start in Excel, but when this message window is displayed, the screen automatically switches to display the VB Editor. You can see the Reset button in the background, but you cannot click it due to the message box being displayed. However, immediately after you click OK to close the message box, you are returned to the Excel user interface instead of being left in the VB Editor. Because this error message occurs quite often, it would be more convenient if you could be returned to the VB Editor after clicking OK.

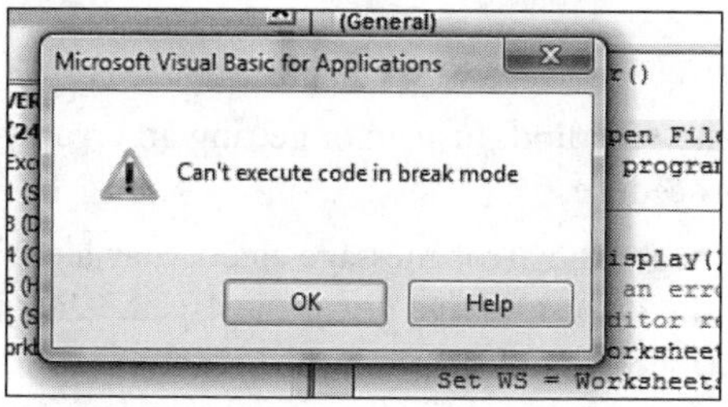

Figure 24.4
This message appears if you forget to click Reset to end a debug session and then attempt to run another macro.

A Misleading Debug Error in Userform Code

After you click Debug, the line highlighted as the error can be misleading in some situation. For example, suppose you call a macro that displays a userform. Somewhere in the userform code, an error occurs. When you click Debug, instead of showing the problem inside the userform code, Excel highlights the line in the original macro that displayed the userform. Follow these steps to find the real error:

1. After the error message box shown in Figure 24.5 is displayed, click the Debug button.

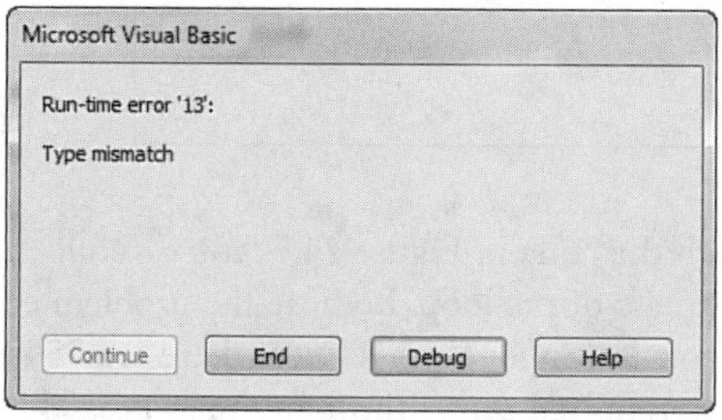

Figure 24.5
Select Debug in response to this error 13.

You see that the error allegedly occurred on a line that shows a userform, as shown in Figure 24.6. Because you have read this chapter, you know that this is not the line in error.

Figure 24.6
The line in error is indicated as the `frmChoose.Show` line.

```
Sub PrepareAndDisplay()
    ' sometimes an error happens in a userform
    ' yet the editor reports it as the next line
    Dim WS As Worksheet
    Set WS = Worksheets("Sheet1")

    FinalRow = WS.Cells(Rows.Count, 1).End(xlUp).Row
    WS.Cells(1, 1).Sort _
        Key1:=WS.Cells(1, 1), Order1:=xlAscending, Header:=xlYes

    frmChoose.Show

    MsgBox "Macro complete"

End Sub
```

2. Press F8 to execute the `Show` method. Instead of getting an error, you are taken into the `Userform_Initialize` procedure.

3. Keep pressing F8 until you get the error message again. Stay alert because as soon as you encounter the error, the error message box is displayed. Click Debug, and you are returned to the `userform.Show` line. It is particularly difficult to follow the code when the error occurs on the other side of a long loop, as shown in Figure 24.7.

24

Figure 24.7
With 25 items to add to the list box, you must press F8 53 times to get through this three-line loop.

```
UserForm
    Private Sub CommandButton1_Click()
        Unload Me
    End Sub


    Private Sub UserForm_Initialize()
        Dim WS As Worksheet
        Set WS = Worksheets("Sheet1")

        FinalRow = WS.Cells(Rows.Count, 1).End(xlUp).Row
        For i = 2 To FinalRow
            Me.ListBox1.AddItem WS.Cells(i, 1)
        Next i

        ' The next line is actually the line that causes an error
        Me.ListBox1(0).Selected = True



    End Sub
```

Imagine trying to step through the code in Figure 24.7. You carefully press F8 5 times with no problems through the first pass of the loop. Because the problem could be in future iterations through the loop, you continue to press F8. If there are 25 items to add to the list box, 48 more presses of F8 are required to get through the loop safely. Each time before pressing F8, you should mentally note that you are about to run some specific line.

At the point shown in Figure 24.7, the next press of the F8 key displays the error and returns you to the `frmChoose.Show` line back in Module1. This is an annoying situation.

At that point, you need to start pressing F8 again. If you can recall the general area where the debug error occurred, click the mouse cursor in a line right before that section and use Ctrl+F8 to run the macro up to the cursor. Alternatively, right-click that line and choose Run to Cursor.

Sometimes an error will occur within a loop. Add `Debug.Print i` inside the loop and use the Immediate pane (which you open by pressing Ctrl+G) to locate which time through the loop caused the problem.

Basic Error Handling with the On Error GoTo Syntax

The basic error-handling option is to tell VBA that in case of an error, you want to have code branch to a specific area of the macro. In this area, you might have special code that alerts users of the problem and enables them to react.

A typical scenario is to add the error-handling routine at the end of the macro. To set up an error handler, follow these steps:

1. After the last code line of the macro, insert the code line `Exit Sub`. This makes sure that the execution of the macro does not continue into the error handler.

2. After the `Exit Sub` line, add a label. A label is a name followed by a colon. For example, you might create a label called `MyErrorHandler:`.

3. Write the code to handle the error. If you want to return control of the macro to the line after the one that caused the error, use the statement `Resume Next`.

In your macro, just before the line that might likely cause the error, add a line reading `On Error GoTo MyErrorHandler`. Note that in this line, you do not include the colon after the label name.

Immediately after the line of code that you suspect will cause the error, add code to turn off the special error handler. Because this is not intuitive, it tends to confuse people. The code to cancel any special error handling is `On Error GoTo 0`. There is no label named 0. Instead, this line is a fictitious line that instructs Excel to go back to the normal state of displaying the debug error message when an error is encountered. This is why it is important to cancel the error handling.

> **NOTE**
>
> The following code includes a special error handler to handle the necessary action if the file has been moved or is missing:
>
> ```
> Sub HandleAnError()
>     Dim MyFile as Variant
>     ' Set up a special error handler
>     On Error GoTo FileNotThere
>     Workbooks.Open Filename:="C:\NotHere.xls"
>     ' If we get here, cancel the special error handler
>     On Error GoTo 0
>     MsgBox "The program is complete"
>
>     ' The macro is done. Use Exit sub, otherwise the macro
>     ' execution WILL continue into the error handler
>     Exit Sub
>
>     ' Set up a name for the Error handler
> FileNotThere:
>     MyPrompt = "There was an error opening the file. " & _
>         "It is possible the file has been moved. " & _
>         "Click OK to browse for the file, or click " & _
>         "Cancel to end the program"
>     Ans = MsgBox(Prompt:=MyPrompt, Buttons:=vbOKCancel)
>     If Ans = vbCancel Then Exit Sub
>
>     ' The client clicked OK. Let him browse for the file
>     MyFile = Application.GetOpenFilename
>     If MyFile = False Then Exit Sub
>
>     ' If the 2nd file is corrupt? Do not recursively throw
>     ' back into this error handler. Just stop the program.
>     On Error GoTo 0
>     Workbooks.Open MyFile
>     ' If we get here, then return back to the original
>     ' macro, to the line after the the error.
>     Resume Next
>
> End Sub
> ```
>
> You definitely do not want this error handler invoked for another error later in the macro, such as a divide-by-zero error.

> **NOTE**
>
> It is possible to have more than one error handler at the end of a macro. Make sure that each error handler ends with either `Resume Next` or `Exit Sub` so that macro execution does not accidentally move into the next error handler.

Generic Error Handlers

Some developers like to direct any error to a generic error handler to make use of the `Err` object. This object has properties for error number and description. You can offer this information to the client and prevent her from getting a debug message. Here is the code to do this:

```
    On Error GoTo HandleAny
    Sheets(9).Select

    Exit Sub

HandleAny:
    Msg = "We encountered " & Err.Number & " - " & Err.Description
    MsgBox Msg
    Exit Sub
```

Handling Errors by Choosing to Ignore Them

Some errors can simply be ignored. For example, suppose you are going to use VBA to write out an index.html file. Your code erases any existing `index.html` file from a folder before writing out the next file.

The `Kill (FileName)` statement returns an error if `FileName` does not exist. This probably is not something you need to worry about. After all, you are trying to delete the file, so you probably do not care whether someone already deleted it before running the macro. In this case, tell Excel to just skip over the offending line and resume macro execution with the next line. The code to do this is `On Error Resume Next`:

```
Sub WriteHTML()
    MyFile = "C:\Index.html"
    On Error Resume Next
    Kill MyFile
    On Error Goto 0
    Open MyFile for Output as #1
    ' etc...
End Sub
```

> **NOTE**
>
> Be careful with `On Error Resume Next`. You can use it selectively in situations in which you know that the error can be ignored. You should immediately return error checking to normal after the line that might cause an error with `On Error GoTo 0`.
>
> If you attempt to have `On Error Resume Next` skip an error that cannot be skipped, the macro immediately steps out of the current macro. If you have a situation in which `MacroA` calls `MacroB`, and `MacroB` encounters a nonskippable error, the program jumps out of `MacroB` and continues with the next line in `MacroA`. This is rarely a good thing.

VBA code to handle printer settings runs much faster if you turn off `PrintCommunication` at the beginning of the preceding code and turn it back on at the end of the code. This trick was new in Excel 2010. Before that, Excel would pause for almost a half-second during each line of print setting code. Now the whole block of code runs in less than a second.

CASE STUDY: OVERLOOKING PAGE SETUP PROBLEMS

When you record a macro and perform page setup, even if you change just one item in the Page Setup dialog, the macro recorder records two dozen settings for you. These settings notoriously differ from printer to printer. For example, if you record the `PageSetup` on a system with a color printer, it might record a setting for `.BlackAndWhite = True`. This setting will fail on another system on which the printer does not offer the choice. Your printer might offer a `.PrintQuality = 600` setting. If the client's printer offers only a 300 resolution setting, this code fails. For this reason, you should surround the entire `PageSetup` with `On Error Resume Next` to ensure that most settings happen but the trivial ones that fail do not cause runtime errors. Here is how to do this:

```
On Error Resume Next
Application.PrintCommunication = False
With ActiveSheet.PageSetup
    .PrintTitleRows = ""
    .PrintTitleColumns = ""
End With
 ActiveSheet.PageSetup.PrintArea = "$A$1:$L$27"
 With ActiveSheet.PageSetup
    .LeftHeader = ""
    .CenterHeader = ""
    .RightHeader = ""
    .LeftFooter = ""
    .CenterFooter = ""
    .RightFooter = ""
    .LeftMargin = Application.InchesToPoints(0.25)
    .RightMargin = Application.InchesToPoints(0.25)
    .TopMargin = Application.InchesToPoints(0.75)
    .BottomMargin = Application.InchesToPoints(0.5)
    .HeaderMargin = Application.InchesToPoints(0.5)
    .FooterMargin = Application.InchesToPoints(0.5)
    .PrintHeadings = False
    .PrintGridlines = False
    .PrintComments = xlPrintNoComments
    .PrintQuality = 300
    .CenterHorizontally = False
    .CenterVertically = False
    .Orientation = xlLandscape
    .Draft = False
    .PaperSize = xlPaperLetter
    .FirstPageNumber = xlAutomatic
    .Order = xlDownThenOver
    .BlackAndWhite = False
    .Zoom = False
    .FitToPagesWide = 1
    .FitToPagesTall = False
    .PrintErrors = xlPrintErrorsDisplayed
End With
Application.PrintCommunication = True
On Error GoTo 0
```

Suppressing Excel Warnings

Some messages appear even if you have set Excel to ignore errors. For example, try to delete a worksheet using code, and you still get the message "You can't undo deleting sheets, and you might be removing some data. If you don't need it, click Delete." This is annoying. You do not want your clients to have to answer this warning; it gives them a chance to choose not to delete the sheet your macro wants to delete. In fact, this is not an error but an alert. To suppress all alerts and force Excel to take the default action, use `Application.DisplayAlerts = False`, like this:

```
Sub DeleteSheet()
    Application.DisplayAlerts = False
    Worksheets("Sheet2").Delete
    Application.DisplayAlerts = True
End Sub
```

Encountering Errors on Purpose

Because programmers hate errors, this concept might seem counterintuitive, but errors are not always bad. Sometimes it is faster to simply encounter an error.

Suppose, for example, that you want to find out whether the active workbook contains a worksheet named Data. To find this out without causing an error, you could use the following eight lines of code:

```
DataFound = False
For Each ws in ActiveWorkbook.Worksheets
    If ws.Name = "Data" then
        DataFound = True
        Exit For
    End if
Next ws
If not DataFound then Sheets.Add.Name = "Data"
```

If your workbook has 128 worksheets, the program loops through 128 times before deciding that the data worksheet is missing.

An alternative is to try to reference the Data worksheet. If you have error checking set to `Resume Next`, the code runs, and the `Err` object is assigned a number other than zero:

```
On Error Resume Next
X = Worksheets("Data").Name
If Err.Number <> 0 then Sheets.Add.Name = "Data"
On Error GoTo 0
```

This code runs much faster. Errors usually make programmers cringe. However, in this case and in many other cases, the errors are perfectly acceptable.

Training Your Clients

Suppose you are developing code for a client across the globe or for the administrative assistant so that he can run the code while you are on vacation. In both cases, you might find yourself trying to debug code remotely while you are on the telephone with the client.

For this reason, it is important to train clients about the difference between an error and a simple `MsgBox`. Even though a `MsgBox` is a planned message, it still appears out of the blue with a beep. Teach your users that error messages are bad, but not everything that pops up is an error message. For example, I had a client who kept reporting to her boss that she was getting an error from my program. In reality, she was getting an informational `MsgBox` message. Both debug errors and `MsgBox` messages beep at the user, and this user didn't know that there's a difference between them.

Train clients to call you while any debug messages they get are still onscreen. This way you can get the error number and description. You also can ask the client to click Debug and tell you the module name, the procedure name, and which line is in yellow. Armed with this information, you can usually figure out what is going on. Without this information, it is unlikely that you will be able to resolve the problem. Getting a call from a client saying that there was a 1004 error is of little help because 1004 is a catchall error that can mean any number of things.

Errors While Developing Versus Errors Months Later

When you have just written code that you are running for the first time, you expect errors. In fact, you might decide to step through code line by line to watch the progress of the code the first time through.

It is another thing to have a program that has been running daily in production suddenly stop working because of an error. That can be perplexing. The code has been working for months, so why did it suddenly stop working today? It is easy to blame the client. However, when you get right down to it, it is really the fault of developers for not considering the possibilities.

The following sections describe a couple of common problems that can strike an application months later.

Runtime Error 9: Subscript Out of Range

You set up an application for a client and you provided a Menu worksheet where some settings are stored. Then one day this client reports getting the error message shown in Figure 24.8.

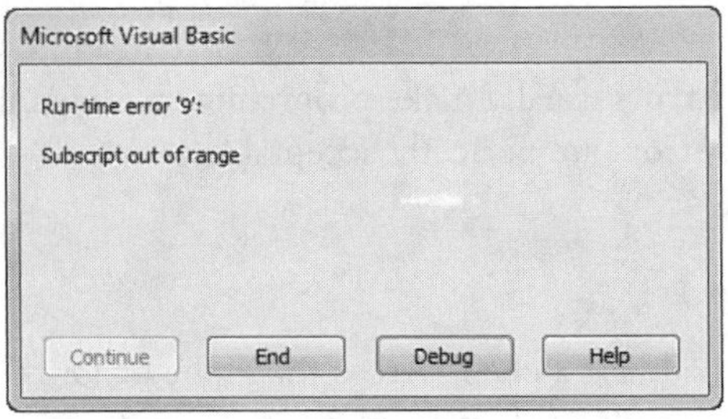

Figure 24.8
Runtime error 9 often occurs when you expect a worksheet to be there, but it has been deleted or renamed by the client.

```
Microsoft Visual Basic

Run-time error '9':

Subscript out of range




   Continue        End         Debug        Help
```

Your code expected a worksheet named Menu. For some reason, the client either accidentally deleted the worksheet or renamed it. When the client then tried to select the sheet, she received an error:

```
Sub GetSettings()
    ThisWorkbook.Worksheets("Menu").Select
    x = Range("A1").Value
End Sub
```

This is a classic situation where you cannot believe that the client would do something so crazy. After you have been burned by this one a few times, you might go to lengths like implementing this code to prevent an unhandled debug error:

```
Sub GetSettings()
    On Error Resume Next
    x = ThisWorkbook.Worksheets("Menu").Name
    If Not Err.Number = 0 Then
        MsgBox "Expected to find a Menu worksheet, but it is missing"
        Exit Sub
    End If
    On Error GoTo 0

    ThisWorkbook.Worksheets("Menu").Select
    x = Range("A1").Value
End Sub
```

Runtime Error 1004: Method Range of Object Global Failed

You have code that imports a text file each day. You expect the text file to end with a Total row. After importing the text, you want to convert all the detail rows to italic.

The following code works fine for months:

```
Sub SetReportInItalics()
    TotalRow = Cells(Rows.Count,1).End(xlUp).Row
    FinalRow = TotalRow - 1
    Range("A1:A" & FinalRow).Font.Italic = True
End Sub
```

Then one day, the client calls with the error message shown in Figure 24.9.

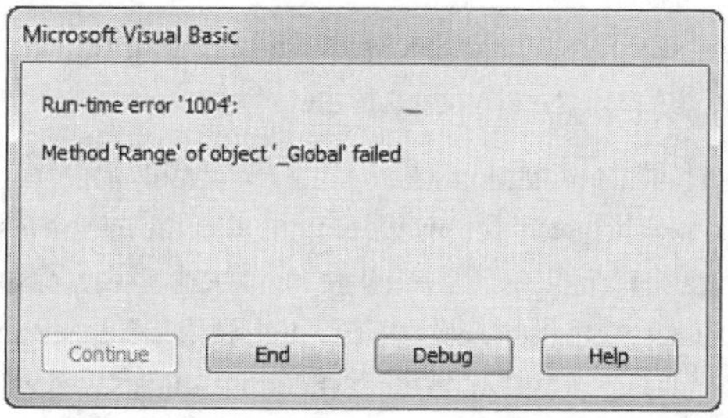

Figure 24.9
Runtime error 1004 can be caused by a number of things.

```
Microsoft Visual Basic

Run-time error '1004':

Method 'Range' of object '_Global' failed

    Continue        End        Debug        Help
```

Upon examining the code, you discover that something bizarre went wrong when the text file was transferred via FTP to the client that day. The text file ended up as an empty file.

Because the worksheet was empty, `TotalRow` was determined to be row 1. If you assume that the last detail row was `TotalRow - 1`, the code is set up to attempt to format row 0, which clearly does not exist.

After an episode like this, you find yourself writing code that preemptively looks for this situation:

```
Sub SetReportInItalics()
    TotalRow = Cells(Rows.Count,1).End(xlUp).Row
    FinalRow = TotalRow - 1
    If FinalRow > 0 Then
        Range("A1:A" & FinalRow).Font.Italic = True
    Else
        MsgBox "It appears the file is empty today. Check the FTP pro-
cess"
    End If
End Sub
```

The Ills of Protecting Code

It is possible to lock a VBA project so that it cannot be viewed. However, doing so is not recommended. When code is protected and an error is encountered, your user is presented with an error message but no opportunity to debug. The Debug button is there, but it is grayed out and useless in helping you discover the problem.

Further, the Excel VBA protection scheme is horribly easy to break. Programmers in Estonia offer $40 software that lets you unlock any project. Therefore, you need to understand that office VBA code is not secure—and then get over it.

If you absolutely need to truly protect your code, invest $100 for a license to Unviewable+ VBA Project from Esoteric Software. This crowd-funded software allows you to create a compiled version of a workbook where no one will be able to view the VBA. For more details, visit http://mrx.cl/hidevba.

CASE STUDY: PASSWORD CRACKING

Password-hacking schemes were very easy in Excel 97 and Excel 2000. The password-cracking software could immediately locate the actual password in the VBA project and report it to the software user.

Then, in Excel 2002, Microsoft offered a brilliant protection scheme that temporarily appeared to foil the password-cracking utilities. The password was tightly encrypted. For several months after the release of Excel 2002, password-cracking programs had to try brute-force combinations. The software could crack an easy password like blue in 10 minutes. However, given a 24-character password like *A6%kJJ542(9$GgU44#2drt8, the program would take 20 hours to find the password. This was a fun annoyance to foist upon other VBA programmers who would potentially break into your code.

However, the next version of the password-cracking software was able to break a 24-character password in Excel 2002 in about 2 seconds. When I tested my 24-character password-protected project, the password utility quickly told me that my password was XVII. I thought this was certainly wrong, but after testing, I found the project had a new password of XVII. Yes, this latest version of the software resorted to another approach. Instead of using brute force to crack the password, it simply wrote a new random four-character password to the project and saved the file.

Now, this causes an embarrassing problem for whoever cracked the password, and I'll explain why.

The developer has a sign on his wall reminding him that the password is *A6%kJJ542(9$GgU44#2drt8. However, in the cracked version of the file, the password is now XVII. If there is a problem with the cracked file and it is sent back to the developer, the developer can no longer open the file. The only person getting anything from this is the programmer in Estonia who wrote the cracking software.

There are not enough Excel VBA developers in the world, and there are more projects than there are programmers. In my circle of developer friends, we acknowledge that business prospects slip through the cracks because we are too busy with other customers. Therefore, the situation of a newbie developer is common. In this scenario, this new developer does an adequate job of writing code for a customer and then locks the VBA project.

The customer needs some changes. The original developer does the work. A few weeks later, the developer delivers some requested changes. A month later, the customer needs more work. Either the developer is busy with other projects or has underpriced these maintenance jobs and has more lucrative work he is attending to instead. The client tries to contact the programmer a few times before realizing he needs to get the project fixed by someone else and calls another developer—you!

You get the code. It is protected. You break the password and see who wrote the code. You have no interest in stealing the new developer's customer. In fact, you prefer to do this one job and then have the customer return to the original developer. However, because of the password hacking, you have created a situation in which the two developers—you and the original one—have different passwords. Your only choice is to remove the password entirely. This will tip off the other developer that someone else has been in his code. Maybe you could try to placate the other developer with a few lines of comment that the password was removed after the customer could not contact the original developer.

More Problems with Passwords

Office 2013 introduced a new SHA-2 class SHA512 algorithm to calculate encryption keys. This algorithm causes significant slowdowns in macros that protect or unprotect sheets.

The password scheme for any version of Excel from 2002 forward is incompatible with Excel 97. If you protected code in Excel 2002, you cannot unlock the project in Excel 97. As your application is given to more employees in a company, you will invariably find an employee using Excel 97. Of course, that user will come up with a runtime error. However, if you locked the project in Excel 2002 or newer, you are not able to unlock the project in Excel 97, which means you cannot debug the program in Excel 97.

Bottom line: Locking code causes more trouble than it is worth.

> **NOTE** If you are using a combination of Excel 2003 through Excel 2016, the passwords transfer easily back and forth between versions. This holds true even if the file is saved as an .xlsm file and opened in Excel 2003 using the file converter. You can change code in Excel 2003, save the file, and successfully round-trip back to Excel 2016.

Errors Caused by Different Versions

Microsoft improves VBA in every version of Excel. Pivot table creation was improved dramatically between Excel 97 and Excel 2000. Sparklines and slicers were new in Excel 2010. The Data Model was introduced in Excel 2013. Power Query was built in to the object model in Excel 2016.

The `TrailingMinusNumbers` parameter was new in Excel 2002. This means that if you write code in Excel 2016 and then send the code to a client with Excel 2000, that user gets a compile error as soon as she tries to run any code that's in the same module as the offending code. For this reason, you need to consider this application in two modules.

Module1 has macros `ProcA`, `ProcB`, and `ProcC`. Module2 has macros `ProcD` and `ProcE`. It happens that `ProcE` has an `ImportText` method with the `TrailingMinusNumbers` parameter.

The client can run `ProcA` and `ProcB` on the Excel 2000 machine without problem. As soon as she tries to run `ProcD`, she gets a compile error reported in `ProcD` because Excel tries to compile all of Module2 when she tries to run code in that module. This can be incredibly misleading: An error being reported when the client runs `ProcD` is actually caused by an error in `ProcE`.

One solution is to have access to every supported version of Excel and test the code in all versions.

Macintosh users will believe that their version of Excel is the same as Excel for Windows. Microsoft promised compatibility of files, but that promise ends in the Excel user interface. VBA code is not compatible between Windows and the Mac. Excel VBA on the Mac in Excel 2016 is close to Excel 2016 VBA but annoyingly different. Further, anything you do with the Windows API is not going to work on a Mac.

Next Steps

In this chapter you've learned how to make your code more bulletproof for your clients. In Chapter 25, "Customizing the Ribbon to Run Macros," you find out how to customize the ribbon to allow your clients to enjoy a professional user interface.

Customizing the Ribbon to Run Macros

25

One of the biggest changes in Excel 2007 was the replacement of command bars and menus with the ribbon, a colorful bar of buttons and drop-downs across the top of the application. Unlike the command bars of old, a ribbon isn't designed via VBA code. Instead, if you want to modify the ribbon and add your own tab, you need to modify the Excel file itself, which isn't as impossible as it sounds. The new Excel file is actually a zipped file, containing various files and folders. All you need to do is unzip it, make your changes, and you're done. Okay, it's not *that* simple—a few more steps are involved—but it's not impossible.

Before beginning, go to the File tab and select Options, Advanced, General and select Show Add-in User Interface Errors. This allows error messages to appear so that you can troubleshoot errors in your custom toolbar.

➡ **See** the "Troubleshooting Error Messages" section, **p. 500**, for more details.

> **┌ CAUTION ──**
>
> Unlike when programming in the VB Editor, you won't have any assistance with automatic correction of letter case; and the XML code—which is what the ribbon code is—is very particular. Note the case of the XML-specific words; for example, for `id`, using `ID` will generate an error.

One thing to keep in mind is that with the change to the single-document interface (SDI) in Excel 2013, the custom ribbon tab attached to a workbook is visible only when that workbook is active. When you activate another workbook, the tab will not appear on the ribbon. The exception is with an add-in; its custom ribbon is visible on any workbook open after the add-in is opened.

➥ See Chapter 28, "What's New in Excel 2016 and What's Changed," for more information on SDI.

➥ See Chapter 26, "Creating Add-ins," for more information on creating an add-in.

> **NOTE**
>
> The original `CommandBars` object in legacy Excel still works, but the customized menus and toolbars are now all placed on the Add-ins tab.

Where to Add Code: The customui Folder and File

Create a folder called customui. This folder will contain the elements of your custom ribbon tab. Within the folder, create a text file and call it customUI14.xml, as shown in Figure 25.1. Open the XML file in a text editor; either Notepad or WordPad will work.

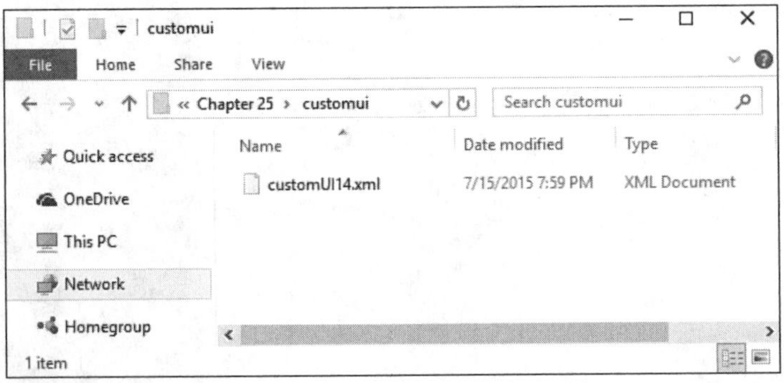

Figure 25.1
Create a customuUI14.xml file within a customui folder.

> **TIP**
>
> My favorite text editor is Notepad ++ by Don Ho (see www.notepad-plus-plus.org). Like the VB Editor, it colors XML-specific syntax after you choose XML as the language you're typing. It also has a lot of other useful tools.

Insert the basic structure for the XML code, shown here, into your XML file. For every opening tag grouping, such as `<ribbon>`, there must be a closing tag, `</ribbon>`:

```
<customUI xmlns="http://schemas.microsoft.com/office/2009/07/customui">
  <ribbon startFromScratch="false">
    <tabs>

      <!-- your ribbon controls here -->

    </tabs>
  </ribbon>
</customUI>
```

`startFromScratch` is optional and has a default value of `false`. You use it to tell the code the other tabs in Excel will not be shown; only yours will be shown. `true` means to show only your tab; `false` means to show your tab and all the other tabs.

> **CAUTION**
>
> Note the case of the letters in `startFromScratch`—the small *s* at the beginning followed by the capital *F* in `From` and capital *S* in `Scratch`. It is crucial that you not deviate from this.

The `<!-- your ribbon controls here -->` you see in the previous code is commented text. Just enter your comments between `<!--` and `-->`, and the program ignores the line when it runs.

> **NOTE**
>
> If you're creating a ribbon that needs to be Excel 2007 compatible, you need to use the following schema: http://schemas.microsoft.com/office/2006/01/customui. Also, where you see customUI14, use customUI.

Creating a Tab and a Group

Before you can add a control to a tab, you need to identify the tab and group. A tab can hold many different controls, which you can group together, like the Font group on the Home tab.

Name your tab My First Ribbon and add a group called My Programs to it, like this (see Figure 25.2):

```
<customUI xmlns="http://schemas.microsoft.com/office/2009/07/customui">
  <ribbon startFromScratch="false">
    <tabs>
      <tab id="CustomTab" label="My First Ribbon">
        <group id="CustomGroup" label="My Programs">

          <!-- your ribbon controls here -->

        </group>
```

```
        </tab>
      </tabs>
    </ribbon>
  </customUI>
```

id is a unique identifier for the control (in this case, the tab and group). label is the text you want to appear on your ribbon for the specified control.

Adding a Control to a Ribbon

After you've set up the ribbon and group, you can add controls. Depending on the type of control, there are different attributes you can include in your XML code. (Refer to Table 25.1 for more information on various controls and their attributes.)

The following code adds a normal-sized button with the text Click to Run to the Reports group and runs the sub HelloWorld when the button is clicked (see Figure 25.2):

```
<customUI xmlns="http://schemas.microsoft.com/office/2009/07/customui">
  <ribbon startFromScratch="false">
    <tabs>
      <tab id="CustomTab" label="My First Ribbon">
        <group id="CustomGroup" label="My Programs">

          <button id="button1" label="Click to run"
              onAction="Module1.HelloWorld" size="normal"/>

        </group>
      </tab>
    </tabs>
  </ribbon>
</customUI>
```

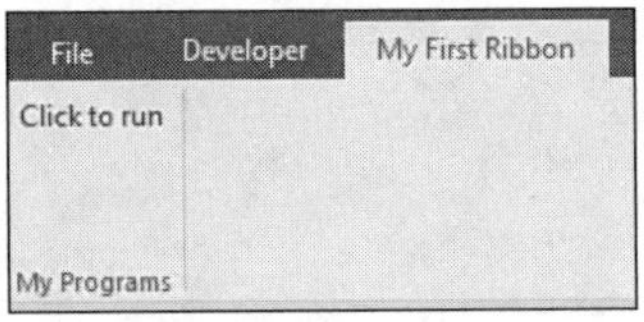

Figure 25.2
Run a program with a click of a button on your custom ribbon.

File	Developer	My First Ribbon
Click to run		
My Programs		

The properties of the button include id, a unique identifier for the control button and label, which holds the text you want to appear on your button. size, which is the size of the button, has a default value of normal; the other option is large. onAction is the sub, HelloWorld, to call when the button is clicked. The sub, shown here, goes in a standard module, Module1, in the workbook:

```
Sub HelloWorld(control As IRibbonControl)
MsgBox "Hello World"
End Sub
```

Notice the argument control `As IRibbonControl`. This is the standard argument for a sub, and it is called by a button control via the `onAction` attribute. Table 25.2 lists the required arguments for other attributes and controls.

Table 25.1   Ribbon Control Attributes

Attribute	Type or Value	Description
description	String	Specifies description text displayed in menus when the `itemSize` attribute is set to `Large`.
enabled	true, false	Specifies whether the control is enabled.
getContent	Callback	Retrieves XML content that describes a dynamic menu.
getDescription	Callback	Gets the description of a control.
getEnabled	Callback	Gets the enabled state of a control.
getImage	Callback	Gets the image for a control.
getImageMso	Callback	Gets a built-in control's icon by using the control ID.
getItemCount	Callback	Gets the number of items to be displayed in a combo box, drop-down list, or gallery.
getItemID	Callback	Gets the ID for a specific item in a combo box, drop-down list, or gallery.
getItemImage	Callback	Gets the image of a combo box, drop-down list, or gallery.
getItemLabel	Callback	Gets the label of a combo box, drop-down list, or gallery.
getItemScreentip	Callback	Gets the screentip for a combo box, drop-down list, or gallery.
getItemSupertip	Callback	Gets the enhanced screentip for a combo box, drop-down list, or gallery.
getKeytip	Callback	Gets the keytip for a control.
getLabel	Callback	Gets the label for a control.
getPressed	Callback	Gets a value that indicates whether a toggle button is pressed or not pressed. Gets a value that indicates whether a check box is selected or cleared.
getScreentip	Callback	Gets the screentip for a control.
getSelectedItemID	Callback	Gets the ID of the selected item in a drop-down list or gallery.
getSelectedItemIndex	Callback	Gets the index of the selected item in a drop-down list or gallery.
getShowImage	Callback	Gets a value that specifies whether to display the control image.
getShowLabel	Callback	Gets a value that specifies whether to display the control label.

25

Attribute	Type or Value	Description
getSize	Callback	Gets a value that specifies the size of a control (normal or large).
getSupertip	Callback	Gets a value that specifies the enhanced screentip for a control.
getText	Callback	Gets the text to be displayed in the edit portion of a text box or edit box.
getTitle	Callback	Gets the text to be displayed (rather than a horizontal line) for a menu separator.
getVisible	Callback	Gets a value that specifies whether the control is visible.
id	String	Acts as a user-defined unique identifier for the control (and is mutually exclusive with idMso and idQ—so specify only one of these values).
idMso	Control id	Acts as a built-in control ID (and is mutually exclusive with id and idQ—so specify only one of these values).
idQ	Qualified id	Acts as a qualified control ID, prefixed with a namespace identifier (and is mutually exclusive with id and idMso—so specify only one of these values).
image	String	Specifies an image for the control.
imageMso	Control id	Specifies an identifier for a built-in image.
insertAfterMso	Control id	Specifies the identifier for the built-in control after which to position this control.
insertAfterQ	Qualified id	Specifies the identifier of a control whose idQ property was specified after which to position this control.
insertBeforeMso	Control id	Specifies the identifier for the built-in control before which to position this control.
insertBeforeQ	Qualified id	Specifies the identifier of a control whose idQ property was specified before which to position this control.
itemSize	large, normal	Specifies the size for the items in a menu.
Keytip	String	Specifies the keytip for the control.
label	String	Specifies the label for the control.
onAction	Callback	Called when the user clicks the control.
onChange	Callback	Called when the user enters or selects text in an edit box or combo box.
screentip	String	Specifies the control's screentip.
showImage	true, false	Specifies whether the control's image is shown.
showItemImage	true, false	Specifies whether to show the image in a combo box, drop-down list, or gallery.
showItemLabel	true, false	Specifies whether to show the label in a combo box, drop-down list, or gallery.

Attribute	Type or Value	Description
`showLabel`	`true`, `false`	Specifies whether the control's label is shown.
`size`	`large`, `normal`	Specifies the size for the control.
`sizeString`	String	Indicates the width for the control by specifying a string, such as `"xxxxxx"`.
`supertip`	String	Specifies the enhanced screentip for the control.
`tag`	String	Specifies user-defined text.
`title`	String	Specifies the text to be displayed, rather than a horizontal line, for a menu separator.
`visible`	`true`, `false`	Specifies whether the control is visible.

Table 25.2 Required Arguments for Other Attributes and Controls

Control	Callback Name	Signature
Various controls	`getDescription`	`Sub GetDescription(control as IRibbonControl, ByRef description)`
	`getEnabled`	`Sub GetEnabled(control As IRibbonControl, ByRef enabled)`
	`getImage`	`Sub GetImage(control As IRibbonControl, ByRef image)`
	`getImageMso`	`Sub GetImageMso(control As IRibbonControl, ByRef imageMso)`
	`getLabel`	`Sub GetLabel(control As IRibbonControl, ByRef label)`
	`getKeytip`	`Sub GetKeytip (control As IRibbonControl, ByRef label)`
	`getSize`	`Sub GetSize(control As IRibbonControl, ByRef size)`
	`getScreentip`	`Sub GetScreentip(control As IRibbonControl, ByRef screentip)`
	`getSupertip`	`Sub GetSupertip(control As IRibbonControl, ByRef screentip)`
	`getVisible`	`Sub GetVisible(control As IRibbonControl, ByRef visible)`
button	`getShowImage`	`Sub GetShowImage (control As IRibbonControl, ByRef showImage)`
	`getShowLabel`	`Sub GetShowLabel (control As IRibbonControl, ByRef showLabel)`
	`onAction`	`Sub OnAction(control As IRibbonControl)`
checkBox	`getPressed`	`Sub GetPressed(control As IRibbonControl, ByRef returnValue)`

25

Control	Callback Name	Signature
	`onAction`	`Sub OnAction(control As IRibbonControl, pressed As Boolean)`
comboBox	`getItemCount`	`Sub GetItemCount(control As IRibbonControl, ByRef count)`
	`getItemID`	`Sub GetItemID(control As IRibbonControl, index As Integer, ByRef id)`
	`getItemImage`	`Sub GetItemImage(control As IRibbonControl, index As Integer, ByRef image)`
	`getItemLabel`	`Sub GetItemLabel(control As IRibbonControl, index As Integer, ByRef label)`
	`getItemScreenTip`	`Sub GetItemScreenTip(control As IRibbonControl, index As Integer, ByRef screentip)`
	`getItemSuperTip`	`Sub GetItemSuperTip (control As IRibbonControl, index As Integer, ByRef supertip)`
	`getText`	`Sub GetText(control As IRibbonControl, ByRef text)`
	`onChange`	`Sub OnChange(control As IRibbonControl, text As String)`
customUI	`loadImage`	`Sub LoadImage(imageId As string, ByRef image)`
	`onLoad`	`Sub OnLoad(ribbon As IRibbonUI)`
dropDown	`getItemCount`	`Sub GetItemCount(control As IRibbonControl, ByRef count)`
	`getItemID`	`Sub GetItemID(control As IRibbonControl, index As Integer, ByRef id)`
	`getItemImage`	`Sub GetItemImage(control As IRibbonControl, index As Integer, ByRef image)`
	`getItemLabel`	`Sub GetItemLabel(control As IRibbonControl, index As Integer, ByRef label)`
	`getItemScreenTip`	`Sub GetItemScreenTip(control As IRibbonControl, index As Integer ByRef screenTip)`
	`getItemSuperTip`	`Sub GetItemSuperTip (control As IRibbonControl, index As Integer, ByRef superTip)`
	`getSelectedItemID`	`Sub GetSelectedItemID(control As IRibbonControl, ByRef index)`

Control	Callback Name	Signature
	getSelectedItemIndex	Sub GetSelectedItemIndex(control As IRibbonControl, ByRef index)
	onAction	Sub OnAction(control As IRibbonControl, selectedId As String, selectedIndex As Integer)
dynamicMen	getContent	Sub GetContent(control As IRibbonControl, ByRef content)
editBox	getText	Sub GetText(control As IRibbonControl, ByRef text)
	onChange	Sub OnChange(control As IRibbonControl, text As String)
gallery	getItemCount	Sub GetItemCount(control As IRibbonControl, ByRef count)
	getItemHeight	Sub getItemHeight(control As IRibbonControl, ByRef height)
	getItemID	Sub GetItemID(control As IRibbonControl, index As Integer, ByRef id)
	getItemImage	Sub GetItemImage(control As IRibbonControl, index As Integer, ByRef image)
	getItemLabel	Sub GetItemLabel(control As IRibbonControl, index As Integer, ByRef label)
	getItemScreenTip	Sub GetItemScreenTip(control As IRibbonControl, index as Integer, ByRef screen)
	getItemSuperTip	Sub GetItemSuperTip (control As IRibbonControl, index as Integer, ByRef screen)
	getItemWidth	Sub getItemWidth(control As IRibbonControl, ByRef width)
	getSelectedItemID	Sub GetSelectedItemID(control As IRibbonControl, ByRef index)
	getSelectedItemIndex	Sub GetSelectedItemIndex(control As IRibbonControl, ByRef index)
	onAction	Sub OnAction(control As IRibbonControl, selectedId As String, selectedIndex As Integer)
menuSeparator	getTitle	Sub GetTitle (control As IRibbonControl, ByRef title)
toggleButton	getPressed	Sub GetPressed(control As IRibbonControl, ByRef returnValue)
	onAction	Sub OnAction(control As IRibbonControl, pressed As Boolean)

25

Accessing the File Structure

Excel files are actually zipped files that contain various files and folders to create the workbook and worksheets you see when you open the workbook. To view this structure, rename the file, adding a .zip extension to the end of the filename. For example, if your filename is Chapter 25 - Simple Ribbon.xlsm, rename it Chapter 25 - Simple Ribbon.xlsm.zip. You can then use your zip utility to access the folders and files within.

Copy into the zip file your customui folder and file, as shown in Figure 25.3. After placing them in the .xlsm file, you need to let the rest of the Excel file know that they are there and what their purpose is. To do that, you need to modify the RELS file, as described in the next section.

Figure 25.3
Using a zip utility, open the .xlsm file and copy in the customui folder and file.

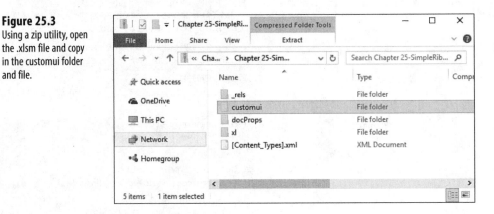

Understanding the RELS File

The RELS file, found in the _rels folder, contains the various relationships of an Excel file. Extract this file from the zip file and open it using a text editor.

The file already contains existing relationships that you do not want to change. Instead, you need to add one for the customui folder. Scroll all the way to the right of the `<Relationships` line and place your cursor before the `</Relationships>` tag, as shown in Figure 25.4. Insert the following code:

```
<Relationship Id="rAB67989"
Type="http://schemas.microsoft.com/office/2007/relationships/ui/_
extensibility"
Target="customui/customUI14.xml"/>
```

`Id` is any unique string to identify the relationship. If Excel has a problem with the string you enter, it might change it when you open the file. `Target` is the customui folder and file. Save your changes and add the RELS file back to the zip file.

➥ **See** the troubleshooting section "Found a Problem with Some Content," **p. 502**, for more information.

Figure 25.4
Place your cursor in the correct spot for entering your custom ribbon relationship.

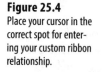

```
📄 C:\Users\Tracy\Desktop\.rels - Notepad++                          —  □  ✕

File  Edit  Search  View  Encoding  Language  Settings  Macro  Run  Plugins  Window  ?      X

custom14.xml  rels

  1  <?xml version="1.0" encoding="UTF-8" standalone="yes"?>
  2  <Relationships xmlns=
     "http://schemas.openxmlformats.org/package/2006/relationships"><Relationship
     Id="rId3" Type=
     "http://schemas.openxmlformats.org/officeDocument/2006/relationships/extended
     -properties" Target="docProps/app.xml"/><Relationship Id="rId2" Type=
     "http://schemas.openxmlformats.org/package/2006/relationships/metadata/core-p
     roperties" Target="docProps/core.xml"/><Relationship Id="rId1" Type=
     "http://schemas.openxmlformats.org/officeDocument/2006/relationships/officeDo
     cument" Target="xl/workbook.xml"/></Relationships>

length : 588  lines : 2      Ln : 2  Col : 516  Sel : 0 | 0        Dos\Windows      UTF-8 w/o BOM      INS
```

> **CAUTION**
>
> Even though the previous code appears as four lines in this book, it should appear as a single line in the RELS file. If you want to enter it as three separate lines, do not separate the lines within the quoted strings and do not use a continuation character as you would in VBA. The preceding examples are correct breaks (not including the line break with the continuation character). The following would be an example of an incorrect break of the fourth line:
>
> ```
> Target = "customui/
>          customUI14.xml"
> ```

25

Renaming an Excel File and Opening a Workbook

Rename the Excel file back to its original name by removing the .zip extension. Open your workbook.

➡ If any error messages appear when you rename an Excel file, **see** "Troubleshooting Error Messages," **p. 500**.

It can be a little time-consuming to perform all the steps involved in adding a custom ribbon, especially if you make little mistakes and have to keep renaming your workbook, opening the zip file, extracting your file, modifying, adding it back to the zip, renaming, and testing. To aid in this, OpenXMLDeveloper.org offers the Custom UI Editor tool, which you can learn more about at http://openxmldeveloper.org/blog/b/openxmldeveloper/archive/2009/08/07/7293. aspx. This tool updates the RELS file, helps with using custom images, and has other useful aids to customizing the ribbon. Another tool I like to use is the RibbonX Visual Designer by Andy Pope, available at http://www.andypope.info/vba/ribboneditor_2010.htm.

Using Images on Buttons

The image that appears on a button can be either an image from the Microsoft Office icon library or a custom image you create and include in the workbook's customui folder. With a good icon image, you can hide the button label but still have a friendly ribbon with images that are self-explanatory.

Using Microsoft Office Icons on a Ribbon

Microsoft has made it fairly easy to reuse Microsoft's button images in custom ribbons. Select File, Options, Customize Ribbon. Place your cursor over any menu command in the list, and a screentip displays, providing more information about the command. Included at the very end, in parentheses, is the image name, as shown in Figure 25.5.

Figure 25.5
Placing your cursor over a command, such as Hyperlink, brings up the icon name, HyperlinkInsert.

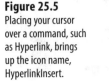

To place an image on your button, you need to go back into the customUI14.xml file and tell Excel what you want. The following code uses the HyperlinkInsert icon for the HelloWorld button and makes it large, as shown in Figure 25.6 (note that the icon name is case sensitive):

```
<customUI xmlns="http://schemas.microsoft.com/office/2009/07/customui">
  <ribbon startFromScratch="false">
    <tabs>
      <tab id="CustomTab" label="My First Ribbon">
        <group id="CustomGroup" label="My Programs">

          <button id="button1" label="Click to run"
            onAction="Module1.HelloWorld"
            imageMso="HyperlinkInsert" size="large"/>

        </group>
      </tab>
    </tabs>
  </ribbon>
</customUI>
```

Figure 25.6
You can apply the image from any Microsoft Office icon to your custom button.

You aren't limited to just the icons available in Excel. You can use the icon for any installed Microsoft Office application. You can download a workbook from Microsoft with several galleries showing the icons available (and their names) from http://www.microsoft.com/en-us/download/details.aspx?id=21103.

Adding Custom Icon Images to a Ribbon

What if the icon library just doesn't have the icon you're looking for? You can create your own image file and modify the ribbon to use it. Follow these steps:

1. Create a folder called images in the customui folder. Place your image in this folder.

2. Create a folder called _rels in the customui folder. Create a text file called customUI14.xml.rels in this new folder, as shown in Figure 25.7. Place the following code in the file (and note that the Id for the image relationship is the name of the image file, helloworld_png):

```
<?xml version="1.0" encoding="UTF-8" standalone="yes"?>
<Relationships xmlns="http://schemas.openxmlformats.org/package/2006/_
relationships"><Relationship Id="helloworld_png"_
Type="http://schemas.openxmlformats.org/officeDocument/2006/ _
relationships/image"
Target="images/helloworld.png"/></Relationships>
```

Figure 25.7
Create a _rels folder and an images folder within the customui folder to hold files relevant to your custom image.

3. Open the customUI14.xml file and add the image attribute to the control, as shown here, before you save and close the file:

```
<customUI xmlns="http://schemas.microsoft.com/office/2009/07/customui">
  <ribbon startFromScratch="false">
    <tabs>
      <tab id="CustomTab" label="My First Ribbon">
        <group id="CustomGroup" label="My Programs">

          <button id="button1" label="Click to run"
            onAction="Module1.HelloWorld" image="helloworld_png"
            size="large" />

        </group>
```

```
        </tab>
       </tabs>
      </ribbon>
     </customUI>
```

4. Open the `[Content_Types].xml` file and add the following at the very end of the file but before `</Types>`:

```
< Default Extension="png" ContentType="image/.png"/>
```

> **NOTE**
>
> If your image is a jpg, you would use the following:
>
> ```
> <Default Extension="jpg" ContentType="application/octet-stream"/>
> ```

5. Save your changes, rename your folder, and open your workbook. The custom image appears on the button, as shown in Figure 25.8.

Figure 25.8
With a few more changes to your customui folder, you can add a custom image to a button.

Troubleshooting Error Messages

To be able to see the error messages generated by a custom ribbon, go to File, Options, Advanced, General and select the Show Add-in User Interface Errors option.

The Attribute "*Attribute Name*" on the Element "*customui Ribbon*" Is Not Defined in the DTD/Schema

As noted in the section "Where to Add Code: The customui Folder and File" earlier in this chapter the case of attributes is very particular. If an attribute is "mis-cased," the error shown in Figure 25.9 might occur.

Figure 25.9
Mis-cased attributes can generate errors. Read the error message carefully; it might help you trace the problem.

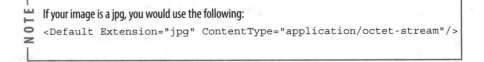

The code in the customUI14.xml file that generated the error had the following line:

```
<ribbon startfromscratch="false">
```

Instead of `startFromScratch`, the code contained `startfromscratch` (all lowercase letters). The error message even helps you narrow down the problem by naming the attribute with which it has a problem.

Illegal Qualified Name Character

For every opening <, you need a closing >. If you forget a closing >, the error shown in Figure 25.10 might appear. The error message is not specific at all, but it does provide a line and column number to indicate where it's having a problem. Still, it's not the actual spot where the missing > would go. Instead, it's the beginning of the next line. You have to review your code to find the error, but you have an idea of where to start.

Figure 25.10
For every opening <, you need a closing >.

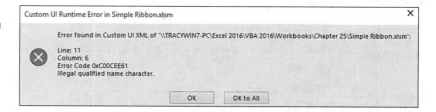

The following code in the customUI14.xml file generated the error:

```
<tab id="CustomTab" label="My First Ribbon">
   <group id="CustomGroup" label="My Programs"
<button id="button1" label="Click to run"
   onAction="Module1.HelloWorld" image="helloworld_png"
   size="large" />
```

Note the missing > for the group line (the second line of code). The line should have been this:

```
<group id="CustomGroup" label="My Programs">
```

Element "*customui Tag Name*" Is Unexpected According to Content Model of Parent Element "*customui Tag Name*"

If your structure is in the wrong order, such as the group tag placed before the tab tag, as shown here, a chain of errors will appear, beginning with the one shown in Figure 25.11:

Figure 25.11
An error in one line can lead to string of error messages because the other lines are now considered out of order.

> Custom UI Runtime Error in Simple Ribbon.xlsm
>
> Error found in Custom UI XML of "\\TRACYWIN7-PC\Excel 2016\VBA 2016\Workbooks\Chapter 25\Simple Ribbon.xlsm":
>
> Line: 7
> Column: 25
> Error Code 0x80004005
> Element '{http://schemas.microsoft.com/office/2009/07/customui}group' is unexpected according to content model of parent element '{http://schemas.microsoft.com/office/2009/07/customui}tabs'.
> Expecting: {http://schemas.microsoft.com/office/2009/07/customui}tab.
>
> OK   OK to All

```
<group id="CustomGroup" label="My Programs">
  <tab id="CustomTab" label="My First Ribbon">
```

Found a Problem with Some Content

Figure 25.12 shows a generic catchall message for different types of problems Excel can find. If you click No, the workbook doesn't open. If you click Yes, you then receive the message shown in Figure 25.13. While creating ribbons, though, I found it appearing most often when Excel doesn't like the `Relationship Id` I have assigned to the customui relationship in the RELS file. What's nice is that if you click Yes in the "Found a Problem" dialog, Excel assigns a new `Id`, and the next time you open the file, the error should not appear.

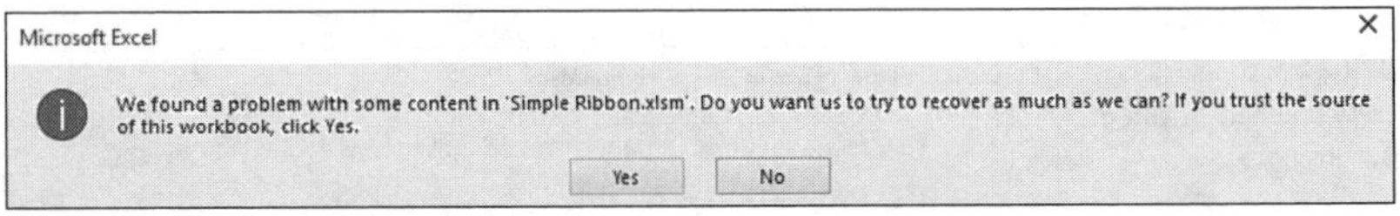

Figure 25.12
This rather generic message could appear for many reasons. Click Yes to try to repair the file.

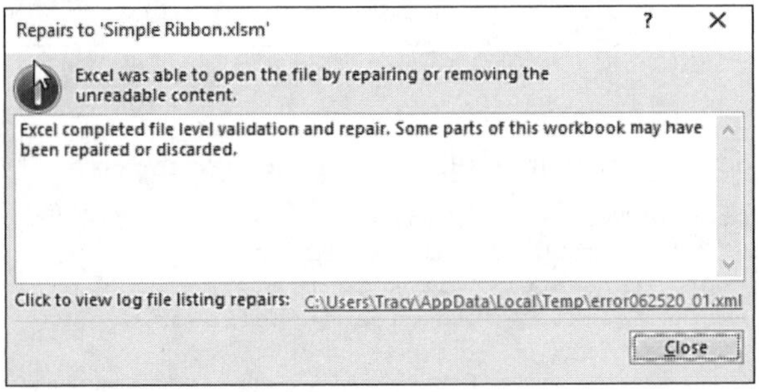

Figure 25.13
Excel lets you know whether it has succeeded in repairing the file.

Here's the original relationship:

```
<Relationship Id="rId3"
Type="http://schemas.microsoft.com/office/2007/relationships/ui/ _
extensibility"
Target="customui/customUI14.xml"/>
```

Here's the Excel-modified relationship:

```
<Relationship Id="rE1FA1CF0-6CA9-499E-9217-90BF2D86492F"
Type="http://schemas.microsoft.com/office/2007/relationships/ui/ _
extensibility"
 Target="customui/customuUI14.xml"/>
```

In the RELS file, the error also appears if you split the relationship line within a quoted string. You might recall that you were cautioned against this in the "Understanding the RELS File" section, earlier in this chapter. In this case, Excel could not fix the file, and you must make the correction yourself.

Wrong Number of Arguments or Invalid Property Assignment

If there is a problem with the sub being called by a control, you might see the error message in Figure 25.14 when you try to run code from your ribbon. For example, the onAction of a button requires a single IRibbonControl argument such as the following:

```
Sub HelloWorld(control As IRibbonControl)
```

It would be incorrect to leave off the argument, as shown here:

```
Sub HelloWorld()
```

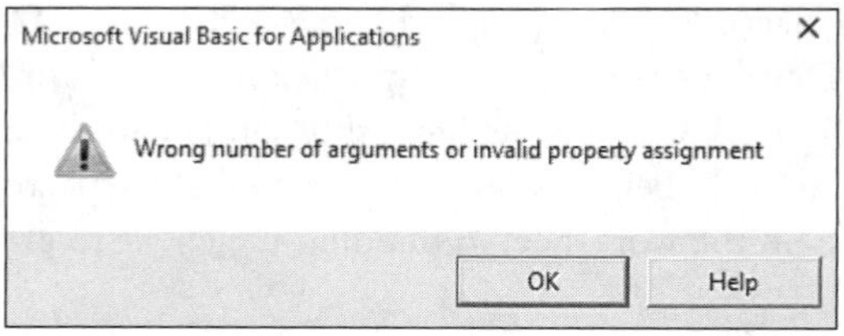

Figure 25.14
It's important for the subs being called by your controls to have the proper arguments. Refer to Table 25.2 for the various control arguments.

Invalid File Format or File Extension

The error message shown in Figure 25.15 looks rather drastic, but it could be deceiving. You could get it if you're missing quotation marks around an attribute's value in the RELS file. For example, look carefully at the following line, and you'll see that the Type value is missing its quotations marks:

```
Type=http://schemas.microsoft.com/office/2007/relationships/ui/extensibility
```

The line should have been this:

```
Type="http://schemas.microsoft.com/office/2007/relationships/ui/extensibility"
```

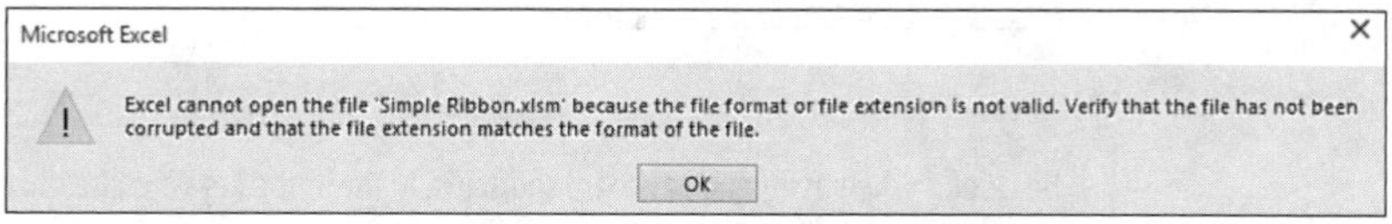

Figure 25.15
A missing quotation mark can generate a drastic message, but it's easily fixed.

Nothing Happens

If you open your modified workbook and your ribbon doesn't appear, but you don't get any error messages, double-check your RELS file. It's possible that you forgot to update it with the required relationship to your custumUI14.xml file.

Other Ways to Run a Macro

Using a custom ribbon is the best way to run a macro; however, if you have only a couple of macros to run, it can be a bit of work to modify the file. You could have the client invoke a macro by going to the View tab, selecting Macros, View Macros, and then selecting the macro from the Macros dialog and clicking the Run button, but this is a bit unprofessional—and tedious. Other options are discussed in the following sections.

Using a Keyboard Shortcut to Run a Macro

The easiest way to run a macro is to assign a keyboard shortcut to it. Open the Macro dialog box by selecting the Developer or View tab and clicking Macros or by pressing Alt+F8. Then select the macro and click Options. Assign a shortcut key to the macro. Figure 25.16 shows the shortcut Ctrl+Shift+H being assigned to the RunHello macro. You can now conspicuously post a note on the worksheet, reminding the client to press Ctrl+Shift+H to clean the first column.

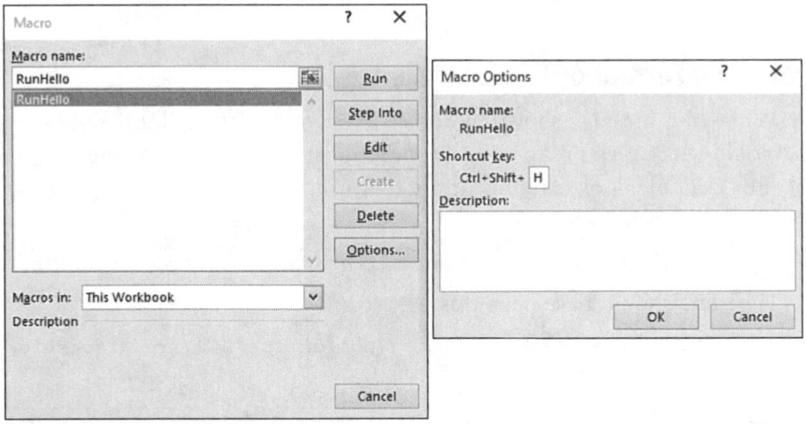

Figure 25.16
The simplest way to enable a client to run a macro is to assign a shortcut key to the macro. Ctrl+Shift+H now runs the RunHello macro.

CAUTION

Be careful when assigning keyboard shortcuts. Many of the keys are already mapped to important Windows shortcuts. If you would happen to assign a macro to Ctrl+C, for example, anyone who uses this shortcut to copy the selection to the Clipboard will be frustrated when your application does something else in response to this common shortcut. The letters J, M, and Q are usually good choices because as of Excel 2016, they have not yet been assigned to Excel's menu of "Ctrl+" shortcut combinations. Ctrl+L and Ctrl+T used to be available, but these are now used to create tables.

Attaching a Macro to a Command Button

Two types of buttons can be embedded in a sheet: the traditional button shape that you can find in the Form Controls section and an ActiveX command button. (You can access both on the Developer tab under the Controls, Insert option.)

To add a form control button with a macro to your sheet, follow these steps:

1. On the Developer tab, click the Insert button and select the button control from the Form Controls section of the drop-down, as shown in Figure 25.17.

2. Place your cursor in the worksheet where you want to insert the button and then click and drag to create the shape of the new button. When you release the mouse button, the Assign Macro dialog displays.

3. In the Assign Macro dialog, select a macro to assign to the button and click OK.

4. Highlight the text on the button and type new meaningful text.

5. To change the font, text alignment, and other aspects of the button's appearance, right-click the button and select Format Control from the pop-up menu.

6. To reassign a new macro to the button, right-click the button and select Assign Macro from the pop-up menu.

Attaching a Macro to a Shape

The previous method assigned a macro to an object that looks like a button. You can also assign a macro to any drawing object on the worksheet. To assign a macro to an Autoshape (which you get by selecting Insert, Illustrations, Shapes), right-click the shape and select Assign Macro, as shown in Figure 25.18.

This method is useful because you can easily add a drawing object with code and use the OnAction property to assign another macro to the object. There is one big drawback to this method: If you assign a macro that exists in another workbook, and the other workbook is saved and closed, Excel changes the OnAction for the object to be hard-coded to a specific folder.

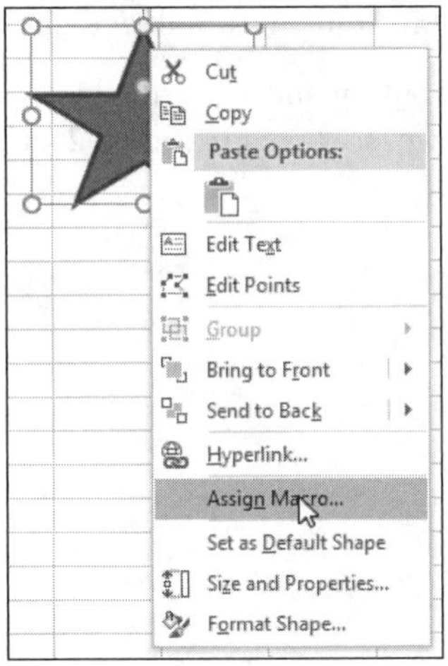

Figure 25.18
Macros can be assigned to any drawing object on the worksheet.

Attaching a Macro to an ActiveX Control

ActiveX controls are newer than form controls and slightly more complicated to set up. Instead of simply assigning a macro to a button, you have a `button_click` event where you can either call another macro or have the macro code actually embedded in the event. Follow these steps:

1. On the Developer tab, click the Insert button and select the Command Button icon from the ActiveX Controls section.

2. Place your cursor in the worksheet where you want to insert the button and then click and drag to create the shape of the new button.

3. To format the button, right-click the button and select Properties or select Controls, Properties from the Developer tab. You can now adjust the button's caption and color in the Properties window, as shown in Figure 25.19. If nothing happens when you right-click the button, enter Design mode by clicking the Design Mode button on the Developer tab.

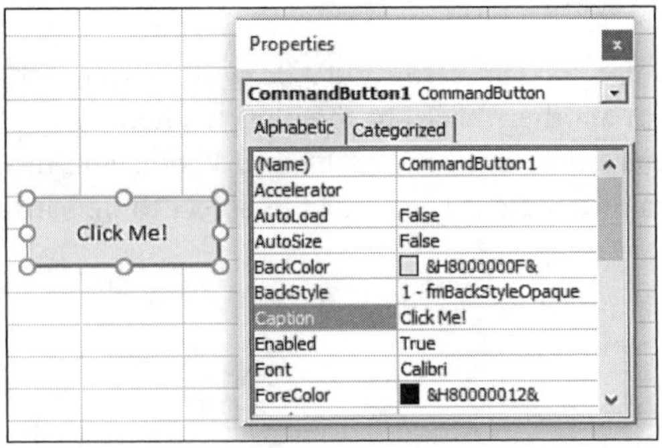

Figure 25.19
Use the Properties window to adjust aspects of the ActiveX button.

4. To assign a macro to the button, right-click it and select View Code. This creates the header and footer for the `button_click` event in the code window for the current worksheet. Type the code you want to have run or the name of the macro you want to call.

> **NOTE**
> There is one annoying aspect of this Properties window: It is huge and covers a large portion of your worksheet. Eventually, if you want to use the worksheet, you are going to have to resize or close this Properties window. When you close the Properties window, it is also hidden in the VB Editor. I would prefer to be able to close this Properties window without affecting my VB Editor environment.

Running a Macro from a Hyperlink

There is a trick you can use to run a macro from a hyperlink. Because many people are used to clicking a hyperlink to perform an action, this method might be the most intuitive for your clients.

The trick is to set up placeholder hyperlinks that simply link back to themselves. Select the cell with the text you want to link to, and from the Insert tab, select Links, Hyperlink (or press Ctrl+K). In the Insert Hyperlink dialog, click Place in This Document. Figure 25.20 shows a worksheet with four hyperlinks. Each hyperlink points back to its own cell.

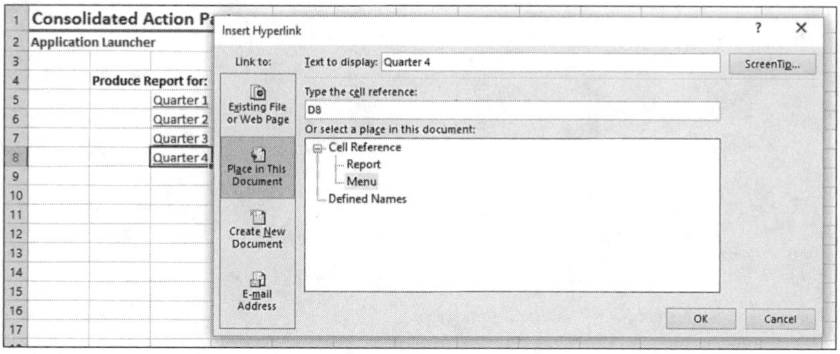

Figure 25.20
To run a macro from a hyperlink, you must create placeholder hyperlinks that link back to their cells. Then, using an event handler macro in the worksheet's code module, you can intercept the hyperlink and run any macro.

When a client clicks a hyperlink, you can intercept this action and run any macro by using the `FollowHyperlink` event. Enter the following code in the code module for the worksheet:

```
Private Sub Worksheet_FollowHyperlink(ByVal Target As Hyperlink)
Select Case Target.TextToDisplay
    Case "Quarter 1"
        RunQuarter1Report
    Case "Quarter 2"
        RunQuarter2Report
    Case "Quarter 3"
        RunQuarter3Report
    Case "Quarter 4"
        RunQuarter4Report
End Select
End Sub
```

Next Steps

From custom ribbons to simple buttons or hyperlinks, there are plenty of ways to ensure that your clients never need to see the Macro dialog box. In Chapter 26, you find out how to package your macros into add-ins that you can easily distribute to others.

Creating Add-ins

26

By using VBA, you can create standard add-in files for your clients to use. After the client installs your add-in on his PC, the program will be available to Excel and will load automatically every time that person opens Excel. This chapter discusses standard add-ins.

Be aware that there are two other kinds of add-ins: COM add-ins and DLL add-ins. Neither of these can be created with VBA. To create these types of add-ins, you need either Visual Basic.NET or Visual C++.

Characteristics of Standard Add-ins

If you are going to distribute an application, you might want to package the application as an add-in. Typically saved with an .xlam extension, an add-in offers several advantages:

- Usually, clients can bypass your `Workbook_Open` code by holding down the Shift key while opening the workbook. With an add-in, they cannot bypass the `Workbook_Open` code in this manner.

- After you use the Add-ins dialog to install an add-in (by selecting File, Options, Add-ins, Manage Excel Add-ins, Go), the add-in will always be loaded and available.

- Even if the macro security level is set to disallow macros, programs in an installed add-in can still run.

- Generally, custom functions work only in the workbook in which they are defined. A custom function added to an add-in is available to all open workbooks.

■ The add-in does not show up in the list of open files in the Window menu item. The client cannot unhide the workbook by choosing View, Window, Unhide.

> ┌ CAUTION ──
>
> There is one strange rule for which you need to plan. An add-in is a hidden workbook. Because the add-in can never be displayed, your code cannot select or activate any cells in the add-in workbook. You are allowed to save data in your add-in file, but you cannot select the file. Also, if you do write to your add-in file data that you want to be available in the future, your add-in code needs to handle saving the file. Because your clients will not realize that the add-in is there, they will never be reminded or asked to save an unsaved add-in. You might, therefore, add `ThisWorkbook.Save` to the add-in's `Workbook_BeforeClose` event.

Converting an Excel Workbook to an Add-in

Add-ins are typically managed using the Add-ins dialog. This dialog presents an add-in name and description, which you control by entering two specific properties for the file before you convert it to an add-in.

> **NOTE**
>
> If you're modifying an existing add-in, you must make it visible before you can edit the properties. See the section "Using the VB Editor to Convert a File to an Add-in" later in this chapter.

To change the title and description shown in the Add-ins dialog, follow these steps:

1. Select File, Info. Excel displays the Document Properties pane on the right side of the window.
2. From the Properties drop-down, select Advanced Properties.
3. Enter the name for the add-in in the Title field.
4. Enter a short description of the add-in in the Comments field (see Figure 26.1).
5. Click the back arrow at the top left of the screen to return to your workbook.

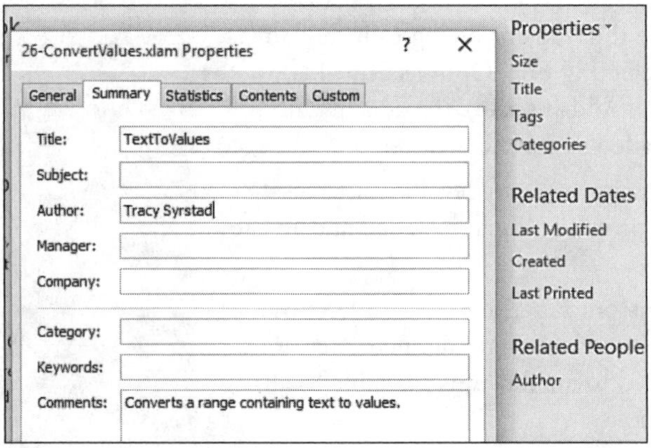

Figure 26.1
Fill in the Title and Comments fields before converting a workbook to an add-in.

There are two ways to convert a file to an add-in. The first method, using Save As, is easier but has an annoying byproduct. The second method uses the VB Editor and requires two steps, but it gives you some extra control. The sections that follow describe the steps for using these methods.

Using Save As to Convert a File to an Add-in

Select File, Save As. In the Save as Type field, scroll through the list and select Excel Add-in (*.xlam).

As shown in Figure 26.2, the filename changes from filename.xlsm to filename.xlam. Also note that the save location automatically changes to an AddIns folder. The location of this folder varies by operating system, but it will be something along the lines of C:\ Users*username*\AppData\Roaming\Microsoft\AddIns. It is also confusing that, after the .xlsm file is saved as an .xlam type, the unsaved .xlsm file remains open. It is not necessary to keep an .xlsm version of the file because it is easy to change an .xlam back to an .xlsm for editing.

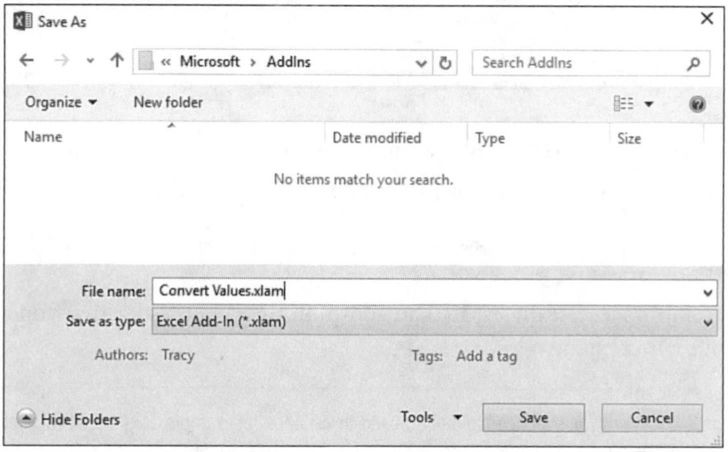

Figure 26.2
The Save As method changes the `IsAddin` property, changes the name, and automatically saves the file in your AddIns folder.

TIP

If, before selecting the add-in file type, you are already in the folder to which you want to save, just click the back arrow in the Save As window to return to that folder.

CAUTION

When the Save As method is being used to create an add-in, a worksheet must be the active sheet. The add-in file type is not available if a chart sheet is the active sheet.

Using the VB Editor to Convert a File to an Add-in

The Save As method is great if you are creating an add-in for your own use. However, if you are creating an add-in for a client, you probably want to keep the add-in stored in a folder with all the client's application files. It is fairly easy to bypass the Save As method and create an add-in using the VB Editor:

1. Open the workbook that you want to convert to an add-in.
2. Switch to the VB Editor.
3. In the Project Explorer, click ThisWorkbook.
4. In the Properties window, find the property called `IsAddin` and change its value to `True`, as shown in Figure 26.3.

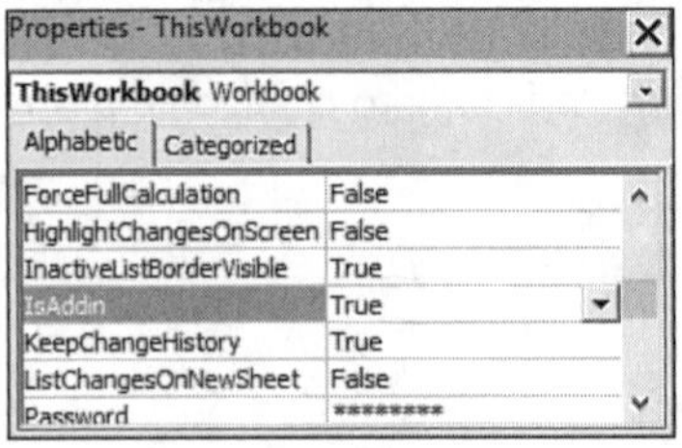

Figure 26.3
Creating an add-in is as simple as changing the `IsAddin` property of `ThisWorkbook`.

5. Press Ctrl+G to display the Immediate window.
6. In the Immediate window, save the file, using an .xlam extension, like this:

```
ThisWorkbook.SaveAs FileName:="C:\ClientFiles\Chap26.xlam", _
FileFormat:= xlOpenXMLAddIn
```

You've now successfully created an add-in in the client folder that you can easily find and email to your client.

> **TIP**
> If you ever need to make an add-in visible—for example, to change the properties or view data you have on sheets—repeat the previous steps except select `False` for the `IsAddin` property. The add-in becomes visible in Excel. When you are done with your changes, change the property back to `True`.

Having a Client Install an Add-in

When you email an add-in to a client, have her save it on her desktop or in another easy-to-find folder. You should tell her to follow these steps:

1. Open Excel and select File, Options. The Excel Options dialog appears.
2. In the left navigation pane, select Add-ins.
3. At the bottom of the window, select Excel Add-ins from the Manage drop-down (see Figure 26.4).

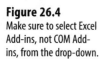

Figure 26.4
Make sure to select Excel Add-ins, not COM Add-ins, from the drop-down.

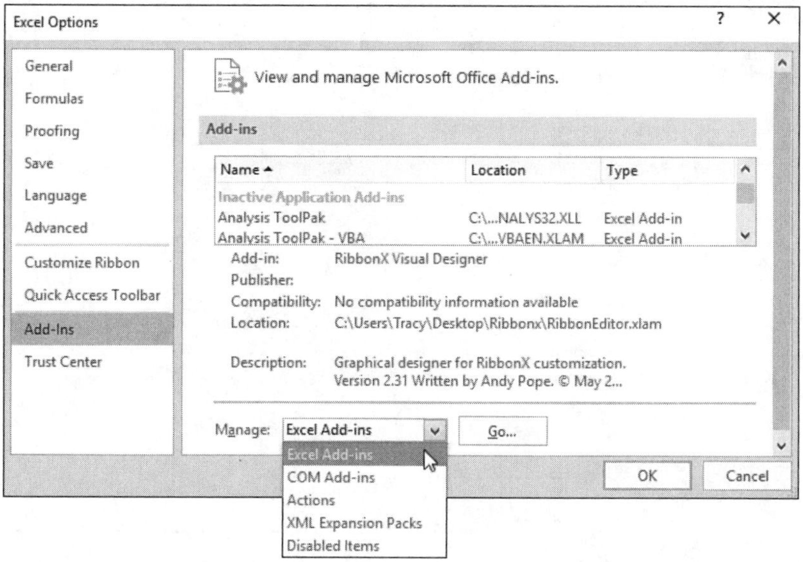

4. Click Go. Excel displays the familiar Add-ins dialog.

5. In the Add-ins dialog, click the Browse button.

6. Browse to where you saved the file. Highlight the add-in and click OK.

> **NOTE** Excel might prompt you to copy the add-in to its AddIns folder. I do not do this because the folder is hard to find, especially if I need to update the file.

The add-in is now installed. If you allow it, Excel copies the file from where you saved it to the proper location of the AddIns folder. In the Add-ins dialog, the title of the add-in and comments as specified in the File Properties dialog are displayed (see Figure 26.5).

Standard Add-ins Are Not Secure

Remember that anyone can go to the VB Editor, select your add-in, and change the `IsAddin` property to `False` to unhide the workbook. You can discourage this process by locking the .xlam project for viewing and protecting it in the VB Editor, but be aware that plenty of vendors sell a password-hacking utility for less than $40. To add a password to your add-in, follow these steps:

1. Go to the VB Editor.

2. Select Tools, VBAProject Properties.

3. Select the Protection tab.

4. Select the Lock Project for Viewing check box.

5. Enter the password twice for verification.

26

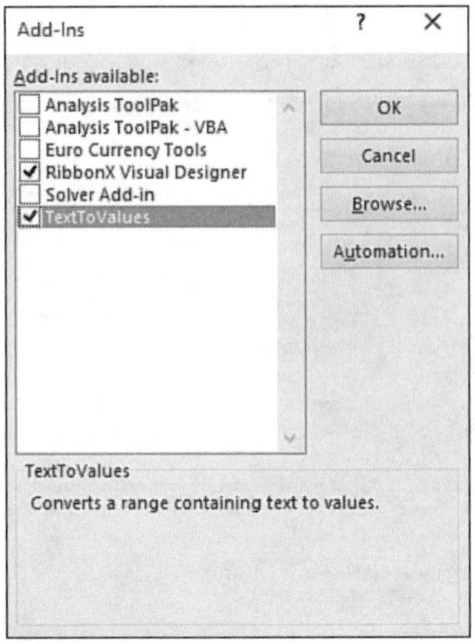

Figure 26.5
The add-in is now available for use.

┌─ C A U T I O N ───┐

If you protect the code and don't include error handling, users won't be able to click the Debug button if an error message appears. See chapter 24, "Handling Errors," for more information on handling errors in code so that the program ends properly and still provides the user with error information that can pass to you.

└──┘

Closing Add-ins

Add-ins can be closed in three ways:

- Clear the add-in from the Add-ins dialog. This closes the add-in for this session and ensures that it does not open during future sessions.
- Use the VB Editor to close the add-in. In the VB Editor's Immediate window, type this code to close the add-in:

```
Workbooks("YourAddinName.xlam").Close
```

- Close Excel. All add-ins are closed when Excel is closed.

Removing Add-ins

You might want to remove an add-in from the list of available add-ins in the Add-in dialog box. There is no effective way to do this within Excel. Follow these steps:

1. Close all running instances of Excel.
2. Use Windows Explorer to locate the file. The file might be located in %AppData%\Microsoft\AddIns\.
3. In Windows Explorer, rename the file or move it to a different folder.

4. Open Excel. You get a note warning you that the add-in could not be found. Click OK to dismiss this warning.

5. Select File, Options, Add-ins, Manage Excel Add-ins, Go. In the Add-ins dialog box, clear the name of the add-in you want to remove. Excel notifies you that the file cannot be found and asks whether you want to remove it from the list. Click Yes.

Using a Hidden Workbook as an Alternative to an Add-in

One cool feature of an add-in is that the workbook is hidden. This keeps most novice users from poking around and changing formulas. However, it is possible to hide a workbook without creating an add-in.

It is easy enough to hide a workbook by selecting View, Window, Hide in Excel. The trick is to then save the workbook as Hidden. With a file that is hidden, the normal File, Save choice does not work. Saving the file can be done from the VB Editor window. In the VB Editor, make sure that the workbook is selected in the Project Explorer. Then, in the Immediate window, type the following:

```
ThisWorkbook.Save
```

There is a downside to using a hidden workbook: A custom ribbon tab will not be visible if the workbook it is attached to is hidden.

CASE STUDY USING A HIDDEN CODE WORKBOOK TO HOLD ALL MACROS AND FORMS

Access developers routinely use a separate database to hold macros and forms. They place all forms and programs in one database and all data in a second database. These database files are linked through the Link Tables function in Access.

For large projects in Excel, I recommend using the same method. You use a little bit of VBA code in the Data workbook to open the Code workbook.

The advantage to this method is that when it is time to enhance the application, you can mail a new code file without affecting the client's data file.

I once encountered a single-file application rolled out by another developer that the client had sent out to 50 sales reps. The reps replicated the application for each of their 10 largest customers. Within a week, there were 500 copies of this file floating around the country. When they discovered a critical flaw in the program, patching 500 files was a nightmare.

We designed a replacement application that used two workbooks. The data workbook ended up with about 20 lines of code. This code was responsible for opening the code workbook and passing control to the code workbook. As the files were being closed, the data workbook would close the code workbook.

There were many advantages to this method. First, the customer data files were kept to a very small size. Each sales rep now has 1 workbook with program code and 10 or more data files for each customer. As enhancements are completed, we distribute new program code workbooks. The sales rep opens his or her existing customer data workbook, which automatically grabs the new code workbook.

26

Because the previous developer had been stuck with the job of trying to patch 500 workbooks, we were extremely careful to have as few lines of code in the customer workbook as possible. There are maybe 10 lines of code, and they were tested thoroughly before being sent out. By contrast, the code workbook contains 3,000-plus lines of code. If something goes wrong with the application, I am almost certain that the bad code is in the easy-to-replace code workbook.

In the customer data workbook, the `Workbook_Open` procedure has this code:

```
Private Sub Workbook_Open()
 On Error Resume Next
    X = Workbooks("Code.xlsm").Name
    If Not Err = 0 then
        On Error Goto 0
        Workbooks.Open Filename:= _
            ThisWorkbook.Path & Application.PathSeparator & "Code.xlsm"
    End If
    On Error Goto 0
    Application.Run "Code.xlsm!CustFileOpen"
 End Sub
```

The `CustFileOpen` procedure in the code workbook could also handle adding a custom menu for the application. Because custom tabs for hidden workbooks are not visible, you have to use the legacy `commandbars` method to create a menu that appears on the Add-ins tab.

This dual-workbook solution works well and allows updates to be seamlessly delivered to the client without touching any of the 500 customer files.

Next Steps

Microsoft has introduced a new way of sharing applications with users: Office Add-ins. These are programs that, simply put, use JavaScript, HTML, and XML to put a web page in a frame on a sheet. Chapter 27, "An Introduction to Creating Office Add-ins," introduces you to what is involved in creating these apps and deploying them over a network.

An Introduction to Creating Office Add-ins

27

With Office 2013, Microsoft introduced Office add-ins, applications that provide expanded functionality to a sheet, such as a selectable calendar, or an interface with the Web, such as retrieving information from Wikipedia or Bing. Like Excel add-ins, once Office add-ins are installed, they're always available. But unlike Excel add-ins, the Office add-ins have limited interaction with sheets and do not use VBA.

An Office add-in consists of an HTML file that provides the user interface on a task or content pane, a CSS file to provide styles for the HTML file, a JavaScript file to provide interactivity to the HTML file, and an XML file to register the Office add-in with Excel. This might sound like a lot of new programming skills, but it's not. I've designed only the most basic web pages, and that was years ago, but I was able to apply my VBA programming skills to JavaScript, which is where the bulk of the programming goes. The language is a little different, but it's not so different that you can't create a simple, useful app.

This chapter introduces you to creating an Office add-in to distribute locally and to the basics of the various programming languages. It is not meant to provide in-depth instruction, especially for JavaScript.

Creating Your First Office Add-in—Hello World

Hello World is probably the most popular first program for programmers to try out. It's a simple program, just outputting the words "Hello World," but it introduces the basics required by the application.

So, with that said, it's time to create a Hello World Office add-in. Follow these steps to create the files for the Office add-in:

CAUTION

A network is used to distribute the Office add-in locally. You cannot use a local drive or a network drive mapped to a drive letter. If you do not have access to a network, you will not be able to test your Office add-in. See the section "Napa Office 365 Development Tools" for an alternative location for creating Office add-ins.

NOTE

In the following steps, you'll enter text into a text editor. Unlike with the VB Editor, there isn't a compiler to point out mistakes before you run the program. It is very important that you enter the text exactly as written, including the case of text within quotation marks.

To open a file for editing, such as with Notepad, right-click the file and select Open With. If you see Notepad, select it; otherwise, select Choose Another App. From the dialog that opens, find Notepad. Make sure that Always Use This App to Open *filetype* Files is *not* selected and then click OK. The next time you need to edit the file, Notepad appears in the quick list of available programs in the Open With option.

Follow these steps to create your Office add-in:

1. Create a folder and name it `HelloWorld`. This folder can be on your local drive while you are creating the program. All the program files will be placed in this folder. When you're finished, you will move it to the network.

2. Create the HTML program by inserting a text file in the folder and naming it `HelloWorld.html`. Then open the HTML file for editing and enter the following code in it:

```
<!DOCTYPEhtml>
<html>
    <head>
        <meta charset="UTF-8"/>
        <meta http-equiv="X-UA-Compatible" content="IE=Edge"/>
        <link rel="stylesheet" type="text/css" href="program.css"/>
    </head>
    <body>
        <p>Hello World!</p>
    </body>
</html>
```

Save and close the file.

3. Create the CSS file to hold the styles used by the HTML file by inserting a text file in the folder and naming it `program.css`. Note that this is the same filename used in the HTML file in the `<link rel>` tag. Then open the CSS file for editing and enter the following code in it:

```
body
{
```

```
    position:relative;
}
li :hover
{
    text-decoration: underline;
    cursor:pointer;
}
h1,h3,h4,p,a,li
{
    font-family: "Segoe UI Light","Segoe UI",Tahoma,sans-serif;
    text-decoration-color:#4ec724;
}
```

Save and close the file.

4. Create the XML file by inserting a text file in the folder and naming it `HelloWorld.xml`. Then open the XML file for editing and enter the following code in it:

> **CAUTION**
>
> The following code sample and others that follow include lines that extended beyond the width of the page, so we needed to add a _ to indicate a line that is continued. Unlike in VBA, in this case you should not type in the underscores. Instead, when you get to an underscore, just ignore it but continue inputting the code after it on the same line.

```xml
<?xml version="1.0" encoding="utf-8"?>
<OfficeApp xmlns="http://schemas.microsoft.com/office/appforoffice/1.0"
    xmlns:xsi="http://www.w3.org/2001/XMLSchema-instance"
    xsi:type="TaskPaneApp">
    <Id>08afd7fe-1631-42f4-84f1-5ba51e242f98</Id>
    <Version>1.0</Version>
    <ProviderName>Tracy Syrstad</ProviderName>
    <DefaultLocale>EN-US</DefaultLocale>
    <DisplayName DefaultValue="Hello World app"/>
    <Description DefaultValue="My first app."/>
    <IconUrl DefaultValue=
        "http://officeimg.vo.msecnd.net/_layouts/images/general/ _
officelogo.jpg"/>
    <Capabilities>
        <Capability Name="Document"/>
        <Capability Name="Workbook"/>
    </Capabilities>

    <DefaultSettings>
    <SourceLocation DefaultValue="\\workpc\MyApps\HelloWorld\ _
HelloWorld.html"/>
    </DefaultSettings>
    <Permissions>ReadWriteDocument</Permissions>
</OfficeApp>
```

Do not close the XML file yet.

5. While the XML file is still open, note the Id `08afd7fe-1631-42f4-84f1-5ba51e242f98`. This is a globally unique identifier (GUID). If you are testing on a private network and not distributing this file, you can likely use this GUID. But if

you're on a business network with other programmers or if you're distributing the file, you must generate your own GUID. See the section "Using XML to Define an Office Add-in," later in this chapter, for more information on GUIDs.

> **NOTE** GUID stands for *globally unique identifier*. A GUID is a unique reference number that identifies software. It's usually displayed as 32 alphanumeric digits separated into five groups (8-4-4-4-12) by hyphens. A GUID has so many digits that it's rare for identical ones to be generated.

6. Move the `HelloWorld` folder to a network share folder if it's not already there. Note the path to the folder and to the HTML file because you will be making use of this information. The path to the folder should be `\\myserver\myfolder`. For example, my `HelloWorld` folder is located at `\\workpc\MyApps\HelloWorld`.

7. Open the XML file for editing and change `<SourceLocation>` (located near the bottom of the code) to the location of the HTML file on your network. Save and close the file.

8. Configure your network share as a Trusted Catalog Address by following these steps:

   a. Start Excel and go to File, Options, Trust Center and click Trust Center Settings.

   b. Select Trusted Add-in Catalogs.

   c. Enter your folder path in the Catalog URL field and click Add Catalog. The path is added to the list box.

   d. Select the Show in Menu box.

   e. Click OK. You should see a prompt indicating that the Office add-in will be available the next time Excel starts (see Figure 27.1). Click OK twice.

   f. Restart Excel.

   > **CAUTION**
   > Only one network share at a time can be configured to show in the catalog. If you want users to have access to multiple Office add-ins at once, the XML for the Office add-ins must be stored in the same network share. Otherwise, users will have to go into their settings and select which catalog to show.

9. Insert the Office add-in you just created into Excel by selecting Insert, Add-Ins, Store. Then, in the Office Add-Ins dialog, select Shared Folder. If you don't see anything when you've selected the link, click Refresh. The Hello World Office add-in should be listed, as shown in Figure 27.2.

> **NOTE** If you still do not see anything after refreshing, there is something incorrect in the files or setup. Carefully review all the code and steps. If you do not see anything incorrect, try changing the GUID.

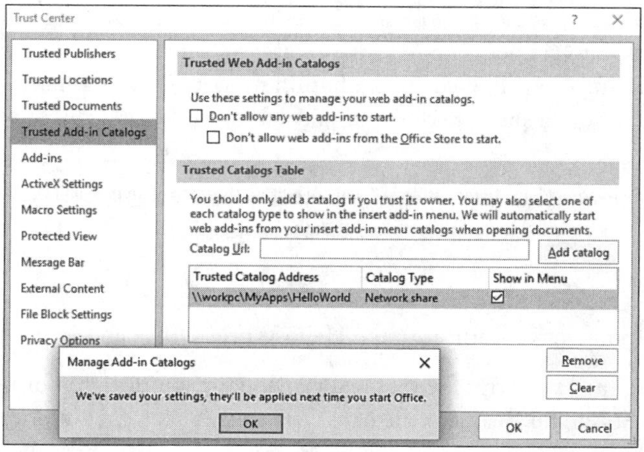

Figure 27.1
Configure the location of your Office add-ins under Trusted Add-in Catalogs.

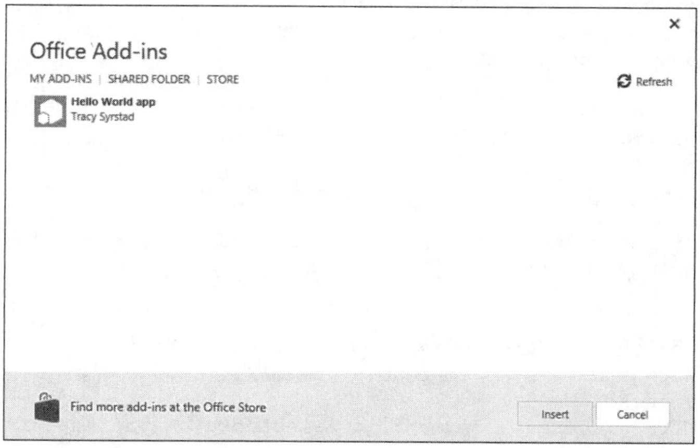

Figure 27.2
The Shared Folder lists any Office add-ins available in the active catalog.

10. Select the Office add-in and click Insert. A task pane on the right side of the Excel window opens, as shown in Figure 27.3, displaying the words "Hello World!"

Figure 27.3
By creating Hello World you take a first step in creating interactive Office add-ins.

Adding Interactivity to an Office Add-in

The Hello World Office add-in created in the preceding section is a static one; it doesn't do anything except show the words in the code. But as you browse the Web, you run into dynamic web pages. Some of those web pages use JavaScript, a programming language that adds automation to elements on otherwise static websites. In this section, you'll modify the Hello World Office add-in by adding a button to write data to a sheet and another button that reads data from a sheet, performs a calculation, and writes the results to the task pane.

> **TIP** You don't have to restart Excel if you are editing the code of an installed Office Add-in. Instead, right-click in the Office add-in's task pane and select Reload.

To add these interactive features to the Hello World Office add-in, follow these steps:

1. To create the JavaScript file that will provide the interactivity for the two buttons Write Data to Sheet and Read & Calculate Data from Sheet, first insert a text file in the Hello World folder and name the file program.js. Then open the JavaScript file for editing and enter the following code in it:

```
Office.initialize = function (reason) {
//Add any needed initialization
}
//declare and set the values of an array
var MyArray = [[234],[56],[1798], [52358]];

//write MyArray contents to the active sheet
function writeData() {
    Office.context.document.setSelectedDataAsync(MyArray, _
{coercionType: 'matrix'});
}

/*reads the selected data from the active sheet
so that we have some content to read*/
function ReadData() {
    Office.context.document.getSelectedDataAsync("matrix", _
function (result) {
//if the cells are successfully read, print results in task pane
    if (result.status === "succeeded"){
            sumData(result.value);
        }
//if there was an error, print error in task pane
        else{
            document.getElementById("results").innerText = _
result.error.name;
        }
    });
}

/*the function that calculates and shows the result
in the task pane*/
function sumData(data) {
    var printOut = 0;

//sum together all the values in the selected range
    for (var x = 0 ; x < data.length; x++) {
        for (var y = 0; y < data[x].length; y++) {
            printOut += data[x][y];
```

```
        }
      }
//print results in task pane
    document.getElementById("results").innerText = printOut;
}
```

Save and close the file.

2. Edit the `HelloWorld.html` file so that it points to the JavaScript file `program.js` and add the two buttons used by the JavaScript code. To do this, replace the existing code with the following:

```
<!DOCTYPEhtml>
<html>
    <head>
        <meta charset="UTF-8"/>
        <meta http-equiv="X-UA-Compatible" content="IE=Edge"/>
        <link rel="stylesheet" type="text/css" href="program.css"/>
<!--begin pointer to JavaScript file-->
        <script src = "https://appsforoffice.microsoft.com/lib/1.0/ _
hosted/office.js"></script>
        <script src= "program.js"></script>
<!--end pointer to JavaScript file-->
    </head>
    <body>
<!--begin replacement of body-->
        <button onclick="writeData()">Write Data To Sheet</button></br>
        <button onclick="ReadData()">Read & Calculate Data From Sheet _
          </button></br>
         <h4>Calculation Results: <div id="results"></div> </h4>
<!--end replacement of body-->
    </body>
</html>
```

In this new code, you've added `<script>` tags and replaced the code between the `<body>` tags. Comment tags, `<!--comments-->`, are included to show where the changes are.

3. Save and close the file.

After creating the JavaScript file and updating the HTML file, reload the Office add-in and test it by clicking the Write Data to Sheet button. It should write the numbers from `MyArray` onto the sheet. With those cells selected, click Read & Calculate Data from Sheet, and the results of adding the selected numbers together will appear in the Calculation Results line of the task pane, as shown in Figure 27.4.

27

Figure 27.4
Use JavaScript to create an Office Add-in that can perform a calculation with data from a sheet.

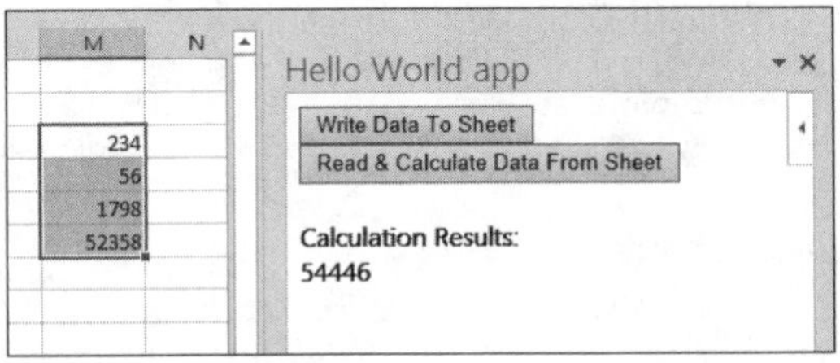

A Basic Introduction to HTML

The HTML code in an Office add-in controls how the task or content pane will look, such as the text and buttons. If you open the HTML file from either of your Hello World files, it opens in your default browser and looks as it did in Excel's task pane (though without any functionality). You can design the Office add-in as you would a web page, including adding images and links. The following sections review a few basics to get you started in designing your own Office add-in interface.

Using Tags

HTML consists of elements, such as images, links, and controls, that are defined by the use of tags enclosed in angle brackets. For example, the starting tag `<button>` tells the code that what follows, inside and outside the tag's brackets, relates to a button element. For each start tag, you have an end tag, which is usually the same as the opening tag but with a slash—like `</button>`—but some tags can be empty—like `/>`. A browser does not display tags or anything within a tag's brackets. Text that you want displayed needs to be outside the tags.

Comments have a tag of their own and don't require your typical end tag. As in VBA, commented text does not appear on the screen. Add comments to your HTML code like this:

```
<!--This is a comment-->
```

A multiline comment would appear like this:

```
<!--This is a multiline comment.
Notice that nothing special is needed -->
```

Adding Buttons

To create the code for a button, you need to label the button and link it to a function in the JavaScript file that will run when the button is clicked. Here's an example:

```
<button onclick="writeData()">Write Data To Sheet</button>
```

The first part, `<button onclick="writeData()">`, identifies the control as a button and assigns the function `writeData` to the click event for the button. Notice that the function name is in quotes and includes argument parentheses, which are empty. The second part, `Write Data To Sheet`, is the text of the label on the button. The label name is not in quotation marks. The line ends with the closing tag for the button.

To change other attributes of the button, you just need to specify those attributes. For example, to change the button text to red, add the `style` attribute for color, like this:

```
<button onclick="writeData()" style="color:Red">Write Data To _
    Sheet</button>
```

To add a tooltip that appears when the mouse is placed over the button, as shown in Figure 27.5, use the `title` attribute, like this:

```
<button onclick="writeData()" style="color:Red"
    title = "Use to quickly add numbers to your sheet">
    Write Data To Sheet</button></br>
```

Use a space to separate multiple attributes. After an attribute name, such as `style`, put an equal sign and then the value in quotation marks. Also notice that HTML is rather forgiving about where you put your line breaks. Just don't put them within a string, or you might also get a line break on the screen in that position.

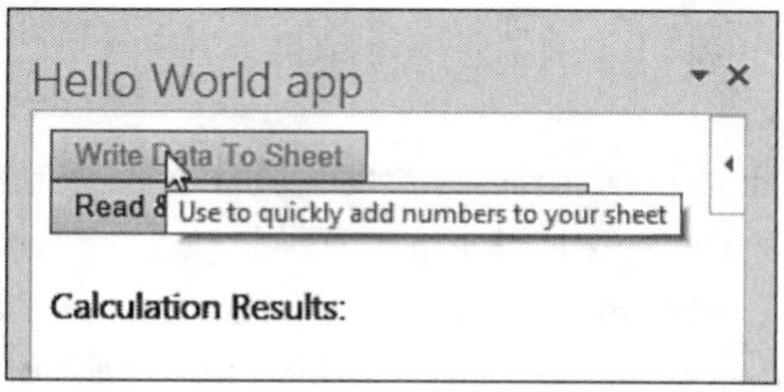

Figure 27.5
Add other attributes to your button to change colors or add tooltip text for users.

Using CSS Files

CSS stands for Cascading Style Sheets. You create styles in Excel and Word to make it easy to modify how text looks in an entire file without changing every single occurrence. You can do the same thing with an Office add-in by creating a separate style file (CSS) that your HTML code references. In the file, you set up rules for various elements of the HTML file, such as layout, colors, and fonts.

The CSS file provided in the Hello World example can be used for a variety of projects. It includes styles for `h1`, `h3`, and `h4` headings, hyperlinks (`a`), paragraph tags (`p`), and bullets (`li`).

Using XML to Define an Office Add-in

XML defines the elements needed to display and run an Office add-in in Excel, including the GUID, Office add-in logo, and location of the HTML file. XML also configures how the Office add-in will appear in the Office Add-ins store and can provide a version number for the program.

> ┌ CAUTION ──────────────────
> XML tags are case sensitive. When you make changes to the provided Hello World sample, be sure you don't change any of the tags but only their values.

Two types of user interfaces are available for an Office add-in: a task pane or a content pane. A task pane starts off docked on the right side of the Excel window, but a user can undock it and move it around the window. A content pane appears as a frame in the middle of the Excel window. Which type you use is up to you. To tell an Office add-in which type of pane to use, set the `xsi:type` value to either `TaskPaneApp` or `ContentApp`.

You should always use a unique identifier when creating an Office add-in. Websites such as http://www.guidgen.com generate GUIDs for you.

In the Hello World sample, the store icon used is an online icon that Microsoft has made available. But you can also use your own .jpg file. The image should be small, about 32×32 pixels. Update `IconURL` with the full path to the image, like this:

```
<IconUrl DefaultValue="\\workpc\MyApps\HelloWorld\mrexcellogo.jpg"/>
```

The `SourceLocation` tag is used to set the full path to the HTML file. If the HTML file cannot be found when the Office add-in is being installed, an error message will appear, stating that the file couldn't be found.

> **NOTE** If you make changes to XML after you've already configured the location of the catalog or installed the Office add-in, be sure to click the Refresh link in the Office Add-ins dialog. For example, if you switch between `TaskPaneApp` and `ContentApp`, the change might not be reflected even if you select to install the Office add-in again. To be safe, refresh the Office Add-ins dialog box.

Using JavaScript to Add Interactivity to an Office Add-in

JavaScript provides the wow factor behind an Office add-in. You can create a very useful reference with just HTML, but to make an interactive Office add-in, such as a function calculator, you need JavaScript. One limitation, though, is that you cannot specify cell addresses. The program interacts with what is selected on the sheet.

The following sections provide basic introduction to JavaScript. If you are already familiar with JavaScript, you can go ahead to "JavaScript Changes for Working in the Office Add-in."

> **NOTE** The `document.getElementById("results").innerText` command used in the following examples is the command for the code to put the returned value in the place reserved by the `"results"` variable in the HTML file.

The Structure of a Function

JavaScript code consists of functions called by HTML code and by other JavaScript functions. Just as in VBA, each JavaScript function starts with `function` followed by the name of the function and any arguments in parentheses. But unlike in VBA, there is no `End Function` at the end; instead, you use curly braces to group the function. See the following subsection, "Curly Braces and Spaces," for more information.

JavaScript is case sensitive, including variable and function names. For example, if you create a function called `writeData` but then try to call `WriteData` from another function, the code does not work because in one case, *write* is in lowercase and in the other it has a capital *W*. JavaScript recognizes these as different functions. Create case rules for yourself, such as initial caps for each word in a variable, and stick to them. This helps reduce troubleshooting of JavaScript code issues.

Curly Braces and Spaces

Curly braces ({}) are characters used in JavaScript but not in VBA. You use them to group blocks of code that should be executed together. You can have several sets of braces within a function. For example, you would use them to group all the code in a function; then, within the function, you would use them to group lines of code such as within an `if` statement.

After you have finished typing a line in VBA and gone to another line, you might notice that the line adjusts itself, adding or removing spaces. In JavaScript, spaces don't usually matter; the exceptions are spaces in strings and spaces between keywords and variables in the code. In the code samples in this section, notice that sometimes I have included spaces (`a = 1`) and sometimes I have not (`a=1`).

Semicolons and Line Breaks

You've probably noticed the semicolons (;) used in JavaScript code. They might have appeared at the end of every line, or maybe only on some lines. Perhaps you've noticed a line without a semicolon or noticed a semicolon in the middle of a line. The reason the use of semicolons appears inconsistent is that, under normal circumstances, semicolons are not required. A semicolon is a line break. If you use hard returns in your code, you are already placing line breaks, and so the semicolon is not needed. If you combine multiple lines of code onto one line, though, you need a semicolon to let the code know that the next piece of code is not part of the previous code.

Comments

There are two ways to comment out lines in JavaScript. To comment out a single line, place two slashes (//) at the beginning of the line, like this:

```
//comment out a single line in the code like this
```

If you want to comment out multiple lines in VBA, you have to preface each line with an apostrophe. JavaScript has a cleaner method. At the beginning of the first line you want to comment out, place a slash and an asterisk (/*). At the end of the last line of the comment, place an asterisk and a slash (*/). It looks like this:

```
/* Comment out
multiple lines of code
like this */
```

Variables

In VBA, you have the option of declaring variables. If you do declare them, you don't have to declare the variable type, but after a value is assigned to a variable, it's not always easy

27

to change the type. In JavaScript, you don't declare variables, except for arrays. (See the later subsection "Arrays" for more information.) When a value is assigned to a variable, it becomes that type, but if you reference the variable in another way, its type might change.

In the following example, the string `"123"` is assigned to myVar, but in the next line, a number is subtracted:

```
myVar = "123"
myVar = myVar-2
```

JavaScript just goes with it, allowing you to change the variable from a string to a number. If you ran this code, myVar would be 121. Note that myVar + 2 would not deliver the same result. See the next subsection, "Strings," for more information.

If you need to ensure that a variable is of a specific type, use one of these functions to do so: Boolean, Number, or String. For example, you have a function that is reading in numbers imported onto a sheet. As is common in imports, the numbers could be stored as text. Instead of having to ensure that the user converts the data, use the Number keyword when processing the values like this to force the number to be a number:

```
Number(importedValue)
```

Strings

As in VBA, in JavaScript you reference strings by using double quotations marks (`"string"`), but, unlike in VBA, you can also use single quotation marks (`'string'`). The choice is up to you; just don't start a string with one type of quotations marks and end with another. The capability to use either set can be useful. For example, if you want to show quoted text, you use the single quotes around the entire string, like this:

```
document.getElementById("results").innerText = _
    'She heard him shout, "Stay away!"'
```

This would be the result in the pane:

```
She heard him shout, "Stay away!"
```

To concatenate two strings, use the plus (+) sign. You also use the plus to add two numbers. So what happens if you have a variable hold a number as text and add it to a number, as in this example:

```
myVar = "123"
myVar = myVar+2
```

You might think that the result would be 125. After all, in the previous example, with -2, the result was 121. In this case, concatenation has priority over addition, and the answer is actually 1232. To ensure that the variable is treated like a number, use the Number function. If the variable it is holding cannot be converted to a number, the function returns NaN, for "not a number."

Arrays

Arrays are required for processing multiple cells in JavaScript. Arrays in JavaScript are not very different from arrays in VBA. To declare an unlimited-size array, do this:

```
var MyArray = new Array ()
```

NOTE If you are unfamiliar with using arrays in VBA, see Chapter 8, "Arrays."

To create an array of limited size, such as 3, do this:

```
var MyArray = new Array(3)
```

You can also fill an array at the same time that you declare it. The following creates an array of three elements, two of which are strings and the third of which is a number:

```
var MyArray = ['first value', 'second value', 3]
```

The array index always starts at 0. To print the second element, second value, of the preceding array, do this:

```
document.getElementById("results").innerText = MyArray[1]
```

If you've declared an array with a specific size but need to add another element, you can add the element by specifying the index number or by using the push() function. For example, to add a fourth element, 4, to the previously declared array, MyArray, do this (because the count starts at 0, the fourth element has an index of 3):

```
MyArray [3] = 4
```

If you don't know the current size of the array, use the push() function to add a new value to the end of the array. For example, if you don't know the index value for the last value in the preceding array, you can add a new element, fifth value, like this:

```
MyArray.push('fifth value')
```

Refer to the section "How to Do a For each..next Statement in JavaScript" if you need to process the entire array at once. JavaScript has other functions for processing arrays, such as concat(), which can join two arrays together, and reverse(), which reverses the order of the array's elements. Because this is just a basic introduction to JavaScript, those functions are not covered here. For a tip on applying a math function to an entire array with a single line of code, see the section "Math Functions in JavaScript."

JavaScript for Loops

When you added interactivity to the Hello World Office add-in earlier in this chapter, you used the following code to sum the selected range:

```
for (var x = 0 ; x < data.length; x++) {
    for (var y = 0; y < data[x].length; y++) {
        printOut += data[x][y];
    }
}
```

The two for loops process the array, data, that is passed into the function, with x as the row and y as the column.

A for loop consists of three separate sections separated by semicolons. When the loop is started, the first section, var x=0, initializes any variables used in the loop. Multiple variables would be separated by commas. The second section, x < data.length, tests whether the loop should be entered. The third section, x++, changes any variables to continue the loop, in this case incrementing x by 1 (x++ is shorthand for x=x+1). This section can also have more than one variable, with commas separating them.

> **TIP**
>
> To break out of a loop early, use the break keyword.

How to Do an if Statement in JavaScript

The basic if statement in JavaScript has this syntax:

```
if (expression){
//do this
}
```

Here, expression is a logical function that returns true or false, just as in VBA. If the expression is true, the code continues and runs the lines of code in the //do this section. To execute code if the expression is false, you need to add an else statement, like this:

```
if (expression){
//do this if true
}
else{
//do this if false
}
```

How to Do a Select..Case Statement in JavaScript

Select..Case statements are very useful in VBA as an alternative to using multiple If.. Else statements. In JavaScript, similar functionality is found in the switch() statement. Typically, this is the syntax of a switch() statement:

```
switch(expression){
    case firstcomparison : {
        //do this
        break;
        }
    case secondcomparison : {
        //do this
        break;
        }
    default : {
        //no matches, so do this
        break;
        }
    }
```

Here, expression is the value you want to compare to the case statements. The break keyword is used to stop the program from comparing to the next statement, after it has run one comparison. That is one difference from a Select statement: Whereas in VBA, after a comparison is successful, the program leaves the Select statement, in JavaScript, without the break keyword, the program continues in the switch statement until it reaches the end.

Use `default` as you would a `Case Else` in VBA—to cover any comparisons that are not specified.

The preceding syntax works for one-on-one comparisons. If you want to see how an expression fits within a range, the standard syntax won't work. You need to replace the expression with `true` to force the code into running the `switch` statement. The `case` statements are where you use the expression compared to the range. The following code is the BMI calculator UDF from Chapter 14, "Sample User-Defined Functions," converted to JavaScript. It compares the calculated BMI to the various ranges and returns a text description to post to the task pane:

```
Office.initialize = function (reason) {
//Add any needed initialization.
}

function calculateBMI() {
    Office.context.document.getSelectedDataAsync("matrix", function _
(result) {
//call the calculator with the array, result.value, as the argument
        myCalculator(result.value);
    });
}

function myCalculator(data){
    var calcBMI = 0;
    var BMI="";
    //Do the initial BMI calculation to get the numerical value
    calcBMI = (data[1][0] / (data[0][0] *data [0][0]))* 703

/*evaluate the calculated BMI to get a string value because we want to
evaluate range, instead of switch(calcBMI), we do switch (true) and then
use our variable as part of the ranges */
    switch(true){
        //if the calcBMI is less than 18.5
        case (calcBMI <= 18.5) : {
            BMI = "Underweight"
            break;
            }
        //if the calcBMI is a value between 18.5 and (&&) 24.9
        case ((calcBMI > 18.5)&&(calcBMI <= 24.9)):{
            BMI = "Normal"
            break;
            }
        case ((calcBMI > 24.9)&&(calcBMI <= 29.9)) : {
            BMI = "Overweight"
            break;
            }
        //if the calcBMI is greater than 30
        case (calcBMI > 29.9) : BMI = "Obese"
        default : {
            BMI = 'Try again'
            break;
            }
    }
    document.getElementById("results").innerText = BMI;
}
```

27

How to Do a `For each..next` Statement in JavaScript

If you have a collection of items to process in VBA, you might use a `For each..next` statement. One option in JavaScript is `for (... in ...)`. For example, if you have an array of items, you can use the following code to output the list:

```
//set up a variable to hold the output text
arrayOutput = ""
/*process the array
i is a variable to hold the index value.
Its count starts as 0*/
for (i in MyArray) {
/*create the output by adding the element
to the previous element value.
\n is used to put in a line break */
    arrayOutput += MyArray[i] + '\n'
    }
//write the output to the screen
document.getElementById("results").innerText = arrayOutput
```

You can do whatever you need to each element of the array. In this example, you're building a string to hold the element value and a line break so that when it prints to the screen, each element appears on its own line, as shown in Figure 27.6. The `MyArray` variable used in this code was filled in the earlier section, "Arrays."

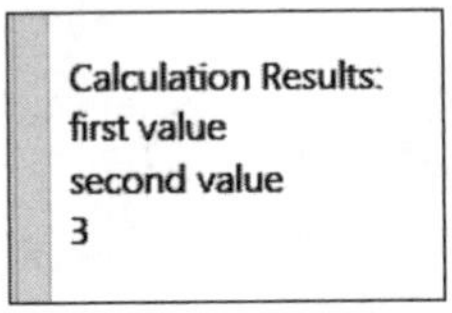

Figure 27.6
JavaScript has its own equivalents to many VBA looping statements, such as `for..in` loop.

```
Calculation Results:
first value
second value
3
```

Mathematical, Logical, and Assignment Operators

JavaScript offers the same basic operators as VBA plus a few more to shorten your code. Table 27.1 lists the various operators. Assume here that x = 5.

Table 27.1   JavaScript Operators

Operator	Description	Example	Result
+	Addition	x+5	10
-	Subtraction	x-5	0
/	Division	x/5	1
*	Multiplication	x*5	25
%	Remainder after division	11%x	1
()	Override the usual order of operations	(x+2)*5	35, whereas x+2*5=15

Operator	Description	Example	Result
-	Unary minus (for negative numbers)	-x	-5
==	Values are equal	x=='5'	True
===	Values and types are equal	x==='5'	False since the types don't match. x is a number being compared to a string.
>	Greater than	x>10	False
<	Less than	x<10	True
>=	Greater than or equal to	x>=5	True
<=	Less than or equal to	x<=4	False
!=	Values are not equal	x!='5'	False
!==	Values and types are not equal	x!=='5'	True
&&	And	x==5 && 1==1	True
||	Or	x=='5' || 1==2	False
!	Not	!(x==5)	False
++	Increment	++x or x++	6
--	Decrement	--x or x--	4
+=	Equal to with addition	x += 11	16
-=	Equal to with subtraction	x-=22	-17
*=	Equal to with multiplication	x*=2	10
/=	Equal to with division	x/=30	6
%=	Equal to with the remainder	x%=11	1

The increment and decrement operators are two of my favorite ones; I wish we had them in VBA. Not only do they reduce your code, but they offer a flexibility that VBA lacks (post- and pre-increments). You might remember the use of x++ in the Hello World program earlier in this chapter. You used this in place of x=x+1 to increment the for loop. But it doesn't just increment the value. It uses the value and then increments it. This is called a post-increment. JavaScript also offers a pre-increment, which means the value is incremented and then used. So if you have x=5, both of the following lines of code return 6:

```
//would increment x then post the value
document.getElementById("results").innerText = ++x //would return 6
//would post the value of x (now 6 after the previous increment) then
//increment
document.getElementById("results2").innerText = x++ //would return 6
```

Math Functions in JavaScript

JavaScript has several math functions available, as shown in Table 27.2. Using these functions is straightforward. For example, to return the absolute value of the variable `myNumber`, do this:

```
result = Math.abs(myNumber)
```

Table 27.2 JavaScript Math Functions

Function	Description
`Math.abs(a)`	Returns the absolute value of a.
`Math.acos(a)`	Returns the arc cosine of a.
`Math.asin(a)`	Returns the arc sine of a.
`Math.atan(a)`	Returns the arc tangent of a.
`Math.atan2(a,b)`	Returns the arc tangent of a/b.
`Math.ceil(a)`	Returns the integer closest to a and not less than a.
`Math.cos(a)`	Returns the cosine of a.
`Math.exp(a)`	Returns the exponent of a (Euler's number to the power a).
`Math.floor(a)`	Rounds down, returns the integer closest to a.
`Math.log(a)`	Returns the log of a base e.
`Math.max(a,b)`	Returns the maximum of a and b.
`Math.min(a,b)`	Returns the minimum of a and b.
`Math.pow(a,b)`	Returns a to the power b.
`Math.random()`	Returns a random number between 0 and 1 (but not including 0 or 1).
`Math.round(a)`	Rounds up or down, and returns the integer closest to a.
`Math.sin(a)`	Returns the sine of a.
`Math.sqrt(a`	Returns the square root of a.
`Math.tan(a)`	Returns the tangent of a.

TIP
If you need to apply a math function to all elements of an array, you can do so by using the `map()` function and the desired `Math` function. For example, to ensure that every value in an array is positive, use the `Math.abs` function. The following example changes each element in an array to its absolute value and then prints the results to the screen, as shown in Figure 27.7:

```
result = 0
arrayOutput = ""
arrNums = [9, -16, 25, -34, 28.9]
result = arrNums.map(Math.abs)
for (i in result){
    arrayOutput += result[i] +'\n'
}
document.getElementById("results").innerText = arrayOutput
```

Figure 27.7
Using arrays is a common way of storing data in JavaScript, which offers many functions for simplifying working with those arrays.

```
Calculation Results:
9
16
25
34
28.9
```

Writing to the Content Pane or Task Pane

After you've processed a user's data, you need to display the results. This can be done on the sheet or in the Office add-in's pane. Assuming that `arrayOutput` holds the data you want to write to the pane, do this:

```
document.getElementById("results").innerText = arrayOutput
```

This code writes data to the Office add-in's pane, specifically to the `results` variable reserved in the HTML code. To write to the sheet, see the later subsection "Reading from and Writing to a Sheet."

JavaScript Changes for Working in an Office Add-in

Not all JavaScript code will work in an Office add-in. For example, you cannot use the `alert` or `document.write` statements. There are also some new statements for interacting with Excel provided in a JavaScript API that you link to in the HTML file with this line:

```
<script src = "https://appsforoffice.microsoft.com/lib/1.0/hosted/office.js">
</script>
```

Like the APIs used in VBA, the JavaScript API gives you access to objects, methods, properties, and events that JavaScript can use to interact with Excel. You've now seen some of the most commonly used objects. For more information on these and other available objects, go to http://msdn.microsoft.com/en-us/library/office/apps/fp142185.aspx.

27

Initializing an Office Add-in

The following event statement must be placed at the top of the JavaScript script:

```
Office.initialize = function (reason) { /*any initialization*/}
```

It initializes the Office add-in to interact with Excel. The `reason` parameter returns how the Office add-in was initialized. If the Office add-in is inserted into the document, then `reason` is `inserted`. If the Office add-in is already part of a workbook that's being opened, `reason` is `documentOpened`.

Reading from and Writing to a Sheet

`Office.context.document` represents the object that the Office add-in is interacting with—the sheet. It has several methods available, most importantly the two that enable you to read selected data and write to a range.

The following line uses the `setSelectedDataAsync` method to write the values in `MyArray` to the selected range on a sheet:

```
Office.context.document.setSelectedDataAsync(MyArray, {coercionType: _
'matrix'});
```

The first argument, `MyArray`, is required. It contains the values to write to the selected range. The second argument, `coercionType`, is optional. Its value, `matrix`, tells the code that you want the values treated as a one-dimensional array.

The method for reading from a sheet, `getSelectedDataAsync`, is similar to the write method:

```
Office.context.document.getSelectedDataAsync("matrix", function (result) {
    //code to manipulate the read data, result
});
```

The first argument, `matrix`, is the `coercionType` and is required. It tells the method how the selected data should be returned—in this case, in an array. The second argument shown is an optional callback function, with `result` being a variable that holds the returned values (`result.value`) if the call was successful and an error if not.

To find out whether the call was successful, use the status property, `result.status`. To retrieve the error message, use this:

```
result.error.name
```

Napa Office 365 Development Tools

You don't need a fancy program to write the code for any of the files used in an Office add-in. The Notepad program that comes with Windows does the job. But when you consider the case sensitivity of some programming languages, like JavaScript, using a program that will provide some help is a good idea. I spent a couple of hours in frustration over some of the samples in this chapter, wondering why they didn't work when the code was perfect. Except the code wasn't perfect. Again and again I missed the case sensitivity in JavaScript and XML.

To help you create distributable Office add-ins, Microsoft has released Napa Office 365 Development Tools. After you sign up for a developer site, Microsoft provides you with space on a SharePoint server and the tools for developing Office add-ins. Go to dev.office. com to get started. Napa Office 365 Development Tools also helps you release your Office add-ins through the Office Add-in store.

Next Steps

Read Chapter 28, "What's New in Excel 2016 and What's Changed," to learn about more features that have changed significantly in Excel 2016.

27

What's New in Excel 2016 and What's Changed

This chapter reviews changes since Excel 2007–2013. In conjunction with reviewing those sections, you should also review information in this book on tables, sorting, and conditional formatting.

If It Has Changed in the Front End, It Has Changed in VBA

If you were using Excel 2003 (or older) before Excel 2016, almost everything you knew about programming Excel objects has changed. Basic logic still works (`for` loops, for example), but most objects have changed.

If you have been using Excel 2007, 2010, or 2013, there are still a few changes to consider, and they are noted in this chapter. For most items, the changes are obvious because if the Excel user interface has changed, the VBA has changed.

The Ribbon

If you have been working with a legacy version of Excel, the ribbon is one of the first changes you'll notice when you open Excel 2016. Although the `CommandBars` object does still work to a point, if you want to flawlessly integrate your custom controls into the ribbon, you need to make some major changes.

➡ **See** Chapter 25, "Customizing the Ribbon to Run Macros," for more information.

Single Document Interface (SDI)

For years, if you had multiple documents open in Word, you could drag each document to a different monitor. This capability was not available in Excel until Excel 2013. With Excel 2013, Excel changed from a *multiple-document interface* to a *single-document interface*. This means the individual workbook window no longer resides within a single application window. Instead, each workbook is in its own standalone window, separate from any other open workbook.

Changes to the layout of one window don't affect any previously opened windows. To see this in action, open two workbooks. In the second workbook, enter and run the following code, which adds a new item, Example Option, to the bottom of the right-click menu:

```
Sub AddRightClickMenuItem()
Dim cb As CommandBarButton
Set cb = CommandBars("Cell").Controls.Add _
    (Type:=msoControlButton, temporary:=True)
cb.Caption = "Example Option"
End Sub
```

Right-click a cell in the second workbook, and Example Option appears right where it should. Right-click a cell in the first workbook, and the option does not appear. Return to the second workbook and press Ctrl+N to add a new workbook. Right-click a cell in this third workbook, and the menu item appears. Go to the first workbook, create a new workbook, and check the right-click menu. The option does not appear.

Now, delete the custom menu. Go to the third workbook and paste and run the following code:

```
Sub DeleteRightClickMenuItem()
CommandBars("Cell").Controls("Example Option").Delete
End Sub
```

The menu item is removed from the third workbook, but when you check the right-click menu of the second workbook, the item is still there. Although Excel copied the menu from the active workbook when creating new workbooks, the logic to remove the menu item does not propagate.

 NOTE   Don't worry about having to delete all instances of the sample menu item. It was created to be temporary and will be gone when you restart Excel.

Another change to keep in mind is that making a change to the window of one workbook, such as minimizing it, doesn't affect the other workbooks. If you want to minimize all windows, you need to loop through the application's windows, like this:

```
Sub MinimizeAll()
Dim myWin As Window
For Each myWin In Application.Windows
    myWin.WindowState = xlMinimized
Next myWin
End Sub
```

Quick Analysis Tool

Introduced in Excel 2013, the Quick Analysis tool appears in the lower-right corner when a range of data is selected. This tool suggests what the user could do with the data, such as apply conditional formatting or create a chart. You can activate a specific tab, such as Totals, when the user selects a range, like this:

```
Private Sub Worksheet_SelectionChange(ByVal Target As Range)
Application.QuickAnalysis.Show (xlTotals)
End Sub
```

Charts

Charts have gone through a few incarnations since Excel 2003, and with those changes to the interface there have also been changes to the object model. In Excel 2013, Microsoft introduced a completely new interface and a new method, AddChart2, which is not backward compatible—not even to Excel 2010. With Excel 2016, Microsoft has introduced six new-style charts; they are not supported by the macro recorder, and the VBA code is buggy. Although Microsoft has promised to update the old charts to the modern charting system and fix the VBA bugs, we don't know when this will happen. Until then, the safest solution is to create your code carefully. With these compatibility issues in mind, Chapter 15, "Creating Charts," provides examples for Excel 2003, 2007–2010, 2013, and 2016.

Excel 2010 introduced a type of minichart, called a sparkline. A sparkline is different from a standard chart in that it can be inserted within a cell. Sparklines are not backward compatible.

Pivot Tables

Excel 2007, 2010, 2013, and 2016 have offered many new features in pivot tables. If you use code for a new feature, the code works in the current version but crashes in previous versions of Excel. See Chapter 12, "Using VBA to Create Pivot Tables," for more information.

Slicers

Slicers were a new feature in Excel 2010 for use on pivot tables. They aren't backward compatible—not even to Excel 2007. They're useful in pivot tables because they allow for easy-to-see and -use filtering options. If you open a workbook with a slicer in an older version of Excel, the slicer is replaced with a shape that includes text explaining what the shape is there for and that the feature is not available.

In Excel 2013, slicers were added to tables. The functionality is the same as that of slicers for pivot tables, but these new slicers are not backward compatible—not even to Excel 2010.

➡ **See** Chapter 12 for more information on pivot table slicers.

28

SmartArt

SmartArt was introduced in Excel 2007 to replace the Diagram feature in legacy versions of Excel. Recording is very limited, but it helps you find the correct schema. After that, the recorder doesn't capture text entry or format changes.

The following example created the art shown in Figure 28.1. The name of the schema used is hChevron3. In this code I changed schemecolor for the middle chevron and left the other two with the default colors:

```
Sub AddDiagram()
With ActiveSheet
    Call .Shapes.AddSmartArt(Application.SmartArtLayouts( _
        "urn:microsoft.com/office/officeart/2005/8/layout/hChevron3")) _
        .Select
    .Shapes.Range(Array("Diagram 1")).GroupItems(1).TextEffect.Text = _
        "Bill"
    .Shapes.Range(Array("Diagram 1")).GroupItems(3).TextEffect.Text = _
        "Tracy"
    With .Shapes.Range(Array("Diagram 1")).GroupItems(2)
        .Fill.BackColor.SchemeColor = 7
        .Fill.Visible = True
        .TextEffect.Text = "Barb"
    End With
End With
End Sub
```

Figure 28.1
The macro recorder is limited when recording the creation of SmartArt. You need to trace through the object's properties to find what you need.

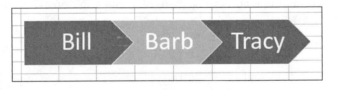

Learning the New Objects and Methods

When you click the Help button in Excel's VBEVB Editor, you're brought to Microsoft's online Help resource. On the left side of the browser window, select What's New for Excel 2016 Developers to open an article that provides an overview of some of the changes. Select Excel VBA Reference, Object Model to view a list of all objects, properties, methods, and events in the Excel 2016 object model.

Compatibility Mode

With the changes in Excel 2016, it's important to verify an application's version. Two properties you can use to do this are Version and Excel8CompatibilityMode.

28

Dealing With Compatibility Issues

Creating a Compatibility mode workbook can be problematic. Most code will still run in legacy versions of Excel, as long as the program doesn't run into an item from the Excel 2007 or newer object models. If you use any items from the newer object models, however, the code will not compile in legacy versions. To work around this, comment out the specific lines of code, compile, and then comment the lines back in.

If your only Excel compatibility issue is the use of constant values, partially treat your code as if you were doing late binding to an external application. If you have only constant values that are incompatible, treat them like late-binding arguments, assigning a variable the numeric value of the constant. The following section shows an example of this approach.

➡ **See** "Using Constant Values," **p. 411**, for more information on using constant values.

Using the `Version` Property

The `Version` property returns a string that contains the active Excel application version. For 2016, this is 16.0. This can prove useful if you've developed an add-in to use across versions, but some parts of it, such as saving the active workbook, are version specific:

```
Sub WorkbookSave()
Dim xlVersion As String, myxlOpenXMLWorkbook As String
myxlOpenXMLWorkbook = "51" 'non-macro enabled workbook
xlVersion = Application.Version
Select Case xlVersion
    Case Is = "9.0", "10.0", "11.0"
        ActiveWorkbook.SaveAs Filename:="LegacyVersionExcel.xls"
    Case Is = "12.0", "14.0", "15.0", "16.0" '12.0 is 2007, 14.0 is 2010
        ActiveWorkbook.SaveAs Filename:="Excel2016Version", _
        FileFormat:=myxlOpenXMLWorkbook
End Select
End Sub
```

CAUTION

Note that for the `FileFormat` property of the Excel 12.0 and newer `Case`, I had to create my own variable, `myxlOpenXMLWorkbook`, to hold the constant value of `xlOpenXMLWorkbook`. If I were to try to run this in a legacy version of Excel just using the Excel constant `xlOpenXMLWorkbook`, the code would not even compile.

Using the `Excel8CompatibilityMode` Property

The `Excel8CompatibilityMode` property returns a Boolean to let you know whether a workbook is in Compatibility mode—that is, saved as an Excel 97–2003 file. You use this, for example, if you have an add-in that uses conditional formatting that you don't want the user to try to use on the workbook. The `CompatibilityCheck` function returns `True` if the active workbook is in Compatibility mode and `False` if it is not. The procedure `CheckCompatibility` uses the result to inform the user of an incompatible feature:

28

```
Function CompatibilityCheck() As Boolean
Dim blMode As Boolean
Dim arrVersions()
arrVersions = Array("12.0", "14,0", "15.0", "16.0")
If Application.IsNumber(Application.Match(Application.Version, _
    arrVersions, 0)) Then
    blMode = ActiveWorkbook.Excel8CompatibilityMode
    If blMode = True Then
        CompatibilityCheck = True
    ElseIf blMode = False Then
        CompatibilityCheck = False
    End If
End If
End Function

Sub CheckCompatibility()
Dim xlCompatible As Boolean
xlCompatible = CompatibilityCheck
If xlCompatible = True Then
    MsgBox "You are attempting to use an Excel 2007 or newer function " & _
        Chr(10) "in a 97-2003 Compatibility Mode workbook"
End If
End Sub
```

Next Steps

If we as authors have done our job correctly, you now have the tools you need to design your own VBA applications in Excel. You understand the shortcomings of the macro recorder yet know how to use it as an aid in learning how to do something. You know how to use Excel's power tools in VBA to produce workhorse routines that can save you hours of time each week. You've also learned how to have your application interact with others so that you can create applications to be used by others in your organization or in other organizations.

If you have found any sections of the book confusing or thought they could have been spelled out better, we welcome your comments and will give them consideration as we prepare the next edition of this book. Write to us:

Pub@MrExcel.com to contact Bill or

ExcelGGirl@gmail.com to contact Tracy

Whether your goal is to automate some of your own tasks or to become a paid Excel consultant, we hope that we've helped you on your way. Both are rewarding goals. With 500 million potential customers, we find that being Excel consultants is a friendly business. If you are interested in joining our ranks, you can use this book as your training manual. Master the topics, and you will be qualified to join us.

Index

D

M

S

T

REGISTER THIS PRODUCT
SAVE 35%*
ON YOUR NEXT PURCHASE!

💻 How to Register Your Product

- Go to quepublishing.com/register
- Sign in or create an account
- Enter ISBN: 10- or 13-digit ISBN that appears on the back cover of your product

🔓 Benefits of Registering

- Ability to download product updates
- Access to bonus chapters and workshop files
- A 35% coupon to be used on your next purchase – valid for 30 days
  To obtain your coupon, click on "Manage Codes" in the right column of your Account page
- Receive special offers on new editions and related Que products

Please note that the benefits for registering may vary by product. Benefits will be listed on your Account page under Registered Products.

We value and respect your privacy. Your email address will not be sold to any third party company.

* 35% discount code presented after product registration is valid on most print books, eBooks, and full-course videos sold on QuePublishing.com. Discount may not be combined with any other offer and is not redeemable for cash. Discount code expires after 30 days from the time of product registration. Offer subject to change.

quepublishing.com